Event Studies

Event Studies is the only book devoted to developing knowledge and theory about planned events. It focuses on event planning and management, outcomes, the experience of events and the meanings attached to them, the dynamic processes shaping events and why people attend them.

This title draws from a large number of foundation disciplines and closely related professional fields to foster interdisciplinary theory focused on planned events. This revised edition has been updated to reflect and examine a number of substantial and important new ideas.

New to the fourth edition:

- new sections on the evolution of design theory, management, planning and marketing theory applied to events, sensory stimulation, leadership, and the nature of crises and security issues;
- new content on critical event studies and what this means for research and practice, the life-cycle model for event programming, and an action plan for how events can be a positive force in sustainable cities;
- new and additional case studies from a wide range of international events, and reviews of the evolving theory of contemporary research in event studies are included throughout.

This will be an invaluable resource for all undergraduate students of event studies throughout their degree programmes.

Donald Getz is Professor Emeritus at the University of Calgary, Canada. He works as a management consultant and also holds guest positions at several universities. In addition to event studies, his areas of expertise include wine and food tourism, evaluation and impact assessment, consumer research and special-interest travel. Professor Getz co-founded and was Editor-in-Chief of *Event Management: An International Journal*.

Stephen J. Page is Associate Dean (Research) and Professor of Business and Management at Hertfordshire Business School, University of Hertfordshire, UK. He holds an Honorary Doctorate from the University of West London and is an Honorary Professor at Cardiff Metropolitan University and the University of Plymouth. He has worked as a tourism consultant with different organizations, including the United Nations World Tourism Organization, OECD, VisitScotland, Scottish Enterprise, Highlands and Islands Enterprise, Harrah's Casinos and Sky Tower, Auckland, New Zealand, among many other clients. He is the author and editor of 43 books on tourism, leisure and events and is Editor of the leading tourism journal, *Tourism Management*.

Books in the Events Management Series

Edited by Glenn Bowdin, Leeds Metropolitan University, UK
Donald Getz, University of Calgary, Canada
Conrad Lashley, Nottingham Trent University, UK

Marketing Destinations and Venues for Conferences, Conventions and Business Events
Tony Rogers and Rob Davidson

Human Resource Management for Events
Managing the Event Workforce
Lynn Van der Wagen

Risk Management for Meetings and Events
Julia Rutherford Silvers

Conferences and Conventions
A Global Industry, 2nd Edition
Tony Rogers

Events Feasibility and Development
William O'Toole

Events Management, 3rd Edition
*Glenn Bowdin, Johnny Allen, William O'Toole,
Rob Harris and Ian McDonnell*

Event Studies, 2nd Edition
Donald Getz

Conferences and Conventions, 3rd Edition
Tony Rogers

Human Resource Management for Events
Managing the Event Workforce, 2nd Edition
Lynn Van der Wagen and Lauren White

Event Studies, 3rd Edition
Donald Getz and Stephen J. Page

Marketing Destinations and Venues for Conferences, Conventions and Business Events, 2nd Edition
Tony Rogers and Rob Davidson

Event Studies, 4th Edition
Donald Getz and Stephen J. Page

Event Studies

Theory, Research and Policy for Planned Events

Fourth Edition

Donald Getz and Stephen J. Page

LONDON AND NEW YORK

Fourth edition published 2020
by Routledge
2 Park Square, Milton Park, Abingdon, Oxon, OX14 4RN

and by Routledge
52 Vanderbilt Avenue, New York, NY 10017

Routledge is an imprint of the Taylor & Francis Group, an informa business

First edition published by Butterworth-Heinemann 2007
Third edition published by Routledge 2016

British Library Cataloguing-in-Publication Data
A catalogue record for this book is available from the British Library

Library of Congress Cataloging-in-Publication Data
Names: Getz, Donald, 1949– author. | Page, Stephen J., author. |
   Routledge (Firm)
Title: Event studies : theory, research and policy for planned events /
   Donald Getz and Stephen J. Page.
Other titles: Events management series.
Description: Fourth Edition. | New York : Routledge, 2020. |
   Series: Events management series | "First edition published
   by Butterworth-Heinemann 2007. Third edition published by
   Routledge 2016"—T.p. verso. | Includes bibliographical
   references and index.
Identifiers: LCCN 2019025272 | ISBN 9780367085629 (Hardback) |
   ISBN 9780429023002 (eBook)
Subjects: LCSH: Special events—Planning. | Special events—Research. |
   Special events—Management.
Classification: LCC GT3405 .G48 2020 | DDC 394.2—dc23
LC record available at https://lccn.loc.gov/2019025272

ISBN: 978-0-367-08562-9 (hbk)
ISBN: 978-0-367-08563-6 (pbk)
ISBN: 978-0-429-02300-2 (ebk)

Typeset in Iowan Old Style
by Apex CoVantage, LLC

Visit the companion website: www.routledge.com/cw/getz

Printed and bound by CPI Group (UK) Ltd, Croydon, CR0 4YY

Contents

Figures

Tables

Events in focus

Expert opinions

Series preface

The events industry, including festivals, meetings, conferences, exhibitions, incentives, sports and a range of other events, is rapidly developing and makes a significant contribution to business- and leisure-related tourism. With increased regulation and the growth of government and corporate involvement in events, the environment has become much more complex. Event managers are now required to identify and service a wide range of stakeholders and to balance their needs and objectives. Though mainly operating at national levels, there has been a significant growth of academic provision to meet the needs of events and related industries and the organizations that comprise them. The English-speaking nations, together with key Northern European countries, have developed programmes of study leading to the award of diploma, undergraduate and postgraduate awards. These courses focus on providing education and training for future event professionals, and cover areas such as event planning and management, marketing, finance, human resource management and operations. Modules in events management are also included in many tourism, leisure, recreation and hospitality qualifications in universities and colleges.

The rapid growth of such courses has meant that there is a vast gap in the available literature on this topic for lecturers, students and professionals alike. To this end, the Routledge Events Management Series has been created to meet these needs and to create a planned and targeted set of publications in this area.

Aimed at academic and management development in events management and related studies, the *Events Management Series*:

- provides a portfolio of titles that match management development needs through various stages;
- prioritizes publication of texts where there are current gaps in the market or where current provision is unsatisfactory;
- develops a portfolio of both practical and stimulating texts;
- provides a basis for theory and research underpinning programmes of study;
- is recognized as being of consistent high quality; and
- will quickly become the series of first choice for both authors and users.

Preface to the fourth edition

While all the fundamentals of the book remain the same, periodic updates are desirable for several reasons. First, the literature on planned events keeps expanding at a rapid pace, particularly with the publication of many new special-topic books and journal articles that add new insights and expand our thinking about event studies. Second, the world keeps changing. Some new trends are emerging, and others identified in the past have become mainstream. Finally, each new edition provides the opportunity for authors to expand on certain topics of great interest and especially to take advantage of research we have undertaken. Each new edition enables these changes, including:

- new research notes (mostly abstracts from published papers) that point to current topics and relevant methods
- new and revised expert opinions that bring additional insights to the discussions
- new figures to supplement the written material
- references to many new articles and books to provide a much greater synthesis and roadmap of the literature on events.

    In this fourth edition there are a number of substantial new ideas examined:

- critical event studies, and what this means for research and practice
- the evolution of design theory, leading to the notion of strategic value co-creation networks and elaboration of event portfolio theory
- elaboration of sensory stimulation, and the concept of sensory mapping
- the life-cycle model for event programming and portfolios
- the scope and nature of management, planning and marketing theory applied to events
- leadership: roles, styles and applications within event management
- the nature of crises, security issues and dynamic crowd management
- elaboration of evaluation and impact assessment, including the classification of the subjects and objects, the roles of logic and theory of change models, and how to identify winners and losers (i.e. the equity issue)
- an action plan for how events can be a positive force in sustainable cities
- a review of review articles with emphasis on how themes and theory development in event studies have been evolving.

Acknowledgements

The following have made a direct contribution to this fourth edition, and we are especially thankful for their help. Their affiliations are in the pertinent Expert Opinion sections: Steve Brown, Matt Frew, Joe Jeff Goldblatt, William O'Toole, Ian Patterson and Ully Wuensch.

We would also like to thank Emma Travis and Lydia Kessell at Routledge, and Stephen would like to thank Jo, Rosie and Toby Page for keeping him entertained whilst writing.

A number of organizations and bodies have provided the authors with permission to reproduce material in the book, and we wish to express our thanks to them. Figure 1.3: T. Pernecky (ed.) (2016) *Approaches and Methods in Event Studies*, p7, with permission from Routledge; Figure 3.2: Human participants and accessibility, in Finkel *et al.* (2019) *Accessibility, Inclusion and Diversity in Critical Event Studies*, p.71; Figure 3.4: Applying psychological ideas to event participation, from Benckendorff and Pearce (2012: 166), reprinted from *The Routledge Handbook of Events*, Page and Connell, Routledge (2012); Figure 4.1: Roles and contributions of the private sector to events, in Stokes (2014: 219). Ryan (2014) for Figure 6.9: Matrix of event meaning and duration of interest, reprinted from *The Routledge Handbook of Events*, Page and Connell, Routledge (2014: 257).

Figures 1.7 and 1.8 and Table 1.2 have been reproduced from Page and Connell's *Visitor attractions and events: Responding to seasonality* (2015) and Figure 10.1 from Tommy D. Andersson and Erik Lundberg's *Commensurability and sustainability: Triple impact assessments of a tourism event* (2013) both published in the journal *Tourism Management*, with the kind permission of Elsevier; Figure 2.2 from Page and Connell's *Leisure: An Introduction* (2010), with the kind permission of Pearson Education; Figure 6.11 from A. Coughlan's *Tourism and health: Using positive psychology principles to maximise participants' well-being outcomes* (2015) published in *The Journal of Sustainable Tourism* and Figure 8.5 from Jackson, Crawford and Godbey's *Negotiation of leisure constraints* (1993) published in the journal *Leisure Sciences*, both with the permission of Taylor and Francis; Figure 9.4 from Getz, Andersson and Larson's *Festival stakeholder roles: Concepts and case studies* (2007) and Table 10.3 from Getz, D.'s *The sustainability of eventful cities: Concepts, challenges, and principles* (2017), both published in the *Event Management* journal, with the permission of Cognizant Communication Corporation; Figures 3.3 and 6.6 from Page's *Tourism Management*, 6th Edition (2015); Figure 4.1, 6.9 and Table 6.3 from Page and Connell's *Routledge Handbook of Events* (2014), Figure 5.2 from Pigram and Jenkin's *Outdoor Recreation Management* (1983), Figures 5.3 and 12.2 from Hall and Page's *Geography of Tourism and Recreation* (2014), all with the permission of Routledge; Table 10.4 from Getz's *Event Impact Assessment* (2019), reprinted with the permission of Goodfellow Publishers. Lastly, Paul Smith at the Thomas Cook archive for permission to reproduce Plate 4.1.

PART I

Introductory concepts in event studies

Introduction and overview of event studies

Upon completion of this chapter, students should know the following:

- the definition and characteristics of event studies as an academic field, and specifically its core phenomenon and major themes or components;
- why students and academics study planned events;
- different perspectives on the study of planned events – foundation disciplines and closely related professional fields;
- three major subdivisions (or discourses) within event studies: the discipline-based or classical, event tourism and events management;
- emerging interdisciplinary theories of planned events;
- major forces shaping planned events, and important trends and issues.

What is event studies?

Event studies is the academic field devoted to creating knowledge and theory about planned events; the scope of events spans individual celebrations and community festivals, sports, business meetings and exhibitions; it also includes mega events, which have largely become the realm of professionals, corporations and entrepreneurs. Within the study of events, an academic field of knowledge requires a unique core phenomenon as the principal focus for academic inquiry. It is the study of all planned events that is the main focus of this book within the field that is known broadly as 'event studies'. As a recent area of growth, event studies encompasses the planning and management, outcomes, experience of events and meanings attached to them, and all the dynamic processes shaping events and the reasons why people attend them.

Event studies draws from a large number of foundation disciplines and closely related professional fields, and the interconnections between these areas of study should foster interdisciplinary theory focused on planned events to better understand why they exist and how we can manage them better to derive positive outcomes as well as minimizing undesirable and unforeseen consequences of hosting planned events. As a growing field of study, event studies brings an exciting and unique set of perspectives to bear on three important discourses on events – event management, event tourism and the 'classical' study of events – within various disciplines that consider the roles, importance and impacts of events in society and culture.

Event studies as a field of study is defined by its holistic approach towards events as a phenomenon, including all the issues surrounding planned events, in addition to their management, design and production. In fact Pernecky (2016: 1) has argued that, 'event studies is whatever researchers invested in the study of events do', reflecting the expanding dimensions of event studies. In this respect, event studies can exist without event management, and in fact it already does. Events have policy implications that cannot be ignored, and they are not the sole domain of event producers and managers. This begins to illustrate why the study of planned events is both a fascinating and essential feature of many post-modern societies with the growth in consumption of events by people as part of everyday leisure time as participants, as spectators and as consumers of fun and entertainment (Page and Connell 2010). So, why should we study events?

Why study planned events?

Many readers of this book will be students interested in a professional or business career related to planned events. The careers potential and entrepreneurship opportunities associated with planned events have grown dramatically, in tune with general trends in the experience economy (see Events in Focus 1.1 for a discussion of the experience economy).

EVENTS IN FOCUS

1.1 The experience economy and events

Pine and Gilmore's (1999) *The Experience Economy* makes an interesting contribution to the study of events because it argues that the experience economy is the next stage in the evolution of society from a service economy. The initial work by Pine and Gilmore suggested that businesses need to create experiences that are memorable, given the increased levels of education of many consumers and their pursuit of value-added elements within the experience they purchase. The essence of the Pine and Gilmore (1999) study was that the production of experiences (also see Sundbo and Sorensen 2016 and Smit and Melissen 2018), such as those which are associated with events, will need to focus on a number of aspects of consumption, including:

- the need to create a sensation;
- the need to personalize the experience; to develop trust and a bond with the consumer which has been embodied in the use of brands.

The experience economy concept suggests that we need to focus on four areas of experience:

- entertainment
- education

- aesthetic (i.e. an ability to immerse oneself in something)
- escapism in what is consumed.

Consequently, events will need to be designed to allow participants and audiences to engage in discrete ways ranging from absorption through to immersion. Such experiences need to be able to accommodate different modes of participation, from passive to very active forms of involvement. They also need to engage all of our senses (hearing, sight, touch, smell and taste).

Source: Adapted and developed from Page and Connell (2010).

Professionals entering public service, or the not-for-profit sector, will encounter events and related issues at some point; they need to know how to relate to events as businesses or as policy instruments.

There are more general, educational reasons for studying planned events. Within the 'experience economy', planned events are a very important and expanding social and cultural phenomenon, which is of considerable interest to students and practitioners in many fields. Events reflect changes in popular culture and continue to make high culture accessible. Whatever one's cultural interests, from entertainment to opera, planned events are an enduring delivery vehicle.

The diversity of perspectives being adopted on planned events is expanding exponentially, and the literature continues to grow and expand accordingly. However, as this book will demonstrate, the study of events has a long and rich tradition within many disciplines, especially within the social sciences where many of the underpinning concepts and approaches we examine can be traced back to the early twentieth century. Therefore, this book provides a major contribution to our understanding of event studies on two dimensions:

- *horizontally* by looking at the depth and richness of its study within specific areas and disciplines;
- *vertically* by embracing the scope and breadth of the subjects and topics now being studied within event studies, disciplines and subject areas.

Education for planned events

In the first edition, a pyramid-shaped model with event studies at the top, resting on a foundation of event management degree and diploma programmes was developed, which in turn existed primarily because of the large 'industry' and career opportunities in the events sector. The principal argument was that event studies would not exist without this foundation, and that it mostly relied on teachers and researchers within the event management field. This is no longer the case, as event studies features in many event management programmes. The study of events can also occur outside event management and tourism-related programmes, as outlined by Barron and Leask (2012), and in due course it will become an accepted interdisciplinary field. Accordingly a new education model is presented here, building on the current thinking around the issues highlighted by Barron and Leask (2012). In this framework (see Figure 1.1), event studies is all-encompassing and interdisciplinary, while the other discourses or fields are applied in nature. It is not necessarily linked to, nor dependent upon, the closely related applied fields, but in practice is closely associated with them through educational programmes where the researchers are situated.

There is an ongoing debate within many vocationally oriented subjects that the focus of study does not necessarily mean it is a distinct discipline. These types of debates have affected many subjects that have grown from the 1960s, such as marketing, which has a number of founding disciplines that contribute to its study (e.g. psychology and sociology). Similar debates have been reiterated in more recent times around the growth of areas like tourism, which have a great deal of synergy with the subsequent growth of event studies.

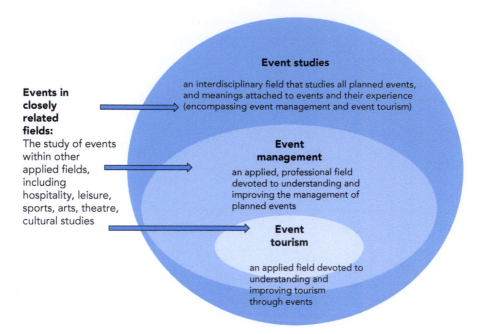

Figure 1.1 Event studies, event management and event tourism

Tribe (2004, 2006) argued that tourism is not a discipline, but a field of study drawing on a number of disciplines which can also be applied to event studies. Accepting that event studies will be a 'social and political construct' (Tribe 2004: 47), one's perspective on, or object of interest in, events will determine which approach one draws upon (as outlined in Events in Focus 1.1). An interest in the impacts of mega events on housing, for example, could draw upon sociology, urban planning and political science. An interest in the nature of festival sustainability will use management theory, social psychology and other sources that contribute understanding. To create event-related knowledge, the contributions of theory and methodologies from multiple disciplines are required. Where a number of disciplines are drawn upon, we can say that the new field of study is multidisciplinary in nature. With time, the interactions might establish a field of knowledge with its own theories and methodologies, and this can be said to be interdisciplinary in nature.

Tribe (2002) tackled the subject of what a higher-level curriculum for tourism should embody and this has relevance to the study of events. Tribe (2002: 338) argues that most tourism studies are vocational and business oriented (just as event management is), but there is a need to produce 'philosophic practitioners' who can deliver 'efficient and effective services while at the same time discharging the role of stewardship for the development of the wider tourism world in which these services are delivered'. Stewardship, in this context, can mean sustainable development. Tribe (2014) re-examined the notion of philosophical practitioners, while Dredge *et al.* (2014) suggested what a core curriculum for tourism, hospitality and events should provide. Tribe (2014: 17–29) referred to Barnett (1990: 202–203) who advocated six basic requirements for any advanced education, each of these being important to students, and they are incorporated in various ways into this book (our thoughts related to this book are parenthesized for each point):

1 a deep understanding of some knowledge claims (this brings ontology into the picture, that is, what we collectively claim to know about planned events);

2 a radical critique of knowledge claims (do not take all claims as given, but challenge them);

3 competence to develop critique in the company of others (being able to engage in various discourses, such as that concerning the meaning and importance of events);

4 self-direction and independent inquiry (knowing where you want to go and how to get there with regard to learning and professionalism; develop lifelong learning capability);

5 self-reflection (intellectuals and professionals always think carefully about what they are doing, why they are doing it, and potential outcomes; do we have enough information or theory? what can we learn from evaluation?);

6 open dialogue and cooperation (being part of a free, professional community and a responsible citizen).

In considering the sometimes divergent directions taken by liberal education versus vocational training in these largely applied fields, Dredge *et al.* (2014) argued that each teaching institution engages in a dynamic process of curriculum design that results in differences, including the potential for innovation. Those teaching event studies or applied event tourism/management should not only combine some elements of training with more theoretical and philosophical subjects, but also develop the student's capability for lifelong learning. Starting with some basic skills and simple concepts, educational programmes can add more complex knowledge and expert practices as appropriate and for competitive advantage. The professional event manager or event-tourism planner has to have more than skills. Professionals must have a broad base of knowledge, together with the ability to reflect upon how it will shape both specific managerial or business decisions and the wider implications of events in society and the environment. They also have to possess a well-developed sense of ethics and professional responsibility, which should be based on a solid foundation that includes philosophy and comparative cultural studies.

However, there are fundamental differences between the paths that tourism studies and event studies have trodden in establishing themselves as fields of study. The growth of tourism education can be traced back as far as the 1930s, and its major boom was in the 1980s. Event studies has a more recent and compressed, even meteoric, growth, and some of the drivers of that growth are shown in Figure 1.2. As Getz (2012a) argued, there were two distinct and potentially complementary approaches to events education:

- an *interdisciplinary approach*, which was based upon the theoretical and intellectual basis of higher education, with a philosophical approach underpinned by traditional disciplines and new subject areas (see Events in Focus 1.2 for a more detailed discussion of approaches towards event studies and more recent developments beyond interdisciplinary approaches);
- the *professional bodies approach*, which is based on competencies and skills, with factual knowledge and problem-solving at the heart of the curriculum.

Figure 1.2 Key drivers of the growth in event education

1.2 Understanding the language of the academic study of events

Pernecky (2016) examined the terms used to depict the study of events within social science, and key features of that debate are discussed here to highlight the problem of trying to draw boundaries around what we are studying and how to describe it. Pernecky (2016), as shown in Figure 1.3, identified a range of approaches to show how knowledge in event studies can be produced from the traditional disciplinary approaches to more diverse approaches. The disciplinary perspectives have generated the vast majority of the studies of events being the long-standing focus of distinct subject areas located in the social sciences and humanities. These subjects are somewhat closed and demarcated by their own theories, models and ideas on how to approach events. In contrast, cross-disciplinary approaches try to synthesize (i.e. bring together and understand different perspectives) the existing disciplinary knowledge which is often a byproduct of successful textbooks that introduce a subject area, drawing together a rich diversity of approaches and ideas. Figure 1.3 then moves to multi-disciplinary approaches which are often where researchers from different disciplines approach a problem or issue from their own perspective, usually with little collaboration. Next are the inter-disciplinary approaches which are based on thinking from

Mode of inquiry	Symbol	Description
Disciplinarity		Disciplinary knowledge is specific to distinct branches of learning – it has its own procedures, methods, concepts and ways of framing research problems.
Cross-disciplinarity		Cross-disciplinary knowledge is the 'viewing of one discipline from the perspective of another' (Stember 1991: 4) or the 'importing' of knowledge from other disciplines.
Multi-disciplinarity		Multi-disciplinarity occurs when 'researchers work in parallel or sequentially from [a] disciplinary-specific base to address [a] common problem' (Rosenfield 1992: 1351).
Inter-disciplinarity		Inter-disciplinarity occurs when 'researchers work jointly but still from [a] disciplinary-specific basis to address [a] common problem' (Rosenfield 1992: 1351).
Trans-disciplinarity		Trans-disciplinarity is the most collaborative approach to research: 'researchers work jointly using [a] shared conceptual framework drawing together disciplinary-specific theories, concepts, and approaches to address [a] common problem' (Rosenfield 1992: 1351).
Post-disciplinarity		Post-disciplinarity weaves a unique inquiry thread. It is an 'escape' from disciplines – marked by flexibility, creative problem-solving and intellectual disobedience.

Figure 1.3 Modes of knowledge production

disciplines but based on collaboration around an issue or problem where the disciplinary walls of their subjects are dropped to contribute to the project or research from their own perspective. But this does not lead to a merging of concepts or methodologies as Pernecky (2016) argues, which is dependent upon the next stage – trans-disciplinary research. Trans-disciplinary research represents the highest level of collaboration in research to try to make a transformational differ-ence from the work which challenges the disciplinary silos in which many academic subjects are embedded. Lastly, Pernecky (2016) points to the post-disciplinary approach as being by far the most contentious because it is based on abolishing disciplinary knowledge with, for example, the creation of new focal points, such as the development of gender studies or cultural studies, that is not rooted in any one discipline by examining the phenomena in question as opposed to being constrained by the methods or modes of inquiry that a disciplinary approach uses (see Jessop and Sum 2001 for more detail on trans-disciplinary developments).

What this shows is a more refined and industry-focused growth in event education, and to a lesser degree research has characterized this expansion to meet the rising demand for events professionals. The industry bodies' ultimate objective was to professionalize a field of study in much the same way as nurse education in many countries, which shifted from colleges to universities. In the case of event studies, the sub-ject arose from many of the collaborations of stakeholders (professional bodies, employers, public-sector agencies, and universities and higher education institutions) to capitalize on the main drivers of growth outlined in Figure 1.2. These drivers range from more macro and global processes around place branding and using planned events to reposition destinations, through to more micro and localized demands for a professional workforce to service the demand for planned events along with meetings, conventions and other events (often called MICE). This has been a second phase of growth for many countries that had expanded their tourism economies and then regarded planned events as the next natural stage of devel-opment in the 1980s and 1990s, to expand their economies around the concept of the growing experience economy as a dimension of increased consumer demand for entertainment and leisure experiences.

These trends have certainly meant that there is and will continue to be a growing need for planners and policy analysts who must deal with complex issues related to events from many different perspectives (e.g. social, cultural, economic, environmental) for whom event studies provides a necessary foundation. Linked to this will be a rising need for higher education and lifelong learning in the profession of event management (i.e. continuing professional development), and educators must ask that anyone with a higher degree, or a professional with advanced standing, should be well versed in theories and methods of this dynamic and fast-changing area. They will be the mentors of the next generation of professionals, and we always expect more of the next generation.

According to Leiper (1981, 1990), if we are to adopt a multidisciplinary approach, it involves studying a topic (for us, planned events) by including information from other disciplines, whereas an interdisciplin-ary approach blends various philosophies and techniques to create a synthesis. What is clear from Events in Focus 1.2 is that a wide variety of approaches are now available and being used to develop the field of event studies, and one of the most recent – critical event studies – is discussed at the end of the chapter. Therefore, building on Echtner and Jamal (1997), a subject should embody the following attributes:

- holistic, integrated research;
- the generation of a theoretical body of knowledge;
- an interdisciplinary focus or alternative approaches (as outlined in Table 1.3);
- a clearly explicated theory/ies and methodology/ies;

- the application of qualitative and quantitative methods, including positivist and non-positivist traditions;
- new research approaches as they emerge from this growing body of knowledge.

This raises the question: are we entering a stage of development where eventology exists?

Eventology

In the English language, 'ology' added to a noun indicates 'the study or science of', so 'eventology' would mean (and you will not find it in the dictionary) the study or science of events. It's an awkward term (imagine 'festivalology' or 'meetingsology' and you get the point), and those in established disciplines like biology do not like newcomers, especially in fields of applied study, taking on the veneer of pure science. Goldblatt (2011) uses the term in a specific way, related to his model of how events foster cultural progression through innovation, and this is a very useful conceptualization. Goldblatt (2011: xii) argued that: 'Eventology is the study of planned events to promote positive societal benefits.' Bringing together people through planned events is said to make societies healthier, smarter, wealthier and fairer, greener, safer and stronger. These can be considered a worthwhile (or normative) agenda, with events as instruments of policy. Goldblatt's expert opinion, later in this chapter, also introduces a mathematical notion of eventology as a subset of probability theory, and this idea has only recently been introduced to planned events. The challenge of science is to establish cause and effect. Consider this problem when we examine the desirability of developing a philosophical approach to 'event services', again under the heading of epistemology and ontology, and finally when we look at outcomes and impact assessment.

A framework for understanding and creating knowledge about planned events

The core phenomenon

What defines a field of study is the 'core phenomenon' – phenomenon means a state or process known through the senses; in other words something that can be 'experienced'. We are studying a universal phenomenon that has importance around the world, in every culture and society. Incidentally, the alternative, more popular definition of 'phenomenon' is that of a 'remarkable occurrence', which can be a synonym for 'special event'!

A three-part core is depicted in Figure 1.4, consisting of:

1 the study of all planned events, and no other discipline or field attempts to do that;
2 the experience of events (by all the stakeholders, even the public at large);
3 meanings attached to events (for example, as institutions or entertainment) and to the experience of events.

This definition of the core of event studies broadens the field considerably and imposes a substantial theoretical and philosophical component.

What do all planned events have in common that justifies their own field of study? They have the following characteristics:

- *timelessness*: events are inherent in all societies and integral to civilization itself;
- *global importance* in terms of public policy, industry and corporate strategy;

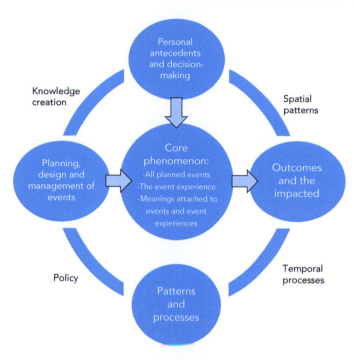

Figure 1.4 A framework for understanding and creating knowledge about planned events

- recent and rapidly *expanding professional practice* of event management, event tourism and event policy careers; business opportunities abound;
- recognition that events are *fundamental to the experience economy*, indeed are essential to the evolving nature of leisure and culture;
- a high level of *student demand*, leading to a proliferation of event management programmes globally, many with specializations, which in turn fosters further academic research and publication to advance knowledge in the field.

The essence of the planned event is that of *an experience that has been designed* (or at least the experience is facilitated), which would not otherwise occur. There are many styles of planned events, produced for many purposes, but in every case there is intent to create, or at least shape, the individual and collective experiences of the audience or participants. New forms are always being created, and this in itself is of considerable interest. According to Hjorth and Kostera (2007), the vital characteristics of an event experience are: immediacy, playfulness, subjectivity and performativity. The latter characteristic has been examined as a key element of events by Rojek (2013) in terms of *performative labour* drawing upon the work of Bryman (2004: 103) as 'the rendering of the work by management and employees alike as akin to a theatrical performance in which the workplace is construed as similar to a stage'. Rojek (2013) expands upon this, highlighting the factors which are affecting the growth of performative labour globally including communications, the media, information flows and the rise of the digital economy that makes things available continuously.

Multiple perspectives on experiences and meaning have to be included in designing events. Obviously there are paying customers or invited guests at planned events, but we also need to recognize the organizers including staff, sponsors and other facilitators (providing resources and support), regulators (e.g. city officials), co-producers, participants (as in athletics events), exhibitors and suppliers (see Morris *et al*. 2012). A further dimension is the pivotal role of volunteers, as numerous events cannot exist without them. Consequently this raises a number of fundamental questions around the experience and meaning of events:

- What motivates all these stakeholders and what different experiences do they have?
- How do all these stakeholders react to the designed experience or at least to the setting and programme of events?

To address these questions, we need to examine a number of key concepts around the experience and meaning of events associated with the study of semiotics and meaning.

Semiotics and the meaning of 'meanings'

A key proposition we need to start with in the discussion of the meaning of events is – *do all events and event experiences have hidden or profound meanings?* Not necessarily, because an experience can be purely hedonistic, which means it gives pleasure without significance or symbolic meaning. In fact, many people would describe such experiences as 'fun' or 'diversions'. Conversely, many experiences, and therefore events as facilitators and packagers of experiences, are *significant* in social, cultural, economic and environmental terms because they generate impacts that are either valued and desired, or are negative and unwanted. Event experiences may also have *symbolic meaning* for participants, host communities and entire nations. To assist in understanding these issues in more depth, we can turn to the field of linguistics and the concept of semiotics.

Semiotics is the study of signs and symbols, and therefore of how meaning is conveyed and interpreted. The symbols can be language, icons (that is, symbols like a logo or brand) or objects, including people. Meaning can also be conveyed through actions, and institutions also hold meanings. The very idea of 'leisure' holds meanings for individuals and groups that are in part socially and culturally determined (Page and Connell 2010). To some, leisure has negative connotations and is to be avoided, and to others it is their reason for being. Therefore, understanding events as part of societal attitudes towards leisure and entertainment, fun and hedonism, is only a partial understanding. Wider studies of the social psychology of events as a leisure experience or business phenomenon are required in order to fully appreciate the individualized nature of meaning and what events convey to individuals and groups (i.e. families and kinship groups and friends). An important step is to consider the symbolic meanings associated with events.

Symbolic meaning refers to *mediated* experiences where an object, sign, word or action means something else, or conveys ideas and feelings beyond itself (Levy 1959). For example, the event is not merely interpreted as entertainment, but it is understood by some or all of the audience that it may be an expression of nationalism or community identity. Allan (2006: 407) explains the way in which the mass media mediates experiences and makes the fundamental distinction between 'mediated experiences [which] are a contrast to social experiences that take place in face-to-face encounters and are created as people are exposed to situations and others with whom they have no direct association through space and time'.

Within the study of symbolic meaning, we also need to be cognizant of the growing importance of how marketing has utilized these mediated experiences to communicate the value of an experience using the notion of branding. Marketing is defined as: 'a social and managerial process by which individuals and groups obtain what they need through creating and exchanging products and value with others' (Kotler *et al.* 1999: 12). To help simplify and create recognizable signs and symbols, marketing as a profession uses the concept of branding, which is about communicating with intended customers using a name, logo, symbol or word to simplify and create awareness or to attract an audience and a perception of quality or value in the intended experience or event.

Therefore, in an event setting, how symbols are used will affect how they are perceived and interpreted. Sometimes organizers will be completely unaware of symbolic meanings attached to their events and actions. But some events deliberately seek to convey meaning, which is the essence of theming. Cities and destinations use events to convey positive images and meanings, so the event itself becomes a symbol and branding is applied to create the value or quality message. This is the essence of hallmark events. Sponsors at events believe that the goodwill generated by the event will attach itself to their brands, and the brand itself is a symbol of quality or value. To illustrate these principles in action, a study by Wooten and Norman (2008) reported that visitors to a coastal shrimp festival placed more importance on the coastal location (the event setting) than the shrimp (the theme or 'object' of the event) when explaining their satisfaction. People attending or participating in an event can attach their own meanings to the experiences, regardless of what others want them to experience. Research Note 1.1, concerning meanings, illustrates a variety of applications and methods.

1.1 RESEARCH NOTES ON MEANINGS

1 Crespi-Vallbona, M. and Richards, G. (2007). The meaning of cultural festivals: Stakeholder perspectives in Catalunya. *International Journal of Cultural Policy*, 13 (1): 103–122.

Traditional and popular culture events in Catalunya, Spain, were examined as to the aims of various stakeholders in the events. Researchers found there was generally a high level of agreement regarding the importance of cultural events in underpinning Catalan identity; however, stakeholders differed in the meanings they attached to identity. Policy-makers placed greater emphasis on economic and political issues, whereas cultural producers were more concerned with social aspects of identity.

2 Wooten, M. and Norman, W. (2008). Interpreting and managing special events and festivals. In A. Woodside and D. Martin (eds), *Managing Tourism: Analysis, Behaviour and Strategy*, pp. 197–217. Wallingford: CABI.

Objects and settings at the Kentucky Arts Festival (Kentucky, USA) were examined for their symbolic meaning to determine if the audience experiences matched what organizers claimed was unique about the event. Results demonstrated a fair degree of congruence, but not on all measures. In other words, the audience might not be getting the full symbolic meaning of the festival that the organizers intended.

3 Kaplanidou, K. and Vogt, C. (2010). The meaning and measurement of a sport event experience among active sport tourists. *Journal of Sport Management*, 24 (5): 544–566.

Researchers aimed to understand how active sport tourists perceive the meaning of a sport event experience, and to develop a scale for that meaning. Results from focus groups suggested that participants attribute meanings related to organizational, environmental, physical, social and emotional aspects of the experience.

Event studies is also concerned about how meanings are attached to planned events by individuals, groups and society. For example, is the event perceived to be a shared cultural experience or personally self-fulfilling? And we also have to examine meanings from different perspectives. Each stakeholder in the process wants, expects and receives potentially different experiences and attaches potentially different meanings to the event. Do they receive the experiences that were planned for them?

Theory on experience and meanings

In social science, which is where event studies are largely located, as we shall show in later chapters, the subject areas seek to develop our knowledge and understanding by building theories which are broadly defined as propositions derived from empirical observations. The resulting theories help us to explain the complexity of the real world and to help guide further research activity. Although there are many debates within social science over what theory is, how you develop it and its purpose, in event studies the interdisciplinary development of the subject means that theories from cognate areas are often used and adapted to the event context to explain how event phenomena occur and develop. In the context of events as experiences, this means we tend to borrow and rely upon theory that has been developed in social psychology and leisure studies so as to begin to understand what event experiences are and how they are constructed.

Therefore a useful starting point in seeking to understand event experiences, and meanings attached to them, is through the use of 'personal and social constructs' (Kelly 1955) based on the study of psychology. The basic argument from Kelly's work is that personal constructs enable an individual to develop an understanding of their own psychology by the constructs they use. These constructs are created by an individual's experiences and their own ideas about reality, based on observations of the real world. For example, when people attend concerts their expectation is to be entertained, and probably also to have fun with like-minded fans in a dynamic social setting. Going to a conference requires that we think in terms of having a learning experience. We are supposed to be happy when we go to festivals, and sad when we attend funerals.

Consumption of all kinds is the social norm, leading to enormous expenditure on entertainment events. So we need theory on both personal antecedents to attending events (including needs, motives, preferences, constraints) and the social constructs that give events broader meanings and importance within societies and cultures.

To a degree, expectations are shaped purposefully by advertising, branding and the media. 'Event experiences' are the hot topic in branding and marketing, so corporations know how to create the experiences necessary to foster positive brand attitudes and increased consumption. This leads us into the world of the psychology of branding (e.g. Evans 2013) and its use to shape expectations and the desire to consume. However, we also need to be aware of whether some event experiences are exploitive and deceiving. Even where the event experience is created by not-for-profits or government agencies, there is the possibility that the meanings we are to attach to the experience are part of some propaganda or social marketing scheme, and several Olympic Games have been accused of such behaviour, none more explicitly than the 1936 Games hosted in Nazi Germany. Rojek (2013) also pointed to the way in which the Rio Carnival has been manipulated by government and the tourism sector to enhance the global image of the country. The very people who the carnival is supposed to represent are being priced out of attending the event and the history of the event is being re-engineered to 'neutralise ethnic divisions' according to Rojek (2013).

To help develop our understanding of event studies and the role of events as experiences, the book is structured thus: Chapter 2 introduces each form of event and talks about the experiences associated with them. Pertinent theory is introduced in the discussion of foundation disciplines and closely related professional fields in Chapters 3–5. Chapter 6 applies and develops theory pertaining to event experiences and meanings, specifically the theory of liminality, drawing from anthropology and the study of rituals. The planned event experience is then modelled as a particular kind of liminal/liminoid zone – a special space and time, a different realm of existence, that has to be symbolically or ritualistically marked for its special purposes. In this liminal/liminoid zone, event-goers are aware of the contrasts with everyday life, and this is an important part of the experience. The concepts of 'flow' and 'peak experiences', drawing from social psychology and leisure studies, which describe how some people feel and act when 'in the zone' – how they get totally involved and lose track of time – are also introduced.

To understand event experiences we also need to look at communication, learning and interpretation theory (i.e. how do we motivate attendance, shape expectations and create the best learning environments?). Theories on 'serious leisure', 'ego involvement' and 'commitment' help us understand event motives, experiences and meanings for those participants who seek out specific event opportunities and the personal benefits they provide.

Chapter 7 examines event design, commencing with a discussion of the meaning of design as both a creative and technical problem-solving process, its theoretical foundations and how design is applied to planned events. The theme, programme, setting, services and consumables are all subjects of design. One major conclusion we wish to stress is that *every event experience will be unique to the individual*, because experiences are internal psychological states. We also interpret our experiences from different frames of reference. Related to that conclusion is the assertion that event planning and design cannot create experiences, but only suggest, facilitate or constrain them. The ability to influence the event, audience demand, is conditioned by antecedents and decision-making by consumers.

Antecedents and decision-making

'Antecedents' include all those factors shaping individual and collective needs or demands for events, and how choices and decisions are made. Theory from a variety of disciplines is useful, particularly from marketing and psychology, and in turn that theory has been adapted by consumer behaviour researchers in leisure and tourism studies (Hall and Page 2014; Page and Connell 2010). In Chapter 8, a framework is provided for organizing the discussion, starting with the personal dimension: personality; needs and motives; personal and interpersonal factors; expectations; and event careers. Both 'intrinsic' (related to free choice and leisure) and 'extrinsic' (related to work and obligation) motives are important in shaping what impacts on the demand for events. Juxtaposed with demand are structural, personal and interpersonal constraints acting against our desires to participate in, or attend, events, which has a long tradition of study within leisure studies as the contributing field (Page and Connell 2010).

The decision-making process starts with how people negotiate through constraints, as some people manage better than others to realize their personal goals by overcoming barriers to participation in events, whilst others may have multiple layers of constraints that coalesce to prevent participation (e.g. a lack of income, inadequate access and knowledge of how to overcome such barriers). Attention is also given to information searching and use, event attractiveness (the pull factors), substitution, loyalty and novelty seeking as key elements affecting the demand for events.

Following event experiences, we have to consider satisfaction with the event, the meanings attached to experiences, and the possibility of personal development and transformation. These factors and ongoing recollection (if indeed the experience was memorable) shape future intentions. Some people clearly become highly 'involved' or engaged in sports, the arts and other lifestyle or leisure interests and are therefore more committed to events. Commitment and resulting 'event careers' can also be work or business-related, which moves into the area of serious leisure we will examine later. Identifying and catering to the 'highly involved' is of particular interest to event designers and marketers and is a focus of marketing strategies, including the increased use of social media.

Planning, design and management

Planned events happen by conscious human design; they are created by organizations with many stakeholders, usually with specific goals in mind. This is largely the event management or business domain, focusing as it does on mobilizing resources, transforming processes, management systems and professionalism. Yet as events are means towards an end (e.g. profit, celebration, branding, political benefits, place marketing), we always must carefully assess goals and take a multi-stakeholder approach, meaning we need to be cognizant of the wider range of objectives and needs of hosting associated with a specific event. This leads us into the realm of event tourism (Getz and Page 2016), wherein events have specific roles to play in attracting tourists, fostering a positive destination image and acting as animators and catalysts within a specific location, region or country. It is also the 'urban imaging' question (part of place marketing) in which, according to Hall (2005: 198), events play a prominent role as places increasingly compete with each other for visitors' attention and event spending.

Chapter 7 is specifically devoted to event design, as it needs to follow directly from the discussion of planned event experiences and meanings to illustrate how to create events that match with expectations and visitor preferences, while the remaining planning and management topics are covered in Chapter 9. Each of the key management 'functions' is discussed in turn, not in a 'how-to' style, but to stress the main topics within each function, their disciplinary foundations and unique issues or applications for events. Examples of event-specific research are provided to illustrate the application of theory in practice.

Outcomes and the impacted

'Outcomes' are a dominant area of growth in event studies research and whilst they appear to follow logically from many of the other themes, they can also be a starting point in their own right for the analysis of events as a phenomenon that affects people and environments. Many events are created or assisted by authorities and sponsors, with intended outcomes clearly expressed. Tourism organizations work backwards from the goals of putting bums on seats or beds, then decide what events to bid on, create or market. Sponsors determine which target segments to build relationships with, or to sell to, then decide on their event-marketing strategies. Government agencies routinely formulate social and cultural policies, then assist the event sector in implementing those policies. Impacts can also be unintended and unmeasured, giving rise to evaluation and accountability problems which make the assessment of impacts an interesting pursuit but intensely political, as different factions seek to interpret the findings for their own political purposes.

In Chapter 10 we discuss evaluation and impact assessment, distinguishing between short-term outputs (goal-attainment that event producers need to measure) and longer-term outcomes or impacts that stem from the intention to make events agents of change. The 'subjects and objects' of evaluation and impact assessment are fully examined, with the 'objects' being social, cultural, ecological, economic and built-environment outcomes, and the 'subjects' being the people, organizations or things that are affected by events and event tourism.

Patterns and processes

The theme 'patterns and processes' represents the broader environmental influences and the dynamic aspects of our event studies 'system': temporal processes; geographical (spatial) patterns; policy; and creating knowledge. Chapter 4 presents the three disciplines of history, human geography and future studies. Together they help us answer questions like 'where do events come from and how do they evolve over time? How are they distributed in time and space, and why? What cultural and political, technological and economic forces shape events?'

Policy is a theme running throughout the book, with Chapter 11 devoted to events and public policy. Policy is a force that both reacts to and shapes the planned event system. Events are increasingly influenced by formal government policy, including funding and regulations. Numerous events are created and marketed for strategic policy reasons, usually economic, but also cultural and social. And as events become larger and generate more substantial impacts, they cannot be ignored by policy-makers and political parties. Specific attention is given to what event-related policy should consist of, in an integrated approach, and how it should be formulated.

Creating knowledge about events is the remaining theme of importance, which is discussed in Chapter 12. The greater the volume of research, theory and management knowledge that is generated, the better we will be at creating meaningful experiences, formulating effective policy, achieving goals, marketing events and preventing or managing outcomes. To accomplish this requires knowledge about knowledge-creation! What is the nature of knowledge and theory, what are the appropriate methodologies and techniques we can use, and how should events-related research be done? Chapter 12 also provides a research agenda for advancing event studies and some specific suggestions for research projects. In Chapter 12 the book's conclusions are presented, emphasizing the big ideas discussed throughout.

A theory of planned events?

It is unlikely that a single, grand theory can be advanced to cover all important aspects of planned events, but a set of interrelated theories that deals with the key elements is within reach. These constructs, assembled in an interdisciplinary fashion from available theories adapted to events, provide substantial explanatory power regarding all the important elements of the framework. This is how many areas of leisure and tourism studies have developed through time, and events seem to be following a similar pathway to harnessing the interdisciplinarity of event studies. We need integrative theory that accomplishes the following:

- explains the roles and importance of planned events in human society and culture (this covers antecedents and meanings, spatial and temporal patterns), addressing a key challenge of how event spaces are transformed through a temporary activity that redefines how people view and enjoy everyday spaces;
- provides deep insight into the evolution of events, including indications of how various forms of events and their functions are developing (this covers policy, strategy and environmental forces);
- explains how event experiences are influenced, and how meanings – at the levels of personal, group and society – are attached to event experiences (this covers the core phenomenon and also planning, management and design, antecedents and consequences);
- suggests ways in which the outcomes of planned events can be predicted and controlled, as in establishment of cause-and-effect-relationships (this covers planning, policy and outcomes).

Throughout this book we will examine many theories and ideas that can help build the integrative sets of theory for planned events and these are brought together in the concluding chapter. Exchange theory provides fundamental insights on why civilization needs and creates events, both in an economic and cultural frame. A 'convergence model' is presented (see the final chapter), which pertains to the tendency for form and function to merge over time, particularly for larger events and when they serve political purposes. 'Serious leisure' combined with 'social world' theory shows us the connections between our leisure interests and events, while the 'event travel career trajectory' extends that line of reasoning to event tourism.

How the literature has evolved

Where do ideas come from, what are the seminal works in our field, and where do we go to get information and ideas? The creation of the first peer-reviewed journal for event studies in 1993 marked a major turning point, not only providing an outlet for researchers but also helping to legitimize the field of studies. At first this and other applied fields were multidisciplinary in nature, drawing from the theories and methodologies of various established disciplines. With the creation of a number of publishing outlets for event-related research, the era of interdisciplinary research began – that is, developing new theories and methods designed explicitly for event studies. All this has greatly hastened the number of researchers and publications, and, more recently, has led to an explosion in specialized book topics. Figure 1.4 shows selected publications prior to 1980 and for the period 1981–1992. The early period included a number of one-off studies, especially from sociological and anthropological perspectives. After 1981 we see an acceleration of event-specific research in the tourism periodicals, then in event-specific journals. Along the way are notable books that helped shape the field.

Several reviews of the research literature have been published, and for a historical overview consult the works of Formica (1998), Getz (2000b) and Harris *et al.* (2001). Hede *et al.* (2003) reviewed special events research for the period 1990–2002. Sherwood's doctoral dissertation (2007) also entailed a large-scale review of pertinent literature and specifically examined 85 event economic impact studies prepared in Australia. A more recent review by Mair and Whitford (2013) concluded that the majority of research had focused on economic impacts, yet even more work on this topic is needed. Mair and Whitford (2013) acknowledged that the most important topics for future research were socio-cultural and community impacts, then environmental impacts and sustainability issues, as well as the policy dimensions of event tourism.

The major Routledge four-volume collection of key studies in the field, *Event Tourism* (Connell and Page 2010 – see Figure 1.5) is also significant because this compendium traced the evolution of key studies back to the 1920s with the Allix's (1922) publication on fairs. One might also argue that the professional field of event management pre-dates the academic study of this phenomenon, as the first convention and visitors bureau (CVB) was established in the USA at Detroit in 1896 (Ford and Peeper 2007). Interestingly, as Ford and Peeper (2007) found, there were also examples, pre-dating Detroit, of attracting meetings and convention business to towns and cities, facilitated by the spread of the railroad in the USA. Therefore, the academic study of the professional events sector has taken several hundreds of years to reach fruition, and if sporting events such as the Olympiad are included, then their management and organization – as opposed to their philosophical rationale – can be dated back to early civilization.

As Formica (1998) observed, there were few articles related to events management or tourism published in the 1970s – he found only four in *Annals of Tourism Research* and the *Journal of Travel Research* (*JTR*). Events were not yet 'attractions' within the tourism system of Gunn's landmark book, *Tourism Planning* (1979), although in passing he did mention 'places for festivals and conventions'. In the 1960s and 1970s, the events sector was not recognized as an area of separate study within leisure, tourism or recreation, all of which were rapidly growing in the academic community and in professional practice.

Ritchie and Beliveau published the first article specifically about event tourism in 1974, the topic being how 'hallmark events' could combat the seasonality of tourism demand. They examined the Quebec Winter Carnival and included the citation of an unpublished study of the economic impacts of this event, dated in 1962. Most of the pioneering published studies were event economic impact assessments, notably Della Bitta *et al.* (1977), who reported on a Tall Ships event. Another early study of the economic impacts of event tourism was conducted by Vaughan in Edinburgh in 1979, where the Tourism Recreation Research Unit at the University of Edinburgh had recently been established.

Event tourism expanded dramatically as a research topic in the 1980s. Two notable research articles from early in this decade were those by Gartner and Holecek (1983), on the economic impact of an annual tourism industry exposition, and Ritchie (1984), on the nature of impacts from hallmark events, which remains a classic in terms of citations and influence. A major study of festival visitors and the economic impacts of multiple festivals in Canada's National Capital Region was conducted in the latter part of this decade (Coopers and Lybrand 1989), followed by a similar major study in Edinburgh (Scotinform Ltd 1991). These remain landmarks in terms of their scope and cross-event comparisons. However, the most recent update of the Edinburgh Festivals Impact Study (BOP Consulting 2011) expands the scope of this important research through a triple-bottom-line approach.

Mill and Morrison's (1985) USA-based text *The Tourism System* explicitly recognized the power of events. The 1985 TTRA Canada Chapter conference was themed 'International Events: The Real Tourism Impact' (Travel and Tourism Research Association and Canada Chapter (TTRA) 1986), with the impetus coming

1922–1980

- Allix, A. (1922). The geography of fairs. *Geographical Review*, 12(4), 532–569.
- Naik, T. (1948). Aboriginal festivals in Gujarat. *Easter Anthropologist*, 2(1), 16–21.
- Boorstin, D. (1961). *The image: A guide to pseudo-events in America*. New York: Harper & Row.
- Turner, V. (1969). *The ritual process: Structure and anti-structure*. New York: Aldine de Gruyter.
- Greenwood, D. (1972). Tourism as an agent of change: A Spanish Basque case study. *Ethnology*, 11, 89–91.
- Ritchie, J. R. B. and Beliveau, D. (1974). Hallmark events: An evaluation of a strategic response to seasonality in the travel market. *Journal of Travel Research*, 14, 14–20.
- Turner, V. (1974). Liminal to liminoid, in play, flow and ritual: An essay in comparative symbology. In E. Norbeck (ed.), *The Anthropological Study of Human Play*, 60, 53–92. Rice University Studies.
- Duvignaud, J. (1976). Festivals – sociological approach. *Cultures*, 3(1), 14–25.
- Della Bitta, A., Loudon, D., Booth, G. and Weeks, R. (1978). Estimating the economic impact of a short-term tourist event. *Journal of Travel Research*, 16, 10–15.
- Vaughan, R. (1979). *Does a Festival Pay? A Case Study of the Edinburgh Festival in 1976*. Tourism Recreation Research Unit, Working paper 5, University of Edinburgh.
- Davidson, L. and Schaffer, W. (1980). A discussion of methods employed in analyzing the impact of short-term entertainment events. *Journal of Travel Research*, 28(3), 12–16.
- Lavenda, R. H. (1980). The festival of progress: The globalizing world-system and the transformation of the Caracas carnival. *Journal of Popular Culture*, 14(3), 465–475.

1981–1992

- Turner, V. (ed.). (1982). *Celebration: Studies in Festivity and Ritual*. Washington: Smithsonian Institution Press.
- Gartner, W. and Holocek, D. (1983). Economic impact of an annual tourism industry exposition. *Annals of Tourism Research*, 10(2), 199–212.
- Ritchie, J. R. B. (1984). Assessing the impacts of hallmark events: Conceptual and research issues. *Journal of Travel Research*, 23(1), 2–11.
- Olds, K. and Ley, D. (1988). Landscape as spectacle: World's fairs and the culture of heroic consumption. *Environment and Planning D: Society and Space*, 6, 191–212.
- Syme, G., Shaw, B., Fenton, D. and Mueller, W. (eds) (1989). *The Planning and Evaluation of Hallmark Events*. Aldershot: Gower.
- Getz, D. (1989). Special events: Defining the product. *Tourism Management*, 10(2), 135–137.
- Hall, C. M. (1989). The definition and analysis of hallmark tourist events. *GeoJournal*, 19(3), 263–268.
- Handelman, D. (1990). *Models and Mirrors: Towards an Anthropology of Public Events*. Oxford: Berghahn Books.
- Goldblatt, J. (1990). *Special Events: The Art and Science of Celebration*. New York: Van Nostrand Rheinhold.
- Getz, D. (1991). *Festivals, Special Events, and Tourism*. New York: Van Nostrand Rheinhold.
- Ritchie, J. R. B. and Smith, B. (1991). The impact of a mega-event on host region awareness: A longitudinal study. *Journal of Travel Research*, 30(1), 3–10.
- Hall, C. M. (1992). *Hallmark Tourist Events: Impacts, Management and Planning*. London: Belhaven.

Figure 1.5 Selected early event studies, 1922–1992

from the planned 1986 Vancouver World's Fair and the 1988 Calgary Winter Olympics. Internationally, the AIEST (1987) conference produced a notable collection of material on the general subject of mega events.

Australian scholars were involved with event tourism very early and their influence has continued, especially with substantial research funding (now terminated) from the Cooperative Research Centre programme in Sustainable Tourism. Prior to the America's Cup Defence in Perth in 1988, the People and Physical Environment Research Conference (America's Cup Office 1987) was held under the theme of the

Effects of Hallmark Events on Cities. Soutar and McLeod (1993) later published research on residents' perceptions of that major event. One of the most influential research projects of that period was the comprehensive assessment of impacts from the first Adelaide Grand Prix (Burns *et al.* 1986). At the end of the 1980s, Syme *et al.* (1989) published a book entitled *The Planning and Evaluation of Hallmark Events*, and Hall (1989) wrote an article on the definition and analysis of hallmark tourist events which noted the need for greater attention to social and cultural impacts.

In 1990, a landmark year in the event management literature, as Goldblatt's book *Special Events: The Art and Science of Celebration* was published, followed by *Festivals, Special Events and Tourism* (Getz 1991) and a year later *Hallmark Tourist Events* by C. M. Hall (1992). In the early 1990s, academics were clearly leading the way, as at that time there were few if any degree programmes and few courses available anywhere that featured event management or tourism. In the USA, George Washington University pioneered event management education, leading Hawkins and Goldblatt (1995), in a journal article, to address the need for event management education. Interestingly, their article also asked how events should be treated within a tourism curriculum. The mid- to late 1990s were the 'take-off' years for the academic institutionalization of event management, and with it a more legitimized advancement of scholarship on event tourism and event studies. This process has been roughly 25–30 years behind the equivalent for tourism, hospitality and leisure. There is also no doubt that tourism, hospitality and leisure provided a large part of the foundation, having adapted discipline-based theory and methodology, supporting event-specific courses, and spinning off event management degree programmes.

The journal *Festival Management and Event Tourism* (later renamed *Event Management*) was founded by Don Getz and Bruce Wicks in 1993, with vital support from Bob Miranda, President of Cognizant Communications Corp. Uysal *et al.* (1993), in the very first issue, began an enduring research theme on why people attend and travel to festivals and events, while Wicks and Fesenmaier (1993) looked at service quality at events and Getz (1993a) examined organizational culture. In the next year, Bos (1994) examined the importance of mega events in generating tourism demand, and Crompton and McKay's (1994) article on measuring the economic impacts of events set the stage for many subsequent impact studies. John Crompton's many contributions also include his research-based book, published by the National Recreation and Park Association in 1999 and entitled *Measuring the Economic Impact of Visitors to Sport Tournaments and Special Events*. In 1997, the *Journal of Convention & Exhibition Management* was launched (renamed the *Journal of Convention & Event Tourism* in 2004), with a broad focus on the convention and exhibition world in contrast to *Event Management*.

A very large number of research projects were commenced in Australia in preparation for the Sydney 2000 Summer Olympic Games. Faulkner *et al.* (2000) reported on this impressive initiative and many papers were subsequently published. As the twentieth century closed, the world celebrated with numerous special events. No doubt this gave a boost to the events sector and its tourism value. Several noteworthy articles were published right at the turn of the century, including state-of-the-art commentary and methodology for conducting event impact assessments by Dwyer *et al.* (2000a, 2000b). These more or less laid to rest any debate on what needed to be done, and how to do it validly, although the Cooperative Research Centre for Sustainable Tourism in Australia continued (through to 2009) to release impact studies and models (notably Jago and Dwyer 2006).

With so much attention having been given previously to the economic dimensions of event tourism, it was to be expected that scholars would seek more balance. Although research on social and cultural impacts of events goes back to occasional anthropological studies like Greenwood (1972), the conceptual overview provided by J. R. B. Ritchie (1984) and a noteworthy piece of sociological research by Cunneen and Lynch (1988), who studied ritualized rioting at a sport event, suggest that the decade beginning in 2000 really ushered in a systematic and theoretically grounded line of comprehensive event impact research. This has led to important discussions on sustainability.

The literature on events has now grown beyond anyone's capability of reading it all, with a number of distinct specializations having emerged. In very practical terms, this probably defines 'maturity' or at least the path towards impending maturity. The longstanding divisions based on types of events remain (especially sports events, business events and festivals), the Olympics will always attract its own scholarship, while world's fairs and other mega events retain an allure, much of which can be dated to major events such as the 1851 Great Exhibition in London that continue to attract scholarly attention from the social science community for the wider impact on society and economy.

The field has evolved to the point where the emphasis is now on specific aspects of event management/ tourism, specific types of events and event-related research and discourses. A summary of recent specialized books, mostly since 2010 (see Table 1.1), illustrates the growing diversity and depth of event studies and provides a handy starting point for students and researchers interested in particular topics or broader themes (also see the Further Reading lists suggested at the end of each chapter).

Table 1.1 A summary of recent specialized books

Book themes	Selected book titles and authors
Arts and culture	Yeoman *et al.* 2004; Du Cros and Joliffe 2014
Audiences and their expectations	MacKellar 2013a
Battlefield events	Reeves *et al.* 2015
Careers	Columbus 2011
Commemorative events	Frost and Laing 2013
Community festivals and events	Jepson and Clarke 2014; Clarke and Jepson 2016
Concepts in events	Silvers 2004
Coordination	Quinn 2013
Design	Monroe and Kates 2005; Berridge 2007; Malouf 2011; Richards *et al.* 2014; Frissen *et al.* 2016
Disciplinary perspective on research	Finkel *et al.* 2013; Pernecky 2016
Enduring festivals	Derrett 2015
Entertainment	Sonder 2003
Entrepreneurship	Olberding 2016
Ethics and social responsibility	Henderson and McIlwraith 2013
Evaluation	Getz 2018
Fashion events	Williams *et al.* 2013
Feasibility	O'Toole 2011
Food/beverage events	Hall and Sharples 2008; Cavicchi and Santini 2014
Future of events	Yeoman *et al.* 2014
Geography	Salazar *et al.* (2016); Hannam *et al.* 2016; Wise and Harris 2017
Handbook of events	Page and Connell 2011
Human resources	Van der Wagen 2006; Van der Wagen and White 2014; Baum *et al.* 2009
Marketing and communications	Hoyle 2002; Masterman and Wood 2006; Preston 2012; Reic 2016

(continued)

Table 1.1 (continued)

Book themes	Selected book titles and authors
Meetings, conventions, exhibitions	Davidson and Cope 2003; Davidson and Rogers 2006; Fenich 2005; Krugman and Wright 2006; Mair 2013; Rogers 2013; Rogers and Davidson 2015
Music	Gibson and Connell 2012
Olympics	Preuss 2004; Roche 2017; Theodoraki 2007; Toohey and Veal 2007; Poynter and MacRury 2009; Gold and Gold 2010; Hiller 2012; Weed 2012
Operations management	Tum *et al.* 2006
Policy	Foley *et al.* 2011
Portfolio management	Ziakas 2013; Antchak, Ziakas and Getz 2019
Power and politics	Merkel 2013; Lamond and Spracken 2015
Project management and logistics	O'Toole and Mikolaitis 2002
Risk	Tarlow 2002; Silvers 2008; Piekarz *et al.* 2015; O'Toole *et al.* 2019; Wynn-Moylan 2017
Rituals and traditional events	Laing and Frost 2014
Social change	Picard and Robinson 2006a, 2006b; Roche 2017
Social impacts	Richards *et al.* 2013; Moufakkir and Pernecky 2014; Taks *et al.* 2017
Sponsorship	Skinner and Rukavina 2003
Sport and events	Solomon 2002; Masterman 2004; Funk 2012; Shipway and Fyall 2012; Preuss 2013; Dashper *et al.* 2014; Tyson *et al.* 2016
Stakeholders	Van Niekerk and Getz 2019
Sustainability, the environment and green operations	Raj and Musgrave 2009; Jones 2018; Goldblatt and Goldblatt 2011; Pernecky and Luck 2013; Case 2013
Theoretical analysis	Rojek 2013
Tourism	Getz 2013a
Urban events	Richards and Palmer 2010; Smith 2012, 2015; Viehoff and Poynter 2015
Value and events	Lundberg *et al.* 2017
Visitor attractions and events	Baum *et al.* 2009; Smith *et al.* 2014
Volunteering	Weidenfeld *et al.* 2015
World's fairs (expos)	Mattie and George 1998; Findling and Pelle 2008; Greenhalgh 2011

Major subdivisions (discourses) within event studies

It is clear that there are three predominant subdivisions (or discourses) concerning planned events. While they tend to run in separate directions, it is essential for event studies to integrate them more fully. An online article by Getz (2010) concerning festivals provides a substantive basis for this interpretation of the literature, with over 400 citations along with more recent syntheses such as the *Routledge Handbook of Events* (Page and Connell 2011), with its wider social science reach.

Discipline-based approaches

Many disciplines contribute to an understanding of the roles, meanings, importance and effects of planned events in society and culture. These disciplines employ their own methodologies and theories, reflecting different research paradigms (i.e. a distinctive approach with its own methodologies, concepts and view of the world), and they all contribute something of value to event studies. The key point is that in each discipline (and in many closely related fields) the focus is not on events – events are one of many phenomena being studied. And the object is not to develop theory about events. Later in this book, each of the foundation disciplines and related fields is examined for their contributions. The best-established lines of pertinent research are from cultural anthropology and sociology, which might be labelled 'classical' discourse, in which some of the important topics are rites, rituals, symbolism and celebration. In particular, these concepts, along with liminality and communitas, play a key part in the model of the planned event experience developed in this book.

Event tourism

'Event tourism' is an applied area within event studies, as it takes an instrumentalist approach. An ontological mapping of the literature (see Figure 1.6) clearly reveals the dominant themes to be the production, attraction and marketing of festivals and events for tourism and other forms of development, with a heavy methodological emphasis on marketing and economic impact assessment. A thorough review of the

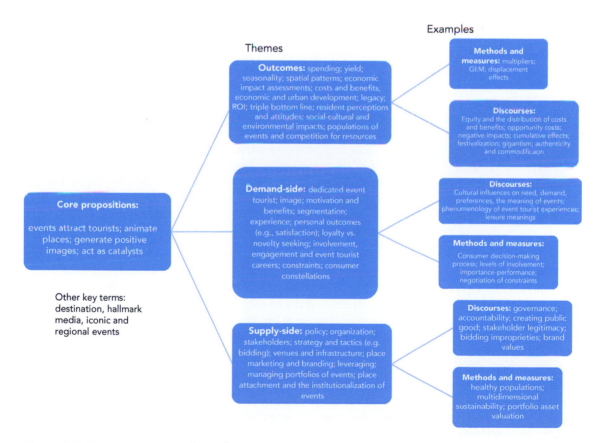

Figure 1.6 Event tourism: ontological mapping

literature within this discourse has been published in an article by Getz (2008) as well as the book *Event Tourism* (Getz 2013a), and is the subject of a four-volume set by Connell and Page (2010).

The roles of events in tourism and development constitute the core propositions that created and delimit this sub-field. They are: (1) events attract tourists (to specific places, and to overcome seasonality); (2) events contribute to place marketing (including image formation and destination branding); (3) events animate attractions and places, which essentially means that anyone with a park or facility is almost automatically in the events business; and (4) events can act as catalysts for other forms of development or improved capacity to attract tourists through infrastructure gains and more effective marketing. These 'propositions' are not theories because it is not possible to use the experience of others or the findings of available research to explain or predict the precise impacts of event-tourism policies, strategies or actions. Rather, the collective wisdom that propels event tourism is the belief, based on experience and analysis, that desired outcomes can be obtained through development and marketing efforts. Accordingly, each 'proposition' must be understood as containing an inherent element of uncertain outcomes.

Ontological mapping is concerned with claims to knowledge within fields of study, and therefore terminology is important. The key terms unique to event tourism include descriptors that explicitly reflect the tourism-related roles of events, namely hallmark, signature, iconic, mega, regional or media. These types of event have a role to play in the planning and management of event portfolios, as assets for destinations to value.

Dominating this discourse has been three themes, each embodying key terminology and concepts that set it somewhat apart from the others. The first theme is that of outcomes, with the emphasis placed on assessment of economic impacts of events and event tourism. Figure 1.6 mentions a number of lines of research, with key topics being event-tourist expenditure and yield, seasonality effects, estimation of gross and net economic impacts, occasionally more comprehensive studies of costs and benefits, return on investment and an interest in leveraging events and planning for long-term legacies such as urban renewal or re-positioning in a place-branding context. The general acceptance of a sustainability paradigm by academics has led to a more triple-bottom-line approach encompassing environmental and socio-cultural impacts, so that resident perceptions and attitudes are now a very important topic, and this has expanded into a multi-stakeholder approach to evaluating outcomes. Moreover, the dominant positivistic emphasis on measuring impacts in monetary terms is giving way to a more interpretive, and sometimes critical, evaluation of the roles, costs and benefits of events, including the matter of exactly who gains or loses. As this matures we can expect to see more research and practical applications of portfolio management (i.e. cumulative and long-term value from events as assets) on the dynamics of populations of events, within which competition for resources and markets is a dominant consideration.

Figure 1.6 also indicates some methods and measures being employed in each theme, some of which are unique to event tourism. Displacement effects are in this category – as an event has the potential to displace other tourists (especially if held in peak seasons) – as is time displacement, which occurs when people alter their planned or necessary travel in order to take in an event. The term 'casual event tourist' refers to those non-residents who attend an event but do not travel because of its attraction. Also indicated in the diagram are various discourses found in the literature, and sometimes they occur politically, with the dominant one being economic or financial justification of public-sector intervention in the events and tourism marketplaces. To justify venues, bidding, marketing and hosting events governments generally require economic impact assessments and measures of public attitudes and support. Academics and certain interest groups like to ask more difficult questions, including those pertaining to the ideal of requiring full cost and benefit disclosure and attention to the distribution of impacts (especially: which elite groups benefit? and which disadvantaged segments pay the price?). Often hidden in event accounts are externalities like security costs and inflation, crime and pollution, giving rise to debates over measurement and disclosure. Opportunity costs are a related concern, as events and tourism are not necessarily the only or best way to achieve policy aims. As events have become standard tools in development, more and more attention and debate can be expected regarding long-term and cumulative impacts (which relates to the concepts of event portfolios and populations).

Theme two is analysis and development of demand. Event-tourism markets can be generally separated into business events, sports, entertainment, festivals and other cultural celebrations. Within each of these markets the emphasis is placed on dedicated event tourists, which are those individuals who travel principally because of an event. Key research topics have included studies of motivation and the benefits sought, the image of events and their venues and host destinations, satisfaction, the overall event-tourist experience and effects on future behaviour including event or destination loyalty.

When it comes to the supply side of the development equation, there are many actors involved within the public, private and not-for-profit sectors. Not all events are produced with tourism in mind, but they might nevertheless attract tourists or entertain casual visitors to a city. Organizers might want tourists as one segment, even if they emphasize appealing to residents. On the other hand are event development corporations that have the explicit mandate of bidding on events, creating them, and marketing destinations through the appeal and imagery of events. Business events – and sports in particular – are capital intensive, generally requiring major facilities; they are often developed by separate organizations such as convention bureaus and sport (tourism) commissions. Cultural celebrations, and especially festivals, are favoured by communities all around the world in part because they are not necessarily capital intensive, can be created anywhere, and tap into both community and tourist desires for authentic social and cultural experiences.

MICE is an acronym for meetings, incentives, conventions and exhibitions (Schlentrich 2008). Often described as an 'industry', it is better thought of as a collection of primarily business events that depend on specific types of facilities called convention and/or exhibition centres. Smaller MICE venues can be described as meeting or assembly venues and are often within hotels, resorts and other facilities. Incentive travel does not quite fit into planned events, although it is possible that a tour arranged as a reward for star employees or leading salespeople can be considered a special event from their perspective. Such a tour might also include small events like parties, seminars and exhibitions.

It is worth noting that theory development in event tourism borrows heavily from economics and consumer behaviour. Much of the knowledge base of this discourse is, however, purely 'factual' (what you need to know in order to develop event tourism) and of the problem-solving kind (how to attract tourists). In looking for event-specific theory, we need to refine the concept of 'attractiveness' as it applies to various events (that is, their drawing power for specific segments) and in the context of combating seasonality of demand and the over-concentration of tourism. Seasonality refers to the way in which destinations see a rise and fall in demand as visitors peak at certain points in time and decline at others.

Connell *et al.* (2015: 285) suggested that:

> As Getz (2010) argues, the strategic development of events and festivals at a destination level has an important role to play in attracting visitors, contributing to place marketing and expanding the economic impact of tourism. Within this positive frame, events are widely positioned as a strategic tool to assist in combating seasonality, a premise established in an early study by Ritchie and Beliveau (1974).

Connell *et al.* (2015) describe how one sector of the visitor economy (i.e. Scottish visitor attractions) sought to harness events to address seasonality, particularly the very concentrated patterns of tourism visitation in Scotland. As Figures 1.7 and 1.8 show, the conceptual framework used by Connell *et al.*

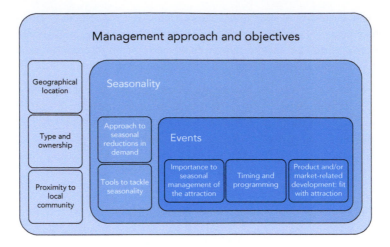

Figure 1.7 Simplified conceptual framework

Source: Connell *et al.* (2015: 285). Reprinted from *Tourism Management*, 46, Connell, J. Page, S. J. and Meyer, D., Visitor attractions and events: Responding to seasonality, 283–298, Copyright (2015), with permission from Elsevier.

- Hartman (1986) argued that the complexity of seasonality is created by the interplay of factors in both origin and destination areas where flows of tourism are conditioned by a wide range of social and cultural factors (e.g. imagery), economic factors (e.g. price) and physical factors (e.g. the availability of skiing in winter periods).
- Seasonality has both a distinct time-based element and a more neglected spatial component. Hartman (1986: 12) defined tourism seasonality as 'temporal variance in the phenomenon of tourism activities' and acknowledged the existence of a spatial element.
- Butler (2001: 5) argued that 'little research has addressed the problem of whether seasonality varies in nature and intensity on a spatial basis either within or between destination areas'. The point is further reaffirmed by Baum and Lundtorp (2001), who argue that there is no concept or theory of tourism seasonality.
- Butler and Mao (1997) recognize that urban tourism is often the least seasonally affected form of tourism; seasonal spatial patterns within destinations are not readily charted and understood.
- Seasonal variations in destination characteristics can act as a magnet for visitors seeking ephemeral experiences linked with climate or nature, such as the autumn market (Spencer and Holecek 2007), as well as economic-driven destination experiences such as Christmas markets (see Haid *et al.* 2006).

Figure 1.8 Perspectives on tourism and seasonality that inform events research

Source: Connell *et al.* (2015: 285).

(2015) demonstrates how the analysis of event tourism has to span various disciplines (i.e. geography, economics, politics and policy analysis and management) to understand the nuances of event activity and its use in specific business contexts. This study also highlights the wider need to understand how substitution of demand from tourism markets can be adapted to include residents and the school markets in terms of building the business opportunities which off-peak events (see Table 1.2) can provide as businesses understand what event themes appeal to visitors. Such research also indicates the notion of an event travel career trajectory for people who become more and more involved in serious leisure pursuits, building an increasing engagement with events as part of holiday and weekly leisure experiences.

Table 1.2 Off-peak seasonal theming of visitor attractions

- Harvest theme, with a focus on harvest produce, local foods and traditional celebrations of food production and rural life, such as Apple Day (September/October).

- Hallowe'en, with a clear focus on attracting families with children for low-scare experiences (e.g. dressing-up, pumpkin carving, storytelling), and for adults/adult groups with moderate scare experiences (e.g. ghost tours, theatrical events and other entertainment) (late October, and corresponding with the half-term school holiday in the UK).

- Christmas preparations/celebrations, often with a primary focus on shopping, where attractions offer a significant retail operation, and special menus in restaurants/cafés. This can help to keep a shop and café open even if the main attraction remains closed (December). Attractions may also offer limited opening for special Christmas events, e.g. in England and Wales, National Trust houses traditionally close in winter for conservation purposes but now offer limited opening with a Christmas theme such as 'dressing the house for Christmas'.

Source: Connell *et al.* (2015: 286).

Olympic and mega event tourism

Mega events have a special appeal, so a great deal of attention is always focused on major sporting events and particularly the Olympic Games. While the basic tourism-related issues are often the same, mega events are quite different in terms of policy, funding and urban impacts. Tourism flows are altered (both positively in the immediate period of the event and often negatively in the lagged effect post-event), but it must be remembered that there are always finite limits to the number of tickets that can be sold to visitors. World's fairs have much more potential to attract large numbers of tourists because of their scale and length. All mega events are viewed as promotional tools, so that image-enhancing effects are potentially much greater than direct tourism impacts. *The Economics of Staging the Olympics* by Preuss (2004) includes an assessment of tourism impacts, while the book *Olympic Tourism* by Weed (2008) pays special attention to the nature of tourism related to the Olympics and how the Games can be leveraged for broader and longer-term benefits.

Education and careers in event tourism

Once the preserve of marketing professionals, now numerous DMOs (Destination Marketing Organizations) and special-purpose event development agencies are employing event-tourism professionals who understand the roles events can play in destination development and marketing. In the UK, People 1st (2010) reported that the majority of graduates produced from event programmes had been absorbed into the industry. The ability to absorb these graduates reflects the scale and significance of this sector in the UK (which is also seen in many other countries):

- Events are worth £42 billion to UK economy
- Some 570,000 jobs in events exist in 25,000 businesses
- The top event destination in the UK is London
- Events attract 85 million attendees a year and around 1.3 million business events are held every year
- The economic value of events comprise:
  1 Conferences and meetings valued at £19.9 billion
  2 Exhibitions and trade fairs valued at £11.0 billion

3 Incentive travel and performance improvement valued at £1.2 billion

4 Corporate hospitality and corporate events valued at £1.2 billion

5 Outdoor events valued at £1.1 billion

6 Festivals and cultural events valued at £1.1 billion

7 Music events valued at £1.3 billion

8 Sporting events valued at £2.3 billion

Source: Eventbrite (2018), https://www.eventbrite.co.uk/blog/academy/
uk-event-industry-in-numbers-ds00/

An educational background in tourism, events and marketing is a suitable basis for employment, but increasingly there will be specializations within event development agencies and DMOs. Table 1.3 presents a number of positions and key associated tasks.

Event management

The first major textbook on this subject was Professor Goldblatt's *Special Events: The Art and Science of Celebration* (first published in 1990, with the seventh edition in 2014), and Goldblatt has remained at the forefront of event management studies and professional development through multiple books. This was followed closely by Getz (1991) with the book *Festivals, Special Events and Tourism*, and a year later came M. Hall's book, *Hallmark Tourist Events* (1992). Raj *et al.* (2008), Allen *et al.* (2011), Bowdin *et al.* (2011) and Shone and Parry (2004) have also produced notable texts. In addition, there are many more practical books from the event practitioners' point of view, such as the series written by Judy Allen (e.g. Allen 2008, 2014).

Table 1.3 Careers in event tourism

Typical functions	Major tasks
Event facilitator/coordinator	Work with events in the destination to help realize their tourism potential (funding, advice, marketing)
	Liaise with convention/exhibition centres and other venues Liaise with sport and other organizations that produce events
Event tourism producer	Create and produce events specifically for their tourism value Stakeholder management (with numerous event partners)
Event tourism planner	Develop a strategy for the destination
	Integrate events with product development and image making/branding
Event tourism policy analyst and researcher	Work with policy-makers to facilitate event tourism
	Conduct research (e.g. feasibility studies, demand forecasting, impact assessments and performance evaluations)
Event bidding	Bid on events
	Develop relationships leading to winning events for the destination
	Conduct risk assessments and feasibility studies for each potential bid
Event services	Provide essential and special services to events (e.g. travel and logistics; accommodation and venue bookings; supplier contacts)

1.1 EXPERT OPINION

The many contributions of Professor Joe Goldblatt to the development of professionalism and education in event management are recognized around the world.

A future for planned events in education

Professor Joe Goldblatt, FRSA, Executive Director, International Centre for the Study of Planned Events, Queen Margaret University, Edinburgh, Scotland

Having spent nearly 30 years in the classroom as a teacher of event management and, most recently, event studies, I am convinced that events are a strong curricular current or stream that must flow throughout the entire curriculum in the future. The strong current that represents event studies is one that impacts every human life both personally and professionally throughout every lifetime.

Recently, the producer of the 2004 Olympic Games Opening Ceremony in Athens, Greece, asked me about the types of students we were producing to ensure a sustainable future for the field of planned events. I answered by describing how my curricular ambitions and outcomes had changed during the past quarter of a century in higher education.

When I first entered the classroom, my goal was to produce the next producer of the Super Bowl Half-Time Spectacular or other mega or hallmark event. However, over time, I have realized that it is far more important to return to the original goal of public education and that is to produce well-rounded citizens who are motivated and prepared to contribute to society. Part of this well-roundedness is the ability to appreciate and support planned events at the local, regional and national level. The legendary original producer of Disneyland's Main Street Electric Parade (Robert Jani, 1934–1989) once told me that 'The size of the event does not matter. What matters most is the integrity of the outcome.'

One example of this phenomenon was exemplified in a meeting I had with a third-year event studies student: 'I want to become a paediatric nurse,' she confided to me. When I asked why she was going to make this career change she answered, 'I have always loved children and everything I have learned in event studies will make me a better nurse.' This type of change of career is not uncommon for the millennial generation and therefore event studies is, I believe, excellent preparation for a lifetime of many different career pursuits. The skills one will learn in organization, time management, establishing aims and objectives, team work and other key workplace tasks will serve every student well, not just for their first job but their last one as well.

Throughout one's lifetime there are innumerable opportunities to attend, fund, support, participate in and even produce planned events. Whether you become a member of a local government council, a corporate officer or an event planner, you will have many opportunities to encourage the development and sustainability of planned events. Within higher education, the very best institutions will recognize this fact and provide you with opportunities to explore event studies as a stream that runs throughout the entire general studies curriculum.

We know now that event studies is the emerging field, as was tourism many years ago. It is based upon many different classic theorems from established disciplines, including, but not limited to, anthropology, psychology, sociology and others. Recently I have even explored and written an article in the field of eventology, with Professor Oleg Vorab of Russia, which is a subset of probability theory within mathematics. Perhaps one day you will be able, through a future scientific model, to help to better forecast or predict the outcome of a planned event and, through manipulation of some independent variables, actually improve the sustainability of the event itself.

Indeed, planned events and event studies have great potential throughout the entire curricular structure of a great modern institution of higher education. By recognizing the importance of events and their impact on everyday life, we may use planned events to incrementally or in some cases actually dramatically change the world within which we live now and in the future.

One day, public bodies and private sponsors may even link their future support to the planned events to positively impact not only the economy but also health, social cohesion, education and, of course, environmental sustainability. Therefore, it is important for institutions of higher education, and the faculty and students who populate these institutions, to recognize that event studies is an opportunity for significant social change.

The Scottish author Robert Louis Stevenson wrote, when describing my adopted city of Edinburgh, 'An *event* strikes root and grows into legend when it finds congenial surroundings.' Through a growing awareness of event studies and the potential planned events within human society, the world may indeed be greatly changed for the better, as you provide through event studies the congenial surroundings to create the stronger roots that indeed will one day grow into even more legendary events. Therefore, as you advance the field of event management to a much greater level in higher education through event studies, you must recognize that it is not as important to produce the next mega event as it is to help extend the roots that will grow our field of study and profession to achieve even greater heights in the future.

EMBOK, the event management body of knowledge (Silvers *et al.* 2006), has been created by practitioners and academics to codify the skills and knowledge required by professional event managers. There are five main knowledge domains: administration; design; marketing; operations; and risk, each with numerous subdivisions. Much of this knowledge base has to come from business or managerial literature. For example, 'marketing mix' and 'stakeholder management' are generic. The managerial and problem-solving skills needed by professionals are stressed, whereas theory is not addressed. EMBOK also has implications for licensing and cross-border job mobility. It tells academics what a full degree programme in event management should cover, but the means of acquiring all the pertinent skills and knowledge has to include on-the-job experience which underpins why the curriculum needs to be almost focused on employability and the link to work. This is even more the case than with predecessor vocation subjects such as sport, leisure and tourism that have contributed to the growth of event education. With the emphasis on organizing, managing, people interaction and operational issues, many curricula are underpinned by substantive placement elements and industry involvement in the delivery and production of degree programmes.

Event management and event studies interrelationships

Against this background of the growth of event education and research, the philosophy embodied in this book is unambiguous: teaching event management requires a blend of management fundamentals (easily obtained from business schools, but usually taught within event management or tourism/hospitality degree programmes) and the specific study of planned events. In this approach, specializations are taught after the fundamentals have been acquired, although we realize there will probably be continuing demand by students and professional bodies for a quick introduction to specialized career paths serviced by conversion Master's programmes, continuing professional development (CPD) and event MBA programmes in due course. The argument presented here is that event management is generic, and the knowledge can be applied to all types of events. But we need to understand the fundamentals of events as planned activities before we can begin to look at managing them.

Traditionally the specializations within events education have been aligned with professional bodies, including those devoted to meetings and conventions, exhibitions, festivals and sports. *We argue that this is now very antiquated thinking*, and it will not survive the rapid growth in event-related career paths that now include policy and analysis positions, private enterprise, new forms of events and the amazing possibilities opened up by global communications and social media for the co-creation of events. In the experience economy, increasingly diverse market segments (that is, social worlds or communities of interest) are generating their own events and event-travel careers. Specialization also occurs by the type of employer, namely venues and corporations, government departments and non-profit associations, all of which have unique perspectives on the roles of events. With generic event management as the foundation, all these possible specializations are open and available – as is the expanding boundaries of events into specialist fields such as facilities management.

In Table 1.4, major career paths in event management are illustrated, with sample job titles and pertinent professional associations. Many countries have their own national-level associations, and there are many certifications offered by educational institutions as well. The book *The Complete Guide to Careers in Special Events* by Columbus (2011) provides practical advice, and plenty of information, for the aspiring professional. See Chapter 9 for a discussion of theory and research on careers in the events sector.

Forces, trends and issues

What explains the rapid growth and expansion of planned events in the modern world? No one who has studied the events sector could conclude anything else, but will this trend continue? The sector has seen an unprecedented growth in the demand for event activity as well as a rise in the supply of event venues and activities since 1945. Ford and Peeper (2007) point to the early nineteenth-century willingness of Americans for association as one factor behind the growth of meetings and conventions. They also point to the willingness to share knowledge in the industrial age (compared to a secrecy culture in Europe) along with the need for people to spread out over a wide geographic area to gather in order to share new ideas and knowledge. Added to this was the need for boosterism by cities to overcome the impact of the 1890s' depression in the USA. This can best be summarized as the need for innovation in a fast-changing society, where industrialization was the powerhouse of the economy. Many of these general trends still remain important today: the desire for people to share ideas and knowledge in face-to-face meetings, with the added elements of consumer consumption and entertainment. What these evolutionary factors illustrate are the implications for the growth of individual events and the entire events sector. If we understand the underlying forces, document the trends and discuss the issues that arise, then surely we will be better able to plan for the future.

Table 1.5 summarizes the ensuing discussion, beginning with an overview of major forces.

Forces

For convenience, force-field analysis often follows the acronym PEST – which can be interpreted broadly to mean Population (including demographics) and Politics (with law), Economy and Environment, Society and Culture (including values), and Technology. While it is fairly easy to suggest powerful forces, these are usually interrelated and often compounding. And there is always tension between those forces propelling growth and those constraining it. So far, the forces that have propelled growth of the events sector are outstripping any resistance factors (also see the section on future studies for a related discussion).

Table 1.4 Careers in event management

Event types and settings	Sample job titles	Sample related professional associations and certifications
Festivals and special events		
Public, private and non-profit sectors Social and private entrepreneurship	Producer (overall responsibility for the festival) Designer (artistic, usually) Manager (general, or functional area) Coordinator (usually at city level)	International Festivals and Events Association (IFEA): Certified Festival and Event Executive (CFEE) International Special Events Society (ISES): Certified Special Events Professional (CSEP)
Meetings and conventions		
Private consulting companies Corporations Associations Government agencies Venues with meeting services and facilities	Meeting planner Event coordinator (at a convention or exhibition facility)	Convention Industry Council (CIC): Certified Meeting Professional (CMP) Meeting Professionals International (MPI): Certificate in Meeting Management (CMP; CMM) Professional Convention Management Association (PCMA): CMP
Exhibitions (trade and consumer shows)		
Companies producing and designing exhibitions Employees of exhibition venues	Exhibition producer/exhibition designer	International Association of Exhibitions and Events (IAEE): Certified in Exhibition Management (CEM)
Sports		
Employee of professional team Employee of amateur league Private company producing events Employee of venue	Sport event manager Sport coordinator	The Certified Sports Event Executive (CSEE) Programme, open only to National Association of Sport Commissions members, *www.sportscommissions.org*
Corporate events		
Employee of corporation Private consultant	Public relations manager Event producer	Generic event or meeting management
Venues		
Employee of facilities Consultant	Facility manager Event coordinator	International Association of Venue Managers (IAVM): Certified Facilities Executive (CFE)
Fairs		
	Fair manager, producer	International Association of Fairs and Expositions (IAFE): Certified Fair Executive (CFE)

Table 1.5 Forces, trends and issues related to planned events

Forces	Trends	Issues
Population		
Migration and diaspora Urbanization; urban stress Generational changes	Rising demand for events of all kinds Events for urban and rural identity, social integration Events reflecting changes in demography, diaspora	Can events relieve urban stresses? Bring diverse groups together? Are there limits to festivalization? What does the next generation want in planned events?
Politics and legal issues		
Country/global/civic (in) stability; protests, riots War, terror Policies affecting travel, culture, leisure and events	Events increasingly viewed as instruments of public policy; as foundations of civil society Increasing regulation and professionalism in the events sector	Education and training; certification of event professionals Danger of events being exploited for reasons of propaganda and ideology Danger zones (for tourists and residents)
Economics		
Wealth and disparity rising together Globalization Financial crises as a threat	Events increasingly viewed as instruments of corporate strategy Event tourism on the rise More events for profit	Commodification vs. authenticity Exclusion of the disadvantaged and dispossessed Elitism (owing to politics, pricing)
Environment		
Climate change Peak oil; renewable energy Water and food shortages	Threats to leisure and travel Threats to prosperity and peace	Need for events that are sustainable; events as social-marketing tools (for environmental change) Will event tourism become impossible?
Society and culture		
Values (favouring change or status quo?) Multiculturalism vs. exclusion	Experiences drive leisure and travel Diversity in event forms and cultural functions Social integration as a policy objective favouring new events; events and civil society	Proving that events solve problems and make things better Supporting sustainable event populations and portfolios
Technology		
Global communications Social media Potential to create and solve problems	Media events on the rise Social media affecting events Technology of marketing, logistics, producing events	Threat of spectacle replacing participation Virtual vs. live event experiences

Population

The world's rapidly growing population not only fuels growth in the demand and need for planned events, it is also a constant pressure on all of the planet's resources, recently giving rise to fears about food and water shortages, and the end of cheap (fossil-fuel) energy. Sustainability issues also arise from global climate change, which is projected to result in the serious displacement of populations and crises for the global economy. These are the main worries or limiting factors. Eventually they will profoundly influence the world in many ways.

Several aspects of population and demographics deserve special attention in the context of planned events. The first is large-scale migration, or diaspora, and the resulting changes in social life and culture. Many once homogeneous societies are now multicultural, and the mix is changing. This often imposes serious strains on the fabric of society, but also potentially enriches life. Most of the world's population, especially migrants, live in cities that are getting larger and more complex. Urban life is a source of many stressors on the environment and on human health. In many places rural areas continue to depopulate, while in others the divisions between rural and urban life have blurred because of lifestyle migrants, tourism and second homes. Events that bring people together and provide identity for persons, groups and places have taken on much greater significance.

Intergenerational differences, and the process of changing values and preferences over time, have not been studied to any extent in the context of events, particularly the contribution to Quality of Life (Jepson and Stadler 2017) and the new methodologies being developed to understand emotion, memory creation and the resulting psychosocial effects of event attendance (Stadler, Jepson and Wood 2018; Wood and Kenyon 2018). We have to borrow extensively from psychology, leisure and tourism studies to provide these insights, but there is no doubt that younger generations are going to have to deal with many more serious challenges, compared with the post-war baby-boomers, and many different opportunities. One of these is ageing as populations across the globe live longer and have more active lives in later life (Rowland 2012). This is also shown in Figure 1.9 with forecasts of the growth of world population to 2100 and the rise in an ageing population globally.

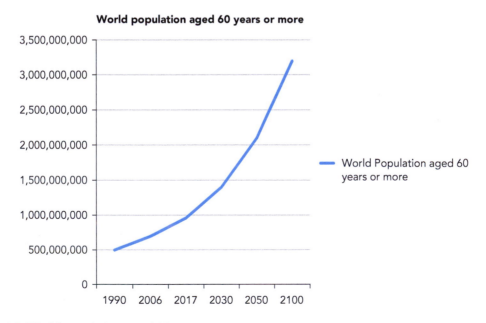

Figure 1.9 World population aged 60 years or more

Changes related to ageing have been described as the *Third Age* by Laslett (1989) in terms of a new stage of later life where one derives personal fulfilment from the activities they pursue. Blaikie (1999) expanded the concept of the Third Age seeing it as a period of independent living in later life preceding the fourth age – one of dependency. One of the key challenges and opportunities for people in the third age is embracing new technology and its rapid adoption that is now influencing habits and preferences in social life, work and leisure. Another generational issue of importance is the continuing decline in exercise and outdoor activity and the resulting contribution towards unhealthy lifestyles, with predictions of obesity epidemics in many developed countries (Bleich *et al*. 2008).

Politics and legal issues

There always seem to be factors such as conflicts, terrorism, disease or civic unrest that have an impact on tourism – and on event tourism in particular – affecting the perception and stability of environments in which to host events. It is easy to cancel conventions, competitions and festivals, and governments seeking to restore order or prevent unrest will often see public gatherings as a threat. But whatever the source of disruption, be it political or a new global pandemic (like swine flu), the effects are usually regionalized, and long-term trends show that global tourism growth has always rebounded. More specifically relevant are the many policies and regulations enacted by governments affecting travel, culture, leisure and events, and these vary from country to country. During the past five decades, such policies have given a major boost to leisure, consumerism, tourism and event development. On the other hand, pressure to deal with climate change results in carbon taxes and, potentially, other measures that could increasingly act to slow growth or impose specific barriers to travel and events. Increasing regulation and professionalism in the events sector also means that advanced education is becoming more and more essential, and inevitably professionals and companies will have to be licensed in order for events to get approvals and insurance. The education, lifelong learning and ever more detailed training of event professionals is necessary both for health and safety reasons and to ensure that companies and governments realize their goals.

Economics and the propelling force of globalization

We know that economic recessions affect demand for many events, and while this is a periodic phenomenon, it has not slowed the long-term growth in travel or planned events. Despite being defined in many ways, globalization is in general a collection of forces resulting in greater integration of economies and cultures. Global communications, transportation advances, capital flows, migration and freer trade are major contributing factors. The world is shrinking in real and perceived terms as people and their lives seem to draw closer; this is described as time–space compression (Warf 2008), as transport and communications have made the world a much easier place in which to communicate and travel. We are all interconnected and global events, even the broadcast of minor events, reinforce these perceptions.

In examining globalization and sport tourism, Higham and Hinch (2009: 18) argued that 'The first general characteristic of globalization is the accelerated compression of time and space.' This is followed by growing interdependence, but with marked inequalities of its costs and benefits. These forces are reflected in the 'spectacularization' of sport mega events like the World Cup and the Olympics. Fans can travel easily to numerous international events, while favouring highly developed economies with modern transport. Both teams and fans are more mobile than ever. Higham and Hinch (2009: 26) continued to argue that 'Sport is ubiquitous as a form of popular culture while maintaining its significance as a form of place-based local culture.'

Globalization has many potential consequences for planned events. Mass global communications make it possible to reach out to everyone, and instant communications encourage people to meet virtually and in person. The democratization of tourism makes it possible for increasingly large numbers of people to attend festivals and events. But there is a concomitant tendency for standardization (as 'global parties' produced for tourism or as the 'live communications' of corporations) that threatens local control and authenticity. The mass movement of people, both migration and business tourism, encourages the spread of ideas. Diaspora (people moving away from their homes in large numbers) leads to a desire to retain or reinvent root cultures through festivals and events.

Globalization is accepted by many as good, or at least inevitable, and is rejected and countered by others. Invariably, anti-globalization protestors show up at international political meetings, concerned over the tendency for wealth to concentrate in rich countries, and the obvious failure of international efforts to eliminate poverty. The term 'glocalization' has been coined to describe a process in which the local culture is preserved (this applies to events) within global systems, but is this mostly wishful thinking? How can it be implemented? Overall, globalization helps explain rapid growth in the planned events sector, as a consequence of more trade and travel, easier communications and mass migrations. Ideas spread quickly. Everywhere we go, cities and nations are competing, corporations are pushing their brands, everything is for sale. This notion leads to a very serious issue: the commodification of experiences and the services we consume.

Environment

Everyone now talks about global climate change, and we know this process carries many threats, including coastal inundation, more severe weather, water and food shortages, political turmoil and resultant mass population displacements. And although oil supply increased and prices dropped in 2015, the threat of diminishing supplies framed around the notion of peak oil production has been reached (see Becken 2015); it is easy to become pessimistic about the future of the planet, not to mention the implications for tourism and events. This is because much of the economy and society in developed nations is dependent upon oil (and also the by-products of oil) for its functioning. Against those negative prospects are the possibilities that technology, especially through renewable energy sources, can prevent or mitigate the effect of oil dependence and its contribution to climate change. But the effects of climate change are already evident, and governments and industry have been very slow to react. These factors all have to be considered when we look at sustainability and the future of planned events.

Society and culture

Values are constantly shifting, and this is reflected in consumer patterns and political upheavals. Some of this is predictable, based on changing demographics (what does Generation 'next' want?), migration (e.g. from Asia to Western nations) and more pluralistic, better-educated and more connected societies. Ideally these shifts will result in an integrated, healthier and creative new society. But we can also expect major public and political reactions to racial and religious mixing, to economic downturn, to food or water shortages, and to environmental problems. How these forces will translate into political and economic action is more difficult to predict and can be country- and city-specific. Keep scanning the media and news for evidence of dominant trends. Probably the biggest global challenges to peace and prosperity are increasing forced migration (i.e. refugees from conflict, poverty, environmental catastrophes or disease) and the widening gap between rich and poor countries (and also between the wealthy class and all others, even within developed nations). These forces will influence many aspects of politics, society and economics.

Technology

Technological changes are at the forefront of thinking about the future and monitoring trends. As the Rapiergroup (2017) observed, the five main trends affecting the future of events and exhibitions are: AI; the Internet of Things; Robotism; Augmented Reality and Virtual Reality. Some particularly relevant forecasts relate to the impact that technology is having on jobs, with many entire categories set to disappear and be replaced by others that are either nascent or not yet invented! The age of specialization is leading to many more careers in which mastery of both knowledge and IT are prerequisite. Advances in technology also bring new opportunities for cultural exchanges and development, and this certainly has implications for the event sector. Yet whilst there is a key need for performative labour, then technology will not entirely replace the human factor in events. The availability of instant, global communications has numerous potential consequences for planned events, and we will consider social media trends in detail. Technological advances, for example, in terms of health, safety, food and water supplies, and carbon storage, offer significant opportunities for planned events. Wearable technology, as one example, is making physiological monitoring of audience biometrics a practical form of consumer feedback and means to monitor audience health and safety.

Major trends

Big trends are easy to spot, and there are many 'trend-spotters' on the Internet, publishing books and advising corporations and governments. Consumer trends are the most closely scrutinized by businesses and organizations, as they directly impact businesses of all kinds including events and tourism. Real value comes from spotting trends early on, so as to prevent something from happening or to capitalize on new opportunities. The following trends are already well established, but within each there are many possible sub-trends that need to be identified and monitored. Consider how each trend reflects the major underlying forces.

Consumer trends

Practitioners and researchers should be aware of the trends but not assume they will continue, especially in the realm of consumerism where conditions change very fast. Here are some consumer trends and forecasts coming from trend-spotters that might have a real impact on the events sector.

- sampling: consumers increasingly want to try something first and pay later (especially true for games, but maybe this applies to co-creating event experiences as well – see Smit and Melissen 2018);
- crowd sourcing: working with unknown others can be an innovation driver in the events and venues design world; this seems to connect to the whole co-creation of experiences concept;
- visualization is replacing text and discussion (why are there so many photo and video sites online? Learn to communicate experiences with pictures and video);
- wearable technology (use it to monitor visitor experiences, including heartbeat reactions to stimuli on sites as the study by Stadler, Jepson and Wood 2018 examined);
- female values becoming established (there is no doubt about the consumer power held by females in the Western world – how is it expressed in event design?);
- bargain hunting: various apps make it possible to find bargains, and consumers always seem to want the best price – what does this do for event ticket prices?;
- instant sharing: social networking means that everyone connects quickly, so that consumer dissatisfaction can quickly translate into a backlash or even a protest or boycott; by the same means, happy event-goers can immediately convince others to share in the experience.

The continued growth of festivals and events

The continued growth and expansion of events around the globe have been commented upon frequently, although it is impossible to quantify on a global scale. Indeed, in most countries there are no statistics on festival/event numbers and growth trends. Long *et al.* (2004: 1) noted that: 'In recent years there has been a clear increase in the number of festivals and events taking place across the world, though it is problematic to put an exact figure to this.' These researchers, all attached to the Centre for Tourism and Cultural Change at Leeds Metropolitan University, provide a number of reasons for the growth and spread of festivals. Long *et al.* (2004: 1) claimed that:

> *international tourism, as an important dimension of the wider concept of globalisation, has in many cases, shifted festivals from being relatively parochial and stable concerns with more or less localised audiences, to events that can attract global audiences, either as tourists, or via other forms of communicative media.*

and growth

> *can be explained in part by an increasing, if not necessarily articulated, desire to re-assert local/ community identities as part of an effort to combat a sense of cultural dislocation associated with processes of globalisation (Manning 1983; Boissevain 1996; De Bres and Davis 2001; Quinn 2003). For others, and in contrast, a number of festivals, such as carnivals and melas, are themselves expressions of globalised and diasporic cultures and identities and are becoming more visible beyond the confines of their 'host' communities as a consequence of their external promotion by festival organizers, the media and tourism marketing agencies, contributing to the building of 'global festival themes'.*

See Research Note 1.2.

1.2 RESEARCH NOTES ON THE GROWTH OF FESTIVALS

1 Janiskee, R. (1994). Some macroscale growth trends in America's community festival industry. *Festival Management and Event Tourism*, 2(1), 10–14.

Robert Janiskee, geographer, was a pioneer in event studies. His landmark analysis in the USA led to the conclusion (1994: 13) that: 'It appears that recurring community festivals increased in number at an average annual rate of approximately 4.6 per cent between 1930 and 1991, with the number of festivals doubling about every 15 years.' His research examined types, locations and timing, and he believed that the observed rate of growth could not be sustained everywhere.

2 Yolal, M., Cetinel, F. and Uysal, M. (2009). An examination of festival motivation and perceived benefits relationship: Eskisehir International Festival. *Journal of Convention and Event Tourism*, 10(4), 276–291.

Growth in festival numbers, size and frequency has been observed in many countries. The paper by Yolal *et al.* (2009: 276) noted how 'small towns and cities across Turkey are increasingly being encouraged to develop and organize festivals and events to improve their images; stimulate urban development; foster economic, cultural, and social life; and attract visitors and investment'. The authors concluded there are more than 1,350 festivals and events held annually in Turkey.

3 Lashua, B., Spracklen, K. and Long, P. (2014). Introduction to the special issue: Music and tourism. *Tourist Studies*, 14(1), 3–9.

A special issue of *Tourist Studies* on music and tourism points to the rapid growth of music festivals and concerts as cultural and touristic phenomena. Topics covered by contributors include the festival experience, fandom, authenticity versus commercialization, self-identity and place marketing.

Sport events and participation trends

Sport participation and events continue to expand. Not all sports are growing, and the trend watcher must never assume that growth will continue or that growth in one area applies across the board. Golf has been in decline for some time, in terms of numbers of North American participants and rounds played, although there has been a small gain in female golfers and it is growing in Asia! If participation declines, you can expect fewer events (and golf courses).

Continued expansion of the entertainment industry

Stein and Evans (2009: 11), discussing the entertainment industry, commented that 'Americans have become obsessed with entertainment and celebrities.' This appears to be the case globally, facilitated by all forms of media. One consequence is that the marketplace is crowded: 'We are saturated with entertainment options. So, for one segment of the entertainment market to grow, another segment must decline' (Stein and Evans 2009: 1). Thus, 'Event planning is a lucrative business within the entertainment industry and can be an ideal career for those who thrive on details' (Stein and Evans 2009: 279). One obvious area of growth has been the number of award shows, as it seems the celebration of entertainers has never been more popular. Rojek (2012) and Williamson (2016) examined this phenomenon as the growth of and celebration of celebrity. Providing fans with the opportunity to vote on something is always popular and has never been easier.

Entrepreneurship and a festival 'industry'

The existence of private festival-producing companies, and a professional class of event managers, makes it possible to 'order' an event to specification. Festivals and other celebrations can now be assembled from various inputs, if the money is available. This makes festivals retail commodities to be created or purchased as needed; successful event producers can go on to produce more events. More experienced customers are demanding ever-higher standards and quality, not to mention more unique experiences. Festivals have been able to provide these, although there must be limits to how much variety can be provided, and there are likely limits within a life-cycle model to how long any given festival can remain fresh. In addition to a private festivals sector, many festivals have been established by 'social entrepreneurs' who create non-profit festivals for a cause (and interesting jobs for themselves). Little is known about these people and their work, but they are vital in the festivals sector. Presumably social entrepreneurs have the option of being profit-oriented, although the scant evidence available suggests that profit-seeking entrepreneurs have to stay in well-defined niches with minimal public-sector and non-profit competition (see Morris *et al.* 2012; Hjorth and Kostera 2007; Olberding 2016 on social entrepreneurship and events). Such entrepreneurs are particularly at a disadvantage in attracting government grants or subsidies, although not – it appears – in terms of attracting volunteers, a theme that has attracted considerable interest alongside wider human resource issues in the event sector (Baum *et al.* 2009).

The experience economy and co-creation of experiences

Advances in the experience economy are relentless, with general recognition now that sophisticated, post-modern consumers want unique, personalized and memorable experiences. This applies especially in the sectors of entertainment, tourism, hospitality and events. Furthermore, many highly involved people, engaged as they are in various 'serious' lifestyle and leisure pursuits, invest heavily in travel and events and they want them to contribute to experiences, participating themselves in experience creation. Event producers therefore must become experienced designers and co-creators. Prahalad and Ramaswamy (2004) called for a strategic approach to experience creation drawing on shared values, allowing customers to co-create in the search for personal growth. Co-creation means that a company (event) and customer (or potential audience) share in the creation of value by allowing customers to shape experiences to suit their needs and desires. This is in stark contrast to the idea of consuming a single product, with experiences shaped entirely by the event producers. It recognizes that personal experiences are always different, and the customer increasingly does not want what everybody else is getting. Therefore, personalization is a key trend. Knudsen *et al.* (2014) argue that since the original study by Pine and Gilmore on the experience economy, the framing of these experiences has evolved whereby the signs and symbols associated with events adds meaning to these experiences alongside the co-production of these experiences by participating consumers.

Is this new ideal possible for planned events? In some cases the design of events can be modified to permit co-creation, and this is a 'liberating' or 'enabling' approach. In others, the format of an event is fixed and consumers are tightly constrained – as in a theatrical performance with everyone in ticketed seats. Outside the event, however, other related experiences can be created, employing social media for discussion and extended dialogue about what should go into an event. At the leading edge of event management, designers are conceiving entirely new forms of events that will enable the liberation of experiences. But more importantly, members of social worlds and the unlimited number of communities of interest are creating their own events.

Gigantism and mega events

Horne (2006) suggested three main reasons for the expansion and growth in attraction of mega events: global audiences generated through satellite and other communications technologies; growth in corporate sponsorship; and place marketing, to showcase cities and countries. Preuss (2009) concluded that mega sport events are now too expensive for host cities, requiring senior government commitments, and argued that 'Increasing event gigantism clearly creates trouble for host cities by demanding infrastructure that is oversized and/or not sustainable for a city in the long term' (Preuss 2009: 132). The increasing size of events in itself reflects a number of forces including globalization through media coverage and global sponsorship, increasing demand for event attendance and justification of the costs in terms of place marketing, and economic and urban development. The events themselves could and should be operated at a smaller scale, but they are no longer simply sport events.

Policy instrumentalism and festivalization

The creation and exploitation of events by public policy-makers can be divided into two general areas: civil society and social/cultural policy on the one hand, and tourism and place marketing on the other. Planned events play an important role in the 'civil society'. This term has multiple, interrelated connotations, so its usage is somewhat confusing. Definitions include the following:

- The totality of voluntary civic and social organizations and institutions that form the basis of a functioning society as opposed to the force-backed structures of a state (regardless of that state's political system) and commercial institutions of the market (Wikipedia).
- Civil society refers to the arena of uncoerced collective action around shared interests, purposes and values (www.traditionalknowledge.info/glossary).
- A society where individuals cooperate with other individuals and with public authority in tackling their individual and social problems. The civil society also ensures representation of those interest groups which cannot represent themselves by using economic and political means of influence (www.mk.gov.lv).

With these three definitions in mind, we can posit that planned events are both institutions of civil society (at least the public and non-profit ones) and instruments of civil society. Governments wanting to strengthen civil society (either because they believe in this form of democracy, or to devolve responsibility for certain 'public goods') create and support events that reflect or promote certain values (this is social marketing), foster voluntarism and, in a number of ways, boost community development. Numerous groups with shared values employ events to promote their own interests, and for the most part, this is a positive phenomenon.

So pervasive are festivals and events as instruments of public policy that some authors have described the process as 'festivalization'. There are several connotations, however, that need to be explored. According to Richards (2007a) this term has recently entered the literature. It appears to have arrived through translation from the writing of two Germans, Häussermann and Siebel (1993). The dominant usage refers to the festivalization of urban policy or politics, presumably following Häussermann and Siebel, who argued that cities competing for cultural consumers create or support festivals for different target markets, and consequently the cities become festivalized (in German the term used was *Festivalisierung*).

Hitters (2007: 282) stated that:

> *The concept of festivalization is a fairly widely accepted phenomenon among analysts of urban policy and cultural trends (Häussermann and Siebel 1993). In this chapter it refers to the increasing use of flagship festivals and large cultural events as a means to market major cities. Furthermore, I will argue that festivalization is not just limited to city marketing objectives but is becoming a new policy paradigm in the field of urban culture.*

Frank and Roth (2000: 237) discussed events and the media, concentrating on forces shaping public discourse surrounding major events. The dominating influences were politics and the cultural sector, leading these authors to conclude that 'non-state actors gain importance in the process of the festivalization of city politics'. Long *et al.* (2004: 8) referred to the festivalization of urban policy as 'it may also be the case that urban development policies themselves are becoming "festivalized" with cultural festival spaces being conceived as a contribution to an urban aesthetic streetscape as part of wider planning, architectural and design processes'. Smith (2014, 2015) explored these issues in relation to public spaces as spaces become festivalized and Belghazi (2006) discussed the festivalization of spaces and whole cities as part of event tourism and place-marketing strategies. Apparently anything can be festivalized, as intimated by Long *et al.* (2004: 3) who discussed the festivalization of advertising and product branding. There appears to be a general negativity associated with the term 'festivalization', as if it were an undesirable process, or at least that it carries risks. In this way it connects to the terms 'commodification' and 'commoditization', which are frequently employed in a derogatory sense to describe the process of festivals losing their cultural authenticity when exploited for tourism or other commercial purposes. This line of criticism specific to festivals seems to have started with ethnographic studies by Greenwood (1972, 1989). To Richards (2007a), festivalization implies commodification and a removal of control from local to national and global, arguing that, increasingly, festivals are aimed at the socialization of communities, rather than tourists and economic development.

Social media and social networking

Although progress in the technology of communications and entertainment is rapid, it is the use of social media that has caught everyone's attention – whether in the context of public uprisings, their role in spawning or facilitating new events (both planned and 'spontaneous') or as social networking tools connected to serious leisure, social worlds, subcultures and related niche events. We have now gone past the age of both broadcasting (i.e. mass media like television, radio, newspapers and magazines with content aimed at a generic 'audience') and narrowcasting (employing the same media for diverse and fragmenting niche markets). Users are now able to create and utilize their own global networks, with no one in charge and everyone a content producer. The basic ingredients are the digital communications devices and networks (i.e. mobile devices plus commercial networks, or at least access to the Internet) and self-forming groups. The groups can share information, and persons in the groups can interact. The evolution of social media and networks is rather difficult to predict, as they are changing and growing at astounding speed. Their exploitation for marketing events has already been well established. How the events sector uses them in the future is still an open question.

What can social media do? Consider the power of these characteristics individually and in any combination:

- instant global communications including virtual events (like a meeting) and live 'netcasting' of events (watching sports in real time);
- marketing events to target communities online (you need your own database or access to various networks of potential users);
- facilitating easy and cheap publication (e.g. event advertising and content);
- tools that make everyone a journalist, such as reporting on event experiences;
- sharing at an enormous scale (articles, ideas, photos, profiles, music, videos at or about events);
- engagement of the audience at an event (see Laurell and Björner 2018);
- real-time collaboration among researchers, events managers, public agencies, institutions and corporations (for the purpose of getting embedded in a support network);
- discussion and public discourse, everywhere and all the time (planning and evaluating events, co-producing the experiences, reporting the 'news' about events) (see Tang and Cooper 2018 and Banerjee 2018);
- social networking or group formation around events or leading to event-related travel; connecting to others with similar interests; virtually experiencing social events;
- amusement (will gaming take the place of live event experiences?);
- shopping (buying tickets and travel packages);
- their use as a research tool to estimate the density of people in event spaces (Gong *et al.* 2018).

The implications of social media are manifold. Organizations and governments can no longer control information and discourse, not even news reporting. Corporations have found that brands are not theirs to exclusively create and manage, as everyone has an opinion and a potential audience. And the event experience can be augmented by pre-, mid- and post-event interactions to foster engagement and increase satisfaction. New niche markets are being created all the time, reflecting real and virtual social worlds; they offer the opportunity to co-create events interactively with online communities (see Research Note 1.3).

1.3 RESEARCH NOTE ON SOCIAL MEDIA

Hudson, S., Roth, M., Madden, T. and Hudson, R. (2015). The effects of social media on emotions, brand relationship quality, and word of mouth: An empirical study of music festival attendees. *Tourism Management*, 47, 68–76.

Hudson and fellow researchers studied the influence of social media on customer relationships regarding music festivals. Results show that social media had a significant influence on emotions and attachments to festival brands, and that social media-based relationships led to desired outcomes, such as positive word of mouth.

Major issues

Commodification

Has everything been commodified, that is, turned into commercialized, profit-making business? Have people disengaged from authentic experiences and resorted to entertainment and spectacle, as suggested by Debord (1983)? It often appears this way, and it is a worrying trend. The French philosopher, building on Marxist traditions, argued that culture had become 'an immense accumulation of images', a sequence of commercial fragments detached from original experience. In this pessimistic interpretation of the modern world people are denied authentic, live experiences such as festivity or celebration and instead are fed a steady barrage of spectacle – things we passively watch instead of experiences we live, in contrast to the historical analysis of Frost fairs in eighteenth-century Britain (Bowen 2018) where the experience was not as commoditized.

The potential dominance of spectacle

Spectacle exists within the realm of the visual as something viewed (by 'spectators', obviously); but it is larger than life, colourful, exciting and novel, otherwise we would perceive it to be ordinary and unremarkable. We are easily seduced by spectacle, otherwise people would tire of fireworks and lasers, parades and outlandish costumes, and it is a substantial part of entertainment in general and events programming in particular as illustrated by Bao *et al.* 2017) in relation to the diffusion of such activity in China. Gotham (2005a) examined spectacle in the context of urban festivals in New Orleans, using Debord's theory of the spectacle and the writings of Henri Lefebvre (e.g. *The Production of Space*, Lefebvre 1991) to examine conflicting meanings assigned to the celebrations. Different stakeholders employed festivals to attract tourists, empower communities or sow dissent. Viewed as spectacle, in the tradition of Debord, a festival is merely one manifestation of everything becoming a commodity as opposed to festivals or carnivals as participatory experiences. Andrews (2006) examined the Disneyization of the National Basketball League and creation of a spectacle to revitalize the audiences using Debord as a theoretical frame of reference.

According to the anthropologist MacAloon (1984), a festival is a joyous celebration of unity, cooperation, accomplishment and excellence, while a spectacle is a grandiloquent display of imagery evoking a diffuse sense of wonderment and awe. Regarding the Olympic Games, MacAloon (1984: 242) argued that of the genres of cultural performance, spectacle and games appeared first, followed by festival and ritual. Spectacles are not only things to be seen, he argued in his 'theory of spectacle', but also possess symbolic codes. Spectacles must be grand, dramatic or huge. There is no spectacle without actors and audience, or performers and spectators. Spectators must be excited by the spectacle, or otherwise emotionally moved. The Olympics, according to MacAloon (1984: 245), 'must be seen, and seen in person, to be believed'. Host cities are transformed and animated through this process (Broudehoux 2017b). The scale and intensity of the overall experience cannot be captured on television (Billings *et al.* 2017). Ritual is a duty, but spectacle is by choice. Outsiders, or uninformed audiences, might mistake ritual for spectacle or not care about the embedded cultural meanings. While 'festival' requires a certain style of celebratory mood, and internal 'special observances', spectacle does not. MacAloon was suspicious of spectacles, as they tend to be 'tasteless' and become a 'moral cacophony'. Although the Olympic Games are proclaimed to be a festival, MacAloon (1984: 250) argued that festival and spectacle are in opposition. Nevertheless, both share one feature – they erect frames of cultural performances around a variety of genres; they both make 'differentiated forms of symbolic action into new wholes by means of a common spatiotemporal location, expressive theme, affective style, ideological intention, or social function'.

In this way the Olympics embodies a ritual organized around the classic rites of passage (that is, opening and closing ceremonies) which introduce liminality, intensification (i.e. victory and medal awards), closure and reaggregation. Using the concepts of van Gennep and Turner, MacAloon (1984: 253) noted that at the Olympic Games 'the assembled thousands and the space that they occupied are released into an extraordinary expression of spontaneous communitas'. MacAloon concluded (1984: 268) by saying that spectacle has destructive effects on ritual, festival and games. These genres of cultural performance bring people together – a 'communitas' – whereas spectacle is just about watching. On the other hand, in societies favouring individualism, spectacle can act to bring people into a festival or ritualistic environment that they would otherwise be suspicious of. Rockwell and Mau (2006) gave historical examples of the power and misuse of spectacle by the Nazis at Nuremberg and the Fascist Mussolini, through his revival of traditional games-festivals to manipulate nationalism. Do contemporary events also seek to manipulate people for political purposes or profits?

The high costs of bidding and hosting major events

Many issues are raised by this trend, not the least of which are the opportunity costs associated with such a vast commitment of resources (see McGillivray and Turner 2017). Particularly when austerity cuts in many European public-sector organizations reduce public spending per se. The opportunity cost of bidding may have very unpalatable local consequences politically. This is because bidding requires significant resources which are 'consumed' by mega events with seldom any consideration of what else society could do with the money and labour. Usually we get only vague promises of benefits in the bidding process, including tourism gains and future events that can be held, or development of sport and housing as a legacy. Post-event accountability is generally lacking, or unconvincing, with benefits not demonstrable and costs rising.

Virtual events and augmented reality

What people usually mean by 'virtual event' is really a form of online and remote communications. This includes teleconferences and online streaming of sports or entertainment. There has been a fear for many years that people will stay at home or in their offices rather than attend meetings, conventions, exhibitions or any entertainment offering. Sadd (2014) argued that the transformational power of technology will impact upon the design of events, and that blended technology fusing the virtual and the real is the way forward, but she also maintained that gatherings of people still need interaction for the co-creation of experiences. Sadd discussed how augmented reality (AR) changes perceptions of reality and permits interaction, and this is a different concept from replacing real events. Planned events are social by nature, and many people will only resort to 'virtuality' when the real thing is not available: this is not necessarily a replacement. It is great to augment events with live streaming and online interconnectivity, and many meetings should be conducted remotely rather than waste energy through travel, but these are not the planned events we want to participate in for social reasons. Event business is better done in person, otherwise exhibitions would have died out long ago, but traditional trade shows have found that they need to add substantial educational and social components to attract exhibitors and customers. Having made the case, however, there are exceptions. Consider the choice between watching sports on television (or your personal communications device) and going to the live event. Some people will prefer the remote experience, as it is cheaper, often easier to see the details, and comes with additional commentary and information.

1.4 RESEARCH NOTE ON TECHNOLOGY

Locke, M. (2010). A framework for conducting a situational analysis of the meetings, incentives, conventions, and exhibitions sector. *Journal of Convention and Event Tourism*, 11(3), 209–233.

Locke (2010) argued that technological advances in information and communication technology 'have had a significant impact on the MICE sector in all parts of the world. Virtual meetings, webcasts, podcasts, teleconferencing, video conferences, distance learning, blogs, and interactive multimedia are becoming increasingly common tools in the corporate world.' Her literature review revealed that the lead time for planning events has decreased, in part owing to communications and information processing software (e.g. for online registration). Venues must provide a high standard of technology. Technology is also employed to improve the experience, as in assisted speaker–audience interaction. Locke also discusses virtual conferencing, noting that some observers believe that technology is changing the ways in which people meet, while others see these as supplementing traditional in-person events.

1.5 RESEARCH NOTE ON VIRTUAL EVENTS

Pearlman, D. and Gates, N. (2010). Hosting business meetings and special events in virtual worlds: A fad or the future? *Journal of Convention and Event Tourism*, 11(4), 247–265.

Pearlman and Gates (2010) discussed trends impacting on events, including economic recession, that have led to increasing interest in technological solutions to business-information challenges. Their research investigated the awareness, acceptance and adoption of virtual reality applications. They found that 'virtual meetings and special events are innovative and viable methods to effectively and efficiently achieve organizational objectives. Still, in the early stages of development, the use of virtual reality within the meetings, incentive, convention and exhibition industry looks promising; however, widespread adoption may be years away.'

Event sustainability

Underlying forces continue to generate growth and diversity in the events sector, and this is likely to continue in the foreseeable future. But there are limiting factors, or threats, that will eventually check growth – especially in event tourism. When and how this will happen is still uncertain. Indeed, the challenge of security issues in events is assuming a much greater significance after terrorist attacks and other targeted attacks on event-goers (Nuñez and Vendrell 2016; Wynn-Moylan 2017; Cassinger *et al.* 2018). From an economic perspective, terrorist threats and violent attacks will damage the sustainability of hosting events. In the concluding chapter, a future scenario based on the end of tourism is presented, enabling some speculation about how events will be affected if dramatic and permanent changes occur to our global environment and economy, including the political stability that affects terrorist attacks. Some commentators argue that attacks on live music venues have shown a sharp increase since 2015, with the Paris attack and a series of other attacks in 2017 and 2018 across the globe targeting people in a leisure setting where their focus is on enjoyment as an audience as opposed to being vigilant citizens concerned about personal security and safety. Such attacks focus on these mass audiences as very soft and easy targets despite the security measures taken at such events.

Environmental sustainability is a broad concept (see Holmes *et al.* 2015), and various threads of this discourse run throughout this book: green operations; ecological footprint and carbon loadings; the future of event tourism; institutionalization; economic viability; managerial competence; population ecology and portfolio management; costs and legacies. Bringing them all together to formulate a clear and integrated measure of sustainability is all but impossible, if for no other reason than multiple stakeholder perspectives on event goals and impacts. It is probably wise to think of sustainable tourism and events as a process of continuous striving for improvement; setting and attaining goals for green operations is likely the starting point for most events, and should not be the end. Through a continuous process of evaluation and strategic planning, all events can pursue a more sustainable path but alongside such assessments of the developments of events, a more critical perspective that is moving thinking to a more theoretical level.

Developments in event studies

Critical event studies

A key strand of recent research on event studies that has emerged has been labelled critical event studies, which questions the existing paradigm (the existing practices and concepts used within a discipline or subject). This emanates from wider developments in social science which are derived from critical social science that argues for a more reflective approach to understanding society and the issues it examines. Many studies point to the influence of the Frankfurt School of critical theory in the 1920s, which stimulated much of the subsequent interest in critical social science (see Bohman 2005 for a more detailed discussion). It used theoretical constructs from social science to create a more critical understanding of individuals' circumstances so that they might be able to emancipate themselves from the structural constraints imposed upon them. Implicit in these arguments was the notion of social movements that people could join to help overcome their domination in society, thereby empowering themselves, popularized by the Frankfurt School and the development of critical theory by Horkheimer, the Director of the School and Professor of Social Philosophy at the University of Frankfurt from 1930–1933, and again from 1949–1958. As Bohman (2005: n.p.) argued, critical theory can be summarized thus:

> It follows from Horkheimer's definition that a critical theory is adequate only if it meets three criteria: it must be explanatory, practical, and normative, all at the same time. That is, it must explain what is wrong with current social reality, identify the actors to change it, and provide both clear norms for criticism and achievable practical goals for social transformation. Any truly critical theory of society, as Horkheimer further defined it in his writings as Director of the Frankfurt School's Institute for Social Research, 'has as its object human beings as producers of their own historical form of life' (Horkheimer 1993: 21). In light of the practical goal of identifying and overcoming all the circumstances that limit human freedom, the explanatory goal could be furthered only through interdisciplinary research that includes psychological, cultural, and social dimensions, as well as institutional forms of domination.

Traditionally these ideas have evolved from political ideologies such as Marxism and more recently the work of Habermas as a proponent of critical social theory. Lamond and Spracklen (2015) illustrate this in their focus on protest as events where critical social science and radical political studies challenges the domination of global capitalism. In this context, their book interprets activism as a form of leisure activity as part of a counter-hegemonic struggle (meaning it is a challenge to the existing status quo in political terms, where hegemony means dominance over something) in pursuit of this mission to liberate oneself from the oppressive features of society. For event studies this means that critical social scientists approach the phenomenon of events from a very different standpoint; as Lamond and Spracklen (2015) point out, events are very much a neo-liberal form of commodified experience. Rojek (2013: xi–xii) summarized the impact for event research where:

> *the professional events literature provides a technocratic view of events. It focuses on the nuts and bolts in the machine and when and where to oil the parts. The crucial issue of who owns the machine, who controls it and what is its purpose are confined to the backwater.*

One of the most useful studies that expands upon this perspective is derived from the critical social theorist Adorno's (2001) critique of the culture industry (in which events can be situated). Adorno (2001) argued that capitalism was responsible for producing and disseminating cultural commodities, principally through the mass media. The creation of popular culture, as Adorno (2001) highlighted, was a means by which people obtained gratification and so were made passive and content and so did not challenge the oppressive features of society even where their economic conditions were poor. Many of these issues are revisited throughout Rojek's theoretical treatise on events which is a good sociological analysis of the critical issues at a variety of scales from the global to the individual. What Rojek's stimulating analysis depicts is a series of key themes that hallmark events exploit from the social psychological characteristics of people:

- *Catharsis* – where people use events as a place where private and public emotions are expressed;
- *Emotionalism* – the desire to perform as part of a team or to do good;
- *Exhibitionism* – the symbolic behaviour where sentiments are communicated and camaraderie is achieved.

These themes provide the uplift for people to temporarily escape the mundaneness of the everyday life albeit in a time-limited setting, reinforcing Adorno's argument about the gratification that events provide as cultural commodities.

The application of critical social theory in event studies has created new directions for research such as gender studies and cultural anthropology as part of the transdisciplinary developments in event studies. Such a critical perspective has also raised criticisms of previous editions of this book (Getz 2012b and Getz and Page 2015) by Spracklen and Lamond (2016: 2) that 'it adopts a political neutral perspective on events'. They use this as a basis to level much broader criticisms of the event literature that 'locate events in a paradigm that is either directly connected to, or influenced by, contemporary capitalism, particularly the variant that is more commonly referred to as neo-liberalism' (Spracklen and Lamond 2016: 8–9). Such critical debates have also arisen in cognate areas such as sports geography (Koch 2016) as part of a wider critical approach to social science. Yet such debate in events is not as new as commentators would suggest – as a new domain for research as many examples abound from the 1990s where studies such as Hall (1992) and Roche (1992) adopt such critiques towards events in their analysis of the impact and meaning of events.

Lamond and Platt's (2016) edited collection of research approaches in events provides numerous illustrations of the methodologies and application of critical event studies from different disciplines such as qualitative methods (Dowse 2016), cultural studies (Ying-Chih 2016), disability studies (Misener *et al.* 2016) and ethnography (Dashper 2016). Other studies such as Finkel *et al.* (2019b) on accessibility, inclusion and diversity in events also expand the domain of critical event studies especially their focus on gender, sexualities, ethnicities, age, class, religion, and the relationship with non-mainstream, non-majority communities. Despite this new emergent critical literature, there are debates within social science on the effect of such debates and who the writers are communicating with. Critics have suggested that radical critiques do not necessarily influence policy unless the issue has reached a key tipping point where public and political support is galvanized. More cynically, researchers who focus on applied research looking at problem-solving and practical outcomes to make a difference work within the neo-liberalist ideology to enact change and so are often interpreted by critical theorists as reinforcing the hegemonic structure by largely maintaining the status quo. Whilst there is a role for academic research that adopts a critical perspective and questions the existing paradigms and status quo, the extent to which such positions can enact radical change depends upon how widely the views are understood outside of the academic community they are communicating with using their terminology and language. Policy-makers look for simple and straightforward interpretations and solutions they can resource to improve the condition of society albeit within the existing neo-liberalist tradition. Critical studies may help to identify inequalities, problems and issues but the solution of enabling citizens to remove all the barriers and oppressive features will occur on a piecemeal basis as capitalist societies have historically reformed themselves from within when the status quo is no longer tenable, as evidenced by the gradual introduction of equality legislation in many developed countries to eradicate inequalities, for example.

STUDY GUIDE

In this first chapter, the student should gain understanding of how and why event studies is defined and justified as a field of academic inquiry. Consideration has been given to why anyone should study planned events, including the obvious relationship to event management and event tourism professional education, but also the importance of events within many other disciplines, fields of enquiry and policy domains.

Study the framework for understanding and creating knowledge about planned events, as this has been important in structuring the book. Each of the components is considered later, in detail, in one or more chapters. Be comfortable in explaining the three major subdivisions of event studies and how they inter-relate: disciplinary perspectives (including the 'classical' social and cultural perspective rooted in sociology and anthropology), event management and event tourism. The last two subdivisions are applied, leading to distinct career paths, whereas the disciplinary perspective is much more theoretical. All three have policy implications for governments concerned with events and their impacts. They are also called 'discourses': each has its own tradition in the literature, in terms of epistemology (underlying theory and methodology) and ontology (bodies of knowledge). Those topics are considered later in the book.

Start to consider the major challenges and issues facing event management and event tourism, as well as the big policy issues for governments at all levels. There are many specific points throughout the book. Careers are introduced here, and there is some theory and research on careers later in the book when we look at human resources. Also relevant is the later discussion on ethics and professionalism.

Be able to answer, in full sentences and paragraphs, the study questions – all are potential exam questions based on this chapter.

STUDY QUESTIONS

- Define event studies and explain why it is, or is not, an academic discipline.
- What is the core phenomenon of event studies, and whose experiences are we interested in?
- How are meanings attached to events and event experiences?
- Explain each component of the framework for understanding and creating knowledge about planned events, and be able to illustrate each of them with specific research examples.
- Outline the three main subdivisions within event studies and how they relate to policy and careers.
- What are the various specializations open to event management and event tourism professionals, and how are the necessary knowledge and skills obtained?

- Discuss major forces shaping planned events and resulting trends and issues.
- How do you think social media are shaping the demand for events, and the event experience?

FURTHER READING

See the References section for all references cited in the book. At the end of each chapter is a short list of books recommended for additional reading that elaborate upon key topics.

Bowdin, G., Allen, J., O'Toole, W., Harris, R. and McDonnell, I. (2011). *Events Management* (3rd edn). Oxford: Butterworth-Heinemann.

Getz, D. (2013a). *Event Tourism: Concepts, International Case Studies, and Research*. New York: Cognizant.

Goldblatt, J. (2014). *Special Events* (7th edn). New York: Wiley.

Page, S. J. and Connell, J. (2014). *Routledge Handbook of Events*. London: Routledge.

2

The world of planned events

LEARNING OBJECTIVES

Upon completion of this chapter, students should know the following:

- definitions and the nature of events and planned events;
- meanings attached to time and how they make events special;
- the critical importance of place and setting;
- how size, length, frequency and periodicity of events are important variables;
- classifications of events in terms of their form, function and experiential dimensions;
- how and why event forms and functions converge;
- differences between planned and unplanned events.

Describing and classifying events

The world of planned events is diverse and exciting, with almost unlimited scope for variety in form, function and event experiences. The meanings we attach to these events, and the importance they have always held in our personal and collective lives, make them fundamental components of culture, business and lifestyles. This chapter commences with a discussion of basic definitions of the term 'event' and 'planned events', including differences between planned and unplanned events, and the question of scale (small versus large events). The inherent temporal and spatial dimensions of events are discussed, as this is fundamental to understanding much of the related theory.

Many adjectives are used in conjunction with the term 'event' and we need to understand how they arise from consideration of either the form or function of planned events. Terms like 'hallmark', 'mega' or 'iconic' refer to the function of events (e.g. for image making and place marketing, their size and significance, and their unique appeal). The comprehensive event typology illustrated in Figure 2.1 is largely based on their form. When we associate specific form, setting and programming with event types like 'festival', 'convention' or 'sport competition', we are really creating and reflecting 'social constructs' that are based on tradition and common, societal expectations. Concluding this chapter is a profile of each of the main types and key subtypes of planned events.

What is an event?

Common dictionary definitions of 'event' stress three points:

> Event: an occurrence at a given place and time; a special set of circumstances; a noteworthy occurrence.

Events, by definition, have a beginning and an end. They are temporal phenomena (i.e. they are time-limited), and with planned events the event programme or schedule is generally planned in detail and well publicized in advance. Planned events are also usually confined to particular places, although the space involved might be a specific facility, a very large open space, or many locations simultaneously or in sequence. As will be argued, what we call planned or special events are a matter of perspective and are social constructs.

When you search 'event' on the Internet, you will encounter its use in many other fields, for example, in finance (events that disrupt the markets or change a business), physics (e.g. 'event horizons'), biology (e.g. 'extinction events'), philosophy (e.g. 'mental events'), climatology (e.g. 'weather events'), medicine (e.g. 'adverse events'), probability theory (e.g. events as 'outcomes of experiments') and computer science (e.g. 'event-driven programming'). In many cases, the temporal dimension is more important than the spatial (i.e. geographical) in most of these usages.

No matter how hard one tries, it is literally impossible to replicate an event; by definition they only occur once, creating a unique experience for the audience or participants. Although planned events might be similar in form, some aspect of setting, people and programme will ensure that the event is always tangibly or experientially different. The expectations, moods and attitudes of guests and participants will always be new, so their experiences will differ regardless of the programme and setting. This uniqueness of events makes them attractive, even compelling, so that cultivating a 'once in a lifetime' image for an event is the marketer's goal. However, these goals have also become very commonplace in other areas of consumer behaviour, as businesses and organizations seek to create unique selling propositions in marketing terms, to delight their customers consuming services and more experientially focused products. All the planned events we talk about in this book are social events: they are for people, and not merely events in our own, personal lives.

Virtual events

All planned events are social in nature, and that is because people have a need to be together – to socialize, celebrate and do business. While online or teleconferenced, events have their place, they are not replacements. In this book we talk about virtual events in several places, but they are not the object of, or at the core of, event studies although there is growing interest in the rise of technology and its potential impact on the conventional notion of the event. The Expert Opinion by Dr Matt Frew examines some of the trends and issues related to technology and virtuality.

2.1 EXPERT OPINION

Future events and technology culture: dreamscapes or dark fantasy?

Dr Matt Frew, PhD, Senior Lecturer in Event Management, School of Tourism, University of the West of Scotland.

Glance over the shoulder of history and you will see a trajectory of technological transformations in the world of work, life and leisure. The impact of technology has always generated patterns of reaction, from Luddite fears and mass fascination, to dismissive fad. Interestingly, events occupy a pioneering place in the discourse of technology. From the conspicuous consumption of industrial innovation in the Great Exhibition of 1851 (Hall 2006) and the Nazi TV propaganda of the 1936 Berlin Olympics to the 2014 Brazilian World Cup, a 'sporting event that has generated bigger TV audiences and more social network chatter than any in history' (Watt 2014), technology and events have a symbiotic relationship.

Today we are in an age of acceleration where, I argue, globally evolving techno-capitalism (Suarez-Villa 2009) and techno-culture (Dijck 2013) are changing not only events but the structuring relations of life, society and the self. Consider for a moment the *last century* and the impact of innovations such as the silent then talking pictures, radio or the masses mesmerized by the magic box of early TV. Now, consider the *past decade* – the explosion of digital and social media, smart technologies, holographics, haptics, brain-to-computer interface, augmented reality and the re-birth of virtual reality (Kaku 2012). The Internet of Things and era of big data has just begun and given that, from the 'dawn of civilisation until 2003, human kind generated five exabytes of data. Now we produce five exabytes every two days' (Schmidt, cited in Booch 2014: 21), the speed and scale of technological transformation is unprecedented. A paradigm shift is at play, where we are swamped by a technological tsunami that is moving so fast and is networked in a daily convergent conversation of billions, that it has become a given. So in this age of accelerating techno-culture what does the future hold for events?

Currently, most events are stuck grappling with techno-cultures of convergence (Flinn and Frew 2014) where the digital lifestyles of consumers represent a new mode of social commerce (Solis 2013) to be mined. The problem is, that while modern events demand a digital heartbeat that engages with and feeds the desire for digital, as much as experiential, distinction, this is only the tip of the technological iceberg. Today's trajectory of technology reveals a shift from an external functionality to the internalization, embodiment and immersion of technologies. This is reflected in the lift and leave of traditional computing, to our constant smartphone companions, to the integrated wearables such as Google Glass and on to the digital layering and animation of the inanimate world through the augmented reality of iOptik. What we are witnessing is a transhuman e-volution, a digital disruption of desire, whereby technologies are, increasingly, challenging the structuring relations of our world, in particular, time, space and subjectivity. Our techno-future is one directed at overcoming those physical laws and, most importantly, frustrations with the embodied state.

Although social, digital, smart-technologies, wearables and augmented reality demonstrate a globally accelerating techno-culture, developments in virtual reality (VR) represent a game-changing future for events. While VR has been around for a few decades, primarily the bastion of gamers, engineering, processor and software advances have catapulted it into the limelight as a pioneering future technology. Currently, while the likes of the University of Southern California's Project Holodeck and major corporations, such as Sony's Project Morpheus and Google's augmented reality project Magic Leap, jostle for position, Oculus Rife is leading the way in immersive VR. Oculus, recently purchased by Facebook's Mark Zuckerberg for $2 billion, produces spectacular off-world constructs where the depth of immersive experiences is designed to achieve 'presence': that feeling of actually being there. With VR and the likes of Oculus the 'end game' is where 'people will spend part of their days virtually teleported if you will, place shifted'. Moreover, when integrated with the sensory, force-feedback of haptics and holography, the visions of VR promise new dreamscapes where the 'warm embrace; the view, sounds, breeze, and smells of the beach' (Schybergson 2014) are possible. The constructing of such dreamscape 'realities', where you will feel 'truly present … share unbounded spaces … not just moments with your friends online, but entire experiences and adventures' (Zuckerberg, cited in Dredge 2014), is of critical importance for future events, if not for life.

Accelerating techno-culture and its VR dreamscapes promise much for the future of events. Time, space and subjectivity are blurred, re-written if not erased. Go anywhere, anyplace, anytime; live and relive past memories; be young, old or assume a new self, a new performativity, and be whoever you want to be. As Schmidt and Cohen of Google put it:

If you're feeling bored and want to take an hour-long holiday, why not turn on your holograph box and visit Carnival in Rio? Stressed? Go spend some time on a beach in the Maldives … Through virtual-reality interfaces and holographic projection capabilities, you'll be able to 'join' these activities as they happen and experience them as if you were truly there.

(2013: 24)

Of course academic enquiry will always hit the pause button for critical reflection. For one thing, technology is far from neutral; there is always a dark side for, as history shows, while we shape technology, technology always shapes us and that leads to critical questions if not resistance (Dijck 2013; Frew 2014). Indeed the ability to 'place shift' us to magical dreamscapes, where we can visit the Pyramids of Giza, enjoy an Olympics or World Cup in real time, rewind and be up front at a Beatles gig, or adopt a new performative persona and take a walk on the festive or sexual wild side, has a magnetic appeal. In an instant, issues of events, tourism or sports such as capacity are overcome, sustainability and environmental impacts radically reduced, inequity and inclusivity claimed, physical disability or age eliminated and, of course, new modes of commerce created (Kaku 2012). However, while future dreamscapes offer promise, they also herald a dark fantasy.

Already concerns are being raised about escapism, exploitation and the possible dystopian nightmare that future techno-culture may produce (Gumbel 2014). After all, if we can achieve immersive 'presence', that feeling of being 'truly there', or, better, recreate self, relive and reboot life itself, why would we ever leave the dreamscape? Moreover, when you do leave, are you faced with a life and self that is fundamentally disappointing, being ever reminded of that new, younger, adventurous performative self of the dreamscape? Undoubtedly, many will shake their heads and dismiss such notions as folly, arguing for a truly human event experience and how the virtual will never replace or be as authentic as lived, embodied reality. I would argue that this is a deflective if not dying debate. Forget privileging the present over the past, real over the virtual experience. While we do not know the detail of the future, what we do know is that these transformational technologies are here. The drive and direction of techno-culture is accelerating, and with VR dreamscapes the very notion of the 'real' and the 'self' is up for grabs.

Interestingly, the leaders of techno-culture and eminent futurists tend to reference movie culture as the template of imagination and inspiration but also as a critical counterpoint to those who insist on a universal notion of the 'real', essentialist or embodied 'self' (Kaku 2012; Kurzweil 2008).

Whether *Star Trek*, *Total Recall*, *Minority Report*, *The Matrix* or *Transcendence*, they point out how we are turning 'popular science fiction concepts into science facts' (Schmidt and Cohen 2013: 5). More importantly, they recognize the problem of how the 'physical and virtual worlds' need to 'coexist, collide and complement each other' and how this accelerating techno-culture 'will greatly affect how citizens and states behave' (Schmidt and Cohen 2013: 31). It is safe to assume that future events will play a central role in the discourse of accelerating techno-culture, as sites offering dreamscape promise or dark fantasy events will become cultural battlegrounds where the moral, embodied and socio-political tensions of the day, as much as notions of the 'real' and the 'self', will be fought out. Future events in future techno-culture will, increasingly, reflect the dissolution of the structuring relations of time, space and subjectivity. To dismiss such ideas as 'fantastical' would, ironically, be correct, for the future is, indeed, now.

No such thing as events!

Having made the case for 'events' as discrete phenomena, it is worth noting that in a Buddhist inter-pretation, everything is interdependent and all events arise from previous events, and in a more general philosophical context 'events' might not actually exist (for elaboration, and perhaps confusion, see the online article by Mansfield 1998). This line of argument posits that events cannot be separated completely from their context, from the flow of what is happening in the world and in our daily lives. What we call a planned event is in reality an integral part of many people's lives and many stakeholders' actions, with various environmental forces acting upon us. Events, therefore, are merely the perceived intersection (in time and/or places) of different people and the consequences of various flows of activity. This makes perfect sense philosophically, and certainly event managers and policy-makers must be experts at assessing environmental forces, but for pragmatic reasons it does not affect our perception that planned events exist, and that event studies is a vital subject. One need only refer to common language (i.e. the vernacular) to know that discrete events are central to most people's understanding of the world and their own lives. We measure time and events, even if it is arguably an illusion, and therefore we need and recognize events to mark important occasions and define periods of activity.

Event-history analysis

This method within social science focuses on socially significant events in the lives of people, such as the various rites of passage. But these events could also be episodes, such as education and unemployment, jobs and relationships as part of the notion of the life cycle. Rapoport *et al.* (1975) in *Leisure and the Family Life Cycle*, building on the classic studies of family life and leisure of Rowntree and Lavers (1951), iden-tified the notion of a family life-cycle model and the interrelationship between stages in the life cycle, work and leisure. This has an important bearing on the stages in an individual's and family's life where events will have specific meaning. Rapoport *et al.* (1975) identified four stages: Youth, Young Adulthood, Establishment, and Later Years, although we also need to include childhood in these stages. The period of establishment, which is the largest in the family life cycle, is where the majority of social events occur (marriage, childbirth and child rearing and maintaining friendships) and work careers. The concept of stages helps to explain how people engage with events and the type of events they will consume in their work and leisure time, including the increasing blurring of work and leisure. This led Stebbins (1982) to observe that 'serious leisure' was evolving, where leisure and work activities overlap. To explain this emergence of 'serious leisure', Stebbins argued that:

> *Leisure in post-industrial society is no longer seen as chiefly a means of recuperating from the travail of the job ... if leisure is to become, for many, an improvement over work as a way of*

finding personal fulfilment, identity enhancement, self-expression, and the like, then people must be careful to adopt those forms with the greatest payoff. The theme here is that we reach this goal through engaging in serious rather than casual or unserious leisure.

(Stebbins 1982: 253)

This has an important bearing on the patronage of events during the establishment stage of the family life cycle if people become engaged with others in various communities of interest (e.g. as event volunteers) or through serious leisure pursuits. And it is worth asking what the planned events are that we have attended that hold special meaning in our lives, some possibly even being transforming experiences, and how these have evolved through time.

Time is of the essence

Time is not a simple concept, and we use expressions of time in many ways – some of which are highly relevant to event studies. First, time is often conceptualized as being 'cyclical', as with the annual calendar. Seasonal changes are important in terms of climate, food production and the very rhythms of social life, and this helps explain the evolution of many rituals and festivals as discussed in Chapter 1 (Connell *et al.* 2015). We tend to mark the 'passage of time' by annual holidays and celebrations, and we particularly look forward to them coming around next year. However, our modern conception of time and how it is defined through the working week, and the distinction between work time and non-work (leisure) time (see Page and Connell 2010), is fundamental to the analysis of events. This distinction between work and leisure is very much a construction of the capitalist period, particularly the Victorian period, and, as recognized by Billinge (1996), time was used geographically to channel leisure activities such as attending events (e.g. football matches) to appropriate times and places outside of formal work time. This created a social necessity for recreation as freedom from work: a non-work activity to recreate body and soul, to be refreshed for the capitalist economic system, with its regulated time discipline of a place for everything, and everything in its place (Billinge 1996). As the capitalist system of production developed and leisure became more defined in non-work time, the working day developed into a more standardized eight-hour phenomenon (Rybczynski 1991; Cross 1986) and a consumer culture also developed alongside leisure (Cross 1993). For time to be available for participation in events, we need to understand the evolution of the modern working week and the rise of the weekend as a leisure setting.

As Page and Connell (2010) illustrated, the five-day working week that has dominated industrial society is now changing in 'post-modern' society, with more blurring of work and leisure time. This is reflected in the reduction in working time from six days, to five and a half, then to a five-day working week. In some societies working on a Saturday is still a routine activity, but the notion of work time and leisure has very important impacts on when events are scheduled and who will attend. Likewise, time also has an important influence when looking at 'biological' time and the individual and family life cycle: the maturing of one's body and mind marks the passage of a life, relative to others going through the same 'life-stage' changes. These various stages are marked by events we celebrate. Events mark life's changes (*rites de passage*, like birthdays and anniversaries), its triumphs (graduation and other formal ceremonies), its fun and joy (festivals, leisure pursuits, family reunions) and even its temporary pains (goodbyes and funerals). Time and its use in contemporary society therefore have a very significant bearing on the nature of events we celebrate and their impact on our work and non-work time.

'SOCIAL AND CULTURAL CONSTRUCTS' OF TIME

As will be seen later, the conceptualization of the liminal/liminoid zone for the planned event experience is a social construct, and will vary from culture to culture. In most Western societies the meanings and values attached to escapism, free time, leisure pursuits, having a good time (e.g. hedonism) and being entertained, reflect the growth of the public and private consumption of leisure time (Page and Connell 2010). Grappi and Montanari (2011) observed that there was a clear link between event-goers' emotions, hedonism and social identity that affected their patronage and the time devoted to events. For Wood and Kenyon (2018) this was reflected in the shared emotional memory of event participants which as a clear time dimension to it as we will examine further in the chapter on event experiences. Events as leisure pursuits can be traced back through history and so they are not necessarily new. What is new is the way in which our post-modern lives and the globalized nature of leisure consumption have impacted upon the production and enjoyment of so many planned events. Indeed such events are not only accepted but expected. The construction of time through capitalist society has led to the social and cultural construction of time outside of work and the perceived 'need' for annual holidays, numerous special days for commemorations (of just about everything) and time for ourselves where we engage in events. Historical analyses of the way the state has legislated to create leisure time over the past 120 years, to create the conditions in which events as experiences can be enjoyed by more people, have democratized the process of event participation as a mass form of consumption. This is especially the case in time–space compression (see Warf 2008), making attending global and mega events more accessible. This reflects the abundance of leisure choices that digitally connected societies now take for granted, and where events allow people to be co-present in a specific time and place.

TIME AS A 'COMMODITY'

Time is precious in our society; therefore it has become a commodity with high value. We gladly pay for 'quality time' with our friends and families, and this often involves event experiences. We will sacrifice more money to have more 'free time'. We hate 'having our time wasted'. We all know that we cannot 'buy time', but we can certainly 'lose time'. These values and attitudes are all shaped by our culture, and perhaps it would be healthier if our cultural perceptions of time changed. How we use, perceive and value time are important considerations in event studies. Events are temporal phenomena, with start and end points, yet the experience of them begins before and possibly never ends! Clawson and Knetsch (1966) conceptualized recreational travel as a multiphase experience, consisting of five major phases: anticipation, travel-to, on-site, travel-back and recollection. Anticipation and recollection can be just as important as the experience itself. In this way, the packaging of events, a key to effective event tourism development and marketing, should be much more focused on the overall experience than on the technical aspects of travel, accommodation and event tickets.

The value of time varies a great deal among people, at various stages in their lives, and among cultures. 'Time is money' and people want value for their 'investment' of time, but how does this apply to planned events? A short, intense event experience can be just what is needed, but people are also willing to give up large blocks of time to travel to events. Can we measure the value of events by reference to the time various people invest in them? Is it possible that people value time differently, and therefore the identical event experience can be much more satisfying to some? This illustrates an important role for research in positive psychology (see Filep and Pearce 2013) with its focus on how individuals and groups can make their normal life more fulfilling through experiences such as events, especially the event participant valuation and meaning of time. In *Faster: The Acceleration of Just About Everything*, Gleick (2000) argued that everybody now expects that everything can and should be done immediately, giving rise to time pressures in our 24-hour society. In fact Cornish (2004) contextualized this, arguing that the pace of change had accelerated to the point that we now live in an age of hyperchange in society. Cornish argued that this hyperchange combines with the range of super trends which affect society (i.e. technological progress, deculturation, the loss of local culture through globalization, environmental decline and deterioration, increased mobility and economic progress leading to increased prosperity).

We need to think of planned events as a respite from this rapidity, a way to escape these time pressures and if not to slow down, at least to savour the moment. The value of time in the event may therefore be escapism from the routines and rigours of everyday life in much the same way that the annual holiday has been evaluated by researchers for many years with a diversity of views and attitudes. This is why understanding the social psychology of event participants, as discussed in Chapter 3, has such an important role to play in revealing how events fit into our complex modern-day lives and the meaning we attach to events.

A time and a place

Planned events occupy and temporarily transform spaces (or venues), and for the duration of the event one's experience of that place is altered. In turn, many events are intrinsically linked to their setting and community. As Hall and Page (2014: 150) concluded, 'Event Studies has been characterized by a comparative neglect of the way in which events and festivals transform places and spaces from what are everyday environments', whereby the event transforms locations 'into temporary environments that contribute to the production, processing and consumption of culture, concentrated in time and space' (Waterman 1998: 54). Hence, place and culture combine within a set timeframe to produce a temporary experience that is bound by place, with patterns and flows of mobility (see Batty *et al.* 2003). Culture varies geographically, so the influence of place and culture on events is reinforcing. Cross-cultural comparisons are necessary to fully appreciate the differences in how events are created, valued, managed and experienced. In turn, events influence the places and cultures in which they occur, especially when mega events are imposed on a culture that has not experienced such investment and media attention.

Attachment to places, and place identity, can be influenced by planned events (De Bres and Davis 2001; Brennan-Horley *et al.* 2007). Place identity and the branding of places via events has become a major area of research interest, with Richards (2017) pointing to their role in place-making (i.e. how organizations create an external image of the place to attract visitors, investors and to meet other societal goals such as re-imaging negative connotations with a place). In the case of mega events, architectural features such as stadia have been used to create a spectacle or attraction. Public bodies may use multi-annual programmes of events, moving away from ad hoc hosting of events to transform the image of a place (Broudehoux 2017a). Powerful marketing and advertising campaigns, such as the Danish campaign during the London 2012 Olympics (Therkelsen 2010), illustrates the global media attention during the Olympic spectacle (also see Fola 2011). Govers and Go (2016) identified the importance of authenticity and uniqueness in the place-making process using events to ensure acceptance by the community, highlighting the significance of a grassroots local community approach. This was a theme expanded upon by Duffy and Mair (2017) in their analysis of the event encounter to understand the importance of conviviality and social relations in community building by using small events and festivals. In the case of Expo events, Hereźniak and Florek (2018) found that citizen involvement enhanced the sense of community after the event. Every nation and community needs its celebrations, events that generate pride and a sense of belonging, and which build development capacity through volunteering, capital investments and improved marketing. Similarly, communities of interest and subcultures express themselves through events, and they need events and event places to identify with, as:

> *the cultural facets of festivals cannot be divorced from the commercial interests of tourism, regional and local economy and place promotion. Selling the place to the wider world or selling the festival as an inseparable part of the place rapidly becomes a significant facet of most festivals.*
>
> *(Waterman 1998: 60–61)*

Hallmark events give identity and a positive image to their host community, while venues and resorts can also have their hallmark events. The exploitation of festivals in place marketing is a worry to many observers fearing commodification, loss of cultural authenticity and over-production of events. Some events achieve 'iconic' status so they can occur anywhere and still be successful, but they always require specific venues and leave some kind of tangible legacy in terms of urban renewal, tourism and transport infrastructure, and social and environmental change. Mega events, including world's fairs, Olympic Games, other major exhibitions and sport events, have all been studied from many points of view, but there has been little attention paid to the question of whether other events can permanently transform a place.

Planned events

We need a specially constructed definition for this book, and for what we are calling event studies. The events we are considering are planned for one or more purposes, they do not just happen, and they are all unique. We have three components to the definitions around the notion of a planned event. Planning an event and the experience of the event are interconnected:

1 'Planned events' are live, social events created to achieve specific outcomes, including those related to business, the economy, culture, society and the environment.

2 Event planning involves the design and implementation of themes, settings, consumables, services and programmes that suggest, facilitate or constrain experiences for participants, guests, spectators and other stakeholders.

3 Every event experience is personal and unique, arising from the interactions of setting, programme and people.

All planned events get 'labelled': as festivals, conferences, fairs, sports or another formal title. These are really social constructs, because when we use descriptive terms like 'festival' or 'convention', most people have an idea of what they mean. To the individual, these events look and feel different, with different intentions, meanings and programmes. The typology illustrated in Figure 2.1 is based primarily on the *form* of the event (i.e. what it looks like and how it is programmed, which means how it is scheduled or scripted for the audience). Even so, any event can fulfil multiple functions, facilitate similar experiences and have many meanings attached to it. To illustrate the complexity in event typologies, du Cros and Jolliffe (2014: 46) use the following categories of events: *inspirational events* (to build creative capital), *affirming events* (for encouraging events that link to cultural identity), *pleasurable events* that offer tourism, leisure and recreational experiences, *enriching events* that facilitate personal growth and *celebratory events* that can celebrate issues such as cultural diversity (e.g. the Opening Ceremony of the Olympic Games for London 2012).

'Form' derives from the combination of various 'programmed elements of style' (discussed in Chapter 7) that make event types different. For example, the hallmark of a sport event is athletic competition, of a conference it is various interactive learning mechanisms, of a festival it is celebration manifested in theme, symbolism and emotional stimulation. Form is therefore a primary concern of event planners and designers, or at least their usual starting point. The basic and generally accepted forms of meetings, sport events, fairs and festivals can be taught, although in each culture there are going to be differences in their style and meaning. Historically, 'form' has shaped professionalization and led to the establishment of many professional associations around each specific event form (e.g. meetings). In this tradition, meeting professionals have become the most organized globally, community festivals and arts festival producers have separate associations, and sport event managers attend their own conferences. Form is equally applicable to unplanned events. Every event has some form that leads us to call it a celebration, protest, riot or party. What exactly are the 'cues'? First, the way people behave, because people assembling for protests obviously behave differently to those getting together to party. A casual meeting of friends or workmates looks and feels quite different from a spontaneous crowd celebrating the home team's victory. Second, we

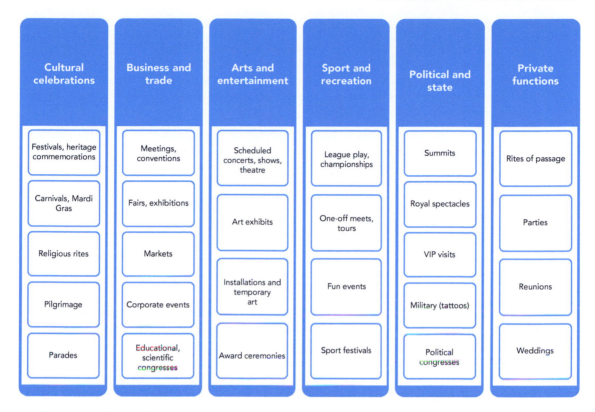

Figure 2.1 Typology of planned events

can ask the people involved what they are doing and why they got together, and this should easily reveal whether the event is a spontaneous discussion or a party. That, of course, leads us to consider experience and meanings. The programme elements of style are not always applicable to unplanned events because they are the tools of event planners and designers. If a celebrating crowd breaks into song and dance, we cannot call that programmed, but it is an activity virtually identical to what happens in many designed event experiences. In other words, the spontaneity and randomness of celebrations and experiences are what make planned events unique and difficult to replicate.

Convergence of forms and functions

It is readily apparent that forms and functions of planned events often overlap, and it appears that they are universally tending to converge. Some of this occurs naturally as cultures change and people experiment, but some of it is quite intentional. For example, the Olympics is ostensibly a celebration of amateur sport (the amateurs are long gone, unfortunately), but they are also mandated by the International Olympic Committee to include an arts festival. Host cities add conventions, exhibitions and many other functions designed to leverage these and other mega events. Television turns the whole thing into entertainment and spectacle, packaged in such a way as to maximize advertising revenue. In the case of London 2012, preceding the Games were four years of Cultural Olympiad, called:

> *the largest cultural celebration in the history of the modern Olympic and Paralympic Games …*
> *a chance for everyone to celebrate London 2012 through dance, music, theatre, the visual arts,*
> *film and digital innovation and leave a lasting legacy for the arts in the UK.*
>
> *(www.london2012.com)*

This culminated in the London 2012 Festival:

> *At the heart of the festival will be a programme of commissions by some of the finest artists in the world in events ranging from pop to film, from visual arts and fashion to theatre, from circus to carnival, from opera to digital innovation … In total, the festival will feature more than 1,000 events, with an estimated audience of more than three million people. Some of the events will be ticketed, some will be free to attend.*
>
> *(www.london2012.com)*

Another good example of convergence is the annual Kentucky Derby Festival in Louisville, Kentucky. This city was the winner of the IFEA award as the top North American Festival City, with a population over 1 million, in 2010. What was once a simple horse race (now iconic in the world of thoroughbred racing) is now something much more, as the following demonstrates from the event's website (http://derbyfestival.org):

> *Mission: Bringing the community together in celebration. The Derby Festival represents the spirit and pride of the community and showcases Louisville at its best. To provide creative and unique entertainment and community service for the people of Greater Louisville, that directly contributes to the aesthetic, cultural, educational, charitable and economic development of the area.*
>
> *The Kentucky Derby Festival's schedule includes over 70 events – most of them occurring in the two weeks leading up to the Kentucky Derby horse race. The annual celebration is kicked off by a day-long air show and fireworks extravaganza – Derby Festival's Opening Ceremonies: Thunder Over Louisville – one of the nation's largest annual fireworks shows. The ensuing two weeks of excitement and entertainment promises something for everyone. For sports fans there is basketball, volleyball and golf. For music lovers the concerts are almost non-stop. With two-thirds of the Festival events free, families can enjoy numerous just-for-kids' activities without stretching their pocketbook. Other highlights include a half and full marathon, hot-air balloon events and live bed racing! The Great Steamboat Race pits historic paddle-wheelers on the mighty Ohio River. The event that started it all, the Republic Bank Pegasus Parade, marches down Broadway on the Thursday before The Run for the Roses.*

The Derby Festival (see Nicolson 2012 for more detail) is one of many 'community festivals' across North America that celebrate community itself. Their appeal is wide, and so their programme is diverse. They defy classification as a single-form event, so convergence is their hallmark. Convergence is also apparent in the nineteenth-century San Antonio fiesta event that has now evolved into a 200-event, ten-day phenomenon (Hernández-Ehrisman 2008); a fiesta-city product has been developed.

Convergence is a powerful argument for a generic approach to event management education. Professionals will have to be increasingly flexible and inventive, not restricted to just being a meeting planner or exhibition designer or festival coordinator. Working for venues means engaging with a diverse range of events. The other important aspects of convergence relate to their meanings and impacts. When conceived as instruments of policy and strategy, events can achieve wider appeal and greater impact by combining elements of style and form. To achieve greater economic benefits, larger and more diverse events are becoming the norm. To generate positive images, more television coverage is required, reaching different and fractured target audiences. To foster social integration, policy-makers have to ensure that events have relevance to many interests. Foley *et al.* (2012) also argue that many events are now decontextualized in time and space, meaning they are inherently portable and capable of being planned at different places. The Formula 1 Grand Prix is one such event – whilst its form remains clear, it exhibits the characteristics of convergence as wider commercial interests and sponsorship combine elements of style and form and it assumes mega-event status. In the final chapter a convergence model is illustrated (Figure 12.2), combined with exchange theory, in an effort to both summarize what is happening in the events sector and to theorize about underlying forces and evolutionary processes. This conceptual model is also fully discussed in the Getz chapter in the book *The Future of Events and Festivals* (Yeoman *et al.* 2014).

Functions of planned events

'Function' moves us into the world of public policy (see Foley *et al.* 2012) for business and professional event management. Why are events held? What is their intended outcome? This is also a key starting point for planned events, and it cannot be left to chance.

Function comes in layers, like an onion. At the outside, superficially, the event might be planned as a community celebration, a festival to involve all residents. But are there also expectations that it will attract tourists? Promote a positive city image? Make money for local charities and businesses? Foster inter-organizational cooperation? The list is potentially endless. Historically, festivals and fairs performed important roles that were not discussed or planned, they just happened because they were needed. Markets and fairs were necessary for trade; parties and celebrations were fitted organically into everyday life; games were not professionalized as sport. But for the most part, that era has passed and most events are planned to meet numerous specific economic, business, social, cultural and other policy aims.

The event planner and designer, therefore, seldom has a free hand. Potentially many stakeholders are involved in determining multiple event goals, and they often conflict. When the goals are made clear, perhaps prioritized, the real work of event design can begin. If the goals are not made explicit, problems are likely to occur. Nevertheless, the designer can at least assume certain things about the event's form as long as terms like 'festival', 'fair', 'tournament' or 'conference' are used – if the stakeholders all agree that the event should be a celebration or festival, specific goals are not absolutely needed to start planning. Again, this is because the types of planned events have become social constructs. Using the example of arts events, du Cros and Jolliffe (2014: 46) identified four specific focal points that may help to classify the function of such events: *a commercial orientation, an industry focus, an individual artist focus* and a *public focus*, although admitting that each type of event will still have to establish the specific focus within each category. What follows are some common terms that pertain to the functions of events. Their definition is not fixed, and they are open to interpretation.

Hallmark events

'Hallmarks' are not only distinctive features but also symbols of quality or authenticity. A significant debate occurred in the 1980s over the terminology of hallmark events following the landmark paper by J. R. B. Ritchie (1984: 2) who defined them as:

> *Major one-time or recurring events of limited duration, developed primarily to enhance the awareness, appeal and profitability of a tourism destination in the short and/or long term. Such events rely for their success on uniqueness, status, or timely significance to create interest and attract attention.*

Ritchie identified a number of different types of hallmark events: world's fairs and expositions, unique carnivals and festivals, major sporting events, significant cultural and religious events, historical milestones (e.g. the five hundredth anniversary of the European discovery of America in 1992), classical commercial and agricultural events, and major political personage events. C. M. Hall (1989) expanded the debate on hallmark events, focusing on the issue of scale, defining them as events designed to attract national and international attention for a destination. However, as Hall (1989) also argued, confining the term 'hallmark' to large-scale events overlooks the community festivals and local celebrations (see Jepson and Clarke 2014 for numerous case studies of such events) which can be described as hallmark given their regional and local significance. Hall preferred to use the term mega events to describe major events such as world's fairs and the Olympic Games targeted at the international tourism market.

Further refinement of the debate over definitions includes a focus on celebration as being the hallmark (or distinctive feature) of festivals. We might also like to consider a hallmark event as belonging to a very special class that represents the best event, one that is authentically embedded in a particular place or culture. These are recurring events that have become so closely associated with their host community or destination that the form is an important part of its image and branding. These events provide, and feed off, place identity. Rio de Janeiro and New Orleans have their Mardi Gras, Calgary has its Stampede, and Edinburgh its Tattoo, all permanent 'institutions' in their cities, full of tradition and generating competitive advantages from a tourism perspective. In the case of Malta, Jones and Navarro (2018) described the influence of the state government in seeking to promote a blue (i.e. water-based) event – the Rolex Middlesea annual event to diversify away from mass tourism to much higher spending marine event attendees, given the country's dependence on mass tourism. For this reason, our definition is more wide ranging and embraces this diversity:

> *Hallmark events are those that possess such significance, in terms of tradition, attractiveness, quality or publicity, that the event provides the host venue, community or destination with a competitive advantage. Over time, the event and destination images become inextricably linked. Hallmark events are, by definition, permanent 'institutions' in their communities or societies.*

If cities or resorts want to design a hallmark event, they need to meet multiple criteria, and should keep in mind the power of convergence in form and function. Hallmark events must attract tourists, generate positive images and be co-branded with the destination. Such events also have to be acceptable to the host community, preferably becoming traditional and institutionalized. The institutionalization of an event was demonstrated by Lavenda (1980) in the political analysis of the Carnival of Caracas, Venezuela, where the old carnival was transformed into a highly organized, European mass event. As Lavenda (1980) illustrated, the wild, rowdy behaviour and attitude of a barbaric event was pilloried in the media to justify the creation of the civilizing model based on the carnivals in Venice, Paris and Rome (i.e. masked and with floats) to create a directed and institutionalized event in which around 30 per cent of the population became involved. To be a permanent institution requires the demonstration of benefits to the residents, including the way the media portrays the negative and positive elements. Finally, hallmark events have to be planned with long-term sustainability in mind. That requires taking a triple-bottom-line approach (see Chapter 10) to their intended outcomes, the involvement of residents at all stages and concern for how impacts are evaluated in a multi-stakeholder manner. A full discussion of the meanings and planning process for hallmark events is available (see Getz *et al.* 2013c).

2.1 RESEARCH NOTE ON RESIDENT RESPONSES TO MEGA EVENTS

Chien, P. M., Ritchie, B. W., Shipway, R. and Henderson, H. (2012). I am having a dilemma: Factors affecting resident support of event development in the community. *Journal of Travel Research*, 51(4), 451–463.

The authors suggest that residents' intention to give or withhold support of hosting an event in the community can be viewed as a social dilemma. They examined the effects of event publicity, perceived fairness of event portrayal and residents' commitment to 2012 Olympic and Paralympic sailing events on residents at Weymouth and Portland in the UK. They concluded that event publicity is linked to residents' supporting behaviours indirectly through commitment. Perceived fairness of event portrayal was identified as a moderator of the event publicity effect; when media reports of the event are considered biased or unfair, the effect of both positive and negative event publicity is attenuated.

Iconic events

An 'icon' is a graphic representation of something, in other words, a symbol. A suitable use would be: Mardi Gras stands for Rio or New Orleans, it is the city's iconic event. The other use of 'iconic event' described earlier is one that has strong appeal all on its own and can be held successfully anywhere. It symbolizes something of potentially global significance. For example, the FIFA World Cup or the Olympics are loaded with symbolic meaning, so that many people want to attend because of what they represent, not where they are. And what they represent (i.e. their meanings) is, of course, of great interest in event studies. Other iconic events that have attracted interest are memorable events such as the destruction of the Berlin Wall which divided East and West Germany (Viol *et al.* 2018). Yet other studies have critiqued the extent to which events are global media spectacles beyond their national borders, as in the case of the American Super Bowl (Dyreson 2017). An interesting analysis of an audience and police riot at the 1996 Brisbane Cybernana event has pointed to its iconic status (Green 2018). However, large events pose major logistics challenges, not least in managing large crowds (Spencer and Steyn 2017). As Jahn *et al.* (2018) noted, when events and festivals are too crowded, people do not return, since it reduces the temporary sense of communitas people feel, where a sense of closeness and camaraderie develops.

In Research Note 2.2 by Getz and McConnell, participants in two 'destination events' are compared. The events are 'iconic' for the target segments, runners and mountain bikers, because of their unique locations in the mountains and their high level of difficulty.

2.2 RESEARCH NOTE ON INVOLVEMENT AND ICONIC EVENTS

Getz, D. and McConnell, A. (2014). Comparing trail runners and mountain bikers: Motivation, involvement, portfolios, and event-tourist careers. *Journal of Convention and Event Tourism*, 15(1), 69–100.

'Amateur trail runners and endurance mountain bikers are compared with regard to motivation, involvement in their sport, competitive-event portfolios and event-travel careers. Because the dominant motivation for both samples, and for both men and women, was personal challenge, it is concluded that for many respondents involvement is directed more towards physically demanding sport than towards a particular kind of sport or event. This involvement has led a majority to develop an event-travel career. Implications are drawn for sport-event management and event-tourism marketing. Recommendations are made for further research to explore the relevance of brand communities and consumption constellations in event tourism.'

Premier or prestige events

These events are defined within specific categories, so that the World Cup is football's 'premier' event; its prestige is unrivalled. All sports and special interests tend to have prestige and premier events, and while some are located in permanent places or venues, many of them move around. Some, like the Boston Marathon, combine elements of iconic and hallmark status, given the media coverage and attention which the prestigious event brings to the location or nation. The bidding process to host these 'premier' events has now become a highly developed activity. In fact Austin, Texas, USA has branded itself as the live music capital of the world and it has a major impact upon visitation, generating around $800 million a year in music-tourism spending. Similarly, Nashville has branded itself as the Home of Country and Western and New Orleans as the Home of Jazz, making it a major platform for music-related events.

Mega events

'Mega' refers to the largest and most significant of events as highlighted under the discussion of hallmark events. The definition and implications of these events were examined in the AIEST (1987) conference proceedings in which Marris (1987) said that mega events should exceed one million visitors and be 'must-see' in nature, while Vanhove and Witt (1987) added that they should be able to attract worldwide publicity. If we equate 'mega' with large size, then they are usually the Olympics, world's fairs and other major sport events. But even a small music festival can have 'mega' impacts on a small town in terms of tourists, economic benefits or disruption as illustrated above in the discussion of hallmark events. The term can also refer to media coverage and impacts on image, as in 'the convention attracted worldwide publicity and put the city on the tourist map'. Therefore, we suggest that:

> *Mega events, by way of their size or significance, are those that yield extraordinarily high levels of tourism, media coverage, prestige or economic impact for the host community, venue or organization.*

The benefit of this definition is that it allows for 'mega events' to be situated within the context of a particular venue or organization rather than using a specific quantitative measure of scale (contrast this with Müller's 2015 debate on defining mega events and the existence of giga-events). In other words, 'mega' is a relative term, not an absolute measure. An interesting article by Müller (2017) outlined six paradoxes (i.e. contradictions) associated with mega events, some of which will be examined later in the book:

- *The universalism paradox*, which suggests that whilst mega events are intended to transcend national differences, they often reinforce them.
- *The compliance paradox*, which implies that to host and run a mega event, one must follow a strict set of guidelines. Conversely, the event cannot occur without violating these rules, often exemplified in the building of Olympic Stadia and the removal of neighbourhoods to make way for construction, compromising local community rights.
- *The winners paradox*, where the winning bid will expect to make a net financial loss on the hosting of the event.
- *The participation paradox*, where events are focused on people as spectators or competitors and yet, as Chapter 3 will show, people are often excluded from the events raising issues of accessibility, inclusion and diversity.
- *The uniqueness paradox*, where the promise of the event is a 'once in a lifetime' experience, yet many events are highly repetitive.
- *The passion paradox*, summarized by Müller (2017) as 'we love them, we hate them', characterizing events as socially divisive activities.

In addition, drawing parallels with Ashworth and Page's (2011) assessment of urban tourism, a further paradox also exists:

- *Events need cities as central locations and spaces capable of accommodating large audiences; but cities do not need events as their diversified economic structure will not necessarily need the event sector as a mainstay of economic activity, but as a supplementary or secondary form of activity.*

Media events

Media events are created primarily for broadcast audiences, such as the 2014 MTV music awards hosted in Glasgow, Scotland, an event which is directly related to the media and the power of television and the Internet to reach global audiences (see Reid 2006 for a review of a previous MTV event). Examples include surfing events that really need to be heavily edited and packaged to make for good viewing, and eco-challenges in remote places over long, arduous courses. However, any event can be packaged for the media, and that might be an essential part of its sponsorship appeal or subsidies from tourism and government agencies. In other words, any event can become a media event – it is a function, not a form.

Cause-related events

These are established to raise money, or to promote a cause, which makes them part of social marketing. While any form of event could perform this function, common types of fund-raisers are gala dinners, concerts, entertainment shows, endurance events (in which donors support participants financially), sponsored sport events (e.g. the UK's annual fun run Race for Life, which has 300 local races to raise money for Cancer Research UK) as well as celebrity sports and auctions.

Corporate events

Any event produced by or for a corporation fits this category, with common types being product launches, meetings, grand openings and publicity stunts. An alternative meaning is the trend for large sport events in particular, like the Super Bowl, to become so tied to corporate sponsors and related hospitality that they in effect become 'corporatized'. A further shift in the events world has been the emphasis on 'experiential marketing' to develop brands and sustain relationships with customers and other corporate stakeholders. The term 'live marketing' has crept into the language to describe the use of events for these purposes. A related concept is the 'brand land', or the creation of venues devoted to 'brand experiences', and of course these corporate monuments have to be animated with events. Ulrich Wuensch gives an expert opinion on corporate events later.

Publicity stunts

Any event designed to garner publicity falls into this broad category, but it is usually associated with politicians and movie stars. Publicity agents should be expert at contriving events or situations that appeal to the media, or to crowds, so that they become 'news'. But to the degree that they are obvious in their intent, or manipulative, they can easily backfire. See elsewhere our discussions of 'pseudo-events' and authenticity.

Special events

Although this term is often used generically for the planned events field, and has been popularized by an important professional association (ISES), what is 'special' about any event is a subjective interpretation by either the producer or the guest. Jago and Shaw (1999) asked adults to describe important attributes of 'special events' and discovered that the number of attendees, international attention given to the event, perceived improvement to image and pride in the host region, and an exciting experience were the main factors explaining perceived specialness.

A long list of factors that can contribute to any event's specialness starts with its uniqueness as we emphasized earlier (see Getz 2005) and includes elements of style (like hospitality, symbolism, festive spirit, theming and authenticity), meeting multiple goals and appealing to different stakeholders and audiences. Two perspectives on 'specialness' have to be taken: is it special to the organizers, or to the participants and customers? Therefore, a special event can comprise the following two features:

1   A special event is a one-time or infrequently occurring event outside the normal programme or activities of the sponsoring or organizing body.

2   To the customer or guest, a special event is an opportunity for an experience outside the normal range of choices or beyond everyday experience.

Spectator and interactive events

'Interactive' events embody person–setting or person–person interactivity, unlike 'spectator' events, which are inherently passive. Interactivity is thought to foster a higher level of involvement or engagement, making it a crucial element in 'experience design'. A study of mega screens in public places in Melbourne, Australia and Incheon, South Korea (Papastergiadis *et al.* 2013) for the presentation of a cultural event – to display public art – illustrates the changing boundaries between spectating and interaction.

Participant events

These are events that are held for people to be involved, not just to spectate. 'Participants' are more than customers or guests, they are necessary for the event to exist. Meetings and conventions do not exist without delegates; there are no marathons without runners; dance festivals need dancers. Exhibitions also require participants, namely the exhibitors. Such events provide 'targeted benefits' (i.e. they are customized experiences), they can be viewed as subcultural manifestations, and are highly sought after by competitive tourist destinations that can either create them or bid on them. For example, Coghlan and Filo (2013) examined participants' experiences and motivation at charity/sport events and the role of adventure philanthropy in such participation.

An events industry?

An industry, in conventional terms, means a sector of the economy that produces the same goods or services, such as the automobile industry. This definition is problematic for events because of their diversity of forms and purposes, as Leiper (2008) observed in relation to tourism. Leiper (2008) used the plural 'tourism industries'. Different kinds of event producers and suppliers feel they are part of a tourism industry, an exhibition industry, even the cultural industry. This last term, cultural industry, is worthy of further discussion; see Events in Focus 2.1; also see Figure 2.2.

EVENTS IN FOCUS

2.1 The cultural industries and events, S. J. Page and J. Connell (Exeter University Business School)

The term 'culture industry' was popularized in the 1930s when the Frankfurt School emerged (the collective name for a group of critical theorists who worked at the Frankfurt Institute for Social Research in the 1920s; also see Chapter 1 and the section on critical event studies). Within that paradigm were theorists such as Adorno and Horkheimer, whose work culminated in terms such as 'culture industry'. Within that term, the focus was on criticisms of the commoditization of art and its reproduction to create repetitive cultural products for mass consumption. The basis of their arguments was the contention that the culture industry was run by capitalism for profit, and so the experiences which the culture industry provided were for popular mass appeal. In stark contrast, such theorists were critical of popular culture. This is because it was interpreted as a form of social control, where popular entertainment socialized the mass population into passivity to make them compliant citizens.

As Page and Connell (2010) demonstrated, a notable transformation in post-modern society is the shift from tangible elements of culture such as the built heritage, museums and monuments to more intangible leisure resources such as image, identity, lifestyle, narratives of the city, creativity and the media. All of these elements enhance the consumer's experience of culture and its consumption in event experiences. For elaboration, see the book *The Arts and Events* by du Cros and Jolliffe (2014).

Hesmondhalgh (2007) is one of the most widely cited studies on the cultural industries and it highlights the context in which events operate as they draw upon the core industries and peripheral sectors (see Figure 2.2 on classifying the cultural industries), all of which coalesce in the formation of planned event experiences in differing degrees and ways. Therefore, one interesting approach to the interpretation of the growth and development of the event sector within a post-modern society is the commoditization, commercialization and creation of consumer experiences around culture (both high and low, with low representing popular culture). The event sector(s) are a clear outcome of the cultural industries' growth in which leisure, tourism and serious leisure have coalesced with work and pleasure to develop what many would label as the event phenomenon.

There are also wider political explanations of why people use the term 'industry' or 'industries' when they want to legitimize their activities and gain government support. Those in the arts seldom think of

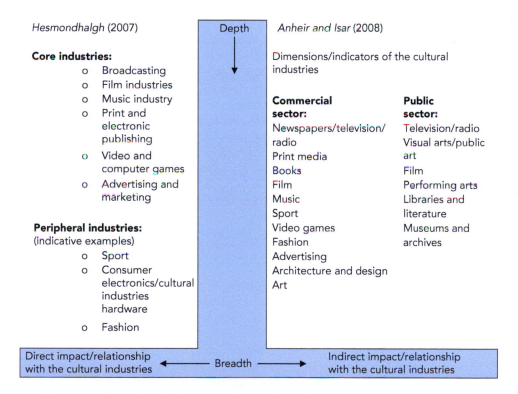

Figure 2.2 Classifying the cultural industries – their scale and scope

Source: Page and Connell (2010: 354). Reprinted from *Leisure: An Introduction*, S. J. Page and J. Connell, Pearson Education (2010).

Developed from Hesmondhalgh, D. (2007). *The Cultural Industries.* London: Sage; Pratt, A. (2008). Locating the cultural economy. In H. Anheir and Y. Isar (eds), *The Cultural Economy.* London: Sage, pp. 42–51.

themselves as being part of an industry, because the word carries connotations of production for economic purposes rather than art for the sake of art. It is also common to talk about the service industry or industries, of which events are clearly a part, and increasingly to view events as being an integral part of the experience economy and creative industries. Numerous private-sector suppliers serve the events sector, creating a kind of 'industry'. Raj *et al.* (2008: 5) said: 'If there is still a case for the existence of an, albeit diverse, events industry, then it is the industry's specialist support services that provide the best argument for it.' Ultimately, it is a matter of perspective and political purpose that leads one to call events of one type, or the entire events sector, an industry. It makes the most sense when speaking of economic goals and outcomes, and the least sense when referring to the social and cultural dimensions of events.

An experiential typology?

Function and form do not predetermine personal experiences, mainly because people create their own experiences within event settings, and will assign meanings to event experiences that can be independent or only loosely related to the event's purpose and programme. Great experiences can be obtained without planned events, but event designers want people to have a great experience at their event. To date, most event designers have had to operate in accordance with established norms (the social constructs again) for event production – such as how to produce an effective meeting, how to programme an arts festival or how to run a tournament. Alternatively, the designer has to work according to instinct, within a creative mentality, and rely on both subtle and overt feedback to determine if the event experience was both pleasant and as intended.

We cannot easily develop a typology of events based primarily on experience, because so many possible experiences can be had at events. Both festivals and sports events can facilitate joy, celebration, excitement, self-fulfilment or aesthetic appreciation. While their form and functions might be completely different, at the experiential level (and to some extent at the level of their meanings) they can be quite similar. That is why a phenomenological research methodology (see Chapter 3) offers considerable scope for a better understanding of event experiences, because it focuses on the individual's state of mind while experiencing the event (for an example, see Ziakas and Boukas's 2013 study of Limassol Carnival, Cyprus). A full range of possible personal and social experiences tied to events is likely not possible, but certainly the major ones people talk about can be identified – as long as we keep in mind the limitations of language and how people express themselves. For example, the section on experiences, and in particular the cognitive, affective and behavioural (conative) dimensions of experiences, expands upon this theme as do the sections on social worlds, involvement and benefits.

Planned versus unplanned events

It might come as a surprise to realize how much of what we see and hear on broadcast media is really about planned events. Consider the attention given to entertainment and sport, both having numerous, dedicated television channels (at least where cable and satellite TV are found). Add the ample coverage given to political events (including news conferences), private events (e.g. famous weddings), food and beverage events, and so on, and it really adds up. Now consider the range of 'unplanned' events that get media exposure, so much so that we wonder if they really are being planned. Indeed, in many cases they are clearly set in motion by people (maybe agitators, publicity agents or social activists) and they have a purpose, but they are categorically different from the events we are talking about when using the terms 'event management' or 'professional event manager'. The distinctions sometimes get blurry, so it is necessary for event studies to encompass both. The only unplanned events we are not including are those that fall under the headings of accidents, forces of nature, wars and insurrections, and other completely unpredictable happenings that hit the news.

'Spontaneous mass celebrations' should be considered. For example, during the Calgary Flames' run for the Stanley Cup in 2003, the 'Red Mile' was created when thousands of fans frequenting bars along the city's 17th Avenue flooded onto the streets. They wore their team's red colours, had a party, attracted news media from all over North America, and were tolerated by the police and civic authorities. This kind of social phenomenon results in events that have a specific duration (as long as the series continues), require some measures and controls similar to planned festivals, yet take on a life of their own. Incidentally, merchants and civic officials decided afterwards that they would not tolerate such a spontaneous celebration in the future, as it posed many risks. Using traffic controls and police action, they prevented it from occurring in 2005. We can interpret this case as a triumph of regulation over spontaneity, which is a theme discussed again in the section on carnivals. Table 2.1 classifies the planned and unplanned events that event studies encompasses. It refers to their purpose or goals, programme or activities, type or degree of control and accountability. Note that these are not always mutually exclusive, as some events demonstrate elements of both planning and spontaneity.

The question of scale

Probably the vast majority of planned events are small and occur in the private or corporate spheres. But most attention focuses on the larger events that are open to the public, covered by the media and generate substantial impacts. So there is a continuum of planned events along the dimension of scale, and the extremes can also be associated with impacts and policy implications (see Table 2.2).

Frequency and periodicity

Does it matter how often an event is produced? In sports, teams play many games during a season and in the arts and entertainment sector concerts or shows are also regularly held. What if a fan or patron goes to many of these events? They can become routine for participants, producers and some of the audience. But we need to remember that every event is still somewhat unique. In fact, many people love sports because the action is infinitely variable and the outcome always unpredictable, making them an

Table 2.1 Planned versus unplanned events

	Planned events (The realm of professional event designers and managers)	Unplanned events (The realm of spontaneity and unpredictability)
Purpose	Goals or outcomes are specified by producers of the event, and are influenced by key stakeholders	Purpose is self-defined; intentions of participants might be unclear, diverse, even contradictory
Programme	Planned and scheduled, usually in detail; designers seek to create 'experiences' for guests, participants and spectators	Spontaneous activities; or, once set in motion by agents, actions become rather unpredictable
Control	Controls are imposed by managers and other formal stakeholders, including governments	No management systems in place, only a degree of normal civic control; sometimes a police response is required
Accountability	Producers and managers are formally held accountable	No organization or legal entity is accountable over all; individuals can be held accountable for their actions, under law

Table 2.2 A question of scale

	Small events	Large events
Form and function	Tend to be single-form events (e.g. a meeting, competition, private function)	Tend to combine elements of style, such as sports becoming festivals, meetings adding exhibitions, or community festivals combining multiple events of all kinds (i.e. convergence)
	Less likely to be planned with tourists or media in mind	More likely to be planned to generate major economic and place-marketing benefits
The event experience	Mostly in the private and corporate spheres of interest The experience might be intensely private or shared with an affinity group	Mostly in the public sphere of interest Crowd dynamics can dominate The event can affect entire communities through media coverage and shared attitudes
Impacts	Collectively they are significant (e.g. weddings, meetings, parties, most sport meets)	Each large event has substantial impacts (e.g. festivals, major sport events, fairs and exhibitions)
Media coverage	Individual, small events seldom attract media attention	The event itself is of interest to the media, or created primarily as a media event
Policy implications	Policies related to venues, and to events in general (e.g. health standards, green operations, permits required)	Policy decisions required for specific events (e.g. decision to bid; infrastructure investments; feasibility studies and impact assessments commissioned)

'authentic' experience when compared with other forms of entertainment like TV and the movies; no actors, musicians or performers can exactly reproduce their efforts from one show to the next so that the audience can return with some expectation of differences. Even frequently attended events can be 'special' to the audience depending on their expectations, mood and experiences. The timing (or periodicity) can also make the event special as in the case of winter festivals, occurring around the festive period.

As Dewar *et al.* (2001: 523) indicated:

> *At low latitudes (northern and southern) winter is a time of suspension. Life slows or stops, days grow shorter, warmth is a warm fire, snow and ice lock the land in a quiet world of white. Winter has been seen as a time of death, famine and fear by many cultures. At the same time it is celebrated as a time of friendship, relaxation, good cheer and festival, a time when the fields are fallow and there is time for play. This paradox is expressed in the ubiquitous winter festival. Christmas, solstice, or whatever the festival is, is a time to hold back the cold and dark with the light of celebration.*

This quotation illustrates not only the special attraction of the festive season but the emotion and surrounding ambience of the season of 'goodwill to all' that makes the Christmas period special; it is often marked in northern climates with Christmas lights, which in many towns and cities have become attractions in their own right.

Thus, frequency is not a defining criterion for inclusion in event studies. We are as interested in scheduled, routine theatre and sports as we are in festivals held only every ten years, as well as what makes the timing 'special'. Periodicity is a key issue, however, as one-time events are usually bid on, are expected to meet very specific objectives (such as attract tourists or generate profit) and might never be seen in an area again. One-time mega events have the greatest impact. Hallmark events by definition should be annual and permanent, as they are co-branded with the destination or community.

Activity or event?

Events contain many activities, but activities are not, by strict definition, events. 'Activity' is defined as the 'state of being active', 'energetic action or movement', 'liveliness' or 'a specified pursuit in which a person partakes'. A leisure or recreation activity is one that is pursued for its own, intrinsic rewards, and a business activity is pursued for its value-creating benefits or out of administrative necessity. Activities within planned events are mostly related to the theme (such as performances at a concert, matches in a competitive sport event or assemblies during a conference). Individual participants and guests at events engage in their own activities, often unscripted and personal (e.g. talking, eating, bodily functions, singing along, cheering, viewing, contemplating) and these also contribute to the overall event experience. Activities at events are influenced by interactions among the setting, the programme and other people.

Even so, the boundaries between activity and event are not really absolute. From the individual's perspective, engaging in a mountain climb, or any other adventure pursuit, might be a planned 'event' with a purpose, design (lots of preparations including a route to the summit), tight schedule, specific setting and the company of others. In this sense the activity of mountain climbing embodies specific events for the participants, but they are highly personal and not open to the public. Many people presumably reflect on their lives and careers as a series of events, and among them will be planned *rites de passage* such as anniversaries.

Length or duration

How long can a single event be? Remembering our earlier discussion about the fact that all events are really part of a continuum of experiences for individuals and a congruence of multi-stakeholder activity, this question of event length is somewhat pointless. If we call it an 'event', then for all practical purposes it is. We frequently see lengthy events, such as the one described by Liburd (2008) with reference to the year-long celebration in Denmark of Hans Christian Andersen's Bicentenary in 2005. The Cultural Capitals movement, which has been spreading globally, is usually a year-long 'event' (see Richards and Palmer 2010). Most of these are promotions, with multiple events packaged within, but they are certainly designed to be perceived as a single, noteworthy event.

Olympic and mega-event studies

People are fascinated by mega events, those that by definition are the largest or most publicized. And so too are researchers, who continue to examine the Olympics, world's fairs and major international sport tournaments from every conceivable angle. For example, social science publishers have developed entire lists of books focused just on the Olympics – in 2014, Routledge had 59 Olympic-titled books on its list and in 2018 this had grown to 88 reflecting the growing research interest in this field. A similar growth is apparent from searching 'Olympics' on Scopus, the academic search engine. In 1976, 12 articles were indexed, rising to 512 in 2012 and dropping to 243 for the year to October 2014, with over 3,600 articles indexed. By 2018, this had exceeded 6,000 items. Therefore, the Olympics as an event phenomenon has developed its own scholarly sub-area within events and sport research. A number of universities have established Olympic research centres in cooperation with the International Olympic Committee, and there are always new articles and books coming out on the Olympics, largely because every winter and summer Olympic Games generates a flurry of interest in host countries (see, for example, Toohey and Veal (2007), who took a social science perspective on the Olympic Games). While the discourse on the Olympics and other mega events stands out in terms of public interest and policy debates, most of the issues are the same as for lesser events. We can separate planned events by types, size, length, periodicity, impacts or whatever, but event studies seeks to unify rather than subdivide. Theory, in particular, should cross all subdivisions, although practical applications will naturally be different.

Description and examples of the major event forms

In this section each of the main forms of planned events is defined and outlined with examples.

Cultural celebrations

'Celebration' has several connotations:

- a joyful occasion; special festivities to mark some happy event; a joyous diversion; to observe a day or event with ceremonies of respect, festivity or rejoicing (such as Thanksgiving celebrations);
- solemnization (the public performance of a sacrament or solemn ceremony with all appropriate ritual, such as to celebrate mass or a marriage);
- to extol, praise or acclaim;
- to make widely known.

Synonyms include: to commemorate, honour or distinguish.

We define 'culture' later, in the section on cultural anthropology, but at this point we can say that 'cultural celebrations' are solemn or joyous events that have cultural meaning. They may include many other types of planned event, but are separated from entertainment by the cultural values being expressed. Consisting of festivals, carnivals, heritage commemorations, parades, and religious rites and rituals, the study of cultural celebrations draws heavily from cultural anthropology. This is one of the oldest and best-established approaches to event studies, focusing on the roles and meanings of festivity and celebration in, and across, cultures.

Festival

Although it does not do justice to the richness and diversity of meanings attached to 'festival', we propose the following simple definition:

> ***Festivals are themed, public celebrations.***

Falassi's (1987: 2) *Time Out of Time: Essays on the Festival* suggested that festivals were a social phenomenon found in virtually all human cultures, and in modern English the term has several meanings:

- a sacred or profane time of celebration, marked by special observances;
- the annual celebration of a notable person or event, or (of) the harvest of an important product;
- a cultural event consisting of a series of performances of works in the fine arts, often devoted to a single artist or genre;
- a fair;
- generic gaiety, conviviality, cheerfulness.

Falassi (1987: 2) continued to argue that in the social sciences, 'festival' means:

> *a periodically recurrent, social occasion in which, through a multiplicity of forms and a series of coordinated events, participate directly or indirectly and to various degrees, all members of a*

whole community, united by ethnic, linguistic, religious, historical bonds, and sharing a world-view. Both the social function and the symbolic meaning of the festival are closely related to a series of overt values that the community recognizes as essential to its ideology and worldview, to its social identity, its historical continuity, and to its physical survival, which is ultimately what festivals celebrate.

The term 'festival' is much overused and misused. Some so-called festivals are nothing more than commercial promotions or parties. Indeed, 'festivity' is often used in the same way as 'having a good time'. Many community or broadly programmed festivals seem to forget what they are celebrating, or at least they do not interpret the meaning. However, Jepson and Clarke (2014: 3) propose the following definition for community festivals as:

Themed and inclusive community event or series of events which have been created as the result of an inclusive community planning process to celebrate the particular way of life of people and groups in the local community with emphasis on particular space and time.

In this sense, 'festival' has often been reduced to a public entertainment programme, or a special time for fun and activities, rather than a celebration (see The *Routledge Handbook of Festivals* for more in-depth discussions of festivals and events, Mair 2018). Even arts festivals are guilty of using the term without paying attention to the meanings and how they are interpreted as we highlighted earlier. Is it a festival if there is nothing more than a series of musical performances?

The reason sociologists and anthropologists have spent so much effort studying festivals is that they reveal much about culture (i.e. the outcome of the socialization process, or learned behaviour, or a way of life that is shaped by religion, mores, traditions and roles) and the functioning of societies. Turner (1982) recognized that people have a need to set aside times and places for celebration where they are co-present, the theory which suggests that other actors may shape individual human behaviour which is rooted in notions of sociality and the company of others, or 'being with'. Eagleton (1981), Hughes (1999) and Ravenscroft and Mateucci (2002) thought festival and carnival provide a socially sanctioned forum for unleashing social tensions that would otherwise prove destructive. Ekman (1999), Farber (1983) and Geertz (1993) saw festivals as socially sustaining devices through which people express identities, connect with their place and communicate with the outside world. Manning (1983: 4) saw festivals as providing a rich 'text', the reading of which provides much knowledge about local culture and community life. His view on 'celebration' was that it is 'performance' entailing the 'dramatic presentation of cultural symbols'. Celebration is also 'public, with no social exclusion', and is therefore 'participatory' entertainment.

The festival experience has been studied in depth, but as Falassi argues.

At festival times, people do something they normally do not; they abstain from something they normally do; they carry to the extreme behaviours that are usually regulated by measure; they invert patterns of daily social life. Reversal, intensification, trespassing, and abstinence are the four cardinal points of festive behaviour.

(Falassi 1987: 3)

This description, however, sounds more like 'carnival' than most contemporary 'festivals'.

The 'building blocks' of festivals can all be considered ritual acts, or 'rites', since they happen within an exceptional frame of time and space, and their meaning is considered to go beyond their literal and specific aspects:

The framing ritual that opens the festival is one of valorization (which for religious events has been called sacralization) that modifies the usual and daily function and meaning of time and space. To serve as the theatre of the festive events an area is reclaimed, cleared, delimited, blessed, adorned, forbidden to normal activities. Similarly, daily time is modified by a gradual or sudden interruption that introduces 'time out of time', a special temporal dimension devoted to special activities.

(Falassi 1987: 4)

Geographical research on festivals has viewed them as contested spaces where symbolic practices (a parade, for example) are used to consolidate or resist prevailing norms and values such as Sydney's Mardi Gras parade, which reveals 'the different ways bodies, emotions, sexuality and spatiality become entwined within the annual rhythms of this mega-event' (Waitt and Stapel 2011: 197). As Hall and Page (2012) argue, 'this [contestation] is especially the case in geographical settings where events characterise the out-of-home forms of leisure (as opposed to the in-home forms except for where they are televised and consumed within the home). What characterizes the event and its significance is the way it transforms everyday living and also serves as a means to reinterpret and represent locality and identity' (also see Cudny 2014 for a recent review of the field). In the case of festivals, Waterman (1998: 56) succinctly conveyed these points, arguing that:

> *a conventional approach to festivals in human geography in which the arts festival was little more than a transient cultural event with a measurable impact on the landscape, environment and economy might simply have been mapped or modelled ... But festivals are cultural artefacts which are not simply bought and consumed but which are also accorded meaning through their active incorporation into people's lives ... They epitomise the representation of contemporary accumulation through spectacle.*

Waterman (1998) highlights the significant role of place in the spectacle of events and their meaning (Olds and Ley 1988), building on the work of Jackson (1988), and the Notting Hill Carnival in London acts as a vehicle for expression of underlying political tensions as one of Europe's largest street festivals. In contrast, Richards (1996) argued that in the 1970s, festivals were recognized as being catalysts for arts development at the local level. Quinn (2006: 291) concluded that in Ireland, festivals over the past 35 years have expanded venue infrastructure, advanced community animation, developed local resources, expanded business in arts and related areas and developed tourist audiences. 'Festivalization', discussed in Chapter 1, is a term used in references to the strategic employment of festivals in place marketing and tourism promotion, as in the 'festivalization' of many historic cities (see, for example, Richards 2007a). Not all observers see this as a positive process.

Robinson *et al.* (2004) discussed how festivals, supposedly reflecting local and ethnic culture, have become part of cultural tourism. However, many are 'placeless' and created just for tourism, giving rise to questions about authenticity and appropriateness. The social meanings of festivals in contemporary economic and cultural life are therefore deserving of more attention. This discourse has been gaining momentum, as indicated in the books *Festivals, Tourism and Social Change* (Picard and Robinson 2006b) and *Festival Places: Revitalising Rural Australia* (Gibson and Connell 2011).

The British Arts Festivals Association (2000, 2002, 2007) provides a typology: music, dance, visual, theatre, film, comedy and street arts, and of course it is possible to subdivide these themes. Other popular festivals pertain to science, food and beverages, literature and arts for children and the family. Festivals with heritage and religious themes are widespread. In North America 'community festivals' are very popular (see Jepson and Clarke 2014 for some examples). These combine many elements of celebration, entertainment, spectacle and sports, often becoming hallmark events and tourist attractions. In essence they celebrate the community itself, provide a sense of identity and hopefully foster social cohesion. Referring to a festival's explicit theme is not always the best indicator of its meanings.

2.3 RESEARCH NOTES ON FESTIVALS

Grunwell, S. and Inhyuck, S. (2008). Film festivals: An empirical study of factors for success. *Event Management*, 11(4), 201–210.

This article reports on a study of film festival attendees that was undertaken to evaluate the success of a regional film festival and assist film festival managers and sponsors in future planning. Attendee characteristics and festival experience were evaluated, as well as the festival's economic impact on the local community. It also includes an overview of what makes film festivals unique as an 'industry', particularly their value in generating economic benefits as well as cultural opportunities for host communities.

Lee, J. (2014). Visitors' emotional responses to the festival environment. *Journal of Travel and Tourism Marketing*, 31(1), 114–131.

The researcher examined how emotions in three Texas-based, agricultural-themed festivals affected post-visit behaviour. 'Results revealed that festival atmospherics had a positive indirect effect on loyalty via positive emotions, satisfaction, and psychological commitment.'

Festivals are evolving

Although the organic forces giving rise to festivals remain intact, springing from a community's need to celebrate, they are evolving quickly in both form and function. It is readily observable that the term itself has been corrupted and commodified, along with the variations 'fest', 'festivity' and 'festive'. They have become commonplace, even trite, and no longer refer exclusively to a cultural celebration – and certainly not to sacred rituals. We can partake in regular 'lobster-fests' at the local seafood restaurant, or become 'festive' for the entire Holiday Season (involving over-consumption of food and drink).

Second, more and more so-called festivals are really entertainment productions, so much so that we argue that many young people only know festivals as outdoor music concerts. The behaviour of attendees is more like carnival, with revelry being the object. There are still festival-like elements to the experience, however, as generators of social communitas. Third, many festivals have been created for their instrumentalist values, such that they are no longer authentic reflections of community or culture, but of policy. O'Sullivan *et al.* (2009) observed that in Wales local/community events are driven by socio-cultural and also economic purposes, when it comes to government involvement. The vast majority are local and oriented towards residents. Economic impact assessments are the dominant form of evaluation, so there is an evident mismatch between stated purpose and impacts measured.

Pop music festivals

Stone (2008) identified the origins of the modern era of outdoor pop music festivals, beginning in the USA in the 1960s with Monterey (1967) and Woodstock (1969) (and the underlying political issues, see Robinson 2016 and McKay 2015). In Britain the earliest were the 1968–1970 Isle of Wight festivals and Glastonbury (1970). The number continues to grow each year in the UK. Stone defines these as recurring performance events with two or more live performances over one or more days, and packaged 'as a coherent whole'. Some are indoors, and some are even free. 'Pop' covers all popular musical genres. They can be competitive (e.g. battle of the bands), for-profit or not, single or multi-venue. The programme might include traditional festive elements like comedy and theatre, dance and merchandizing. Summer is the festival season, and success often depends upon good weather. Stone asserts that the audience has been growing and widening, it's not just young people or ageing hippies. And they are increasingly expensive entertainment options. Those who identify with sub- and counter-cultures are unhappy with the increasing cost, commercialism, professionalism and regulations imposed by governments.

Various experiences are associated with pop music festivals, including camping and communitas (communitas is how people come together – see Chapter 3 for a more in-depth discussion of the concept). Stone (2008: 223) argued that: 'Uniquely, many festivals serve as adult playgrounds, representing marginal, liminal zones devoted to hedonism and largely uninhibited play and fun.' People are also motivated to attend by the need for identity-building and affirmation, linked to the accumulation of 'popular culture capital'. In other words, it's the thing to do. Stone (2008) lists recent trends in the form and themes of pop music festivals (also see Jones (2015) on their historical evolution since the 1960s), and Events in Focus 2.2 provides the example of UK music tourism and the role of such festivals. This is a reflection of diversity, targeted live communications and the power of social media to attract audiences. These festivals include religious, urban, holiday-destination, premium, secret, teen's, deliberately constrained, boutique, women's, green, family, dual-location, economy, political, no-camping and virtual festivals.

EVENTS IN FOCUS

2.2 UK music festivals – scale and impact

In 2013, UK Music produced its report *Music Tourism: Contribution to the UK Economy*, in which it outlined the impact of the music tourism industry on the UK. Music festivals play a major role in this industry, where:

- music tourism contributed £ 2.2 billion to the UK economy in 2012;
- £ 1.3 billion was spent by music tourists, of which £ 6.5 million was from overseas tourists visiting the UK;
- 41 per cent of the market for music tourism was based around live events;
- music visitors attended a diversity of music venues such as arenas, festivals, live performances in parks and stadia; London alone has 349 live music venues.

2.4 RESEARCH NOTE ON MOTIVATION TO ATTEND MUSIC FESTIVALS

Tkaczynski, A. and Rundle-Thiele, S. (2013). Understanding what really motivates attendance: A music festival segmentation study. *Journal of Travel and Tourism Marketing*, 30(6), 610–623.

Attendees at an Australian Christian music festival were studied and segmented using TwoStep cluster analysis. Religion was a dominant motivator, and while religious music was the main attraction, additional motivations were also important including the opportunity to *socialize with others* and *to spend time with friends*. While *headline artists* and *feature artists* were both essential, other activities such as *shopping* were also relevant. Most respondents purchased the *three-day pass*, which implies that the visitors came to the festival for the whole experience rather than seeing only one performer on a particular day.

Carnival

Carnival is a celebration preceding Lent and is associated with feasting, costumes, parades and revelry. Mardi Gras, or Fat Tuesday, is the last day within carnival season. People go to carnivals and Mardi Gras events for fun, play and revelry (even debauchery), enhanced or manifested through role reversal in masquerading, parades and costume balls. People love to dress up (or down), have a party, and suspend the social norms and even laws that govern everyday life. Turner (1974) and other anthropologists and sociologists have paid considerable attention to carnivals, often distinguishing between the 'sacred' elements of traditional, religiously grounded festivals, and the 'profane' side of carnivals. Carnival remains a popular subject for academic researchers, including books by Riggio (2004) on carnival in Trinidad, and by Harris (2003) on folk theology and performance associated with carnivals. Nurse (2004) reported on the Trinidad Carnival from the points of view of tourism and the 'cultural industry'.

Carnival is the 'profane' side of festival. It is an integral part of civilization, embodying revelry, masquerading (and masks), role reversal, social licence and spectacle. To some it is a sanctioned form of mild civil disobedience, to others it is something to forbid or repress. Ritual, festivity, revelry and ecstasy perform a variety of roles, some say as safety valves, and might actually counter depression and lead to social health. In Europe, carnival remains a strong tradition in many countries, especially where Roman Catholic populations are large, and the Federation of European Carnival Cities (www.carnivalcities.com) is the related professional association. According to FECC, there are at least nine types of European carnival, among them the Samba or Caribbean form that is popular in the New World, including Rio de Janeiro. Carnivals have a very long history. They can have distinctive styles, but tend to feature masquerade or costume balls, parades, theatrical productions, feasting and partying. From the Carnival of Venice website (www.carnivalofvenice.com) comes this reminder:

> *The Carnival in Venice is no 'goof', no 'consumerist ceremony' as some people complain, but sincere, wonderful heartfelt tradition that goes back in time almost a millennium, and despite its age, still shows its vitality to whom participates to it in person or in spirit.*

> *Carnival in Venice is believed to have become official in 1296, lasted six weeks or longer, and built on an already established tradition of mask wearing. By the 18th Century it was a famous event embodying balls, spectacles, masks and theatre.*
> *(For the detailed programme, visit the official website www.carnevale.venezia.it)*

Carnival continues to evolve. In cold climates 'winter carnivals' are flourishing, such as Quebec's Winter Carnival, which has become the city's hallmark event. 'Midsumma Carnival' in Melbourne, Australia, is an example of the numerous gay and lesbian Mardi Gras or carnivals held around the world, many of which have become major tourist attractions (Pitts 1999). As the following quote from the 'Midsumma' website explains:

> *Carnival transforms Treasury Gardens into the queerest park in Australia. Carnival is wearing her brand new Treasury frock so come and tell her she's beautiful and experience a spectacular hub of queer games, hot music, bump-your-booty dancing and sporting prowess as we celebrate the closing of Midsumma.*

> *(www.midsumma.org.au)*

According to Ehrenreich (2006) 'collective ecstasy', a part of carnival and akin to dancing in the streets, has been a part of human civilization from the very beginning. There is an age-old conflict between control exerted by social hierarchies and the desire for freedom of expression and behaviour. Religion and politics conspire to suppress natural tendencies. Ehrenreich points to the carnivalization of sports, and says that protest movements constantly reinvent the carnival. Turner's notion of 'communitas' in *The Ritual Process* (1969) and Durkheim's (1965) notion of 'collective effervescence' are related concepts. To

Bakhtin (1993), carnival is something people create for themselves (i.e. it is a liberating force) in contrast to the spectacles that those in power prefer. Debord (1983) in *Society of the Spectacle* argued that it occurs in 'an epic without festivals'. In other words, spectacle (in which audiences are passive spectators and consumers, rather than participants in experiences) is associated with power and control, while carnival or festivity fosters 'inclusiveness'. Gotham (2005a), in a review of urban spectacles associated with carnivals, highlighted the conflict and struggles over the meaning in such celebrations, while Addo's (2009) anthropological review examined the way in which spectacle had become ritualized by festival practices.

Laing and Frost (2014) examine how 'traditional events and the identities they support are increasingly being challenged and rituals may be lost'. Reacting against the homogenizing effects of globalization, many communities and events are recreating or inventing rituals, sometimes borrowing from others, in the pursuit of uniqueness and authenticity. Mardi Gras in New Orleans is one of the events examined in this context. It has been studied by many authors, including the work of Gotham (2005a, 2005b; see Research Note 2.5).

2.5 RESEARCH NOTE ON MARDI GRAS

Gotham, K. F. (2005b). Tourism from above and below: Globalization, localization and New Orleans's Mardi Gras. *International Journal of Urban and Regional Research*, 29(2), 309–326.

'This article uses a case study of the Mardi Gras celebration in New Orleans to explain the connections between global forces and local actions in the development of urban tourism. It argues that the globalization and localization of Mardi Gras are occurring simultaneously with the result being a mix of homogenizing and particularizing influences in New Orleans. It develops this argument by distinguishing between "tourism from above" and "tourism from below", a distinction that helps to explain how tourism can help undermine as well as promote local differences. "Tourism from above" refers to the global-level forces of commodification, standardization and rationalization that affect all cities. "Tourism from below" refers to the ways in which local groups and individuals resist the homogenizing effects of globalized tourism and use tourism to anchor Mardi Gras in place and create new carnival traditions.'

Heritage commemoration

These are memorial services, specific ceremonies or broader events (even festivals) designed to honour the memory of someone or something. Most commonly they are marked in the context of national days, birthdays of kings and queens, battles or wars (through Remembrance Days and varying national emphases according to Van der Auwera and Schramme 2014). Programmes must include something symbolic and interpretive about the event or persons being remembered. Frost and Laing (2013), in the book *Commemorative Events: Memory, Identities, Conflicts*, emphasized that they are all about remembering and are held on the anniversaries of significant past events, either annually or after significant time periods. Such events provide fascinating insight into how societies see themselves, their heritage and their identity. These events, however, carry high propensity for controversy as memory and identity are highly subjective and other stakeholders hold different views of what should be commemorated and why. 'Heritage' is open to interpretation, often being a politically charged term. It means more than historic, and implies a value judgement as to what is important. McCarthy (2012) examined the 1916 Easter Rising in Dublin (also see Grayson and McGarry 2016) – which sparked off a series of events culminating in 1922 with the creation of the Irish Free State – and traces the historiography of the celebration of the event that challenged the British government whilst it was fighting the Great War. A further addition to the events literature is by Frost *et al.* (2008) in Research Note 2.6.

> ## 2.6 RESEARCH NOTE ON COMMEMORATIONS
>
> Frost, W., Wheeler, F. and Harvey, M. (2008). Commemorative events: Sacrifice, identity and dissonance. In J. Ali-Knight, M. Robertson, A. Fyall and A. Ladkin (eds), *International Perspectives of Festivals and Events: Paradigms of Analysis*, pp. 161–171. Oxford: Butterworth-Heinemann.
>
> This chapter reviews commemorative events literature and considers its sometimes contested meanings. The authors studied three annual events of significance to Australians, all of which related to conflict. They identified themes that also apply to many other commemorations. The first is sacrifice, for example of young people in war. Festive elements might be included, but the events are largely commemorative and emotional in nature. Multiple stakeholders with conflicting ideas about organization and meanings are the norm, sometimes leading to gatekeeping and exclusion of groups; in some cases different segments of attendees are in conflict. All these actors make for a politically charged environment. Finally, some attendees view their participation as a pilgrimage, as in the case of Australians who travel to the site of Gallipoli battles in the First World War for Anzac Day.

Parades and processions

The expression 'everyone loves a parade' seems to be a universal and age-old truth. Parades are usually an organized, celebratory procession of people, and the most popular ones are mobile spectacles of entertainment and celebration. As a planned event, parades and other processions are unique in that the entertainment, or other objects of the spectator's gaze, go past the audience in a dynamic progression. City streets are often the stage, and reclaiming them from vehicular traffic is part of the pleasure of viewing parades. They can be events all on their own, or part of broader festivals and sport celebrations. The experience should be one of joy and wonder (especially for children), merriment, socializing on a big scale and an appreciation of the arts, skills, symbols and heritage objects on display.

There are a number of important variations, including flotillas (of boats), cavalcades (of horses), religious processions (often with objects of reverence) and military marches including weapons of warfare. Some parades consist of just people, but frequent elements include floats, marching bands, entertainment units (like dancers or flag-wavers) and important people (the parade marshal, beauty queens). In Chapter 4, there is a profile of one of the biggest and oldest parades ever recorded, and it leads one to conclude that nothing much has changed in thousands of years! From a sociological perspective, Tomlinson (1986) found small-town parades to be full of imagery and symbolism reflecting community values like purity, beauty, humour, religion and politics. Parades are performances for both residents and outsiders. Other examples of scholarship related to parades include the book *Macy's Thanksgiving Day Parade* by Grippo (2004) and Darian-Smith's (2011) history of agricultural shows and festivals in rural Australia and their inclusion of parades. Pojani (2014) examined the use of public space in Tirana, the capital of Albania, through different political transformations and how events and processions link to urban design, power and ideology. In contrast, Olson (2017) undertook a content analysis of the 780 pride events held in the USA and Canada that celebrate sexual diversity.

Religious events and pilgrimage

Festivals and other celebrations often include religious ceremonies, but primarily religious events embody solemn rites and rituals, and are considered to be sacred within the context of specific religions. Some, like Mexico's Day of the Dead, have become national holidays (literally, holy days). The Japanese *matsuri* are a type of religious event, generally community-based, produced by volunteers and celebrating a variety of religious or spiritual themes. Certain events such as Saint Patrick's Day celebrating the Feast of Saint Patrick is a religious celebration which has become a major celebration by Irish diaspora globally. The event has a long history (e.g. see Cronin and Adair 2004), and one of the largest spectacles is the New York City parade, which can be dated back to 1762; it attracts around two million spectators.

Pilgrimage is a journey for religious or spiritual purposes; it reinforces collective religious and cultural values and generally focuses on places and events of significance. Shackley (2001: 102) called pilgrimages 'linear events', in which the journey might be as important as the destination in terms of visitor motivations and experiences. Pilgrimage is a quest, a journey and the experience of a sacred place. For many it is a duty. The entire pilgrimage can be conceptualized as a special event in a person's life, a rite of passage and a transforming experience, but there are often well-defined events associated with religious pilgrimages. The largest events are the Hajj in Mecca, attracting millions of visitors annually (the Saudi Arabian government imposes limits), and Kumbha Mela (mela means sacred-site festival) in India which is held four times in every 12 years and was said to attract over 28 million pilgrims in 2001 (Singh 2006: 228).

2.7 RESEARCH NOTES ON PILGRIMAGE

Shinde, K. (2010). Managing Hindu festivals in pilgrimage sites: Emerging trends, opportunities, and challenges. *Event Management*, 14(1), 53–67.

Pilgrimage sites are repositories of religious culture and traditions. Festivals held at such sites in India bring together organizers, pilgrims and tourists. At the Holi festival, Shinde observed a hierarchy of spaces: the private space of temples and ashrams accessible only to the gurus, priests and religious institutions for conducting rites and rituals; semi-public space where patronage relationships occur among religious functionaries, pilgrims, devotees and visitors; and public space accessible to all, wherein civil authorities must maintain law and order. Religious tourism is discussed in this context, including cultural change processes.

Cheng, T.-M. and Chen, M.-T. (2014). Image transformation for Mazu pilgrimage and festival tourism. *Asia Pacific Journal of Tourism Research*, 19(5), 1–20.

Concerning pilgrimage in Taiwan, the researchers determined that tourists' perception of unique images (such as the ten major ceremonies) is enhanced with information stimulation and tourists' actual visitation.

In a review of pilgrimage and tourism, Collins-Kreiner (2010) compared sacred and secular pilgrimage. Non-religious places and events that hold symbolic meaning do attract visitors who might or might not experience anything spiritual, but still find the experience rewarding. Cusack and Digance (2009), for example, explored the ways in which attendance at Australia's Melbourne Cup (a horse race surrounded by festivity) has become quasi-religious or 'spiritual'. Observance of the event's linked traditions (sweepstakes, ceasing work for the duration of the race, champagne breakfasts) can be understood as post-modern consumerist rituals for Australians, thus reinforcing personal identity.

Political and state events

Any event produced for or by governments and political parties falls into this category. Such events always seem to be in the news, including the following examples:

- the G8 summit of leading industrialized nations;
- royal weddings and events (see Laing and Frost 2017);

- papal tours and related religious festivals;
- VIP visits (e.g. heads of state);
- inauguration of the American President;
- investiture of a prince;
- political party conventions.

Most political and state events are security challenges. When leaders assemble or governments meet, or when a VIP tours, the media pay close attention – and so do people who want to protest or disrupt.

An interesting theoretical analysis of inaugurations and other events like the Super Bowl led Chwe (2013) to argue that common knowledge is the basis of what makes public ceremonies work, because each member of the audience has a common understanding of what the others know. Clearly, it takes a huge effort, at great cost, to mount these kinds of events, and increasingly there are unintended elements of entertainment or disaster associated with their spectacle. Research by Watson and Yip (2011) highlighted the difficulties of estimating the size of the crowds at such events and the challenge this presents to crowd management. In the case of the Hajj, Al-Kodmany (2013) outlined technological solutions to make the event safer when dealing with very large crowds.

Arts and entertainment

Almost any activity, sport, artistic display or event can be viewed as 'entertainment'. Many forms of popular culture fit into this category, including music concerts, award ceremonies, theatre, art exhibitions and dance shows. The activities that are frequently part and parcel of cultural celebrations can certainly be viewed as entertaining, but the underlying purpose is different. To be precise, it has to be emphasized that entertainment is usually passive, something one experiences for pleasure without the need to think about its cultural/historic significance or the values being expressed. In that sense, entertainment is largely in the realm of hedonistic consumption, not cultural celebration. This explains why anything called 'entertainment' is a business, part of a huge industry, and often exists outside government social policy or policy for the arts and culture. 'Theatre' is a very broad category of planned event, encompassing drama, music and other performances usually scripted and in a 'staged' environment. Principles of theatre are regularly applied throughout the events world. We will examine theatre studies and types of theatre and performance later, but it is necessary here to distinguish between the major forms of art.

Performing arts

By definition, almost all performances are planned events. There can be spontaneous performances by individuals and groups, such as singing and chanting, but we would normally not call these 'events' or 'entertainment'. Performing arts traditionally involve musicians, singers, dancers or actors, in front of audiences. In what is often called 'high culture', there is symphony, ballet, opera and traditional theatre for plays. In 'popular culture' we can add every form of musical concert (from jazz to new age, pop to hip-hop), dance (modern, tap, jazz) and alternative performances such as busking and illusion (magic), and the relationship with events was highlighted earlier in relation to pop music events. Film and television involve entertainment based on indirect (not in-person) performances. Fashion could be considered part performance (the fashion show) and part visual art (see the case studies in Williams, Laing and Frost 2013).

Other criteria for classifying arts events include:

- professional versus amateur artists;
- competitive versus festive;

- mixed or single genre (e.g. just jazz, or many music types);
- single or multicultural;
- paid or free performances;
- regularly scheduled, periodic or one-time;
- temporary (i.e. visual art created with a limited life expectancy, or a one-time only performance) versus permanent.

Festivals and music concerts provide many people with their only performing arts experiences. DiMaggio and Mukhtar (2004) in reviewing the evidence for declining arts participation in the USA referred to increased competition with home forms of entertainment as a plausible reason.

Literature

Literature consists of the printed word, including books, magazines, even web-logs ('blogs'). We only call this 'art' if it is meant to entertain or is written in a style (like poetry) that results in aesthetic appreciation. Festivals and other planned events that feature poetry or written works are common, and these can include 'readings' that are in fact performances. Storytelling festivals are a variation, and in this context Walle (1994) studied a Cowboy Poetry Gathering. Hoppen *et al*. (2014) have evaluated literary tourism as a part of destination competitiveness, and it is common for events to be the first and foremost method of implementing this form of tourist attractiveness or branding.

Visual arts

Painting, sculpture and handicraft are the most common visual arts, and touring or one-time 'shows' or 'exhibitions' of visual arts are planned events. For example, Berryman (2013) traced the evolution of the public 'blockbuster' exhibition in 1970s Australia as a national event. 'Installation art' is a cross between an exhibition and a special event. Architecture is a visual art, and other media like computer games and the Internet have become popular for visual artistic expression. Any of these art forms can be the theme of planned events. In a contingent valuation study in Singapore, Chang and Mahadevan (2014) found that a long-running performing arts festival was a well-established event, whereas visual arts festivals seem to be more of a fad. Jain (2016), however, has traced the growth of large arts events in South Asia.

Touring entertainment: circuses, carnivals and other shows

Before the age of mass travel, entertainment had to come to the consumer in the form of travelling shows. Although these forms of art and entertainment reflect a bygone age, they remain popular and continue to evolve. Perhaps the oldest form is the circus (for a history see Simon 2014), which was popular in the ancient Roman Empire (including activities that are no longer acceptable) and which has more recently given rise to animal-free entertainment like Cirque du Soleil. In a classic study, Easto and Truzzi (1973) examined the nature of 'carnivals' in the USA, 'as an entertainment with side shows, rides, games and refreshments, usually operated by a commercial enterprise'. Easto and Truzzi tracked the historiography of research to reviews dating to 1881 and 1932, which clearly differentiated carnivals from circuses. These carnivals ranged in scale from small events to those employing up to 800 staff, with 45 railroad cars to transport the event around the USA. Easto and Marcello estimated that in the 1950s, these events attracted 85 million visitors a year.

Business and trade events (MICE)

You will often hear this large sector of planned events referred to as the MICE industry, or meetings, incentives, conventions (including conferences and congresses) and exhibitions. The fundamental purpose of this type of event is to promote, market or directly engage in commerce, or otherwise meet corporate objectives. Farmers' markets, fairs and exhibitions (trade and consumer shows) are clearly based on marketing and selling. World's fairs, or expos, represent national place marketing and foster international trade and tourism. Meetings and conventions are mostly related to the affairs of associations and corporations and might involve learning, morale building and making policies. Individual companies produce or sponsor many types of events for both internal purposes (e.g. training) and with an external orientation (e.g. grand openings, exhibits and sales at festivals). Incentive travel is the questionable component, as they might include business meetings but often they are just tours. For example, Christmas markets are a common feature in Europe, with 157 larger markets and 2630 smaller markets which generate over 493 million visits a year (Brida *et al.* 2017) given the cultural and business focus of these annual events.

We should not overlook the fact that corporate and other private events may also possess cultural significance (e.g. a ginseng fair in Korea becomes a major annual festival), or be of political interest (countries competing for attention and reputation at world's fairs). Many business and trade events are closely associated with hotels, resorts, convention and exhibition centres, and are thereby important elements in the tourism and hospitality industries, with a variety of stakeholders (Jin *et al.* 2012). When events are developed and marketed as tourist attractions or destination image-makers, they enter the realm of place marketing. Mair (2012) reviewed 144 articles from the business-event literature for the period 2000 to 2009, the vast majority of which were published in the *Journal of Convention and Event Tourism*. Major themes include the meeting planner, technology, economic impact assessments, venue selection, evaluation of satisfaction, the role of destination image on attendance and the decision-making processes of attendees.

Meetings and conventions

People assemble for many reasons, and have always done so, but according to Spiller (2002) the modern convention industry grew in concert with industrialization and trade in the late nineteenth century and throughout the twentieth. A parallel movement was the growth of trade, professional and affinity associations of all kinds. The first convention bureau in the USA was established in 1896 in Detroit, and at that time hotels were the main suppliers of venues. 'Conferences' are assemblies for the purpose of conferring and discussion, and should be small enough to facilitate interaction. Rogers (1998) argued that conferences are often one-time only, with no tradition necessary. Academics hold numerous, themed conferences on specified topics or themes of broad interest within a field of study. 'Conventions' are generally large assemblies of people from associations, political parties, clubs or religious groups. Often convention delegates must go through a screening process. In Europe the term 'congress' is generally used instead of convention, although it typically connotes an international meeting.

Corporations and associations employ meeting or convention managers to handle their business get-togethers (for a look at how decisions are made on association conferences, see the article by Comas and Moscardo 2005). Numerous meeting-planner firms exist, some of which have expanded into the special events field. Hotels, resorts and convention centres also employ professionals whose jobs cover the marketing and hosting of meetings and other events. Meeting Professionals International (MPI – http://www.mpiweb.org/) distinguishes between association, corporate, scientific and incentive meetings, but 'meeting' is a generic term applicable to an assembly of people for any purpose. However, it usually connotes a small, private business affair. The 'corporate' segment is different in a number of ways. Companies hosting large numbers of meetings and conventions are likely to employ their own event managers or meeting planners, although large associations also do this. Corporate events are also likely to be more diverse than those initiated by associations, including training, hospitality, product launches, motivational assemblies, retreats, publicity events, grand openings and team-building exercises. There is a strong tendency for corporate clients to repeatedly use the same venues, and strong links have been forged between corporations and specific hotel and resort chains for this purpose. There is also a growing debate on the future role of technology in the hosting of such events (see Pearlman and Gates 2010; Fenich *et al.* 2011).

Exhibitions (trade and consumer shows)

Morrow's (1997) *The Art of the Show* (produced for the International Association for Exposition Management – IAEM) highlighted the core purpose of 'trade' and 'consumer' shows, as they 'provide a time sensitive, temporary marketing environment where the buyer comes to the seller'. 'Consumer shows' are open to the public, often with an admission fee, and popular themes are linked to automobiles, travel and recreation, pets, electronics, gardening, arts and crafts or other hobbies. The producer, usually a private company, moves the show from place to place so that it is typically annual in any community. Venue owners might also produce their own. Manufacturers test new products at shows, retailers try to sell and the consumer is searching for both ideas and entertainment. Gottlieb *et al.* (2013) evaluated consumer behaviour at such events and concluded that entertainment, product/industry research, and the facilitation of purchase decision-making processes and problem resolution are the key objectives for consumer attendees. Research by Rittichainuwat and Mair (2011) isolated two clusters at travel shows, the first being shoppers whose major motivation is purchasing, and the second called 'Total Visitors', whose motivation combines information searching and learning about trends.

'Trade shows' are usually for invitees only, based on specific business needs or association membership. Manufacturers or suppliers exhibiting at these events are trying to sell their products and services, or at least trying to inform potential customers. Common types are industrial, scientific and engineering, or health care. Many include educational presentations or seminars. Frequently they are attached to association conventions, such as when suppliers to the events industry exhibit at trade shows attached to professional association meetings. 'International trade fairs' are a special class. Typically they are at the large end and are targeted at a global or multi-country audience; they are, therefore, usually held in cities with major airports and exhibition halls. The Center for Exhibition Industry Research (www.ceir.org) exists to provide data to the industry. According to CEIR, 'Attendees rate exhibitions as the number one most useful source of information with which to make a buying decision.' Professionals attend trade shows to learn about new products and meet face to face with suppliers. Often competitive products can be evaluated side by side, which helps explain why people go to consumer shows where many manufacturers exhibit side by side. And the entertainment and social aspects of shows must not be underestimated – attendees should have fun while learning. Exhibitions have a seasonal rhythm, with the lowest month (in North America) for show-starts being December and the peak two months being (almost equally) October and March. Summer (July and August) constitutes the second low season. Part of the growth in venues is attributable to the shortfall of space during the two peak exhibition seasons (see Frost and Laing 2017 for a detailed review of exhibitions and trade fairs).

2.8 RESEARCH NOTE ON EXHIBITIONS IN CHINA

Jin, X., Weber, K. and Bauer, T. (2010). The state of the exhibition industry in China. *Journal of Convention and Event Tourism*, 11(1), 2–17.

This paper discusses the rapid growth and structural evolution of China's exhibition industry. It is Asia's largest exhibition market, and cities like Guangzhou have invested heavily in venues and marketing. 'China is still regarded as a key emerging market internationally. Thus, experiences and lessons learned from its exhibition development can serve as a useful reference to other emerging markets and should be of interest to both academics and practitioners.'

Fairs

This is another word with multiple, and often confusing, meanings. Dictionaries recognize the following:

- a gathering held at a specified time and place for the buying and selling of goods (i.e. a market);
- an exhibition (e.g. of farm products or manufactured goods, usually accompanied by various competitions and entertainments, as in a state fair); exhibitors may be in competition for prizes;
- an exhibition intended to inform people about a product or business opportunity;
- an event, usually for the benefit of a charity or public institution, including entertainment and the sale of goods (also called a bazaar).

The term 'festival' is sometimes used as a synonym of 'fair', but fairs have a long tradition of their own, as periodic exhibitions and markets. Waters (1939) traced the history of fairs from the earliest days of human barter and trade. Although North Americans associate the word 'market' with a place to do shopping, fairs were originally occasional markets. Every society had to have fairs, where goods were sold and traded at specific times, and usually in specific places that became markets or fairgrounds. The Latin word *feriae*, meaning holy day (which evolved into holiday), is the origin of the English word 'fair'. They were often scheduled on church-sanctioned holy days. Although fairs were often associated with religious celebrations, and now usually contain entertainment and amusements, fairs have more to do with productivity and business than with themed public celebrations. Indeed, Abrahams (1987) argued that fairs and festivals are like mirror images. But he also suggested that in modern, urban society they have become almost synonymous because the old ways of production, as celebrated in fairs, have faded.

The IAFE (International Association of Fairs and Expositions) website (www.fairsandexpos.com) provides some history. Most traditional fairs in North America are the numerous county and state fairs which are held annually on the same site, most of which continue to reflect rural and agricultural themes. Some are called 'exhibitions' or 'expositions', reflecting their educational orientation. Most fairs are operated by independent boards or agricultural societies, though many have close links with the host municipality. Typical elements of agricultural fairs and exhibitions include agricultural demonstrations and contests, sales and trade shows (farm machinery, etc.), amusements of all kinds, eating and drinking, parades and a variety of entertainment. Education is also a vital programme element, with close ties to 4H clubs as an example. This type of fair is often called a 'show' in the United Kingdom, Australia and New Zealand. The lines between types of shows, fairs and markets are sometimes hard to distinguish. For example, Morgner (2014) examined the development of art fairs as a kind of trade show to sell and distribute art.

World's fairs

'World's fair' has a very specific meaning, derived from an international agreement in 1928 and regulated by the Bureau International des Expositions (BIE) in Paris. BIE sets the policies for bidding on and holding world's fairs, which are often called expos. Their nominal purpose has always been educational, with particular attention paid to technological progress, but some authors have described them as glorified trade fairs (Benedict 1983). Findling and Pelle (2008) provided a comprehensive review of 100 countries and the world's fairs held since 1851 in their *Encyclopedia of World's Fairs and Expositions*. A detailed analysis of Vancouver's world fair was completed by Olds and Ley (1988), and De Groote (2005) traced the evolution of world's fairs, focusing on the 1992 Expo in Seville, Spain.

There is a large body of literature on world's fairs, reflecting both their significance in economic and social terms and their popularity among expo lovers. Competition to host them is often fierce, as cities and countries see them as an opportunity to attract attention and tourists, typically in concert with urban renewal or other development schemes. World's fairs are almost always accompanied by controversy, owing to their large costs and environmental and social impacts. Governments have shamelessly used them (and other mega events) for their own purposes, leading Hall (1992) to call them political tools. Most of them have generated a permanent built legacy (especially symbols like the Eiffel Tower) through planned urban renewal or development, while heavy tourism promotion has not always succeeded in generating sufficient attendance. Nostalgia for world's fairs is rampant, judging by websites devoted to their images and trading in memorabilia. Some, like Montreal's Expo '67, achieved iconic status – it will always be remembered as a nation-defining event (and one that left Montrealers with decades of debt).

Corporate events

Any event produced by or for a corporation falls into this large category, but it is generally associated with a range of events aimed at the public or for business-to-business purposes – that is, for external audiences (see Mishra *et al.* 1997). Saget (2006: 13) suggests that the essence of corporate events is relationship marketing: 'With events, you can connect with your customer in some physical form on a real level and establish a relationship that you can follow up with a combination of personalized phone calls, scheduled appointments, and one-on-one email communications.' Saget distinguishes between event managers and event marketers. Event marketers have to ask: what messages are we trying to convey to our customers? Are we trying to get the audience to buy something? How will the event impact on sales?

There is also an evolving debate about the wider motives for corporate event sponsorship as Seguin *et al.* (2010) highlight in terms of corporate social responsibility. This is also a theme which Babiak and Wolfe (2006) examined in relation to the Super Bowl and more generic themes (Babiak and Wolfe 2009). More recent analysis has also focused on the theme of corporate social responsibility and sport as a tool for development in less developed countries (e.g. see Levermore 2010) as well as more generic overviews (e.g. Slack and Thurston 2014). Further discussion of corporate events is provided by Ulrich Wuensch in Expert Opinion 2.2.

2.2 EXPERT OPINION

Corporate events

Professor Dr Ulrich Wuensch is President of the SRH University of Popular Arts (a University of Applied Science) in Berlin, Germany. He is both a practitioner and academic (in the field of media and communication science, media aesthetics and audience research), specializing in corporate events and scenography.

Books: Wuensch, U. (2008). *Facets of Contemporary Event Communication – Theory and Practice for Event Success*. Bad Honnef, Germany; Wuensch, U. (2015). *Handbuch Event-Kommunikation* (2nd edn). Berlin; Wuensch, U. (ed.) (2015). *Atmosphären des Populären*. Berlin.

This text will very briefly touch upon some aspects of a special form of corporate activity: the event. These undertakings of companies in order to reach out to a public (being understood as consumers or as employees) within a sphere of face-to-face encounters are often labelled as live communication or experiential communication. The expression draws the line between two-dimensional mass communications, also defined as a communication of 'one-to-many', and the so-called real-time and real-space engagement as a form of 'some-to-some' or group communication.

Corporate events arose with the dawn of industrialization (around the 1850s) before mass media were the main channels of communication. In the late nineteenth century, innovative entrepreneurs such as Heinz (USA), Michelin (France) and Lingner (Germany) employed various innovative forms and formats (such as product characters in festivities, product shows on a pier, political demonstrations and more) to interest their consumers. In the 1920s, Mr Procter and Mr Gamble realized that the first personal contact with a product (the so-called 'Moment of Truth', (a) on the shelf and (b) at the first usage) was one crucial point within the marketing cycle. Experiences stemming from intimate encounters were then, and are today, the key to purchasing decisions. The experience economy, a term coined in the late 1980s, only focuses on this finding in highlighting that in a saturated market, something beyond price is needed to trigger the action to pay for something.

Corporate events come in many formats, all reaching back to the original live communication activities of humankind: ritualistic festivity and staged entertainment. Today exhibitions, conferences, product launches, promotion undertakings, incentives, and more and ever newly developed forms such as ambush and guerrilla marketing events are being employed to reach out to external or internal target groups. Two figures may signify the volume of the event market, where every third stay in a hotel is business-travel induced: meetings in Canada amount to C\$ 76 billion (2006) including hotel cost, transport, entertainment, catering, etc. and the turnover of the exhibition market in Germany is € 2.9 billion (2006).

Whether the event industry is an industry in its own right, or part of the advertising industry or the tourism industry, will become clear in the future. The fact that companies start to develop and brand their own events being staged in public on common ground (for example, Red Bull, with its various sport formats, or Guinness Brewery, with Saint Patrick's Day) seems to point out that an 'own' branch closely connected with media and entertainment is emerging.

Events are being employed in corporate attention management to provide extraordinary experiences. Experiences as such produce only unfocused attention and are the product of the ongoing activity called 'living'. Thus the design process is focused on the forefront of event production, not the organization of events. For event studies, this means that beyond the basic economic and project management research mainly undertaken so far, the humanities become more and more valid. To produce economically successful events one has to understand human beings and employ findings of sociology, aesthetics, religious studies, psychology, biology and more.

With the rise of the digital society, new forms of entwinement of the 'real' and the 'virtual' beyond the Internet and email will arise. The ability of human beings to be immersed (the attention, brain and the self being focused on a world in a dream, a movie, a book, a computer game) will lead to combinations of virtual reality events only dreamt of by science fiction writers so far. Yet it is around the corner, that Google Glass is developed further and that we will have meetings in virtual reality rooms, which we experience as real life meetings. Events will have to evolve and corporations are at the forefront of this evolution.

To illustrate a corporate event, the example of the activities and concept of Bayer's (the global chemical and pharmaceutical industry corporation stemming from Germany) corporate jubilee is briefly described. The 150th anniversary of Bayer occurred in 2013. In 2011, the communication department started to plan. In 2012 the operations to produce a year-long global event were under way. The first and main target group was the company's 100,000 employees, followed by the general public and special-interest groups such as politicians, the media and consumers of products and services of Bayer. The claim 'Science for a Better Life' had to be portrayed as mandatory. It was clear that the events were not a single solution. Integrated communication was the goal, and the cross-fertilization of media and messages that arose formed one event core idea produced in various forms and distributed via various media. Germany as the mother market plus 100 daughter companies worldwide had to be integrated into the event year. Activities such as 30,000 employees forming the world's largest living Bayer cross (the official company logo) on the lawn of a stadium at the headquarters in Leverkusen were planned. A 41-metre long Bayer 'blimp' (zeppelin) travelled around the globe in 2013, stopping in London, New York, Toronto, Tokyo and Mexico City to name just a few destinations. Interested employees created a new Bayer song, which was played at all jubilee events in 2013. A big cultural show, with paintings from Bayer's art collection spanning 150 years, was curated and on display at Berlin's main museum for three months. A new corporate film was shot; science research activities for youngsters were funded and integrated into a special completion of ideas; a science symposium was held. Social sponsoring and donations for local projects and communities were integral parts of the concept. Festivals for employees were held globally on 29 June, Bayer's founding day; German Chancellor Angela Merkel showed up for the main event. On Celebration Day a festive jubilee menu was served to Bayer employees worldwide, starting in New Zealand with the new day. In Germany alone 3,000 litres of tomato soup and 1.5 tons of couscous salad were served. The goal, to reach out to the public and put Bayer on the map worldwide, was successfully reached via 16 million PR and TV contacts, which Bayer did not have to pay for – though Internet contacts on a special anniversary site were not included. All this was steered by a core team of three leading event creators and planners in Leverkusen, Germany, plus an array of consultants and external agencies, artists and workers. Bayer's CEO was satisfied, even though the amount of money put into the event was noteworthy. Yet the results – employer loyalty and public awareness – were convincing.

Educational and scientific events

Often considered as a subset of business and trade events, these are nevertheless different because of their emphasis on creating and exchanging knowledge. Academic and professional symposia, and conferences on specific themes, are the main components of this category of planned event, although numerous small, private meetings are also held for these purposes.

Education, including participative styles as well as demonstrative training, is the hallmark experience of these events. But that is no reason why they should not also be social and fun events. It is obvious that most people attending scientific and academic conferences are searching for knowledge and some cities such as Glasgow, Scotland, have deliberately targeted these events as key sectors in event and conference strategies. Such events also have wider appeal in an increasingly globalized academic community in terms of networking and socializing with old friends and colleagues. This is likely to be an age-related variable.

Sport events

'Sport' is a physical activity involving large muscle groups, requiring strategic methods, physical training and mental preparation and whose outcome is determined, within a rules framework, by skill, not chance. Sport occurs in an organized, structured and competitive environment where a winner is declared.

(Government of British Columbia, Sport Branch)

By definition, sport events are the actual games or meetings during which sport activity occurs. There are many sport event formats (see, for example, Solomon 2002), and one classification includes:

- professional or amateur;
- indoor or outdoor (and other differences in their need for special venues);
- regularly scheduled (league play, plus play-offs or championships) or one-time (exhibition or friendly matches);
- local, regional, national or international in scope;
- for participants, for spectators or both;
- sport festivals (a celebration of sport, often for youth, involving many sports);
- single or multi-sport events.

Another classification approach is to look at the format of sport events:

- the regularly scheduled game, race or competition (in a league);
- scheduled tournaments and championships (for leagues or invitationals);
- one-off sport 'spectaculars' (media or spectator oriented);
- exhibition games with touring or invited teams;
- sport festival (emphasis on celebration and usually youth);
- multi-sport events (e.g. Olympics, Masters Games).

This is an enormous category, given the huge number of sport events occurring around the world all the time, not to mention the increasing diversity of sports and forms of sport event. The influence of the media has been profound, creating a whole category of 'media events' that probably would not otherwise exist.

Graham *et al.*'s (1995) *The Ultimate Guide to Sport Event Management and Marketing* noted there were millions of jobs in sports in the USA, including a growing number specific to the production, managing and marketing of events. These authors argued (1995: 8) that sport events and other special events share commonalities, including their service orientation, the incorporation of celebration and drama, media coverage and similarities in organizing and operations. Motivations of customers and travellers might also be similar, especially with regard to the ritual of attendance and related traditions. Traditional sport events like the Olympics always incorporate ceremonies and festivals, and it has now become commonplace to build a programme of special events around a sport meet to create a festival or special event with heightened appeal. An insight to this process is outlined in Research Note 2.9.

2.9 RESEARCH NOTE ON SPORT EVENTS

Morgan, M. and Wright, R. (2008). Elite sports tours: Special events with special challenges. In J. Ali-Knight, M. Robertson, A. Fyall and A. Ladkin (eds), *International Perspectives of Festivals and Events: Paradigms of Analysis*, pp. 187–204. Oxford: Butterworth-Heinemann.

The authors have observed considerable growth in elite sporting events involving touring by teams. They assess the special challenges involved in crossing regional and national boundaries. The logistics are complicated, as matches or longer stages occur at a succession of venues, with teams and often supporters (fans) following. From the host community's perspective, these are one-time events, and sometimes mega events with international media coverage. Examples include car rallies, cycling tours, tours by national rugby and cricket teams, and some championships. Other major challenges include choice and scheduling of venues, need for inter-regional or international tourism planning, unpredictable patterns of demand and the changing nature of the sports tourism experience.

Recreational events

Recreational events are generally produced by parks and recreation agencies, non-profit organizations and affinity groups (like churches, schools and clubs) for non-competitive reasons, and are often playful in nature. Hence we need social-psychology, play and leisure theory to help understand the event experiences and their benefits. Such events might be informal in their production and management, and they may even be self-organized by groups. If only individuals are involved, we will have to call it 'activity' and not an event. Examples of recreational events are really unlimited in number and scope, from card games to pickup football, from dance and exercise classes to impromptu concerts. Many of them will not meet our definition of 'special', as they are regularly scheduled and hardly unique, while others are at the margin in terms of being planned versus spontaneous.

Private events

Every life is marked by *rites de passage*, varying enormously across cultures, and these are all a form of planned event. From the industry perspective, they are often termed 'functions' when held in venues that cater to individual and small-group clients. From weddings to birthday celebrations, bar mitzvahs to funerals, holiday theme parties to church socials, they might require professionals or be entirely arranged by the participants. The experience is both personal and social, with multiple meanings possible. Most can be considered as celebrations in which a theme and emotional stimulation are essential. Quite a few practitioner-oriented books have been devoted to the planning and design of weddings, parties and other private functions. Weddings are such a universally important event that they have become big business and the subject of serious study (e.g. the book *Cinderella Dreams: The Allure of the Lavish Wedding*, by Otnes and Pleck 2003). Shone and Parry (2004) in their book *Successful Event Management* provided details of the UK wedding 'industry'. The Reunion Network (www.reunionfriendly.com) claims there are 10,000 reunions annually in the United States, including those produced by the military, schools, churches and affinity groups. There is also a venue, hotel and restaurant management literature that examines the case of banquets, parties and other events held in formal settings.

Events at the margin

There is also a category of event which is at the margins of what we mean by 'planned event'. The purpose is to show that definitional boundaries are often blurred and that 'planning' is a matter of degree. Each event certainly creates a novel experience, and some are completely self-created experiences.

Flash mobs

These events are somewhat spontaneous and anti-establishment, even anarchist in their origins or intent. Walker (2013) produced a historical, cultural and philosophical analysis of the flash mob as a performance event, and Molnár (2014) traces its expansion as a feature of youth culture globally. Grant (2016) examines its use as a form of guerrilla marketing in entertainment. The flash mob depends upon personal communications devices to a large extent, which explains why it is largely a recent phenomenon. Attendees assemble in response to a message to be somewhere at a specific time, to do something strange or outrageous.

These recently emerged social phenomena have a purpose, a place and a short time duration, but no real programme – only activity. They are usually frivolous, but some do try to make a point. An individual, or a group, has to initiate the flash mob, but there is no real organization or responsibility for it. If something goes terribly wrong, who gets the blame? The assertion that some flashmobbers are trying to reinvent public spaces is interesting, and fits into the general pattern of carnivalesque behaviour and dancing in the street. This is also something like the 'valorization' process noted by Falassi, which is used to turn settings into temporary festival and event spaces, only the goal of flashmobbers is presumably to show that the space 'belongs' to the people. Or perhaps the purpose is to demonstrate that any space can be made festive or act as a performance setting. But how can you have a liberating, non-conforming event if at the same time it becomes institutionalized around the world?

There are always risks from unplanned events or mobs. This newspaper account tells a sad story.

> *Philadelphia Moves to Nip Flash Mobs in Bud: Mayor Calls for Parents to Monitor Teens' Texts After Incidents of Mob Vandalism: Comments by Vicki Mabrey and Ted Gerstein, 23 April 2010 (http:// abcnews.go.com).*
>
> *Flash mobs initially involved dancing in the streets, freezing like statues or even giant pillow fights. But then something else happened. Bicyclists in San Francisco and Los Angeles started blocking traffic to protest lack of respect from motorists. A spontaneous snowball fight during the winter's epic snowstorm in Washington, D.C., went sour when a plainclothes policeman pulled out a gun. And, then, two weeks ago in Philadelphia, touristy South Street was the scene of a flash mob gone bad. Foot traffic on the street changed in minutes from normal Saturday date night to an onslaught of mostly young people seemingly intent on destruction.*

Protest! Demonstrate! Riot!

It seems that not a political or economic summit goes by without protests and even riots, and often they appear to have been orchestrated. In fact, they are planned events and certain websites (perhaps forbidden to general searches) provide advice on how to organize a demonstration or riot. While the rationale that people have a right to peacefully assemble is fine in most democratic nations, it is not a universally shared value. Furthermore, there is always the risk that those seeking disruption and violence will sabotage those with peaceful intent.

Marches and demonstrations have a long social history (see Rojek 2013 on protest and events), accompanying every war, union–company conflict and political movement. Currently, a favourite rallying cry is 'anti-globalization', which appears to attract many diverse interest groups (see Body-Gendrot 2016). Common types of protest activities include:

- *vigils*: tend to be solemn and reflective;
- *picket lines*: marked by chanting, marching, holding up signs, blockading entrances to factories;
- *marches*: a large march, like a parade, can have public entertainment value, as well as being a show of strength;
- *non-violent civil disobedience*: by definition these are illegal, and often consist of sit-downs and chaining people to objects; participants expect to get arrested, so involving celebrities will maximize media coverage.

As Chapter 1 highlighted, political protest and events has attracted academic research from critical event studies and numerous studies now exist, among the most recent being de Jong (2017), Lundman (2018) and Duignan *et al*. (2019). Prashizky and Remennick (2016) analysed alternative wedding ceremonies in urban spaces as a form of protest amongst immigrant partners unable to marry in rabbinical courts.

Recreational rioting

This term seems to have emerged in the news media, reporting on events in Northern Ireland. Here is a snippet from 14 July 2010, BBC News Northern Ireland (online):

The phrase 'recreational rioting' was made in Belfast to describe the traditional outbreak of street disturbances once the summer school holidays begin.

After a third consecutive night of trouble, Fr Donegan said: 'I pulled stones out of the hands of children. It was a bit like a Euro Disney theme park for rioting. It was ludicrous.'

Most of the young rioters were simply bored kids looking for some excitement in an inner city area where they complain of having nothing else to do.

Children as young as eight years old have been involved in the violence.

Whether the provision of other leisure and event opportunities would put an end to recreational rioting, or whether or not this is an appropriate term at all, is an open question. But it is a disturbing phenomenon, right alongside the occasional destructive behaviour of sports fans.

STUDY GUIDE

This chapter examined the nature of planned events, with some emphasis on their temporal and spatial dimensions. By looking at a number of 'events at the margin', such as flash mobs, we observed that planned and unplanned events can embody similar activities and experiences, which helps us understand human events in general. Professionals and business people are concerned with planned events, whereas policy-makers and researchers might find unplanned events equally as important and interesting.

It is important to distinguish between events (and related terminology) by referring to their forms, functions and experiences. A typology based on event form was presented, and the main types discussed. These types of events are actually 'social constructs' that emerged through tradition and common expectations of what, for example, a festival or convention consists of. By referring to their functions, a number of events were identified – such as iconic, hallmark and mega – that can actually describe many types of event. It was argued that events cannot easily be classified by reference to experiences, because multiple experiences are possible within any event form.

In reviewing each of the main types of planned event, from cultural celebrations to private functions, we introduced some important clues about the nature of the event experiences, their multiple meanings, and how they are designed and programmed. Later chapters explore these topics in greater detail. Be able to make the connections to outcomes and policy as well. Start thinking about the kinds of research appropriate for each type and function of event.

STUDY QUESTIONS

- Define 'event' and 'planned event'.
- What are the temporal and spatial dimensions of events? Does length, frequency, size and periodicity matter to the event manager? To guests? To the community?
- Explain how form, function and experience can be used to classify events (i.e. typologies) and discuss the problems associated with each approach. Give examples.
- Why are the planned events in the typology used in this chapter referred to as 'social constructs'?
- Describe the essential differences between each major type of planned event, including any fundamental differences in experiences and programmed elements of style associated with them.
- Why should event studies also be concerned with unplanned events and 'events at the margin'? Give some examples to compare planned and unplanned events.
- Will the differences between event types and functions become less important because of convergence? Discuss factors leading to convergence.

FURTHER READING

Du Cros, H. and Jolliffe, L. (2014). *The Arts and Events*. London: Routledge.

Falassi, A. (ed.) (1987). *Time Out of Time: Essays on the Festival*. Albuquerque, NM: University of New Mexico Press.

Frost, W. and Laing, J. (2013). *Commemorative Events: Memory, Identities, Conflicts*. London: Routledge.

Jepson, A. and Clarke, A. (eds) (2014). *Exploring Community Festivals and Events*. London: Routledge.

Laing, J. and Frost, W. (eds) (2014). *Rituals and Traditional Events in the Modern World*. London: Routledge.

Mair, J. (2013). *Conferences and Conventions: A Research Perspective*. London: Routledge.

Mair, J. (ed.) (2018). *The Routledge Handbook of Festivals*. London: Routledge.

Müller, M. (2015). The mega-event syndrome: Why so much goes wrong in mega-event planning and what to do about it. *Journal of the American Planning Association*, 81(1), 6–17.

Rogers, T. (2013). *Conferences and Conventions: A Global Industry* (3d edn). Oxford: Butterworth-Heinemann.

Weed, M. (2008). *Olympic Tourism*. Oxford: Butterworth-Heinemann.

PART II

Foundation disciplines and closely related fields

The contribution of anthropology, sociology, philosophy, religious studies and psychology to event studies

Upon completion of this chapter, students should know the following:

- contributions of these five foundation disciplines to understanding the roles, meanings, importance and impacts of events in society and culture;
- key theories and methodologies from anthropology, sociology, philosophy, religious studies and psychology (including social and environmental psychology) that contribute to event studies;
- for each discipline, specific contributions to understanding the nature and meanings of events, antecedents, experiences, outcomes, patterns, processes and policy.

Introduction

This chapter and the ensuing two chapters are devoted to examining the contributions to event studies of core social science disciplines and closely related fields of study. Research notes make specific links to event studies, and figures are provided for each discipline and field that provide a short description of its focus and major contributions to the nature and meaning of event experiences, antecedents, planning and producing events, outcomes and patterns and processes (i.e. see our framework from Figure 1.4). A good starting point is anthropology, as this discipline has a long history of studying planned events and makes substantial contributions to our understanding of experiences and meanings.

Anthropology

Anthropology is primarily about the study of humans and societies with sub-fields of study such as ethnography and social and cultural anthropology, with distinct approaches and research methods used to understand people in past and present-day settings. A landmark study of the anthropology of public events by D. Handelman (1990) identified many of the key features that characterize the anthropologist's interest in events, as shown in Figure 3.1.

Cultural anthropology makes a fundamental contribution to event studies, helping us to understand the reasons for festivals and celebrations and for providing the theoretical framework of rituals and liminality that we adapt to explain the rationale for planned events in general. In contrast, the biological origins and variations of humans are the subject of 'physical anthropology'; cultural evolution is the focus of archaeology, which specifically examines physical remains of civilizations and human artefacts. Sometimes cultural anthropology is called social or 'socio-cultural anthropology', or 'ethnology'. Sociology and anthropology developed as disciplines at the same time and share a common interest in social organization (Schultz and Lavenda 2005: 8). Both disciplines study social structures and institutions, while anthropologists are the ones who examine 'symbolic representations' of culture like art and myths. Ethnology is also defined as the systematic comparison of cultures.

Culture

Cultural anthropology's core phenomenon is 'culture', which Schultz and Lavenda (2005: 4) defined as 'sets of learned behaviour and ideas that human beings acquire as members of society'. Culture is learned

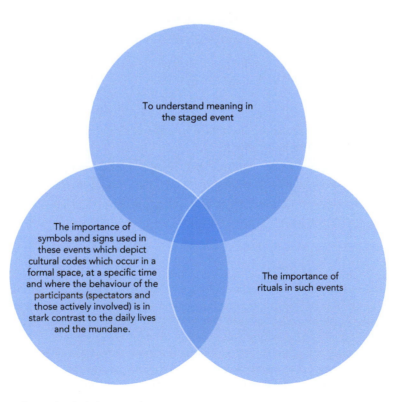

Figure 3.1 The anthropologist's interest in events

and passed on; it evolves, and takes on different dimensions reflected in belief systems, symbols and ritualistic behaviour. Culture is 'central to the explanations of why human beings are what they are and why they do what they do' (Schultz and Lavenda 2005: 4). 'Holism' is the principle of studying cultures as complex systems, the implication being that the study of events has to be placed in a very broad context. For example, events may contain highly symbolic representations of importance to a culture (see Table 3.1).

Culture, and its study, is often contested – even becoming highly political or involving conflict. Who speaks for disenfranchised groups, and how does history judge the winners and losers of war or colonization? Indeed, some anthropologists have a mission, or at least a particular agenda. Mitler *et al.* (2004), in their text on cultural anthropology, insist that this discipline should be 'relevant' to contemporary issues. Their book takes an applied approach, with an emphasis on understanding social inequality and cultural change processes. Some of the issues they examine include poverty and gender inequality. Issues raised by globalization are relevant to cultural anthropologists, and this could include the 'homogenization' of events through corporate sponsorship and media manipulation, or a loss of authenticity because of adopting a tourism orientation.

Many people distinguish between 'popular' and 'high culture', as discussed in Chapter 2, in relation to the cultural industries. This is not a clear differentiation, and some would deny it exists, but from both public policy and practical marketing perspectives there are important differences. 'High' culture is associated with theatre, opera, ballet, the symphony, serious literature, art galleries and museums, all of which tend to be considered national assets and thereby attract government subsidies. They are associated with the cultural elite, sophistication, and of course people with money. In contrast, 'popular' culture consists of what ordinary people prefer and do. This is the realm of consumerism, with private companies providing sport, entertainment, various communication media and many other 'products' for sale to the masses. There is more standardization of products and experiences in this realm of popular culture; most people relate to it on a day-to-day basis without even thinking about it as representing 'their' culture.

Table 3.1 Anthropology

Anthropology	Nature and meanings; the event experience	Antecedents to attending events
Definition: The study of human origins and evolution, language and culture		
Cultural anthropology • Studies the nature, functions and systematic comparison of cultures • Studies social organization with a focus on symbolic representations of culture	Cultural importance and meanings of celebration • Rites, rituals • Symbolism • Pilgrimage • Liminality • Authenticity • Communitas	Cultural influences on attending events (e.g. consumerism, traditions, perceived freedoms)
Planning and producing events	Outcomes and the impacted	Processes and patterns
• Cultural programming • Culturally defined elements of style	Cultural impacts (e.g. host–guest interactions; cultural authenticity; sustainability of traditions)	Cultural trends and forces (e.g. values; globalization) affecting events • Cultural policy

Such invisible distinctions mean we have festivals that are mostly entertainment for popular consumption, and festivals that are highbrow celebrations of culture. When private companies provide money to popular culture it is generally in the form of sponsorship, with expected marketing benefits, while giving money to 'high' culture can be viewed as philanthropy and being a good corporate citizen. Booth (2016) examined diasporic Asian cultural events in New Zealand and how these were developed through time for minority groups to display and celebrate their culture.

Rites and rituals

Cultural anthropologists (and a number of sociologists, for example see Schnell and Pali's 2013 discussion of pilgrimage as a ritual) have often focused their attention on cultural expressions within the realm of planned events, specifically festivals and carnivals (see Andrews and Leopold 2013). Rites and rituals are full of cultural meaning and can also be viewed as building blocks (or programmed elements of style) for event programmers. Rituals and rites are 'patterned forms of behaviour' (Mitler *et al.* 2004: 293) or prescribed ceremonies. Many have religious or mythological significance, while others relate to politics and group identity. 'Periodic rituals' include harvest festivals and annual commemorations such as national anniversary days. It is always worth thinking about the themes of celebrations and what they symbolically stand for. An interesting example, which Greenwood (1989) studied, is the Alarde in the Basque country, Spain, which was used to promote tourism in the region. As a result of too many visitors, the local organizers decided to stage the event twice, leading local people to view the event as a commoditized performance for visitors; as a consequence they did not visit the event.

'Life-cycle rituals' are also called *rites de passage*. Persons and groups mark important life stages with ceremonies and parties, sometimes sacred and often secular. According to van Gennep (1909: 21; emphasis in original) they occur in three phases, namely separation, transition and reincorporation:

> *I propose to call the rites of separation from a previous world, preliminal rites, those executed during the transitional stage liminal (or threshold) rites, and the ceremonies of incorporation into the new world postliminal rites.*

Turner (1969) detected three stages in many life-cycle rituals, namely separation of the individual from normal life (emotionally or symbolically, sometimes physically), transition (the 'liminal' stage where one might have to learn something new or perform specified acts), and finally reintegration (involving a welcome back and new status). Later Turner (1979) applied the concept of liminality to pilgrimage, and the related concept of the 'liminoid' to carnivals.

'Rituals of reversal' occur when normal social roles and behavioural standards can be turned inside out, such as during carnival or Mardi Gras. The masquerade, wearing masks at balls or in parades, is one way people try to protect their identity, or dignity, when they act up at carnival time. Falassi (1987: 4–6) discussed the above types of ritual and several others. His full classification is as follows:

- '*Rites of purification*': a cleansing, or chasing away of evil, such as practised in Japanese *matsuri*, by fire or holy water, sacred relics and symbols.
- '*Rites of passage*': marking a transition from one stage of life to another, such as initiations.
- '*Rites of reversal*': through symbolic inversion, including the common wearing of masks and costumes at carnivals, gender misidentification, role confusion, using sacred places for profane activities.
- '*Rites of conspicuous display*': objects of high symbolic value are put on display, perhaps touched or worshipped; often used in processions where the guardians and social/political elite display their powers.
- '*Rites of conspicuous consumption*': food and beverages are consumed in feasts; gifts are showered upon guests (gift or 'loot bags' at parties and award ceremonies); the ancient Potlatch of west-coast natives); sacred communion is a special form.

- *'Ritual dramas'*: the retelling of myths and legends, or historical re-enactments.
- *'Rites of exchange'*: from commerce (buying and selling) to gift exchanges and charitable donations.
- *'Rites of competition'*: games, sports, contests of all kinds, either highly unpredictable and merit-based or ritualized and predictable.
- *'De-valorization rites'* take place at the end of the event. Normal time and space have to be restored, as in closing ceremonies and formal or informal farewells.

Rituals and related symbolism are found in most planned events, and they can be used as programmed elements of style. For example, venues dedicated to conventions or exhibitions have to be transformed in order for an event to occur. In what Falassi referred to as a framing ritual, the entry has to be demarcated and regulated so that one first 'arrives' at the correct time and place, then is allowed entry to the event. It is already defined as a special place, but the growing rumble of conversation, a flurry of preparations, the anticipation of the programme, the seeing and being seen, all add to the sense of specialness in time. As an example, Anand and Watson (2004) examined the performative elements of the Grammy Awards in terms of the rites and ceremonies within the event.

If the meeting planners or venue staff have done even a basic job of preparation, there will also be a realization that the empty space has been transformed: symbolism (flags, corporate banners, association logos, sponsors' exhibits), music, food and beverages, other sensory stimulation (lighting, smells), the grand entry of speakers and dignitaries, and finally the opening ceremonies are all expressions that this particular event is only for these special attendees. While the opening words of a meeting or convention might not carry the cultural weight of a religious blessing (i.e. 'sacralization'), they do perform the 'valorization rite' that conveys clearly 'we have begun' and this place, empty a few minutes ago, is now ours to enjoy.

Liminal, liminoid and communitas

Victor Turner's works on pilgrimage (1979; Turner and Turner 1978), liminality and communitas (1974) (which draw from van Gennep) have had tremendous influence on tourism and event studies, including direct incorporation into this book's model of the planned event experience. Whereas 'liminal' experiences are associated with ritual and the 'sacred', 'liminoid' experiences are part of the 'profane' everyday life, including festivity and carnivalesque, revelry and role inversions. Liminality and communitas can occur independently of rites of passage according to Turner, thereby making a clear connection to festival and carnival. He also differentiated between two models of human interrelatedness:

> *The first is of society as a structured, differentiated, and often hierarchical system of politico-legal-economic positions with many types of evaluation, separating men in terms of 'more' or 'less'. The second, which emerges recognizably in the liminal period, is of society as an unstructured or rudimentarily structured and relatively undifferentiated comitatus, community, or even communion of equal individuals who submit together to the general authority of the ritual elders.*
>
> *(Turner 1969: 96; emphasis in original)*

'Communitas' is Latin for people helping people, or people coming together for the good of the community. Turner stressed unstructured togetherness and a feeling of equality. Communitas can be spontaneous, erupting through joy and celebration, or a more permanent structuring of society – something akin to civil society notions. Turner (1969: 132) distinguished between three forms of communitas:

- *existential or spontaneous communitas*: the transient personal experience of togetherness;
- *normative communitas*: communitas organized into a permanent social system;
- *ideological communitas*: which can be applied to many utopian social models.

Of these three forms, the first or existential occurs at events, and is desired by many people who attend events. An interesting element of the ability of events to achieve this was reviewed by Stevens and Shin (2014) in terms of the geographical space within public event settings and the meaning derived from these. The degree to which event space is organized and the interaction of people within such spaces affect the encounters and engagement with the event which in turn affects the ability to achieve communitas. People want and need to come together in harmony, and this is reflected in Turner's (2012) *Communitas: The Art of Collective Joy*. This leads us to a key question: can events therefore be a springboard or building block to a higher level of societal communitas?

Anthropological exchange theory

In anthropological exchange theory the focus is on symbolism, such as the symbolic value of events in a cultural context. Ritual is symbolic by definition, covering religious rites, the display of sacred objects – including flags – ceremonies that convey deep meaning about the nature of an event (e.g. the Olympics as a global celebration of youth and amateur sport, and of goodwill among nations) and awards that convey excellence, prestige or triumph.

This theory is in opposition to economic exchange theory, which emphasizes rational choices. In anthropological exchange theory social order and the pursuit of individual advantages arise from underlying ritual and the symbolic nature of exchanges between people – which are often obligatory in nature. When exchange processes break down, social disorder or conflict results. According to Marshall (1998), this anthropological approach:

> *draws on Durkheim's claim that not everything in the contract is contractual, that is, rational (business) exchange cannot itself be the source of settled, morally regulated social order, but instead presupposes it. Social sentiments must be embodied in symbols (or collective representation) of society's obligatory rules and commands which define the scope remaining for the pursuit of individual interest.*

A more contemporary and extremely important form of symbolism is that of branding, with events fulfilling place-marketing functions. In one way they stand for the country, city or destination, with the event conveying attractive images and meaning. For example, the destination can be conveyed as exciting, romantic, sophisticated or modern, all through the lens of the event. Also, the symbolic content of the event, read as a text, might operate subliminally to affect judgement. Symbolism also applies in important ways to individuals and communities of interest. Events often stand for something important to many social worlds and subcultures.

Research traditions and methods

Both 'deductive' (the formulation and testing of hypotheses in a positivistic tradition) and 'inductive' (use of grounded theory, or based on discourse) methodologies are employed in cultural anthropology. We will return to these in Chapter 12, where we take a detailed look at research paradigms, methodologies and methods, but at this point it is pertinent to focus on the research tradition most associated with cultural anthropology.

Ethnography

Fieldwork, often an ethnographic description and analysis of one cultural group, still dominates cultural anthropology. Traditional 'ethnography' involved living among peoples to gain a deep understanding of their culture and ways of life. Although the early development of this discipline was marked by a distinct bias, separating 'civilized' cultures from 'primitive', today's anthropologist values 'cultural relativism' – the belief that cultures should not be studied, let alone devalued, through the lens of their own belief system. Holloway *et al.* (2010) reviewed the use of ethnographic methods in event studies, arguing for a more qualitative approach to experience-related research. Ethnography enables researchers to better explore structures and interactions within their cultural context, as well as the meanings people give to events and their environment. Such research is inductive, often starting without a theoretical perspective or proposition, and often including case studies, participant observation and interviews. Purposive sampling is favoured over random sampling, in order to talk to or observe the people of specific interest.

The contemporary literature is rich with anthropological studies of festivals in particular (see Merkel 2013). Another good example to examine is Cavalcanti's (2001) ethnographic study of the Amazonian Ox Dance Festival, published in the journal *Cultural Analysis*. In Research Note 3.1, Philip Xie uses participant observation and other methods to examine tourism and cultural performance among traditional people in China, and a number of case studies in Jepson and Clarke (2014) outline anthropological studies of festivals as community events. Dashper (2016) illustrated a variation of anthropology – autoethnography which 'uses highly personal, often emotional and (hopefully) evocative accounts to try to engage the reader in the event experience using, for example, personal stories' (Dashper 2016: 212). This is described by Dashper (2016) as a method of self-narration to adopt a reflexive perspective of the interactions around event experiences. Autoenthrography has its roots in storytelling, exploring event experiences from inside, adopting a perspective that characterizes events as *emic* experiences. This means that the experience of the person is studied in relation to the event, focusing on the person's culture, their social group as an inward-looking approach. An alternative approach is the *etic* perspective, where the researcher adopts an external view, outside of the social group. What Dashper (2016: 217) concludes is that 'ethnography also remains an under-used method in event research although a growing number of scholars are turning to this approach to explore and understand the meaning of event experiences for different groups and individuals'.

3.1 RESEARCH NOTES ON ETHNOGRAPHIC RESEARCH

Xie, P. (2003). The bamboo-beating dance in Hainan, China: Authenticity and commodification. *Journal of Sustainable Tourism*, 11(1), 5–16.

Xie's methodology consisted of fieldwork involving interviews with key informants, including 102 dance performers at eight selected folk villages as well as with ethnic researchers. Participant observation was undertaken to gain greater understanding of the context and meanings attached to places. Xie documented how the government, tourism, tourists and Li communities had appropriated, promoted and manipulated (to make it more entertaining) the traditional dance, which had evolved with tourism development. Symbolic aspects remain, but original meanings were lost. Xie determined that the original ritual meaning of this dance has been turned into a celebration. It acquired new meaning and has become part of aboriginal cultural identity.

Stadler, R., Reid, S. and Fullager, S. (2013). An ethnographic exploration of knowledge practices within the Queensland Music Festival. *International Journal of Event and Festival Management*, 4(2), 90–106.

Reflexive ethnography was employed as an interpretative methodology for researching knowledge practices within festival organizations. Through participant observation and in-depth interviews the researchers concluded that knowledge management practices and processes are often invisible to festival staff when they are embedded within a cohesive organizational culture. Ethnography enables the researcher to make explicit the tacit and normalized ways of working that contribute to the success (and failure) of festival organizations to manage knowledge. The immersion of the researcher in the ethnographic process provided a rich understanding of the relational dimension of knowledge management that would be difficult to elicit from in-depth interviews alone.

Table 3.2 Progress in event studies: recent examples of studies on anthropology and events

Testa, A. (2014). Rethinking the festival: Power and politics. *Method and Theory in the Study of Religion*, 26 (1), 44–73.	This study examines theories of power in historical and contemporary festivals
Pop, C. (2013). The modern Olympic Games: A globalised cultural and sporting event. *Procedia – Social and Behavioral Sciences*, 92, 728–734.	This article examines the link between culture and social rituals in the Olympic Games and the impact of such events on the urban anthropology of host cities
Ziakas, V. and Boukas, N. (2014). Contextualizing phenomenology in event management research: Deciphering the meaning of event experiences. *International Journal of Event and Festival Management*, 5 (1), 56–73.	This article examines the meaning in event experiences using a phenomenological approach
Jaimangal-Jones, D. *et al.* (2010). Going the distance: Locating journey, liminality and rites of passage in dance music experiences. *Leisure Studies*, 29 (3), 253–268.	This study examines visits to music events as an act of a journey and pilgrimage

Ethics

A standard code of conduct has been adopted by the American Anthropological Association, which also provides resources for teaching ethics (see http://www.aaanet.org/cmtes/ethics/Ethics-Resources.cfm). Ethical issues include protecting the confidentially of informants, and the risk that studying a group might change it. If the researcher believes in applied anthropology, then 'action research' might be appropriate. In action research the aim is to cause a change, and to evaluate and shape the change process while learning and theorizing from it. Holloway *et al.* (2010) noted the ethical problem of dealing with gatekeepers when conducting ethnographic research (although such people might be important in quantitative research as well). Gatekeepers, allowing access to an event, a database or a group of people, might place conditions on the work, or actively seek a positive outcome – from their perspective. Many researchers believe that informed consent and active participation by all respondents is the only ethically correct method, and this would apply to observation techniques such as videography. The special case of netnography (online research) should also be considered. While many people post material on the Internet that can be freely accessed, especially in open blogs, the researcher might consider whether quotations can be traced back to people. Participatory or active netnography involves greater issues, as the researcher should make it clear that interactions are being observed or recorded, and particularly if discussions are being directed in certain ways. A selection of recent studies on the anthropology of events can be found in Table 3.2, which illustrates a wide range of research methods and approaches.

Sociology

Sociology is concerned with interactions between people, or 'social life', including a focus on how relationships are patterned in the form of groups, organizations and whole societies. Social rules and process are examined, together with social behaviour, and large-scale social processes. Social behaviour is mostly learned, and sociologists study the totality of behaviour as influenced by all facets of life including economic and political systems, family and friends, institutions and entertainment. The subject has a wide-ranging impact and influence upon the study of events.

According to the online source www.sociology.org.uk, major themes in this discipline include the following (see Table 3.3):

- 'socialization process': learning how to become human and to behave in ways that accord with the general expectations of others (in short, to be socialized);
- the structure of 'social life': values, norms, roles and status (social controls);
- 'values': beliefs that we have about what is important, both to us and to society as a whole;
- 'norms': expected, socially acceptable, ways of behaving in any given social situation;
- 'role': social roles we expect people to play;
- 'status': earned or assigned;
- 'social groups': the nature of family, peers, institutions, nations, communities of interest; relationships within groups;
- 'culture and identity': influencing factors on cultural identity include age, gender, ethnicity and regionalism;
- 'subcultures': groups sharing a particular way of life.

Research traditions and methods

Sociologists use the scientific method and have a long tradition of 'positivistic' methodology. However, there has also been a long tradition of 'humanistic sociology', which stresses the understanding of cultural values, meanings, symbols and norms. Multicultural comparisons are important. Both quantitative and qualitative methods are used, as is ethnography – which is very much akin to cultural anthropology. There are several clear perspectives or theoretical approaches that shape both research methodology and what is studied by sociologists. Alternative, competing traditions of research are now widespread in sociology (Veal 2006).

Veal (2006) assessed the evolution of sociological research pertaining to leisure and tourism, and concluded that the early modelling/prediction emphasis, based on large-scale social surveys and quantitative

Table 3.3 Sociology

Sociology	Nature and meanings; the event experience	Antecedents to attending events	Planning and producing events	Outcomes and the impacted	Processes and patterns
The study of human interactions, or social life; patterns of relationships including groups, organizations and whole societies – how they emerge and function	Social meanings of events Social experiences at events Symbolic interaction	Social factors influencing demand (e.g. family, race, religion, culture, community, social worlds, subcultures)	Implications for design and crowd management Organizational behaviour of event-producing bodies and stakeholders	Impacts on social groups and society as a whole Resident perceptions of, and attitudes towards, events	Social trends and forces (e.g. population and demographics, migration) that impact on the event sector Social development policy Diffusion of innovations

analysis (within the 'functionalist' tradition), had not worked well. More qualitative methods became fashionable in the 1970s and 1980s, with a shift towards learning more about why people did what they did, and what it meant to them, rather than just measuring and forecasting what they did. This era gave rise to research and theory development on leisure benefits and constraints.

Critical social theory

This approach starts with the premise that social 'reality' is historically constituted through social, cultural and political forces (Habermas 1973). The role of the critical researcher is therefore to reveal conflicts and contradictions and help eliminate the causes of alienation or domination. According to 'critical theory', the structure of capitalistic society marginalizes certain people and removes choices from them, which of course flies in the face of leisure being defined in terms of freely chosen, intrinsically motivated uses of time. 'Conflict theorists' emphasize conflicts in society, specifically between social classes, between men and women, and between different ethnic groups. The Marxist tradition has largely fallen out of favour, but it is obvious that many conflicts do remain.

One area of change which Richards *et al.* (2013: 219) acknowledge in the area of social theory is the work of Castells and the Network Society. Castells pointed to the growing global networks that co-exist alongside face-to-face communication in local communities and events creating dispersed social networks. These networks create more opportunities for rituals of co-presence (see Chapter 2), where geographical proximity is not the only determinant of meeting and contact. Hence events do retain attributes as physical spaces for events, but virtual spaces also become important as nodes of and a focal point for virtual networks to meet. Castells (2010) also maintained that power resides in networks, and this idea connects to other important concepts like social media, social worlds and the co-creation of experiences.

Functionalism

From this perspective, everything in society has a purpose or function. The basic values of this perspective emphasize the idea of harmony and social consensus, based around shared values. Functionalists are likely to interpret everything in terms of large-scale social structures.

Symbolic interactionists

Within social psychology, 'symbolic interactionists' concentrate on the way people understand one another. They tend to focus on the individual, looking in particular at the way we create the social world through our behaviour (rather than looking at how society creates the individual). A key issue is the set of symbols and understandings that have emerged which give meanings to interactions. Leisure and work take on meanings from social interactions, so that what we mean by work or leisure is in part determined by our social lives. Certain events might connote either work (say, a conference) and others leisure (a concert or festival). As well, the 'festival' for many people is symbolic of culture, while the trade show is symbolic of commerce. These are social constructs in the same way that we expect planned events to have a certain form and take place in certain settings.

Two books by Goffman (*The Presentation of Self in Everyday Life*, 1959 and *Frame Analysis: An Essay on the Organization of Experience*, 1974) are of particular relevance to event studies. Goffman used the imagery of the theatre to show how people are social 'actors'. In any given social interaction, there has to be an agreed-upon definition of what is happening, otherwise there is no congruence between the 'performers'. 'Actors' usually foster impressions that reflect well upon themselves. In communication theory and sociology, 'framing' is a process of selective control over media content or public communication. Framing defines how media content is packaged and presented so as to allow certain desirable interpretations and rule out others. However, there are also important differences to note in this type of framing and the framing rituals discussed by Falassi.

Social and cultural capital

The sociologist Bourdieu (1972, 1986) distinguished between economic, social, symbolic and cultural capital. Economic capital refers to a command of cash or other assets that can be invested for profit, while social capital consists of the possession of resources that derive from group membership, relationships, networks of influence and support. Cultural capital consists of knowledge, skills, education and other advantages possessed by a person that result in higher social status. Parents are said to transmit such advantages to their children. Symbolic capital accrues to individuals as resources on the basis of honour, prestige or recognition – that is, some people stand out as icons. These concepts are in tune with a long tradition of philosophical thought and sociological theory on the value of networks, and the need to foster social cohesion through institutions and policy. There are clear conceptual links to notions of civil society and the power of communitas through celebration. In other words, social networking has value, and festivals and events can foster it – they also lead to the establishment of events for many social worlds and groups.

Reciprocity and trust are the foundations of 'social capital', and to some extent these qualities of social life are found in all communities and societies. Where social capital is high, people are more likely to be polite, talk to strangers, interact as equals and perform random acts of kindness. In other words, we 'invest' social capital in our community and expect others to do the same (this is similar to 'social exchange theory'). Voluntarism can be viewed as a form of social capital at the community level, as can community-based decision-making, informal business transactions and spontaneous celebrations. Putnam (2004) placed more emphasis on benefits accruing to the community, while others (e.g. Bourdieu 1986; Coleman 1988, 1990) conceptualized social capital at the individual level. When a person develops a substantial 'social network' of friends, allies and collaborators, their social capital increases and when 'invested' or 'spent', it can result in a variety of economic, social, psychological and emotional benefits. Some people pursue the accumulation of social capital through deliberate networking, while others acquire it unconsciously. This is epitomized by the recent monograph by Richards *et al.* (2013) in which social capital is a dominant theme in many of the chapters, including case studies from the event spectrum from European Capital of Culture programmes to sport events.

3.2 RESEARCH NOTES ON SOCIAL CAPITAL

Finkel, R. (2010). Dancing around the ring of fire: Social capital, tourism resistance, and gender dichotomies at Up Helly Aa in Lerwick, Scotland. *Event Management*, 14(4), 275–285.

Finkel interprets this Shetland Islands traditional festival (Viking themed) in the light of community, tourism, traditions of the place and gender. Sacred places are created 'where the whole community can come together on a ritually repeated basis'. Over a thousand volunteers work on the festival each year, and it is a focal point for community cohesion – even though females are excluded from performing the Viking fire-drama. Some residents resist the commercial orientation promoted by tourism authorities, although others appreciate having an audience. In a world where top-down, instrumentalist policy towards festivals prevails, the author claims that this event is a good case of community initiative that generates social capital.

Williams, P. W. and Elkhashab, A. (2012). Leveraging tourism social capital: The case of the 2010 Olympic tourism consortium. *International Journal of Event and Festival Management*, 3(3), 317–334.

Researchers explored social capital emerging from the collective set of activities pursued by a network of stakeholders leveraging tourism benefits from the 2010 Vancouver Winter Olympic and Paralympic Games. Aspects of bonding, bridging and linking social capital creation were examined. Varying levels of confidence, trust, mutual respect, personal ties, shared values and human capacity were generated through the consortium's activities. This social capital was perceived as a valuable but fragile legacy capable of nurturing increased leadership and organizational capacity particularly when tackling issues confronting the industry's overall sustained prosperity.

Social worlds

Unruh (1980: 271) used the term 'social world' to describe 'the notion that actors, events, practices, and formal organizations can coalesce into a meaningful and interactional important unit of social organization for participants'. Involvement in social worlds is voluntary, even though 'guidelines, expectations, and rules certainly exist' (1980: 277). It can be partial, so that order within a social world is negotiated and its bounds are those of the 'universe of discourse'. Total involvement in one social world is highly unlikely, given that leisure choices can lead to multiple affiliations. Interactions are mediated because of reliance on various channels of communication rather than spatial, kinship or other formal ties. Nevertheless, some meeting places are usually important (these can be events), and some places are associated with social worlds because of their concentration of actors, practices or events (a destination could become a mecca for runners, for example). Communication centres are vital, being the points where a great deal of the involvement is focused; communication sets limits on the extent of the discourse that defines a social world. Withdrawal from social worlds might carry a cost in terms of loss of one's interpersonal contacts. Unruh provided a very useful framework for assessing social worlds. The analysis examines participants ('actors'), what they do ('practices'), important events in their social-world activities, and organizations involved in or influencing social worlds.

Actors

People can belong to a variety of social worlds in a fluid, evolving process that takes place over their lifetimes. Unruh (1980: 280) identified types of involvement. 'Strangers' are characterized by marginality, detachment and superficiality, but act as points of reference and comparison with other social worlds. 'Tourists' get involved out of curiosity but lack long-term commitment to a social world. These 'tourists' are not literally travellers; rather they are transitory members of social worlds and remain so as long as the community provides them with some rewards such as entertainment or profit. 'Regulars' (1980: 282) are 'habitual participants who are integrated in the social world's ongoing activities'. This represents a significant amount of commitment. Finally, 'insiders' are the most committed, have intimate knowledge of social-world activities, determine prestige, value and relationships, recruit new members, organize activities, and have the most to gain or lose from the success or failure of the social world.

Events

In Unruh's schema, 'events' are personal occurrences that are important to people involved in a social world, such as their first or most prestigious race. However, these can also be planned events that participants attend, including those events planned specifically to attract members of specific social worlds. It is likely, however, that many event organizers are not consciously appealing to communities of interest. However, it is also clear that events are produced by the insiders themselves; this was the case observed by Green and Chalip (1998) regarding the subcultural identity of female flag footballers.

Practices

There is a behavioural dimension to 'practices' – specifically what members of the social world do. This can include travel to events, participating in clubs, buying and selling, and corresponding. There is also a symbolic and ritualistic dimension reflecting the values or ethos of the social world, including signs of membership and status, and prescribed or desired ways of speaking and doing things. Subcultures and other communities of interest tend to develop their own language.

Formal organizations

Many organizations can play a role in shaping social worlds and facilitating networking among members: governing bodies and associations that are often hierarchical in nature; corporations intent on building brand communities for their own marketing purposes; clubs and teams; tourist organizations attempting to attract groups; events catering to special interests; and magazines and e-zines focused on special interests.

Unruh also developed levels of social-world analysis, from local to regional, dispersed, and social-world systems. A local or regional social world might have boundaries, but that is not what defines it – it only shapes that social world's scale and scope. Globally dispersed social worlds have grown enormously since Unruh's treatise, facilitated by travel, a proliferation of planned events (periodic and one-time), and the power of the Internet and other forms of interpersonal communication to bring together people with similar interests. It is important to consider how social worlds link to the concepts of communitas, the power of networking, the formation and use of social capital, and special-interest tourism.

Integrating emerging discourses from critical event studies: accessibility and inclusion in event practices

The discussion in Chapter 1 highlighted the emergence of the critical event discourse, with particular concerns from sociology about key themes focused on events in society. Rojek (2013) and Horne (2015) use the concept of economic and political power which events create for certain stakeholders to the detriment of some groups. This has created a focus on societal issues that has generated a sharper focus on three fundamental concepts:

- *Accessibility*, which Finkel *et al.* (2019a: 2) define as 'the measures put in place to address participation by those with impairments, both permanent and temporary, as well as both physical and mental, including perceived class and cultural barriers'.
- *Inclusion*, with a focus on removing barriers to participation which often has an interventionist dimension to address wider equality issues within a civil society paradigm, where all people are encouraged to participate in society.
- *Diversity*, which Finkel *et al.* (2019a: 2) define as 'individual and community diversity, such as those relating to gender, sexualities, ethnicity, age, religion …'.

What Finkel *et al.* (2019a) rightly recognize is that while these three domains of accessibility, diversity and inclusion have a clear societal focus, and multiple social science and humanities subjects are engaging with these issues. At a practical level, the broader concern with accessibility 'has become a priority at a global

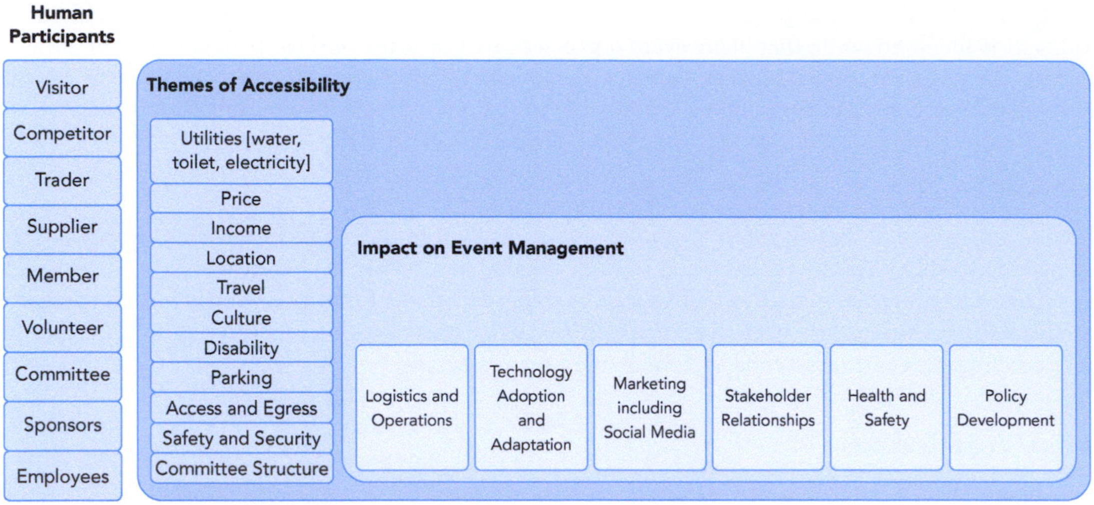

Figure 3.2 Human participants and accessibility

Source: Wiscombe (2019: 71), reproduced with permission from Routledge.

level, taking into account, that by 2050 it is expected that 6.25 billion people will be living in urban centres, 15% of whom will be persons with disabilities' (Barrera-Fernández and Hernández-Escampa 2019: 22). This has generated studies that we use checklists to assess the accessibility of venues and sites (e.g. Doshi *et al.* 2014) and similar studies which conceptualize the scope of human participation and accessibility issues and the management issues (Figure 3.2). More detailed checklists such at Table 3.4 expand upon Figure 3.2, particularly with respect to prior to an event and during its hosting.

Further studies of these issues can be found in Walters and Jepson (2019) where the focus of their book is on marginalization and events by different groups of people.

3.1 EXPERT OPINION

The mediating roles of social worlds on event tourism

Dr Ian Patterson is Associate Professor in the School of Tourism, the University of Queensland. The research he describes has been published: Getz, D. and Patterson, I. (2013). Social worlds as a framework for event and travel careers. *Tourism Analysis*, 18(5), 485–501.

We used Unruh's social-world framework to examine the pertinent events, travel behaviour and related preferences of those who engage in a variety of special interests. The idea was to compare various forms of serious leisure, namely amateur sports, arts, lifestyle pursuits and hobbies. Passive netnographic analysis has demonstrated the relevance of this approach, and substantial evidence has been found to support the notion of event-travel careers.

New understandings of how social worlds lead to, and mediate, participation in events and travel in general have been established. Evidence was clearly available on motivations, covering passion, self-identity, lifestyle, self-esteem and health. Evidence was also available on events, travel, networking and communications, portfolios of activities, specialization and beginning a career.

Our searches yielded variable results that probably can be expanded upon in further research. To this end, a series of questions was created to analyse the netnographic evidence and these could be used or modified when conducting further interviews and larger-scale surveys, or through the use of interactive netnography.

Social worlds act to mediate the travel preferences and patterns of members in at least two major ways. Involved individuals can, of course, elect to make their own travel plans, either to special-interest events or for other social-world experiences. However, many organizations seek to influence these decisions, and peer-to-peer networking also has an impact. Understanding these processes will have profound marketing implications, but there are also other theoretical consequences.

Clear evidence has been found that these different leisure and sporting pursuits all generate and sustain interest in travel and lead to hierarchies of participatory, celebratory and competitive events, and other experiences involving social-world networking. It is also likely that some members of these social worlds were attracted in the first place by their interest in travel and the event dimension.

Many formal organizations are seeking to influence their members, some through their legitimate role as clubs, associations, governing or event organizing bodies, that makes them part of their social world. Others are employing advertising or other promotions, such as event and tour sponsorships, to increase memberships. Another possibility exists, and that is clandestine participation in social networking, which raises both legal and ethical questions.

To further advance research and theory on social worlds and event-tourist careers, a set of propositions has been developed. It is proposed that social worlds moderate travel patterns and references in the following ways:

1 Online and remote interaction among members stimulates interest in specific events and social opportunities (i.e. real-life sharing experiences) that creates travel demand.

2 Events present opportunities for personal and group development and identity-building, and reinforce social-world values.

3 Events can develop (or be assigned) symbolic/iconic appeal to members of social worlds.

4 To be effective, commercial organizations that market specific travel products and events to social worlds must reflect and enable the values and motivations of their members.

5 Events that are social as opposed to competitive in nature have quite a different appeal to various social worlds, and this can only be understood in the context of values and practices.

Subcultures

This is a somewhat vague and flexible term, with some scholars viewing them as deviants, and others associating them more with distinctive styles of dress and symbolic actions. In this book, emphasis is placed on social worlds and people involved in various leisure pursuits leading to interest in events and travel.

Social network theory

Analysing social networks (see Freeman *et al.* 1992; Scott 2000) is a very useful way to examine stakeholder relationships surrounding event policy and management. A 'social network' consists of individual

Table 3.4 Checklist of accessibility measures asked of officials and people with reduced mobility

Venue	Guelaguetza auditorium City centre El Llano park La Danza square Other
Dissemination before the event	Texts in braille Printed materials in large print and good contrast Audio narration Sign language interpreter Subtitles in real time Accessibility symbols included in leaflets Websites meet accessibility standards Specific contact information
During the celebration of the event	Texts in braille Materials in large print and good contrast Hearing aid devices Audio narration Sign language interpreter Subtitles in real time Accessibility symbols included in leaflets
Accessibility of the place Staff	Accessible transport to get to the venue Accessible parking Access for wheelchairs Access for wheelchairs through the main entrance Dedicated signage All areas accessible or people available to offer assistance Elevators, where available, have accessible buttons Reserved spaces for wheelchairs Reserved spaces for wheelchairs located in all sitting areas Aisles are wide enough Good lighting Good visibility of the stage from a wheelchair People with hearing disabilities have dedicated seats near the stage Accessible toilets nearby and well signed Electrical cables or cords are covered Hearing aid devices are arranged when requested Accessible public telephones Guide dogs are allowed to enter Pavement lines or changes in floor textures Glass signage Direction and areas signage Signage is simple, bright and colourful Stage is accessible and adapted for performance of people with reduced mobility Staff given training in needs and requirements of people with different disabilities Staff provide information on accessible toilets and emergency exits Staff have clearly visible clothes Staff know how to proceed in case of emergency

Source: Barrera-Fernández and Hernández-Escampa 2019: 26), reproduced with permission from Routledge.

'actors' and the ties between them, either formal or informal. In one sense, it can be said that the more ties an actor has (e.g. the event organization), the more social capital it will accumulate. But, more importantly, the network itself gains capital and might assume a political life of its own, similar to the concept of a 'political market square' in which the actors negotiate to direct the future of a festival (see Larson and Wikstrom 2001; Larson 2002). Networks can be powerful determinants of policy and strategy. In the network society described by Castells, power resides in networks and in the modern world they are primarily electronic in nature.

Diffusion of innovation theory

Innovations, including both technology and ideas, are communicated through various formal channels and social networks (Rogers 1995). Individuals and organizations do not equally adapt innovation, rather there are the 'innovators', 'early adopters', 'early majority', 'late majority' and 'laggards'. When it comes to innovations that can provide competitive advantage or increased effectiveness, it can pay to be the innovator or the early adopter, but of course there are costs and risks associated with being first.

In the events sector, we can observe innovation and diffusion in terms of new types of events and how they spread globally, usually through the influence of mass media. It is also clear that event producers copy ideas, which to a degree can be good, but without systematic benchmarking this can simply lead to standardization. And if every city and destination pursues the same event-tourism strategy, leading to 'festivalization', this has potentially negative consequences.

3.3 RESEARCH NOTES ON INNOVATION AND FESTIVALS

Hjalager, A. (2009). Cultural tourism innovation systems – the Roskilde Festival. *Scandinavian Journal of Hospitality and Tourism*, 9(2–3), 266–287.

'Since 1971, Roskilde Festival (Denmark) has developed its role as a leading element in an emerging cultural innovation system. Festival organizers maintain long-term, dense and multifaceted relations. Funds from the (non-profit) festival are efficiently channelled into cultural and sports facilities, enhancing the attractiveness of the region. To keep ahead in the festival market, innovators in the field of managerial systems, technologies and services are deliberately invited to use the grounds as test benches for new ideas. ... Since 2001 especially, wider-ranging organizational structures have been constructed and politically enforced with the aim of nurturing spin-offs, and including strong representation within the educational and research sectors.'

Jóhannesson, G. (2010). Emergent Vikings: The social ordering of tourism innovation. *Event Management*, 14(4), 261–274.

The author discusses how Iceland has experienced a rapid growth of tourism, which has increasingly been taken up as an option for economic development. Innovation in this field has been promoted by public actors. In one such tourism innovation project, the Gísla Saga project, in the small fishing village of Þingeyri, the local village festival, Dýrafjarðardagar, has been related to the innovation project. Using Actor-Network Theory, the researcher argues that it is important to follow the enactment of diverse styles of ordering for gaining insight into the emergent cultural economy of tourism. By tracing the practices through which the project is established, the article illustrates some of the ways in which tourism innovation relates to the social ordering of local communities.

Innovation and diffusion are not necessarily good or bad, but understanding how they work is important in terms of strategy and marketing. In particular, marketers want to learn who will be the first to adopt their products and services, then spread the word to other potential customers.

Social exchange theory

'Social exchange theory' (Hormans 1958) suggests that social action is different from straightforward economic actions within a marketplace (i.e. buying and selling), because social actors expect and receive rewarding reactions. Resource exchanges (as well as the bestowal of prestige or support) are, in this context, the result of free, personal choice based on the assessment of expected costs and benefits. People can feel pressure to give, but exchanges should balance out over time. The theory also embodies the concepts of power and dependency within relationships and social networks. In the context of event studies, this theory has been used to explain variation in resident perceptions of, or attitudes towards, events. For example, people benefiting from event tourism will tend to be positive in their attitudes towards the event and its continuance, while people perceiving no benefit tend to be more critical and less supportive.

Contributions of sociology to event studies

It is highly relevant to note that Cohen's (1988a) article entitled 'Traditions in the qualitative sociology of tourism' identified three principal traditions that all have importance for the study of festivals and events, namely those associated with the seminal works of Turner (see section on Anthropology, p. 100), Boorstin (see History, p. 176) and MacCannell. MacCannell's (1973, 1976) sociological thesis on the tourist mainstreamed the discussion of authenticity and the notion that it is sought out because of the inauthenticity of modern life. His work employed the notions of Goffman (1959) on dramaturgy, and suggested that 'staged authenticity' was all that modern tourists could expect to find. This term gained enduring popularity, similar to 'pseudo-events', and his work directly stimulated early articles on 'spurious' festivals (Papson 1981), as well as Buck's (1977) notion of using events for 'boundary maintenance' between tourists and sensitive cultural groups.

Within the tourism literature, commodification and authenticity have been important, festival-related themes. Greenwood (1972, 1989) first suggested that tourism commoditized culture, and particularly festivals, leading to the event's loss of meaning among residents. Cohen (1988b) defined commoditization as a process by which things become valued in monetary terms, or exchange value. Cohen's concept of 'emergent authenticity' applies to festivals; Cohen described how a re-created, tourist-oriented festival could become accepted as being authentic, over time. Thus, commoditization might lead to a festival acquiring new meanings for both tourists and residents. Quinn (2013: 2) discusses authenticity as one of the 'Key Concepts in Event Management'. Drawing from Olsen (2002), authenticity is viewed not as the quality of an object (e.g. asking the question 'is that an authentic performance or setting?' implies there is a correct, truthful interpretation), 'but as a cultural value constantly created and reinvented in social processes'. Festivals and other cultural celebrations both create and proclaim cultural meanings to themselves and outsiders. In this context, Richards (2007b) suggested that residents are more likely to emphasize a 'constructive authenticity' based on familiar cultural norms like traditions and language, whereas visitors tend towards 'existential authenticity' related to their own enjoyment and socializing. We return to this important authenticity theme later in the book.

Duvignaud's (1976) conceptual article on the sociology of festivals and festivity documents how these phenomena have been 'explained', including the dialectic between those, like Durkheim (1965), who viewed festivity as an 'intensification of the collective being' and those who see festivals as being inherently subversive. Duvignaud also discussed festivity as play and commemoration, concluding there was no one correct interpretation. Much of the pertinent sociological theory comes to event studies indirectly through leisure studies, and also through social psychology. Particular themes to explore in this discipline include:

- societal trends and forces shaping values and leisure;
- social change (e.g. globalization and homogenization);
- life-stage influences on event interests and attendance;
- population and demographic factors;
- human ecology (crowds, fads, trends);
- effects of family, gender, race, culture, community, and social class on demand and behaviour;
- social worlds, virtual communities or brand communities (of considerable interest to sponsors and corporations owning events);
- social behaviour at events; conflict theory;
- deviance (certain types of events, deviant behaviour at events);
- social costs and benefits (crime, prostitution, sport or art participation, civic pride, belonging and sharing, integration, cohesion);
- economic development and social inequality (power structures reflected in events).

More specific applications to event studies can be reviewed within the following sub-fields.

Sport sociology

Current research areas within sport sociology include: sport and socialization; sport and social stratification; sport subcultures; the political economy of sport; sport and deviance; sport and the media; sport, the body and the emotions; sport violence; sport politics and national identity; sport and globalization. In a special supplement to the *Sociological Review*, Horne and Manzenreiter (2006: 1) discussed the sociological study of sport as including 'ritualized, rationalized, commercial spectacles and bodily practices that create opportunities for expressive performances, disruptions of the everyday world and affirmations of social status and belonging'. Roche (2000) argued that mega events have become much more central to urban modernity.

Environmental sociology

This is the study of societal–environmental interactions, including the causes of environmental problems and their impacts, ways to solve problems and even how conditions come to be viewed as problems. We could ask, for example, how the creation of social representations comes about, such as: 'mega events are environmentally destructive', or 'festivals are a means to change attitudes about the environment'.

Events and urban sociology

Mega events in particular can have profound impacts on urban forms and life, but the effects of many small events, individually and cumulatively, should not be overlooked. Consider the following research by Harry Hiller (see Research Note 3.4).

3.4 RESEARCH NOTE ON URBAN SOCIOLOGY

Hiller, H. (2000a). Toward an urban sociology of mega-events. *Research in Urban Sociology*, 5, 181–205.

Hiller's contention is that 'from street festivals, parades, and pilgrimages to riots, marches of resistance and demonstrations, such expressive and instrumental activities have been among the most observable aspects of urban social life'. In defining mega events, Hiller (2000a: 183) says 'From the perspective of an urban analyst, any large-scale special event can be considered a mega-event if it has a significant and/or permanent urban effect – that is, if it is considered so significant that it reprioritizes the urban agenda in some way and leads to some modification or alteration of urban space which becomes its urban legacy.'

He assesses mega events as to their part in shaping urban processes – as change factors – and in that respect identifies and discusses roles: catalysts for change; land use changes; creativity in urban planning; mobilizing funds; supporting projects otherwise considered too expensive or ambitious; forcing an agenda by requiring completion at a set date; infrastructure improvements in select domains, like transport; producing signature structures which redefine urban space.'

Events and rural sociology

Janiskee's studies (1980, 1985, 1991; Janiskee and Drews 1998) of rural festivals revealed their importance in social life and tourism, as well as their seasonal and geographic distribution. Rural communities are particularly vulnerable to social disruption caused by tourism, or large influxes of new residents seeking amenities. On the other hand, events and tourism can help to foster community development and self-reliance. Events are one of the few tourism 'products' that even the smallest of communities can produce, without large amounts of capital. However, the volunteer and leadership base might be inadequate for long-term sustainability. In *Festival Places: Revitalising Rural Australia* (Gibson and Connell 2011), various authors explore themes relating to the roles of festivals and events in rural life, including economic development, place identity, tradition (and what it means to be living in the country), social integration (especially in an era where lifestyles and tourism bring newcomers to small towns) and community development. Davies (2011), for example, argues that rural festivals are a catalyst for leadership development, social networking and capacity-building – all of which are essential to preserve or revitalize threatened rural communities. Therefore, the social dimension of events has a major impact upon the development and direction event research follows; this is illustrated in Events in Focus 3.1, which sets out a number of emerging research agendas.

EVENTS IN FOCUS

3.1 Emerging research agendas in the social analysis of events

According to Richards *et al.* (2013) there are a number of emerging research agendas that coalesce into the following themes:

- events as generators of social capital to increase social identity and interaction for event participants and the local community;
- business models to support events, given the increasing demand from public authorities for a better justification of the social benefits accruing from hosting events;

- events as politics and policy, where events are used in the political arena in an emancipatory manner, in a dictatorial context or for economic reasons. Increasingly, the social outcomes from event hosting and political ambitions need to be better understood. For example, issues of social inclusion and exclusion are key areas for analysis (see Vanwynsberghe *et al.* 2013 and Tomlinson 2014 on Olympic legacies which often remain elusive). In fact, a recent study of the Glasgow Commonwealth Games by Gray and Porter (2014) illustrates how the use of compulsory purchase orders to create the athletes' village displaced working-class neighbourhoods based on a political mantra of 'necessity';

- management of event design issues to create a social dimension often called 'imagineering' (see Chapter 6 for more detail) along with the growing scale of events and their wide-ranging impacts on communities;

- co-creation, whereby both producers and consumers collaborate to develop events, which is changing the boundaries between producers, organizers and participants.

A number of key research challenges include:

1 problems of measurement in terms of accessing and using social indicators that measure concepts such as social capital;

2 a need for longitudinal research, to understand continuity and change induced by or related to events despite the difficulties of isolating causality in how events shape social phenomena;

3 the social dimension of events has largely been examined through community and local events and festivals where social consequences can be identified, and where the impact of business events has largely been focused on the corporate social responsibility objectives of sponsors and events hosts as opposed to the wider social effects of hosting different types of events;

4 collective as opposed to just individual experiences of events need greater attention, as much of the research effort has been directed towards understanding individual experiences of events rather than group experiences;

5 the use of social media to understand the networked society and the social implications in event research, including the development of Big Data approaches to capture and analyse event participation and satisfaction;

6 the changing role of different stakeholders and publics in shaping the social dimensions of events where research needs to be triangulated to capture the differing experiences of stakeholders rather than relying upon singular studies of one element of stakeholder experiences of events;

7 identifying the social dimension of events through the 'community' of networked and physically co-present people and stakeholders;

8 shifting event research from a focus predominantly on management, impacts and policy to more comparative and longitudinal studies of where the social impacts and benefits of events accrue.

Source: Developed from Richards, de Brito and Wilks (2013).

Philosophy

Philosophers use reasoning, not empirical research, to theorize about the meaning of life and belief systems. But the nature and scope of philosophy are subject to influence by changing societal values and scientific discoveries. People who contemplate the meaning of life generally fall into two categories: those who adopt religious or spiritual meanings, and those who search elsewhere, inside their own mind and value sets. Philosophy is concerned with the nature of religion and spiritualism, but does not embrace

Table 3.5 Philosophy

Philosophy	Nature and meanings; the event experience	Antecedents to attending events	Planning and producing events	Outcomes and the impacted	Processes and patterns
Critical thought on the nature of experience, the meaning of life and belief systems Aesthetics Ethics Phenomenology Hermeneutics	Aesthetic experiences Experiences that shape one's world-view How we give ethical meaning to experiences	The quest for the meaning of life as a motivator (self-discovery) Desire for aesthetic experiences as a motivator World-view as it shapes preferences	Values and ethics as a basis for producing and managing events (e.g. sustainability) A philosophy of event service	Evaluation of aesthetics Impacts on values and ethics at personal or social levels	Changing value systems affect event planning and policy

faith or divine revelation, only reasoning. However, philosophy provides a firm foundation in the analysis of event phenomena, particularly around the themes in Table 3.5 and in the meaning of event experiences.

The nature of experience (phenomenology and hermeneutics)

What is experience, and how can we study it? These two key questions lead us to consider the critical role of 'phenomenology', being the method used to study people's consciousness and behaviour simultaneously, for example, Jackson *et al.* (2018) adopted a phenomenological approach to music events, informed by specific philosophical methodologies. Applied to event experiences, we could ask people at various times before, during and after the event to describe and explain their actions and thoughts. How does the event appear to them? What meanings are they attaching to their experiences and behaviour? How does it affect them emotionally, intellectually, spiritually? There is great scope for advancing our understanding of the planned event experience through phenomenological methods, as demonstrated in Research Note 3.5.

3.5 RESEARCH NOTE ON PHENOMENOLOGY

Chen, P. (2006). The attributes, consequences, and values associated with event sport tourists' behaviour: A means–end chain approach. *Event Management*, 10(1), 1–22.

A phenomenological study of highly involved members of a fan club was conducted, in order to reveal important personal constructs of the meanings attached to their fan-related experiences. Means–end theory (see Olson and Reynolds 2001) provided the foundation for proceeding from an examination of the concrete (attributes of being a sport fan) to consequences of the event and travel experiences (functional and psychological outcomes) to the abstract (values or goals, like self-fulfilment). Means–end is designed to elicit non-verbal communications, hidden feeling and thoughts, and deeply held constructs and their interrelationships. Chen concluded that socialization was one of the most important, indeed essential aspects of the fans' experiences, consisting of developing one's sense of self-being through friendships, social support and identification with a group. This led to enjoyment, well-being and balance in life.

Hermeneutics

This is a Greek word for interpretation; it has become a branch of philosophy concerned with human understanding and the interpretation of 'texts'. All writing and symbolic communication (including performances and sports) can be viewed as 'text', and that text can be interpreted. What the researcher says about people or real-world phenomena is open to interpretation in two fundamental ways: has the researcher found the truth (if there is a single truth), and what does the analysis say about the researcher? If the researcher claims to have the truth, the researcher is likely a positivist schooled in certain traditions and making use of standard methods.

Aesthetics and art

Tastes and aesthetic appreciation are not absolutes, they are personal and vary a great deal. We can examine taste and aesthetic appreciation from a scientific perspective, considering cognition, sensory receptors and emotional responses, but this will never explain what we mean by 'art' or 'beauty'. While it is a philosophical issue at heart, aesthetics is also the realm of event designers. They learn what pleases and what does not, and how to solve practical problems with personal style.

Where exactly is the art in event design? Many festivals and exhibitions are within the domain of 'the arts' (see du Cros and Jolliffe 2014). That is, they are themed around a variety of arts, with most festivals featuring performing arts like music and dance and most exhibitions displaying visual arts like painting and sculpture. But are the events themselves a form of art? Where is the creativity in them? Is the aesthetic appreciation confined to the objects of the event (i.e. the arts on display, the performers) or do people gain aesthetic benefits from the form of the event itself?

Certainly party and wedding planners take pride in the art of the decorations (from flowers to table arrangements), while chefs generally present meals at least partially as art – not merely as something to eat. Art might be found in the lighting, sounds and smells of an event, or in the costumes and performances of the staff and volunteers (remembering Disney's dictum that staff are 'cast members'). But extending this aesthetic appreciation to the design of the whole event presents conceptual and practical problems. It is unclear whether most event planners and designers view their events, as a totality, as an art form. Certainly there is art in the design, but can we definitely state that a festival or event is a work of art in the same league as, say, a performance of a symphony orchestra?

3.2 EXPERT OPINION

Event as art

Dr Steve Brown is an event designer. He is Head of Tourism, and Course Coordinator of the Festival and Event Design and Management programmes. This is his take on event as art:

John Tribe writing about aesthetics and beauty argues that art 'attempts in different ways to capture the spirit of things freeing us from the conventional limitations of words and language and offering poetic, visual and musical representations that can engender deeper and different engagements with their subjects' (Tribe 2009: 11). In my role as an Event Designer, my intent is to capture and engage the audience to provide experiences that free them from the conventional and offer 'poetic, visual and musical representations'. Event design is sometimes called an 'art' but it is more a philosophical approach that is audience-centric that, if applied correctly, *can* turn a simple event into a work of art.

Ethics

What is right or wrong, good or bad, and how do we judge behaviour or policy? This is the realm of ethics, and is also called 'moral philosophy'. Certainly political ideology and religious beliefs enter the picture, as both of these give people a moral code or set of values to live by. Others develop their own morality and ethics through philosophical means, but always with reference to other people and society in general. We cannot be ethical or moral in isolation. Ethics applies to professional conduct, and no event management programme can be complete without instilling the need for ethical and legal behaviour. Students might ask, however, is 'legal' the same as 'ethical', and should the various professional codes of conduct govern us completely and without question? What place is there for personal and situational ethics, where you or I make the rules as we go?

Goldblatt (2011: 412) discusses ethics, noting that typical event-industry ethical issues include:

- breach of confidentiality (often covered in contracts, but sometimes implicit in professional dealings);
- gifts versus bribes (do gifts influence decisions? are bribes illegal?);
- sexual harassment (a legal issue in many countries with clear policies and training to address the issue);
- poaching clients (staff members who move and take clients with them or go back and poach them);
- taking credit for others' work (i.e. not clearly identifying who is responsible for work produced);
- theft of ideas (which is the same as plagiarism, theft of intellectual property; secure copyright protection).

Henderson, and McIlwraith in their book *Ethics and Corporate Social Responsibility in the Meetings and Events Industry* (2013) take a broad view of ethics, suggesting that green practices, sustainability and corporate social responsibility are all interconnected (also see Tzanelli 2015 on Brazil's 2014 World Cup and ethics). While many see the MICE sector as being simply about business, these authors want practitioners to always consider the harm or good that events can do both immediately (in the setting or community) and in the long term for the planet.

Is event tourism an ethical issue?

We know that tourism has a high carbon footprint, yet every city and country wants more of it! Is this simply a practical problem, with the solution lying in alternative energy sources? Or is it an enduring ethical issue? How much event tourism should we be encouraging or accepting? Page (2015) addresses a similar range of issues related to the growth of global tourism, in which travel related to events is a contributor. Page (2015) posits that some parts of the world with fragile environments should be free of tourism and this raises a whole range of issues, not least where travel to fragile environments becomes an 'event' in someone's life, with access to that opportunity available purely through being able to pay a premium price. Mueller *et al.* (2018), examining small-scale events in the outdoor environment, highlighted a 'Leave no trace' philosophy which was in stark contrast to Wang *et al.*'s (2018) analysis of an urban event and the lack of greening in specific areas of the supply chain and venue (also see Boggia *et al.* 2018 on event greening).

In the absence of clear-cut solutions to such problems, it is difficult to justify a particular ethical position. The problem with this particular dilemma is that there is no obvious solution, meaning that any point of view or political position will find some degree of support and legitimacy, plus there is a huge lobby for continued growth and development. Alternative energy might very well solve the problem – some day – but it is not yet within reach, despite new philosophical paradigms around notions such as the green economy, which aim to facilitate development while reducing carbon use and environmental impacts as illustrated in Figure 3.3 with reference to tourism. But this can equally be applied to events where the

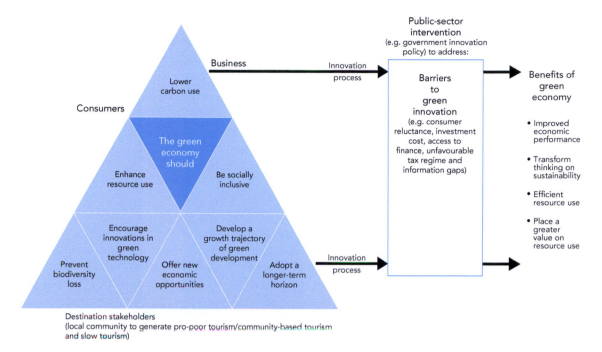

Figure 3.3 Principles of green economic growth

Source: Page (2015: 446), developed from OECD (2013) *Green Innovation in Tourism*, OECD. Paris. Reprinted from *Tourism Management, 5th Edition*, S. J. Page, Routledge (2015).

destination stakeholders are the local community and businesses who can potentially benefit from a new approach towards event development that adopts these principles.

Economic forces might also solve the pollution/global-warming problem by making fossil fuels too expensive, but the resulting economic disruption could destroy countless jobs around the world, which is one of the attractions of the green economy paradigm since it builds economic growth around green principles. Taxing fuels and travel will similarly have an inevitable economic and social cost, probably with inequitable results that allow the rich to continue doing whatever they want and forcing the poor to stay at home. In short, taking an ethical position on event tourism will not solve the problem, and there is a need for such debates to establish workable solutions.

A philosophy of event service

Other applied professional fields incorporate philosophical positions, such as that found in 'leisure service'. If we view leisure and events as a public good, which was the basis for their provision in many Western countries from the mid-nineteenth century onwards (see Page and Connell 2010), then providing leisure, cultural and event services to people becomes a public-sector function. Certainly this philosophical position is embedded within many leisure and culture programmes that remain today, despite cuts in many public-sector budgets, although it is seldom made explicit regarding the events component.

The following questions must be addressed in developing any philosophical position about 'event service':

- Are all planned events fundamentally good?
- Under what conditions is public support justified?

- Must all events be environmentally sustainable in every possible way?
- Should all events contribute positively to individual and community health?
- What obligations to society and the environment do event professionals hold? (consider morality and ethics).
- What is the value of art events? What events are in bad taste? How should we judge beauty? (this is aesthetics).
- What can we learn about the event experience and the multiple meanings attached to events? (such as through hermeneutic phenomenology).

Religious studies

The study of religion includes attention to its origins and evolution, the comparison and analysis of belief systems, and the evaluation of impacts on society. The rites, rituals and celebrations of various religions are scrutinized, including the use of anthropological methods, and this has direct relevance in event studies (see Table 3.6). 'Theologians' hold religious belief systems and apply their specific beliefs and related values to interpreting or criticizing all aspects of human society. Since so many events are religious in origin or theme, or contain programmed elements that hold religious meaning (even something as common as an opening prayer or blessing), theology contributes to event studies. In some societies it is more a matter of spirituality, or even mysticism, that one finds reflected in modern events (see Events in Focus 3.2 on pilgrimages). According to Melton (2011), globally there are 800 celebratory occasions amongst the world's main religions but 'only rarely have religious holidays been singled out for systematic study' (Melton 2011: XIX). Salamone (2004) observed that rituals and festivals with a religious dimension which occur in public include life-cycle rites associated with birth, coming of age, marriage and death (also see Fuller 2004).

Table 3.6 Religious studies

Religious studies	Nature and meanings; the event experience	Antecedents to attending events	Planning and producing events	Outcomes and the impacted	Processes and patterns
The study of religions, emphasizing human society and behaviour Religious life and experience	Sacred experiences (religious rites, symbols, and celebrations) for believers Pilgrimage	Religious motivations for attending or rejecting events Quest for spiritual meaning as a motivator for belonging to religious groups	Ritual and symbolism incorporated into event programming	Religious trends and forces (e.g. the influence of religious lobbies)	Spiritual effects on the individual Impacts on religion Impacts on individual belief systems or faith

EVENTS IN FOCUS

3.2 Pilgrimages as events in early modern society

Pilgrimages can be dated to the ancient Greeks and travel to the Olympic City of Olympia. Pilgrimages became widely associated with Christianity at around the fourth century, initially with trips made on a voluntary basis or as a form of penitence. Trips were initially very localized in scale; they became more long distance during the First Crusade, when pilgrimages to Jerusalem took place. The period from the eleventh to the thirteenth century saw pilgrimages encouraged in Christian countries, with trips by nuns and priests permitted by their superiors; they were popularized in Geoffrey Chaucer's *The Canterbury Tales* and often involved visits to the shrine of Thomas Beckett, who had been murdered in Canterbury Cathedral. Other notable locations in Europe, such as Santiago de Compostela in Spain, were among a number of popular destinations for Italian pilgrims (see Schnell and Pali 2013, for an analysis of religious motives associated with modern-day pilgrimages on the same route). By the fourteenth century, changing attitudes towards pilgrimages began to develop and by the fifteenth century, the spread of the Black Death and labour shortages saw a slowing down of pilgrim traffic in Europe. By the sixteenth century, pilgrimages were being challenged by thinking associated with the Protestant reformers of the Reformation – who opposed the cult of saints – driving much of the activity underground. The difficulties of early pilgrim travellers should not be underestimated; diary accounts outline the problems of travel on unmade roads, the threat to life posed by bandits, the limited availability of accommodation, disease and the time involved to make such perilous journeys – as outlined by Theilmann (1987).

These patterns and motives for undertaking pilgrimages are still very much in evidence today as the study by Raj *et al.* (2015) illustrates, since religious events do have a significant economic effect on the localities hosting them (see Schultz *et al.* 2016).

Source: Theilmann, J. (1987). Medieval pilgrims and the origins of tourism. *Journal of Popular Culture,* 20(4), 93–102.

In Japan, annual *matsuri* are held at or in conjunction with Shinto shrines, on fixed dates. They symbolize a community's well-being and are particularly related to rice harvests. *Matsuri* in modern Japan often include large-scale, public celebrations like carnival, complete with masks, parades with traditional, iconic floats, sports and (to a Western eye) outrageously dangerous behaviour such as playing with fire. Plutschow (2013) in the book *Matsuri: The Festivals of Japan* described and classified these local celebrations according to the deities being represented, and the related rituals.

3.6 RESEARCH NOTE ON RELIGION

Greenfield, G. (2010). Reveillon in Rio de Janeiro. *Event Management,* 14(4), 301–308.

'While Carnival remains the city's most popular event, *Reveillon,* the New Year's Eve celebration on Copacabana Beach in honour of the sea goddess, *Iemanjá,* has become a major tourist draw. A familiar personage in Brazilian popular culture, *Iemanjá* is a major deity in African-Brazilian religions. African and African-Brazilian beliefs, historically associated with lower-class and mixed-race people, were long scorned by Brazilian elites as the superstitious practices of ignorant people. The majority of practitioners of African-Brazilian religions in contemporary Brazil are lower class and visibly of mixed race. The *Reveillon* evokes and commodifies Brazil's preferred national image as a multicultural, multiracial democracy free of the Western stain of racism. As such, the celebration serves as a confirming ritual for Brazilians while, at the same time, packaging and presenting that image to tourists.'

Psychology

The study of the human mind, thought and behaviour constitutes psychology. There are many sub-fields and specialized applications, such as you will encounter in education and interpretation (the 'psychology of learning') and 'industrial psychology', applied to management. There are also divisions in psychology, notably 'humanistic psychology', represented by the works of Maslow, which take a phenomenological approach that is in direct opposition to the scientific or positivistic paradigm that dominates the subject area. In this section we examine two mainstream branches, 'cognitive psychology' and the psychology of personality, then we turn to two blended sub-disciplines of particular relevance to event studies: environmental psychology and social psychology. Their significance in the wider debates on the contribution of psychology to event studies is demonstrated by Benckendorff and Pearce (2012: 165), who provide the most comprehensive review of the field and address the principal question facing psychologists:

> *What kinds of people seek to involve themselves in events and what motivates them to do so? The research in psychology which can assist in answering these questions derives from a combination of applied expertise in personality assessment and the study of social motivation.*

This illustrates the principal challenge for event research – the different ways people become involved in events and how we explain their motivation for that involvement (see Table 3.7). Whilst psychology remains a key discipline in understanding these issues, other interdisciplinary developments and new research agendas, such as experiencescapes (i.e. the on-site experience of events emanating from the work of Pine and Gilmore (1999) on the experience economy (see Chapter 1) and O'Dell's (2005) work on

Table 3.7 Psychology

Psychology	Nature and meanings; the event experience	Antecedents to attending events	Planning and producing events	Outcomes and the impacted	Processes and patterns
Explaining human personality and behaviour	Personal needs, motives, preferences	Effects of age, gender, education, life-stage, income, on demand	Design for personal experiences and transformation	Impacts on personality, values, attitudes	Emergence of 'experience economics' as a major force
The study of perception, memory, feeling, knowing and thinking	Perceiving and experiencing events	Consumer behaviour	Implications for marketing and communications	Influence on future actions	
	Abnormal behaviour	Ego involvement			

experiencescapes as fluid spaces in which people consume experiences (see Chapter 6 for more detail)), have a key role in contextualizing the application of psychology to event studies. This is because:

The design of experiencescapes includes not only the setting but also the sensory, symbolic, temporal and meaningful aspects of experiences ... An understanding of event experiencescapes therefore needs to consider cognitive, conative and affective responses to the setting, theme, programming, personal interactions and provision of services and tangible goods such as food, beverages and merchandise.

(Benckendorff and Pearce 2012: 174)

Therefore, what is discussed in this chapter should not be separated from the discussion of other themes shaping event research throughout the book, particularly the discussion of event experiences in Chapter 6.

The contribution of psychology to event studies has been considerable, and some of the most significant recent studies are outlined in Events in Focus 3.3, which demonstrates the richness of the contributions and themes they typically examine (see Table 3.7). More specifically, Benckendorff and Pearce (2012) provide some key concepts related to how psychology can be applied to event participation by spectators and attendees, performers and participants, and elite participants in the pre-, on-site and post-event experience stages (see Figure 3.4). Approaches used to understand these human experiences are framed around personality, motivation, involvement, different theories associated with participation in events (e.g. role theory, identity, liminality, flow), satisfaction and self-actualization from different fields of psychology. The origin of different approaches to psychology and events and the use of such theories will be examined throughout this section.

EVENTS IN FOCUS

3.3 Recent studies on the psychology of events

The most significant synthesis of the field is in:

Benckendorff, P. and Pearce, P. (2012). The psychology of events. In S. J. Page and J. Connell (eds), *The Routledge Handbook of Events*, pp. 165–185. London: Routledge.

Other more specialized studies that focus on specific areas of the psychological analysis of events include:

	Pre-experience		On-site experience		Post-experience
Spectators and Attendees	Personality, motivation and involvement	+	Role theory, identity, liminality, experience analysis	→	Satisfaction, loyalty
Performers and Participants	Personality, motivation and involvement	+	Role theory, identity, liminality, experience analysis	→	Satisfaction, self-actualization, personal development, quality of life
Elite Participants	Personality and motivation	+	Flow, mindfulness, emotional and performative labour	→	Superior performance

Figure 3.4 Applying psychological ideas to event participation

Source: Benckendorff and Pearce (2012: 166). Reprinted from *The Routledge Handbook of Events*, S. J. Page and J. Connell, Routledge (2012).

Ballantyne, J. *et al.* (2014). Designing and managing music festival experiences to enhance attendees' psychological and social benefits. *Musicae Scientiae*, 18(1), 65–83.

Gyimóthy, S. (2009). Casual observers, connoisseurs and experimentalists: A conceptual exploration of niche festival visitors. *Scandinavian Journal of Hospitality and Tourism*, 9(2–3), 177–205.

Kendrick, V., Haslam, R. and Waterson, P. (2012). Planning crowd events to achieve high participant satisfaction. *Work: A Journal of Prevention, Assessment and Rehabilitation*, 41(1), 3223–3226.

Lee, J. and Kyle, G. (2013). Segmenting festival visitors using psychological commitment. *Journal of Travel Research*, 53(5), 656–669.

Deng, Q. and Li, M. (2014). A model of event–destination image transfer. *Journal of Travel Research*, 53(1), 69–82.

Cognitive psychology

Mainstream psychology is largely positivistic and well known for using experimental research designs (both laboratory and field based). The dominant theoretical framework is 'cognitivism'. *Cognition* involves the integration of memory, experience and judgement, derived from perception, to help us think about the world or about specific stimulants in the environment. Cognition therefore applies to how we perceive, think about and make sense of stimuli or whole events.

Perception is the process of acquiring, interpreting, selecting and organizing sensory information. How do sensory organs and the brain receive and interpret stimuli? People are not passive, they actively explore the environment and in many cases seek out specific forms of stimulation. People create 'mental models (or constructs)' to help with perception and knowledge creation. If we have no experience or 'mental map' as a frame of reference, we might not perceive a stimulus at all. Accordingly, the more experience we have with certain types of planned event experiences, the better we should become at perceiving and interpreting all their nuances.

Experience is more than perception – it requires exposure or involvement and has a transforming effect on the individual. The more we experience, presumably the better we should be at assimilating new knowledge (i.e. 'learning'). But experience can also change us holistically in terms of attitudes, values and personality, resulting in behavioural changes.

Memory entails encoding and storing, retaining and recalling information and experiences. We know that memories can be imperfectly formed, fade over time and be lost or hard to recall. So what makes for a memorable experience? And how do memories, pleasant or otherwise, shape future behaviour? We examine this further in Chapter 6 where the thoughts of Moscardo (2010) are elaborated upon.

'Thinking': the higher-order mental processes we tend to call thinking include 'reasoning' (making sense of things), 'creativity' (or imagination, innovation), 'judgement' (such as determining right from wrong, dangerous from risk-free) and 'problem-solving' (i.e. solving a puzzle, figuring out how to navigate a space). Thinking is based on how we use stored knowledge and how experience has shaped our processes and abilities. Knowledge and experience hopefully lead to 'wisdom' (being 'wise' is a relative term, or a self-perceived quality) and to greater effectiveness in whatever we choose to do.

Ego, identity, self-concept and ego involvement

Who do you think you are? Seriously, are you ordinary or special, smart or dull, an intellectual or a party-animal? And what ideally would you like to be? Something better or different than you are now, perhaps more like someone else that you admire? These are questions about your ego and alter ago.

Ego is a basic psychological concept, especially in Freudian theory, comprising that part of our personality that encompasses conscious awareness. It helps us make sense of the world, including separating reality from imagination. Our main interest is with personal identity, that is, who we think we are. As a 'loner', you might not connect with many people, but as a 'joiner' you likely belong to a number of social worlds and engage heavily in social networking. How we identify ourselves, say as a member of a particular sport or interest group, reflects our ego. We can seek and confirm identity through social arrangements and that very much includes social events.

Self-concept means the beliefs held about our self, including who we think we are in relation to how others view us and how we would like to be viewed. When we drive a certain kind of car, we want it to reflect our self-concept, or the image we have of ourselves as 'sporty'. This also applies to being a sports fan, a runner, an artist or any other form of leisure that generates an interest in planned events. Marketers know how to aim their products and services at people holding specific self-concepts, and clearly these also relate to social-world involvement. Funk (2008) employs self-concept in his approach to studying consumer behaviour for sports and events, namely as an integral part of the 'psychological continuum model' (see also Funk and James 2001, 2006). Awareness, attraction, attachment or allegiance are the progressive steps open to consumers and participants. Self-concept connects specifically to identifying with a sport, event or team.

Ego involvement is another closely related psychological construct much used in leisure research, and it is an integral part of developing theory on the 'event travel career trajectory' (see Chapter 8). Obviously one does not get highly involved with a brand, leisure pursuit (see 'serious leisure'), event, sport or social world unless it reflects our self-construct. An interesting illustration of ego enhancement was observed by Lee *et al.* (2013) in their analysis of the motivational factors affecting volunteer intentions for involvement in local events in the United States. They found that ego enhancement was one of the principal motivations, along with altruism and concern for the community in volunteering.

Personality

Psychologists speak of the 'big five' personality characteristics or factors that are believed to 'differentiate individuals in a somewhat permanent way and across most if not all situations' (Mannell and Kleiber 1997: 156). Personality as it affects leisure has been scrutinized, but little has been done to connect personality to event-related behaviour and a number of critical concepts affect event-related behaviour including:

Extroversion: This factor includes traits such as assertiveness, gregariousness and excitement seeking, leading to the label 'high-energy people'. Extroverted people often pursue sports and take risks. 'Introverts', in contrast, have a low threshold of arousal and do not need as much stimulation. They are more likely to play computer fantasy games. Studies have found that travel preferences and styles correlate with extroversion or introversion (Plog 1972; Nickerson and Ellis 1991). Extroverts are also sensation seekers who are more likely to participate in adventurous, intense activities, and want greater variety (Zuckerman 1979).

Agreeableness: Traits associated with this factor include trust, straightforwardness and altruism, and it is contrasted with hostility, indifference and self-centredness. 'Agreeable' people seek social settings, and are more likely to volunteer. Self-indulgence and escape are more associated with low levels of agreeableness.

Conscientiousness: Order, dutifulness, achievement striving, self-discipline and deliberation are associated with this characteristic of personality. Managers might want staff who are high on this factor, as it is typically manifested in reliability, responsibility and being organized. Stebbins (1992) thought that conscientiousness was associated with a strong goal orientation and 'serious leisure'. However, being high on this factor might also result in lower levels of spontaneity and higher compulsiveness. If one is low on this factor, impulsiveness and seeking immediate gratification are likely to result.

Neuroticism: A general tendency to experience distress is associated with neuroticism. Anxiety, hostility, depression and self-consciousness are likely to accompany this factor. Dislike of playful leisure experiences might result from being neurotic. People with this trait might get less pleasure and enjoyment from both individual and social experiences by reason of discounting the positive aspects of their own lives.

Openness to experience: This is associated with aesthetic sensitivity, the need for variety, unconventional values, flexibility of thought, cultural interest and educational aptitude. Such people are likely to seek out sensory stimulation.

Personality traits have been studied in leisure, although some researchers have concluded that personality has more of an influence on the extent of participation than on the choice of sport or activity (Mannell and Kleiber 1997: 163). There is yet no research evidence to show the connection to planned events, but readers will see the possibilities for examining event-related behaviour and experiences in the context of the following personality dimensions:

- *Locus of control*: How important is it to perceive that you are in control or have freedom to choose? Does this define your perception of what is leisure or enjoyable work?
- *Attentional style*: How do you typically process or deal with environmental and social stimuli? Can you easily get into the 'flow' of deep involvement in an activity or mental process?
- *Type A behaviour*: Some people are driven to compete and succeed, are always worried about getting things done; they feel they are running out of time and so they get impatient with others. How can they relax? How do you get them to pay attention?
- *Playfulness*: Are you a playful person, also curious, creative and joyful? Can males and females be playful together, or are there social constraints?
- *The Autotelic personality*: These people 'are able to find intrinsic interest and enjoyment in almost everything he or she does' (Mannell and Kleiber 1997: 174).
- *Shyness*: Shy people may feel the lack of control over their lives and have low social competence, therefore have a more difficult time finding satisfying experiences.

Leung and Law (2010) reviewed the literature on how personality theory has been applied to tourism and hospitality, and much of this relates to event studies. They concluded that four main areas of application were related to consumer behaviour, human resource management, leisure and education. Most researchers had examined one or more of seven dimensions of personality, grouped as follows:

- *personality traits*, most commonly the big five;
- *biological factors* that influence or are influenced by personality (extroverts and introverts, with extroverts being sensation seekers; can include compulsions or impulsive behaviour);
- *factors within the mind that influence behaviour*; includes needs and motivation;
- *the cognitive domain*: understanding of perceptions, thoughts, feelings, desires (underlying stable motives and other conscious experiences from an individual's point of view; includes locus of control and self-image);
- *the social and cultural domain*: the public aspects of personality and relationships (social psychology);
- *the adjustment domain*: related to mental health and how people cope; self-efficacy and pathological behaviour are included;
- *brand personality* (how brand values connect to self-constructs; involvement).

Applications of personality theory to planned events are less common. Certainly it is relevant to volunteer and employee selection and behaviour (stress, motives, relationships, conscientiousness). Event marketers will want to understand personality as it relates to information searching and buying behaviour, event and destination choice, and this encompasses psychographic segmentation such as that employed in ego-involvement scales. Other useful applications relate to perceptions of event quality, learning preferences at conferences or taking risks (as in many sports). Spirituality is increasingly considered as a motivator for travel and event participation, as is creativity. Personalities of leadership have been studied, but not for events. The personality of event brands related to consumer self-concept has not been examined.

Aggression and anti-social behaviour at events

All too often celebrations and sport competitions get out of control, resulting in fighting, riots or crime. Some protests are organized to achieve these results. Can events be designed and managed to prevent bad behaviour? Moyer (1968) identified seven forms of aggression, with the following pertaining to social behaviour:

1 *Inter-male aggression*: competition between males of the same species over access to females, dominance, status, etc. (watch particularly for males who get drunk at parties and carnivals).

2 *Fear-induced aggression*: aggression associated with attempts to flee from a threat (e.g. crowd reaction to a gunshot, fight or fire at an event).

3 *Irritable aggression*: aggression directed towards an available target induced by some sort of frustration (e.g. impatience and stress caused by waiting or discomfort, resulting in overt hostility towards event organizers).

4 *Territorial aggression*: defence of a fixed space against intruders (as when gangs interact, or incompatible market segments are forced to mix).

5 *Instrumental aggression*: aggression directed towards obtaining some goal, maybe a learned response to a situation (the example of institutionalized rioting at some events).

'Ritualized aggression' helps explain our fascination with competitive team sports, especially when cities and countries are playing against each other. This can be useful in reducing tensions, but it periodically gets out of control and results in fighting and rioting in the audience. A great deal of attention has been given to combating 'hooliganism' in soccer (see Stott *et al.* 2001). In fact Deery and Jago (2010) found that anti-social behaviour has the power to undermine the positive effects of events. This is because the media often focus on drunken, rowdy behaviour and vandalism, and the community might become opposed to events that tolerate or engender these negative social impacts. Community pride can easily be damaged in this way. For this reason, Events in Focus 3.4 focuses on a neglected area of research around the perception of crime and events.

EVENTS IN FOCUS START

3.4 Crime and events: a neglected relationship?

Whilst anti-social behaviour may be a problem associated with events and, in some instances, may lead to crime, this raises important issues on wider debates about the perception of both residents and event participants related to the impact of events on community and visitor safety. As Barker *et al.* (2003) found, there are a few studies that have examined the perceived impact of crime on the community (e.g. Lankford 1996; Pizam 1978; Rothman 1978; Snaith and Haley 1999). One consequence is that the influx of visitors associated with an event can lead to residents perceiving a decline in the level of safety. As Barker *et al.* (2002) indicated, concern for such impacts has generated a range of studies that examine residents' perceptions of special events in the host community, including the impact of crime (e.g. America's Cup Office 1987; Ritchie and Lyons 1990; Soutar and McLeod 1993), whilst visitor perceptions may also impact upon event attendance.

As Barker *et al.* (2003) suggest, there is limited literature on the impact of crime on events, but the findings of such studies confirm that where events attract large numbers of people and generate hedonistic activities such as alcohol and drug consumption, this may lead to conditions which can exacerbate crime. An increase in criminal activity arising with tourism has been noted during the seasonal phenomenon of special events (Burns and Mules 1989; Hall *et al.* 1995) and holiday periods (Barker 2000; Rothman *et al.* 1979; Walmsley *et al.* 1983). Studies of the America's Cup hosted in 1999–2000 by Barker *et al.* (2001, 2002) highlighted the impact of improved visitor safety at events through environmental design as well as a displacement of crime due to an increased police presence during the duration of the America's Cup, which was intended to saturate the area and avoid crime hotspots developing. This illustrates what Barker *et al.* (2002) observed in relation to hotspot theory, which suggests that predatory crime is associated with certain types of geographical areas such that a relatively few locations, or 'hotspots', are associated with a high percentage of crimes. This means that during events, crimes will be directed to the areas where people attending are likely to congregate as participants and as an audience, potentially increasing an individual's risk of victimization from crime. For example, Hall and Selwood (1989) found an explicit relationship between the hosting of the 1987 America's Cup in Fremantle, Australia and an increase in petty crime. Personal crimes of sexual and common assault and robbery increased, combined with significant increases in minor offences (e.g. traffic infringements, drunkenness and disorderly behaviour) (Hall *et al.* 1995). Similarly, results were found by Barker *et al.* (2002, 2003) in their comparative study of the America's Cup in Auckland, and Getz (1997) also observed that social problems such as crime, anti-social behaviour or rioting can become institutionalized at events. Interestingly, a study by Baumann *et al.* (2012) examined the impact of sporting events and franchises on local crime rates in the USA, but found no evidence that these led to any major change in crime rates. However, they did observe that around a 10 per cent increase in property crimes occurred with hosting the Olympic Games, while hosting the Super Bowl actually saw a 2.5 per cent decrease in violent crime.

Therefore, in order to understand the wider experience of events, it is important to recognize that external factors such as perception of and victimization through crime and anti-social behaviour can have a bearing when seeking to understand different dimensions of how people perceive their safety – which leads us to consider the contribution of environmental psychology.

Psychological research paradigms

Within the field of leisure and tourism, most psychological research is positivistic and deductive, and a great deal of it employs research methods that study small experimental groups, often students, and uses self-completion questionnaires (Veal 2006: 30). Consumer behaviour in general, and with regard to tourism in particular, is heavily dependent on theories from cognitive psychology within the wider field of environmental psychology.

Environmental psychology

Environmental psychology has considerable potential for enhancing event studies as it has tourism research (Fridgen 1984). It is an interdisciplinary field focusing on the perception and cognition of natural and built environments (see Moser and Uzzell 2003 for an explanation of its scope and application to leisure). Bell *et al.* (2001: 6) defined it as 'the study of molar relationships between behaviour and experience and the built and natural environments'. 'Molar' means the whole is greater than the parts, or a *gestalt* approach. 'Units' of environment and behaviour are studied, such as the festival place, sport arena, banquet hall or conference centre. Specific topics include arousal, stimulation, stress, adaptation, approach-avoidance behaviour, environmental design, wayfaring, work and leisure environments.

The environment is viewed as both the context for behaviour and a determinant of behaviour. Environmental psychologists also examine the consequences of human behaviour on the environment. Taking a festival place as an example, environmental psychologists would look at how people interact with the setting, how it can be designed or modified to reflect its purpose. Specific considerations would include capacity and crowding, personal space, noise and light, temperature and air flows. For example, Christou *et al.* (2018) examined the importance of emotional dynamics among event attendees and its impact upon satisfaction. Koenigstorfer and Ulrich (2009) examined the effect of atmosphere on emotions at major sporting events, based on approaches from environmental psychology. Would changing the lighting, for example, result in a more subdued audience? Would music enliven the place? Of course, event designers often know the answers from experience, but environmental psychology uses experimental and other research methods to develop both practical solutions and general theories. Although laboratory experiments are sometimes used, more popular methods are field experiments, descriptive and co-relational studies, and simulations (see Table 3.8).

De Young (1999) noted these important environmental psychology research themes:

- *Attention*: how people notice the environment; response to environmental stimuli;
- *Perception* and *cognitive maps*: how people imagine the natural and built environment; formation of mental maps;

Table 3.8 Environmental psychology

Environmental psychology	Nature and meanings; the event experience	Antecedents to attending events	Planning and producing events	Outcomes and the impacted	Processes and patterns
Perception and cognition of natural and built environments Environmental design Wayfaring Behavioural settings and environmental stressors Personal space Crowding	How people perceive, make sense of, and value the event setting Environmental cues as to appropriate behaviour Feeling crowded or comfortable	Preferences for certain environments Fear of crowding and environmental risks	Implications for event setting design and management (e.g. legibility; facilitating interaction, setting the mood, flow)	Environmental factors directly impact on personal health, safety and satisfaction	Environmental preferences and fears are culturally shaped and evolve Event venue development, and use of places for events, constantly presents new opportunities and ideas about the environment

- *Preferred environments*: people tend to seek out places where they feel competent and confident, places where they can make sense of the environment, while also being engaged with it;
- *Environmental stress and coping*: common environmental stressors include noise and climatic extremes; coping with stress can involve a change in physical or social settings, or seeking to interpret or make sense of a situation.

The 'Integrative Model of Environmental Psychology' from Bell *et al.* (2001: 21) can be adapted to event studies (see Figure 3.5). This model provides an overview of environmental psychology topics and their interrelationships. We start with environmental conditions, which for events means purpose-built venues or sometimes natural settings. Human–environment interactions are influenced by both biological (e.g. our need for occasional solitude, or the fear of heights) and learned factors (e.g. we are taught to respect nature or to show respect for others' property). Then we have to consider perceptions of the environment, or how we employ our senses to detect and give meaning to conditions in the setting (this is cognition). 'General effects of the environment' on behaviour include the study of sensory stimulation through noise, light, smell and colour, the effects of general environmental conditions (weather, pollution) and impacts of social interaction (personal space and crowding).

Closely linked to the general factors are the 'behavioural and experiential influences' of specific event settings. Their design, programming and management are explicitly intended to create, suggest or facilitate desired moods, behaviours and experiences. We need to examine all the common and unusual event settings, from sport arenas to parks, from convention centres to city squares. How does each factor alone and in combination with others affect, for example, the behaviour and mood of an audience at a concert? We need to be aware that event settings are often purpose-built, with their intended uses and appropriate behaviours known by convention, while some are unusual and have to be valorized for temporary event purposes. 'Setting affordances' and 'constraints' are those characteristics of the venue or place that suggest and/or allow for various activities and experiences, or which constrain them.

'Changing environmental cognitions' refers to learning from experience and the resultant changes in perceptions and motives. In terms of events this can encompass how people perceive and attach meaning to event settings and design elements. With education, event experiences can also lead to positive shifts in

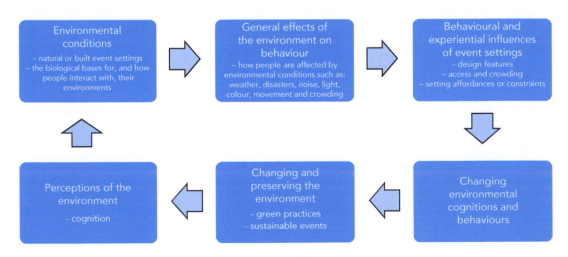

Figure 3.5 Environmental psychology and planned events

Note: Adapted from Bell *et al.* (2001).

attitudes towards the environment, such as support for green operations and sustainable development. Finally, the interactions in this model include changes to cognition in general, or how we perceive our environment.

Environmental preferences

According to Kaplan (1987), humans examine the contents and the spatial configuration of scenes. We have to process a lot of information gained by our senses, in a hurry. Kaplan showed that people prefer scenes or settings that are 'coherent', 'legible', 'complex' and contain some degree of 'mystery'. Legibility and mystery require more cognitive processing. Complexity and mystery together appear to stimulate involvement, or the desire to explore and comprehend the scene. Our responses to event settings and their design reflect certain predispositions, some of which are culturally influenced and some that are highly individual.

In Research Note 3.7 from Pettersson and Getz (2009) another kind of hotspot is featured, in contrast to cold spots at events, and these are related to experiences other than crime.

3.7 RESEARCH NOTE ON EVENT SETTINGS: HOT AND COLD SPOTS

Pettersson, R. and Getz, D. (2009). Event experiences in time and space: A study of visitors to the 2007 World Alpine Ski Championships in Åre, Sweden. *Scandinavian Journal of Hospitality and Tourism*, 9(2–3), 308–326.

'The spatial and temporal nature of event experiences was studied through interviews, participant observation and photography at a major sporting event. Results contribute to a better understanding of how visitors interact with the event setting and with each other, and help build theory on experiences, their design and management. Event tourists were observed spatially and temporally while enjoying various elements of the host village and four event arenas, while photographs and notes made by participant observers enabled a more focused evaluation of positive and negative experiences. Results identified the importance of social factors, as visitors wanted to be where the others were, revealed that surprise created positive experiences, and identified the existence of experiential "hotspots" defined in both time and space. It is concluded that positive experiences are more important than negative ones in terms of overall satisfaction. Implications are drawn regarding the nature of event experiences, their design and management, and on related methodological development.'

Hotspots and cold spots reflect event-goers' perceptions of the event or community environment related to both their expectation (e.g. the place should be exciting, animated, interesting) and the nature of the event (where will the entertainment be located, the races, the food?). These can be shaped by design, and can be changed as the event proceeds (if it is long enough). There is also the possibility that cold spots might be created or tolerated as a crowd management device – to keep people moving, or change their patterns, in order to avoid congestion and negative social or environmental impacts.

The behaviour setting

According to Barker (1968), places have culturally defined purposes and behavioural expectations. The setting and appropriate behaviour are perceived to be an integrated unit, or 'behavioural setting'. Outdoor settings are sometimes more ambiguous than indoor facilities, although this depends on many design and management factors. Certainly people attending a fair in an open area receive different 'cues' and exhibit different behaviour when compared with those attending an art exhibit indoors. Do guests intuitively understand the norms and limits? To be effective, we rely on conventions, or 'standing patterns of behaviour' in Barker's words, which in themselves are culturally determined. A study by Wickham and Kerstetter (2000: 167) argued that 'as individuals' attachment to their community increases so too do their positive feelings about crowds. These results challenge traditional notions about crowding and provide insight to festival managers interested in enhancing their relationship with the host community', since crowds have been associated with negative connotations of event experiences. This raises important issues about the behaviour and experience of individuals, which leads us to the area of social psychology.

Social psychology

Mannell and Kleiber (1997: 25) wrote that 'Social psychology is the scientific study of the behaviour and experience of individuals in social situations.' Its historical evolution is outlined by Allport (1937). Baron and Byrne (2000) defined social psychology as 'the field that seeks to understand the nature and causes of individual behaviour and thought in social settings'. For the purposes of event studies, social psychology helps us understand the nature and causes of behaviour at events, based on studying the relationship between the mind, groups and behaviours. Social psychology has a range of theories and concepts it uses to study these themes (see Table 3.9).

Self-determination theory

Self-determination theory (see Deci and Ryan 1985, 2000) is concerned with human motivation, specifically the development and functioning of personality within social situations. Within leisure, this approach asks if people really engage in actions with a full sense of choice. The social environment can either assist or hinder a person's striving for growth, development and a coherent sense of self through the satisfaction of basic human needs. When needs are unmet, or thwarted, people can suffer in terms of general well-being and psychological health.

Table 3.9 Social psychology

Social psychology	Nature and meanings; the event experience	Antecedents to attending events	Planning and producing events	Outcomes and the impacted	Processes and patterns
Studies the behaviour and experience of individuals in social situations	Events as social experiences Social role schemas Subjective meanings attached to events through social interaction (i.e. events as social constructs)	The influence of social reference groups Social needs (seeking and escaping)	Design for environment–group interactions and dynamics Creating a social atmosphere; belonging and sharing	Satisfaction of social group needs	Changes in family, social groups and social norms affect events

Social cognition and social cognitive theory

Bandura (1977, 1986) provided a framework for understanding, predicting and even seeking to change human behaviour – individually and collectively. The theory states that behaviour is a result of the interaction of personal factors, behaviour and the environment. Social factors influence our beliefs and cognitive competencies. The environment modifies human behaviour, and in turn people seek to change it. The same set of stimuli might result in different behaviour because people construe the situation differently.

'Self-efficacy' is one of the key personal factors involved in Bandura's theory. It refers to a person's belief in their ability to perform a given behaviour successfully, which is different from a person's actual competency. Self-efficacy influences motivation and leisure behaviour. We are more likely to engage in activities that we think will produce desired outcomes, and this depends in part on our assessment of how well we can do the activity. Self-efficacy also affects how people respond to failure. In contrast, a person with high efficacy will attribute failure to external factors, where a person with low self-efficacy will attribute failure to low ability. People with high self-efficacy are generally of the opinion that they are in control of their own lives, while those with low self-efficacy see their lives as being shaped by others, or by destiny.

There are implications for education and training. Self-efficacy, or belief in one's own abilities, increases through mastery or success, and diminishes with failure. It can also be increased through example, by learning from others (especially peers and respected persons) how to accomplish a task. Positive encouragement is also important.

'Social cognition' is how we interpret, analyse, remember and use information about the social world. Baron and Byrne (2000: 80) said that we employ schema which are 'mental frameworks centring around a specific theme that help us to organize social information'. 'Social role schemas' apply to our expectations for the behaviour of ourselves or others in social situations, such as how lecturers act at a conference, how the master of ceremonies behaves at a gala dinner, or what a group of performers does at a concert. Schemas affect three basic processes of social cognition, as shown in Figure 3.6.

Schemas act as filters, saving us time and energy when we size up a social situation, and they are obviously based in part on experience and on cultural conventions. They have perseverance, generally lasting a long time. But they can also result in misconceptions and inappropriate behaviour if the cues we expect are not present or are misleading. They can have the effect of 'self-fulfilling prophecy' in that they can cause us to behave in ways that confirm them. We tend to notice only the cues consistent with our mental schemas, causing us to act in ways that confirm their validity.

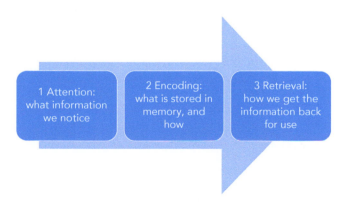

Figure 3.6 The process of social cognition

Theory of planned behaviour

Originating with the work of Ajzen (1985, 1991), this very influential theory posits that behaviour is driven by 'behavioural intentions' (for example, 'I fully intend to go to that concert'). Intentions are a function of the person's (a) attitudes towards the behaviour, (b) subjective norms and (c) perceived behavioural control. The theory states that a person's intention to do something is the most immediate determinant of behaviour.

'Attitude' towards the behaviour is defined as the person's feelings about the behaviour (positive or negative), and this stems from beliefs concerning the possible consequences of the behaviour and the desirability of those impacts (e.g. 'I think rock concerts are cool places to meet and be with friends, and that is top priority for me'). 'Subjective norms' are the individual's perception of what others will think, such as if one's peers will approve of the behaviour (e.g. 'all my friends think the X concert is going to be the best, and I want to be accepted by them').

'Perceived behavioural control' refers to feelings of choice (including having skills, resources and the opportunity to do something). As in leisure constraint theory, people who perceive they do not have the skills, resources or opportunities are unlikely to form strong intentions to go to events.

'Theory of planned behaviour' applies only to uncoerced, rational behaviour, but not all event attendance or participation will meet those criteria. As we know, extrinsic motives also apply to many events, such as work and social obligations. Irrationality might enter into the decision to attend events when, for example, people are in very strange circumstances (such as foreign cultures) or suffering from altered mental states due to such factors as alcohol, drugs, stress or illness. Research note 3.8, by Lee *et al.* (2014), examines the intention–behaviour gap associated with a mega event.

3.8 RESEARCH NOTE ON MEGA EVENTS

Lee, C. K., Mjelde, J. W., Kim, T. K. and Lee, H. M. (2014). Estimating the intention–behaviour gap associated with a mega event: The case of the Expo 2012 Yeosu Korea. *Tourism Management*, 41, 168–177.

Demand (attendance) forecasts are often based on respondents' intentions to attend an event or purchase a product. People, however, do not always act on their intentions; an intention–behaviour gap exists. This study investigates the intention–behaviour gap based on a national survey using a quota sampling method (*N* = 2015) in the realm of visiting the 2012 Yeosu Expo. Results reveal that approximately 50 per cent of the respondents who had intentions to visit the Expo actually visited the Expo. The stronger the intentions are to visit the Expo, the larger the percentage of respondents who acted on their intentions. The researchers found that time and travel distance had a significant bearing on attendance, and that older, more educated respondents were more likely to follow through on intentions to visit.

Expectation-confirmation theory

Oliver (1977, 1980) reasoned that consumer satisfaction is determined by the interactions of expectations and perceived performance, mediated through positive or negative disconfirmation between expectations and perceived performance. In other words, if the guest expects a high level of service, but perceives it to be poor, it will lead to dissatisfaction. A dissatisfied customer is unlikely to be loyal or to say good things about the service providers.

This theory lies at the heart of SERVQUAL and other approaches to defining and measuring satisfaction, which have their origins in consumer behaviour research within marketing (Baron *et al.* 2014). Many researchers, however, believe that it is more practical and just as valid to measure 'post-hoc satisfaction', without a pre-measurement of expectations. Getz *et al.* (2001) used the 'post-hoc satisfaction approach' in evaluating a surfing event. One convincing argument is that many people show up at events without clear expectations of service or product quality, but they can always determine afterwards if they were satisfied or not. On the other hand, the more experienced the consumer, the more likely they are to hold firm expectations. We return to the quality issue in Chapter 7 when examining event design.

3.9 RESEARCH NOTE ON EVENT QUALITY

Tkaczynski, A. and Stokes, R. (2010). FESTPERF: A service quality measurement scale for festivals. *Event Management*, 14(1), 69–82.

The study addresses the question of what elements of performance-based research apply to event service quality. 'Results of this study at an Australian Jazz and Blues Festival led to the creation of FESTPERF, a three-factor solution that differed from the generic SERVPERF instrument and did not replicate the SERVQUAL factors. Two of these factors, Professionalism and Environment, predicted visitor satisfaction that may, in turn, lead to repurchase. The third factor, Core Service, did not predict intent by festival goers to revisit. A practical implication of this research is the availability of an event-specific model of service quality for further testing at other types of music festivals (e.g. rock, gospel, or pop, or at other special events).'

Audience and fan studies

One of the unifying topics in event studies, involving various theoretical perspectives covered in this and subsequent chapters, is that of the audience. Mackellar (2013a) presents a spectrum of audience types that clearly connect to identity, involvement, serious leisure, subculture, communitas and values. She describes 'socializers', 'dabblers', 'enthusiasts' and 'fanatics' in terms of what benefits they seek in attending events or participating in other ways. Jones (2015) expands upon this, tracing the evolution of the Big Day Out in Australia and its transformation from an independent to a multiscene festival and the loss of its festival identity. Within the sport-related literature the fan is a topic of great interest, particularly in terms of determining motivations and styles of sport-event travel and behaviour. When the audience is a focus of research, many different perspectives can be taken to increase understanding and lead to improved design and management. These themes will be evident in the remainder of this book.

STUDY GUIDE

As a field of study, event studies must use and adapt theories, methodologies and research methods from many foundation disciplines, especially those in the social sciences. The potential for drawing on them to expand our knowledge base in event studies is almost unlimited, and it should result in interdisciplinary theory of and for planned events.

For each of the foundation disciplines in this and the next chapter, students should be able to summarize the main topics they cover, their core theories and methodologies, and types of research methods used. These can be illustrated by the research notes throughout this book. They also have direct bearing on the later discussions of experiences, outcomes and policy. Use the figures provided for each discipline as starting points for tracing various themes that run through the book. In particular, link the classical anthropology and sociology theories to the model of planned event experiences in Chapter 6.

STUDY QUESTIONS

- Are all planned events cultural phenomena? Are they all authentic?
- Explain ethnography and phenomenology in the context of research for events.
- What are social and cultural capital and how are these concepts useful in event studies?
- In what ways can we use social exchange theory in event studies?
- Connect social worlds and social network theory to the need for events.
- Where do ethics come from? (Link religion, philosophy and professionalism.)
- Are all pilgrimages religious in nature?
- Tie expectation–confirmation theory to event quality.
- Show how cognitive psychology supports our understanding of the planned event experience and why people attend events (be sure to include personal constructs).
- Describe the big five personality traits and explain why theory about personality is important for event marketing.
- Explain the Integrative Model of Environmental Psychology as adapted to event studies.
- Link the concept of behaviour settings to event design.
- Why are identity, self-cognition and self-efficacy theories important to understanding audiences and the planned event experience?

FURTHER READING

Ehrenreich, B. (2006). *Dancing in the Streets: A History of Collective Joy*. New York: Metropolitan Books.

Henderson, E. and McIlwraith, M. (2013). *Ethics and Corporate Social Responsibility in the Meetings and Events Industry*. Chichester: Wiley.

Mackellar, J. (2013). *Event Audiences and Expectations*. London: Routledge.

Picard, D. and Robinson. M. (eds) (2006). *Festivals, Tourism and Social Change: Remaking Worlds*. Clevedon: Channel View.

Quinn, B. (2013). *Key Concepts in Event Management*. London: Sage.

Turner, V. (ed.) (1982). *Celebration: Studies in Festivity and Ritual*. Washington, DC: Smithsonian Institution Press.

Chapter **4**

The contribution of economics, management, political science, law, history, human geography and future studies to event studies

LEARNING OBJECTIVES

Upon completion of this chapter, students should know the following:

- contributions of these seven foundation disciplines to understanding the roles, meanings, importance and impacts of events in society and culture;
- key theories and methodologies from economics, management, political science, law, history, human geography and future studies;
- for each discipline, specific contributions to understanding the nature and meanings of events, anteced-ents, experiences, outcomes, patterns, processes and policy.

Economics

According to the *Encyclopaedia Britannica*, economics is a 'social science that seeks to analyse and describe the production, distribution, and consumption of wealth'. This is expanded by Craven (1990: 3), who argued that within economics the principal challenge is how we allocate resources given that many resources are scarce; therefore economists look at how these resources need to be allocated and the ways in which they are distributed. A key term in this debate is 'scarcity', meaning that most resources in society are finite and decisions have to be made on the best way to use and sustain them. Economists define resources in terms of:

- natural resources (e.g. the land);
- labour (e.g. human resources and entrepreneurship);
- capital (e.g. synthetic aids to assist in producing goods).

Collectively these resources constitute the factors of production that are used to produce commodities. These commodities can be divided into:

- goods (e.g. tangible products such as an aircraft);
- services (e.g. intangible items such as an event experience).

The total output of all commodities in a country over a period of time, normally a year, is known as the national product. As the production of goods and services can only satisfy a small fraction of consumers' needs and choices in society, we have to allocate resources to determine which goods and services to produce. The way in which goods and services are divided amongst people has been examined by economists in terms of the distribution of income and the degree of equality and efficiency in their distribution.

Macro- and microeconomics

Many of these issues are dealt with under the heading of 'microeconomics', which focuses on the firm, the consumer, production and selling, the demand for goods and the supply of goods. In contrast, macroeconomics examines:

> the entire economy and interactions within it, including the population, income, total unemployment, the average rate of price increases (the inflation rate), the extent of companies' capacities to produce goods and the total amount of money in use in the country.
>
> (Craven 1990: 5)

Meaning that a key focus within macroeconomics is how the national economy operates, employment and unemployment, inflation, national production and consumption, and the money supply in a country.

Macroeconomics has considerable importance for event studies, being concerned with the entire economic system (the study of which is sometimes referred to as 'political economy'). Governments and international agreements set the parameters within which economies operate, including the establishment of trading blocs (e.g. the European Union). Whilst most modern economies are more or less in the free-market mode, meaning that 'laws' of the marketplace are allowed to prevail, specific trading blocs do provide more favourable market conditions for members of that grouping; those outside blocs sometimes have to pay tariffs if they wish to trade with bloc members. Many governments intervene in the marketplace to some extent in order to achieve social, cultural and environmental goals. Investment in event tourism and grants for the arts represent two important policy interventions of concern in this book, and they have dominated much of the research literature (e.g. see Foley *et al.* 2012; Hall 2014).

One area of economics, 'welfare economics' (which is a branch of macroeconomics), has specific concerns with the evaluation of public policy in relation to its impact on the well-being of the population or specific groups within society. This concern in human geography also created an interest in welfare geography, focused on who gets what, where and why. D. M. Smith (1977) has examined the concept of social well-being and welfare geography, arguing that concepts of territorial justice obscure the social and economic processes, whereby distributional justice by social groups is neglected and access to public goods is constrained. This is why most countries, for example, impose higher income taxes on the wealthy, and tax corporations, in effect enabling the transfer of wealth from the rich to the poor to address these social inequalities. How that government revenue from taxes is spent is a matter for party politics and public debate. 'Welfarist' political parties want government funds to be spent in ways that benefit the poor and disadvantaged, resulting in a high degree of government involvement in the economy. Conservative parties prefer to spend less, as their ideology suggests we should use resources to enable individuals rather than governments to make most economic choices. Accordingly, a welfarist government might justify direct production and subsidization of cultural festivals as a contributor to public good, while a conservative government might be more inclined to reduce income taxes in order to give consumers more choices (in other words, a 'supply-side' approach). Page and Connell (2010) review these policy choices in the context of the UK in relation to leisure and cultural policy, observing that in parallel with many other states, major shifts in policy occurred: the emphasis has shifted from state subsidy to a greater role for the private sector, with a corresponding growth in private-sector, profit-led events operated on a commercial basis.

These changes reflect the difficult decisions that governments have had to make in welfare economics. Is it possible to justify a policy that benefits some at the expense of others? Many people do support redistribution measures such as sliding tax scales, and modern governments like to take regular polls of voters to determine the popularity of various options, or to assess attitudes towards existing programmes. The difficulty is that, if a redistribution measure actually hurts some people to benefit others, is that justifiable? Of course these serious policy questions are not generally decided with planned events in mind (see Palma *et al.* 2013 and their discussion of cultural economics and events), but do get raised when public expenditures and subsidies for events are at issue, with events being the outcome of the policy decisions taken. Therefore, as Table 4.1 demonstrates, economics and the politics of how resources are allocated have a clear bearing on the event domain.

Below these macroeconomic issues, microeconomics affect individuals and their consumer behaviour, as well as specific business decisions and how supply and demand finds equilibrium in specific markets. In classical economics, 'laws of supply and demand' govern these processes. Important microeconomic questions regarding planned events are:

- What determines the price of an event and of the resources used to produce it?
- How are event buyers and sellers brought together in a functioning market? (This is crucial in the context of bidding on events: see Getz (2004) for an assessment of the marketplace and how it works both in theory, and in practice, for tourism agencies that bid on events.)

Table 4.1 Economics

Economics	Nature and meanings; the event experience	Antecedents to attending events	Planning and producing events	Outcomes and the impacted	Processes and patterns
Macroeconomics (or 'political economy'): the functioning of whole economic systems Microeconomics: the economics of consumers, and of doing business (by firms or other organizations)	The experience and meanings of consumption Perceived value for money, as it shapes the event experience	Economic incentives and barriers to consumption or participation Supply factors (e.g. cost of travel; alternatives)	The event's business model and economic feasibility Forecasting demand Economic development policy as it affects the event sector	Measuring economic impacts and externalities Costs and benefits evaluated (including their distribution)	Economic trends and forces (competition; globalization)

- How is the economic or financial feasibility of a proposed event assessed?
- What are the differences between types of event organizations in terms of how they operate (i.e. governmental, non-profit and for-profit)?

Economic exchanges: rational choice theory

This theory underpins microeconomics and consumer behaviour. People are assumed to act rationally and make rational choices when it comes to obtaining the benefits they want; they are acting as if they consciously and intelligently balance costs against benefits, even though we know that is often not true. If indeed people (and firms) are always able to maximize personal or corporate advantage – in every transaction – then the economic system is presumed to work most efficiently. Unfortunately, 'rational behaviour' in this context might include unethical or illegal behaviour, and so the system cannot be allowed to function without regulation. There are some obvious exceptions or complications that need to be discussed.

Theory of choice

Firms desiring to make a profit have difficult choices to make; they face a number of constraints regarding their necessary inputs (supplies, labour, rents paid). One combination of inputs will minimize costs, but will it permit the production of an attractive event? If profit is not the goal, a different set of inputs can be justified and in fact if a loss can be incurred (because of subsidies or debt forgiveness), the producers can afford to be rather careless in their use of resources. Little research has been done on how event producers make such choices, but some research employing stakeholder theory has addressed the issue of relative power between event organizers and their suppliers, and how this impacts on non-profit festival viability (see Andersson and Getz 2007).

Theory of allocation

When a business or institution has multiple goals for events, there has to be some kind of prioritization – it is generally not possible to commit resources to fulfil all goals equally. The necessary allocation of resources to meet each goal can be measured, then linked to its priority or 'weighting', and from that analysis an optimal strategy can be determined which will provide the company or agency with the best 'return' on its investment. In this context a key question becomes: how does one determine the relative value of committing resources to events versus other programmes, or one type of event compared with another?

Opportunity costs

Opportunity costs are also a key economic concept. Whatever resources a company or government devotes to events, they could be spent elsewhere. Are events worth the investment in terms of culture, health or tourism? This becomes a serious policy matter, because other opportunities always exist for meeting business and societal goals. So-called 'merit' goods and services are deemed by governments to require subsidies or direct government provision because of their importance and the inability or unwillingness of the private sector to fill the need. Thus, some governments justify the provision of festivals and sport events, or other forms of entertainment, for the 'public good'. Preuss (2009) found that economic analyses of mega sport events usually focus on the positive effects and legacies, while ignoring opportunity costs and the efficiency of using scarce resources. Preuss uses the measure 'efficiency' (i.e. the ratio: output/ input) of alternative investments, making it clear 'that the decision to stage a mega sport event cannot be taken in isolation and that there are many factors that need to be considered'. The argument put forward is based on a stakeholder's perspective and a spatial differentiation of interest groups.

Demand for goods and services

Demand, in economics, is a function of the relationship between price and the quantity 'demanded' for a good or service in specific circumstances. For each price, the demand relationship tells the quantity the buyers want to buy at that corresponding price. Consumers derive 'utility' (such as survival, pleasure, happiness, satisfaction) from spending their limited disposable incomes. Consumers always have choices, especially when it comes to entertainment and travel, and various economic methods of analysis exist in consumer behaviour to model these choices (e.g. see Louviere and Hensher 1983 and the use of multi-attribute choice behaviour modelling to identify how consumers make choices). A 'consumer surplus' can be created when the utility derived from an event exceeds the cost to an individual, or when a free or subsidized event is produced for an appreciative public (e.g. my expectations were exceeded; I would have gladly paid more for that experience; they should have charged an admission fee, it was so wonderful!).

The more one values an event the more one is willing to pay for it, up to a point. So demand rests on certain assumptions about consumer utility, choices and preferences embodied in economic methods of analysis such as willingness to pay (see Burgan and Mules 2001). The principle of 'diminishing marginal utility' says that consumers will eventually get less and less satisfaction from going to events, or any specific type of event, and therefore the benefits derived will at some level of consumption cease to justify the effort or cost required. In terms of supply and demand, there are two related 'elasticity' functions to consider.

Income elasticity: As incomes rise, there is more for consumers to spend on goods and services, therefore overall demand for leisure, travel and events is directly linked to disposable incomes. But will events be 'preferred goods' that people want to spend more on? We know that as countries develop a middle class with rising incomes, more and more is spent on leisure and travel (in effect, there is high 'latent demand' for these goods).

Price elasticity: As price rises, overall demand should fall, so that when an event charges more, it can generally expect to attract fewer paying customers – or to attract different types of customer. Some events might be considered to be 'luxury goods' that attract customers who care little about rising prices, or are even attracted by the exclusivity that higher prices imply. In a free marketplace, supply and demand should eventually reach 'equilibrium', where no more events are produced than can be justified by what consumers are willing to spend. This does not happen, however, for reasons discussed below. In fact, the events sector is so oriented to government subsidies and non-profit values that it is difficult to apply any economic laws, except for the purpose of making comparisons to other sectors or revealing the extent of market distortions.

Economic demand for events

The normal assumptions made by economists regarding demand for goods and services often do not apply in the events sector. Consumers have multiple event choices, some of which are free or subsidized. All events that attract people for personal reasons (i.e. intrinsic motives) are in themselves substitutable with other forms of entertainment or activities. We should expect price elasticity, for example, to apply mostly to events that must be held (a wedding? an association meeting?) and for which supply alternatives abound. In a competitive environment, suppliers must always be wary of price increases.

Nevertheless, when setting the price for event admission, organizers do have to consider how it will affect potential demand. Price elasticity generally means that as price increases, demand will decrease – for the obvious reason that money is a scarce resource, but also because consumers have many alternative opportunities. Tribe (2005: 76–77) shows how elasticity is modified by the necessity of having the good or service, the number of substitutes, addictiveness of the good or service, consumer awareness and the time period (e.g. are tickets bought well in advance?). Furthermore, some goods and services are so useful and so cheap that increases in price will be too small to affect demand.

The income elasticity of demand also must be considered. Generally people spend more on leisure and travel as their disposable incomes rise, and corporations and governments also 'demand' more events as their profits or revenues increase. In part it is a matter of financial feasibility, but it is also a matter of preference. Indeed, events (as leisure) can be considered preferred goods or services because people love to travel and be entertained. And civil servants as well as business people love to meet! Economics therefore provides a basis for demand forecasting, which, in the context of events, often means attendance forecasting. The inherent difficulty is that demand for, or interest in, many events is only partially influenced by the cost.

Willingness to pay

Willingness to pay is a useful economic concept to help determine event demand and to help set prices. Ask yourself how much you would be willing to pay for a choice ticket to a popular concert, then how much more or less you would be willing to pay for a ticket to a community festival. People are often unable to say exactly how much they would pay for any given opportunity, but they can at least compare it to other, normal purchases – we can call these 'value propositions'. For example, we often spend money to attend the cinema or rent a movie, so how much more is it worth to attend that concert? Twice as much? Three times? Market researchers use these value propositions to find a range within which most of their target segment would make a purchase.

A problem with willingness to pay is that some people will mislead you! Well, of course they will. Why volunteer that you would pay a lot of money for something that is currently free or cheap? Won't 'they' just use that information to raise the price? So researchers have to expect that expressed willingness to pay yields under-estimates of what people will actually pay. On the other hand, researchers have to recognize that if the price is raised, some people might indeed decide to stay away or be unable to afford the new price.

Tourists, it is often found, will pay more for events than locals. Studies of festivals in Canada's National Capital Region (Coopers and Lybrand 1989) found that those who travelled to the city especially for the events were willing to spend more than the residents. This happens because the event is the reason for their travel, and they are likely to attend just once. For example, see the study by Whitehead and Wicker (2018) on willingness to pay to attend a cycling event. Residents have plenty of chances to attend (or go to other local events) and might want to attend more than once, so they are less willing to pay higher prices per visit. Tourists therefore often represent a higher-yield segment, but in smaller volumes. In one study, Barros (2006) employed willingness to pay (WTP) to examine demand for the EURO 2004 football event and determined there was a small proportion of the population who were prepared to pay for the event. Their WTP was positively related to the number of times that the individual attends a soccer game during the season and to the education level of the respondent, but negatively related to household income, being a fan of the team and to the perception that the event would be prestigious for the country. Barros concluded that Euro 2004 did not qualify as a 'Pareto improvement of the public good', since the aggregated willingness to pay was lower than the estimated total costs of the event. It should be kept in mind, however, that WTP is only one possible measure of 'public good'.

Pricing

Pricing strategies and tactics are a management and marketing function, but how people react to prices requires both economic and psychological theories. Only a few researchers have dealt with event-related pricing issues. Crompton and Love (1994) analysed the history of demand for a themed event (Dickens on the Strand in Galveston, Texas) as well as responses to questions about substitution opportunities, strength of reference price, distribution of trip costs, affluence of the target market and value for money.

The researchers determined that attendance was mostly related to the life cycle of the event and its need to find new markets. Price could be raised without reducing demand, as each year 50 per cent were first-timers and regular residents could either get discounts in advance or free admission through dressing in period costumes. Demand was inelastic.

Examining many of the issues surrounding major-event ticketing, Happel and Jennings (2002) noted that few entertainment events, such as concerts, employed extensive price discrimination. It was common in the arts (e.g. symphony and opera), where there were often 25 or more ticket prices depending on event quality and seat location. At sport events, ticket prices usually remain the same across all games in a season, regardless of the quality of the teams playing. Happel and Jennings looked for reasons, and suggested that perhaps the arts institutions understood their customers better, or it was more important in the arts to be close to the performers. Sport might also employ a loss-leader strategy to get people into cheaper seats, then make a profit on merchandise and refreshments. Boyd and Boyd (1998: 169) challenged many of the conventional economic rules on pricing, arguing that:

> the pricing of tickets to professional sporting events often appear to be inconsistent with traditional profit-maximising behaviour. For example, the existence of scalpers and 'ticket agents' who sell game tickets at prices significantly in excess of face value could suggest that teams set prices too low for profit maximisation.

And it is known that some performers insist on keeping ticket prices as low as possible in order to be fair to their fans. Changing market conditions, and new technology, are likely to cause changes in event pricing. For example, being able to book and trade tickets online will alter consumer behaviour. In the context of leisure services, Crompton (2011) discussed the concept of the 'zone of tolerance', which is a price range in which consumer resistance might be minimized for new services or price increases. This has apparently not been tested for planned events, but relates closely to the WTP discussion.

Direct and induced demand

'Direct' demand for events consists of those people who pay to attend, or in other words the customers. As price goes up, normally direct demand will fall. If the event is free, direct economic demand cannot be measured, but 'willingness to pay' can be researched to get a 'value' for the event. Forecasting demand for an event is notoriously difficult (see, for example, Teigland 1996; Pyo et al. 1988; Spilling 1998; Mules and McDonald 1994), and so it is normal for many years of research on awareness, interest levels, market areas and segmentation, penetration rates and demand to precede mega events. The principal difficulty with forecasting event demand is in obtaining accurate and reliable data.

'Induced demand' is something quite different. It occurs when an event generates additional awareness for a destination, improves its image, and thereby attracts additional visitors. They might come before a major event to see the developing facilities, or simply because so much attention has been given to the area. Increased capacity is another factor to consider when explaining any tourist gains following an event, as new venues and hotels, better marketing, and heightened political support for tourism and other events are potential consequences.

Olympic cities have found that years before the big event, they attract many more meetings and conventions than otherwise would select them. After the event there should also be a 'halo effect' attracting increased numbers, but it will fade over time. However, many external variables can interfere with induced demand, making it a risky proposition upon which to base forecasts of economic impacts. Kang and Perdue (1994) concluded that the 1988 Seoul Olympics did have a long-term, positive impact on tourist demand for Korea, and they believed this effect would be more pronounced for developing as opposed to established tourist destinations. A more long-run analysis of hosting mega events on tourism (including the Olympics) from 1950 to 2006, by Fourie and Santana-Gallego (2011), found that these events generally promote tourism but the periodicity (e.g. season in which they are held) affects the benefits.

Events and economic development

'Development' can mean economic growth, but it can just as easily refer to urban development and renewal, social and cultural development or sustainable development, with its heavy emphasis on environmental concerns. A number of paradigms, or schools of thought about development, have influenced government policies – including those pertaining to events.

'Modernization' refers to the process of becoming more like Western, industrialized societies through infrastructure development, industrialization and changing attitudes and patterns of work, a feature observed in the examples in Chapters 2 and 3. The all-too-eager development of tourism in many developing nations reflects a desire to be more modern, and tourism (generally requiring foreign investment and many economic concessions made to investors) has produced quick and obvious results. Mega events in particular fit into this approach because they are bold, globally communicated symbols of development. For example, Korea has effectively employed mega events in its modernization schemes (directed by central government) and China is following suit. China embarked on a very ambitious process of modernizing its industrial base, accompanied by airports, motorways, convention and exhibition centres and tourism resorts.

World's fairs were, right from the first, associated with modernization – both as a way for nations to show off their technological developments and to attract visitors to a special place that symbolized progress. Hosting international conventions and exhibitions is still viewed as a method for fostering trade and gaining valuable knowledge about economic development.

Dependency theorists stress the problems associated with development in developing countries, or poor regions within rich countries, typically by referring to 'core–periphery' models (for structural reasons, including foreign ownership, the core always dominates) and neocolonialism (economic power is exerted rather than direct military power, in order to keep developing areas subservient). In this approach, events can be viewed as the exploitation of host cultures, as part of the 'pleasure periphery' for rich foreigners, or as inappropriate users of precious local resources to further an unwanted development model where the former colonial powers are replaced by exploitative forms of development by these visitors (see Britton 1982 for a critical discussion of this concept).

Economic neoliberalism has been the dominant development paradigm since the 1970s, typified by less direct government involvement and an emphasis on freeing up market forces, as mentioned earlier with reference to leisure policy. The 'supply-side economics' of neoliberalism favours consumerism, free trade and private development, not government intervention or centralized planning. Taken to an extreme, the absence of government intervention will certainly result in inequities and problems, so what we see today is varying degrees of government involvement in the market. Critics of globalization argue that neoliberal policies result in the poor getting poorer and the rich getting richer, while local cultures and ways of life disappear.

In Canada and other countries, neoliberal policies have resulted in less funding for the arts and events in general, a rise in corporate sponsorship and influence over the events sector, and quite possibly a decline in creativity because of the need for arts institutions and non-profits to stress commercially viable 'products'. An emphasis on tourism as industry, and events as new, competitive products, fits into the neoliberal way of thinking, so that any government funding is likely to be tied to specific Return on Investment (ROI) forecasts. The value of events in image development, place marketing and branding are aspects of neoliberal thinking.

Hall and Wilson (2011) point to the rise in neoliberalism in the public sector as a change to the relationship between the state and the private sector (i.e. the market). They argue that what constitutes the public good changes, whereby public-sector funding is used to benefit private-sector interests, with an expectation that this will have public benefits (e.g. in the subsidization of or support for major infrastructure projects such as stadia development).

Alternative development focuses on human needs and the human consequences of development, including concerns of gender equity, indigenous rights, physical, mental and social issues, and sustainable development. Empowerment and local involvement, with an emphasis on the process of involving local people in development so they benefit, are hallmarks of this approach (Scheyvens 2002).

The 'triple-bottom-line' approach to event-tourism planning and impacts is a related concept. Hede (2007: 13) argued that 'the Triple Bottom Line (TBL) ... borrowed from accounting and finance, amalgamates the social, economic, and environmental aspects of activities into one framework'. Within the context of special events, the TBL has been particularly linked to their evaluation. The considerable interest in developing 'green' events (Jones 2010) combined with the TBL fits within this paradigm.

A movement towards stressing the cultural and social value of events, and evaluations that treat these factors equally with economic impacts, may be one direction in which alternative thinking develops around state policy towards events in a post-modern society. For example, Whitford (2004a) argued that event policies in the Gold Coast and Brisbane, Australia, had city policies towards events which were predominantly underpinned by 'alternative', not classical economic development paradigms (namely modernization, dependency and neoliberalism). Whitford determined that these approaches were also becoming more widespread across Australia, using 'policy content analysis' to evaluate the internal and external factors influencing policy formation and contents, or the impacts of those policies. Indicators of an 'alternative' paradigm included the development of events not merely for tourism and branding, which is common in Australia and elsewhere, but for promoting cultural diversity, enhancing local ways of life and preserving heritage. Community development was another justification found in the Gold Coast and Brisbane for people's involvement in events. Whitford concluded that governments needed to be much more cognizant of the ideological focus within policies so that the goals and objectives of their event policies were better understood in terms of what they set out to achieve.

However, if an economic paradigm is as well established and accepted as neoliberalism has been in many countries, there is generally no such critical thinking. Rather, events, sports, the arts and business have all adapted to the new realities and compete on the basis of meeting the goals of neoliberalism or globalization. Paradigms change very slowly. Some very practical and valuable advice from Whitford is that researchers have to investigate the effectiveness of development-oriented policies that encompass events, so that policies are founded on fact, not dogma.

Claims made regarding the long-term, developmental benefits of mega events have to be treated with extreme caution. Research is seldom conducted longitudinally (see Chapter 3), and it is always going to be difficult to 'prove' that holding an event caused economic growth or social development. One thorough study, by Spilling (1998), concluded that the 1994 Winter Olympics in Lillehammer, Norway, had produced 'rather marginal' long-term impacts on the host region's economy. The benefits were largely confined to tourism, particularly for hosting new events! Spilling decided that the games could not be justified on economic grounds alone.

The economics of sustainability

There are substantial economic issues associated with any discussion of sustainability, or the related concepts of social responsibility, TBL and green events. In neoclassical economics, the world's natural resources are viewed as unlimited, or easily substituted through increased investment in capital or labour. We know this to be false, but it is extremely difficult to change the pro-growth paradigm that governs global economics. The most basic principle of sustainable economics is that natural resources (i.e. the planet or global ecosystem and all things we call useful) should not be diminished. As articulated by Stallworth *et al.* (n.d.), 'The general consensus on sustainability among economists is based on the "constant capital rule" – the notion of living off interest or income and not consuming capital.' In so-called 'strong sustainability' there is no substitution for natural capital; it must be preserved. The 'precautionary principle' suggests that when in doubt, we act to conserve resources, not exploit them.

Hall (2012) scrutinized mega events from the perspectives of three frames of sustainability. In the economic approach, policy is narrowly focused on economic growth and image enhancement, with insufficient attention given to opportunity costs and long-term impacts. In the 'balanced' approach, Hall claims that little attention is given to equity issues and decisions to hold mega events are still largely based on purported economic gains. Third, in the 'steady-state' approach to sustainability, grounded in ecological considerations, more emphasis is given to natural capital and quality of life. In this paradigm, or world view, mega events are not justifiable. Hall concluded (2012: 129) that, 'Instead, sustainable events are more likely to be found in the smaller localized community based events that run over the longer-term or at least help maximize the use of existing infrastructure.'

Of course there are major impediments to implementing strong sustainability principles, not the least of which is the prevailing attitude that growth is necessary and good. However, also consider the case of energy and fossil fuels – can we continue to extract them until they are gone? If we do so, there will be a major cost relating to air quality and global warming, but (a) we continue to discover more oil and gas all the time (leading to a glut and cost reductions in 2014–2015) and (b) there will certainly be alternatives when they are gone – it's more a matter of cost than of a finite energy supply. There are very good reasons for events and tourism to strive for sustainability in all dimensions (the TBL), but exactly what is or is not sustainable will likely always be open to debate. The authors believe that 'sustainable events' is a matter of context, and that sustainable events or sustainable tourism is a process, not an end-state. We can always improve on the resource impacts associated with hosting events.

Justifying market intervention, or the subsidizing of events

Market economies are based on the premise that it is best to leave most decisions to independent firms and consumers, as government intervention usually results in distortions and often negative, unforeseen consequences. However, in the case of many policy fields – including social, environmental and cultural fields – intervention is frequently justified. In terms of economics, the following concepts are important in this context.

Market failure is a situation in which markets do not efficiently organize production or allocate goods and services to consumers, or where market forces do not serve the perceived public interest. It was frequently cited in Scotland by Scottish Enterprise as its justification for intervention around tourism, where perceived market failure existed and so state investment would help to address this imperfection, especially if it supported innovation (Franchetti and Page 2009). Mules and Dwyer (2006) noted that hospitality and travel firms cannot capture all of the benefits generated by events, so they will not fund them. Consequently, the tourism industry (through Destination Marketing Organizations – see Pike and Page 2014 for a detailed review) often funds events collectively, although this allows for 'free riders' who get benefits without paying. The free-rider problem is why the industry often asks for events to be publicly funded, because government tax revenue comes from every company.

If events of any type are deemed to be a 'public good', then free-market forces cannot be allowed to operate. These are goods from which everyone can simultaneously obtain benefits. Public goods retain the characteristics of 'non-rivalry' and 'non-excludability'. Non-rivalry means that one person's benefit does not reduce the benefit available to others, and non-excludability means that there is no effective way of excluding individuals from the benefit of the good, once it comes into existence (thereby creating the free-rider problem). Due to the free-rider problem, it is not profitable for a private firm to provide a public good.

Economic efficiency is a valid reason for bidding on and creating events, to the extent that they provide revenue or other tangible benefits for publicly owned and subsidized facilities and parks. To the extent that surplus capacity exists (i.e. resident use does not normally fill the venues) the marginal cost of producing events might be much less than the new income realized. Indeed, many facilities and parks are established with this tourist revenue in mind.

A related efficiency issue is that of attracting tourists to events. Andersson (2006) recommended creating surplus capacity in resident-oriented events in order to make it possible to attract tourists. This can often be done without imposing new costs on residents, and will likely generate tourist income that is of value to residents directly (through lower event charges for them) or indirectly (higher taxes for local authorities, and increased economic prosperity in the region).

Economic impacts of events

It is vital to distinguish between 'economic contribution', 'economic impacts' and 'net benefits' when evaluating events. As stressed by Dwyer *et al.* (2010: 11), 'It is widely acknowledged that both domestic and international tourism make an "economic contribution" to a destination, that tourism has positive and negative "economic impacts", and that it brings "benefits and costs" to a destination.' Event tourism can definitely bring new money into an area, but we must always ask at what cost, and who pays or benefits? Many studies have narrowly focused on the new money brought into a destination by tourism and have ignored the other crucial issues.

How is value created?

If we think in terms of an event 'industry', certain economic implications arise. First, economists will measure the economic value of the industry in such terms as jobs created, export earnings (i.e. through event tourism) or wealth created for residents. On the other hand, being an industry might suggest that government intervention is unwarranted and the private sector can take care of demand. Indeed, governments tend to want to meet basic needs, while industry aims to satisfy economic demands expressed through purchasing power. Governments are often big winners from events and tourism, depending upon what services and goods are taxed (e.g. hotels, restaurant meals and alcohol usually generate huge tax revenues) and which level of government gets the benefits. Taking a more balanced view of 'value' beyond economic impacts (since these do not equal value) means embracing a multi-stakeholder approach where different perspectives of value are considered (see Getz *et al.* 2017; Lundberg *et al.* 2017).

Social and cultural value often require completely non-economic indicators of value, such as social integration and cultural development, although it is possible to employ the consumer surplus concept and willingness to pay method – or contingent valuation (see Andersson and Lundberg 2013; Armbrecht 2014) to estimate a monetary value for events or cultural institutions. Environmental value might be treated the same way, but in the context of events, it is also possible to connect value to these efforts: awareness and education; recycling; energy and waste savings; reduced travel so as to generate a smaller carbon footprint; and positive monetary or labour efforts regarding conservation and restoration. The 'ecological footprint' method (see Collins and Flynn 2008; Collins *et al.* 2009) is a more complex method for estimating costs of events, but it can also be a value measure when applied to efforts to reduce an event's footprint.

Another important concept is that of 'externalities'. Normal, free-market economics often fails to take into account effects that are external to a specific business, exchange or event. For example, the air pollution, noise and accidents caused by traffic related to a tourist-oriented event are frequently excluded from an accounting of economic impact. They should, however, be included in a comprehensive evaluation of the costs and benefits of the event. The problems associated with assessing economic impacts of events are summarized in Events in Focus 4.1.

EVENTS IN FOCUS

4.1 Problems associated with the assessment of the economic impacts of events

Dwyer and Jago (2012: 130) identified three main types of criticisms associated with the assessment of the economic impacts of events:

In recent years, a growing number of researchers have been critical of the approach taken to assessing the economic contribution of special events. Three main types of criticism have been advanced:

1 Some argue that the economic contributions of events are often exaggerated. Many of the problems in event assessment arise due to exaggeration of event participant numbers and/or their expenditure (Crompton and McKay 1994; Delpy and Li 1998). Only that proportion of expenditure which represents an injection of 'new money' into a destination is relevant to the calculation of the economic impacts. A number of critics (e.g. Porter 1999; Dwyer *et al.* 2000a, 2000b; Matheson 2002; Matheson and Baade 2003; Crompton 2006) have highlighted inappropriate practices in event assessment (for example, inclusion of residents' expenditure as 'new money', exaggerating visitor numbers and expenditure, abuse of multipliers, inclusion of time switchers and casuals), as well as the tendency to ignore the various costs associated with special events, such as opportunity costs borne by the local community and displacement costs.

2 Other researchers have argued that the standard model used in event assessment needs a re-examination. Economic impact analysis involves estimating the additional expenditure generated by the event, and then using some form of economic model to estimate how this expenditure translates into increased income and employment in the destination. At issue is the relevance of Input-Output (I-O) modelling which, until recently, has been the standard technique for converting event expenditure data into economic impacts. These critics argue that the economic assessment models used for estimating the economic impacts of major events should reflect contemporary developments in economic analysis, particularly regarding the use of Computable General Equilibrium (CGE) modelling. They argue that in most cases, I-O modelling does not provide an accurate picture of the economic impacts of events and is thus incapable of informing event-funding agencies or governments of the 'return on investment' estimated from event funding (Dwyer *et al.* 2005, 2006a, 2006b; Blake 2005; Madden 2006).

3 A third group of researchers argues that event assessment which focuses only on economic impacts is too narrow in scope to provide sufficient information to policy-makers and government funding agencies and that, where practical, a more comprehensive approach should be employed to embrace the importance of social and environmental impacts in addition to economic impacts. These critics highlight the potential importance of cost-benefit analysis (CBA) in event evaluation (Fleischer and Felsenstein 2002; Shaffer *et al.* 2003; Mules and Dwyer 2006; Jago and Dwyer 2006; Victorian Auditor General 2007; Dwyer and Forsyth 2009).

Source: Dwyer and Jago (2012: 130).

In Chapter 10 we return to many of the issues raised in this section related to the measurement of economic impacts and the question of benefits, costs and value; in Chapter 11 the related policy considerations are featured.

Management

Management is a very broad field of studies, with strong disciplinary connections to sociology, psychology and economics (Table 4.2). Four spheres of management that are applicable to events (profit, not-for-profit and governmental events, and the management of destinations which host events) have to be considered. Some will argue that management is a field of studies, not a discipline, because it is really the application of knowledge from a variety of disciplines. However, it is one of the crucial foundations of event studies and, unlike the other closely related professional fields that all have core phenomena, management applies to every field of human endeavour.

Business management

Many companies exist to produce or supply services to planned events, and they are profit-making businesses (see Lapsley and Rekers (2017) study of west end musical companies). We contend, however, that every event should be viewed as a business with the aim of making money. Money is needed to support the organization and improve the event, and it can be in the form of profit (to make individuals money) or 'surplus revenue' allocated to re-investment. If events are run as business propositions, it means that the owners/producers have to follow sound management principles and be focused on the long-term viability of the event. In other words, events need professional management to ensure their sustainability. An

Table 4.2 Management

Management	Nature and meanings; the event experience	Antecedents to attending events	Planning and producing events	Outcomes and the impacted	Processes and patterns
Profit, not-for-profit, governmental and destination management Theories of the firm Institutional theory Management functions (leadership, organizing, leadership and planning) Organizational ecology	Consumerism (events as entertainment products) Commoditization of events	Effectiveness of marketing Image and branding	Project and strategic planning Management effectiveness and efficiency Human resource management (managing people as resources and visitors)	The impacted as stakeholders	Evolution of management theory and practice Changes in factors that influence businesses and entrepreneurship (e.g. business development policy) Shifts in the competitive environment

interesting observation by Kelly and Fairley (2018), using contingency theory (which suggests a one-size fits all strategy may not always be appropriate) found that we need to take into account the size of event organizations and their varied sizes in developing business strategies, especially for small events.

A business exists for several reasons, and if the event is seen as a business venture, the following factors apply:

- making money for those who invest in them (i.e. public or private 'enterprises');
- meeting needs or filling market gaps (i.e. consumers, sponsors and grant givers will pay for the event).

Neither of these criteria negates any social or cultural value attached to events. Indeed, many not-for-profit event organizations are established to create public goods or meet social needs, yet they still have to function as independent firms. Why do for-profit event-production companies exist, and why do not-for-profit event organizations occupy such an important place in the events sector? Each is a kind of firm, or independent organization that provides goods or services in exchange for money/resources.

Entrepreneurship can be explained in part by the following motivations, with examples specific to the events sector:

- independence (e.g. hands-on work; being one's own boss; escaping from the mundane; taking risks);
- creativity (e.g. pursuing an art or craft through events; the act of establishing something that has value and/or creates wealth; working with like-minded people);
- profit (getting rich, or just making a living).

Both private companies and not-for-profit event organizations are set up by 'entrepreneurs'. In either case they have to make a living. Many not-for-profit festival organizations, for example, are established by persons who want to create both an event and a career for themselves. In their case studies of Calgary festivals, for example, Getz *et al.* (2007) interviewed several festival creators who were clearly acting entrepreneurially, and without their initiative and leadership the events would not have existed.

Stokes (2014: 215) summarized the all-embracing role of the private sector in events:

> *At the macro-level, the vision and resources of corporate leaders impacts on both national and local portfolios of events. Sponsorship resources from the private sector and philanthropic contributions of business leaders provide a significant proportion of the funds needed to grow arts, sports and business events. Apart from the political and strategic leverage of corporate leaders and the provision of dollars through sponsorship and philanthropy, the private sector also brings entrepreneurial vision to the design and creation of events. Event organizers and promoters who are involved in staging, producing and marketing events make up a highly specialized industry globally that is gaining increased professionalism and credibility. At the micro-level, a complex network of businesses provide event-specific services (e.g. planners, promoters, venue owners/managers, entertainers, merchandise and licensing firms) while many others provide event support services (travel and transport, tourist attractions, accommodation, retail and professional services). In effect, the private sector is both a recipient of revenue from events as well as the provider of direct and in-kind sponsorship.*

Figure 4.1 from Stokes (2014) illustrates the strategic and enabling role of the private sector in events, through destination-level inputs, event-specific inputs (e.g. event vision and concept creation), event planning, organization and management, the provision of event support services and event impact management and sustainability. Tum (2014) adds to this, arguing that the main challenge of event management is in managing uncertainty. However, explaining the theoretical basis of the firm as an organizational structure for event management requires discussion of the key areas of management theory associated with how such organizations develop, function and can contribute to event development. Carlsson-Wall

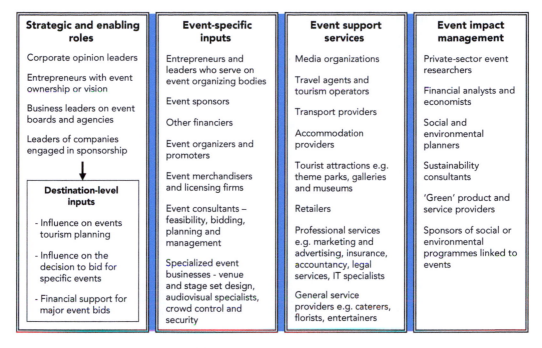

Figure 4.1 Roles and contributions of the private sector to events

Source: Stokes (2014: 219). Reprinted from *The Routledge Handbook of Events*, S. J. Page and J. Connell, Routledge (2014).

et al. (2017) described the peculiarities of event organizations as pulsating, where they build up to an event and require additional staffing (sometimes including volunteers) making the management and control of the organization complex and challenging.

Resource-based theory of the firm

Firms and organizations should possess rare and valuable resources that give them sustainable competitive advantages by protecting against resource imitation, transfer, mobility or substitution (Penrose 1959; Barney 1991). Many events fall into the category of 'serial reproduction', where the same concept is replicated elsewhere. Applied to events, these rare and valuable resources could be intellectual capital (creativity, knowledge), committed stakeholders (see 'stakeholder theory'), a special venue or an endowment, just as long as other events or organizations cannot do the same thing with their resources. Fostering innovation and maintaining authentic traditions are also vital in this context.

Knowledge-based theory of the firm

In this variation of the resource-based theory of the firm, organizations that possess, learn and retain valuable knowledge and capabilities, embedding them in their culture, management systems and stakeholder networks, can sustain competitive advantages and achieve superior performance (Barney 1991; Grant 1996). Information systems also provide advantages. Applied to events, managers should develop unique and inimitable knowledge or capabilities and make certain they are both retained and constantly developed. Consider, for example, the synergies to be gained through blending creative/artistic and business/management knowledge.

Stakeholder and network theory

'Stakeholder theory' (Freeman 1984; Donaldson and Preston 1995; Mitchell *et al.* 1997; Jawahar and McLaughlin 2001) has been thoroughly examined for application to events and tourism by van Niekerk and Getz (2019). The theory helps explain the origins, operation and evolution of events, and provides direction to owners and managers on how to manage their internal and external stakeholder relationships (Izzo *et al.* 2012; Cavicchi and Santini 2014). Stakeholders are those persons or groups who can influence the organization, or are influenced by it. Core stakeholder attributes, according to Mitchell *et al.* (1997: 865–867), are:

- 'Power': 'The ability of a party that it has or can gain access to impose its will in the relationship.'
- 'Legitimacy': 'A generalized perception or assumption that the actions of an entity are desirable, proper, or appropriate within some socially constructed system of norms, values, beliefs, and definitions.'
- 'Urgency': 'The degree to which stakeholder claims call for immediate attention.'
- 'Stakeholder salience': is a function of possessing the other three stakeholder attributes: power, legitimacy and urgency.

There is also a moral aspect to stakeholder theory, which argues that managers should also work with all those affected by the organization, as in the case of events working with their community and special interest groups (Ziakas and Costa 2010b), regardless of their power to influence the organization. Todd *et al.* (2017) provided a useful classification of stakeholder types: organizing, participating, attending, supplying and supporting.

Using the analogy of a 'political market square', Larson and Wikstrom (2001) and Larson (2002) examined several Swedish events. Stakeholders played 'power games' and negotiated from varying positions of power. They formed alliances to realize their goals for the event and the organization producing it. Critical roles identified among the stakeholders included those of 'gatekeeping' (deciding who gets in), negotiation, coalition-building, trust- or legitimacy-building, and identity-building for the event in general. Larson (2009b) later analysed event networks and concluded that they resulted in three different categories of Political Market Squares, which she labelled the jungle, the park and the garden; these represented tumultuous (i.e. jungle), dynamic and institutionalized event networks. The institutionalized network (i.e. the park) was often prescribed for stable event organizations. Larson called for more research on understanding tumultuous and dynamic event networks.

Merrilees *et al.* (2005) used stakeholder theory to analyse how the Goodwill Games were 'branded' in Brisbane, Australia. In this instance, building trust and legitimacy was crucial. Miffling and Taylor (2007) employed stakeholder theory in assessing the success of a youth-oriented event. To sustain itself in the long term, the organization has to manage its stakeholder relationships effectively, and if successful it might become a permanent 'institution' in its community. This means it has the support it needs to survive crises and to solve the social problems it exists for (Getz *et al.* 2007). In another application of stakeholder theory, Spiropoulos *et al.* (2006) examined the 20th Greek Festival of Sydney. The stakeholder environment of this event was closely tied to ethnicity, which suggests the value of examining social networks.

'Network theory' is closely related to stakeholder theory. 'Social networks' are often important for entrepreneurs, especially when obtaining the resources and support required to start an event. 'Social capital' in this sense means the network of people and organizations you can rely on to help you. Organizational networks obviously involve all the stakeholders, but there is an emphasis in network theory on 'centrality' as an attribute, their degree of 'connectedness' and 'bridging' organizations.

Prebensen (2010) examined value creation that arises from a result of stakeholders' participation, using network and co-creation frameworks. The study analysed seven stakeholder groups and their purposes for, and structures in, joining an event in the High North of Norway. In addition, the study examined the stakeholders' evaluation of values created through their own and others' participation in the event (i.e. value co-creation). The stakeholders include both organizations and individuals. The findings reveal that the various groups entail numerous reasons for participating in the event, classified as autotelic and instrumental value experiences.

4.1 RESEARCH NOTE ON STAKEHOLDERS AND NETWORKS

Izzo, F., Bonetti, E. and Masiello, B. (2012). Strong ties within cultural organization event networks and local development in a tale of three festivals. *Event Management*, 16(3), 223–244.

(This paper was the recipient of the second biennial Donald Getz Award for Outstanding Research in Planned Events. The paper was selected from hundreds of submissions by a blue-ribbon panel of international scholars chaired by the editor-in-chief of *Event Management*, an international journal. The recipients received a financial award of $500.00 from the publisher of *Event Management*, Mr Robert Miranda of Cognizant Communications Corp. The Getz Award was established in 2010 at Queen Margaret University by the International Centre for the Study of Planned Events, under the leadership of Professor Joe Jeff Goldblatt.)

'In particular, this study addresses two research questions. First, how does network structure affect the success of the event and its outcomes on local development, other than in economic terms? Second, which main capabilities does the 'network orchestrator' need to promote the effectiveness of the event network? By analyzing three different Italian cultural festivals – 'Festivaletteratura' ('Festival of Literature' – Mantua), 'Festival della Scienza' ('Festival of Science' – Genoa), and 'Festivalfilosofia' ('Festival of Philosophy' – Modena, Carpi, Sassuolo) – this article sheds light on: (a) the features of successful event networks, (b) the dynamics linking network structure and the social outcomes generated, and (c) the typical bundle of relational capabilities that network orchestrators need. Then we draw some implications for management and offer some remarks to stimulate further research in the field of special events.'

Collaboration theory

Collaboration theory relates to how various stakeholders get together in partnerships, alliances or other joint efforts (see Wood and Gray 1991; Jamal and Getz 1995). In true collaborations each partner gives up some degree of control to work with others in achieving common goals. For example, events form professional associations which can be called alliances, but generally do not give up any independence in doing so. Events can partner with other events or with tourist organizations for joint marketing, again without giving up any real power. But if events agree to work closely with each other, perhaps sharing offices, staff and resources, this collaboration entails a loss of independence and poses some risks that must be balanced against the gains. Most often collaborations work in 'policy domains' such as tourism and culture, or for major projects. Long (2000), for example, studied co-operation between tourism and the arts developed for the UK Year of Visual Arts. These were contractual and short-lived, as opposed to more permanent federations. Long concluded that lessons from this and other examples of collaboration and partnership can be applied to relationships with sponsors, reconciling goals, achieving economic efficiencies or dealing with political interests. Stokes (2004) examined inter-organizational relations of public-sector events organizations in Australia, where all states have events development companies or departments. She identified the relationships and knowledge used in event strategies, and identified the importance of shared knowledge as an incentive for participating in networks. Stakeholders included community representatives, public-sector managers, such as events and tourism agencies, corporate leaders, events managers and tourism industry suppliers. Key elements in 'sociospatial knowledge networks' are activity spaces, place inventories and information nodes. A corporate orientation among stakeholders mostly applied at the state level, where emphasis was on tourism development such as bidding for major events. There was more of a community orientation at the regional level, as tourism-related outcomes were considered. For staging major events formal alliances and collaborations were created, but not for strategy in general. Mariani and Giorgio (2017) observed how Destination Management Organisations collaborated with stakeholders to procure events for their destination and introduced the term meta-event where the collaboration spanned different geographical entities. Their use of the term meta-event was used to describe:

> *... a collection of coordinated, synchronised and intertwined events, occurring in a wide geographic area and encompassing two or more nearby competing destinations, which collaborate to better market themselves and/or to reposition themselves in the marketplace. It is part of the event portfolio of two or more DMOs and allows them to collaborate to conjointly garner the benefits of event tourism. It addresses both the tourists and the hosting communities of the destinations involved.*

(Mariani and Giorgio 2017: 101)

Resource dependency theory

All firms require resources, but some are better at getting and holding them. Success is defined, in this context, as maximizing the organization's power (Pfeffer and Salancik 1978; Pfeffer 1981), which can come from reducing one's own dependency or making others dependent on you. Firms lacking essential resources will seek relationships that provide them, resulting in dependency. This is a form of 'social exchange theory' and it seems to work well for events faced with competition for scarce resources and uncertainty in resource availability.

Event failures might arise from a poor 'fit' with the environment, as in the case where a festival is not able to attract interest and support from its host community because of cultural differences, a lack of key contacts or internal management deficiencies. According to Donaldson (1996), 'fit' stems from how an organization adapts to accommodate environmental contingencies. Additional considerations relate to the scarcity of resources (what are the alternative sources?), the nature of the event's operational environment (are there competition or symbiotic relationships among resource users?), certainty versus fluctuations in resource availability (e.g. is long-term support guaranteed?) and variability in resource needs (are the same resources needed every year?).

To deal with these resource issues, a number of strategies are available. Events can attempt to secure resources from many sources, store resources for hard times (i.e. a reserve fund) or switch to new resource suppliers. They can try to reduce their need (e.g. cost reductions), influence the resource providers (e.g. through policy lobbying) or decide to work with, or compete against, other organizations seeking resources.

This theory has been used together with stakeholder theory by Getz *et al.* (2007) to help explain both failure and the institutionalization of events. Other ecological and institutional theories of organizations also view the organization or firm in terms of its internal dynamics, environmental interdependencies and competing interests. Andersson and Getz (2007) examined the financial position of a tourism-oriented street festival in Sweden within the context of resource dependency and stakeholder management theory. Using data from a five-year period, they revealed how costs associated with the strongest stakeholders (that is, with the greatest bargaining power) greatly increased relative to costs associated with weak stakeholders. The festival was also more able to increase its revenues from weak stakeholders than from those in strong bargaining positions.

Competitive and comparative advantages

A 'comparative advantage' means that some events or event organizations have been endowed with better resources or appeal. This advantage could be in terms of support from their communities, which is a stakeholder issue, or in terms of their location. It could consist of 'tradition' or 'authenticity'. 'Competitive advantages' accrue from wise management of whatever you possess, such as by providing target segments with services (events) that they are willing to pay for, and doing it better than competitors. Adapting Porter's (1980) classic model of competitive forces, many events are revealed to be in a relatively weak position. An event has to first assess its competitive environment as to threats: it is generally easy to set up events so that competition is always likely to increase, and events are often substitutable by other events or other forms of entertainment and marketing. Both buyers (companies and customers) can go elsewhere unless there are few events or event-producing firms available. So how should events compete?

Porter's strategies for achieving and sustaining competitive advantage include a focus on costs (keeping costs low and passing savings on to the buyer), focusing on specific target markets, or on differentiation (being unique within the events sector). Competing on price is possible for events, even if their costs are high, when subsidies and sponsorship support are available to compensate. Competing through differentiation makes a lot of sense, but unfortunately numerous events exist for rather general purposes and many producers find it difficult to target in a narrow sense.

In event studies, little attention has been given to competitiveness among events or event companies, particularly how this manifests itself geographically where different regions host events that compete and may split market shares. Research on this important topic has to connect with stakeholder, institutional and population ecology theory, as well as with marketing and positioning strategy.

Agency theory

In 'agency theory' we consider how owners and managers/contractors interact. 'It is assumed that both parties are motivated by self-interest, and that these interests may diverge' (Scott 2001: 105). Sometimes managers know more about what is going on than owners; an example of this situation is when staff are intimately involved in an event and directors are remote. This results in 'information asymmetry' and the owners have to initiate inspections or incentives to ensure their policies are implemented. A central question raised by agency theory is: *do managers or subcontractors always act in the best interests of those who retained their services?* What if event managers ran their events to make more money, or preserve job security for themselves, rather than to meet the aims of the founders or key resource suppliers? This problem can arise in other situations, such as an event put out to tender by a government agency, or a charity hiring a production company to raise money through events.

There are other potential applications of agency theory in event studies. It relates to organizational culture and the role of founders and leaders (do they always get their way?). The processes of professionalization, bureaucratization and institutionalization might very well increase agency problems as more and more managers become involved and possibly begin to feel the event exists for their personal or collective benefits.

Organizational ecology theory

This theory, or interrelated group of theory fragments (Hannan *et al.* 2007), looks at whole 'populations' of organizations within their environment. While most management theory teaches that sound practice and adaptive strategies can ensure success, ecological models suggest that organizations are also likely to succeed or fail in response to environmental factors. The dynamics of populations of festivals and events must be considered, as well as the efforts of individual event organizations. Seminal works in organizational ecology include: Hannan and Freeman (1977, 1984); Carroll (1984); Hannan and Carroll (1992); and Baum (1996). The original question posed by Hannan and Freeman (1977) was: why are there so many forms of organization? Looking back at the subsequent research efforts, Carroll and Hannan (2000) concluded that, clearly, organizational diversity has important consequences for individuals and social structures. Ecological theory seeks to explain the rates of birth, growth and mortality of a 'population' of organizations in any given environment. Baum (1996) noted that all such theories begin with three observations. First, diversity is a property of aggregates of organizations, not of specific organizations. Second, organizations often have difficulty changing fast enough to adapt to uncertain environmental conditions. Third, organizations arise and disappear regularly, like the birth and death of animals.

Populations of events

In nature, a 'population' is defined by its 'species', as in the human population, but not so in organizational ecology. Baum and Oliver (1996) describe the concept of a population as follows:

> *A set of organizations engaged in similar activities and with similar patterns of resource utilization constitutes a population. Populations form as a result of processes that isolate or segregate one set of organizations from another, including technological incompatibilities and institutional actions such as government regulations.*

In other words, we should not assume that all festivals, or all periodic sport events, are alike, because they might have quite different activities (or services offered) and resource dependencies. The vast diversity of festival forms and styles (e.g. performing and visual arts, humour, spectacle, rituals, commemorations), variations arising from ownership (profit, non-profit, public) and differences attributable to size and location all make it very difficult to view them as a single 'species'. It might make more sense to consider performing arts festivals as a species, and other festivals as close cousins, but this analogy means little in practical terms.

There are two perspectives on events that make them resemble a single population, for both public policy and tourism-industry strategy. This is because the variations among festivals are not as important when considering what festivals can do for policy and strategy, from social marketing to place marketing. As instruments of policy, events are fit into 'portfolios' (see Getz 2005; Ziakas 2013) that must meet specified goals and account for their resources, especially if public money has been provided to them. Within a whole population of events in a given area, it might not matter if single events fail or change in some dramatic way, but within a managed portfolio it might cause a serious problem.

Within ecological theory, individual organisms (i.e. events) share space and resources with other organizational populations and the dynamics of this 'community' affects all its members. For example, festivals might have to share venues and grants with other cultural institutions and tourist attractions. 'Communities' are those species sharing the same 'ecosystem', which can be defined as a city or nation. The ecosystem analogy could take on a number of interesting dimensions when applied to festivals or events. Many interactions with their environment can be analysed, not the least of which must be stakeholder relationships, marketing, ownership and decision-making.

Managed portfolios of events

In a tourism context, the idea of a managed portfolio of events is to develop and manage events as destination assets, although the same concept applies to a venue, company or agency. The key is to shift emphasis from single events (through bidding and the marketing of existing events) to multiple events managed strategically. According to Getz (2013a: 23), 'A full portfolio will consist of various types of events, for different target markets, held in different places, and at different times of the year, in pursuit of multiple goals.' Portfolio management enables longer-term strategies to prevail, thereby fostering sustainability of the events sector, and it facilitates synergies such as enhanced economic benefits and the fostering of social and cultural capital. 'In a portfolio approach the types of events, and their host or owners, will often be of less importance than the cumulative effects' (Getz 2013a: 23). Although it is likely that competition for events through bidding will remain intense, if portfolio thinking prevails, there will be more attention paid to the long-term, sustainable values obtained by creating and supporting hallmark events that are co-branded with destinations, as well as a range of highly targeted, iconic events for special interest groups.

Ziakas (2013: 14), in *Event Portfolio Planning and Management: A Holistic Approach*, defined a managed portfolio in the following manner:

> *An event portfolio is the strategic patterning of disparate but interrelated events taking place during the course of a year in a host community that as a whole is intended to achieve multiple outcomes through the implementation of joint event strategies.*

This view on portfolios seeks to integrate tourism with other policy domains, and is therefore a broader conceptualization. Synergies can be fostered between economic, social and environmental policies through events.

Key concepts within organizational ecology

A basic step is to measure and keep track of 'vital statistics', that is, the demographics of the population. These data are seldom available, mainly because no agency keeps track of new events such as births, deaths, failure, growth rates and the overall health of the population (we will look at 'health' later). Unless there are policies and goals, the overall population and its health do not even become issues in most areas.

STRUCTURAL INERTIA

Organizational ecologists make a strong case that organizations tend towards 'structural inertia' – that is, they cannot adapt to changing conditions, and that is a major reason for failure. Change in the population therefore occurs through (in part) 'selection', a natural process of winnowing those organizations that do not hold a viable niche or which cannot adapt to change. Indeed, a case has been made that society imposes strong demands on organizations for accountability, and rewards reliability and predictability, thereby increasing the tendency towards inertia. The key concept here, in line with institutional theory, is that organizations must occupy a niche that ensures them resources and support.

COMPETITION VERSUS COOPERATION

Research supports the position that, in common with other non-profit sectors, most festivals and events would gain by pursuing a strategy of collaboration and sharing, however difficult this might be to implement. The barriers arise from the very nature of the sector, which is often dominated by small and volunteer-managed organizations. As an example of empirical support, Baum and Oliver (1996: 1421) found that the comparative success of the non-profit sector resulted in part because:

1 non-profits were more inclined to cooperate than compete, facilitating their expansion;
2 non-profits' greater social legitimacy made them more formidable competitors, impeding the expansion of for-profits; and
3 non-profits invested in institutional links that stimulated further non-profit growth.

Many event managers do not believe they compete directly with other events or institutions, but this is a fallacy. Within organizational ecology theory, the ecosystem has a finite resource base and the community or different organizations tend towards growth until limits are reached. The study of how events compete for resources, including audiences, sponsors, grants and audiences, is in its infancy, with evidence to date coming from research on festival management and stakeholders.

AGE DEPENDENCE

According to this theory, there is a greater risk of failure when an organization is either new or old. Older, more generalized organizations have a better chance of survival because the reliability of their performance encourages others to supply resources. The contrary position is that as periodic events age, there is an increased risk of obsolescence, in a competitive sense, and of senescence (or managerial failure), often due to complacency or a conservative culture that resists adaptation or resists compromise, which is needed to secure stakeholder support. New event organizations will often have a difficult time getting adequate resources and learning how to survive. When events can be set up in a free-market environment, as opposed to a heavily regulated setting, it seems likely that many will begin, without adequate resources, to survive a crisis. A key variable is the initial endowment or committed resources available to the event – how long can it last without becoming financially self-sufficient? Many festivals do expire, and failure is often linked directly to inadequate resources.

NICHE THEORY

Within an ecosystem, a 'niche' is occupied by a species that has evolved in such a way that it has a competitive advantage in securing particular resources. But in organizational ecology, a single entity can also occupy a niche. The festival that occupies a 'narrow' niche is a 'specialist' organization that maximizes its exploitation of the environment by catering to a narrow audience or relying on one or a few key resources suppliers. They are often successful as institutions, but risk failure from unpredicted changes in the environment, such as new government policy. On the other hand, 'generalist' events work strategically to secure resources from many sources, to become financially self-sufficient and to avoid over-dependency. They usually prefer many small sponsors to one or a few big corporate supporters. They try to balance grants, sponsorships, ticket sales and other income. Generalist organizations accept a lower level of exploitation in return for greater security (Hannan and Freeman 1977: 948). If environmental forces are subject to frequent change, the sustainable event will want to become a generalist. 'Niche width' defines the resource or market space an organization could potentially occupy, if environmental conditions change. For example, do specialist organizations have any more resources to draw upon, or audiences to tap, if they face financial threats?

RESOURCE PARTITIONING

This concept relates to generalist versus specialist organizations. It makes predictions about founding and mortality rates among organizations as a function of market concentration, with generalist and specialist organizations sometimes being able to separate themselves – in effect partitioning the available resources. Carroll concluded that 'more available resources should translate into better chances of success for specialists when they operate in the more concentrated market' (Carroll 1985: 1272). Archibald (2007) found that for both commercial and non-commercial organizations, control of resource niches is important. A few large generalist organizations in a population tend to use all a sector's resources, but this leaves room for specialist organizations. In the context of events, both the human population and its economic prosperity must be considered, as cities should offer more opportunities for specialization.

DENSITY DEPENDENCE

This theory postulates that vital rates in the population are a function of the number of entities (i.e. events) in an area (Hannan and Freeman 1977). As density increases, there is likely to be an increase in both 'legitimation' (i.e. the process of festival/event creation is accepted as being natural) and competition for resources, which are opposing forces. At higher densities, the competition force is hypothesized to be stronger, thereby leading to reduced founding rates and higher mortality rates. This dynamic tension is suggested to result in an inverted U-shaped curve to describe founding rates (i.e. new, start-up events) and a normal U-shaped curve to describe mortality rates, over time. It also seems appropriate to consider how Butler's (1980) notion of 'critical limits to growth', from his destination life-cycle model, might apply in terms of whole populations of organizations. This has been added to Figure 4.2, providing a hypothetical model of event development within a given environment.

Alternatively, it can be hypothesized that in some environments (say, in a city with a proactive policy to grow the festival sector), resources available to festivals can be deliberately increased (e.g. more grant money) or competition decreased (through collaboration), thereby resulting in a temporal extension of the U-shaped curve and a larger event population. In that kind of facilitating, supportive environment, individual event organizations might also have a greater chance of both growth and institutionalization.

RELATIONAL DENSITY AND NETWORK THEORY

An additional element of organizational ecology theory is the concept of 'relational density' (Baum and Oliver 1992), which refers to the number of links tying organizations to institutions in the environment. This is also called 'embeddedness' in institutional theory and is related to social network theory. An example of high relational density would be the city in which government policy seeks to grow and nurture the festival sector, resulting in more formal and stronger links between festival organizations, between the festival sector and politicians, and possibly between those key stakeholder groups and corporate sponsors and other grant givers. There has been little work undertaken on whole populations of events, and theory development utilizing organizational ecology as a framework for event studies is only

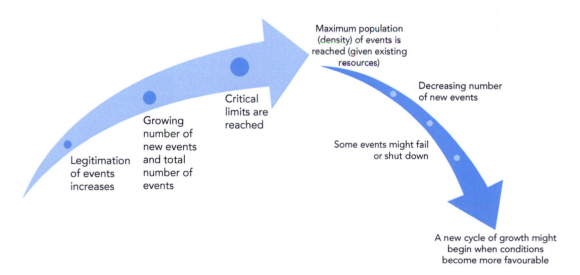

Figure 4.2 Organizational ecology – density dependence

Source: Adapted from Hannan and Freeman (1977) and Butler (1980).

beginning. In Research Notes 4.2 work from Norway on festival populations reveals a number of unique considerations, but also tends to support density dependence theory.

4.2 RESEARCH NOTES ON THE STUDY OF A WHOLE POPULATION OF FESTIVALS

Jaeger, K. and Mykletun, R. J. (2009). The festivalscape of Finnmark. *Scandinavian Journal of Hospitality and Tourism*, 9(2/3), 327–348.

'The diversity of festivals in Finnmark, Norway, was researched with the aim of creating a festival map of the county's Festivalscape. Data were collected by questionnaires to the registered festival managers. It was concluded that Finnmark is a festive county where 72,000 people share close to 60 festivals arranged annually in 19 municipalities across the county. The festivals were categorized as either music, arts, sports or market festivals; however, the largest group were named thematic festivals, as they are each built around rather unique themes, thus representing a diverse example of festival variety and creativity. Even so, live music and food sales are found at most festivals, and all festivals have more than one main activity.'

Andersson, T., Getz, D. and Mykletun, R. (2013). Sustainable festival populations: An application of organizational ecology. *Tourism Analysis*, 18, 621–634.

'Data from whole populations of festivals in three Norwegian counties were examined. Analyses of festival start-ups demonstrated that the number of events in each county had risen faster than population growth before plateauing, and changes were correlated significantly with trends in the Norwegian gross domestic product. Data on festival age, theme and other variables were also considered in the light of whole population dynamics. It was concluded that the fundamental tenets of density dependence theory were empirically demonstrated insofar as rapid growth in the festival populations was not sustainable when resources diminished, but no data were available on festival failures. It appears that the hypothetical legitimation of festivals helps to explain rapid growth, as festivals became popular instruments of public policy.'

What is a healthy population of festivals?

The coming and going of festivals and events is often ignored, especially in countries where a free market is assumed and many players are at work in this sector – from diverse government agencies and non-profits to corporate sponsors and for-profit event companies. However, the growing exploitation of events for place marketing, tourism development and many social/cultural policy initiatives, means that festivals and events are coming under increased scrutiny, both individually and collectively. The question then arises, do we have a healthy population or portfolio of events in our area? Is there a need for strategy and/or intervention?

A population has to be able to sustain itself, given available resources. This might result in growth or decline as necessary, or as judged to be appropriate. In times of resource scarcity, adjustments to population size will have to be made consciously or through natural selection (i.e. the weak will be allowed to perish). A directed or coordinated open-system of organizations has to be able to adjust to its environment – or if possible influence external forces – in such a way as to sustain equilibrium, that is, the level of resource consumption that will keep it healthy. This might require planned adjustments to population size or a reduction in resource consumption by all members.

However, festivals and other event-producing organizations are typically not able to achieve population equilibrium because they are not coordinated, nor is their sector directed by any agency. Owing to the special nature of festivals as manifestations of fundamental social, cultural and economic needs, and as instruments of policy and strategy, the health of festival populations requires additional and essentially goal-dependent considerations. Other periodic events, mainly sports in terms of numbers, can be given similar treatment insofar as they implement event-tourism policy and strategy or sport development and human health.

The International Festivals and Events Association (IFEA) (http://www.ifea.com/p/industryawards/worldfestivalandeventcityaward) annually awards 'festival city' status, and its evaluative criteria suggest what it takes to sustain a healthy population of events. Their main criteria are:

- Community overview: population; venues available and their capacity; infrastructure and parking availability; tourist numbers attributed to events.
- Community festivals and events: numbers, types and dates; budgets; sponsorship support; volunteer numbers and hours worked; attendance; target markets and numbers achieved; awards received; professionals with certification.
- City/governmental support of festivals and events: policies and support programmes; direct funding given; city roles and process in approval of events; coordination.
- Participation by city/politicians in events; regulations affecting events; training provided.
- Non-governmental community support of festivals and events: volunteer involvement in the event sector; total sponsorship provided; media support; support from DMO, Chamber of Commerce and other organizations; incentives to events from venues; access to local suppliers; direct industry involvement in the events sector.
- Leveraging 'community capital' created by festivals and events, such as: branding; tourism marketing; corporate recruiting; media coverage and public relations; enhancing exposure to the arts; encouraging social integration or celebration; better use of facilities or parks; long-term legacies of events.
- Extra credit for actions such as: skills development; availability of certificate or degree programmes in event management; sharing among festivals; efforts to recruit new events to the city.

Public administration

Our discussion of public policy and law in this book represents aspects of public administration. Governments do not have to obey the laws of the marketplace, such as supply and demand. They can create and subsidize events for a multitude of reasons and not worry about profits or break-event points. Our discussion of 'public goods', 'equity' and 'failure of the marketplace' provides the justification. Since many events are produced by, or subcontracted by, government departments and agencies, some attention to public administration is required in event studies. If the event functions as a programme within a governmental agency, then it is clearly an instrument of policy. Under some circumstances the event could be managed as an enterprise, either to make money or at least break even, in which case it has to operate like a business. This often means that a standalone event organization or division of a public-sector body is created to handle the event activity, with clear legal parameters of what it can do and its remit for event development and management.

Not-for-profit management

Festivals and sport events are often produced by not-for-profit organizations that are either in existence for other reasons, or are set up specifically to manage the event (see Ruperto and Kerr 2009; Edwards

2012). 'Not-for-profit' is a more accurate term than 'non-profit' to describe them, because they can make surplus revenue (and should aim to) but must use it to sustain and improve the organization and their events. Grant writing, fundraising, governance issues (especially with volunteer boards), service provision, needs assessments, volunteer recruitment and management and programme evaluation are topics of particular interest in this sector as well as not-for-profit marketing (see Taylor and Shanka 2008). Another relevant concept in terms of not-for-profit events is the notion of social entrepreneurship and population ecology (especially related to social movements). Social entrepreneurship has a focus on not-for-profit objectives where the wider issues of community and population well-being assume a greater role than a simple focus on profit.

Destination management

Destinations are really 'policy domains', defined for specific purposes of tourism marketing, and comprising the '4As' of attractions, accommodation, accessibility and ancillary services represented by the diverse range of stakeholders and organizations that coalesce to form the tourism sector. Events can be classified as attractions if they animate the destination as Connell *et al.* (2015) noted. There is a considerable debate about whether the organizations often created by public-sector bodies, collaborative public–private partnerships or private-sector organizations in fact 'manage' destinations as postulated by Pike and Page (2014), who argued that 'The term management implies control, and the authors here argue that very few DMOs have either the mandate or resources to effectively manage their destination even though stakeholders in the broader tourism industries.'

DMOs are usually limited in what they can achieve in terms of management, with many practical and logistical issues being controlled by local authorities (e.g. car parking, street cleaning, waste removal, control of crowds and visitors by the police during special events, and environmental issues) (Pike and Page 2014: 204). Consequently, these organizations predominantly market the destination and have a wider liaison role in 'management'.

Destination management is rather unique, because it exists for both public good (economic development) and private gain (members or partners such as hotels) to improve the competitiveness of the destination. As event tourism is now so well established, and globally competitive, how destinations plan, bid for, and in some cases produce and manage events is of considerable interest in event studies. The following Research Note 4.3 illustrates how destination marketing organizations view events.

4.3 RESEARCH NOTE ON LEVERAGING EVENTS

O'Brien, D. (2005). Event business leveraging: The Sydney 2000 Olympic Games. *Annals of Tourism Research*, 33(1), 240–261.

Business Club Australia was established to foster business networking and international trade development surrounding the 2000 Summer Olympic Games. O'Brien reported that accumulated knowledge was being institutionalized and applied in other event situations. The steps taken by the Club included generating public- and private-sector support for networking, and facilitation of networking between Australian businesses and visiting international business leaders (or politicians) before, during and after the event. Australians had to be convinced that the benefits of the event could be spread throughout the country.

Institutional theory and 'institutionalization'

Within organizations, 'institutional theory' refers to processes by which rules and norms become guidelines or controllers of behaviour. For example, how does an event's approach to stakeholder relationship management become 'institutionalized' over many years? This ties in with organizational culture and social network theory, with direct relevance to planning, decision-making, coordination and control systems. However, we are more interested here in what an 'institution' is, and how an event can become one.

Regarding the organization as an 'institution', Scott (2001) suggested that it is a social structure with a great deal of resilience; it provides meaning to social life, connotes stability and is taken for granted. Others believe an institution has to exist for a specific purpose, which is to achieve important societal goals or solve crucial societal problems.

The following criteria appear to be important factors determining event institutionalization, and should be tested through a variety of comparative research studies on different types of events:

- An event that is an 'institution' solves important social problems or meets important community goals.
- Society or the community cannot be without it – failure is unthinkable.
- Permanence is taken for granted.
- Support is assured – sponsors and agencies will always give it money.
- It is highly visible – everyone knows about it – the event has a strong, positive brand.
- It is expert in managing its stakeholder relationships.
- Key stakeholders have been internalized.

Fuller understanding of institutionalization also requires linkage with population ecology, resource theories of the firm and stakeholder theory. Chapter 9 explains the process in more detail.

Critical success factors for managing events

Is there a formula for event success, or at least a well-established list of critical success factors (CSFs)? Such a formula would be great, but experience is probably necessary to ensure the success of any venture, and researchers have not come up with a universal recipe. What works in one situation might not work in another, and over time conditions always change – a feature observed by Connell *et al.* (2015) in relation to visitor attractions and how they use events to extend the season in Scotland.

One attempt to develop CSFs through research was conducted by Jordan (2006), based on a study of planning for the Cricket World Cup of 2007, which was held in the West Indies. Her factors pertained to executive management (decision-making and project planning), collaboration and communication, community participation and involvement, and learning from past mistakes. Joliffe *et al.* (2008) also identified CSFs for a new event: community involvement; new partnerships and alliances in trade and tourism; branding of coffee and the destination; media coverage; new product (tours); and building business for local enterprises. A major goal of researchers is to aid managerial and planning decisions, in an effort to increase the likelihood of success. But this can never be assured by following a formula. That is why we have concepts and theories that can inform and guide, but cannot be employed deterministically.

Political science

Political science is the theory and practice of politics, political systems and political behaviour. Political scientists study government and its processes, public institutions, power and policy-making, politics, intergovernmental and international relations (see Table 4.3). 'Political philosophy', on the other hand, is more concerned with values and political ideas, such as the differences between Marxism and capitalism, or the meanings of rights and justice (from *Encyclopaedia Britannica Online*).

According to Hall (2014: 186–187):

> *politics is about power: who gets what, where, how and why ... The conception of politics and the political is important because it shapes the questions that researchers do or do not consider as well as assumptions made when undertaking research ... Some of the most widely used definitions of politics are:*
>
> - *Politics is the exercise of power.*
> - *Politics is the public allocation of things that are valued.*
> - *Politics is the resolution of conflict.*
> - *Politics is the competition among individuals and groups pursuing their own interests.*
> - *Politics is the determination of who gets what, when, and how.*

As Hall (2014) suggests, each of these different definitions revolves around the notion of actors (individuals, interest groups, and public and private organizations) each of whom are involved in a struggle for power. Hall (2014) points to the relative lack of research on the politics of events, aside from his seminal studies on politics and events (Hall 1989, 1992) and the politics of tourism in which events also feature (Hall 1994a). There are many political reasons for staging events, and politics often influences their management and marketing. Ideological reasons lie behind many mega events, wherein the dominant power in society seeks to demonstrate and reinforce its values, or to win support (Hall 1994a).

In many countries there are substantial, party-based differences in approaches to policy that impinge on the events sector. These are generally rooted in philosophy and traditional voting bases, such as Labour versus Conservative, but they also express the more mundane necessity of opposing the party in power. It is always worth asking if a 'party-political platform' reflects fundamental philosophical differences between parties, or if the opposition is simply trying to appear to be different. One might expect, for example, that a left-leaning party would stress equity issues and government interventions, such as

Table 4.3 Political science

Political science	Nature and meanings; the event experience	Antecedents to attending events	Planning and producing events	Outcomes and the impacted	Processes and patterns
The study of governments, public policies and political behaviour	Events may take on political significance Attendance can be a political statement	Political motives to attend or stay away	Creating events as a political statement (e.g. protest; party loyalty; nationalism) Government policy and programmes re: events	Effects on politics, government, political parties and law	How politics and policies influence event development and attendance

making the arts accessible to everyone, while right-leaning parties would stress free-market economics and privatization.

Government intervention in the events industry is often justified, for reasons discussed previously (i.e. public goods and failure of the marketplace). But these arguments can disguise underlying political motivations, such as getting re-elected, spreading party-specific values (this is correctly termed 'propaganda') or catering to interest groups that support the party in question. As examples, Baker and Rowe (2014) focused on multiculturalism and the need for events to pay attention to this growing global trend, while Allen and Cochrane (2014) debated the corporatist politics surrounding London's hosting of the 2012 Olympic Games and the more place-specific politics manifested locally.

Interest groups and elites

Who supports public involvement with events, and why?, is a question too infrequently asked. Often the answer is disturbing, because getting the government to produce, subsidize or bid on events obviously benefits some more than others. The tourism industry benefits directly when major events are produced, but the arguments put forward in support of mega-event bids typically emphasize the public goods, such as more jobs, economic development, new infrastructure and enhanced civic pride.

It is usually easy to identify the elite groups, or at least their interests with regard to events and particularly related to the decisions made concerning the bidding on and hosting of major events. For sports, elite athletes and the organizations representing them (e.g. Olympic committees) can gain tremendously from major events and new facilities for sport; they often frame major events as mechanisms for increasing participation, with imputed health benefits, without much or any proof being available. Those engaged in property development and the supply industry gain, hospitality and tourism usually benefit, and so do politicians who associate themselves with popular events. Of course one might argue that if so many benefit, surely society as a whole gains. That proposition requires a detailed cost and benefit evaluation which is seldom conducted or made public.

Jennings (2013) argued that public events and big capital projects are 'an ideal vehicle for "high politics" and the predilection of policy-making elites for grand, iconic and schematic visions that offer high-profile policy successes and historic legacies'. The political rewards, however, should be set against the risks and especially the frequent failure of official economic forecasts to be realized.

Political attitudes and voting patterns

Political scientists often study elections and underlying voter attitudes and behaviour, including how political campaigns and specific messages affect the voter. When it comes to events, the most closely related approach has typically involved measures of resident or tourist perceptions of event impacts, and attitudes towards them. But such research has more of a sociological orientation than political science. More research is needed on how perceptions and attitudes translate into political action or voting patterns, and how interest groups lobby for and achieve their event-related goals. This is similar to stakeholder theory.

International relations

Events often involve international relations, both as a reflection of trade, power and cultural exchange. Consider the importance of hosting a mega event for national pride and the legitimacy of governments, the importance assigned to using events to foster trade and economic development, and the value of showcasing one's cultural and economic accomplishments in a global forum. Santos (2014) discussed how mega events were used to strengthen Brazil's position in global affairs, while Grix (2013) assessed how mega events use the promise of legacies to attract support. In Qatar, Brannagan and Rookwood (2016) examined the role of acquiring the 2022 World Cup and how it was linked to the country's foreign policy.

Policy formulation

According to Page and Connell (2014: 226), 'the term "policy" is frequently used to denote the direction and objectives an organization wishes to pursue over a set period of time'. And in the view of Turner (1997), the policy process is a function of three interrelated issues:

- the intentions of political and other key actors;
- the way in which decisions and non-decisions are made;
- the implications of these decisions.

The policy context affecting events, and how events shape policy, have been receiving considerable attention. In their book *Event Policy: From Theory to Strategy*, Foley *et al.* (2011) argued that in the urban entrepreneurial policy environment of the previous decades, events were increasingly deemed unsupportable unless they achieved economic, social, cultural and environmental goals. For example, Higgins-Desbiolles (2018) examined the challenge of balancing these goals in event policy formulation. Contemporary planned events have to fulfil multiple functions, which has changed the nature of events and their roles in society. With Scotland as their reference point, Foley *et al.* have evaluated how two quasi-, non-governmental bodies, EventScotland and Creative Scotland, have played a significant role in attracting event-based tourism visitation to the country.

The ways in which event-related policies are formulated and implemented are still deserving of greater study, especially in terms of cross-cultural comparisons. Certainly we are all aware of how many tragedies at events gave rise to health and safety regulations and policies are formulated post-hoc to prevent a reoccurrence as well as increasing concerns about public security at major events (e.g. see the special issue of *Urban Studies* (Giulianotti and Klauser 2011) which reviews security and surveillance at sport mega events). But what went into the decision of the Canadian government (and other nations) to ban tobacco sponsorship at events? Will the same happen to alcohol sponsorship? How did events lobby and why were they successful, or not? As the event management profession and industry become better established and more professional, it can be expected their lobbying efforts will increase and become more effective. But who sets and steers that agenda?

An interesting, events-related theme in policy-making is that of irrational decision-making. Elites, holding influence and power in society, tend to get what they want. It's a mutually reinforcing process! So when a mega event is desired, or perhaps a subsidy for certain types of event, rational decision-making can get in the way. Zimbalist (2015) critiques the bidding for mega events and the gamble this often involves around subsidies and politics. Accordingly, various spurious arguments about tourism impacts or infrastructure gains are used to make it seem like a rational decision. Those who use rational arguments to oppose such decisions are then branded as being unpatriotic, irresponsible or stupid. This is how power gets abused.

A kinder explanation is that emotions get the better of people. Consider how emotional a country can get when it is bidding for the Olympics against a rival country (does London versus Paris 2012 come to mind?). In a highly charged, emotional context, irrational decisions are more likely to be made. How can that be prevented or ameliorated? Should it be?

Power and resources

Much of politics can be construed as a struggle for power, and power means control of resources. When elections are held, the balance of power shifts: lobbyists have more or less influence, funds are reallocated, and new policies become possible. Political science deals with how power and the economy are interdependent, and in the events context this requires studying how various parties (political or otherwise) exert influence to get what they want. In his examination of *Tourism and Politics*, Hall (1994a) pointed out the negative side of using events to achieve political goals. Events not only can be used as an excuse for overriding normal planning and consultation processes, but can displace powerless groups – especially in the inner city – in the name of urban renewal and economic development. He rightly argued that mega events are almost always sought after by the community's elite who stand to benefit the most, whereas ordinary residents are seldom consulted. Hall noted that proponents of the successful Sydney, Australia bid for the 2000 Summer Olympic Games regarded opponents as 'unpatriotic' or 'unAustralian' and that the public was consulted only by means of polls.

In *Power, Politics and International Events: Socio-cultural Analyses of Festivals and Spectacles*, Merkel (2013: 4) defines politics as being about social relations and decision-making processes that involve power and authority. Power is either of a collective nature, in which groups seek to achieve their common goals, or of a distributive nature, meaning who has power over whom, and what. This clearly relates to the resources issue, which is of singular importance regarding mega events and mega projects, being who gets what, and who pays. Merkel also notes how many events reflect or celebrate the four main sources of power: military, ideological, political and economic. This perspective on power links to the notion of events as 'texts' that can be read. In the accompanying Research Note 4.4, Bonthuys analyses a very specific policy debate that often surrounds major events.

4.4 RESEARCH NOTE ON POLICY CONTROVERSY

Bonthuys, E. (2012). The 2010 Football World Cup and the regulation of sex work in South Africa. *Journal of Southern African Studies*, 38(1), 11–29.

'While the South African government expected the 2010 Football World Cup to stimulate economic growth and infrastructure development, and to foster a sense of national unity amongst its citizens, members of the public and the media anticipated an increased demand for commercial sex. The call, in 2007, by the National Commissioner of Police to legalize sex work for the duration of the tournament stimulated debates on the legal status of sex work. Media reports show how advocates for sex workers' rights used the publicity around the event to argue for the legalization of sex work and the protection of sex workers' human rights. However, these calls were persistently overshadowed by claims that up to 40,000 foreign women would be trafficked into the country for sex work, and that many children would be abducted or trafficked for the same purposes. Similar claims have been made in the past in relation to other large sporting events, especially the 2006 Football World Cup held in Germany. However, these fears have not materialized elsewhere, nor did they do so in 2010. Fears of sex trafficking represent a form of moral panic which, while purporting to focus on the well-being of trafficked sex workers, often instead provides justification for the harassment and punishment of sex workers. This happened at the German World Cup and such fears were used to similar effect in the Cape Town Metro. The preoccupation with trafficking and child sexual abuse distracts attention from more important issues in debates about sex work, such as the ways in which the state, global and local commercial interests, and beliefs about sexuality in the wider society, construct and uphold women's economic dependence on men and the routine exploitation of women's sexuality. These factors create and sustain the conditions which force women to resort to sex work, both in the formal sex work industry, and in "informal" sex work transactions.'

Do people have a right to hold and attend events?

In some countries, the right to public assembly, and particularly for the purpose of protest or demonstration, is severely curtailed. The 'right' to attend an event might also be absent, given that in many societies there are barriers that cannot be surmounted, including cost, social status, or the availability of tickets that are rationed and channelled to the elite (also see Chapter 3 on inclusion). The Olympic movement, and other elitist event owners, ensure that the best and often the most tickets go to those on the inside of the movement, to those politically connected, and of course to the top sponsors, leaving the public to enter lotteries for the 'privilege' of having a chance to win a ticket-purchase opportunity! Veal (2010: 98) concluded that human rights are political in nature. If it can be said that people need leisure and sport, or travel, then it is more legitimate to claim a right to travel, to attend or hold events. Veal believes that statements about 'need' are value-based, not scientific, and that in this context need and rights are the same thing. These debates are running in parallel to the discussion in Chapter 3 on social inclusion/exclusion and accessibility and Baker and Rowe (2014 provide an interesting discussion of the cultural politics of multiculturalism and event attendance in Australia.

Research on the political science of events

Both humanistic and scientific methodologies are employed in political studies. Political scientists use methods and techniques that relate to the kinds of inquiries sought: primary sources such as historical documents and official records, secondary sources such as scholarly journal articles, survey research, statistical analysis and model-building. Hall (1992: 99) argued that 'emphasis should be placed on the allocation of resources for events and the manner in which interests influence this process, particularly through the interaction of power, values, interests, place, and the processes of capital accumulation'. Research by Hiller (2000a) provided a look at the politics of event bidding, namely the people and organizations backing Cape Town's campaign to win the Olympics. Events, given their image-making potential, present attractive opportunities for propagandizing and blatant political messages. At its worst, this can lead to manipulation or control over media coverage – either to hide some elements or to highlight others. Event boycotts have occasionally been used as political tools, especially at the Olympics. The use of 'boosterism' by politicians to achieve political goals via events is examined by Roth and Frank (2000).

Law

Governments at all levels pass a multitude of laws, each of which is enforceable by the police or other formal action. Laws either forbid actions or mandate them. They govern how persons and organizations interact, and what happens in cases of violations and disputes. There is a vast legal system for law making and law enforcement, including layers of courts, the law profession and law enforcers (see Table 4.4). A central tenet of democratic societies is 'the rule of law', in which 'justice' is based on law and the courts rather than arbitrary decisions. This is all supposed to prevent abuses and protect 'fundamental rights', but of course all these concepts are value laden and change from one country to another as illustrated in Events in Focus 4.2.

Events operate within political and legal systems that at once facilitate, constrain and hold accountable the people and organizations producing them. What events can be held, and what activities allowed, is a legal matter. Every event producer understands the need for obeying laws, satisfying the regulatory agencies, involving the police in security matters and obtaining the advice of lawyers when it comes to contracts, risk assessment and many other technical matters. Event-producing organizations need to be legally sanctioned or incorporated. Taxes have to be paid and audits filed. One source is Becker (2006), *The Essential Legal Guide to Events*. However, the legal system and the laws it creates and enforces are different in every country.

Table 4.4 Law

Law	Nature and meanings; the event experience	Antecedents to attending events	Planning and producing events	Outcomes and the impacted	Processes and patterns
The legal system, including legislators, courts and police Specific laws and regulations	Events as real and implicit contracts Event experiences shaped by social/legal differences	Perception of legal implications as a factor in the decision to travel or attend events	Laws and regulations pertaining to event production Legal considerations for event management	Interpretations of justice Legal recourse for loss or injury at events	Changing laws and regulations; accountability

EVENTS IN FOCUS

4.2 The political impacts of hosting the 2010 Commonwealth Games, Delhi, India

Stephen J. Page and Joanne Connell (2014)

In October 2010, Delhi in India hosted the Commonwealth Games (CWG) amidst a public focus on the poor state of the preparation of the infrastructure prior to hosting the event. A very insightful and detailed report by the organization Equations (2010) published in the lead up to the CWG identified the history of the Games' approval process and the public policy environment associated with the event. It highlighted the major public subsidies which the event has required as costs spiralled out of control, and as media reports suggest it rose to over £ 3.8 billion (or may even rise higher as some estimates suggest) which is 114 times the original cost budgeted for in 2002. This is a huge cost for a country which has extremes of wealth and poverty. Up to 2007, Equations (2010) pointed to 300,000 people evicted and displaced to create the space for the Games, while it was predicted that demand for prostitution during the event would rise. The government restricted the number of street vendor licences available in 2010 to try and reduce the visual impact of street traders for visitors. Equations (2010) pointed to comparative data for other mega events where 720,000 people were forcibly evicted to make way for the 1988 Seoul Olympics, 1.25 million in Beijing and 30,000 in Atlanta due to the process of gentrification. Equations (2010) argued that the development of Games infrastructure and projects did not follow established environmental impact assessment guidelines, noting the huge impacts on natural resources of hosting the Games (i.e. in terms of demand for water and power, sewage discharge and solid waste management). These issues are not simply issues for developing countries, as subsequent studies of Olympic Games persistently highlight the displacement of poorer people to accommodate venues and development as illustrated most recently with Scotland hosting the Commonwealth Games discussed in Chapter 3.

Justice

'Distributive justice' is a principle that applies to economic development and impact assessment, raising the question of who benefits and who pays?, and within welfare geography it adds the additional concept of territorial justice whereby who benefits and pays has the added dimension of who is affected, where and why (see Pavoni 2018). The issue of distributive justice is illustrated in Events Focus 4.2, concerning the Commonwealth Games. 'Legal justice' is another concept altogether, and is tied closely to constitutions and the courts. If something goes wrong, can the aggrieved party find justice?

Legal considerations influencing demand, experiences and meanings

Do people assess legal liabilities and risks when making decisions to attend events? They should, given all the things that can and do go wrong, which are often followed by police action or lawsuits. As events exist within a legal environment, does this actually shape the experience or meanings attached to them? For example, attending a protest certainly carries with it some expectation of confrontation, possibly even civil disobedience. Going to a party and engaging in some form of elicit behaviour (drugs, drinking, sex) absolutely places the participant and others in a potentially dangerous situation. Even the most ordinary event experiences like attending a concert, convention or exhibition entail some form of risk, some degree of legal constraints on one's behaviour, and moral if not legal obligations in the case of emergencies. How do guests, consumers and participants feel about these issues? Although advice is readily available on risk management and contracts for event management, little research has been undertaken on the legal side of events. There is a need to examine event organizations and the law, the marketing functions from a legal perspective, and the event experience as impacted by all the stakeholders' perceptions of liability. It has to be asked if the fear of litigation is seriously altering the practice of event management and the range of event experiences available. Certainly it can be observed that many forms of organizational and individual risk taking are declining. However, compliance with the growing range of legal requirements in many countries around accessibility, diversity and equality mean that statutory measures now have to be built into the hosting of events in these countries, as illustrated in Chapter 3.

History

Superficially, history is about dates and chronologies, but historical facts are only the starting point. According to the American Historical Association (www.historians.org), history studies the human condition and social change. The ability to assess evidence, and to assess conflicting interpretations, is essential to what historians do. Because historians are usually researching a topic or theme, and often from a disciplinary perspective, it is common to speak of 'historical geography', 'historical sociology', etc. All of the disciplines we talk about in this book can be studied through the lens of historical fact-finding and interpretation (see Table 4.5).

Historiography

Who chronicles the evolution and determines the importance of events through history, and on what evidence? Historical method is often focused on finding and understanding documents, determining their veracity, comparing the information with other sources and interpreting the meanings. There are standard issues concerning the accuracy of documents or witness testimony, the perceptual abilities of observers, the possibility of bias or outright lies. A search for the truth, or at least a consensus on what happened and why, is at the heart of much historical research. Many historians write about historical 'facts', whereas others are concerned with how history is researched and interpreted – these people are 'historiographers'.

Table 4.5 History

History	Nature and meanings; the event experience	Antecedents to attending events	Planning and producing events	Outcomes and the impacted	Processes and patterns
Documentation and analysis of human evolution and historic events Historiography evaluates historical evidence and interpretations	Importance of events through history Changing meanings attached to events Changes in how people experience events	Historical patterns and trends in demand for, and consumption of events Changes in why people attend and what they want from events	Evolution and life cycle of events Changes in the supply of events and event types Changes in planning and designing events	Historical evidence of impacts Analysis of long-term impacts	History of specific events and of event types Evolution of planned events in different cultures History reflected in, and commemorated through, planned events

To appreciate why events are a key area of research, we need to try to understand the different elements that combine to shape how people consume events – from a business activity through to their much wider use in leisure time. Cross (1993: 2) argued that:

> *to understand when and why leisure behaviour took major changes of course ... since the 16th century ... Perhaps the greatest problem is that historians have seldom shown much interest in the question of explaining people's use of free time ... In recent years, social history has frequently filled the gap left ... social historians have explored those private sides of history, family, community, and work that had been so long neglected; and they have increasingly linked these social spheres to popular culture, much of which is leisure.*

This quote highlights the importance of neglect by historians, as well as the link to popular culture, in which events are firmly anchored as they have played a key role in the evolution of society.

In any historical overview of events, two underlying themes are important: continuity and change. Continuity means that leisure has continued to be an important process, which remained influential in the pursuits of certain social classes. Change on the other hand characterizes the evolution of events through the ages, since events are a dynamic ever-changing phenomenon. Much of this change is based upon the interaction between the demand for, and supply of event opportunities through time.

In this sense we can speak of both the history of planned events and the historiography of writing about event history. Indeed, there has been much criticism about historical analysis. Post-modernists and critical theorists often argue that too much history has been written by and for elites, from a dominant positivistic perspective, often ignoring or devaluing minority groups, the exploited or losers of wars. If we get history wrong, then our contemporary values and attitudes might also be wrong. Consequently, there has been a shift in thinking within social history and its development as a field of inquiry so that the voices of minority or hidden groups get heard and documented where evidence exists. One important development from the mid-1970s was the emergence of oral history and the recording of historical experiences amongst such groups, so they were not lost. An example of the historical analysis of an event can be seen in the Events in Focus 4.3 – The Great Exhibition of 1851.

EVENTS IN FOCUS

4.3 The 1851 Great Exhibition: event studies in a microcosm

McDowell and Skillen (2016) highlight the lack of historical research on events and the importance of archival research in reconstructing historical analyses of events. Much of the research activity has arisen from sports and leisure researchers where historical analysis and interpretation has a long tradition with specific journals that focus on the area (e.g. the Journal of Sport History). Yet a critique of mega events such as the 1851 Great Exhibition demonstrates that many of the current themes which researchers are pursuing as areas of study can be discerned in the hosting of historical events. Many varying interpretations exist around the hosting of the Great Exhibition as a grand spectacle that showcased the state of technology and the state of capitalism (Purbrick 2001). However, as Davis (1999) argued, the genealogy of major exhibitions in Europe can be traced to the Middle Ages and trade fairs and markets which were focused on selling goods. Such exhibitions in the Victorian period, as Davis (1999) argued, were a result of a philosophical position in European society that education was a means of personal advancement and an essential route to developing both people and society as illustrated by some of the creations of literary and scientific societies such as the Royal Society. The Great Exhibition was a major trade exhibition which had an educational element in which technological developments were on display (see Hunt 1851 for a list of the 100,000 exhibits and 13,737 exhibitors) and promoted technological inventions and innovations from companies across the globe, especially the British Empire (Gold 2004). This tradition of trade exhibitions was very much an eighteenth-century innovation in European capitals with several sponsored by the state prior to the UK's decision to host the Great Exhibition. The Great Exhibition is credited with 'marking a definite advance into the contemporary age of industrial society' (Short 1966: 193).

The event was a global spectacle akin to the interest now shown in modern Olympic Games and it also marked the development of mass travel by train to visit the Exhibition with companies such as Thomas Cook providing their services on organized excursions such as from York to London (Plate 4.1). The planning of the event and depositions made to a Royal Commission (see https://www.royalcommission1851.org/) outlines the purpose of the Exhibition to 'increase the means of industrial education and extend the influence of science and art upon productive industry' which was housed in Paxton's Crystal Palace built in Hyde Park for the duration of the Exhibition. As the Royal Commission hearings found in 1849, residents of the Belgravia and Kensington area of London were opposed to such a scheme due to the perceived impact on property prices and potential increase in crime, issues which can often be seen in communities' opposition to hosting major events. The Lord Chancellor attempted to get the event cancelled or at least moved from central London, to no avail. Evidence used to support this challenge was derived from experience of fairs and mass gatherings in London as outlined in Charles Dickens' *Sketches by Boz* (see Dickens 1995), where the Greenwich fair was described as 'three days of fever' with raucous behaviour as Leapman (2001) illustrated. More sinister concerns were also raised about having a large public gathering after the experience of 'the mob' (Mullan 2001) and riots in other European capital cities in 1848 (Hobsbawm 2010) and the resulting revolutions that occurred. In London, concerns were also raised about the activism of the Chartist movement (Walvin 1984; Walton 1999) and there were wider concerns about the behaviour and likely actions of the working classes when the event was staged (Short 1966). Despite opposition, the event was held between May

Plate 4.1 Great Exhibition poster

and October 1851 and it hosted 6556 overseas exhibits and 7381 British exhibits which were oversubscribed. The event posed a challenge for event management and the logistics of hosting such large numbers of visitors. For example, daily attendance at the event was over 10,000 visitors which rose to over 200,000 when reduced priced tickets of a Shilling (5p) were offered (Leapman 2001). Many of the common complaints around event attendance were noted in the newspapers of the time including the food and beverages available, mischarging by unscrupulous taxi drivers along with the need for crowd management measures by the police such as bringing in a one-way system for queuing and traffic. Caricatures by the magazine *Punch* highlighted the juxtaposition of the expensive entry prices at the outset of the Exhibition of one pound which were then reduced to a shilling whereby the affluent and less affluent classes mixed under the cartoon heading of 'Whoever thought of meeting you here'. HMSO (1981) noted the social mixing which occurred at the Exhibition, evidenced in their compilation of statistics of attendance from the event. These statistics were also published in popular newspapers of the time such as Weekly Dispatch with its painstaking analysis of visitation on a daily, weekly and monthly basis which were graphically represented (see Anon 1852). The Exhibition received over 6 million visitors, with £775,776 being generated from season ticket holders, £1042 from £1 entries, £245,389 from 5 shilling entries, £579,574 from 2s 6d entries and £4,439,428 from the 1 shilling entries. The greatest number of admissions was 93,224 towards the end of the Exhibition, on 7th October 1851, when ticket prices were reduced. Here the Victorian managers of the event understood the significance of yield management and the event was managed by 350–400 police officers on a daily basis. Overall, the event was seen as a positive economic success, with the building costing £335,742 and receipts from entry of £552,174 generating a surplus of £186,437 which was a significant achievement given the lack of experience of hosting a major event of this scale. From the analysis of the archival sources and contemporary accounts of the event, there are numerous opportunities to apply the approaches and methods of analysis used by different disciplines and approaches to event studies. It is clear from this brief discussion that many of the diverse issues which researchers examine in contemporary events are not new – what is new is the perspective and analysis which is now being applied to understand these issues which illustrate a degree of continuity and change through time.

A historical interpretation of events in America

In his book *The Image: A Guide to Pseudo-Events in America* (1961: 79), historian Daniel Boorstin opened a lasting debate about events and authenticity by claiming that life in America was full of 'pseudo-events'. They are staged, scripted and counterfeit – just like many celebrities and tourism products:

> *The modern American tourist now fills his experience with pseudo-events. He has come to expect both more strangeness and more familiarity than the world naturally offers. He has come to believe that he can have a lifetime of adventure in two weeks and all the thrills of risking his life without any real risk at all.*

According to Boorstin, a pseudo-event is:

- not spontaneous; it comes about because someone has planned or incited it;

- planned primarily, but not always exclusively, for the purpose of being reported or reproduced, and its occurrence is arranged for the convenience of the reporting or reproducing media;

- ambiguous in terms of its relation to the underlying reality of the situation; whether it is 'real' or not is less important than its newsworthiness and ability to gain favourable attention;

- usually intended to be a self-fulfilling prophecy (in terms of public relations, if we produce an event to show that something is good, we expect that the claim will be accepted).

And why are they so popular? Boorstin suggested the pseudo-event is appealing because it is scripted and dramatic, includes a cast of interesting characters, and produces iconic images such as impassioned crowds, hugging families or rainstorms of patriotic balloons. It is designed to be reassuring, create the illusion that we who watch it are 'informed', and it leads to an endless number of other pseudo-events.

Boorstin particularly criticized public relations professionals, and they remain sensitive to the issue of manipulation through pseudo-events. Journalists are rightly concerned about pseudo-events, fearing they are being manipulated and that their reporting of a staged event actually makes a falsehood appear to be true. Judith Clarke observed this problem in an article entitled 'How journalists judge the "reality" of an international "pseudo-event": A study of correspondents who covered the final withdrawal of Vietnamese troops from Cambodia in 1989' (Clarke 2003: 50). She said:

> As proxy information-gatherers for their audiences, journalists often cover 'pseudo-events', whose purpose is to present to the world a version of reality set up by the organizers. These are usually people with links to wealth and power but they can also be out-groups trying to get their 'real' news noticed. For reporters the challenge is whether to cover these events at face value or delve deeper to find the truth.

History through the lens of planned events

Many people remember history through the lens of events, both news and planned events. A history of the world (or any corner or aspect of it) has to include major planned and spontaneous events, particularly social history. Wars might or might not be planned, but victory celebrations and remembrance commemorations certainly are. A simple listing of dates and events is one way that people remember the flow of history. Some of those events just happened, others were planned. Increasingly, it seems that planned events are more central to our recollection and interpretation of history and geography.

Planned events now seem to occupy more space and time in the media, they enjoy a larger element of our attention, and they seem to have more impact on how we perceive ourselves and our place in the world. Whilst we do not want to discount the significance of wars and natural disasters, after a while – unless we were personally affected – they all seem to blur. But our memories of personal involvement in special events, of the big celebrations and shows we see on television, of the landmark meetings we went to – of the world getting together for 'The Games' or a Millennial party – those seem to endure.

There are good reasons why planned events mark and give meaning to history. First, we need to relate more to accomplishments and good times than to disasters and conflicts. Who really wants to remember death and destruction when it constantly repeats? We grow weary of it. Those desiring to keep alive the memory of dark parts of history have to go to great lengths to create historical places and events, even giving rise to what has been called 'dark tourism' (Lennon and Foley 2000).

And there is a diversity and creativity to planned events that signifies invention, rebirth, exploration, and other great triumphs of the human spirit. They help us to transcend our personal lives, to become fulfilled. Ordinary news hardly ever does that, and when we do feel satisfaction from a news story, how often is a story derived from or about a planned event? Think of sports, the arts, education, trade – all require events to generate news.

Several examples can be cited to show the range of historical interpretations that are being placed on events and their place in society and culture. Kachun's (2003) book *Festivals of Freedom, 1808–1915* examined the development of African-American freedom festivals following the abolition of slavery. This period of celebration marked an important process of adaptation and formation of an African-American consciousness. Johnsen (2009) focused on cultural heritage tourism in southern Norway, specifically maritime history, through the lens of two festivals. The researcher believed that recent growth in this form of tourism and celebration reflects the community's response to 'economic deprivation' (a relative term), population decrease and industrial decline.

Life-cycle research

The evolution and 'life cycle' of events is an important historical topic with management implications. Every consumer 'product', including events, has a life cycle. A life cycle is not fully predictable, nor is the model deterministic. Stages in the life cycle are not always clear, but events do have a birth, they grow and mature, and many die or require rejuvenation. This temporal aspect of events, and factors shaping the life cycle, have been studied by several researchers (Getz and Frisby 1988; Getz 1993a, 2000a; Frisby and Getz 1989; Walle 1994) (also see the discussion on organizational ecology).

Sofield and Li (1998) examined an 800-year-old festival in China from a historical perspective and showed how politics and tourism influenced its transformation in recent years. Despite the changes, the researchers believed it retained its cultural authenticity. Sofield and Sivan (2003) showed how Hong Kong's famous Dragon Boat Races had shifted from culture to sports tourism in their orientation, with tourism helping to preserve the tradition. For an account of the history of a category of event in its cultural context, see Brewster *et al.* (2009) on the Highland Games.

Beverland *et al.* (2001) compared the organization and evolution of several New Zealand wine festivals, concluding that all of them had changed in terms of organizational structure, programme, strategy or consumers, and indeed each stage had been marked by crises. In fact this seems to be an emerging theme, that sustainable events learn and adapt from crises, and that they have to rejuvenate themselves to avoid decline. In Chapter 9, more attention is given to sustainability and the institutionalization of events.

A history of event producers and managers

Many people share our fascination with reading about events in ancient history. What's more, many of the forms and styles of planned events have continued uninterrupted through thousands of years! But there is one question apparently few have asked: who planned and produced these ancient events? Were they revered and rich professionals? Did any historian record their stories? What can we learn from them?

The ancient Romans, although fond of their events, were contemptuous of slaves, prostitutes, actors and the procurers of gladiators. So perhaps the job of event producer was reviled, even while the rich sponsors were elevated in society by their largesse. Nevertheless they had a big job, and it must also have been dangerous. Consider the shows in which ferocious wild animals were turned loose on captives, or slaughtered; or the miniaturized sea battles requiring artificial lakes. Disasters were reported, such as crazed elephants rampaging through the crowd, and the collapse of temporary wooden seating. Standards were set for safety. And hooliganism was also known, with parochial rivalries among spectators resulting in riots, so much so that games had to be cancelled. It all sounds so familiar. (There are many websites devoted to ancient Roman and Greek games, such as www.roman-empire.net.)

The greatest parade ever?

What is amazing about the Grand Procession of Ptolemy II Philadelphus is not just its scale, but the familiarity of many of its elements to modern observers of parades and festivals (Rice 1983). The historian/travel writer Athanaeus described the great tent decorated with elaborate care, then details of the parade which was full of religious symbolism and spectacle. Elements of modern parades were in evidence, including floats, numerous animals, soldiers and cavalry. One notable feature was the dispensation of free wine to the onlookers! Some historians believe the motivation for the grand procession was political, in order to legitimize the regime (http://ancientcelebration.blogspot.ca/2011/04/grand-procession-of-ptolemy.html).

There is an apt expression in French: *'plus ça change, plus c'est la même chose'* ('the more things change, the more they stay the same'). It certainly appears to apply to the world of events as highlighted above in terms of the twin points of focus on continuity and change in the history of events. Their forms, and many of their meanings, have endured in most civilizations for thousands of years. Their historical analysis has also been the focus of several seminal studies in human geography (e.g. Allix 1922 and the geography of fairs, and Zelinsky's 1994 analysis of conventions in the USA and changes since the 1960s) to which our attention now turns.

Human geography

According to Hall and Page (2014: 149):

> *The study of geography has a long and rich history in the social sciences and its hallmark features are its concern with place, space and the environment. Its distinctive contribution to these three elements (and geography of course does not have a monopoly on their analysis) is the way in which the synergies are examined focusing on the spatial elements (i.e. locational issues of where, why and more importantly who and what) exist in relation to human and physical phenomenon.*

In the study of events, the predominant focus is from human geography with the focus on people and their activities (see Table 4.6) although there is also a role for physical geography, with the growing interest in environmental sustainability and the impact of hosting events on the natural environment and in resource use such as our carbon footprint and climate change.

Geographical analysis can be linked directly to any of the other social sciences, and what is particularly relevant to the study of events can be described as economic/developmental, cultural/social, historical, political or behavioural geography. Geographical analysis can also be applied to almost any form of human endeavour or particular environment, so that we can also speak of urban and rural geography, or event geography. Links to physical geography, or the environmental sciences, are always present. And a feminist or welfarist/Marxist perspective can be taken on geographic studies, as epitomized in studies published in the journal *Antipode*.

Table 4.6 Human geography

Human geography	Nature and meanings; the event experience	Antecedents to attending events	Planning and producing events	Outcomes and the impacted	Processes and patterns
Studies human-resource interactions, especially spatial and temporal patterns of human activity and including impacts on the environment	Linking events to resources, culture and human activity (e.g. harvest festivals; seasonality factors) Interaction with the event environment and sense-making	Demand linked to distance and accessibility The influence of religion and culture across regions	Event settings Locational analysis	Environmental impacts analysed spatially	Spatial/temporal patterns (rural distribution; growth of events as part of urban renewal schemes)

Among the key event themes geographers analyse are:

- Events as spatial phenomena (i.e. they are not permanent landscape features and so they are a transient event, such as carnival).
- How places are transformed by events, particularly the role of scale in event analysis.
- Critical debates on event – place – space relationships such as who gets what, where? Why and when? Who can access? Who is excluded? As Hall and Page (2014: 149) observed, these critical debates 'focus on consumption (as well as the production) of event related phenomena as a critical issue was already well established in the geographical analysis of tourism by the 1980s, especially with respect to the role of mega-events as spectacles of consumption'.

Behavioural geography draws mostly on psychology and focuses on the cognitive processes underlying spatial reasoning, decision-making and behaviour (see Table 4.6). Topics of relevance to events include 'wayfinding' (how people move around, including the development of new technologies such as GPS tracking research – see Pettersson and Zillinger 2011), the construction of 'cognitive maps' (our mental maps of places like event sites), 'place attachment' (our emotional connections to communities), the development of attitudes about space and place, and decisions and behaviour based on imperfect knowledge of one's environment. There is clearly a close connection to 'environmental psychology', as discussed in Chapter 3.

Historical geography studies geographical patterns through time, such as the evolving distribution of events in a region as well as their growing attraction in scale and time. How people interact with their environment creates 'cultural landscapes', and this can include a variety of resource-based, place-specific events given the growth in research within cultural geography informed by the cultural turn which connects the discipline to developments across other areas of social science. Similarly other developments such as the 'new economic geography', with its focus on globalization, have a key role to play in understanding how events have become global phenomena and part of the pursuit of cultural infrastructure as regions compete for inward investment to redevelop former industrial economies in a post-modern world.

Economic geography is the study of the location, distribution and spatial organization of economic activities. Questions asked might include: do economic 'laws' determine resource use, settlement patterns or the distribution and evolution of events? What unique, local or national political and cultural forces shape event formation, sustainability and density?

Development geography is a related field of inquiry, focusing on various factors that shape economic and social development, or population and demographics focused on less developed and developing countries.

Welfare geography is also closely related, as highlighted in Chapter 3 and earlier in this chapter. Why are some people disadvantaged, and what does this have to do with resource use, urban form, or the distribution and nature of planned events? Welfare geographers tend to be 'critical' in their methodologies.

Cultural geography looks at the relationships between environment and culture. For example, it is clear that cultures are shaped by the places in which they developed, featuring climate and resources, and by trade and other external contacts, related to politics, accessibility and evolving communications. Cultural tourism is closely linked, especially in terms of assessing the distribution of cultural attractions or resources, consideration of cultural regions and place identity or distinctiveness.

Spatial and temporal patterns of events

The spatial and temporal distribution of events is clearly a topic for geographers with the focus on space, place and time. Event distribution patterns are at least partially dependent on the natural resource base, such as those themed or derived from agricultural products or other primary economic activities like mining. But the pattern of events in the landscape has been changing dramatically in response to powerful forces such as globalization and their use for political purposes. Specifically, the resource base of events has shifted away from natural resources and they are now created strategically.

Janiskee's many contributions to the geography of events deserve special recognition. For example, Janiskee (1980) examined the themes, locations, timing, programme of activities, reported attendance and benefits of rural festivals in South Carolina. In Janiskee's (1991) paper, he looked more carefully at festival history in the state, including when festivals were established, and their spatial distribution over time. Janiskee (1994) documented how his 'Fest List' database was compiled from various published sources and interviews and presented an analysis of growth in festival numbers. He saw clearly in graphical format an almost exponential growth rate, with exploding numbers of new events after 1970. In his (1996) study he examined the monthly and seasonal patterns of community festivals in the USA, making it clear that their numbers are relatively low in winter, late autumn and early spring. Although regional patterns are different, across the country a huge number occurs on the July 4 weekend. In the conclusions to this paper he raised the issue of saturation, and asked how many festivals can be held at any one time. It has been observed by other authors that growth in event numbers, and their concentration in certain areas or times of the year, could result in event failure (Jones 1993; Richards 1996). Most contemporary festivals are held in summer or fair-weather months (also see Ryan *et al.* 1998, regarding New Zealand events), although it should be stressed that other types of events, like business meetings and conventions, peak in the spring and autumn and some sport events are most frequent in winter. Cultural factors and traditions help keep certain seasons dominant for specific types of events, but many are now being created specifically to overcome the traditional seasonality pattern of tourism. One study of event tourism seasonality was undertaken by Yoon *et al.* (2000), who examined the event market in Michigan. Wicks and Fesenmaier (1995) found summer to be the most popular for travelling to events in the US Midwest, with autumn being the next most popular.

Event tourism: the geographical perspective

Supply–demand interactions are fertile ground for event geographers and the most recent review of the field is provided by Hall and Page (2014), who review many of the themes we have discussed so far. Analysis and forecasting of demand for a particular event or a region's events will in part depend on population distribution, competition and intervening opportunities.

Bohlin (2000) used a traditional tool of geographers, the 'distance-decay function', to examine festival-related travel in Sweden. He found that attendance decreased with distance, although recurring and well-established events have greater 'drawing power'. Getz (1991) illustrated several models of potential event tourism patterns in a region. One option is clustering events in service centres, as opposed to dispersing them over a large, rural area. These are related to the concept of 'attractiveness' and also have implications for the distribution of benefits and costs.

Analysis of the zones of influence of events has been undertaken by Teigland (1996) specific to the Lillehammer (Norway) Winter Olympics, and this method has implications for event planning, especially regarding mega events with multiple venues. The elements of these zones of influence are the gateways, venue locations, tourist flows, transport management and displacement of other activities.

Connell and Page (2005) modelled the spatial impacts of the World Medical Games hosted in Stirling, illustrating the spatial distribution of business impacts; as those researchers noted, the city centre locations benefited disproportionately compared with outlying districts, despite many of the venues being located outside of the city centre. This illustrates the importance of seeking to match demand with the available infrastructure and facilities when decisions are made to host events. In policy terms, two main outcomes were sought from this event: first, to showcase the ability of the city to host an event and thereby develop its role as an event location, and second, to assess the extent to which the wider Stirling region and its tourism sector could benefit from such activities led by the public sector. This theme of evaluating impacts in time and space was developed further by Tyrrell and Johnston (2014).

Event attractiveness

Arising from numerous event visitor studies, it can be concluded that most events rely on local and regional (day-trip) visitors, not long-distance tourists. Even world's fairs and Olympics must sell most of their tickets to residents. The concept of tourist 'attractiveness' must therefore be assessed for each event. How powerful an attraction is the event for various target segments? Who will travel and stay overnight?

Lee and Crompton (2003) assessed the drawing power of three events located in Ocean City, New Jersey. Three festivals in one city in one year (held in May, late September and November–January) were compared in terms of the number of tourists attracted specifically because of the event, and the distances travelled (i.e. the 'market areas'). All three proved to be valuable in drawing tourists (41–55 per cent of attendance) and generating economic benefits, although attendance was much higher at the September event. McKercher *et al.* (2006) considered the tourist attractiveness of festivals in Hong Kong, concluding that only a few people would travel for them, but they generated general image and cultural value.

Hierarchies of event places could be determined through analysis of existing events and event venues, leading to implications for place marketing. Improved measurement of the spatial distribution of event tourist activities and spending will aid in forecasting event impacts, as will studies of 'time switching' and 'displacement'. Analysis of event patterns in time and space is essential to gaining a better understanding of event trends and potential competition. One technique deserving wider application was used by Verhoven *et al.* (1998). Their 'demand mapping' enabled them to examine patterns of travel to festivals.

Time switching and displacement

There is no doubt that people alter their travel plans because of events. For example, they are going to a certain destination for business or pleasure anyway, but decide to time their visit with an event because it provides additional value to the trip. This 'time switching' is an important limitation in estimating the economic impact of events, because the spending of time-switchers cannot be attributed as a benefit of the event itself (Dwyer *et al.* 2000a, 2000b). Switching is more likely to occur in major cities and resorts that have considerable drawing power all year round, as opposed to small towns and rural areas where an event might be the only reason for people to make the trip. Accordingly, economic and image-related impacts of events can be expected to be greater in smaller population centres.

Another theoretical and methodological concern when conducting impact evaluations is the matter of 'displacement'. Regular tourists can be displaced when events take up available accommodation, and it is therefore often counter-productive to hold major events in the peak tourist season. For example, Hultkrantz (1998) was able to demonstrate that the World Championship of Athletics held in Gothenburg, Sweden in 1995 had the effect of displacing as many expected tourists as were attracted by the event, resulting in no gain in tourist volumes. Of course, it is possible that event tourists generate greater economic impact owing to their spending patterns, and there is also the publicity value to consider. Major events also motivate people to travel to one place as opposed to another, so that during the World's Fair (Expo) in Vancouver, Canada (1986) normal travel patterns were disrupted – Vancouver and British Columbia gained, but the rest of Canada lost traffic (Lee 1987). The spatial distribution of costs and benefits is of particular interest in event geography, and so too are issues of social equity. Two very specific geographic questions are those of defining the region for which economic benefits are to be estimated, and measuring the spatial distribution of spending by visitors.

Economic geography and central place theory

This classic construct of economic geography – central place theory – has largely been ignored in the field of event studies. Basically it postulates that settlements emerge in a hierarchical pattern, with many small ones and few large ones. The larger settlements provide higher-order services. Consequently, events will tend to locate in the larger centres, with a central location, if they have good transport access and infrastructure. As Terzi *et al.* (2013) found, conference planners give a great deal of credence to such locational issues. Modern reality, of course, is quite different from the original, rural-based model, but there remains some basic truth in the differentiation of settlements by their ability to host tourists. Daniels (2007) applied central place theory to a sport event, finding that the economic benefits were quite different in the two adjacent counties that were co-hosts. The larger population centre received most of the economic benefits because it was able to accommodate the service requirements of visitors. An important implication is that smaller towns have a tougher time generating economic benefits from events. They will have to co-brand and cooperate with nearby cities.

Event places

In terms of theory building, a crucial question is the extent to which certain types of events are resource dependent or rooted in specific environments. The matter of authenticity should be explored more from a geographic point of view, such as addressing the issue of how – for example – a food festival can both emerge from and reinforce a distinct sense of place. While economic and environmental impacts of events and event tourism have been explored by many, there is still a need for attention to the process by which events help shape and define urban environments, particularly in the context of urban renewal, mega events and event venues. More attention should also be paid to explaining, rather than mapping, spatial and temporal variations in events. What are the relative contributions of resources, culture, policy and economics in accounting for patterns? All events require a venue (often specific facilities, but sometimes a street or open space), people to organize and manage them, customers to pay, and often sponsors to subsidize them. As communities and destinations become more competitive for tourism and investment, more economic resources are committed to events. So the nature and distribution of events is increasingly shaped by policy.

The study of event places has barely been addressed in the literature. Traditionally, many events have been associated with specific places that take on, at least temporarily, special cultural significance. Historically town squares and parks, even streets, have fulfilled this important civic function, but in recent decades the trend is to purpose-build festival and event places, including multipurpose sport and arts complexes, festival squares and parks, and waterfront facilities for community event programming. The results of these capital and social investments are special places that can be identified by their monuments, special-purpose buildings, attractive landscape and vistas, and frequent ceremonial use. They definitely attract visitors who view them as must-see, urban icons. Several authors have reported on the roles of events in urban renewal projects (Hughes 1993; Mules 1993), and it can be concluded that event programming and the creation of event places has become a necessary element in urban development.

What is the nature of an event place? Getz (2001) examined festival places, comparing a number in Europe and North America. A conceptual model was developed, but its testing and elaboration will require collaboration from the fields of environmental psychology, urban design, arts, event management and sociology. The model focuses on the interdependence of elements of setting (location and design), management systems (including the programme) and people. An important issue for researchers is to examine the interactions of event places with tourists and residents. The capacity of sites or communities to host events is an important topic in need of further research. While crowds often add to the appeal of events, how much is too much? One study (Wickham and Kerstetter 2000) examined the relationship between place attachment and perceptions of crowding in an event setting. Abbott and Geddie (2000) argued that effective crowd management techniques can reduce management's legal liability. At the site level, attention is frequently given to the spatial component in estimating event attendance, such as through aerial mapping of crowds (Raybould *et al.* 2000) or spatial stratification in sampling (Denton and Furse 1993).

Event clusters

Certain locations have competitive advantages when it comes to developing new experiences for tourists, such being the case in food and wine clusters. As detailed in the book *Foodies and Food Tourism* (Getz *et al.* 2014), events play a critical role in branding clusters and in providing opportunities for direct visitor–supplier interaction. Cluster development involves the geographic concentration of attractions and services, and it can evolve naturally, based on unique terroir and pioneering entrepreneurship or through a concerted effort to establish more of them. Related to wine and food, this clustering process entails building the value chain to include tourist consumption and (hopefully) resulting exports. Even though seaports with fishing fleets and agricultural areas with unique produce have some advantages, from a demand-side point of view, it can be said that there is much more potential within cities, resorts and other places where visitors naturally concentrate. That is why some cities hold successful food and wine events of international renown. These principles have been widely used in the design and development of visitor attraction complexes, where a major attractor will underpin destination development and the hosting of events adds further vitality and interest alongside the flagship attraction project that is designed to act as a draw card for visitation. This embodies many of the principles of human geography on achieving agglomerative benefits from the spatial concentration of visitors and events at key accessible locations. Bathelt and Spigel (2012) illustrated the agglomeration benefits achieved at American trade fairs as relational events which brought producers, users, suppliers and businesses together to form and renew partnerships which are vital to business success.

Geographical methods applied to events

People often associate geography with mapping, but this is only one method of examining human interactions with their environments. Technological advances have made it possible to discover individual and micro-level interactions, as illustrated in Research Note 4.5. Other studies, such as Ristea *et al.* (2018) and the analysis of crime during hockey game days illustrated the relationship between sporting events and crime in time and space.

4.5 RESEARCH NOTE ON GEOGRAPHICAL ANALYSIS OF EVENT VISITORS

Pettersson, R. and Zillinger, M. (2011). Time and space in event behaviour: Tracking visitors by GPS. *Tourism Geographies*, 13(1), 1–20.

'Research on tourist mobility in combination with the tourists' experiences has been rare to date. Previous studies focusing on the activities of tourists in time and space have most often used the method of time–space diaries. However, an important flaw in this method is that these recordings depend on the respondents' personal observations and notes. This disadvantage is avoided by using Global Positioning Systems (GPS) devices, which record their carriers' movements directly, thus replacing personal notes. This new method was used to study the time–space movements of visitors during the Biathlon World Championships 2008 in Östersund, Sweden. In addition to the GPS devices, questionnaires were used to study the tourists' movements and experiences. In trying to combine methods to support the event analysis, the aim of the study is to evaluate the practicability of GPS devices during an outdoor sports event. Movements and experiences in time and space are studied. In order to answer questions regarding the visitors' movements on a macro-level, these methods were combined with bird's-eye view photographs taken of the race arena every minute.'

Future studies

Human fascination with the future is at least equal to our curiosity about the past. Visioning and goal-setting is totally future oriented. When we talk about planning events, we are actually seeking to shape the future. General research enables us to say more about probable future conditions, while marketing research gives us greater confidence that our plans will succeed. It is no wonder, then, that 'futurism' and 'future studies' have become so popular.

Future studies (Table 4.7) is not prophecy, as in predicting the future, nor is it science fiction in terms of letting one's imagination run wild. It is an interdisciplinary approach to gaining understanding of how today's conditions and trends will likely shape the future (in part, it is therefore impact forecasting), and how future conditions could be shaped by policies and actions taken (or not taken) today – as in how we need to reduce greenhouse gas emissions to avoid the worst effects of global warming. Trend analysis, forecasting, environmental and future scanning and scenario making are tools of future studies.

The future is a social construct

The future is by definition unknown, and somewhat unpredictable. Even the ways in which we think about it, and the language we use, is a social construct. To some, 'the future' is full of science-fiction images, to others it is the great unknown, and for entrepreneurs it is opportunity.

We incorporate the future into our daily lives when we say things like: 'it's a good investment' (i.e. I will be richer in a few years), or 'I will wait for the price to come down' (technological innovations are always

Table 4.7 Future studies

Future studies	Nature and meanings; the event experience	Antecedents to attending events	Planning and producing events	Outcomes and the impacted	Processes and patterns
Future thinking (can we know or shape the future?) Trend analysis Environmental and future scanning Forecasting and scenario making	How we think about time affects our experiences and the meanings we attach to them	How do people plan for future events? Will virtual reality replace live event experiences?	Environmental and future scanning applied to the event sector	Predicting event impacts Future scenarios (likely and desired future states)	Changes in how we think about time and the future What do we envisage about the future of events?

expensive at first, then consumers see the price fall rapidly). Indeed, because technological progress is so fast, and most innovations have already been predicted (or pre-sold through exhibitions and TV programmes), we are no longer surprised by the next innovation – we are only surprised that it is not yet cheap to purchase! In other words, the future is already imagined and partially consumed.

The future is becoming an obsession, and this has direct policy implications. Politicians promise not just a better future, but actual deliverables. We begin to take for granted that it will get better, not worse, and that what has been promised will become reality. One of the key research methodologies employed in future research is scenario planning.

Futures Research Methodology

A generic source on future studies is Futures Research Methodology Version 3.0, edited by Jerome C. Glenn and Theodore J. Gordon (http://millennium-project.org/millennium/FRM-V3.html). A detailed review of such techniques and their use in tourism can be found in Page *et al.* (2010).

Trend analysis and extrapolation

A basic method is trend analysis and extrapolation, in order to demonstrate what will likely happen if current forces and trends continue. This is a useful starting point for discussions about the future. A related issue is to separate fast-paced, but short-lived fads adopted by specific groups from slow-growth but persistent trends that affect whole societies. According to the article on future studies in Wikipedia, there are three major types of trend. 'Mega trends' extend over many generations, consisting of complex interactions between many factors (e.g. major social trends such as the growth and globalization of event tourism). 'Potential trends' are possible new trends arising from innovations, projects, beliefs or actions that have the potential to grow and eventually go mainstream. Somebody has to identify these in the early stages, and they might get it wrong.

Once a mega trend is identified, many 'branching' or interrelated trends can be detected and evaluated. For example, the whole event tourism trend has many niche-market trends spinning off, including marathon running, food and wine events, etc. One can then look at trends in the market segments for each type of event, such as gender-based, linked to levels of involvement, or destination choices.

Delphi

This method has traditionally been a technique aimed at building consensus about an opinion or future conditions. Multiple rounds of surveying are typically required, both to identify trends and possible future consequences, and to assign probabilities and consider implications. As expert panels are usually recruited for Delphi, it is also a way to create new knowledge, or at least to synthesize the knowledge and opinions from many experts.

Ideally, through multiple rounds, the weight of evidence leads to a consensus or at least a dominant evaluation of what is likely to happen and its consequences. Enduring minority views are also of interest, as they describe alternative scenarios that might have to be taken into account by planners.

Its use in the events sector has been limited, but Carlsen *et al.* (2000) employed Delphi to examine event evaluation practice and needs, while Weber and Ladkin (2005) used the expert panel to identify and assess trends affecting the convention industry.

Scenario making

We can imagine the future in one of two ways. In the first we ask 'what might happen, and how can we prepare for it?' This approach includes the options of combating or opposing trends that lead to undesirable future states. It involves working backwards from a predicted or alternative future state. In the second approach, we ask 'how can we ensure the future that we desire?' This approach leads to strategies and actions intended to shape the future to our liking, such as policies and events that will achieve desired social or economic impacts. All future scenarios begin with an understanding of history, current forces and conditions, and trends. Scenarios emerge from understanding, not dreaming. The more you know about the world of events, the better you will be at scenario-making and strategic planning.

According to Page *et al.* (2010: 123), 'scenario planning is a process that provides the organisation with the capability to think about the future and provides it with the skills needed to manoeuvre the organisation and, over time, to create change'. De Geus (1988) called this 'Adaptive Organisational Learning', where the organization 'creates a capability to understand, create and manage change that leads to competitive advantage'. As Chatterjee and Gordon (2006: 255) suggest:

> *In scenario planning the aim is to develop distinctive depictions of the future. Alternative scenarios are developed from the present situation for a desired time horizon. In a scenario planning exercise a number of driving forces will be identified. By making different assumptions about these driving forces or key influences, different 'stories' are formulated about how these interact. The scenarios are effectively those issues.*

As Page *et al.* (2010) suggest, scenario planning has a rich history dating to the 1960s. According to Ling (1998), within scenario planning there are a range of hard to soft techniques used in research, each having a variety of objectives ranging from intuitive and learning outcomes for the organization, focused on ambiguity, with softer techniques, through to more analytical techniques aiming for certainty. The softer techniques typically incorporate the following: informed fiction writing, behavioural simulation and scenarios (which are predominantly qualitative, embrace uncertainty, clarify risk, and enable organizational adaptive understanding). Harder techniques range from economic modelling and forecasting with a focus on certainty in the future, with quantitative precision and the use of single point projections.

Main themes in events-related futures

Specifically related to events, the book to consult is *The Future of Events and Festivals* (2014) edited by Ian Yeoman *et al.* The editors explain that some of the chapters are in the nature of predictions, and that making explanatory claims about the future must be based on knowledge and expertise (Yeoman *et al.* 2014: 4). Others are 'what-if' scenarios, which lead to questions on how to attain this future, or prevent it from happening. In the conclusions to the book, Yeoman *et al.* develop a set of cognitive maps to capture core concepts from the various authors' contributions. They conclude that three future views are predominant, focusing on consumer values and identity, political reasons and power, and the role of technology. Figure 4.3 is adapted from Yeoman *et al.* (2014) in order to illustrate the main themes and perhaps give ideas to students and researchers for futures research in event studies.

Global challenges

In the periodical *The Futurist* (May–June 2011) two futurists (Halal and Marien) provided four scenarios and two perspectives on what they called the Global MegaCrisis. A number of trends are depicted as leading to the crisis, including global climate change leading to food and water shortages, and a lack of political willpower to deal with the causes. They foresaw a general economic worsening, in part owing to institutional failures (i.e. the global financial crisis). Other threats include terrorism and cyber attacks and weapons of mass destruction. Making use of some expert input they evaluated the perceived severity of the threats and then developed four scenarios ranging from pessimistic to optimistic. While these futurists believed there would be severe challenges and problems facing the planet, eventually they thought a new order would emerge – one based on global information technology and artificial intelligence.

Figure 4.3 Themes associated with the analysis of event futures

Source: Developed from Yeoman *et al.* (2014).

An influential futures perspective is the report *2013–14 State of the Future* by Jerome C. Glenn *et al.*, published by the Millennium Project (http://millennium-project.org/millennium/201314SOF.html). The '15 Global Challenges' as defined through a Delphi panel approach and tracked since 1997 by the Millennium Project are a springboard for thinking about event-specific challenges. For each of the following, readers are invited to develop at least one event-specific research topic:

1 *How can sustainable development be achieved for all while addressing global climate change?*

2 *How can everyone have sufficient clean water without conflict?*

3 *How can population growth and resources be brought into balance?*

4 *How can genuine democracy emerge from authoritarian regimes?*

5 *How can decision-making be enhanced by integrating improved global foresight during unprecedented accelerating change?*

6 *How can the global convergence of information and communications technologies work for everyone?*

7 *How can ethical market economies be encouraged to help reduce the gap between rich and poor?*

8 *How can the threat of new and re-emerging diseases and immune micro-organisms be reduced?*

9 *How can education make humanity more intelligent, knowledgeable, and wise enough to address its global challenges?*

10 *How can shared values and new security strategies reduce ethnic conflicts, terrorism, and the use of weapons of mass destruction?*

11   *How can the changing status of women help improve the human condition?*

12   *How can transnational organized crime networks be stopped from becoming more powerful and sophisticated global enterprises?*

13   *How can growing energy demands be met safely and efficiently?*

14   *How can scientific and technological breakthroughs be accelerated to improve the human condition?*

15   *How can ethical considerations become more routinely incorporated into global decisions?*

(http://millennium-project.org/millennium/challenges.html).

According to the Millennium Project, global challenges are interdependent and cannot be dealt with individually. Collaborative action is required, bringing together the efforts of governments, international organizations, corporations, universities, non-governmental bodies (NGOs) and creative individuals.

STUDY GUIDE

Each discipline has been discussed because of its existing and potential contributions to event studies, and students should be able to demonstrate applications from economics, management, political science, law, history, human geography and future studies. Find major themes running through this book that connect the discipline-based theory to management issues, event design, public policy-making and event tourism. For example, economic theory connects both to event pricing and justifications for governments to support and bid on events.

STUDY QUESTIONS

- What is meant by economic demand for events? How is it measured?
- Explain how rational choice theory fails to explain all decisions made regarding event demand.
- How does ideology shape event policy?
- What is power, and how does it affect decisions made about events?
- Why should policy-makers and tourism strategists be concerned with whole populations of events? What theory is applicable?
- Demonstrate how both stakeholder and network theory contribute to event management.
- How can an event become an institution? What are the implications?
- Discuss Boorstin's notions of 'pseudo-events' and authenticity.
- What themes and issues are explored in 'event geography'?
- Define the 'attractiveness' of events in geographic terms. How can it be measured?
- What research methods are used in future studies? How can they be used in strategic planning and policy-making?

FURTHER READING

Becker, D. (2006). *The Essential Legal Guide to Events: A Practical Handbook for Event Professionals and Their Advisers.* Self-published.

Dwyer, L., Forsyth, P. and Dwyer, W. (2010). *Tourism Economics and Policy.* Bristol: Channel View.

Foley, M., McGillivray, D. and McPherson, G. (2011). *Event Policy: From Theory to Strategy.* London: Routledge.

Hall, C. M. and Page, S. J. (2014). *The Geography of Tourism and Recreation: Environment, Place and Space* (4th edn). London: Routledge.

Merkel, U. (ed.) (2013). *Power, Politics and International Events: Socio-cultural Analyses of Festivals and Spectacles*. London: Routledge.

Page, S. J. (2019). *Tourism Management* (6th edn). London: Routledge.

Yeoman, I., Robertson, M., McMahon-Beattie, U., Backer, E. and Smith, K. (eds) (2014). *The Future of Events and Festivals*. London: Routledge.

Ziakas, V. (2013). *Event Portfolio Planning and Management: A Holistic Approach*. London: Routledge.

Chapter 5

The contribution of closely related professional fields to event studies

Upon completion of this chapter, students should know the following:

- why and how events are important in closely related professional fields;
- the theoretical and methodological contributions from other fields to event studies;
- common interests in the nature and design of event experiences.

Introduction

There are a number of closely related professional fields that involve, contribute to and can benefit from event studies. Although professionals in these fields might not call themselves 'event managers', the coordination, production or marketing of events is sometimes an important part of their work. Leisure studies is the most advanced in terms of developing its own interdisciplinary theory, and possibly has the most to contribute to event studies. Similarly, tourism and hospitality are also very closely related, especially because of the importance of planned events as 'products' or 'attractions' and in view of the consumption of events in the leisure time of tourists and non-tourists. This chapter also reviews some new and emerging fields of relevance, including visitor studies, in which events are one part of their scope.

Leisure studies

The history of leisure studies has been reviewed by Page and Connell (2010), with landmark studies identified in Page and Connell (2006). Its modern-day roots can be traced to the parks and recreation movement in North America in the mid-nineteenth century. Through the encouragement of Christian churches, wholesome and socially responsible activities such as outdoor recreation and camping, community sport and supervised children's play were encouraged in North America. This was achieved through the provision of public parks and open spaces, as well as recreation and sporting facilities to counteract idle activity, juvenile delinquency, drinking and gambling. It soon became apparent that the growth of parks and recreation services required professional training at the college and university level. In Europe, a different growth trajectory exists for leisure, which emerged from the early sociological investigations of the habits and behaviour of the population of urban industrial cities and their living conditions. The pursuit of different forms of leisure research informed by sociology continued from the early twentieth century into the growth of interest in the 1920s and 1930s as Page and Connell (2010) outlined. Subsequent development of the outdoor ethos towards recreation saw a significant boom in Europe in the early twentieth century, albeit constrained by the availability of leisure time.

In the USA, recreation and park management professionals are responsible for the provision and management of parks, recreation facilities, and leisure programmes and services. Their skill sets range from venue planning, management and marketing to community development and therapeutic recreation programming. Commercial recreation requires knowledge of business management and tourism. Hospitality services are often integrated in leisure facilities, and events are both users of these facilities and elements in leisure programming. Parks and recreation facilities and services are found within all levels of government, numerous not-for-profit organizations, educational and religious institutions, private clubs, the military and private corporations. Most towns and cities run sport facilities that host numerous events and parks that provide spaces for festivals and other public gatherings. Increasingly, they employ professional event managers to produce their own events, or event coordinators to oversee the events strategy and portfolio. Many are also explicitly involved in event tourism.

As Godbey and Shim (2008) and Page and Connell (2010) noted, leisure studies emerged from European sociology departments, with concern focused on free time within industrial societies. Early leisure scholars paid attention to work/leisure patterns and time use, and later they examined leisure and social class, suburbanization, impacts of technology, community life and the effects of work arrangements on leisure; these remain key themes in the twenty-first century. It was not long before academics from the newly emerging leisure and recreation field of study began to apply theory from the foundation disciplines to formulate and test possible theories within a social sciences framework. Indeed this theory building and testing continues apace as the example of Flinn and Frew (2014) illustrates, where they explore the interconnections between the experiential dimension of Glastonbury music festival, mystical and fantasy narratives and the political contestation of festivity, focusing on the narratives created through multi- and social media. Their theoretical analysis is underpinned by the theoretical developments around experience and the experience economy (see Chapter 6).

What is leisure?

Much debate occurs over how to define leisure (also reviewed in Page and Connell 2006, 2010). Figure 5.1 identifies some of the principal features to consider in seeking to understand what leisure is. Therefore, leisure is often conceptualized as a component of lifestyle. To some it is activity, free time, meaningful and satisfying experience, or combinations of these. Certainly we take it for granted that leisure is based on free time and free choice, so attending events for their 'intrinsic worth' is leisure (this is a social construction of both leisure and many types of event). When people attend events for 'extrinsic' reasons (i.e. compulsion, the requirements of work or of social obligation) that is not necessarily leisure; although we still want them to have a memorable and rewarding experience. Some of the principal approaches to leisure and events are outlined in Table 5.1.

Stockdale (1985) listed three approaches to leisure:

- as a period of time, or focused on an activity or a 'state of mind' in which choice is the dominant feature; therefore, leisure may be a form of free time for an individual;
- in an objective sense, where leisure is perceived as the opposite of work and so leisure time is construed as non-work or residual time (i.e. that time left after all of the normal obligations have been fulfilled);
- in a subjective manner, where leisure is viewed as a qualitative notion, so that leisure activities only take on a meaning in relation to the perceptions and belief systems of individuals, but these activities can occur at any time and in any context rather than being bound by time and work issues.

Herbert (1988) extended these three perspectives, arguing that leisure is related to the time an individual exercises choices and is able to undertake activities in a voluntary manner, free from other constraints.

Glyptis's (1981) concept of leisure lifestyles highlighted the key role of individual perceptions of leisure.

Consequently a range of key issues needs to be taken into account in defining leisure:

- the role of time;
- freedom from constraints or obligations;
- an individual's state of mind and perception of leisure;
- the significance of work and non-work (or for those with domestic responsibilities, the importance of the domestic routine) since Durant (1938: 31) recognized that the work ethic was the foundation of society, but 'Only when this division ceases, where leisure is complementary and not opposed to work' will the balance between leisure and work be better understood;
- the lifestyle of individuals.

Figure 5.1 Principles to consider in approaches to leisure

Source: Extracts from Page and Connell (2010: 11).

Neulinger's 'leisure paradigm' has been very influential in trying to identify the key elements of leisure. To Neulinger (1974), the defining criterion of leisure was 'perceived freedom'. That is, the individual must believe they have a choice in whatever they are doing, and they want to do it for its own reward. Neulinger developed a model in the form of a diagram consisting of four cells labelled 'pure job' (constrained and extrinsically motivated), 'pure work' (constrained but intrinsically motivated), 'leisure job' (freely chosen but extrinsically motivated) and 'pure leisure' (intrinsically motivated and freely chosen).

We all recognize that various constraints (i.e. barriers to leisure) always apply to our choices and actions, and that none of us is completely 'free' to do whatever we want, whenever we want. Chapter 4 also outlined the wider issues of barriers to accessibility and participation in events. As well, there are often combinations of intrinsic and extrinsic motivations for work and pleasure. So it is more appropriate to think of free versus constrained as a continuum, and intrinsic versus extrinsic motivation as not being diametrically opposed. 'Lifestyle' can be defined as a pattern of living, or as a set of values and actions reflecting personal preferences. There is no doubt that leisure and travel figure prominently in our lifestyle choices, to the point where we speak of the 'life of leisure' or say things like 'he is a globe-trotter, a jet-setter'.

How do we define our lifestyles? By our material possessions, but also by reference to:

- where we live (coastal, mountain, suburban, urban) and what that means for recreation and event opportunities;
- what we do (hobbies, interests, travel – all connected to special-interest events);
- whom we associate with (social networks, including events attended);
- our tastes and how we express them (art, music, food and wine, and the related events we attend).

Table 5.1 Parks and recreation management: leisure studies

	Nature and meanings; the event experience	Antecedents to attending events	Planning and producing events	Outcomes and the impacted	Processes and patterns
Parks management					
Parks managed for recreation, aesthetics and environmental protection	Communing with nature The outdoors experience as therapy	Parks are attractions and popular event settings Outdoor events have a special appeal	Planning for events as a park use Site planning	Impacts have to be evaluated across environmental, social and personal dimensions	Changing demand and political support for public parks Changes in resource availability and quality
Recreation management					
Public recreation Therapeutic (special needs) recreation	Events as fulfilling social and personal experiences Well-being and health from recreation	Recreation facilities are needed for certain types of events The facility as an attraction	Programming of recreation venues	Impacts on the person and society	Shifts in demand and political support for public recreation
Leisure studies					
Theories of play and leisure Intrinsic motivation Leisure constraints	Events yield leisure benefits Serious leisure Optimal arousal and flow Lifestyle meanings Leisure philosophy	Leisure motives for attending events Leisure constraints and negotiation Recreation specialization Ego involvement Commitment	Implication of theory for design and planning of programmes, venues and events	How to measure the benefits of leisure (e.g. health, self-fulfilment, social integration) Leisure careers	Leisure trends, fads

Two observations are important at this juncture because there has been a debate that in the post-war period, society in many Western countries changed and the transition to a consumer society led to the growth in leisure and consumptive lifestyles. The first major wave of growth in consumer spending in many Western countries after 1945 was in home ownership, then in car ownership, and then in accessing tourism and international travel. The impact of car ownership made people far more mobile and able to attend events and activities on a more spontaneous basis. As Page (2015) illustrates, many countries have also seen the amount of leisure time and paid holiday entitlement for their workers increase in the post-war period so that workers now have the opportunity to engage in the new forms of leisure consumption such as planned events. These changes have been described as being part of what has been termed the 'leisure society', a term coined in the 1970s by sociologists although long hours of work in many developed societies challenge whether this term ever really developed. One aspect of the leisure society marked by economies in developed countries has been a shift from a reliance upon manufacturing and production to new service-related employment, followed by an emphasis on experiences.

Page (2015) suggests that as society has passed from the stage of industrialization to one now described as post-industrial, where new technologies and ways of communicating and working have evolved, sociologists such as Baudrillard, in *The Consumer Society: Myths and Structures* (1998), have argued that we have moved to a society where work and production no longer dominate, having been replaced by leisure and consumption. Within wider notions of leisure, people are also seeking new forms of consumption that enable them to acquire cultural capital. As Page and Connell (2010) argue, the rise of technology, combined with the pursuit of cultural capital from visiting places and events, means that people are looking for more from their event experiences than simple enjoyment and entertainment at the point of consumption. They are looking for lasting memories and objects and tangible features, and these will be re-examined in Chapter 6 on issues around leisure experiences and the experience economy. Consequently, events have a more deep-meaning role in the consumptive activities of people than as passive spectators or participants. This marks a shift in the philosophical basis of leisure within society from the simple conception that it is non-work.

Leisure philosophy

Pieper (1952) and others were concerned that mere idleness should not be construed as leisure. In terms of Pieper's religion-grounded philosophy, true leisure consists of contemplative celebration, and festivals in his framework are of necessity spiritual in nature (that is, religious rituals). Some contemporaries stress that leisure exists as fun, pleasure or hedonism, including deviant and dangerous behaviour (Rojek 1995). More recently, Rojek (2005: 17) defined leisure as 'voluntary behaviour', with 'choice, freedom and voluntarism as the basic components in the narration of leisure'. Rojek's interpretation is based on how people speak of their voluntary behaviour, which can include work. Within a discourse on power and civil society, Rojek argued for leisure as a positive component in the life of 'active citizens'.

If one defines leisure as being more than just free time, or voluntary behaviour, then it tends to become a value-laden or ideological construct. Many people believe leisure has to be socially acceptable behaviour, that is, healthy and renewing of body and spirit. Others think that the very concept of leisure ties in to capitalist ideals and crass consumerism, reflecting who has power and money in society. Historically, as analysed by Veblen (1899), only certain social classes (being coercive or exploitive) had leisure, or could live a life of leisure, and they engaged in conspicuous consumption (materialism) and conspicuous leisure (wasting time). Critics rightly point out that who has leisure, and what they can do with it, is still highly differentiated within societies and between economies.

A prevailing philosophical position is that recreation and leisure are basic human needs (after Maslow 1968), thereby justifying public leisure services. Concomitantly, leisure generates numerous benefits for individuals that lead to broader societal benefits. The Academy of Leisure Sciences (White Paper No. 7) categorizes these benefits as: economic; physiological; environmental; psychological; and social. In recent years a great deal more attention has been given to the links between leisure, physical activity and health. Associated with the work of Driver (see Driver *et al.* 1991), benefits-based management stresses the provision of services that deliver the benefits desired by consumers. Certainly benefits exist in marketing terms, as consumers are obviously willing to pay for many tangible and experiential benefits, but are there not also benefits that justify public investment and subsidies? Is this philosophy transferable to event studies? Can we in fact talk legitimately about event services? Or is that merely another element in leisure? There is no doubt that in many jurisdictions, events are viewed as legitimate 'public goods' in their own right, especially when it comes to cultural celebrations. Amateur sports are often assigned the same status, primarily for health reasons. Business events, however, tend to be viewed narrowly as part of economic development and tourism.

Ultimately it boils down to people with belief and commitment. First, ask yourself why you believe it is important to produce or support festivals and events. Is it something that should be debated in public and worked into public policy through political processes? Where will support come from – the business community, arts and cultural groups, neighbourhood committees, other social services? Do people have a right to public celebration and to a choice in attending events for business and pleasure? What is likely to happen, in line with leisure services, is that some events will be judged to be public goods and others will be considered private, that is, left to the free market. The balance will vary from place to place, and evolve over time (see Table 5.2).

Leisure experience

Experience is a fundamental concept in leisure. According to Mannell and Kleiber (1997: 11): 'Success is based on structuring the leisure environment in such a way as to create or encourage predictably satisfying experiences ... it has become apparent that an understanding of the psychological or experiential nature of leisure must be developed.' What a person perceives, feels, learns or remembers – in a word, his or her experience – is often inferred from behaviour. Mannell and Kleiber also suggested that we have to examine experience through the interplay of internal psychological dispositions (e.g. perceptions, feelings, emotions, beliefs, attitudes, needs, personality characteristics) and situational influences that are part of an individual's social environment (e.g. other people, group norms, human artefacts and media). As Kleiber (1999) argues, leisure can provide a basis for self-expression and potentially improve the human condition, particularly where the needs and barriers are addressed, and so it is potentially enabling for individuals.

To study leisure experiences, researchers have looked at what people are doing (the behavioural or 'conative' dimension), moods, emotions and feelings (the 'affective' or evaluative components), and thoughts and images (the 'cognitive' component). Related studies also focus on concentration, focus of attention and absorption, self-consciousness, self-awareness and ego-loss, sense of competence, sense of freedom, arousal, activation and relaxation, intensity and duration. More work has been undertaken on emotions than on cognition.

'Optimal experiences' are states of high psychological involvement or absorption in activities or settings. For example, Maslow's (1968) notion of the 'peak experience' ('moments of highest happiness and fulfilment') and Csikszentmihalyi's (1975) 'flow' ('the best moments of people's lives') occur 'when a person's body or mind is stretched to its limits in a voluntary effort to accomplish something difficult and worthwhile' (Csikszentmihalyi 1990: 3). Is this equivalent to the vernacular expression 'being in the zone'? Can it not apply equally to work or any other challenging or rewarding experience?

Table 5.2 Meanings and philosophies of leisure applied to event studies

What is leisure?	Selected applications in event studies
Leisure as freedom from work, enabling contemplation and the arts without ulterior purpose; leisure as philosophy, the pursuit of understanding (de Grazia 1962)	Most planned events fall within a broad definition of leisure experiences; many events are in the business/economic realm but organizers still want attendees to have enjoyable experiences
Free time/non-work (Neulinger 1974)	Extrinsic motivators appear to apply to many events, yet attendees still usually retain the right to decline to attend
Freely chosen activity/intrinsically motivated pursuits (Kelly 1987)	Events directed at learning and aesthetic appreciation fit the Greek philosophy
Leisure as voluntary behaviour (Rojek 2005)	
Leisure as contemplation and spiritualism (Pieper 1952)	This philosophy applies to religious events and pilgrimages, and to sacred rites and rituals within many events
Play (Huizinga 1955; Ellis 1973)	Play and hedonism are essential in carnival and festivity
Hedonism, fun and pleasure (Rojek 1995)	Play is essential to events based on games and competition
	Playfulness as an expected state of mind at many events
	Numerous entertainment and consumption events (e.g. food and wine) cater to hedonism
Lifestyle 'Conspicuous leisure/consumption', or a lifestyle of leisure by an exploitive social class (Veblen 1899)	Events can become central to serious leisure lifestyles (involvement; commitment; specialization) leading to event travel careers
	Attendance at events as a status symbol
	Prestigious events advocated and sponsored by the elite
Leisure as experience (pleasurable, satisfactory, memorable, transforming)	A phenomenological approach to understanding planned event experiences
	Experiential sampling and other methods to understand planned events and their meanings
	Events in the experience economy
	Experience design applied to events

Much of the 1960s research in outdoor recreation still has a significant bearing on the notion of leisure and travel as experience. The Clawson and Knetsch (1966) model (Figure 5.2) suggests the leisure experience is a largely social psychological construct that involves the following elements: anticipation, the experience on site and value derived from the experience.

This led Page and Connell (2010) to summarize the main focus of leisure researchers where the experience concept has generated the following three germane areas of study:

- *The form of the leisure experience, particularly the activity undertaken or where it is undertaken (the setting)*

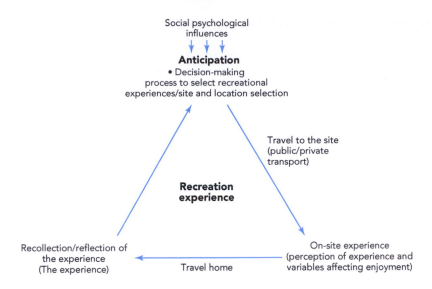

Figure 5.2 The Clawson five-phase model of the recreation experience

Source: Pigram (1983) in Page and Connell (2010: 175). Reprinted from *Outdoor Recreation Management*, J. Pigram and J. Jenkins, Routledge (1983).

- *The immediate experience of leisure at the place of consumption, which is evaluated at the time of experience and during the actual participation of leisure*
- *The experience of leisure after the event, to ask people to reflect on the experience.*

(Page and Connell 2010: 173)

More recently, researchers have begun to refer to the leisure experience as multidimensional in nature and characterized by the variety of experiences that can occur. For example, Lee *et al.* (1994) referred to the transitory, dynamic and complex nature of leisure experiences. To most people, leisure is seen as a mixture of pleasurable (sometimes unpleasurable) experiences that are generally characterized by feelings of fun, enjoyment and relaxation. As a result of the application of social psychological theory, leisure and event researchers are now more heavily focused on studying the feelings, attitudes and motivations of people's leisure and event behaviour, rather than concentrating purely on participation rates or future leisure or event trends. In other words, the variety, frequency and quality of the 'experience' has become more important to study as a measure of overall life satisfaction rather than the actual type of leisure or event that a person participates in (Smith and Godbey 1991).

Applied to the study of planned events, there is an obvious first question to ask: do events provide leisure experiences? There is definitely an assumption made within event management and event tourism that most events exist to provide leisure experiences, in the form of entertainment, hedonism, celebration, games (including sport), cultural performances and self-development (including learning and aesthetic appreciation). These are believed by event designers to be in the leisure realm. Events that are primarily business related add the above-mentioned leisure elements to their programmes in order to make them more appealing or memorable. Working with tourism authorities, conventions and exhibitions often add tours and other add-on experiences to the event package to build in attractive leisure components to enhance the delegate experience.

Event researchers have increasingly focused on the experience of participants. Agrusa *et al.* (2008) studied runners in the Honolulu Marathon in 2006 and concluded that they valued the 'experience'; they also had a significant economic impact on the state of Hawaii's economy. First-time competitors placed a greater value 'on the experience' of participating and spent more than repeat runners; as well, the Honolulu Marathon satisfied their sensation-seeking personality trait. However, this declined with repeated exposure. Atkinson (2008) examined how triathletes learned to physically manage, socially perform and individually reflect upon the endurance sport of triathlon as a leisure experience. They found that triathletes come together as a mutually recognized 'pain community' of like-minded actors, who learn to relish the physical and mental suffering from the sport. Atkinson (2008) discussed how they ritually punish their bodies in triathlon races which can induce a 'liminal' state for many participants. The triathlon as a planned event was described as physiologically exhilarating and novel for most competitors at first, and it became even more exciting when the triathletes started to push their body harder and longer. Group runs, rides and swims were seen as social occasions where these athletes could inflict further suffering on their bodies.

Leisure over one's life (the life-stage approach)

Overall, leisure participation decreases with age, and we can assume (in the absence of any specific evidence) that this also applies in general to attending and travelling to planned events as part of leisure. There are bound to be exceptions, however, and these will be worth studying. Do retired people suddenly attend more social events? How does the life cycle relate to the concepts of 'involvement', 'serious leisure' and 'travel careers'? Leisure researchers have also noticed that people's interest in variety or change also varies over a lifetime, with experimentalism (novelty-seeking and trying things out) being strongest in youth. The social environment is changing rapidly as we mature, and young people are flexible in adapting to changes. Iso-Ahola *et al.* (1994) found that 'the tendency to seek novelty through new leisure activities declines with advancing life stages, whereas the tendency to maintain stability through old and familiar activities increases with life stages'.

Leisure careers and leisure socialization

Roberts (2006: 156) argued that 'The best predictor of any individual's future uses of leisure is the same person's last behaviour.' People are conservative, and become more so as they age. We tend to stick to routines, and we take fewer risks. It is therefore useful to longitudinally examine leisure careers, and this relates to other concepts like serious leisure, recreation specialization and involvement. Early involvement in the arts, particularly within the family socialization context, explains lifelong involvement with 'high culture' (Roberts 2006: 157). It is unlikely that adults will show interest in opera or ballet if they were not socialized into these interests early in their lives. But early participation in sports does not necessarily lead to lifelong sport careers. It is much easier for committed people to stay involved with sports than to restart after a lapse.

Self-determination theory

Deci and Ryan (1985) proposed this theory to explain how intrinsic motivation works. Intrinsically motivated behaviour occurs in the absence of any apparent external reward and when people have free choice. The activities, or events, are chosen out of interest in those events. The resulting experiences are optimally challenging and result in flow. Intrinsically motivated behaviour is based on the innate psychological need for competence, relatedness (love and meaningful social connections) and self-determination.

Self-construal (see also self-concept)

Self-construal refers to an individual's sense of self in relation to others (Markus and Kitayama 1991). In collectivist cultures people tend to be more interdependent, whereas in more individualistic cultures they tend to be more independent. Self-construal is believed to affect cognition, emotion and motivation. Walker, Deng and Dieser (2005) argued that cultural differences must be taken into account when theorizing about intrinsic versus extrinsic motivation and the nature of free choice and leisure. Asian and other cultures with interdependent self-construals assign greater value to belonging and maintaining harmony, as opposed to individualism. Relatedness might be more important than autonomy and free choice, so that the basic assumption that leisure is based on free choice seems to be a 'Western' construct. These cultural differences should be considered when designing events, in communicating their benefits, and when considering event impacts on individuals and communities. Benefits to persons and groups have to be evaluated separately. In fact Gabrenya and Hwang (1996) observed that in Chinese culture, annual festivals and spectator sports facilitate social interaction outside normal social hierarchies and networks, thereby releasing people from usual constraints on behaviour.

Leisure constraints

Leisure researchers and theorists (e.g. Jackson *et al.* 1993; Jackson 2005) want to know why people participate, and what prevents them from doing what they want to do. Generic categories of constraints have been identified, including the intrapersonal (one's perceptions and attitudes), interpersonal (such as a lack of leisure partners) and structural (time, money, supply and accessibility). How people negotiate through constraints is an important issue. These are examined in more detail in the Antecedents chapter (Chapter 8) and have remained a major area of leisure research to date, as they can determine the level of involvement and engagement in leisure.

Leisure involvement

Based on psychological theory, Havitz and Dimanche (1999: 123) defined leisure involvement as 'an unobservable state of motivation, arousal or interest toward a recreational activity or associated product'. With regard to leisure, travel and lifestyle pursuits, it has been confirmed that people's preferences, behaviour and satisfaction are affected by their level of involvement with products and pursuits. How one actually becomes involved is another question, and is more difficult to answer. Many researchers utilize the Zaichkowsky uni-dimensional 'Personal Involvement Inventory Scale', but Kyle and Chick (2002) suggested that there is a general consensus that leisure involvement is best conceptualized as a multidimensional construct with the following dimensions being most important:

1 'Attraction': perceived importance or interest in an activity or product, and the pleasure derived from doing or consuming it (for example, running offers certain benefits, but what is the additional pleasure derived from participating in a marathon?).
2 'Sign': unspoken elements that the activity or product consumption conveys about the person (such as the prestige associated with certain events).
3 'Centrality' to lifestyle: referring to both social contexts and the role of the activity or product in the person's lifestyle (people who are highly involved in the arts will demonstrate quite different levels of interest in certain art events, and will look for different benefits from their attendance).

Risk is sometimes included in involvement scales, such as those employed by Getz and McConnell (2011) to test participants' level of involvement with mountain biking. The risk element deals with the fact that highly involved event tourists place a higher value on well-run events because they invest so much of themselves (and their money and time) in making event and travel decisions. They really hate it when events are poorly run, and this presumably applies to the risks associated with any of their decisions. To someone less involved, the risk of a bad experience might be the same, but not the psychological consequences. Kyle *et al.* (2007) later revised their scale to give much greater emphasis to the social aspects of 'enduring leisure involvement'; their new scale included dimensions of attraction, centrality, social bonding, identity expression and identity affirmation. Identifying with a social world is thereby linked to involvement, as well as finding one's identity, or re-affirming it through leisure and travel pursuits.

An application of involvement theory to travel and events can be found in Ryan and Trauer (2005). They studied a major participant-based, multi-sport event, for which they believe location was a secondary consideration for sport tourists. Masters Games attract a large core of sport 'enthusiasts' who invest heavily in their athletic pursuits – including travel – and also those who only participate at the local level. Ryan and Trauer talked about a 'career' that leads from local to international competitions. 'It can be hypothesized that participants form a degree of involvement with games participation that in part is a confirmation of self-identity as an exponent of a particular sport' (Ryan and Trauer 2005: 179). The highly involved participants who are willing to travel may be critical for the success of events.

Involvement was the core concept employed in a major study of 'foodies' and their food-tourism behaviour and preferences (Getz *et al.* 2014). That research demonstrated the critical importance of event attendance in defining the highly involved foodie, and thereby revealing the necessity for employing a range of events in attracting food tourists. The most highly involved, those whose personal and social identities were significantly linked to food, attended the most food-related events and preferred the most specialized, hands-on event experiences. While all foodies tend to enjoy food festivals, and food at other events like ethnic and multicultural festivals, it is the highly involved foodies who are most likely to seek out experiences that connect them to each other (i.e. communitas), to experts (the chefs are important) and to learning about food and its cultural heritage.

Recreation specialization

Bryan (1977: 175) described specialization as 'a continuum of behaviour from the general to the particular, reflected by equipment and skills used in the sport, and activity setting preferences'. As experience in an activity increases, it is theorized that people will progress from more general to specialized behaviour and related patterns of consumption. Their identification with the activity will also change. Characteristic styles of participation emerge, so that beginners can often be easily distinguished from the more experienced participants. The theory has been applied to many activities, and to comparison of participants in terms of their motivation, setting preferences, involvement, attitudes towards management and the use of information. It is clearly related to the concepts of ego-involvement, commitment and serious leisure. Burr and Scott (2004) argued that the recreational specialization framework could be applied to understanding visitors to the Great Salt Lake Bird Festival. They used a random visitor intercept and a mail-back survey, and site visits to observe the festival. Specialization (in 'birding') of those attending this festival was measured in terms of their behaviour, commitment and level of skill. Only a small fraction was found to be highly specialized or serious about bird watching, and these people were less satisfied with the event – which suggests the need for careful segmentation. Most visitors seemed to have an interest in birds, but they combined that interest with other leisure pursuits and enjoyed the general festival programming. To the organizers, this also helped them meet their aims of increasing awareness and improved conservation efforts. The authors suggested that specialization can be usefully applied to other types of events to increase understanding of motives and behaviour.

Commitment and serious leisure

'Commitment' is a social-psychological construct, used to explain consistent behaviour. In the context of leisure it has been defined by Kim *et al.* (1997: 323) as 'those personal and behavioural mechanisms that bind individuals to consistent patterns of leisure behaviour'. Those authors sought to explore commitment in terms of dedication, inner conviction, centrality, costs and social considerations. Becker (1960) used the term 'side bets' to describe what would be lost if an individual discontinued something he or she was committed to, such as loss of friendships, personal investments of time and money, as well as consideration of the absence of alternatives. Kim *et al.* (1997) determined that commitment (conceptualized as centrality to lifestyle) and social-psychological involvement scales were highly interrelated among a sample of birdwatchers, and that behavioural measures of involvement were more useful in predicting behaviour. According to these same researchers, involvement is likely an antecedent of commitment and might be at the root of 'serious leisure'.

Stebbins's concept of 'serious leisure' (1982, 1992, 2001, 2006) appears to be closely related to commitment and involvement constructs. Serious leisure is (1992: 53):

> *the steady pursuit of an amateur, hobbyist, or career volunteer activity that captivates its participants with its complexity and many challenges. It is profound, long-lasting, and invariably based on substantial skill, knowledge, or experience, if not on a combination of these three.*

It is like pursuing a career, but without remuneration. Serious leisure participants 'typically become members of a vast social world, a complex mosaic of groups, events, networks, organizations, and social relationships'. The rewards of serious leisure include 'fulfilling one's human potential, expressing one's skills and knowledge, having cherished experiences, and developing a valued identity'. According to Stebbins, characteristics of serious leisure include:

- perseverance (learning to overcome constraints);
- developing a career (includes stages of achievement or reward; may be assisted by experts; may include a progression of events leading towards the highest level of participation);
- significant personal effort is required (acquiring knowledge and skills; travel);
- durable benefits as outcomes (e.g. self-fulfilment, enhancement of self-concept, self-esteem; social identity);
- an ethos associated with the social world (common interests and inter-communications related to the 'social object' of interest to the group, such as sport, art, wine);
- social identification with the activity (a subculture).

Shipway and Jones (2008) adopted an 'insider's' perspective on experiences at the 2007 Flora London Marathon (FLM) using the concepts of serious leisure and social identification to explore the experiences of 'serious' participants travelling to take part in this event. An ethnographic research design was utilized using a combination of interviews, observation and participant observation. Data collection commenced four months prior to the marathon and involved monitoring the experiences of participants, all of whom viewed their activity as a 'serious leisure' pursuit. This was followed up with a number of semi-structured interviews with participants in the two-week period after the event. The key finding was the strength of identification that participants had with the activity of running. The salience of this identity was heightened by the act of travel to, and residence in, London both before and after the marathon. A number of themes emerged from the data that were seen as consequences of this sense of identification, these being the unique ethos, language and behaviours of participants, the need for significant personal effort to complete the event, the perseverance of participants in the activity, both in terms of training and competing, the durable benefits obtained by the runners through participation, and the 'career structure' associated with distance running. Participants also followed behaviours prescribed by a particular prototype associated with the running subculture, resulting in homogeneity of dress, behaviour and values among the group.

Mackellar's (2013a) *Event Audiences and Expectations* presents a model called the 'event audience spectrum' (Mackellar 2013a: 70), which is a form of benefit segmentation based on increasing levels of interest, commitment, knowledge and skills. This continuum owes its foundations to Stebbins and to the work of Brotherton and Himmetoğlu (1997); it starts with 'socializers' and progresses through 'dabblers' to 'enthusiasts' and 'fanatics'. Her SERPA model, for 'serious participation at events' (MacKellar 2013a: 77) combines elements of social-identity motivation with various psychological factors, including personal identity and commitment, that help explain serious participation in events and event-related travel. This model connects well with the foodies and food-tourism findings of Getz *et al.* (2014) and can form the basis of special-interest segmentation and the development and marketing of iconic events targeted at the highly involved.

Research methodologies and methods in leisure studies

The North American approach to the leisure studies field, in common with social psychology in general, has been largely positivist and quantitative, but there has been growing interest in values, beliefs, and the application of theory to practical social problems and policy issues (Mannell and Kleiber 1997: 27). This is in direct contrast to the European tradition that has been more theoretical and conceptual, and informed by sociology. Leisure researchers in North America have frequently used large-scale surveys, experiments and time diaries to observe and measure leisure quantitatively and to develop or test theories. More qualitative and interpretive methods include participant observation and unstructured interviews, case studies and introspection.

Researchers can observe experience by asking people what is on their minds. A full understanding of behaviour can only be obtained when we know what it means to the person – which is phenomenology. 'Experiential sampling' (Csikszentmihalyi and Csikszentmihalyi 1988) is the related method used in leisure studies, and we will revisit it later in this book.

At the nexus of leisure and event studies, Patterson and Getz (2013) conclude that leisure studies has a great influence on event studies, as both fields are focused on experience and related meanings from multiple perspectives, including personal and societal. Event managers might also do well to adapt the notion of leisure philosophy and leisure services to the planning and delivery of events, with an emphasis on benefits sought and realized. However, they argued that within leisure studies, the planned event will undoubtedly remain a minor concern, one of many activities or 'experiencescapes' worthy of consideration by leisure policy-makers and parks/recreation practitioners.

Tourism studies

Tourism has evolved as a subset of leisure and it developed into a distinctive field of study in the 1970s and 1980s – initially in Europe and North America – but it is now emerging globally. Tourism is often studied as an industry, alongside hospitality, with related educational programmes stressing professional career preparation. But, like leisure and events, academics also want to study tourism as a social, cultural and economic phenomenon, and to consider all its potential impacts. Tourism, like leisure, has a major stake in planned events and has evolved along similar lines from a management orientation to a full-fledged field of studies with its own advanced degrees. When defining tourism, scholars tend to separate the industry-oriented approach from the broader 'tourism studies' approach that relies on multi- and interdisciplinarity. However, the blurring of boundaries is illustrated in Figure 5.3, which sets out the interconnections between leisure, tourism and recreation.

Leiper (1981) argued that a multidisciplinary approach was an impediment to tourism education, and that what is needed is an interdisciplinary approach that integrates concepts from other disciplines and fields (also see Hall and Page 2010 on the wider contribution of Leiper to this debate). Tribe (1997), on the other hand, recommended that there is nothing to be gained by disciplinary status, and that tourism studies does not qualify. Rojek and Urry (1997) asked: where does tourism begin and leisure studies end?

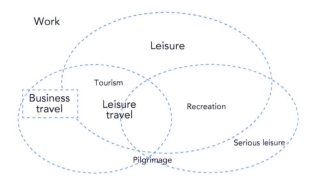

Figure 5.3 The relationships between leisure, recreation and tourism

Source: Hall and Page (2014). Reprinted from *The Geography of Tourism and Recreation* (4th edn). S. J. Page and C. M. Hall, Routledge (2014).

What is clear aside from these tautological propositions on what tourism and leisure are (see, for example, Hall and Page 2014 and Page and Connell 2010 on distinguishing between these areas) is that tourism has a clear role to play in event studies (Table 5.3).

Leisure and tourism studies clearly overlap if one views tourism as a social phenomenon taking place within leisure, and they overlap at the business and management level because numerous enterprises exist to deliver recreational/travel experiences; Figure 5.3 illustrates this interdependence. Event studies sits at the intersection (or nexus) of tourism, leisure and recreation, since it can occur within all of these areas, and some studies have lamented the decline of leisure studies as a subject, as event studies has taken centre stage (Spracklen 2014). Events can be viewed as a subset of this leisure/tourism interdependence illustrated in Figure 5.3, but neither leisure nor tourism studies deals centrally with the planning, design, experience and management of events within these interdependent areas. Rather, in tourism and leisure, events are treated as attractions, activities, or aspects of some larger tourism/leisure construct, such as business travel, pilgrimage or serious leisure as illustrated in Hassan and Sharma's (2018) examination of tourism and events in Asia.

Event tourism, the destination perspective

As with any niche market, or special-interest travel segment, we can define 'event tourism' from two perspectives – the consumer's and the destination's; a substantial review of the event-tourism field can be found in Getz (2008) and Getz and Page (2016). Here we look at event tourism as a destination strategy to develop and market events for their specific tourism and economic benefits. The five main roles played by events in tourism are discussed below.

Events as attractions

Although many tourism organizations stress international tourism, there is no doubt that most festivals and events are dependent on local and regional audiences. But whether events are true tourist attractions (i.e. motivating overnight or non-local travel), or a reason for visitors already in an area to stay longer, they can have tourism value. Events can also have the effect of keeping people and their money at home, rather than travelling outside the region. Event 'drawing power' or 'attractiveness' can be measured by how many tourists will be attracted, and how far or frequently they will travel. Important goals are to use events to overcome the seasonality problem, and to spread demand geographically throughout a country

Table 5.3 Tourism studies and event tourism

	Nature and meanings; the event experience	Antecedents to attending events	Planning and producing events	Outcomes and the impacted	Processes and patterns
Tourism studies					
The study of travel and the tourist experience, and of the tourism industry					
Event tourism					
Travel related to planned events Destination development and marketing through events	The overall event travel experience Tourism roles of events: attractions; place marketing; image creation; animators Iconic events for various social worlds Event travel career trajectories	General travel demand affects event travel demand Specific motivators for event tourism Media coverage and media events influence demand Increasing supply of tourist-oriented events	Marketing for event tourists Packaging Events produced primarily for tourists or destination image enhancement Destination event portfolios	Event tourism impacts Economic impacts and EIAs Cost and benefit evaluations	Event tourism trends (e.g. changing demand for long- or short-haul event trips)

or region. Destinations often classify events according to their drawing power, scale or tourism potential. Bos (1994) reported on classification in the Netherlands, and the Economic Planning Group and Lord Cultural Resources (1992) developed a system for the Canadian province of Ontario. Often these are intended to assist in funding decisions, but it is a practice that entails some difficult decisions. Is it current or potential attractiveness that should be the main criterion for receiving assistance? How are events of different types to be compared? Should peripheral locations receive special consideration?

Resources for event tourism consist of more than just events. An inventory of resources has to include organizations capable of producing events, companies that sponsor them, agencies to assist, all possible resources (human, financial, natural, political) and themes. One issue to consider is that cultural and environmental 'resources' are often in the public domain and anyone can 'exploit' them without compensation or regard to impacts. The 'law of the commons' applies here, as a community and its resources could become damaged by too many events, too much event tourism or by poorly managed events. This is a strong argument for public policy and regulation of events, encompassing the principles of resource stewardship and sustainability.

The goal should not be to maximize event tourism volumes, but to develop a manageable and balanced portfolio of events that meet multiple goals and generate many benefits as discussed in Chapter 4 (see Chapter 12 for more details too). An emphasis on event tourist quality, that is, attracting high-yield, dedicated event tourists, is preferred. Strategies employed in event tourism have not generally been evaluated for effectiveness. A substantial part of the event tourism business is bidding on events. This process has been described as a special-purpose marketplace by Getz (2004), who studied the event-bidding goals, methods and attributed success factors of Canadian DMOs. Bidding has also been studied by Emery (2001), Persson (2002), Westerbeek *et al.* (2002), Berridge (2010) and Foley *et al.* (2012). Lockstone-Binney *et al.* (2014) have extended this rather neglected line of research by focusing on the roles of ambassadors in the bidding process.

Other destination development strategies include starting (and sometimes owning) new events for tourism purposes, using events in theme years, cultivating and improving many local and regional events, developing one or more events into 'hallmark' status, and hosting the occasional mega event. An interesting example of developing events as attractions was studied by Brown (2010), examining the visiting friends and relatives (VFR) market in Cape Breton, Canada. The study examined how VFR tourists attended local festivals and events, with Brown concluding that it was an important tourist and event segment, and that marketing directly to residents (i.e. the local hosts) is the key.

Events as animators

Resorts, museums, historic districts, heritage sites, archaeological sites, markets and shopping centres, sports stadia, convention centres and theme parks all develop programmes of special events. Built attractions and facilities have everywhere realized the advantages of 'animation' – the process of programming interpretive features and/or special events which make the place come alive with sensory stimulation and appealing atmosphere.

The potential benefits of animation through events are of major importance to facility and attraction managers:

- to attract people who might otherwise not make a visit because they perceive the facility or attraction itself to be uninteresting;
- to encourage repeat visits by people who might otherwise think that one visit is enough;
- to attract publicity for the site or facility, including the highlighting of historical events associated with the site;
- to encourage longer stays and greater spending;
- to target groups for special functions.

Venues are almost automatically in the events business, out of necessity. Pearce (1998) examined how attractions in different countries were adding events and integrating with festivals and events in their marketing. Whitfield (2009) documented the rise of meetings and conventions seeking unusual venues, and how various attractions were adapting their facilities and marketing to cater to this planned-event market.

Events and place marketing: co-branding

Kotler *et al.* (1993) in *Marketing Places* identified the value of events in enhancing the image of communities and attracting tourists. They demonstrated how places compete for investments, quality people and tourists, all in pursuit of more liveable and prosperous communities. 'Place marketing' provides a framework within which events and event tourism find multiple roles, as image-makers, quality-of-life enhancers and tourist attractions. More traditional approaches to economic development stressed industrialization and the provision of physical rather than cultural infrastructure, and downplayed the economic value of tourism.

'Co-branding' between events and destinations is one strategy gaining popularity (Brown *et al.* 2001; Chalip and Costa 2006). Jago *et al.* (2002, 2003) argued that there was substantial potential for events to be used in destination branding but that neither event nor destination managers do a good job in harnessing that potential. The intent is to reinforce the destination's brand with compatible events, a transferral of positive images, with a classic case being surfing competitions in Surfers Paradise. This is because most destinations contain an array of events, largely beyond the control of the state, and for that reason it might be wise to focus on one or a few well-imaged 'hallmark events' to achieve place-marketing and branding goals.

Gibson and Davidson (2004) examined the application of place marketing through events, and related political debates, in the context of how Tamworth became Australia's self-proclaimed country music capital. Andersson and Niedomysl (2010) focused on how, why and what Swedish cities hope to achieve by engaging themselves in hosting the try-outs to the Eurovision Song Contest. The study relied on stakeholder interviews and found that local authorities did more collaboration than competition for the events. Various motives for bidding applied, including demonstrating that the town or city was interested in hosting events. The try-out itself was viewed by locals as little more than a good party.

Events as image makers

It is apparent that major events can have the effect of shaping an image of the host community or country, leading to its favourable perception as a potential travel destination. With global media attention focused on the host city, even for a relatively short duration, the publicity value is enormous, and some destinations will use this fact alone to justify great expenditures on attracting events. For example, Wang and Gitelson (1988: 5) observed that the annual Spoleto Festival in Charleston, South Carolina does not appear to be economically justifiable, 'but the city holds it every year to maintain a desirable image'. Cameron (1989) noted the role of festivals and events, and cultural tourism in general, in altering the image of the Lehigh Valley in Pennsylvania.

Hede and Jago (2005) placed the discussion in the context of theory about planned and reasoned action (Ajzen and Fishbein 1973; Fishbein and Ajzen 1975; Fishbein 1980; Ajzen 1985, 1991) in which positive perceptions created by the publicity surrounding events (or viewing the events, or reading about them) leads to positive attitudes, intentions to travel there and eventual travel. This theory, or belief, underlies a great deal of destination promotion. Hudson *et al.* (2004), however, in conceptualizing (with a graphic model) the process by which events might influence travel choices, concluded that there were many intervening factors separating perception from travel behaviour, and that watching events – especially sport events – might lead to travel elsewhere to participate in the sport. Indeed, many sport event broadcasts do not provide much in the way of destination imagery or information. Longitudinal studies of the impact of hosting the 1988 Winter Olympic Games in Calgary (Ritchie and Smith 1991) showed how a definite positive image boost grew, peaked and started to decline afterwards. This life cycle of image enhancement related to one-time events has also been noted by Mackellar and Nisbet (2014). But additional gains in tourism infrastructure and the legacy of enhanced tourism marketing and organization can potentially sustain the effect.

Pertinent research has been mostly on how events might change destination image (e.g. Chalip *et al.* 2003; Hede 2005; Li and Vogelsong 2005; Mossberg 2000; Shibli and the Sport Industry Research Centre 2002; Ritchie *et al.* 2006; Smith 2005; Ferreira and Donaldson 2013; Kim *et al.* 2012, 2014). Results have been mixed. The somewhat limited research on media impacts suggests that enhanced image is difficult to obtain, let alone prove (Mossberg 2000). A study by Boo and Busser (2006) concluded that the festival under study did not contribute to a positive destination image among participants. Indeed, it appeared to have a negative impact owing to poor marketing and quality. The researchers pointed out the necessity for further research on the imputed connections between events and image enhancement. Hede (2005), however, concluded that Australians who viewed telecasts of the Athens 2004 Olympics did change their overall attitude toward Greece as a destination. Ritchie *et al.* (2006) concluded that media broadcast of events helped change images of Canberra, and they recommended that events be part of any promotional strategy for national capitals. Chalip *et al.* (2003) examined the effects of different media (destination and event advertising, and event telecasts) on nine dimensions of destination image and intention to travel to the host destination (Gold Coast, Australia) from New Zealand and the USA. They found that different media had different impacts in foreign countries, not all of which were positive, and that different media could do more or less to attract tourists. For example, some media exposure convinced respondents that the event might have negative impacts on the Australian natural environment.

Gripsrud *et al.* (2010) demonstrated the interrelationships between hosting an international mega-sport event, country image, product image and purchase intentions for the Winter Olympics in Turin, Italy in 2006. A quasi-experimental design was employed, based upon two samples of undergraduate students in Norway. Data were gathered both before and after the Olympic Games took place. The study indicates that dimensions of country image for those who are very interested in sports may be changed by hosting a megasport event. However, there is no guarantee that the image of the host country will improve. It may actually deteriorate. This finding underscores the importance of managing international sport events properly.

Proactive media management is generally necessary to secure desired media coverage and communication of the desired image for events and destinations (Getz and Fairley 2004). For example, Andrew Smith (2008, 2009) examined the use of major events to promote peripheral urban areas and concluded that it is very difficult to intervene with the media to secure desired outcomes for places. Jutbring (2014) analysed exactly how brand values of the destination can be encoded in media coverage of events. Chen (2012) examined how the hosting of major international events provided the government with opportunities to boost its image among the Chinese population. Xue *et al.* (2012) indicate that hosting events can be both a positive enhancement to a country's image as well as a useful public relations tool (see Research Note 5.1).

5.1 RESEARCH NOTE ON HOSTING EVENTS

Xue, K., Chen, X. and Yu, M. (2012). Can the World Expo change a city's image through foreign media reports? *Public Relations Review*, 38(5), 746–754.

'Hosting global events like the World Expo is a new form of public relations for cities, but few studies have been conducted to explore the extent to which they can change the content of media reports and media attitudes toward city image. We conducted a content analysis of all Shanghai-related news reports from November 2009 to April 2011 in 30 English newspapers in 10 countries. We found a few interesting discoveries. First, the Shanghai Expo 2010 did affect newspapers' agenda-building, with the Expo being the topic of most reports and the most important news before and during the Expo. Second, the Expo brought changes to the news frames of newspapers, but the changes were still constrained by media practices. Third, the Expo improved newspapers' attitudes towards Shanghai's city image, particularly towards the city's potential. Finally and most importantly, global events such as the Expo do have a significant impact on the content and attitudes of newspaper reports, but a single event cannot produce long-lasting effects. Therefore improving city image requires "better actions than just better words".'

What happens when negative publicity strikes a destination? To a degree, bad news events can be managed: both to minimize the negative impact and to fight back. Ahmed (1991) argued that negative images can be turned into positive ones by organizing festivals and commemorations of the event, although this is restricted mostly to natural disasters and entails the risk of stirring up unhappy or controversial memories.

Although it can be concluded from the evidence that events can potentially have an image-change effect, the measurement of media effects remains a difficult problem for evaluators. Advertising-equivalence measures are predominant, with the major shortcoming of only considering quantity and content, not impact. Alternatives include more reliance on expert opinion from target market areas and a fuller analysis of social media. The power of social media to empower citizens to create alternative narratives to the official media responses to events has become a new area for research on events (see McGillivray 2014).

Events as catalysts: leveraging and the legacy

Mega events, such as world's fairs and Olympic Games, have been supported by host governments in large part because of their role as catalysts in major redevelopment schemes (Wise and Harris 2017). The Knoxville World's Fair was conceived as a catalyst for urban renewal through image enhancement and physical redevelopment, and left a legacy of infrastructure, a convention centre, private investments, a better tax base and new jobs for the Tennessee city (Mendell *et al*. 1983). Dungan (1984) gave a number of examples of the indirect and direct physical legacies of major events. Atlanta's 1996 Summer Olympic Games generated two billion dollars in construction projects in Georgia, including sport facilities, an urban park in central Atlanta, housing improvements and educational facilities (Mihalik 1994). Major events tend to attract investment into the hospitality sector, especially hotels and restaurants. Sometimes these additions have been brought forward in time, while others represent new infrastructure related to expected longer-term increases in demand. Sport events generally lead to new or improved facilities which can be used to attract events in the future, and improvements to convention or arts centres can have a similar effect. In this way, a community can use the event to realize a 'quantum leap' in its tourism development, accelerating growth or jumping into a higher competitive category.

'Leveraging' events is a related concept. The idea is to exploit or 'leverage' events for broader business benefits, through enhancing event tourist spending at the event and elsewhere in the destination, and through building new relationships (Faulkner *et al*. 2000). Chalip and Leyns (2002) showed how events can be leveraged for enhanced local benefits by working with businesses, and Chalip (2006) expanded this concept with regard to the social leveraging of events – that is, tying events to social and educational causes.

The 'legacy' of events is also part of the 'catalyst' role, to the extent that it is planned. Ritchie (2000) deduced ten lessons from two Winter Olympics for getting the most out of the investment in the long term. See Chapter 10 on 'Outcomes' for more discussion on these topics.

Ziakas's (2014) review of mega-event leveraging derived a list of ten key research themes for further study, namely:

- *Equity and sustainability*, so that distributional justice is achieved and through triple bottom line accounting, the outcomes might be better distributed.
- *Social capital and diversity*, so that mega events can be used to transfer social capital to more civic gatherings and bridge the gaps within communities around diversity.
- An ability to accommodate a *diversity of meanings* associated with the event and to transcend divisions across borders.

- *Localization of leveraging benefits and capacity building,* to grow the collaboration and ability of the area to host such events by harnessing the latent potential through collaboration and coordination.
- *Inclusiveness and co-creation,* especially through a participative planning process and the wider engagement of publics in the process.
- *Authenticity* in the event, avoiding over-commercialization and protection from politics.
- *Cultural revitalization,* with local communities being empowered with the opportunity to devise their own leveraging plans.
- *Accountability and evaluation,* with a holistic overview of the leveraging plans.
- *Holistic strategy development,* with a cross-leveraging strategy to encompass event portfolios.
- *Ideology and marginalization,* understanding the processes which lead to people being marginalized through event leveraging strategies.

Whilst this list of areas for research is laudable for readers, it is somewhat devoid of the reality of how leveraging works in practice – especially the highly politicized nature of decision-making in the real world – and detached from the mechanisms that shape mega-event development. Such a socially inclusive agenda for mega-event development is probably very idealistic and fails to acknowledge the dynamics of the bidding and implementation process where costs and benefits are not reviewed against a social checklist to enhance the public good. Typically the prime purpose is for area development within an economic setting, whereby the investment from the public sector has an overriding focus on employment growth and cultural strategy to elevate the image and commercial appeal of a destination. The social outcomes tend to be by-products of the wider economic strategies to replace lost employment in areas that have been transformed through the loss of local industries in global economic restructuring. This has been expressed in some critiques as the entrepreneurial city or location, seeking to engage in new economic opportunities, sometimes at a major cost.

Cities competing as event capitals

Any city can call itself an event capital, but what does it mean? In a highly competitive international marketplace, cities will inevitably want to brand themselves in such a way as to attract attention and respect. Gothenburg, Sweden has often referred to itself as a European event capital, and Edmonton, Canada has identified itself as a festival capital. Singapore wants to be the events and entertainment capital of Asia (see Foley *et al.* 2008). Increasingly there are awards to be won! Edinburgh won IFEA's World Festival and Event City award for 2010 and was declared the 'most outstanding global entry' (www.ifea.com). IFEA said: 'There is a real sense of magic in the transforming power that a truly great festival brings to a city. The intensity of that magic in Edinburgh is not from one festival, but twelve.' Melbourne, Australia won the 'Ultimate Sports City' award from *Sport Business* magazine (www.sportbusiness.com), competing against 24 other cities, for the third time in a row. Criteria included the number of annual sports events held, major events held or hosting rights secured between 2006 and 2014, numbers of federations hosted, facilities/venues, transport, accommodation, government support, security, legacy, public sports interest and quality of life.

Hospitality studies

This professional field is focused on hotels, resorts and food and beverage services (e.g. catering, restaurants and bars) and often encompasses elements of the travel and tourism industry. Some diploma and degree programmes specialize in clubs, business and industry dining, leisure services, campus dining, convention facilities, transportation, theme parks, state and national park operations, and casino operations.

Increasingly convention and event management is included within hospitality curricula. Frequently hospitality and tourism programmes are integrated within business schools, and in some cases with sport and leisure as well.

Hotel, club, convention-centre and restaurant managers are responsible for the events or 'functions' markets in their properties, while many resorts specialize in festivals and sport events suited to their recreational amenities and beautiful settings. The most common 'functions' held in hotels, restaurants and other hospitality venues are:

- weddings with banquets;
- private parties (graduations, bar and bat mitzvahs);
- meetings and conventions;
- consumer and trade shows;
- entertainment events;
- corporate functions like product launches.

For hospitality establishments to enter the conventions or exhibitions market they must have special-purpose facilities, equipment and services above and beyond the usual catering competencies. An important trend is the use of unique, non-traditional venues for meetings and conventions, such as museums, historic houses or even zoos. Most hospitality programmes are applied in nature, usually requiring hands-on training and job experience. At the university level, there is increasing emphasis on hospitality studies, or the academic bases for a professional career in hospitality. This foundation has to include general business management, services management and marketing, the special management challenges of hospitality venues, and events or functions – often tied to catering (see Table 5.4).

As its core phenomenon, hospitality studies deals with formal, usually commercialized, host–guest interaction and interdependence. To be a 'host' in this context entails legal and social responsibilities, and requires an understanding of service provision both as a business, a technical skill and a fundamental aspect of human nature. Service quality is a major theme in hospitality studies, and the related theory and methods are directly applicable to event management. Customer-to-customer interaction is important in shaping the experience and perceptions of quality, and to a degree this interaction can be facilitated by managers. Levy (2010) argued that in the design and programming of hedonic service settings such as events, managers can facilitate positive social interactions between guests. Levy's study outlined the effect of managerially facilitated consumer-to-consumer interactions on Asian and Western consumer evaluations and behavioural outcomes. A field experimental methodology was employed within the cultural group tour context. Asians are found to benefit from management facilitation of social interaction at higher levels than Westerners. There is also a growing concern about the waste generated by the hospitality sector driving events, as studies model the amount of waste produced per person at large events (Abdulredha *et al.* 2018).

Education and interpretation

Education and informal learning are embodied in many types of planned events, notably meetings and conventions, but little attention has been paid to the educational roles of events in general and research in leisure offers a number of observations on how we examine such experiences (Dattilo and Howard 1994) as a dynamic phenomenon. A study by Gitelson *et al.* (1995) was a rare look at the educational objectives of an event, and related effectiveness. Sponsors and social marketers are very concerned with how to best get across their messages to event audiences. We also need to be concerned with how events themselves can be interpreted, for example to explain symbolic and culturally significant elements to visitors, and to engage visitors more through learning opportunities at events. The event designer and programmer

Table 5.4 Hospitality management and hospitality studies

	Nature and meanings; the event experience	Antecedents to attending events	Planning and producing events	Outcomes and the impacted	Processes and patterns
Hospitality management					
Hotel, resort, restaurant management; service provision; gastronomy; events as 'functions'	Receiving hospitality at events (being a guest) Corporate hospitality as a unique event experience		Service quality Atmospherics Technical considerations (lighting, sound, safety, health)	Business impacts Client and guest satisfaction	The competitive environment for events is dynamic Rising expectations for quality
Hospitality studies					
Studies host–guest interactions and interdependencies The nature of hospitality and service	Service quality as a determinant of future demand Growth in demand for corporate and private events as professional services				

therefore has to draw upon the education and interpretation fields, including their understanding and use of cognitive psychology and learning styles.

Learning theory

'Learning' is a process requiring the active involvement of the learner – knowledge cannot simply be transferred to people by teachers or any other means. 'Experience' is often said to be the best teacher, and certainly graduates are fond of saying they learned more in the first week of employment than they did in their entire academic career (teachers dispute this). In addition to basic knowledge, the learning process can be focused on physical or problem-solving skills, or shaping one's values and attitudes. Teachers generally emphasize that their job is to enable students to become lifelong learners – to learn how to learn (Table 5.5).

'Bloom's Taxonomy' (Bloom 1956: 201–207) divides the learning process into a six-level hierarchy, where knowledge is the lowest order of cognition and evaluation the highest:

1 'Knowledge' is the memory of previously learnt materials such as facts, terms, basic concepts and answers.

Table 5.5 Education and interpretation

	Nature and meanings; the event experience	Antecedents to attending events	Planning and producing events	Outcomes and the impacted	Processes and patterns
Education					
What is knowledge? Didactics (teaching) Learning styles	Events as learning experiences	The influence of education levels on demand Desire for learning as a motive to attend events	Programming and design for learning (e.g. seminars, speakers, clinics)	What participants learn (i.e. measures of educational effectiveness)	Rising education levels affect motives and demand
Interpretation					
Theories and practice of interpretation in various settings (e.g. heritage sites, museums, events)	Interpretation through events Interpretation of the meanings of events	Availability of interpretation as it affects demand	Programming with interpretation (styles of interpretation)	Measuring the effectiveness of interpretation	Growing demand for profound experiences leads to greater need for interpretation

2 'Comprehension' is the understanding of facts and ideas by organization, comparison, translation, interpretation and description.

3 'Application' is the use of new knowledge to solve problems.

4 'Analysis' is the examination and division of information into parts by identifying motives or causes. A person can analyse by making inferences and finding evidence to support generalizations.

5 'Synthesis' is the compilation of information in a new way by combining elements into patterns or proposing alternative solutions.

6 'Evaluation' is the presentation and defence of opinions by making judgements about information, validity of ideas or quality of work based on a set of criteria.

How do people learn? The four main styles of learning can be adapted to meetings, conventions and other educational events as follows (they are not mutually exclusive, and some people learn best by one style or several combined):

1 'visual' (learn by seeing): use movies, graphics, performances;

2 'verbal/auditory' (learn by hearing): use speakers, discussants, panels, tapes;

3 'reading/writing' (learn by processing text): use readings and printed material; have attendees write things, make notes;

4 'kinaesthetic' or 'experiential': involve people in creating or discussing; take field trips; get people to participate in events; run experiments; combine observation with reflection and discussion/writing.

Meeting Professionals International (MPI 2003: 62), in their *Planning Guide*, advised members they must know how adults learn. They discussed how learning can be influenced by a number of event-related facets including emotional stimulation, socializing, setting and conference programme. 'Tools of the trade' for meeting planners to foster learning experiences include case studies, lectures, discussions, poster sessions, demonstrations, participatory workshops and 'experiential learning' (i.e. learn through doing). Hilliard (2006: 46) noted that 'education is the most consistent function of associations' but there has been little research devoted to how adult learning principles should be applied at conventions. Hilliard therefore discussed how meeting planners can better achieve their goal of educating association members. Common challenges include an over-emphasis on content, rather than delivery, and a one-way flow of information rather than the creation of an interactive learning environment.

Packer and Ballantyne (2005) found that the social dimension is an important aspect of museum learning. Many visitors report having discussed or shared information with their companions. There is also evidence, however, that some museum visitors prefer to visit alone or to learn by themselves. This study explores qualitative and quantitative differences in the nature and outcomes of solitary and shared museum learning experiences. Forty solitary adults and 40 adults visiting in pairs were observed and interviewed during their visit to a museum exhibition area, and a proportion of participants were contacted by telephone four weeks after the visit. The findings challenge the supposition that social interaction is more beneficial to learning than a solitary experience and suggest that, for adult learners, solitary and shared learning experiences can be equally beneficial, but in different ways.

Interpretation

This can mean language interpretation, or the interpretation of signs and symbols (i.e. semiotics), but we are interested here in the forms of education or other communications designed to reveal meanings and relationships. Interpreters work for parks, heritage sites, zoos, museums, galleries, aquariums, theme parks and tour companies with the purpose of making certain their visitors truly understand what is being displayed, observed or otherwise experienced. The National Association for Interpretation (www.interpnet.com) is international in its membership and proclaims that 'interpretation is a communication process that forges emotional and intellectual connections between the interests of the audience and the meanings inherent in the resource'.

With regard to parks and heritage interpretation, Tilden (1957) is considered to have had the greatest influence. His six Principles of Interpretation are widely used:

1 Any interpretation that does not somehow relate what is being displayed or described to something within the personality or experience of the visitor will be sterile.
2 Information, as such, is not interpretation. Interpretation is revelation based upon information. But they are entirely different things. However, all interpretation includes information.
3 Interpretation is an art, which combines many arts, whether the materials presented are scientific, historical or architectural. Any art is in some degree teachable.
4 The chief aim of interpretation is not instruction, but provocation.
5 Interpretation should aim to present a whole rather than a part, and must address itself to the whole man rather than any phase.
6 Interpretation addressed to children (say, up to the age of 12) should not be a dilution of the presentation to adults, but should follow a fundamentally different approach. To be at its best, it will require a separate programme.

Bramwell and Lane (1993) have argued that interpretation is a cornerstone of sustainable tourism, but they identified a number of related issues or pitfalls. One concern is that interpretation can alter the meaning of cultural assets, such as by emphasizing economic roles. Deciding on what to interpret for visitors is an issue, as only a few themes or stories can be told, and this can be a political or even divisive process. Should only the unusual or spectacular be interpreted? There is also a danger of aiming interpretation only at the educated elite, while ignoring the needs of mass tourism.

Thematic interpretation

Based on cognitive psychology, 'thematic interpretation' is based on a key premise: that people remember themes far more easily than they remember facts. If event designers tap into universal belief systems, they can more easily communicate with audiences, and audiences both need and want meaningful experiences as opposed to simple entertainment. Thematic interpretation aims to create visitor experiences that have lasting impact, translating into higher levels of satisfaction, positive word of mouth, sales and repeat visits. It is best described as strategic communication.

Professor Sam Ham of the University of Idaho is most closely associated with developing and applying thematic interpretation within parks, heritage and tourism. Dr Ham, Anna Housego and Betty Weiler together authored the *Tasmanian Thematic Interpretation Planning Manual* (May 2005: available online at www. tourismtasmania.com), as part of that Australian state's innovative Experience Strategy. We can adapt their planning process to events. A convenient starting point is their definition and explanation of theme:

> *A theme is a take-home message; it's the moral of the story or main conclusion a visitor takes away.*
>
> *(Ham et al. 2005: 3)*

> *A theme is a whole idea ... is the way you express the essence of the message you and others in your organisation want to impart to visitors; it is not necessarily the set of words you would use in direct communication to visitors ... when a moral to the story really matters to the visitor then it touches them in lots of ways, and that's when it really sticks.*
>
> *(Ham et al. 2005: 13)*

If an event theme is thought of merely in terms of decoration or entertainment, which is appropriate at many events, then interpretation is not really required. But at cultural celebrations, religious ceremonies, arts festivals and many other planned events, we want the visitor to be emotionally and cognitively affected; we want a memorable, even transforming experience. While event guests and customers might not remember all the activities or information provided, they should be provoked into reflection and involvement by the main theme so they can make their own meanings from, and about, the event, the place and the time they spent there. Using both tangibles and intangible elements (such as symbols and emotional engagement) in interpretation makes for more powerful theming.

Ideally, the theme and various interpretive media (or tools) are targeted to various audiences depending on their levels of interest, the extent and nature of their participation, and how managers want to influence them, thereby requiring a fairly sophisticated research and evaluation process. Higher levels of effectiveness can probably be achieved through greater investment in planning and research. Evaluation of results will have to include measures of actual behaviour at the event and afterwards, questions about more intangible emotional and cognitive outcomes and effects on other people through word of mouth.

Interpretation tools

Interpretation of, and at, events can include the following tools; they can be thought of as different 'media', each with their own application depending on audiences and situations as shown in Figure 5.4. As Arellano (2011) observed within a commemorative festival with 'street culture', producers get people

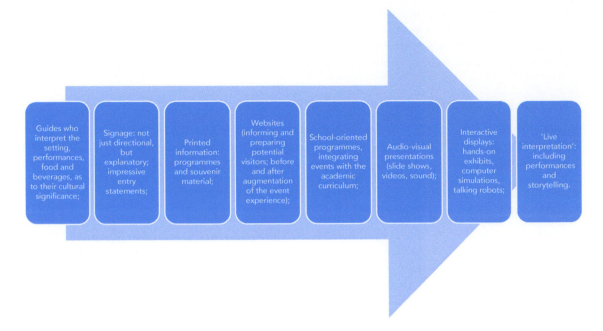

Figure 5.4 Forms of interpretation

to join in, and not just watch the spectacle. 'The festival goers are more than just a passive audience; they are confronted with several layers of dramatization and interpretation. Reconstruction proper, where the actor plays a historical character in the first person ... uses spectacle to convey a passive vision.' But interpretation is also interactive, with some performers explaining to the audience what they are doing, both meanings and roles of historical characters, generating a dialogue. 'In addition to dressing in period costume and interacting with the players and actors, visitors are incorporated into the historical performance, through improvising and directing the performance, which encourages active learning, learning by doing ...' This links with the discussion of dramaturgy which we will return to in the next chapter on the event experience.

Communications, media and performance studies

Communications can be defined as the exchange of meanings between people through a common system of symbols, such as – and especially – language. Jaworski and Pritchard (2005: 2) noted that communication 'refers to the practices, processes and mediums by which meanings are provided and understood in a cultural context'. This field covers a wide range of topics and issues, particularly speech and rhetoric, intercultural communication, information theory, public relations, propaganda and mass communications technology. It is often considered to include broadcasting, media and performance studies. Events can be considered as communication tools or artefacts, both from the point of view of event marketing (i.e. sponsors' messages at events) and as a means to interpret culture (Table 5.6). Elsewhere we have examined interpretation as a form of communication and education.

Information theory, at its most basic, is concerned with the communication process between a 'sender' (e.g. the event or some element of it) and a 'receiver' (a person or a broader audience). Masterman and Wood (2006: 4) described how the event organizer tries to convey 'messages' through specific 'media', and these messages are 'encoded' through selection of certain images, words or symbols. The target

Table 5.6 Communications, media and performance studies

	Nature and meanings; the event experience	Antecedents to attending events	Planning and producing events	Outcomes and the impacted	Processes and patterns
Communication studies					
Theories of information; symbols and semiotics; discourse Problems and methods in communications	Events as symbols and communications tools	Symbolic representations of events can encourage 'consumption'	Communication effectiveness Branding Interpretation Edutainment	Evaluation of marketing effectiveness resulting in changes in attitude or behaviour	Technological and media trends (TV coverage, virtual reality, Internet)
Media studies					
Studies the nature and influences of mass media on individuals and society Media content and representations The audience New media	Homogenization of events through mass media effects Virtual experiences	Effects of advertising on decision-making	Events designed for media audiences, both mass and segmented	Global audiences Displacement of indigenous forms of communication/events	Trends in mass media affecting the event sector
Performance studies					
The study and uses of performances, including planned events	Events as expressions of sub- and counter-cultures Create your own event experience	Desire for alternative experiences	Actors and audience merge	Personal and group identities	Values and attitudes toward performance styles

audience might fail to get the messages, owing to environmental 'noise' (i.e. all the competing stimuli and messages), or might incorrectly 'decode' (i.e. misinterpret) the messages because of ambiguity, social or cultural biases. Unless this process is monitored and evaluated, the senders could be wasting their efforts.

There are many communications and information issues: is the message clear, accurate and compelling? Does the receiver get the intended message, and act upon it in accordance with the sender's intent? Are there cultural differences that affect the communication process? Are certain channels or media more effective? These issues have obvious event-marketing implications. Communications can also be ritualistic, as with events that hold meanings such as pilgrimage and *rites de passage*. Information has to be communicated in certain ways, and perhaps only the initiated understand the true meaning. Events, in this context, can hold both superficial appeal as entertainment and deeper cultural meanings for participants.

Media studies

Media studies covers the nature and effects of mass media upon individuals and society, as well as analysing actual media content and representations. The pioneer scholar in media studies, McLuhan (1964), in *Understanding Media* stated 'the medium is the message', which is probably one of the most misunderstood popular phrases of all times. Our interpretation of McLuhan's dictum is that planned events are not merely communications tools, but are media for change. And we will understand events only by examining those changes, intended or otherwise. So we should not be distracted by the Internet or social media, but look always to the content and what it is changing.

The study of the effects and techniques of advertising forms a cornerstone of media studies. 'Critical media theory' looks at how the corporate ownership of media production and distribution affects society, and this can be applied to the events world by examining how sponsorship and media coverage can convert a local production into a global event, or how mega events have been converted into advertising platforms and instruments of cultural influence. As Dean (1999) noted, three advertising cues – third-party product endorsement, brand popularity and event sponsorship – have a powerful impact on how consumers perceive an event, including its esteem value. McPhail's (2006) theory of 'electronic colonialism' has gained international recognition. He argued that mass media over time will impact upon more and more individuals, primarily using the English language, resulting in greater similarities. Indigenous films and artefacts become marginalized by high-quality and mass-produced media. Perhaps this can be called the Hollywood effect.

Performance studies

Schechner (2002) combined the study of anthropology with performance of all kinds, including ritual, drama, environmental theatre, political rallies, dance and music, thereby creating an intellectual-artistic field of studies. Performances, including planned events and their various performative elements, are studied from multiple perspectives in terms of their contribution to society. Wikipedia defined performance studies thus:

> *This field of study engages performance as both an object of study and as something to be experienced, practiced, enacted. Events are more than their face value. A sporting event, a ceremony, a protest are all performances in their own right. Events have specific actors, costumes, settings and audiences. Within these performances are more minute performances of self: of gender, of societal role(s), of age, of disposition(s). Examining events as performance provides insight into how we perform ourselves and our lives.*

According to Deighton (1992), consumers and events/performances interact in the following ways:

- People attend performances (passive spectators);
- People participate in performance (active roles);
- Consumers 'perform' with products (they buy goods that have symbolic meaning and use them with others, to impress them, for example, which becomes a performance (see Goffman's 1959 book *The Representation of Self in Everyday Life*));
- Products 'perform' for consumers: this is a metaphorical use of the term, as performance here means meeting technical specifications; but the marketer uses the analogy of theatrical or event performance to help sell the product (e.g. car ads that feature speed, glamour, etc. in a way that clearly suggests that buying the car will positively impact on your lifestyle).

Deighton also assessed how people assign meaning to their experiences. Photography is often a record of the good aspects of the trip or event, not the bad. When the photos are viewed at a later date, especially when shared, they are a record of the good times experienced. Given the imperfections of human memory, it is possible that we remember our remembrances (through photos and stories) more than the real experience. Telling stories – a 'narrative' – is the other common way that people assign meaning to experiences. This leads to several research methods, including asking people to construct a narrative, or analysing what people are saying on blogs. These narratives are 'social constructions' and can be heavily influenced by cultural/social conventions and interactions with fellow event-goers. They can also be quite unique, with different meanings assigned to exactly the same tangible experience.

When it comes to evaluating the quality of performances, Deighton argued that they must be considered in a different light from other goods and services. The event-goer might very well ascribe satisfaction to his or her participation or mood, or to others in the audience, rather than to the event organizers or performers. As well, surprise must be considered – people's expectations can be met and exceeded through good marketing and event design, but surprising people introduces a whole new set of factors. Is the audience delighted with the surprise, or angered?

As a consequence of temporality, people asked to evaluate satisfaction levels or quality during an event are likely to consider benefits that have not yet accrued to them, such as how they anticipate they will feel when it is over. Even when it is officially over, there is the possibility that event-goers need a lot of time to really come to a conclusion about how the event affected them, and what it means – if anything – in their lives. A good event designer also has the opportunity to educate the audience during the event, so that their evaluations at the beginning, mid-way and end might be quite different. For example, if the audience is not familiar with a particular form of interpretation, art or contest, they will need time and instruction before they can pass any judgement about the event's quality and their own satisfaction with it.

Deighton analysed performance failures related to the intention behind the performance. Expectations are a big issue. If the audience feels deceived in any way, such as if the performance was quite different from what was advertised, the quality of the performance becomes rather irrelevant to them. The skill level of performers might be judged incompetent (lip-syncing rather than live singing; rigged outcomes rather than unpredictable). A lack of originality can lead to the failure of a performance; if it is highly predictable there will be no surprise. In thrill events (races) the audience might conclude that risks were minimal, or were manipulated. Finally, if the audience is not brought into a festive event, if it lacks involvement, the organizers are likely to be blamed. Deighton concluded that a 'show frame' rather than a 'skill frame' should be created for certain performances so that audience expectations are not disappointed as, for example, when athletes at all-star games or exhibition matches do not put everything into the contest. In the 'festive frame' organizers have to involve the audience and a certain amount of spontaneity should result. In a 'thrill frame' the risks have to be perceived to be real. Many implications for marketing and communications follow from this conclusion. As in the SERVQUAL model, consumer expectations directly impact on their evaluation of satisfaction and quality.

Performance (or 'live') art

Performance art consists of the impermanent actions of an individual or a group at a particular place and in a particular time, which of course also defines an 'event'. Presumably there has to be an audience, for can there be art without appreciation? Busking can be viewed as performance art. Martin *et al.* (2012) examined the engagement of young people with such art performances. In an extreme case, if you take away the audience, you have a flash mob, with the immediate and short-lived experience for participants overriding any concern for art.

Installation art

Sometimes artists are commissioned by governments or companies to enliven a space, get media attention or realize tourism and place-marketing aims. The installation artist can use a variety of media, and the installation is always temporary. The idea is to modify a space in terms of our tangible experience or concept of it. Most art installations are indoors, often in galleries. When they are outdoors they can attract a lot of attention, like a planned event but without a programme. Hu *et al.* (2013) examined the use of technology in creating interactive installations. Social connectedness among visitors can be facilitated and attractiveness of the experience thereby heightened, although the use of art is not without its critical role as Adese (2016) highlighted with native artists and their resistance of the Vancouver Olympics.

Arts and cultural management

Superficially, arts and cultural management (or administration) is the application of management, including business practices and theory, to the operation of arts and cultural organizations and their work. It gets more complex, however, when we hear that many people in the arts or cultural sectors do not think that what they do is a business, or that normal management functions like marketing should apply. Why? The arguments are largely framed around notions of 'artistic integrity' that should not be diluted or commercialized by business methods – that audience development and accessibility are more important than pricing for profit, or that cultural tourism erodes authenticity (see Table 5.7 on this field of study). Degree programmes in arts administration present one means of getting professionally involved with events, especially arts festivals and events held in art and cultural venues such as theatres, concert halls, museums and galleries. This is also a pathway into community outreach to foster art and cultural appreciation. In these programmes business management is applied to governmental and not-for-profit organizations that produce or commission events. Community building is covered, including outreach programmes, fundraising, volunteerism and partnership-building, all of which is useful to the event manager. Perhaps more importantly, the student will get an appreciation of the importance and roles of arts and culture in community life.

Cultural studies

The meanings and practice of everyday life are the subjects of cultural studies, a field that draws from anthropology, sociology and theory about all the forms of art and communications. Cultural practices comprise the ways people do particular things (such as watching television or eating out) in a given culture. Researchers examine how art, or popular activities like watching television, relate to matters of power, ideology, race, social class or gender. There can be a heavy Marxist bent to cultural studies, or a

Table 5.7 Arts and cultural management

Arts and cultural management	Nature and meanings; the event experience	Antecedents to attending events	Planning and producing events	Outcomes and the impacted	Processes and patterns
Management of arts and cultural organizations Community building through the arts and culture	Events as artistic and cultural expression Fostering appreciation and interpretation of arts and culture	Audience-building efforts generate demand for events	Management of arts and culture organizations that programme venues and produce events Volunteerism at events Partnerships for the arts/culture	Evaluating satisfaction with venues and performances Cultural impacts on society	Changing cultural norms Elitist perspectives on what is important The distribution of venues, events and organizations

Table 5.8 Cultural studies

Cultural studies	Nature and meanings; the event experience	Antecedents to attending events	Planning and producing events	Outcomes and the impacted	Processes and patterns
Critical study of popular culture and ordinary life	The appeal of art and entertainment events Importance and nature of cultural performances High and popular culture Cultural policy	Cultural capital Extrinsic motives to attend events	Linking the event sector to power and politics, gender and inequality	The distribution of costs and benefits	Culture is dynamic Cross-cultural comparisons and interactions

more neutral attempt to understand mass culture and how consumers attach meanings to forms of cultural expression. Hermeneutics is therefore employed to study the various 'texts' of cultural productions or artefacts (see Table 5.8 for an overview of the field). As Chapter 1 outlined, events are often subsumed under the broader notion of the cultural industries, a feature which is explored in more detail in Oakley and O'Conner (2015).

Sport management and sport studies

Sport management focuses on sport organizations, such as professional clubs and public facilities, with specific interests in sport marketing, human resources, finance, organizational structure, organizational behaviour, ethics, information technology, policy development and communications (North American Society for Sport Management; www.nassm.com). NASSM's *Journal of Sport Management* carries articles on sport events and sport tourism, which are of particular interest to event studies. The importance of events in sport management is reflected in several handbooks on sport management in general (Robinson *et al.* 2013), sport event management (Parent and Smith-Swan 2013, Parent and Chappelet 2015) as well as in other studies (Viehoff and Poynter 2015; Mallen and Adams 2017).

Sports by nature involve competitions, both regularly scheduled and one-time, so the coordination, production or marketing of events is usually an essential part of the job. This generally applies in athletics departments of educational institutions, international sport federations, professional sport clubs and leagues, sport facility and fitness club management, recreational sports (for parks and recreation departments or associations), sports commissions (city-based agencies active in event tourism development) and sport marketing firms. Graham *et al.* (1995), in their book *The Ultimate Guide to Sport Event Management and Marketing*, described this sector in detail, including types of careers and specific sport-event issues. In the book *Profiles of Sport Industry Professionals* by Robinson *et al.* (2001), numerous contributors describe their career paths and jobs, many of which involve events. The wider contribution of the subject to events is outlined in Table 5.9, with a number of these themes covered in Masterman's (2004, 2014) strategic analysis of sports event management.

Sport studies

'Sport psychology' is primarily concerned with the athlete, but the sport fan is also studied. Why does 'hooliganism' plague football, and why do fans celebrate to excess? Are there differences in motives between male and female fans and sport tourists? 'Sport sociology' relates more to event studies in that it focuses on groups and organizations engaged in sport, including those that produce and consume events. Studies of particular interest include sport subcultures, sport politics and national identity, sport and the media, violence, and sport influenced by gender, class, race or ethnicity. 'Sport anthropologists' are interested in the cultural importance of sport, and cultural differences reflected in sport.

Sport economics covers the economics of sport organizations, teams and events. Although sport-for-all and amateur athletics are often publicly supported to encourage healthy pursuits and socialization, subsidies for professional sport venues and teams have been quite controversial. Similarly, the bidding on and construction of facilities for sport events (i.e. sport tourism) almost always generates debates on costs and benefits.

Sport history includes the history of events and venues, with a great deal of attention having been paid to the Olympics; many interesting contributions can be found in the *International Journal of Sport History*. 'Sport geographers' examine the spatial distribution of sport events, and where athletes come from. The diffusion of new sports and of sport events combines the spatial and temporal dimensions and a number of interesting perspectives emerge from the work of key sport geographers (e.g. Bale and Dejonghe 2008) and the analysis of sporting events as cultural phenomena (e.g. Ferbrache 2013).

Sport tourism has emerged as a sub-field as illustrated by the *Journal of Sport and Tourism*, particularly because it has become a major element in destination competitiveness.

For example, Funk *et al.* (2007) outlined the attraction process within the Psychological Continuum Model (Funk and James 2001, 2006) to develop and examine five hypotheses related to motives of international participants who registered for a hallmark Australian running event. Structural equation modelling

Table 5.9 Sport management and sport studies

	Nature and meanings; the event experience	Antecedents to attending events	Planning and producing events	Outcomes and the impacted	Processes and patterns
Sport management					
Management of sport organizations, venues and events	Sport is both big business and public good Sport for health, fitness, mastery Sport as a social phenomenon	Unique motives for competing in or spectating at sport events Demand for sport tourism	Sport venue managers produce and host events Competitions produced by leagues and clubs Sport events bid on as part of sport tourism	Sport tourism impacts Personal well-being and social benefits of participation in sport events	Sport trends, fads (e.g. the diffusion of new sports) Sport development policy
Sport studies					
Sport psychology, sociology, history, geography	Sport as entertainment		Social structures, patterns and organizations engaged in sport		Sport history Sport geography (patterns of sport and sport events)

revealed that registration for the event is motivated by prior running involvement; the desire to participate in organized running events; favourable beliefs and feelings toward the host destination; and perceived travel benefits of escape, social interaction, prestige, relaxation, culture experience, cultural learning and knowledge exploration.

Venue, club and assembly management

Events are often held in single- or general-purpose arenas, convention centres, stadia or theatres, all of which can belong to the International Association of Venue Managers (www.iavm.org). When you own or manage a venue, events are at the forefront of your mind: there are sometimes clients who pay to use the facility, and sometimes events are bid on or created to fill gaps. Hotels, clubs, restaurants and many other facilities with function spaces are also in this business. Clubs are usually private, owned by members or based on paid membership, and often closely tied to sports (e.g. golf or yacht clubs), fitness and health. Not-for-profit associations, including ethnic groups, often run clubs with facilities. The magazine *Club Management* is aimed at professional club managers, and their association is Club Managers Association of America (www.cmaa.org). Entertainment and catered events are common at clubs. Their 'events directors' might have responsibility for booking entertainment, arranging caterers or hiring decorators (see Table 5.10).

Table 5.10 Venue, club and assembly management

Venue, club and assembly management	Nature and meanings; the event experience	Antecedents to attending events	Planning and producing events	Outcomes and the impacted	Processes and patterns
Design and management of event settings	Club membership generates expectations and participation Experience is shaped by the venue and its management	Some venues are attractions in their own right Big events usually require big arenas	Venues produce and host events Policy and regulations affecting venues and clubs	Private versus public access to venues and events Small, private events versus large, public events	Venue technologies and design Popularity of types of clubs Locational patterns (supply and demand factors)

Some of the pertinent research includes the study of Preda and Watts (2003) on capacity constraints in moving people at sport-event venues. Yeoman *et al.* (2004) discussed event visitor management, including demand, flow, capacity, queuing and service.

Theatre studies

Theatre studies are liberal arts programmes that typically encompass acting, production, technical aspects of theatre and the history of theatre. At New York University's Tisch School of the Arts, the theatre studies programme aims 'to give students the artistic and intellectual foundations necessary for a successful professional life in the theatre and allied disciplines. The intensive and rigorous training received in studio is contextualized within and enriched by a knowledge of the theatre as an art and an institution, with a history, a literature, and a vital role in culture' (http://drama.tisch.nyu.edu/object/dr_theatreStudies.html). Theatrical productions are events. While they are typically produced as the regular business of theatrical companies, in regular seasons or programmes, they are also produced in festivals. And plays or other theatrical productions can certainly be viewed as special events from the perspective of the audience. More importantly, the very concepts of theatre and performance, steeped in tradition and culturally distinctive, lie at the foundation of event design. And theatre is relevant to all forms of event, from sports (especially 'professional' wrestling, which hopefully everyone recognizes as being staged), to meetings (the 'drama' of debate and the 'staging' of presentations), to festivals ('rites and rituals performed' for the audience and including the audience) to trade shows (replete with entertainment and 'showmanship'). Many opening performances of Olympic Games are also carefully choreographed examples of theatre on the global stage, as McKinnie (2016) found.

Scripting events

The metaphor of events as theatre is good only to a point. First, theatres are production houses (business or not-for-profit) that create programmes of scheduled events. Second, while many event producers have a theatrical background, only certain types of planned events can be fully staged and scripted. Pine and Gilmore (1999) used the framework of Richard Schechner from the book *Performance Theory* (1988). The base is 'drama', which can be any form of story or tragedy. Drama depicts the theme of the performance, and can be expressed through different media. For a conference, the drama is the collective mission and discourse of those in attendance; for a gala banquet it can be a historical theme. The 'script' tells performers what to do, and it can include precise instructions or general directions. A script can incorporate elements of surprise or improvisation (see Table 5.11).

Theatre, in this framework, is the event itself – the performers implementing their script. Staff members, even volunteers at events, are performers in this theatre because they have such an important role to play in creating the desired experience. Accordingly, everyone has to have a script. What Pine and Gilmore (1999) wanted to stress is that work, in the workplace, should also be thought of as theatre. And of course if the theatre is interactive, involving the audience by way of activity and mental/emotional immersion, the experience will be that much more unique and memorable. Finally, Schechner (1988) defined 'performance' as being dependent on having an audience. Performances are perceived or simply enjoyed. An interaction has to occur, but the 'audience' does not necessarily have to appreciate that they are part of a performance or being influenced by a script.

Forms of theatre

Schechner (1988) also differentiated between four basic forms of theatre (see Table 5.12), each embodying varying degrees of being scripted in combination with stable or dynamic performance. The first is 'improvisation' (or 'improv'), a form of theatre in which the script is very flexible and the outcomes unpredictable. It is most used for comedy, but also seems to describe many flash-mob events. Improvisation actually requires preparation and many skills to be effective as theatre or to be used in a special event. Audiences should quickly appreciate that they are part of an experiment and the journey they are taking with the performers is going nowhere in particular, or inevitably will result in surprises. At a minimum, 'improv' events need a premise or a scenario, a starting point or concept. They offer great scope for audience involvement. In stark contrast to the 'improv' is the 'platform' theatre, which we associate with plays and musicals. The performance is generally fully scripted (memorized and rehearsed) and the

Table 5.11 Theatre studies

Theatre studies	Nature and meanings; the event experience	Antecedents to attending events	Planning and producing events	Outcomes and the impacted	Processes and patterns
Professional preparation for theatrical productions	Professional theatre applied to events	Cultural traditions shape demand for theatre	Creativity Scripted performances Setting design (staging)	Personal versus societal benefits Theatre as a business	Arts and cultural policy Changing societal values
Drama Acting History and types of theatre	Events as entertainment or social commentary Cultural meanings	Demand shaped by opportunity (supply) Unique theatrical productions motivate travel			

Table 5.12 Schechner's (1988) four forms of theatre

Street theatre	Improv theatre
Dynamic performance	Dynamic script
Stable script	Stable performance
Platform theatre	Matching theatre
Stable performance	Dynamic script
Stable script	Dynamic performance

performers clearly separated from the audience. In these types of event, the guest is seldom motivated to attend twice, unless the excellence and subtleties of the show encourage a desire for deeper understanding; unless it is so enjoyable that experiencing it again is more enjoyable!

'Matching theatre' is edited, like a film or television show. Someone has to put it together to create a coherent whole. The audience can be asked to move about a venue, as in some murder mystery performances, trying to form a mental picture of everything that is happening, despite discontinuities in both space and time.

'Street theatre', otherwise known as 'performances by buskers or travelling minstrels', can be informal and highly individualistic or packaged within festivals. The entertainers have to put on a show, first drawing the audience then engaging them sufficiently to secure a voluntary financial reward. Ordinary space has to serve as a stage, and in some cases can be incorporated into the act, becoming really unique, temporary event settings. Their script has to be relatively stable, after all they are jugglers or fire-eaters, or singers or clowns. But each performance is also going to be a unique blend of audience–performer interactions, setting (imagine the street noise) and programme (they have to possess an adaptable repertoire in terms of specific acts, and be able to alter their sequence and timing). A. Rogers (2012), a geographer, examined in a review article how the performing arts of dance, theatre, music and live art have become established means through which cultural geographers can examine how people experience and make sense of their everyday worlds. This is a very similar theme to that of connecting festivals and events to place identity, as articulated by De Bres and Davis (2001) regarding festivals and Ramshaw and Hinch (2006) in the context of sports events.

Health studies

Mass assemblies, from a health perspective, present a huge risk and there are many historical examples such as the flu pandemic of 1918–1919 that saw such gatherings avoided (Johnson 2006). Increasingly we are seeing attention given to events from health and related fields, often combining elements of risk management, security, customer service and regulations. Event tourism is obviously impacted by disease, real or threatened (see Table 5.13), and this highlights the major role of travel medicine in informing event management and hosting (Page 2009; Al-Tawfiq and Memish 2012; Memish *et al.* 2014). A great deal of attention must be given to mass gatherings such as the Hajj, and the visitors' well-being. One such examination of events and health was undertaken around the Athens Summer Olympics of 2004 (Tsouros and Efstathiou 2007). The main risks were identified as disease (transmitted through food, water, travellers); accidents and injuries; terrorism and crime; and weather and other environmental threats. These are broadly similar to the continuum of traveller problems identified in the scientific literature on travel medicine. Where travellers come from is a concern, as well as how many, density in and around venues, visitor flow and turnover.

Table 5.13 Health studies

Health studies	Nature and meanings; the event experience	Antecedents to attending events	Planning and producing events	Outcomes and the impacted	Processes and patterns
The study of injury and illness: causes, prevention, treatment	Events as factors contributing to health and well-being Safe and healthy experiences Experiences and behaviour modified by drugs and alcohol	Fear of injury and illness is a constraint Health concerns can motivate attendance at certain events (e.g. healthy living expos) Some events have a drug/alcohol culture	Health and safety regulations affect design and management Restrictions on travel or activities Need for security	Health effects of events and related activities on persons and populations Events that gain bad reputations in the community	Events and the spread of illness Statistics of injury and illnesses at events, over time

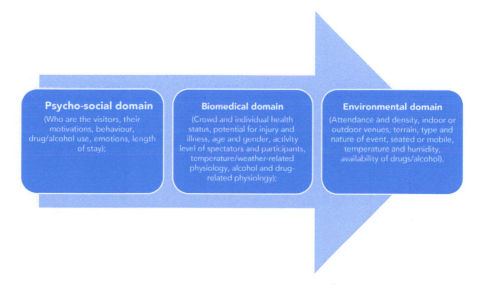

Figure 5.5 Planning model for events and health concerns

Three main areas of concern are illustrated in Figure 5.5, which can form the starting point for planning.

Health-care specialists want to assess the risks, the need for response services and the ways in which prevention or minimization can be implemented. The potential for a major incident is particularly important, including violence and the outbreak of serious disease. One important consideration when contemplating the hosting of a large-scale event is the host region's capability of dealing with a resulting disaster.

5.2 RESEARCH NOTES ON HEALTH AND EVENTS

Lee, J.-E., Almanza, B. and Nelson, D. (2010). Food safety at fairs and festivals: Vendor knowledge and violations at regional festivals. *Event Management*, 14(3), 215–223.

The concern is for food-borne illnesses at events. Researchers studied violations, and food vendors at Indiana festivals were tested. They were found to be mostly knowledgeable of regulations. Training implications were discussed.

Memish, Z. A., Zumla, A., Alhakeem, R. F., Assiri, A., Turkestani, A., Al Harby, K. D. and Al-Tawfiq, J. A. (2014). Hajj: Infectious disease surveillance and control. *The Lancet*, 383(9934), 2073–2082.

'Religious festivals attract a large number of pilgrims from all over the world and are a potential risk for the transmission of infectious diseases between pilgrims, and to the indigenous population. The gathering of a large number of pilgrims could compromise the health system of the host country. The threat to global health security posed by infectious diseases with epidemic potential shows the importance of advanced planning of public health surveillance and response at these religious events. Saudi Arabia has extensive experience of providing health care at mass gatherings acquired through decades of managing millions of pilgrims at the Hajj. In this report, we describe the extensive public health planning, surveillance systems used to monitor public health risks, and health services provided and accessed during Hajj 2012 and Hajj 2013 that together attracted more than 5 million pilgrims from 184 countries. We also describe the recent establishment of the Global Center for Mass Gathering Medicine, a Saudi government partnership with the WHO Collaborating Centre for Mass Gatherings Medicine, Gulf Co-operation Council states, UK universities and public health institutions globally.'

Urban and community studies

Urban and community studies, and its closely related professional field urban (or town) planning, deals with a variety of issues concerning the development and planning of cities and communities as well as related policy issues. It is interdisciplinary and draws heavily from geography, history, economics, sociology, architecture, design, cultural anthropology and political science and is a very productive area of research on events; its scope is illustrated in Table 5.14. Event studies fits into any number of urban and community topics, particularly since most large-scale events and event venues are located in cities (the exception being large music festivals located in rural areas such as Glastonbury that do not require fixed infrastructure like a stadium). Figure 5.6 provides examples from the recent research literature on urban studies to illustrate the important interface between urban and event studies; the journal *Urban Studies* is an important source. One of the most influential studies on mega events and urban policy was by Roche (1994), who reviewed the influence of planning, political and urban contextual processes and factors on mega-event production. Roche illustrated these themes through a discussion of comparative event research and a case study of Sheffield's Universiade 1991. This study indicates the important influence of contextual societal change, urban leadership and non-rational planning in event production processes. Subsequently Quinn (2003) reviewed the existing literature on urban festivals and argued that city authorities tend to disregard the social value of festivals and to construe them simply as vehicles of economic generation or as 'quick fix' solutions to city image problems. Quinn argued that if arts festivals are to achieve their undoubted potential in animating communities, celebrating diversity and improving quality of life, then they must be conceived of in a more holistic way by urban managers.

Table 5.14 Urban and community studies

Urban and community studies	Nature and meanings; the event experience	Antecedents to attending events	Planning and producing events	Outcomes and the impacted	Processes and patterns
Urban development and dynamics Communities Place identity Planning, development and design	Events as urban cultural experiences Relationship to the urban setting (e.g. heritage) Larger crowds affect urban events Venues are mostly urban	Desire to escape city environments Proximity to many event venues Increased opportunity for urban-dwellers Subcultural and community influences (desire for identity and sharing)	Urban planners and designers create spaces for events, and spaces that need the animation of events Event offices within city administrations Urban-based tourism and cultural agencies	Effects of events on urban form, housing, design, liveability	The festivalization of urban policy (within the context of development and place marketing) The geography of events within cities The history and evolution of events within cities

Cornelissen, S. (2011). Mega event securitisation in a third world setting: Glocal processes and ramifications during the 2010 FIFA World Cup. *Urban Studies*, 48(15), 3221–3240.

Dawson, M. (2011). Putting cities on the map: Vancouver's 1954 British Empire and Commonwealth Games in comparative and historical perspective. *Urban Geography*, 32(6), 788–803.

Kontokosta, C. (2012). The price of victory: The impact of the Olympic Games on residential real estate markets. *Urban Studies*, 49(5), 961–978.

Macbeth, J., Selwood, J. and Veitch, S. (2012). Paradigm shift or a drop in the ocean? The America's Cup impact on Fremantle. *Tourism Geographies*, 14(1), 162–182.

Rota, F.S. and Salone, C. (2014). Place-making processes in unconventional cultural practices. The case of Turin's contemporary art festival Paratissima. *Cities*, 40, 90–98.

Smith, A. (2014). 'Borrowing' public space to stage major events: The Greenwich Park controversy. *Urban Studies*, 51(2), 247–263.

Smith, A. (2015). *Events in the City: Using Public Spaces as Event Venues.* London: Routledge.

Taylor, T. and Toohey, K. (2011). Ensuring safety at Australian sport event precincts: Creating securitised, sanitised and stifling spaces? *Urban Studies*, 48(15), 3259–3275.

Vanwynsberghe, R., Surborg, B. and Wyly, E. (2013). When the games come to town: Neoliberalism, mega-events and social inclusion in the Vancouver 2010 Winter Olympic Games. *International Journal of Urban and Regional Research*, 37(6), 2074–2093.

Wang, M. and Bao, H. (2018). Mega-event effects on the housing market: Evidence from the Beijing 2008 Olympic Games. *Cities*, 72, 207–216.

Weller, S. (2013). Consuming the city: Public fashion festivals and the participatory economies of urban spaces in Melbourne. *Urban Studies*, 50(14), 2853–2868.

Figure 5.6 Recent examples of progress in urban studies and events research

Gelder and Robinson (2011: 140) emphasized the importance of arts and festivals in particular in urban policy as:

> *Arts and cultural projects have played an increasingly important role in British urban regeneration since the mid-1980s; however, the focus has shifted over the years to the capability of arts activity in supporting community-led renewal, rather than on capital projects.*

These can also be harnessed more fully in year-long cultural events, such as the European Cities of Culture, as outlined by Richards and Palmer (2010).

Rural studies

Hall and Page (2014) argue that the term 'rural', based on G. M. Robinson's (1990) synthesis, has remained an elusive one to define in academic research, although a number of popular conceptions of rural areas are based on images of rusticity and the idyllic village life.

However, Robinson argued that:

> *defining rural … in the past has tended to ignore common economic, social and political structures in both urban and rural areas … In simple terms … 'rural' areas define themselves with respect to the presence of particular types of problems. A selective list of examples could include depopulation and deprivation in areas remote from major metropolitan centres; a reliance upon primary activity; conflicts between presentation of certain landscapes and development of a variety of economic activities; and conflicts between local needs and legislation emanating from urban-based legislators. Key characteristics of 'rural' are taken to be extensive land uses, including large open spaces of underdeveloped land, and small settlements at the base of the settlement hierarchy, but including settlements thought of as rural.*
>
> *(Robinson 1990: xxi–xxii)*

Therefore, within events research, the term 'rural' will have a wide range of meanings and uses, ranging from very remote rural areas through to those located on the urban fringe of towns and cities. Rural areas are diverse and vary in their degree of ruralness and their attributes, but they do have an important role to play in event studies, especially given the rural lifestyle, economy and landscape (see Table 5.15).

Agricultural festivals and events as manifestations of rurality are an obvious theme (see the various studies by Janiskee), but so too is the contribution of events to rural identity and economic development. The book *Festival Places: Revitalizing Rural Australia* (edited by Chris Gibson and John Connell 2011) covers the many connections between festivals and other events and rural communities.

5.3 RESEARCH NOTE ON EVENTS AND COMMUNITIES

Gibson, C., Waitt, G., Walmsley, J. and Connell, J. (2009). Cultural festivals and economic development in nonmetropolitan Australia. *Journal of Planning Education and Research*, 29(3), 280–293.

'Examining a database of 2,856 festivals in Australia and survey results from 480 festival organizers, the authors consider how nonmetropolitan cultural festivals provide constraints as well as opportunities for economic planners. Cultural festivals are ubiquitous, impressively diverse, and strongly connected to local communities through employment, volunteerism and participation. Despite cultural festivals being mostly small-scale, economically modest affairs, geared around community goals, the regional proliferation of cultural festivals produces enormous direct and indirect economic benefits. Amid debates over cultural and political issues (such as identity, exclusion and elitism), links between cultural festivals and economic development planning are explored.'

Table 5.15 Rural studies

Rural studies	Nature and meanings; the event experience	Antecedents to attending events	Planning and producing events	Outcomes and the impacted	Processes and patterns
Rural development and dynamics The nature of ruralness and rural communities Place identity Planning	Events as rural cultural experiences Relationship to heritage, colonialism, settlement patterns, migration, agriculture Venues are more likely to be outdoors	Need for entertainment and socializing Often must travel to towns and event venues Tradition and an annual events calendar (especially connected to agriculture)	Heightened need for leadership Resources for events might be scarce (financial, human) Limited choice of venues Traditional use of show/fair grounds Use of events for positioning and tourism	Effects of events on community viability and the environment are paramount concerns	The festivalization of rural and regional policy (within the context of development and place marketing) The geography of events within large regions The history and evolution of events within rural areas

Reid (2007) identified a range of social consequences that occur as a result of hosting events, especially within rural communities. She resisted a classification into positives and negatives and looked at how impacts were socially constructed. By taking an event stakeholder perspective within three rural communities of Southwest Queensland, Australia, Reid found a number of consequences that were often ignored in the event impact literature, including trust- and respect-building, breaking down social barriers, forgetting hard times and being affiliated with a success.

Recent progress in rural studies and events is outlined in Figure 5.7, where subject-specific journals such as the *Journal of Rural Studies* have a key role to play in the theoretical development of the field.

Aboriginal, ethnic and multicultural studies

This grouping could be subsumed under cultural anthropology and cultural studies, but there are specific and important implications of aboriginal, ethnic and multicultural studies for planned events. The study of anthropology and events has a long tradition, exemplified in India with the research dating back to the nineteenth century. Indian anthropologists of the twentieth century (e.g. Naik 1948) examined the event phenomenon at a time of dramatic change within the structure of Indian society. Numerous festivals and events are produced by, and have themes tied to, specific cultural groups, while in many countries the multicultural (or international) festival is a well-established format. Topics of concern to those who study native peoples and ethnic groups include identity (self-perception and that of others), preservation of their heritage and special challenges facing them (such as discrimination, and native land ownership and other rights). Multiculturalism is but one approach, sometimes formalized, to bringing people together as outlined in Table 5.16. There are many connections between festivals, events and the specific cultural manifestations of ethnicity, particularly in an era of global migration and diaspora. Ethnicity can be expressed through performances (including music, costumes, song and dance), consumption (food and beverages, arts and crafts), literature, language and religion (rites and rituals).

Blichfeldt, B. S. and Halkier, H. (2014). Mussels, tourism and community development: A case study of place branding through food festivals in rural North Jutland, Denmark. *European Planning Studies*, 22(8), 1587–1603.

Bob, U. and Majola, M. (2011). Rural community perceptions of the 2010 FIFA World Cup: The Makhowe community in Kwazulu-Natal. *Development Southern Africa*, 28(3), 386–399.

Capriello, A. and Rotherham, I.D. (2011). Building a preliminary model of event management for rural communities. *Journal of Hospitality Marketing and Management*, 20(3/4), 246–264.

Gibson, C. and Davidson, D. (2004). Tamworth, Australia's 'country music capital': Place marketing, rurality, and resident reactions. *Journal of Rural Studies*, 20(4), 387–404.

Holloway, L. (2004). Showing and telling farming: Agricultural shows and re-imaging British agriculture. *Journal of Rural Studies*, 20(3), 319–330.

Li, M., Huang, Z. and Cai, L. (2009). Benefit segmentation of visitors to a rural community-based festival. *Journal of Travel and Tourism Marketing*, 26(5/6), 585–598.

McHenry, J. A. (2011). Rural empowerment through the arts: The role of the arts in civic and social participation in the Mid West region of Western Australia. *Journal of Rural Studies*, 27(3), 245–253.

Perić, M., Durkin, J. and Wise, N. (2016). Leveraging small-scale sport events: Challenges of organising, delivering and managing sustainable outcomes in rural communities, the case of Gorskikotar, Croatia. *Sustainability*, 8(12).

Rich, K., Bean, C. and Apramian, Z. (2014). Boozing, brawling, and community building: Sport-facilitated community development in a rural Ontario community. *Leisure/Loisir*, 38(1), 73–91.

Figure 5.7 Recent progress in rural studies and events research

Table 5.16 Aboriginal, ethnic and multicultural studies

Aboriginal, ethnic and multicultural studies	Nature and meanings; the event experience	Antecedents to attending events	Planning and producing events	Outcomes and the impacted	Processes and patterns
The identity of racial and cultural groups Preserving cultural heritage Special challenges facing groups Aboriginal rights	Expressions of identity The desire for sharing and understanding between groups Celebration of diversity	Groups with a need to preserve or rediscover their roots and identity Learning about other cultures (search for authenticity)	Reserving sacred rituals from public view Who is in control? The need for interpretation	Threat of commodifying traditions Tourism impacts Intercultural understanding	Geographical spread of festivity and ritual Creation of new traditions and forms of events Influence on cultural and multicultural policy

Often the intent is to share, foster mutual understanding and encourage social integration, rather than to have a party just for one group. Carnegie and Smith (2006) provided a showcase of ethnic cultures, or an expression of 'Indianness'; the Mela in Edinburgh, and elsewhere in Europe, increasingly involves festivity with others. According to the authors, it has become a mainstay of the city's summer festival season. It helps both Scots and Indians in the community to reflect on identity and togetherness. However, Carnegie and Smith suggest that the more successful it becomes as a tourist attraction, the less likely it is to remain tied to a local community. Burdseya (2008) provided a case study of the Amsterdam World Cup, an annual amateur football competition and multicultural festival. Placing the event within the context of Dutch integration policy, it examines the differing and contested conceptions of identity, community and multiculturalism articulated by participants and organizers and, more broadly, the role that 'alternative' events play in resisting or reinforcing dominant political ideologies. Other papers specific to ethnicity include those by Cheska (1981), Sofield (1991), Spiropoulos *et al.* (2006) and Brewster *et al.* (2009).

'Aboriginal' events (encompassing all native peoples) have special significance in cultural terms, raising issues of authenticity (e.g. are performances commodified for tourists?), the need for preserving the sacred by keeping certain rituals hidden and using public events to make political statements. Many native groups want to attract tourists for reasons of both cultural understanding and economic development.

Figure 5.8 provides a sample of aboriginal studies related to events. For example, Phipps (2011) provided a case study of Australia's 'most prominent Aboriginal festival', called the Garma Festival, which highlights the desires of its aboriginal producers for both equality of opportunity (necessary to redress many disadvantages) and to preserve and pursue their distinctive culture. Phipps describes such celebrations as cultural politics.

Chang, J. (2006). Segmenting tourists to aboriginal cultural festivals: An example in the Rukai tribal area, Taiwan. *Tourism Management*, 27(6), 1224–1234.

Forsyth, J. (2016). The illusion of inclusion: Agenda 21 and the commodification of Aboriginal culture in the Vancouver 2010 Olympic Games. *Public*, 27(53), 22–34.

Hinch, T. and Delamere, T. (1993). Native festivals as tourism attractions: A community challenge. *Journal of Applied Recreation Research*, 18(2), 131–142.

Jackson, I. (2008). Celebrating communities: Community festivals, participation and belonging. *The Australian Centre, School of Historical Studies*, 161–172.

Lee, T. H. and Hsu, F. Y. (2013). Examining how attending motivation and satisfaction affects the loyalty for attendees at Aboriginal festivals. *International Journal of Tourism Research*, 15(1), 18–34.

Phipps, P. (2011). Performing culture as political strategy: The Garma Festival, northeast Arnhem Land. In C. Gibson and J. Connell (eds), *Festival Places: Revitalising Rural Australia*, pp. 109–122. Bristol: Channel View.

Slater, L. (2010). 'Calling our spirits home': Indigenous cultural festivals and the making of a good life. *Cultural Studies Review*, 16(1), 143–154.

White, L. (2011). The Sydney 2000 Olympic Games bid: Marketing indigenous Australia for the Millennium Games. *International Journal of the History of Sport*, 28(10), 1447–1462.

White, L. (2013). Cathy Freeman and Australia's indigenous heritage: A new beginning for an old nation at the Sydney 2000 Olympic Games. *International Journal of Heritage Studies*, 19(2), 153–170.

Whitford, M. and Ruhanen, L. (2013). Indigenous festivals and community development: A sociocultural analysis of an Australian indigenous festival. *Event Management*, 17(1), 49–61.

Figure 5.8 Sample research studies on aboriginal events

Visitor studies

Visitor studies is an interdisciplinary theme and a set of methods, with its own professional association and research journal. The Visitor Studies Association (www.visitorstudies.org) focuses on all facets of the visitor experience in settings like museums, zoos, nature centres, visitor centres, historic sites, parks and other informal learning settings. The purpose of related research and evaluation is to understand and enhance visitor experiences in informal learning settings. Obviously tourism, hospitality, leisure, arts and event studies are all concerned with visitors and their experiences. The potential for synergies is great (see Table 5.17). Delbosc (2008) suggested a number of lines of research that bring event studies and visitor studies together, as summarized in Research Note 5.4.

Table 5.17 Visitor studies

Visitor studies	Nature and meanings; the event experience	Antecedents to attending events	Planning and producing events	Outcomes and the impacted	Processes and patterns
Understanding and enhancing visitor experiences Interpretation and exhibition design and methods (including signage) Learning and behavioural outcomes of experiences and interpretation	Events as learning experiences Enhanced events through interpretation	Demand for learning experiences Special needs and preferences of tourists	Venues produce exhibitions and other events The effects of various settings on experiences	Measuring the effects of interpretation on visitors	Efficiency policies dictate the use of events as interpretive devices and means to attract visitors

5.4 RESEARCH NOTE ON FESTIVALS AT MUSEUMS

Delbosc, A. (2008). Social identity as a motivator in cultural festivals. *Visitor Studies*, 11(1), 3–15.

Delbosc argued that 'as museums continue to broaden their offers and attract increasingly diverse audiences, it becomes ever more important to understand how motivations for visitation can vary between different cultural groups. This article explores some of the reasons people visit cultural festivals at the Immigration Museum in Melbourne, Australia, combining data from five different festivals with a total sample of 414. The audience of these festivals contains a mix of 74 per cent cultural community members and 26 per cent non-community members, and their reasons for visiting the festivals differ in distinct ways. Among these distinctions, it was found that social identity played a role in why people chose to visit, especially for community members and at the festivals of communities that were relatively new to Melbourne.'

STUDY GUIDE

Closely related professional fields were discussed as to their links with, and contributions to, event studies. These fields all involve events to some extent, so the discipline of event studies, as it develops, can feed back important concepts to them. Note how each field has to draw upon foundation disciplines for theory and methodology, and how the ways in which they apply theory suggests possibilities and direct applications for event studies. Leisure studies offers the most in terms of theory and philosophy, because that field is specifically concerned with events and experiences. Several leisure theories and methods are vital in helping to explain motivations to attend events and event tourism. They have also developed a philosophy of leisure service that might be applicable to events.

STUDY QUESTIONS

- Are all planned events opportunities for leisure experiences?
- Distinguish between intrinsic and extrinsic motivations as they apply to events.
- Discuss the relevance of serious leisure, recreation specialization, involvement and commitment to event studies – and specifically to event tourist careers.
- In what ways can all planned events be considered part of cultural tourism?
- Is sport tourism mostly concerned with events? What else is pertinent?
- How can events contribute to destination image enhancement?
- Why exactly are venue managers and hospitality professionals involved with planned events? What can their field contribute to event studies?
- How can learning theories be applied to events?
- Discuss the meaning and applications of thematic interpretation.
- Show how to apply information theory to the study of events, and for event marketing.
- What are the fundamental principles of performance? Link performance to social interaction theory.
- Distinguish between cultural management and cultural studies.
- Apply Schechner's four forms of theatre to other forms of planned events.
- In terms of experiences, are all planned events similar to theatre?
- What are the health concerns most applicable to mass gatherings?
- How are events important to both urban and rural place identity?

FURTHER READING

Dwyer, L. and Wickens, E. (eds) (2013). *Event Tourism and Cultural Tourism: Issues and Debates*. London: Routledge.

Gibson, C. and Connell, J. (eds) (2011). *Festival Places: Revitalising Rural Australia*. Bristol: Channel View.

Gibson, H. (ed.) (2006). *Sport Tourism: Concepts and Theories*. London: Routledge.

Page, S. J. and Connell, J. (2006). *Leisure: Critical Concepts in the Social Sciences,* 4 Volumes. London: Routledge.

Page, S. J. and Connell, J. (2010). *Leisure: An Introduction*. Harlow: Pearson Education.

Schechner, R. (2002, 2013 3rd edn). *Performance Studies: An Introduction*. London: Routledge.

Stebbins, R. (2006). *Serious Leisure: A Perspective for Our Time*. Somerset, NJ: Aldine Transaction Publications.

PART **III**

Framework for understanding and creating knowledge

Chapter 6

The event experience and meanings

Upon completion of this chapter, students should know the following:

- the cognitive, affective and conative dimensions of event experiences;
- leisure experiences versus work (and intrinsic versus extrinsic motivation);
- the concepts of liminality and the liminoid in the context of cultural anthropology and as applied to event experiences, with specific reference to rites and rituals;
- 'communitas' and its importance in event experiences;
- how event experiences can be different for customers/guests, spectators or participants, volunteers, organizers/staff, and other stakeholders;
- meanings attached to event experiences;
- experiences associated with planned event types, and the meanings attached to those experiences by individuals and societies;
- why some experiences are memorable or transforming;
- the scope for, and limitations related to, designing event experiences;
- the meaning of co-creation of event experiences;
- differences between constraining and liberating experiences;
- service dominant logic.

Defining 'experience'

This chapter concerns the core phenomenon of event studies – planned event experiences – and meanings attached to them. If we cannot clearly articulate what the event experience is, then how can it be planned or designed? If we do not understand what it means to people, then how can it be important? Our starting point is a discussion of definitions, noting different meanings of 'experience' and how it can be used as both a noun and a verb. We recall the interpretation of 'leisure experiences' and then return to the 'experience economy' we introduced in Chapter 1 and how the corporate world has been developing 'experiential marketing' to commercialize the experience economy, whereby two-way relationships are built with consumers and businesses beyond the conventional model of consumer marketing. The basic premise is to engage the consumer much more deeply with a focus on their emotions and in a far more personal manner than is achievable by mass-marketing methods. The significance of experiential marketing as a dimension of consumer behaviour led Miller and Washington (2011) to argue that in the USA, around $37 billion is spent annually on such forms of marketing, illustrating its significance in engaging consumers.

Following a discussion of these issues around the experience economy, the chapter presents a model of the planned event experience, derived from anthropology, leisure and tourism studies. The notion of 'liminal' and 'liminoid' experiences, and the creation of special places and times, are central to the model. Specific types or forms of events are revisited, looking at the experiential dimensions associated with each, and how people might describe them. Each stakeholder group is also examined, from customers to volunteers, in order to demonstrate substantial differences in event experiences and how they are obtained. Meanings attached to event experiences are examined from the perspectives of individuals, society, culture and the corporate world.

'Experience' defined generically

In normal conversation, people might use the term 'experience' in several ways, either as a noun or a verb. In each of the immediately following examples 'experience' is used as a noun. These statements illustrate key points, so a little commentary is attached to each.

> *'I had an intellectually stimulating experience at the meeting.'*

This statement describes the experience both in terms of cognition (i.e. learning) and affect (attitude, or emotion).

> *'The marathon was a challenging and exhausting experience, but I was exhilarated by my success!'*

The runner describes her/his experience in terms of:

- physicality (exhausting), which is the conative or behavioural dimension of experience;
- feelings about it (exhilaration is an emotional state);
- 'challenging', in this context, can relate either to the physical experience (they had to push themselves extra hard to complete the race) or to a post-event assessment of meaning, in which case the runner might be saying they felt a sense of accomplishment or mastery in the achievement of personal goals.

> *'I am a person with lots of event experience.'*

(i.e. I have been to many events and learned a lot about them; there has been an accumulation of knowledge or skill).

> *'The experience of attending my first World's Fair was a highlight of my life; I will never forget it!'*

The person is talking about being at the event, involving direct observation and a stream of consciousness; there is also profound, transforming meaning attached.

We also use 'to experience' (the verb) in different ways. Here are event-related examples:

'As an event manager, I have experienced (i.e. lived through) many near disasters.'

This a simple statement about something that happened, not a value judgement, emotional reaction or inference of meaning.

'I want to experience the excitement of a Rolling Stones concert!'

This use of the verb is loaded with emotion or feelings, and it refers to the knowing and feeling that comes only through direct participation, or 'being there'.

'You have to get experienced in many tasks at real events before you can become a competent manager.'

Here it means to undergo a change, an accumulation of transformative experiences, becoming more knowledgeable and skilled.

Referring back to these examples and Chapter 3, we need to remind ourselves that the 'conative' dimension of experience describes actual behaviour, the things people do including physical activity. The 'cognitive' dimension of experience refers to awareness, perception, memory, learning, judgement and understanding or making sense of the experience. This is likely to be dominant in meetings, conferences, scientific forums and some business and trade events, where education or sharing ideas and knowledge are the main goals. The 'affective' dimension of experience concerns feelings and emotions, preferences and values. Describing experiences as fun or giving pleasure reflects emotions, while many social aspects of experience reflect values – including being with friends and family, and a sense of sharing and belonging to a wider community.

How people describe event experiences as they occur, and talk about them afterwards, remains in large part a mystery and therefore must be of considerable interest to event researchers (some researchers look at these journeys through an event experience retrospectively, for example) and producers. It is certainly possible that events satisfy those in attendance at one level, but at the same time fail to achieve the organizers' intended experiences (such as learning, cultural appreciation, social integration, increased brand identity). It is also quite possible that events are determined to be successful in terms of desired outcomes (e.g. money earned, attendance, brand recognition), but the experiences of guests are unsatisfactory, even negative. For this reason, it is useful to briefly examine how psychology (and other disciplines) have contributed to the way we conceptualize experience as a key element of event studies.

The concept of 'experience': its development and constituent elements

The development of psychology in the late nineteenth century, particularly the work of the Leipzig School and the work of Wundt, in establishing psychology as a distinct discipline (see Wundt 1896) *Grundriss der Psychologie* (Outline of Psychology) helped stimulate debate about the concept of experience (see Jantzen 2013 for a detailed history of the evolution of the psychologists' study of experience). Other studies, such as Bentley (1924), continued this trajectory of research on experience noting that 'experience is complex. It is complex in both its temporal course and in its momentary phases' (Bentley 1924: 50). Bentley (1924) outlined the constituent of experience (which we have touched upon in previous chapters) around the concept of stimuli (i.e. things that stimulate the experience) and receptors (i.e. our senses that receive and help formulate our experience). Bentley (1924) pointed to the sensational elements of the human experience that are grouped around:

- *Visual qualities* of what we see, that are affected by colour and light;
- *Auditory* (i.e. hearing) elements that are affected by the concept of tones;
- *Taste and smell*;
- *Touch*;

and the body's ability to receive messages about each of these elements. A study by Toraldo (2013) highlighted the paucity of research on sensory issues and events, particularly the impact on experience and hedonism. Toraldo (2013) indicated that many sensory differences between humans are socially and culturally conditioned and understanding these sensory issues in events hinges upon one key concept – anticipation. The event experience is dependent upon the expectation and anticipation of the experience and whether it is met (see Sugathan *et al.* 2017 for a discussion of attribution theory, which is based on the reasoning associated with our emotional states and what stimulates a behavioural response, either positive or negative). As Jantzen (2013) argues, in any theorizing about experience, we need to recognize the reversal from one state of mind (i.e. relaxation) to another (e.g. excitement) and how our senses may arouse our emotions to a particular state. Jantzen (2013: 167) recognizes that 'experiences are a universal feature of human existence' and are central to understanding events as part of the experience economy, in which human experiences are dynamic and the human emotional state affects behaviour with reference to events. Such arguments can be recognized when trying to summarize the factors which contribute to success or failure in events, where experiential elements are writ large (see Table 6.1).

As Table 6.1 demonstrates, many success/failure factors can directly and indirectly be attributed to experiential factors which event organizers need to be cognizant of. Yet the experience of events is not just about the point of consumption as many studies have focused on (e.g. Stricklin and Ellis 2018). We also need to consider how past experiences of events are constructed by humans as these can often affect the propensity to return to events. Some studies (e.g. Hulst) have pointed to various concepts such as 'experiencescape' that have evolved from human geography and the concern with event places and spaces to understand how an event experience is delivered (see Dahlgaard – Park *et al.* 2010 – for a discussion). This embraces the atmosphere in the event space which influences the event-goers overall event experience. For example, sensory elements such as smelly portaloo toilets, excessive noise impact upon the aesthetic dimensions of what is consumed (Toraldo 2013). For this reason, understanding your audience and its motivation to attend an event are crucial to create the type of sensory experience they desire. Two contrasting examples of musical events illustrate this: Pitts' (2005) study of a chamber music festival found attendees to be committed, involved and self-aware and that the individual experience of the event was central to their motivation to attend. In contrast, in a large music festival context, Pegg and Patterson (2010) observed that despite being unified by an interest in music, attendees had very diverse needs even though this was a niche market.

Kim and Jang (2016) observed that past event experiences were key to returning to events, focusing on the methodologies used to understand memory-retrieval of events. Their study outlined the two principal ways that memory is researched:

- *the semantic memory*, where the context of the memory is based on our knowledge we have accumulated during our lifetime, affected by the experiences we have had over a life course;
- *the episodic memory*, which is a more autobiographical accumulation of events (e.g. the times and places along with contextual information and more in-depth detailed past experiences).

The episodic memory has been the focus of most event research studies of memory, with key concepts of communitas, desire and belonging examined in these past experiences. However, the memory alone cannot be the sole focus for understanding the event experience as there is a growing recognition that fulfilling the anticipation someone has is fundamental to providing a fulfilling experience. Recent developments in

Table 6.1 Factors affecting the success or failure of events

Success factors	Factors attributed to failure in events
The creation of a sense of community	A lack of corporate sponsorship
Social interaction	Weather-related issues (e.g. being rained off)
The variety in the event programme	Over-reliance upon one source of funding
The event atmosphere	Poor marketing and promotion
Unexpected outcomes (i.e. surprising the audience)	An absence of professional advice or lack of strategic planning
Merchandising	The event becomes a social and financial burden on the host community
Safety and good service	Unintended consequences of hosting the event (e.g. anti-social behaviour and crime)
Event organization and effective event management	Over-commercialization of the event
Technical aspects of the venue and its ability to provide a unique event experience	Locals being priced out of the event
Information and marketing	
Market orientation to meet demand	
Brand equity (i.e. having a good brand name and recognition).	

Source: Developed from Kinnunen and Haahti (2015); Getz (2002); authors.

psychology, neuroscience and chemistry, according to Beard and Russ (2017), have illustrated how event experiences can be made more compelling. They point to the importance of four chemicals that drive the cognitive elements (serotonin, oxytocin, dopamine and endorphin). Stimulating these can be a means by which positive emotions are created (although there are also concerns that over-stimulation on a regular basis can lead to addictive behaviours).

As Beard and Russ (2017) demonstrate, the approach to understanding event experiences needs to understand the way an event is constructed:

- *Socially* (i.e. the interaction with other people);
- *Psychologically* (i.e. how this affects the self);
- *Emotionally* (i.e. our feelings);
- *Cognitively* (i.e. how it affects our mind);
- *Environmentally* (i.e. the importance of place).

Other studies point to the importance of key drivers or a focal point in making the event experience unique or special. For example, Rockwell and Mau (2006: 14) portray this vividly where:

> *An empty stadium, an open field or a busy urban thoroughfare – each one a public space – undergoes an alchemical process when transformed by spectacle.*

As we have discussed previously, spectacles (see Table 6.2) may provide the unique ingredients that help to create the transformational changes and experience as 'spectacles are an alchemical act – a moment [as] cities become stages; people are remade as audiences, actors, atmosphere' (Rockwell and Mau 2006:

Table 6.2 Examples of spectacles

Event	Year	Number of people estimated to attend	Location	Purpose
Kumbh Mela	2001	70 million	India	Religious festival held every 12 years.
Athens Olympics	2004	22,000 attended opening ceremony 2,428 volunteer performer 11,999 athletes 4 billion watched the games on television	Greece	Event which is a quadrennial international multi-sport with historical roots dating to the Ancient Greeks but hosted on a regular basis since the 1896 *Games of the Olympiad.*
Macy's Thanksgiving Parade	Annual	2–3 million with a further 40 million plus watching it on television	Manhattan, New York, USA	An annual event first held in 1924 characterized by large outdoor theatre and designed to celebrate the Thanksgiving, a blessing given to celebrate the previous year's harvest. It has large inflated balloons in special designs.
Brussels Flower Carpet	Biennial event held on Assumption Day	Tens of thousands	Grand Palace, Brussels, Belgium	First established in 1971, the event weaves a carpet using almost 1 million begonias that are grown in Belgium.
Harbin Ice and Snow Festival	Annually in January–February	2 million	Northern China	2,000 workers carve out 176,000 cubic feet of ice to create sculptures and living exhibits such as an Ice Hotel and buildings. This is based on a 300-year winter lanterns tradition from Mongolian culture and lasts for a month.
Burning Man Festival	Annual	25,000–30,000	Nevada, USA	An alternative event where a city of people assemble in the inhospitable desert environment to celebrate the Summer Solstice and surviving whilst living in a communal mode. The philosophy is to leave no trace.
National Association of Stock Car Auto Racing (NASCAR)	Annual event	75 million attendees over a racing season (up to 186,000 each weekend)	USA	Racing events at 32 race tracks across the USA which have the highest sporting event attendance figures globally. It is often focused on the Daytona circuit in Florida as the home of NASCAR which was founded in 1947 and the first race occurred at Daytona in 1948.
Speech and Protest as Spectacle	Ad hoc	250,000–500,000	USA	The National Mall in Washington has developed as the site of free speech in America. Most events are on-off. Two notable events: the 1963 Civil Rights March (250,000 attendees) and the 1971 Vietnam War Protest event (500,000). See https://en.wikipedia.org/wiki/List_of_rallies_and_protest_marches_in_Washington,_D.C.

Events as compiled from Rockwell and Mau (2006) and other sources by the authors

153). This alchemical process can be attributed to the culmination of different processes we explore in this book. For example, as the subsequent chapters will show, one key element in making the event experience is how the audience is created by breaking down barriers to turn people into event-goers (i.e. the removal of physical, psychological, social and other barriers such as a lack of information) (Maitland 1999). Whilst spectacles are the ultimate event experience, we also want to acknowledge that other chapters will demonstrate that five types of event audience exist (i.e. mass event audiences epitomized by major spectacles; special interest audiences; community event audiences; incidental event audiences who did not intend to be there but have become fortuitous attendees; and the media events) (see MacKellar 2013a). Each of these audiences will have different requirements in terms of what makes their experience unique or special.

Other research studies such as Loeffler and Church (2015) point to the importance of creating an exceptional experience, based on people drawing upon experience from Disney, which is acknowledged as a world leader in creating exceptional experiences from the Disney model of customer care. They point to the First Care principles of customer care, where the experience is an interface between the client and provider, and to create the 'Exceptional Experience' they must follow certain care principles (Figure 6.1). Based on studies of the Fortune 500 companies in the USA, Loeffler and Church (2015) found that experience levels among consumers were extremely low, as Figure 6.2 demonstrates, so taking the service and experience to the next level and achieving the exceptional was the main challenge.

These underpinning concepts of experience have also been developed in specific contexts such as leisure, tourism and marketing to seek to explain how the experiences are constructed and how they are special, to which attention now turns.

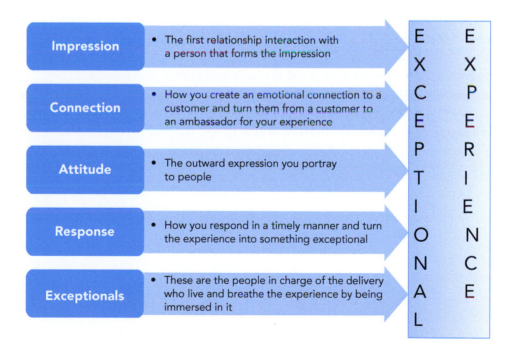

Figure 6.1 The five principles of Disney service

Source: Developed from Leoffler and Church (2015).

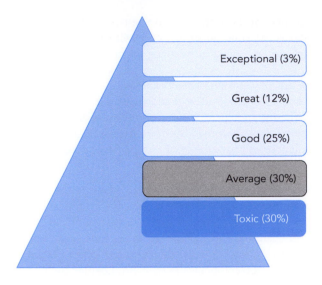

Figure 6.2 Experience levels

Source: Developed from Loeffler and Church (2015).

'Leisure experience' (intrinsic motivation and freedom of choice)

As Chapter 5 illustrated, Mannell and Kleiber (1997) discussed leisure experiences using the concept of 'immediate conscious experience' (or stream of consciousness) which, to understand it, requires the monitoring of real-time behaviour. To be 'leisure', the experience should be accompanied by a sense of freedom, and of competence and control. For this reason we need to understand the immediate conscious experience at events based on:

- anatomy of the experience (what happened to you? intensity; duration);
- moods, emotions, feelings (self-evaluation of the experience); intensity, relaxation, arousal, activation (bored/excited; energetic/tired; active/passive; alert/drowsy);
- involvement: perceived duration; narrow focus of attention; ego-loss;
- cognitive components (ideas, beliefs, thoughts, images/imagination, meanings attached);
- sense of competence/control;
- sense of freedom.

We will return to this approach when talking about experiential sampling, the phenomenological method used to study experiences.

The 'experience economy'

One of the most profound trends in the world of events has been the corporate sector's embracing of the desirability of using the concept of 'experiences' for purposes of marketing and branding. This has occurred because of the readily observed rise of demand for experiences rather than products, and the power of events and other 'experiences' to emotionally connect with consumers, while traditional methods of marketing have declined in impact. All of this has given rise to what some are calling the 'experience economy' and a host of 'creative industries' as we introduced in earlier chapters. Mossberg (2006: 51) suggested that 'The growth of these industries can be explained by new consumption patterns, new technology, and the need for meetings, caring, entertainment and delight.' In fact Jens (2009) identified a number of megatrends that were driving the growth of the experience economy, notably:

- globalization;
- world trade;
- technology;
- individualization;
- the search for authenticity.

There has been an explosion of literature on the 'experience economy' and 'experiential marketing'. This was, as Chapter 1 illustrated, stimulated by Pine and Gilmore who, in their influential book *The Experience Economy* (1999: 3), claimed that 'companies stage an experience whenever they engage customers, connecting with them in a personal, memorable way'. As Smidt-Jensen *et al.* (2009: 849) argue, the experience economy as conceived by Pine and Gilmore suggests 'that economic actors gain an advantage in the market by staging and selling memorable experiences that are enjoyable and personally engaging for the customer' which has redefined many elements of capitalist economies in the developed world. Smidt-Jensen *et al.* (2009: 849–850) argue that, 'This new economic evolution is argued to be based on the fact that customers are generally becoming more open to experiences and more willing to take greater risks and spend larger sums of money to experience something new, because basic goods and services no longer satisfy customers sufficiently.' This growth in industries to meet this need, focused around the cultural industries, and those offering experiences we can consume, are directly aligned with planned events. Conceptually, Sundbo and Bærenholdt (2007: 11) divided the experience economy into two distinct sectors:

- *a primary experience* sector that is composed of companies and institutions that have the production of experiences as the primary objective;
- *a secondary experience* sector where experiences are add-ons to artefacts or service.

For events the co-presence of the event producer and consumer need to be co-located for the experience to be realized. In their economic geography of the experience economy in Denmark, Smidt-Jensen *et al.* (2009) identified the growth of employment in these sectors that clustered around the main towns and cities.

When the customer becomes part of the interplay (i.e. a co-performer), the experience becomes individualized. Four 'realms' of experience were suggested by Pine and Gilmore (1999), derived from two intersecting dimensions as noted in Chapter 1. From an event perspective, the horizontal dimension in the Pine and Gilmore model is a simple active–passive dichotomy, reflecting the activity level of the customer or event-goer. The vertical dimension is much more interesting, reflecting the connection between customer and event. People are 'absorbed' in the experience when the performance occupies their attention and is brought into their minds. 'Immersion' is when the person is physically or virtually 'into' the experience.

Pine and Gilmore (1999: 31) referred to the *Oxford English Dictionary* to define 'entertainment' as 'the action of occupying a person's attention agreeably; amusement'. They suggested that it is one of the oldest forms of experience. In 'aesthetic' experiences (Pine and Gilmore 1999: 35) 'individuals immerse themselves in an event or environment but themselves have little or no effect on it, leaving the environment (but not themselves) essentially untouched'. Thus, 'passive participation' in the Pine and Gilmore model equates with entertainment or aesthetic experiences, while 'active participation' equates with education and escapism.

Education, according to Pine and Gilmore (and many educators), should be interactive, with the onus on the learner to become involved and on the educator to facilitate it. Mental engagement is probably more difficult to realize than physical engagement, as in outdoor pursuits and recreation. Hence, physical engagement is often used to promote the mental side. As well, making education fun, as in 'edutainment', is an effective approach.

'Escapist' experiences require much greater immersion than either educational or entertainment experiences, according to Pine and Gilmore (1999: 33). 'Rather than playing the passive role of couch potato, watching others act, the individual becomes an actor, able to affect the actual performance.' This approach is counter to most theatre or concert events as entertainment, and most closely resembles the festival, party or flash mob, which all depend upon interactivity. The theoretical elements we can observe in the four-realm model of Pine and Gilmore are the basic 'seeking–escaping' motivators identified by Iso-Ahola (1980, 1983) that apply to all leisure and travel, as confirmed in many studies of the motivations of event-goers. It is a very useful model in stimulating thought about the nature of designed experiences, but it is short on making explicit the theoretical underpinnings.

Pine and Gilmore on designing experiences

The Experience Economy (Pine and Gilmore 1999) provides details on how to create experiences, and those authors' guidelines resonate well with event professionals – although they were originally aiming their process mostly at retailers. The first task is to establish the 'theme' of the experience, including the scripting of a 'participative story' to unify all the elements (Pine and Gilmore 1999: 48). Themes should alter the guests' sense of time, place and reality. Themes are made tangible and memorable through 'positive cues' that leave lasting impressions, notably high-quality customer service, design elements, the entertainment, food and beverages, and various other sensory stimulations. Remember how smell triggers memories! Negative cues must be eliminated. Guests should be given, or be able to purchase, memorabilia of their experience.

Surprise is a big element in the Pine and Gilmore approach, by which they mean 'staging the unexpected' (1999: 96). Surprise has to be built on customer satisfaction (basically, delivering what was promised) and eliminating customer 'sacrifice' (i.e. the difference between what they expect and what they perceive they received, often a deficit). Surprise can mean departing from the script or including seemingly bizarre elements into it. Surprise can come from the juxtaposition of contrasting elements of style, out-of-context performance or display, humour and even fright. It will often require a preformulation of guest expectations. And it can be risky!

Taking the theatrical analogy further, Pine and Gilmore discussed the various roles and actors required for a theatrical production, all of which are directly pertinent in the events business. There are producers who financially back the event, and directors who are in charge of the actual production. 'Dramaturgs' act as interpreters of the theme or story, and in the events business they might be consultants from various backgrounds as diverse as theatre, education/interpretation, sport or commerce. Scriptwriters have to prepare the written script or other forms of directions for performers. In dance they are choreographers. In sport they are coaches and in athletics they are trainers. Singers require songwriters and voice trainers.

A host of technicians make essential services happen, whilst set designers make the setting work visually. In the events world, set designers and technicians can be the same, as in making a spectacle from fireworks and lasers, creating intriguing sound and light effects, or decorating tables. Chefs have to both cook and create interesting, tasteful delights. Flower and balloon arrangers stress aesthetics, but must know what will work in various circumstances. Good set designers know about environmental psychology, whether or not they have studied it formally. Prop managers, costume designers, stage crews and casting companies are also needed.

The final topic covered in *The Experience Economy* is 'transformation'. Pine and Gilmore argued that events are 'produced experiences', but transformations occur within the guest or customer. Many event designers seek to facilitate or guide such transformations, specifying outcomes in terms of health and well-being, learning, self-actualization and happiness. These arise from meaningful experiences and may be cumulative. 'When you customize an experience you change the individual' (Pine and Gilmore 1999: 165).

If an event is merely intended to inform or sell, entertain or amuse, achieving transformations will not be a goal of the designer. Increasingly, however, events are planned explicitly for this purpose. Companies want employees to become committed and achieve their full potential, so their corporate functions are intended to transform attitudes and behaviour. Governments and cause-related organizations want the public not only to give money, but to become healthier, wiser, more involved citizens. A key study which explains the experience economy that develops the pine and Gilmore contribution further is Sundbo and Sørensen (2013) *Handbook on the Experience Economy* which is an excellent source of further reference on this area. A key element in the experience economy is co-creation.

Co-creating experiences

'Passive participation' in the Pine and Gilmore model equates with entertainment or aesthetic experiences, while 'active participation' equates with education and escapism. As an extension of this line of reasoning, we need to consider the ideas of co-creation, and liberating experiences. An experience continuum is suggested, and it clearly links to concepts of involvement, engagement, serious leisure and travel careers.

Level 1

Pure entertainment is passive, as in spectating at sports or watching a performance, with no engagement or activity ('couch potato' comes to mind!). Along these lines, spectacle is intended to overwhelm the senses, especially the visual, leaving little room for engagement or learning. Aesthetic appreciation of art is a little different, as it requires an emotional response. It is worth recalling that anything can be perceived as entertainment, especially if no interpretation of meaning is provided.

Level 2

Engagement: participation as an athlete, performer, volunteer or organizer requires engagement with the event and co-creation of its meanings. Meanings of the experience can be mediated and facilitated, but not created by the producers. Interactive audiences provide at least partial engagement, if only at the emotional and cognitive levels (e.g. conference participants, aesthetic appreciation of performances and exhibits).

Level 3

Co-creation: user innovation is part of the event production process. Experience meanings are fluid, as the concept and event progresses. While the event might be mostly entertainment in concept, co-creators feel engaged. A degree of unpredictability must be accepted.

Level 4

Liberating experiences: people reject formal planned event organization as being overly restrictive and engage in their own, possibly spontaneous 'happenings'. In this context, entertainment is a state of mind (self-entertainment), not a production. Van Limburg (2008) examined co-creation as innovation in pop festivals, indicating that it adds a new dimension into the marketing policy of a company, and the research identified a seven-step model that festival managers can use to implement co-creation in their festival. This is explored further in Research Note 6.1. Co-creation has emerged as a recent research theme in event studies as different approaches have been developed to understand the various elements of event experiences.

6.1 RESEARCH NOTE ON CO-CREATION

Van Limburg, B. (2008). Innovation in pop festivals by co-creation. *Event Management*, 12(2), 105–117.

'Co-creation adds a new dimension into the marketing policy of a company, thus developing the ultimate product or service … First the trends within this branch were identified. The next steps were to locate the lead users and then to analyse their experiences. Useful tools within this explorative research are communities, which are used to gain information on lead users. The experiences of lead users in the multiday pop festival branch showed the problems and needs in this branch. These findings are both scientific and practical. The scientific contribution is the question for more research of co-creation stimulating environments. The other scientific finding is the quest for research in order to make the lead user a better lead user and so more of value to a firm. The practical contribution is the delivery of a seven-step model festival managers can use to implement co-creation in their festival.'

Approaches to event experiences

Tourism experiences

Ooi (2005: 53) identified six approaches to identifying and studying tourism experiences. The first derives from cognitive psychology and relates to leisure theory. Preconceived ideas, expectations and perceptions affect how tourists consume, evaluate and experience tourism 'products'. The second approach reflects a great deal of tourism literature, all based on the assumption that travel generates positive experiences; tourism is a means to an end, resulting in learning, happiness and nice memories. In the third approach (again from leisure studies) researchers concentrate on state of mind and the depth of engagement, or 'flow' and 'optimal experiences'. The fourth approach is the 'phenomenological' as proposed by Li (2000) to describe the immediacy of personal touristic experiences through rich, reflexive and intimate data. In the fifth approach, Urry's (1990, 1995, 2002) concept of the 'tourist gaze' is employed, focusing on how travellers notice differences from their own environment and daily life. But because the visitor lacks local knowledge, their experience is a reflection of their own background. In the sixth approach, the theatrical analogy is used, as by Pine and Gilmore in *The Experience Economy* (1999), arguing that 'engaging experiences' depend on the degree to which tourists interact with the 'product'. Ooi (2005: 54) also suggested that tourist experiences are enriched or shaped by 'mediators', including guides, Destination Marketing Organizations and the information available. These help to catch the attention of travellers and even to manage their experiences. Ooi argued that (2005: 55): 'Tourism mediators craft tourism experiences by controlling and directing tourists' attention.' People can only pay attention to one thing at a time, and we are easily overwhelmed by too much information or too many stimuli. When attention shifts, our experience is altered; individuals are both drawn to different stimuli, and react differently to the same stimuli (see Campos *et al.* 2018 for a detailed review of the tourism experience literature and concept). A further development of the experience notion is the contribution made by marketing, particularly experiential marketing.

Event experiences and marketing

Within the growth in marketing research, the experience economy has been embraced as a major area for research. This has emerged from a tradition of services marketing outlined by Baron *et al.* (2014) in their review of the field. As research on services developed, this review highlighted key phases of growth – with different strands of work – one of which was the shift from a measurement and analysis of customer service and quality issues (SERQUAL) to that known as 'service dominant logic' that has contributed to the work on the experience economy as illustrated in Figure 6.3 (see Vargo and Lusch 2004, 2006, 2008 for the basic principles, and Crowther and Donlan 2011 for a discussion of service dominant logic and events). O'Sullivan and Spangler's (1998: 5) *Experience Marketing: Strategies for the New Millennium* stated that in the 'experience economy', there are three types of actors. 'Infusers' are manufacturers who infuse their products with experiences for marketability. 'Enhancers' are service providers who use experiences to heighten satisfaction levels, to differentiate from competitors. And 'experience makers' are service providers who create experiences as the core of their business. To O'Sullivan and Spangler (1998: 3) event experiences involve the following:

- participation and involvement in the consumption;
- the state of being physically, mentally, socially, spiritually or emotionally engaged;
- a change in knowledge, skill, memory or emotion;
- the conscious perception of having intentionally encountered, gone to or lived through an activity or event;
- an effort directed at addressing a psychological or internal need.

They also identified five 'parameters' of experience (O'Sullivan and Spangler 1998: 23):

1 stages: events or feelings that occur prior to, during and after;
2 the actual experience: factors or variables that influence participation and shape outcomes;

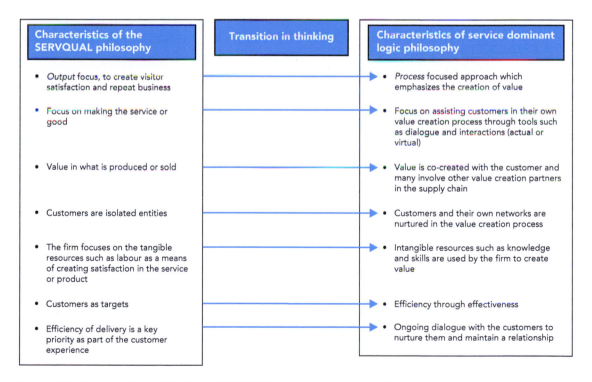

Figure 6.3 The paradigm shift from SERVQUAL to service dominant logic

Source: Page (2015: 321). Reprinted from *Tourism Management, 5th Edition*, S. J. Page, Routledge (2015).

3 needs being addressed;

4 roles of the participant and other people involved (personality, expectations, behaviour) in shaping outcomes;

5 roles of and relationships with the provider of the experience (ability and willingness to customize the experience, control it).

O'Sullivan and Spangler ask a lot of pertinent questions about the event experience. To what extent is the experience real versus virtual, customized or mass produced, unique or commonplace? Is it focused on people, an attraction, a facility, equipment or performance? Does the event experience consist of concrete or disconnected episodes? Is the guest or customer participant or spectator, facilitated or self-directed? Does the event create a temporary or transforming change, or result in pleasure or preservation? What is the level of authenticity?

Co-creating event experiences

One of the main developments emanating from marketing research on the experience economy is the interest in co-creation, as outlined in Figure 6.3 as part of the service dominant logic paradigm. As Van Winkle and Bueddefeld (2016) argued, it focuses on how satisfying event experiences are constructed based on the concept of value. Holbrook (1999) identified eight experiential types of value (see Figure 6.4) while Rihova (2013) examined the six practices of co-creation observed at music festivals as illustrated in Figure 6.5.

What Figure 6.5 demonstrates is the importance of sociality in how festival goers co-create event experiences. This tends to reaffirm Verleye's (2015) argument that people put more effort into the activity they undertake because of the return they expect to receive, based on social exchange theory. The consequence as Verleye (2015) found is that people may expect various types of experience as a result of participation

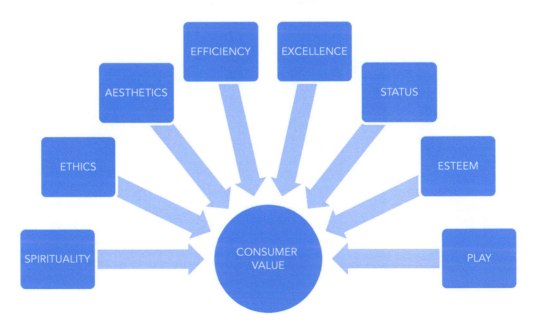

Figure 6.4 The concept of the eight types of consumer value

Source: Developed from Holbrook (1999).

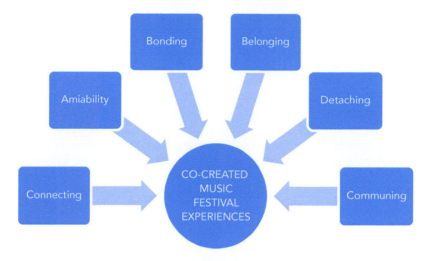

Figure 6.5 The six practices of co-creating event experiences

Source: Developed from Rihova (2013).

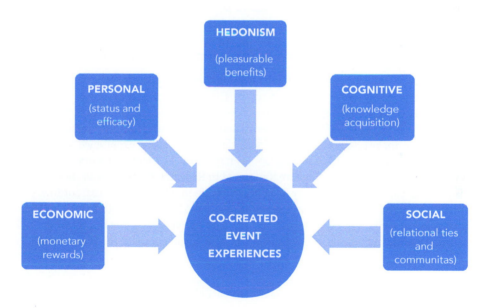

Figure 6.6 Expected benefits from co-creating experiences

Source: Developed from Verleye (2015); authors.

as reflected in Figure 6.6, which are impacted by technology, the connectedness with other people as well as the nature of these interactions which shape hedonistic behaviour in relation to events.

Whilst Verleye (2015) recognizes that a co-created experience is a multidimensional construct, 'despite its acknowledged importance, empirical work about the outcomes of co-creation is limited' (Verleye 2015: 322), even given recent literature reviews of the co-creation area (see Campos *et al.* 2018). Nevertheless, criticisms of event studies research as being descriptive and lacking theoretical grounding by Gyimóthy and Larson (2015) do not hold ground in terms of the rigour with which recent studies of co-creation and events demonstrate.

The 'guaranteed' and safe experience

How do we explain the popularity of theme parks and entertainment events – including cultural productions? One answer is that they provide 'guaranteed' and safe experiences. Their predictability, combined with perceived personal security, assures the customer that they will get what they expect, even though their expectations are limited. In contrast, travel and many event experiences are somewhat unpredictable, with plenty of risks. If people are willing to sacrifice spontaneity, cultural authenticity and surprise for the safe and mundane, that is their business. The more highly 'involved' traveller, plus the many novelty seekers of the world, will certainly continue to seek out special experiences.

The WOW! factor

Event designers strive hard to impress the visitor. Citrine (n.d.) held that the 'WOW! factor' is a guiding principle for event designers. Visitors, Citrine argued, should be 'dazzled' when they arrive and leave. Is this the same as saying event designers seek to create really special, emotionally engaging and memorable experiences? Much of what goes into 'WOW!' is art and *spectacle* (as discussed earlier) – a visual impression which Page and Connell (2010) observed in relation to visitor attractions. Sound and smell can also be combined with decor, lighting and other programmic elements of style, so 'WOW!' can be a complete sensory reaction. Clearly this can be designed. But can you have a 'WOW!' experience in terms of learning, cultural authenticity or perhaps physical mastery? That's a little more difficult to conceptualize, let alone to design or programme.

Considerably exceeding expectations, and building in elements of surprise, could achieve the 'WOW!' reaction. This was discussed earlier in relation to the Disney model and customer satisfaction, so that the expectation is exceeded and exceptional experience is created. So too could disappointment and failure, giving rise to the wrong kind of 'WOW!' (as in, that really stunk!). An interesting study by Morgan (2008) entitled 'What makes a good festival? Understanding the event experience' explored the nature of extraordinary experiences through a netnographic analysis of the views of committed attendees at the 2005 Sidmouth Folk Festival. The findings are illustrated in Research Note 6.2, and they support the view that festivals provide a space and time away from everyday life in which intense extraordinary experiences can be created and shared, a theme we will return to below. Allen *et al.* (2008) point to the concept of extraordinary experiences in marketing research building on psychological constructs around achieving an extremely happy state through events where the social interaction is one of the main stimuli.

6.2 RESEARCH NOTE ON EVENT EXPERIENCES

Morgan, M. (2008). What makes a good festival? Understanding the event experience. *Event Management*, 12(2), 81–93.

'This article explores the nature of extraordinary experiences through a netnographic analysis of the views of committed attendees at the 2005 Sidmouth Folk Festival. … To provide a framework for analysing these responses, a holistic prism model was developed from the literature to bring together the main external and internal elements of the festival experience: "Design and Programming", "Physical Organization", "Social Interaction", "Personal Benefits", "Symbolic Meanings" and "Cultural Communication". This was used to analyse the messages and explore the way in which festival-goers evaluate their experience. The findings support the view that festivals provide a space and time away from everyday life in which intense extraordinary experiences can be created and shared.'

A model of the planned event experience

This conceptual model (Figure 6.7) is based largely on the social and anthropological literature discussed earlier, especially pertaining to rituals and communitas. It is not intended as a design model, but you can see general design implications. At the core of our model is a distinct experiential zone called 'liminal/liminoid'. It is a zone that must be delineated in both spatial and temporal terms. This is a 'special place' because of programming and how it is designed, all in preparation for the guests, viewers or participants. Designers can make it special through decor, entertainment, activity and sensory stimulations of all kinds, and they should use Falassi's (1987) 'valorization' concept to make event-goers aware that they are entering a space/time that has been set aside for their special purposes.

Meaning is conveyed through opening ceremonies, symbolism such as banners or logos, and the theme. Some event experiences can be called 'sacred' (religious, spiritual) and others 'profane' (fun, escapist). However, it should always be a 'time out of time', to use Falassi's terminology – that is, it should be perceived to be outside the normal, beyond routine, unique. To the extent possible, all those involved with the event should experience the belonging and sharing that defines 'communitas'. An interesting explanation of meaning and its role in events can be found in Events in Focus 6.1. This begins to lead us towards building a model to explain the type of factors to incorporate into a planned event experience.

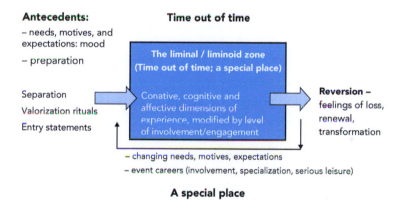

Figure 6.7 A model of the planned event experience

EVENTS IN FOCUS

6.1 Understanding event experiences in the experience economy, event meaning and event duration: new research directions

According to Kociatkiewicz and Kostera (2012), the key features of the experience economy that we need to understand in relation to events include the immediacy, subjectivity, playfulness and performativity of the experience economy. Within the context of events, their research also highlighted a number of other key concepts shaping the meaning of the event experience, notably the speed of the event and scale which begin to shape two key elements of the resulting experience – the immediate and memorable (see Figure 6.8). This provides a basis on which to begin to focus on the meaning in the experience and what key concepts will help to identify what shapes these experiences.

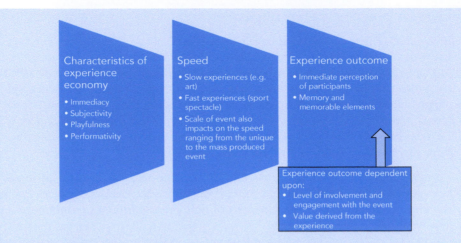

Figure 6.8 The experience economy, scale and speed in event experiences

According to Ryan (2014: 250):

> First, the event is perceived as having meaning for the individual. There is something about an event with which the attendee identifies – it reflects degrees of interest that at the time of the event is deemed significant. Attributed significance to the nature of the event however may be either temporary or enduring, and is to be distinguished from the significance of the experience as being temporary or enduring, although the two are linked.

Ryan (2014: 251) highlighted identifiable concepts in the analysis of meaning in event experiences:

- *Enduring meaning*, something which emerges when the person attending the event has an ongoing interest with the event.

- Attachment and identification arguing that:

> The more closely is one's association with an event through interests or personal connections, the more one identifies with the desired success of the event. Identification is a two-way process, and as evidenced by the literature relating to serious leisure … so one's own sense of being is reinforced by association with being present at, or playing an organising role in the event.
>
> (Ryan 2014: 251)

- *Anticipation* as determinant of the experience and the key role of media in informing and in the build up to the anticipation.

- Events as *liminal experiences*, since they are outside of the everyday and ordinary life experiences.

- The role of the event in stimulating *emotional responses* especially communitas when being with others and other signifiers such as tee shirts, football shirts and insignia.

This led Ryan (2014) to develop Figure 6.9, based on the level of meaning in an event and the duration of interest in the event with four types of event participant identified in each of the four quadrants. In fact studies such as Scott (1995) emphasize how important many of the concepts highlighted are for event attendance in terms of meaning, with sociability and family togetherness (including communitas) and escape from routine, event excitement and curiosity noted

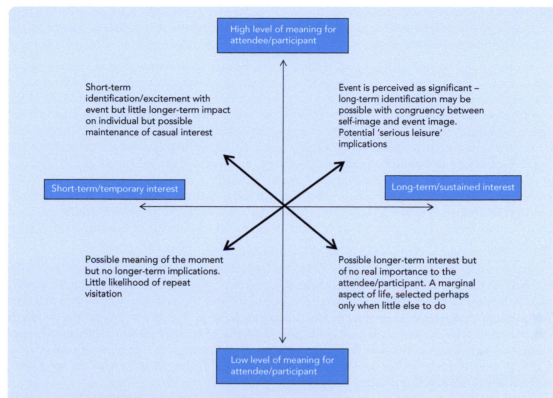

Figure 6.9 Matrix of event meaning and duration of interest

Source: Ryan (2014: 257). Reprinted from *The Routledge Handbook of Events*, S. J. Page and J. Connell, Routledge (2014).

as frequent facets underpinning the experience and meaning derived from events. Research by Ziakas and Boukas (2014) has suggested that we may need to adopt phenomenological research approaches to begin to understand experiences and meaning in events, understanding what is memorable, why and over what duration that memorability is retained. Additional approaches from cultural and environmental economics using valuation methods to understand the value of events to people have used the Triple-Ex approach looking at experience, extent of visit (duration) and visit expenditure (Andersson and Ambrecht 2014). More traditional research methods around notions of service quality that emanate from marketing have also been applied (e.g. Song *et al.* 2014) in relation to the experience economy, observing that aesthetics and entertainment were amongst the most important experiential elements of Expo visitors. Manthiou *et al.* (2014) found similar results when examining loyalty and vivid memories of attending events, with the entertainment and aesthetics elements shaping loyalty to visit. Sit and Birch's (2014) review of events in shopping malls also identified some of these components in the family-oriented events staged that were rated as relaxing and entertaining.

It is easy to think of a special place as an event venue, like an arena, theatre or convention centre. But it can also be a temporary event space, or a whole community. The question of scale is important (as illustrated in Events in Focus 6.1) along with speed, because as we move from venue to large public space to entire community, we have a much more complex and difficult job of design and programming and a different type of experience evolving from the slow to fast type. Nevertheless, many communities manage to make themselves festive throughout, or at least operate as important entrances and meeting places, during the time of special events.

Before we get to the event, there is preparation and anticipation. Most people go to an event having some expectations of the experience to be obtained (or partially self-created), or at least some foreknowledge that an event is about to be experienced. Much research has been conducted on motivation to attend events, especially festivals, and it mostly confirms the 'seeking–escaping' theory, suggesting that people clearly anticipate that an event is going to be out of the ordinary. You could stumble upon an event and be surprised, but even so there will be a sense of having left somewhere and arrived at some special place. Even where expectations are completely absent, that is, the event-goer never gave it any thought at all, there still has to be the 'entering into' event that marks a transition from ordinary to extraordinary. Seeking to capture these elements and measure them remains a challenging process around the concepts in Events in Focus 6.1 (such as emotion, mood (Hull 1990), surprise (Vanhamme and Snelders 2001)), using in situ research methods or techniques around reminiscing or focusing on triggers such as nostalgia.

Csikszentmihalyi's theory of 'flow' (1975, 1990) fits into this model. It suggests that people seek 'optimal arousal', leading to 'flow' experiences which can be characterized by deep involvement, intense concentration, lack of self-consciousness and transcendence of self. These are intrinsically rewarding experiences. To the extent that designers can facilitate 'flow', event-goers can be expected to report exhilaration (from fantasizing or total immersion in music or activity), a sense of accomplishment (athletic achievement, mastery of a skill, intellectual stimulation) or transformation (through an intense emotional or spiritual process). How to foster a high level of involvement is the real challenge, and events that provide mere entertainment will find this illusive.

'Liminality' is not strictly dependent upon the type of event or venue. This space/time exists in the minds of the attendees and participants, not within the programme or venue itself. It can therefore be entered through the pathways of 'fantasy' (the heart of many theme parties), a willing suspension of the ordinary to play a role (as in carnival), engagement in new ideas and processes (such as discourse, clinical learning, team projects), participation with others (like celebration) or any kind of higher-than-usual level of involvement.

In the case of 'flash mobs' and other events at the fringe, it is the participants who, according to some unwritten script or external prodding, largely make their own experiences. They are temporarily using (or 'liberating') a space for their purposes, perhaps making a social or political statement in doing so, but quickly returning it to the ordinary. 'Reversion' to normal life should be accompanied by a sense of change, going from the special to the ordinary. There might be a feeling of accomplishment, renewal, transformation, relief or loss. It is important to feel something at the end, otherwise what was special or memorable about the experience? It may be possible to feel a sense of loss at the end of conferences, not necessarily because the stimulating programme is over, but because of separation from friends and colleagues. It is the loss of 'communitas', and it leads to the drive to attend future events. Anyone who is highly 'involved' or emotionally moved by events will experience this loss. It gives meaning to the event and to our ordinary lives.

To the extent that people enjoy events, or at least derive some benefits from attending, they might very well develop an event career. Similar to Pearce's 'travel career', we learn from events and perhaps desire more of the same (the loyal festival-goer), or we crave the uniqueness, even surprises that come from many different types of event (the cultural event tourist), or we want ever-increasing challenge (the amateur, competitive athlete). In fact nostalgia has a clear role to play, as demonstrated by Fairley and Gammon (see Research Note 6.3).

> ## 6.3 RESEARCH NOTE ON LIMINAL EXPERIENCES AND NOSTALGIA
>
> Fairley, S. and Gammon, S. (2006). Something lived, something learned: Nostalgia's expanding role in sport tourism. In H. Gibson (ed.), *Sport Tourism: Concepts and Theories*, pp. 50–65. London: Routledge.
>
> Fairley and Gammon suggested that for many sport fans there is a nostalgic desire to re-enter the liminoid space they associate with events and with the group experience of travelling to events. This space involves a strong sense of community or shared subcultural identity, and resembles the carnival in its acceptance of abandoning social norms. There is also the appeal of escape from everyday life. Nostalgia, in this context, fuels a career of event-related travel, and it relates to volunteers at events as well.

O'Dell (2005: 133) argued that we must not over-emphasize the disjuncture from ordinary life when we consider 'liminal' or 'liminoid' experiences. His point is that touristic and event experiences can only be special or exceptional when considered in light of one's ordinary life and experiences. He said: 'To a large extent people learn the ropes of "experiencing" through their daily consumption patterns. We also need to develop competencies for experiencing, and this is embodied in the concepts of serious leisure, specialization, and self-efficacy.'

What makes an event experience rewarding and memorable?

Moscardo (2010) summarized the literature on effective and rewarding customer and tourist experiences, and this body of knowledge is easily adaptable to event design (see Table 6.3). Her discussion is in the context of the importance of storytelling and themes for tourist experiences. Stories are one form of thematic interpretation. Compare Moscardo's factors to the list of features that help make events 'special', to the 'elements of style', and discussions of ego involvement and serious leisure; consider which of these reflect generic versus targeted benefits. In Table 6.3, a number of event-specific references have been added. In fact a useful study that has a bearing on the memorable nature of the event experience is mindfulness. Van Winkle and Backman (2009) examined visitor mindfulness at a cultural event that revolves around the concept of mindfulness, which is a state of being that requires individuals to engage in active information processing, enabling them to be adaptive and responsive to information in their surroundings. This is explored further in Research Note 6.4.

Table 6.3 Factors associated with effective and rewarding customer and tourist experiences

Factors (*Source:* Moscardo, 2010)	References specific to events (or highly applicable)
Theme: strong, clear and consistent, supported by design and 'servicescape'	Themed events: Goldblatt 2011: 108; Targeting through theming: Getz 2005: 321. Developing the theme: Van der Wagen 2008; Getz *et al.* 2001, on service mapping/servicescapes; Bruwer and Kelley 2015.
Story or narrative: allows customers to play a desirable role or create their own stories to tell others	Deighton 1992, on narratives in performance; Cruikshank 1997, on a storytelling festival; Mossberg 2008, on storytelling in hospitality; Moscardo 2010.

(Continued)

Table 6.3 (continued)

Factors (*Source*: Moscardo, 2010)	References specific to events (or highly applicable)
Perceived authenticity: access to real objects, places and people (i.e. objective authenticity); genuine interactions with others in the setting; and opportunities for activities that reflect one's true self (i.e. existential authenticity)	Boorstin 1961; Greenwood 1972, 1989; Buck 1977; Papson 1981; Cohen 1988b; Getz 1998b; Sofield and Li 1998; Wang 1999; Robinson *et al.* 2004; Xie 2003, 2004; Picard and Robinson 2006a; McCartney and Osti 2007; Knox 2008; Brida *et al.* 2013; Robinson and Clifford 2012.
Interactive, participatory and engaging: customers as co-creators of the experience	Hilliard 2006, on meeting planning; Harvey *et al.* 1998, on exhibits; Ralston *et al.* 2007; Pine and Gilmore 1999; Bjorner and Berg 2012, on co-creation.
Uniqueness: rarity, novelty and surprise	On surprise: Schechner 1988 (theatre); Pine and Gilmore 1999; Pettersson and Getz 2009. On uniqueness: Nicholson and Pearce 2001; Ralston *et al.* 2007; Getz 2005; Foster and Robinson 2010.
Easy to access: easy to get to, move around and understand (i.e. legibility)	On accessibility: Severt *et al.* 2007; for disabled: Darcy and Harris 2003; on legibility and site design: Getz 2005.
Multisensory	Harvey *et al.* 1998, discovered they could more than double the time visitors spent at exhibits by making them interactive and multisensory.
Emotive	Botterill and Crompton 1996: emotional states are integral to 'optimal experiences'; Russell and Lanius 1984: the same stimulus can generate widely different affective appraisals of settings; Matheson 2008; Nelson 2009; Huang *et al.* 2012 on mood.
Opportunities to be social	Fairley and Gammon 2006, on nostalgia and shared experiences of sport fans; Coghlan and Filo 2013 on connectedness.
Personal relevance: making connections to personal history; can be personalized; total immersion in the setting	Van Winkle and Backman (2009): mindfulness at events. Harvey *et al.* 1998: The influence of museum exhibit design on immersion and psychological flow; Berridge 2012a.
Learning opportunities	Lee and Back 2009: the importance of learning at conferences; evaluation of an event's educational goals: Gitelson *et al.* 1995; visitor desire for interpretation: Xie 2004.

6.4 RESEARCH NOTE ON MINDFULNESS AND EVENT EXPERIENCE

Van Winkle, C. and Backman, K. (2009). Examining visitor mindfulness at a cultural event. *Event Management*, 12(3/4), 163–169.

'Mindfulness is considered a state of being that requires individuals to engage in active information processing, enabling them to be adaptive and responsive to information in their surroundings.

Mindfulness is believed to result in more learning, high satisfaction, greater understanding, and greater feeling of control over behaviour. Event managers must find ways to enhance visitor satisfaction as well as minimize negative impacts that result from events, and encouraging visitor mindfulness could contribute to these outcomes. This study took place over a two-week period in July 2005 at the Winnipeg Fringe Theatre Festival in Winnipeg, Manitoba, Canada. Results presented demonstrate that the more interested visitors were in the festival, the higher they scored on the mindfulness scale. Visitor level of mindfulness was positively related to their satisfaction with the event and their feelings of control over their own contribution to impacts. Implications for event managers are discussed.'

Generic and specific types of planned event experiences

If we return to the earlier discussion of how our planned event typology is based on event forms, which are social constructs, it suggests they are not based on unique experiential components. Not only is it difficult to describe experiences, but any event can conceivably engender many different experiences. The following discussion is an attempt to show that there are both generic and specific experiences associated with types of events, but this is not the same as formulating an experiential typology of events.

Generic event experiences

'Generic experiences' are those which can occur at any event, and therefore have more to do with the individual's state of mind and particular circumstances than with the event theme, programme or setting. We are convinced that many people attend events for generic personal benefits such as entertainment and simple diversion (we can call this 'escapism') and 'having fun' is probably how most people would describe the experience (see Table 6.3). Meanings attached to these experiences would not normally be profound. We cannot expect them to be memorable or transforming, but that is possible. More important are the generic social motivations and benefits associated with leisure and travel in general, which apply to intrinsically motivated event experiences – especially to have quality time with friends and family, and to enjoy that sense of belonging and sharing we call 'communitas'.

Social experiences can occur whenever and wherever people get together, but planned events definitely facilitate them. Indeed, social and cultural groups create events specifically for this purpose, or find that certain events are good at facilitating it.

Uysal and Li (2008) presented a critical literature review of empirical studies of festival and event motivation. They identified that the most frequently mentioned dimension was socialization (24.0 per cent), followed by family togetherness (18.8 per cent), novelty (19.0 per cent) and escape (15.7 per cent). The other major dimensions were cultural exploration (5.0 per cent), entertainment (5.8 per cent) and attractions (4.1 per cent). The key role of social factors was also identified by Foster and Robinson (2010) focusing on the motivational factors that influence event attendance in family groups. The study of families with children confirmed the overriding importance of family togetherness, followed by socializing and then excitement in motivating family attendance at special events. The study concluded that families are willing to compromise on individual motivation and attend events that children will find satisfying. Families were not interested in novelty or uniqueness, they just wanted to spend time together. Similarly, Ko *et al.* (2010) examined consumer satisfaction and event quality perception at a US Open Taekwondo Championship. Their study found that 'social interaction' was a motivator for spectators at the martial arts event. We will return to this important discussion in Chapter 8, specifically dealing with festival motivations where a model is presented showing essential services, generic and event-specific benefits.

Specific event experiences

In this section we examine the kinds of experiences that can and should be associated with certain types of planned events.

Cultural celebrations

Cultural experiences in general are all about seeking knowledge, learning and understanding something new, and appreciating some aspects of culture – both the traveller's and that of the destination. The cultural tourist or cultural event-goer wants to engage emotionally and cognitively with places, people and dimensions of lifestyle, including tangible things like historic sites, cultural performances, food and beverages, or meeting local people, and with intangible aspects including the symbolism of art and architecture. Simply sightseeing, or enjoying entertainment or spectacle, does not constitute a cultural experience. Celebrations and commemorations in general reflect and foster belonging and sharing among a family, social group, community or nation. Values come to the fore, and a clear sense of place is usually present. The event's theme suggests what is to be celebrated, although in many cases it is the community itself that is the object of celebrations. In all cultural events, we should be concerned with the notion of 'authenticity' and what that means in experiential terms. A detailed discussion of authenticity follows, in the section on meanings.

Festivals and carnivals

Festivals and carnivals, as discussed previously, are meant to be joyous experiences. But they can range from solemn and sacred festivals to profane carnivals marked by wild revelry. Role playing and inversion (including masquerading) are found in many carnivals. They usually embody rituals and symbolism that act as cues in suggesting the appropriate mood and emotions (see case studies of these issues in Laing and Frost 2014). These experience domains have been studied in depth by sociologists and anthropologists, such as Turner and Falassi. Many so-called 'festivals', however, seem to provide little more than packaged entertainment and a party atmosphere, leaving it up to the audience and others involved to create their own, deeper experiences – if possible. Thematic interpretation can help communicate what is culturally significant about events, including their setting (the place), symbolic elements and historic context. One area of interest among researchers is the area of music festivals. For example, Pegg and Patterson (2010) examined visitor motivations and experiences sought; they found that visitors' love of country music was the primary reason for attending the festival. However, the overall results indicated that it was the variety of activities and festival atmosphere that were considered by visitors as being the most important aspects of their participation. The atmosphere was repeatedly mentioned as a reoccurring theme, and, in particular, they stressed the casual, relaxed, family-friendly atmosphere. Visitors also commented on the welcoming feelings that they received from people who were living locally. This reflects a sense that the event attracted people with desires similar to the visitors, that is, to have a safe and enjoyable time together. Further insights are provided by Ballantyne et al. (2014) in their analysis of the music festival experience.

In contrast to the Tamworth (Australia) festival mentioned above by Pegg and Patterson (2010), consider this radically different experience described by an anonymous blogger who attended a drugs-infested concert:

> *Take how many times you have been offered drugs and multiply that times 1,000 and that's how many times you will be offered drugs a day at .... People walking around with backpacks shouting 'coke, x, molly, nugs, doses!' and every other drug you can think of. I walked by a table where people were selling nitrus in balloons. What I learned throughout this was that the people who are carrying around all of these drugs were there to screw you over and take your money. There is*

a system with the ... drug world its either bring your own or make friends with hippies because they have the best stuff. We were exchanging food and beer for getting smoked up and acid.

Religious and spiritual experiences

Sacred and spiritual experiences are not necessarily the same. 'Sacred' generally refers to established religious dogma (e.g. the Holy Scriptures are sacred; communion is a sacred rite). Spiritual experiences could be non-religious in nature, consisting of feelings of transcendence (e.g. 'I felt completely removed from, even raised above, the worries of daily life') or self-discovery ('I was on a different plane of existence where I felt connected to everything and everyone'). Timothy and Olsen (2006: 271) argued that there are significant differences between being religious and being spiritual. Spiritual refers to personal belief, a search for meaning in one's life, and so any tourist could have a spiritual experience in a sacred place or alongside religious pilgrims. Rapture, ecstasy, transcendence and revelation are terms used in conjunction with intense religious or spiritual experiences. Is this what is supposed to happen at a church service or during a papal tour? Can these experiences be designed or facilitated at religious events? Certainly there is often the intent to do so, as when a preacher calls upon people in the congregation to come forward to repent. There is also a special dimension of 'communitas' in religious events, as highlighted by the rite of 'communion'.

Reisinger (2006) saw possibilities for spiritual experiences being incorporated into, or modifying, many common forms of tourism, from nature tours to attending farm shows and harvest festivals, food and wine tastings to spa visits. While often associated with visits to sacred places, spiritual experiences are also realized through meditation, exploring and performing rituals. In this sense the search for meaning in life can propel, almost invisibly, many leisure and travel activities.

Pilgrimage

Pilgrimage is a quest, a journey and the experience of a sacred place. For many it is a duty. The entire pilgrimage can be conceptualized as a special event in a person's life, a rite of passage and a transforming experience, but there are often well-defined events associated with religious pilgrimages. Pilgrimage occurs in stages. To prepare for the Hajj in Mecca, Muslims are to put their earthly affairs in order and become spiritually prepared. The event itself involves a number of rituals, including those of purification, praise, repentance and sacrifice. Upon completion of the Hajj, one becomes 'hajji' and gains special status, making it a transforming process, at least in symbolic terms. Raj and Morpeth (2007) described the activities and experience of the Hajj, emphasizing that it was not a touristic experience, but a religious obligation, and a beautiful, once-in-a-lifetime experience.

Singh (2006: 232) argued that Hindu pilgrims 'enjoy sacred journeys as an earthly adventure from one place to another that entails the combined effects of a spiritual quest and physical hardship'. But could that not also describe the experience of a long-distance runner? Certainly the key elements that make religious quests and experiences different from other spiritual or emotionally uplifting experiences are participation in specified rituals or ceremonies that have deep meaning to the devoted and faithful. The place itself is crucial, but unlike a secular event venue, the meaning of sacred places is permanent, traditional and sanctioned by official religious bodies.

Virtual and secular pilgrimage

Only Muslims can experience the Hajj in person, but others may visit websites that provide a simulacrum of what it is like to be a pilgrim. Many tourism scholars now speak of secular pilgrimages, such as a golfer's pilgrimage to St Andrews in Scotland (the generally recognized birthplace of the game) or a wine lover's pilgrimage to the regions in which favourite wines are produced. Gammon (2004: 40) argued that pilgrimage 'will include a journey of some kind to a place (or places) which holds personal and/or collective meaning to the "pilgrim"'. The experience might provoke 'awe and wonderment', whether at a sport, shrine or holy event. Within special interest groups, or subcultures, certain events have prestige and become must-see, must-do 'icons'. For example, marathon runners strive to qualify for the Boston Marathon, making participation in that event almost like a pilgrimage. Does this apply to music concerts or other types of events? Could consumer researchers identify a set of events that people just have to attend because of their symbolic value?

Political and state events

Many political and state events will have a high degree of formality, pomp and ceremony attached to them. Terms like stately, regal or dignified might be used to describe the mood. What you will experience at such events can vary greatly, depending on why you attended (to protest, participate or report on?), what access you have to the VIPs and how you interact with security. For the politicians in attendance, there should be dialogue, negotiation and public displays of diplomacy. A study by Digance (2005) examined the impact of the Commonwealth Heads of Government (CHOGM) meeting.

Arts and entertainment experiences (including the aesthetic)

By labelling entertainment an 'industry', society has created a social construct that depicts many forms of planned events (especially concerts, award shows and sports, but even festivals and art exhibitions) as entertainment. Events, for many, have become legitimate outlets for consumerism, where we spend our time and money oblivious to, or unwanting of, any deeper experience or meaning than short-lived amusement. This, of course, is a dangerous thing for anyone concerned about the arts, cultural authenticity or social values. 'Aesthetic judgement' concerns art and beauty, but is value laden and relative. What one person finds attractive, another might describe as boring or disgusting. An aesthetic experience, however, is one in which we find something to be pleasing to our senses. It can be the aesthetic appreciation of paintings, food, fashion or music. Hence it is intensely personal, which leads to the expression 'you can't please everyone'. Designers take note: aesthetic experiences are valued, and they motivate a great deal of travel and consumption, but you cannot guarantee satisfaction. For most appreciators of fine art, food, music or whatever, it is the exploration and sense of discovery that matter most.

Limited research has been reported on art exhibitions (see du Cros and Jolliffe 2014 for a review), but Axelsen and Arcodia (2004) argued that they should be viewed in the context of special-event motivation and experience. A review of the literature suggested that people attend art galleries for reasons of learning, social interaction, status and novelty. Smith (2006) discussed the rise of 'new leisure tourism', linking it to the increasing blurring of work and leisure, and to 'de-differentiation' or the breakdown of boundaries between previously distinct activities. New leisure tourists are engaging in escapism, looking for fresh experiences, wanting fun and high-quality entertainment. Novelty-seeking is a key aspect of this trend, leading Urry (2002) to suggest that people are becoming insatiable in their quest for novelty because reality never matches their expectations.

Youthful, hard-working consumers, brought up on music videos and computer entertainment, seem to have a very limited attention span and are constantly seeking stimulation. Smith (2006: 224) concluded that new leisure tourists are not interested in culture, but want playful, event-fantastical experiences. Contrived, simulated, even obviously fake settings can provide this. Interactivity is desired, but in a technological sense. Fascination with celebrities is part of this new experiential realm. Industry has responded (in the spirit of the 'experience economy') with theming, overtly catering to hedonism, celebrity endorsements, and what is being called 'shoppertainment'.

Competitive sport/recreation event experiences (for athletes)

It has to be more than just winning! Although competitive sports superficially involve games played by persons or teams with the intent of winning, that in itself does not constitute the entire experience or meaning. Many people compete for very personal reasons, such as to gain fitness and mastery, while others compete for social reasons – to be part of a group and to enjoy a social event. Bouchet *et al.* (2004) reviewed the literature on sport-tourist experiences and concluded there are four theoretical streams evident. From a 'behavioural theory' perspective, group activities and interactions are the focus. For example, Green and Chalip (1998) found that strong subcultural meanings were attached by participants to a women's sport event. From cognitive psychology comes attention to needs, motives, values and risk taking. A third approach combined the psychological and behavioural roles of travellers, and the fourth is the experiential model.

Bouchet *et al.* (2004) advanced their own approach to analysing the sport-tourist experience, encompassing considerations of self-worth (perceived risk, optimal stimulation, variety and novelty-seeking), spatial variables, or the place (including functional components and a post-modernist view of how visitors create their own experiences and living space), and interpersonal variables (new relationships and 'communitas').

What particularly distinguishes competitive sport experiences from any other event experiences is the structure (venues, rules and team versus single play), all of which are specific to each sport. Either this structure appeals to a person or it does not, and the diversity of sport gives rise to an almost infinite variety of experiential possibilities. Some are less combative than others; some require brute strength, others demand finesse and artistry. Sport is both highly personal (what the athlete accomplishes on their own) and social (the team, the community of athletes, the whole event organization).

The sport spectator and sport-fan experience

In the report *Travelers Who Attend Sport Events* (Travel Industry Association of America 1999), sport-event tourism was depicted as a major social and economic phenomenon, where 84 per cent of the American adults who had travelled for sport reasons had been spectators. Many of these were parents or grandparents going to watch children play in competitions. In other words there is a huge family market within sport-event tourism. Only 16 per cent travelled to participate, and some of them also spectated. Gibson (1998, 2006b) found in her research that the 'active sport tourist' was mostly a male with college education and higher income. This segment, she concluded, will likely continue to travel for participation in their favourite sports well into retirement.

Attending a sport event can be motivated by a desire for entertainment and spectacle (i.e. simple diversion), the desire for emotional stimulation or having a social outing. Being a sport spectator is a role we can all play, and most spectators know that it is generally more interesting (certainly more emotionally exciting) to be at a live event as opposed to watching on TV. Being a sport 'fan', however, is something quite a bit more engaging. Wann (1995) and Wann *et al.* (1999) developed a 'sport-fan motivation scale' that covers both intrinsic and extrinsic motivation. It consists of eight common reasons for watching sport, and these can also be conceptualized as desired experiences: escape, 'eustress' (i.e. stress evoked by emotions or events, here considered to be positive stimulation), aesthetics (appreciation of the beauty of sports), self-esteem, group affiliation, family, entertainment and economic (e.g. betting). Chen (2006) provided a review of the literature on sport fans, in a paper devoted to a phenomenological study of event sport-fans' behaviour, experiences and values.

Studies of sport fans have taken psychological and social-psychological approaches (see, for example, Wann 1997; Smith and Mackie 2000). Specific attention has been given to 'affect and emotion' (Dietz-Uhler and Murrell 1999; Wann *et al.* 2002; Madrigal 2003), motives (Trail and James 2001; James and Ridinger 2002), 'identification' (Laverie and Arnett 2000), gender differences (Dietz-Uhler *et al.* 2000; James and Ridinger 2002), factors influencing fan behaviour (End *et al.* 2003) and loyalty (Mahony *et al.* 1999, 2000; Tapp 2004). Some fans can be considered to be engaging in 'serious leisure' (Gibson *et al.* 2003). It has even been determined that highly 'committed' sport fans spend more in destinations than casual fans. A summary of the motives of sport spectators can be found in Table 6.4.

Chen concluded that most studies suggest that personally relevant values (from needs and the benefits sought), and 'identifications' (such as social identity) most explain why fans become highly involved and committed to teams (see also Wann and Branscombe 1993; Madrigal 1995; Bristow and Sebastion 2001). Chen's (2006) study determined that 'personal balance' and 'socialization' were the essential parts of the experiences being sought, and these were obtained through volunteering, being at events, travel with other fans and the team, 'pilgrimages' to places with special meanings, and non-related social and touristic activities in destinations.

Exhibition experiences

According to Mair (2013) conferences and exhibitions continue to play a major role in the world of business and trade, despite the rise of social media and technology-enabled communication (e.g. Skype) for facilitating face-to-face meetings of customers and clients. A study by Jung (2005) on exhibition attendee perceptions of service quality gave some insight on desired experiences, namely the importance assigned

Table 6.4 Motives of sport spectators

Authors	Framework	Motives
Wann (1995)	Sports Fan Motivation Scale (SFMS)	eustress, self-esteem, escape, entertainment, economic (gambling), aesthetic, group affiliation, family
Milne and McDonald (1999)	Motivation of Sport Consumers (MSC)	risk-taking, stress reduction, aggression, affiliation, social facilitation, self-esteem, competition, achievement, skill mastery, aesthetics, value development and self-actualization
Trail and James (2001)	Motivation Scale for Sport Consumption (MSSC)	achievement, acquisition of knowledge, aesthetics, drama, escape, family, physical attraction, physical skills of players, social interaction.
Funk and James (2001), Funk *et al.* (2002, 2003)	Sport Interest Inventory (SII)	family bonding, friends bonding, drama, entertainment value, escape, excitement, player interest, role model, socialization, team interest, vicarious achievement
James and Ross (2004)	-	entertainment, skill, drama, team effort, achievement, social interaction, family, team affiliation, empathy
Mehus (2005)	Entertainment Sport Motivation Scale	social, excitement
Koo and Hardin (2008)	-	vicarious achievement, team performance, escape, family, eustress, aesthetics, entertainment value, social opportunities.

Source: Benckendorff and Pearce (2012: 170). Reprinted from *The Routledge Handbook of Events*, S. J. Page and J. Connell, Routledge (2012).

to the number of exhibitors, quality of goods and services exhibited, and the seminars, conferences and other events that were part of it. These are all product quality items that reflect the learning and marketing content of the event.

Convention and meeting experiences

It is probably assumed that people attend conferences and meetings for extrinsic reasons, because it is part of their business or job description, so very little pertinent research has been done. Certainly event marketers need to know more about how to attract and satisfy their clientele, while in event studies we want to know if these experiences are categorically different from those at other events. An interesting perspective to engage the audience at conferences is the use of drama – described by Nelson (2009) as dramaturgy. The purpose here is to enhance the experience through using creative and emotional cues that introduce a dramatic element to the experience as illustrated in Figure 6.10.

Oppermann and Chon (1997) discussed the decision process, constraints, and both extrinsic and intrinsic motivations for convention attendance by members of associations. They observed both push and pull factors, and noted that many people were annual attendees. Van Riper *et al.* (2013) focused on one of the key motives for conference attendance – social networking (see Research Note 6.5).

Much choice exists so intervening opportunities, locational factors and destination image play a role. Davidson (2003) discussed the benefits to destinations and convention-goers in adding pleasure to their business trips. A convention might represent a rare or once-in-a-lifetime opportunity to visit an attractive area. Spouses and other family members often want to come along.

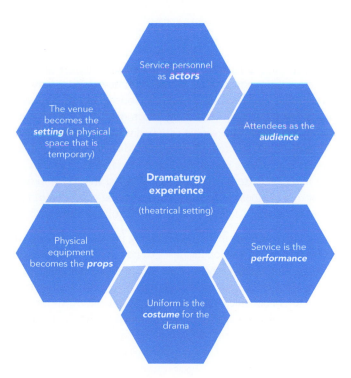

Figure 6.10 The elements of dramaturgy in conferences
Source: Developed from Nelson (2009).

6.5 RESEARCH NOTE ON SOCIAL NETWORKING

Van Riper, C. J., van Riper III, C., Kyle, G. T. and Lee, M. E. (2013). Understanding how social networking influences perceived satisfaction with conference experiences. *Annals of Leisure Research*, 16(1), 103–114.

'Social networking is a key benefit derived from participation in conferences that bind the ties of a professional community. Building social networks can lead to satisfactory experiences while furthering participants' long- and short-term career goals. Although investigations of social networking can lend insight into how to effectively engage individuals and groups within a professional cohort, this area has been largely overlooked in past research. The present study investigates the relationship between social networking and satisfaction with the 10th Biennial Conference of Research on the Colorado Plateau using structural equation modelling. Results partially support the hypothesis that three dimensions of social networking – interpersonal connections, social cohesion and secondary associations – positively contribute to the performance of various conference attributes identified in two focus group sessions. The theoretical and applied contributions of this paper shed light on the social systems formed within professional communities and resource allocation among service providers.'

Rittichainuwat *et al.* (2001) determined that attendees at a hospitality educator/researcher conference were motivated primarily by self-enhancement, business and association activities, and sightseeing. The work of Severt *et al.* (2007) reveals that different types of conferences and meetings will be associated with different motivators and experiential dimensions. They studied the motivations, satisfaction and behavioural intentions of a group of small business owners and managers attending a regional-level conference with exhibitions produced by a national trade association. Their most important motivations for attending, in order, were: education; educational information at exhibits; reasonable travel time to the event; networking opportunities; and business activities. Four of these five are clearly experiential in nature, while accessibility is a facilitating/constraining factor. Attendees were very satisfied with the educational component, ranking it highest. Those most satisfied with education were the most satisfied overall, and the most likely to both return and tell others to attend the conference. The Centre for Exhibition Research (CEIR 2003) research confirms that face-to-face interaction is vital in marketing, and this will ensure the continuance of live events despite the impact of social media on networking people virtually. Indeed, it appears that although business events are the first to be cancelled in times of troubles (terrorism, pandemics and natural disasters), they bounce back very quickly and continue to grow in number.

Mair (2013) reported that many countries in Asia were facing possible over-capacity issues in venue construction as destinations have raced to develop localities to host major conferences. Even so, Page (2015) highlighted the scale of growth in the conference and convention market using the International Congress and Convention Association data as illustrated in Figure 6.11. What this illustrates is that the demand for conferences and conventions continues apace, and the ICCA data also illustrates that the USA and Europe dominate the market for events. Clearly the rise of social media has not dampened enthusiasm for meeting face-to-face: it may have even expanded the appetite for such meetings. There really is no 'virtual event' that can simulate symbolic interaction, socializing or having fun while doing business. People love to travel and meet, and always will.

According to ICCA (2018), in the period 2013–2017, Europe's market share of the meeting's market was 53.6 per cent with Asia increasing its share to 18.5 per cent, with North America having a 11.7 per cent share and Latin America with 9.6 per cent share. However, ICCA data shows that of the 65,000 meetings

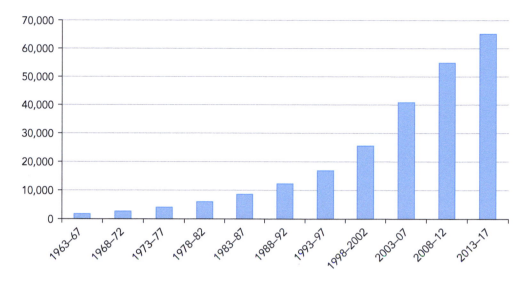

Figure 6.11 Number of ICCA meetings 1963–2017 (based on five-year aggregated data)

Source: ICCA data.

held annually, the countries which dominated as hosts were: the USA, Germany, the UK, France and Spain in the top five rankings. In contrast, between 2013 and 2017, the top five cities for meetings were: Paris, Vienna, Berlin, London and Barcelona. The trend in number of participants per meeting is dropping from 1,263 in 1963–1967 to 409 in 2013–2017. At the same time, the number of meetings has tripled over the same period. This is reflected in the ICCA's data which shows that in 1963–1967, the total number of participants at all the meetings was 2 million. By 2013–2017, this had risen to 25 million, despite the reduction in the average meeting size. Similarly the average meeting length has dropped from just under six days in 1963–1967 to 3.6 in 2013–2017 according to ICCA (2018).

The experiences of different stakeholders

Table 6.5 lists many of the principal event stakeholders, from guest and customer to the media and general public, each of which can have quite different experiences from the same event. The event experience is always at least partially dependent upon the expectations and attitudes of those involved (as inferred above with reference to dramaturgy), and on one's willingness to enter into the spirit of the occasion. As well, different stakeholders will be directly or indirectly affected (on-site versus off) and dependent on their roles (organizers and volunteers). Accordingly, we need more understanding of the expectations people bring to events, and how they describe their experiences. Most of the experiences shown in this table are, of course, attainable by many of the stakeholders in many event settings. What Table 6.5 sets out to list are those attributes that could be different or special, for each stakeholder – not their full range of potential experiences.

Paying customers

Many events charge admission and attract paying customers who will expect delivery of the promised product or experience to a high standard. They are entitled to complain if they do not get their perceived consumer benefit, to use the consumer behaviour concept. Marketers might be content with determining satisfaction levels, as that is the simplest measure of experiential effectiveness in a commercial context.

Table 6.5 The experiences of different stakeholders

Groups having event experiences	Subcategories	Unique or especially important experiential dimensions
Paying customers	Sport spectators	Escaping, being entertained
	Concert audience	Belonging and sharing
	Exhibition and conference attendees	Authentic cultural experience
		Emotionally involved and loyal fans (also nostalgia)
	Festival tourists	
		Socializing and communitas
Guests	Persons invited to a private event	Learning, and seeking self-actualization
		Socializing, networking
	The public at free events	Being part of a community or family
	Guests of sponsors	Subcultural identity
		Being treated as honoured guests, VIPs
Participants	Athletes at competitions	Challenge and mastery
	Performers in arts competitions	Communitas and subcultural expression
Media audience	Remote TV viewers, radio listeners, webcast participants	A virtual entertainment experience shaped by the media
Performers	The entertainers at events	Professional competence, mastery self-esteem
	Buskers, street performers	
	Professional athletes	Ancillary enjoyment of the event
Producers and organizers	Owners	Might be similar to staff and volunteers
	Directors	Need to be responsive and reflective
	Managers	
Very Important People (invited VIPs)	Politicians	Doing their duty
	Celebrities	Protocol shapes their experience as 'performers'
	The Olympic 'family'	
	Investors	Being treated with honour and respect
		Gaining self-esteem
		Ancillary enjoyment of the event
Officials	Referees, timekeepers and stewards	Professional conduct and responsibility defines their involvement
Regulators	Police, fire, health inspectors, etc.	Professional conduct and responsibility defines their involvement
Sponsors and grant givers	With their own hospitality component or as VIPs	Business success, networking
		Providers of hospitality to their own guests (the event is still the attraction)
		Or same as VIPs
Suppliers and vendors	External suppliers	Contractual relationships define their involvement
	Or on-site vendors	Ancillary enjoyment of the event

Table 6.5 (continued)

Groups having event experiences	Subcategories	Unique or especially important experiential dimensions
Volunteers	Board members (may be workers or VIPs at the event)	The 'cast', part of the experience for others
	Unpaid workers at the event	
		Enjoyment of the event
		Communitas among volunteers
		Self-fulfilment
Paid staff	Paid workers at the event	Paid employment defines their experience
	Security staff, after hours	Ancillary enjoyment of the event
The media	Official (as sponsors)	Might want a VIP experience
	Unofficial media	Professional competence
The public	Indirectly experiences the event (overspill effects or vicarious experiences)	The public's experience can range from 'psychic benefits' to being inconvenienced or harmed

'Fans' might have other experiences on their mind, including loyalty, communitas and nostalgia (see Fairley 2003 on nostalgia). Cultural tourists might stress belonging and sharing, an authentic cultural experience and a learning experience. Satisfaction levels do not provide much insight to the event experience. Deeper inquiry can reveal how memorable the event was, its meaning to the customer (especially in terms of personal and social constructs), and whether or not the customer had a transforming experience in any way. These phenomenological measures could be potentially valuable for improving the event.

Guests

This term, 'guests', implies that the event-goer is there because they are wanted. The guest will expect to be treated like a personal guest, with hospitality being a key service quality. Guests expect to be greeted and honoured by their hosts. While guests at private parties know they were invited, which shapes their expectations about hospitality and possibly about service levels, making paying customers feel like guests is a real challenge. The guest 'experience' will inevitably include a strong social component, because they are part of an invited group. 'Communitas' is often presupposed in this context, with all guests having an existing affiliation, but it also might have to be facilitated when strangers are in the mix. The use of esoteric rituals and symbols known only to 'insiders' is one form of bonding that designers can use.

Participants

This group consists of the athletes in sports or recreational events, dancers in dance festivals, musicians in music competitions, and to a degree the delegates attending conventions. The event is all about them; it does not exist without their participation. They are likely to feel that the event is for their benefit and its organizers should respect their needs and wishes. Participants also might feel a personal responsibility for the success of the event, but that is contingent on factors such as who owns or sponsors it. To understand participants' experiences requires knowledge of their motives, expectations, activities, emotions and cognitive processes in the specific context of the event. The full range of planned event experiences can apply, but participants are typically looking for mastery through meeting challenges, learning opportunities, and subcultural identity or communitas.

Media audience

Presumably most 'virtual' experiences of planned events, especially TV coverage of sports and concerts, award ceremonies and spectacles, would be described as entertainment. A key question for event studies researchers is whether or not media experiences can be the same as live experiences in terms of emotional engagement and cognition. Can they be as memorable or transforming? We will have to rely on media studies for answers. With the ascendancy of webcasts, there is a need for researchers to examine interactive media experiences, as observed in Chapter 3.

Performers

This group consists of paid entertainers or athletes, all part of the show that customers want to experience. They have quite different motives for being at the event, and gaining a sense of professional accomplishment has to be important. If their experience is bad, it can negatively impact on the overall event quality and customer satisfaction. Producers generally know how to treat professionals with dignity and respect, and to look after their tangible and emotional needs. If the opportunity arises, some performers can also get to enjoy parts of the event themselves.

Producers/organizers

Sometimes the producers/organizers are also involved, working alongside other volunteers; in other events they are completely detached from the experiences they are seeking to create and therefore need to be responsive, and reflective on what they are doing and the feedback they are getting.

VIPs

Whether they are politicians, royalty or celebrities, being a Very Important Person by definition means that event organizers will be giving them special treatment, honour, respect and a lot of security, with protocol often determining what can and cannot be done. Their experience cannot possibly be the same as other guests or customers, and indeed they might become part of the spectacle, temporarily becoming performers. Despite these considerations it might be possible to segregate VIPs enough that they can enjoy part of the event.

Officials and security

Professional conduct and specific responsibilities govern the event experiences of referees, stewards, timekeepers and other officials. They might be almost invisible, or play an important and highly visible role in the event. Their experiences will perhaps include off-duty enjoyment of part of the event, otherwise their main concerns are purely technical. The experience of security personnel is restricted by their need for vigilance.

Regulators

This category of stakeholder (e.g. building and health inspectors) attends events to supervise and ensure compliance, but also have to be made comfortable, kept safe, and have their basic technical and human needs looked after. Professional conduct defines their roles, but might they not take a little time to actually enjoy the event? Perhaps some of them deserve to have VIP status.

Sponsors and donors

Unless they see themselves as regulators, these 'facilitating' stakeholders should be given VIP treatment at events. Corporate sponsors often want specific hospitality services for themselves and their guests, even to the point of having private and exclusive areas and mini-events. Business has to be done, and that is an experience realm that does not have to be divorced from having fun. In addition to enjoying the event, which might be of secondary importance, facilitators also have a vested interest in its success and might therefore play the role of supervisors or evaluators. Some might want status as producers or owners. Needless to say, their overall, multidimensional experience has to be made satisfactory.

Suppliers and vendors

Often these contracted service and goods providers are brought into the event as sponsors as well, giving them a vested interest in its success. They might also find time to enjoy the event. Yet they have specific, professional functions to complete which have to be supervised and evaluated by event management. That means there is a risk of 'split personality' when it comes to the event experiences of contracted suppliers. Health and safety will always be top priorities for suppliers and vendors.

Volunteers

To the extent that they interact with other people at the event, they are both helping to create, and share in, the experiences. Volunteers should have a unique perspective on the overall experience and how others are enjoying the event and have become a specific field of research within events (see Stebbins and Graham 2004 for an overview) especially in the public/not-for-profit sector. Volunteers have to be satisfied or they will not continue to volunteer. Johnston *et al*. (2000) found that sport involvement led directly to volunteering at sport events, which suggests that participants want an experience related to that sport, such as contact with its stars. Saleh and Wood (1998) found some unique motives held by volunteers at a multicultural festival (namely sharing their culture and maintaining cultural links). Elstad (1997) studied student volunteers at the Winter Olympic Games in Lillehammer, Norway, and determined that satisfaction with their experience related most strongly to expanding personal networks, being part of the event atmosphere and achieving job-related competence. In another study, Elstad (2003) found that the top reasons for event volunteers to quit were workload, lack of appreciation and poor organization, all of which suggest experiential implications.

Ralston, Lumsdon and Downward (2005) reviewed the literature on event volunteers, covering motivation, profiles, satisfaction studies and theory. The reasons why people volunteered clearly pertained to the experiences they sought, including excitement, uniqueness (the chance of a lifetime), meeting interesting people and being part of a team. Meanings attached to the experience included supporting sport, doing something useful for the community, helping the city, region and country, and using their skills. A review of the event-volunteer phenomenon by Schlenker *et al*. (2014) noted the episodic nature of event volunteering related to their timing and frequency, and this also has major implications for the use of paid staff.

Paid staff

Hanlon and Jago (2014) reviewed the nature of human resource needs in event management, observing the pulsating nature of events and the unusual demands this places on human resourcing, which needs to pay particular attention to the staffing demands illustrated in Figure 6.12. As Figure 6.12 shows, there might be quite different experiences for staff (and this applies to many volunteers as well) depending on their level of involvement through the entire planning and de-commissioning cycle. Most paid staff will be able to have some direct experience of the event, if only when off-duty, but some, like overnight security, will not. All paid staff have specific duties, so they have to be supervised and evaluated, with event enjoyment being an ancillary goal, and (ideally) secondary to the experience of professional accomplishment. There can be overlap, of course, between the roles and experiences of volunteers, paid staff and performers. This will depend on the extent to which these groups are part of the show (as 'cast members') and how dependent guests/customers are on each group for their experiences.

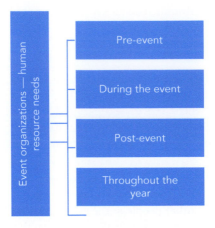

Figure 6.12 The human resource needs of event organizations

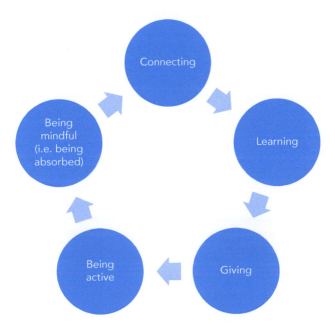

Figure 6.13 Predictors of well-being

The media

Hopefully most media people attending the event are official sponsors, in which case they require technical support and VIP status. But there are also likely to be unofficial media whose access to the event might be restricted. Conflicts could occur between the two groups of media, between media and VIPs or performers, and between media and organizers/staff. Media relations has become a major task at events and cannot be left to chance. If people have a bad personal or professional experience, the event's image could consequently take a negative hit. In addition to the media and event experience, Dayan (1994) examined the televising and live broadcasting of historic events such as the Olympic Games. These were described as festive television or media events; such events are therefore viewed not as routine but as cultural performances, and are exceptional planned events with the power to reach global audiences.

The public at large

There might be spillover effects from events, such as noise, light, traffic, smells, crowds and bad behaviour, all of which can cause bad feelings among neighbours and the wider community. The media like to focus on all these issues. The public at large, even those not attending and not interested, can nevertheless gain 'psychic benefits' from their vicarious experience of events, such as increased community pride and perceptions of economic and other impacts. Our discussion of resident perceptions and attitudes in Chapter 10 elaborates on these points.

Meanings attached to planned event experiences

Event experiences can mean as little to us as fleeting entertainment (not important and not memorable), or as much as profoundly transforming. To a community or society, events can have simple commercial meaning (as part of the 'entertainment industry') or they can be significant economic and place-marketing forces. From a cultural perspective events can be reinforcing or threatening. From an economic and tourism point of view, events are products to sell, and they must generate tangible as well as image benefits. And to corporations that sponsor or produce events, they have importance in terms of marketing, branding and corporate responsibility.

Meanings attached to planned events are at once anticipatory (as in, 'we are going to the festival to celebrate our heritage'), evolving (e.g. 'the event itself was responsible for changing everyone's attitudes toward the arts') and reflective (such as, 'looking back, it was clearly an event with great economic and political impact'). Historians and critical researchers help to attach meanings to events. So do political ideologies and the interactions of all the stakeholders involved. Meanings that are political and societal might not impress the individual, who is, after all, able to formulate personal interpretations and meanings for any event. But, if events have little or no meaning of importance to people, they will not attend. If events lack social, cultural and economic meaning, who will support them?

Personal meanings

The meanings that individuals attach to event experiences are 'personal constructs', which can be defined as a level of cognitive significance that represents how we understand the world around us. In effect, we construct reality in our minds to explain experiences. 'Personal construct theory' posits that people attribute meanings to their experiences, and each person therefore has different experiences. Kelly (1955) theorized that a person's experiences consist of 'a set of personally construed events' that are not necessarily valid. That is, we might not get it right – they are subjective and subject to change. Based on our experiences we can anticipate and predict future experiences, which of course influences what we expect from a planned event. Epting and Neimeyer (1984: 2) argued that these personal constructs 'serve not only as interpretation of past events but as hypotheses about events yet to be encountered'. Botterill and Crompton (1996) used personal construct theory to examine leisure/tourist experiences and concluded that emotional states are integral to 'optimal experiences' as defined by interviewees. At one level, we can say that personal meanings relate directly to personal needs, the motives expressed for attending events, and the anticipated benefits to be obtained through the planned event experience. Ask yourself how you give meaning to your life through work, leisure and family. Where do events fit into that meaning system? The rites of passage that mark our lives are bound to be memorable, and full of personal meaning, helping to define who we are. But most of them, like birthdays, anniversaries, weddings and graduations, are also social occasions, with substantial meaning to families and wider social networks.

Experience marketers have also realized that they must engage consumers in events that hold meaning for them. Diller *et al.* (2006: 3) in *Making Meaning* concluded:

> *Our own work in the field has led us to the conviction that for companies to achieve enduring competitive advantage through experience design, their innovations cannot be based simply on novelty. Increasingly, they must address their customers' essential human need for meaning. To do this, companies must first understand the role that meaning plays in people's lives, how products and services can evoke meaning, and then how to identify the core meanings they should target with their own offerings. For companies facing both globalization and the end of the mass market, 'making meaning' is one of very few strategies that will work.*

The personal benefits and meanings can include any of the following, derived from earlier discussions as well as the contribution of Diller *et al.* (2006: 320):

- communitas (as a result of belonging and sharing, from reaffirmation of roots or of connections and values);
- esteem: validation of oneself in the opinions of others; self-worth; prestige and reputation (such as may be realized through competitive or intellectual accomplishments);
- learning, enlightenment (for example, from new cultural experiences or a connoisseur's appreciation of food, art or music);
- self-discovery, self-actualization, understanding, wonder;
- transformation (religious, spiritual, personality or character, renewed, motivated);
- redemption and atonement (from failure or sins);
- mastery (from skills, physical triumph);
- accomplishment or success (from business, trade, commerce, networking, creativity, artistic expression);
- creativity or innovation (making a lasting contribution);
- fulfilment of responsibility (professionalism, or as a dedicated sport fan, or from getting involved as a volunteer);
- health and well-being (through physical activity, learning);
- security (living without fear);
- duty (military or civic) fulfilled; patriotism and loyalty to a cause;
- truth, honesty, integrity (a meaning given to relationships and to one's own behaviour);
- beauty or aesthetic appreciation;
- freedom (acting without constraint; intrinsically rewarding pursuits);
- harmony (with nature or others) and oneness (belonging, unity);
- justice (fairness and equality; democratic expression).

People might not be able to articulate the meanings they assign to event experiences; they might not think of meanings at all. You could ask them what benefits they expected and derived from the experience, and that comes close. They can be asked to respond to a list of statements or adjectives about the event to see if they found it memorable, transforming or meaningful in terms of the above-mentioned dimensions. People want to give meaning to their experiences and to their lives in general, but expressing those meanings requires deep thought and a good vocabulary! This is a real challenge for researchers and theorists. Events in Focus 6.2 highlights how positive psychology may make a significant contribution to this area.

EVENTS IN FOCUS

6.2 Using positive psychology in designing events

Coghlan, A. (2015). Tourism and health: Using positive psychology principles to maximise participants' wellbeing outcomes – a design concept for charity challenge tourism. *Journal of Sustainable Tourism*, 23(3), 382–400.

A recent study of event design by Coghlan examines how to harness the key tenets of positive psychology into the design principles for events to achieve eudomonic states (i.e. the state of mind where an individual can flourish and be happy) so that their sense of well-being is enhanced. Coghlan points to five predictors of well-being that have been identified as enhancing eudomonic states as shown in Figure 6.13.

What this study emphasizes is the importance of participation in an event, and using the example of a charity event, Coghlan illustrates the underpinning principles that need to be designed in to achieve these well-being principles combined with the theory of positive psychology. Within the literature on positive psychology, Coghlan illustrates that five principles have to be incorporated into the event to leverage the well-being benefits as illustrated in Figure 6.13.

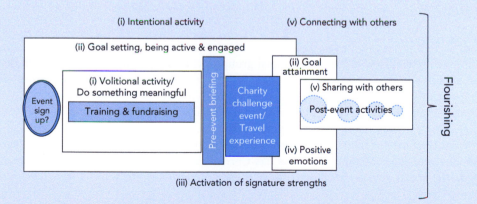

Figure 6.14 Integrating the science of positive psychology into the design of tourism experiences: a conceptual model

Source: Coghlan (2015: 388). Reprinted from *The Journal of Sustainable Tourism*, 23, A. Coughlan, Tourism and health: Using positive psychology principles to maximise participants' wellbeing outcomes, Copyright (2015), with the permission of Taylor and Francis.

What Figure 6.14 shows is that the following principles are significant:

- *Intentional activity*, which is derived from the literature in leisure where physical activity makes a contribution to happiness (especially where combined with something like a charity event which Coghlan studied) and so this feature has to be able to derive meaning for the participant.

- *Motivation and goal attainment*, where the event has the ability to motivate an individual's intrinsic motivation so as to achieve self-set goals which can be attained (as well as setting mini goals within the event, such as reaching half-way).

- *Signature strengths*, which Coghlan describes as the thoughts, feelings and behaviours of individuals that can contribute to the reward of participation, such as endurance, a sense of community, leadership and so forth. The event needs to leverage these signature strengths to engage the participants to enhance their positive benefit from involvement.

- *Positive emotions and gratification*, where positive emotions help to achieve a state of authentic happiness, which may be displayed through enjoyment, engagement and satisfaction with the event.

- *Sharing positive events*, where individuals recount and reminisce about events in the past, has the potential to achieve what Coghlan describes as capitalization, where the retelling of the event provides an opportunity to relive it.

Summarizing the findings of the study, Coghlan highlights the value of appropriate forms of event design to incorporate these principles, whereby the intentional element can be achieved from the point of sign-up to the end of the charity event; connecting with others, setting goals and achieving a meaningful involvement and activating the signature strengths as well as reminiscing all have very good positive psychological benefits and a contribution to well-being. The study lays the groundwork for the further development of well-being and event research which may expand our understanding of this important area in the future.

Social meanings

These are meanings given to events by social groups, communities and society as a whole. Individuals are affected by these meanings, but are also able to make their own interpretations of events. Event types or forms, as previously discussed, are to a large extent 'social constructs', with collectively assigned and generally recognized meanings. Abrahams (1987) noted that the way we frame or attach meaning to experiences is embedded in social and cultural order. Our most popular religious holidays and civic celebrations have generally accepted meanings. For many people, the sacred might have given way to the profane for holidays like Christmas; nevertheless society as a whole recognizes and needs the social and personal benefits of these holidays, despite some differences in meanings attached to them.

Forms of events, like festivals and sport competitions, are expected to conform to widely held expectations regarding where and when they are held, who attends, accepted and expected behaviours, and even their programmic elements. Going beyond the norms, as innovative event designers are wont to do, risks alienating or at least mystifying elements of the potential audience. If the changes are accepted, perhaps over a long period of time, then they are added to the social constructs we hold. We can call this process the making of tradition, or the establishment of social norms and conformity.

Social and political constructs

Roche (2000: 7; see also Roche 2006) saw events, like the global Millennium celebrations, acting as 'important elements in the orientation of national societies to international or global society'. Indeed, many countries have used mega events to gain legitimacy and prestige, draw attention to their accomplishments, foster trade and tourism, or to help open their countries to global influences. This is much more than place marketing – it is more like national identity building. And Whitson and Macintosh (1996: 279) argued that countries and cities compete for mega-sport events to demonstrate their 'modernity and economic dynamism'.

Julie Russell (2004) examined the political meanings attached to the National Eisteddfod of Wales, which has a tradition dating back to 1176. She found that this annual competition of music and poetry is simultaneously an arena for performing arts, a forum for preserving the Welsh language, a tourist attraction, a trade fair and a platform for political acts of Welsh significance. 'As an arts and cultural festival … the Eisteddfod also delivers the wider range of economic and socio-linguistic benefits which embrace the interests of the Wales Tourist Board, the Arts Council of Wales, the Welsh Language Board, local authorities and others.'

Sense of community and sense of place

Derrett (2004: 48) discussed how communities share their culture through festivals and events, and how the interdependencies of residents, place and visitors help establish a valued sense of community and place:

> They celebrate a sense of place through organizing inclusive activities in specific safe environments. They provide a vehicle for communities to host visitors and share such activities as representations of communally agreed values, interests and aspirations. Thirdly, they are the outward manifestation of the identity of the community and provide a distinctive identifier of place and people.

On the other hand, 'commodification' or 'festivalization' of culture is a threat. Duffy (2000) examined the sense of place achieved through popular music festivals, and a body of work within environmental psychology has focused on the theme of place attachment (the bonding of an individual with an environment they value) and the meanings ascribed to places, which can be adapted to the notion of planned events. Scannell and Gifford (2010) reviewed the various definitions of the concept and synthesized them into a three-dimensional organizing framework. According to those authors, the 'person dimension' of place attachment refers to its individually or collectively determined meanings, the 'psychological dimension' includes the affective, cognitive and behavioural components, and the 'place dimension' emphasizes the spatial level.

Cultural meanings

Quinn (2000: 264) concluded that:

> If at the heart of every festival are a place and a place-based community actively reproducing its shared values and belief systems, there is an important sense in which these cultural meanings are intentionally produced to be read by the outside world.

A related challenge stems from the fact that meanings are easily and often contested, based on different values and belief systems within the same community. So while the festival is a 'text' on culture, to be interpreted, it is often an ambiguous one. In fact studies from anthropology (e.g. Rotenberg and McDonogh 1993) illustrate the significance of a body of knowledge around spatial meanings in urban studies. However, the principal challenge for event research is that these environments are essentially temporary; they pose different research problems for understanding spatial meaning.

Sport as cultural expression

'Games and sports, like religious rituals and festivals, can be interpreted as reflections of broader social relationships and cultural ideals' (Mitler *et al.* 2004: 348). To Geertz (1993) they are models of culture depicting key values and ideals, such as fair play or friendly competition. Sport can also have more sinister or controversial significance, reflecting or encouraging aggression and dominance of one group over another, or territoriality and cultural imperialism. Many people see elements of a national culture in their sports, and in the emphasis they place on sports. We should be asking, does policy regarding sport reflect or shape culture?

Cultural authenticity

There has been a great deal of debate about what an 'authentic' experience or event really is, and if it is even desired or understood by tourists or event-goers. We are speaking here of cultural authenticity, which is really the cultural meaning attached to an event. Boorstin's famous (1961) description of 'pseudo-events' was really a commentary on mass tourism, as he believed that culture was being commoditized and that many events were created to cater to tourists' expectations. This belief contrasts with those of MacCannell (1973) and others, who believed that people sought out authentic cultural experiences because they lived shallow or uninteresting lives. Cohen (1979) argued that different types of tourists required different experiences, which hold different meanings, all of which are mediated by culture. He distinguished two major streams – those searching for authenticity (or on a spiritual quest) called 'modern pilgrimage', and those seeking pleasure.

Wang (1999) identified three types of authenticity. 'Object-related authenticity' pertains to the true nature of the event as a cultural expression. In this context, event producers have to ensure that their performances, design features and other programmic elements are genuine reflections of the culture being displayed. But who is to judge this?

'Constructive authenticity' is projected onto the event in terms of images, expectations, preferences and beliefs. Visitors might be fooled, and they might not care if the event is not a true cultural expression. Event producers have considerable scope for entertaining people, but should they be concerned about meanings attached by visitors? Does the event producer have an obligation (moral, or in terms of marketing) to ensure that the event is not misperceived?

To Wang 'existential authenticity' occurs because whatever the nature of the event (authentic in cultural terms, or not), event consumers might have their own, meaningful experiences which they interpret as being authentic. The theory is that authentic experiences enable discovery of one's true self. This presents a real challenge for the event producers, as they must acknowledge that their programme is (merely?) a setting or background for desired, highly individualized experiences. In a variation, Timothy and Boyd (2006) discussed 'relative authenticity', saying that authenticity is a subjective notion varying from person to person, depending on our social conditioning. Meaning is not derived from the event, in this interpretation, but from the interaction of event and visitor-created meanings.

The conclusion we are left with is that 'cultural authenticity' is a theoretically difficult concept. Our position is that when it comes to determining what is authentic or not, only the cultural groups being represented, or doing the performance, are qualified to judge. Within cultures there often rages a debate about whether modern performances are authentic and justifiable, but surely outsiders cannot be expected to decide.

There is a completely different approach to 'authentic' experiences, one that has wider application. Consider this: are sport events authentic? Not in cultural terms, but as events deserving of trust and belief in them? Despite the occasional scandal arising from gambling or bad refereeing, sports are generally considered to be authentic because the outcome is unpredictable, the players give their best, and talent plus hard work is rewarded. Many other forms of entertainment are widely thought to be contrived and unbelievable. Even so-called television 'reality shows' appear to be nothing more than stylized, scripted theatre. More research on event-consumer beliefs and on mass-media experiences related to 'authenticity' is warranted.

Contested culture, stakeholders and legitimacy

Will all stakeholders in a community agree on core values and what is to be celebrated? In fact, culture and its representations are often contested. To examine this issue, Crespi-Vallbona and Richards (2007) interviewed many stakeholders in Catalonia, finding that there were common issues surrounding festivals in that region. Cultural identity was the strongest and most common theme, reflecting this region's long struggle to establish a national identity. This was a binding factor, even though differences in meanings were evident. Nevertheless, the researchers observed tension between the local and global perspectives on events, and there was concern for preserving cultural integrity when events were also expected to serve political, economic and social goals. They observed that:

> *stakeholders tend to differ more in the meanings attached to concepts such as identity, with policy makers exhibiting a greater emphasis on economic and political issues, whereas cultural producers are more concerned with social aspects of identity. However, the general consensus on the social role of cultural events between the different stakeholders may be one explanation for the relatively vibrant festival culture in Catalunya.*
>
> (Crespi-Vallbona and Richards 2007: 103)

Differences in meanings attached to festivals are related to claims to power, legitimacy and urgency by the various stakeholders involved in the policy process.

Economic meanings

To a large extent, we have already defined the economic meanings attached to events by looking at event tourism and the roles of attraction, catalyst, animator, image-maker and place marketer. These meanings are shaped by politicians and industry, rather than the general public or travellers themselves. Many events are also considered to be part of the 'entertainment or culture industries', or perhaps the 'creative industries', and these represent economic meanings. Within the context of 'popular culture', using the term 'industry' is likely to imply commercialization and mass consumption.

Although many events are within the realm of arts and culture, they do have to be managed as businesses. This introduces a tension between the values of arts/culture on the one hand, and the potential for hard-nosed management or commercialization on the other. Ideally the economic and arts/cultural meanings can be brought into balance. Sports as 'big business' is a recurring theme. For example, Rozin (2000) described Indianapolis as a 'classic case' of how sports can generate a civic turnaround. Sports Business Market Research Inc. (2000: 167) observed that in the 1980s and 1990s, American cities 'put heavy emphasis on sports, entertainment and tourism as a source of revenue for the cities'. Gratton and Kokolakakis (1997) believed that in the UK, sport events had become the main platform for economic regeneration in many cities.

Berridge (2007) observed that:

> *The discipline of events is expanding significantly from its cultural and celebratory origins and the role of events in business is changing as its effectiveness in 'brand marketing' is more clearly understood and the levels of investment increase as a result.*

Within the corporate world, it is now fashionable to think of a brand in terms of relationships, with 'live communications' or 'event experiences' building and sustaining these relationships between company and customer. In this context, planned events are brand-building tools, and the experiences have to be evaluated in terms of how they meet corporate marketing aims. There is growing competition to attract and 'engage' customers this way, so events will tend to have a short life cycle. Something new will always be needed.

When companies practise corporate responsibility, their participation in events takes on new meanings. To the extent that corporations show commitment to the community and the environment out of altruism or necessity, events can be expressions of that commitment. Contemporary consumers and lobby groups expect companies to behave responsibly and that should lead to something of a reversal in the trend towards viewing participation in events as just marketing. In this context it seems reasonable to suggest that 'authenticity' and commercialism are incompatible. What do you think?

STUDY GUIDE

It is essential to be able to explain the planned event experience, and meanings attached to it – this is the core phenomenon of event studies. This chapter first explored the meaning of 'experience', including how it is conceptualized in leisure theory and within the context of the 'experience economy'. To develop a model of the planned event experience also required drawing upon anthropological theory, particularly to employ the notions of 'liminal', 'liminoid' and 'communitas'. Different event stakeholders will have different motives, experiences and meanings, so producers have to understand how, for example, paying customers are different from invited guests or VIPs. Consider how the material in this chapter aids in event design, making events 'special', and in marketing events to specific target audiences.

STUDY QUESTIONS

- What are the behavioural (conative), emotional (affective) and mental (cognitive) dimensions of 'experience'?
- What do intrinsic and extrinsic motivations have to do with event experiences?
- Why are corporations so interested in event experiences, within the context of the 'experience economy'?
- Explain why service dominant logic is a compelling new approach to experience design and event planning.
- Describe the model of planned event experiences, and specifically define 'liminal' and 'liminoid' in this context, drawing on anthropological theory.
- Discuss the concept of 'communitas' as it applies to event experiences, including why it can be a 'generic' event experience.
- How do the concepts of 'optimal arousal' and 'flow' relate to the planned event experience?
- In what ways can event experiences be 'memorable' and 'transforming'?
- What is the 'theory of spectacle' and how does it apply to event experiences?
- Give examples of how different types of planned events can facilitate both 'generic' and 'event-specific' experiences.
- Show how different stakeholders experience events in different ways, related to their motives and functions.

- Use the concepts of 'personal construct' and 'social construct' to explain various meanings attached to events.

- What is meant by 'cultural authenticity' and why is it important in event studies?

FURTHER READING

Baron, S., Warnaby, G. and Hunter-Jones, P. (2014). Service(s) marketing research: Developments and directions. *International Journal of Management Reviews*, 16(2), 150–171.

Diller, S., Shedroff, N. and Rhea, D. (2006). *Making Meaning*. Upper Saddle River, NJ: Pearson.

Gilmore, J. and Pine, J. (2007). *Authenticity: What Consumers Really Want*. Boston, MA: Harvard Business School Press.

Morgan, M., Lugosi, P. and Ritchie, J. R. B. (2010). *The Tourism and Leisure Experience: Consumer and Managerial Perspectives*. Bristol: Channel View.

Pine, B. and Gilmore, J. (1999). *The Experience Economy: Work Is Theatre and Every Business a Stage*. Boston, MA: Harvard Business School Press.

Sundbo, J. and Sørensen, F. (eds) (2013). *Handbook on the Experience Economy*. Cheltenham: Edward Elgar.

Timothy, D. and Olsen, D. (eds) (2006). *Tourism, Religion and Spiritual Journeys*. London: Routledge.

Verleye, K. (2015). The co-creation experience from the customer perspective: Its measurement and determinants. *Journal of Service Management*, 26(2), 321–342.

7

Event design

Upon completion of this chapter, students should know the following:

- the meaning, practice and evolution of design;
- the roles of design as applied to event form, experiences, and value-creation networks;
- designing meaningful experiences;
- the orchestra model for event designers;
- creativity and innovation; what they are and how to foster them;
- design for generic event settings: assembly, procession, linear-nodal, exhibition and sales, and open spaces;
- event staging and events as theatre;
- sensory stimulation and sensory mapping;
- cognitive mapping and wayfinding;
- crowding, crowd management and controls;
- theme and programme design;
- programme and service quality; importance-performance measurement;
- service blueprinting and evaluative mapping;
- events as restorative or instorative environments;
- programmic elements of style and the life cycle;

- research and evidence-based design;
- liberating versus constraining experiences.

What is design?

Design is neither pure science nor art; it is both a technical and creative act. Increasingly design is viewed as a collaborative process for value creation. Creativity is therefore an integral part of design, which means consideration of tools that have been used to foster creativity or innovation. This takes us into the arts, but design also draws from science and engineering, and increasingly from sociology applied to the network society.

Shedroff's *Experience Design* (2001) and *Making Meaning: How Successful Businesses Deliver Meaningful Customer Experiences* (Diller *et al.* 2006) are key studies in this area. The definition of design is derived from Shedroff (www.nathan.com):

> *Design is a set of fields for problem-solving that uses user-centric approaches to understand user needs (as well as business, economic, environmental, social, and other requirements) to create successful solutions that solve real problems. Design is often used as a process to create real change within a system or market. Too often, Design is defined only as visual problem solving or communication because of the predominance of graphic designers.*

Shedroff distinguishes several fields of design applications including 'environmental design' for structures or settings, and 'experience design'. Experience, to Shedroff, comprises:

> *The sensation of interaction with a product, service, or event, through all of our senses, over time, and on both physical and cognitive levels. The boundaries of an experience can be expansive and include the sensorial, the symbolic, the temporal, and the meaningful.*

Brown and James (2004: 59) argued that: 'Design is essential to an event's success because it leads to improvement of the event on every level.' The 'core values' of the event provide the starting point: why is an event held, and for whom? What is its substance and intended outcomes? Brown and James identified five design principles for events:

- scale
- shape
- focus
- timing
- build

Underlying these principles is the need for creativity and uniqueness in event design, as generic events offering the same benefits are unlikely to endure. This can be accomplished, in part, by incorporating the rituals and symbols of the host community. Silvers (2004: 5) summarized the issue thus: 'Remember that you are packaging and managing an experience. This means that you must envision that experience, from start to finish, from the guest's point of view.'

Berridge (2007) discusses the field of 'experience design' stating that the subject is in its infancy. Unfortunately, the term is being used to describe the design of everything from websites (digital media) to storytelling, theme parks and corporate 'brand events'. Berridge argued that the purpose of event design is to create desired perceptions, cognition and behaviour. Building and maintaining relationships is at the core, and stimulating emotional connections through engagement is the vehicle. Berridge (2012b: 278) also argued that it might be useful to distinguish between 'event architecture', which largely encompasses the technical, problem-solving functions of design, and the 'artistic or aesthetic design and creation' processes, both of which must be combined to create successful event experiences. Many creative challenges exist for the event experience designer, including concept and theme, entertainment, staging, ambience, decoration, and food and beverage. We often associate 'design' with fashion, aesthetics or visual graphics. Events do require aesthetic design, particularly to create the right atmosphere, but there is much more to it. Perhaps we need to think more about industrial design, with its emphasis on problem solving. A chair has to be designed for efficiency and comfort, plus it has to be pleasing to the eye. An event, both its *tangible setting* (the site and venue), *the atmosphere* (with sensory stimulations of all kinds) and its *programme* combine to create the 'experiential components', and also have to be designed, both with the producer's goals in mind and the needs, preferences and desires of the audience or customers. If design is separated from goals and real-world needs, we are left with art for its own sake.

A paradigm shift in design thinking

Orefice (2018 – see the research note) has examined the evolution of design thinking and applied new ideas about design to events. Drawing upon service-dominant logic (Chapter 6) and co-production, to create value this is expressed in Figure 7.1 as the 'event design ladder'. Figure 7.1 illustrates how stakeholders are engaged at different levels, or different conceptualizations of design applied to events. In event production, this remains a matter of 'form', in which the emphasis is on theming, décor, and creative application of many elements of style. Achieving the 'wow' response from guests and clients (i.e. the consumers) is an explicit aim in this paradigm, placing them in the position of passive recipients.

Step two reflects the 'experience economy' paradigm, in which 'experience design' and 'return on experience' have entered the lexicon and are currently the dominant perspectives. Customers and guests are co-creators of experience in this frame, recognizing that services and experiences cannot be fabricated like mass-produced goods. Value propositions are offered by event producers, and the customer or guest will

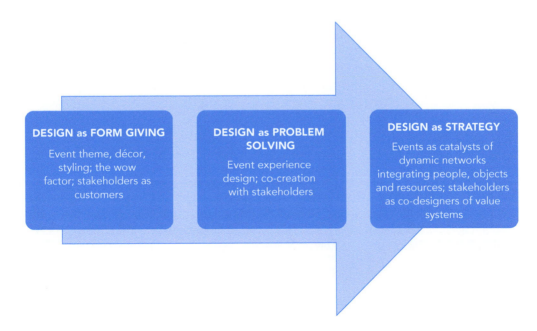

DESIGN as FORM GIVING

Event theme, décor, styling; the wow factor; stakeholders as customers

DESIGN as PROBLEM SOLVING

Event experience design; co-creation with stakeholders

DESIGN as STRATEGY

Events as catalysts of dynamic networks integrating people, objects and resources; stakeholders as co-designers of value systems

Figure 7.1 The evolution of design thinking, applied to events

Sources: Adapted from Orefice (2018), Danish Design Centre (2007), Ramirez and Mannervik (2008)

bring their own needs, wants and level of engagement into the experience and, more importantly, give it meaning. More and more thought is being given to how social media shapes the experience before, during and after an event – or any other type of service encounter.

Step three, reflecting the most recent theorizing about design and marketing, views design in a strategic manner. At this level, stakeholders collaborate within dynamic networks to create value systems. Picture a single event not as an entertainment, learning, fund-raising, challenging or celebratory opportunity, but as a creator of value for individuals, communities, cultures, the economy and environment. Events conceived as agents of change (or as social marketing vehicles) fit this paradigm. This idea is most relevant to event portfolio planning. If events within a city or destination are conceived as a value system, rather than an ad hoc or unregulated population of independent entities, then creation of synergies and long-term, cumulative outcomes (the benefits, or value to be created) becomes the strategy. What has to be given a lot of thought, however, is the fact that many value perspectives are applicable, and stakeholders must at some point agree upon strategies, goals and the methods and measures for evaluation. That is a political process.

7.1 RESEARCH NOTE ON THE EVOLUTION OF DESIGN THINKING

Orefice, C. (2018). Designing for events: A new perspective on event design. *International Journal of Event and Festival Management*, 9(1), 20–33.

Abstract: The purpose of this paper is to contribute to the paradigm shift towards event design predominant research by presenting an analysis of how the concept of event design has developed in the events literature and by exploring a new perspective based on its contribution to value co-creation. Design/methodology/approach – Theory from design management and service design is discussed to provide insights on the role of event design as contributing to the creation of value in social systems. Findings: A new framework for categorising the role of event design is proposed, called the Event Design Ladder. Event design is no longer considered as a problem solving activity, but as a contributor to value creation and an on-going pursuit carried out over time and space. Stakeholders become co-designers of value systems.

Service design and design management literature offer interesting potential for event researchers to advance the conceptualisation of event design. Considering events as platforms for long-term stakeholder engagement implies that the concept of design becomes strategic. Design as strategy is identified as a new area of event research.

This paper proposes a new perspective on events considered as catalysts of value systems, where the role of design is not only to orchestrate meaningful experiences but to facilitate collaboration across projects, integrating resources and building on stakeholders' skills and knowledge. Theories of practice are explored as a way to theorise and carry out research on how value is co-created by actors.

Figure 7.1 adapts several sources on the evolution of design thinking, applied to events. It is increasingly recognized that event portfolio management is a collaborative effort involving close-working networks of stakeholders to create multiple benefits (i.e. the value proposition) for communities and destinations, and that is what design as strategy is all about.

Can experiences be designed?

The Wikipedia definition of experience design states:

> *Experience design is the practice of designing products, processes, services, events, omnichannel journeys, and environments with a focus placed on the quality of the user experience and culturally relevant solutions. A meta discipline, experience design draws from many other disciplines including cognitive psychology and perceptual psychology, linguistics, cognitive science, architecture and environmental design, haptics, product design, strategic design, information design, information architecture, ethnography, marketing and brand strategy, strategic management and strategy consulting, interaction design, service design, storytelling, agile, lean startup, technical communication, and design thinking.*

In this context, 'haptics' refers to the sense of touch and is concerned with applying the sense of touch to user interfaces (such as computer keyboards).

At this point, you may find it helpful to go back to the previous chapter and re-read the definitions of 'experience', look again at how meanings are attached to experiences and think about that long list of stakeholders (much more than guests or the audience) who are experientially influenced by planned events. It is possible to get people involved, have them do specific things and receive desired stimuli, but it is not possible to guarantee or predict what individuals actually 'experience' cognitively and emotionally as an outcome. Nor can the event designer know for a certainty what meanings will be attached to those event experiences, or whether they will have any transforming impact.

'Experienced' event producers build up an understanding of what seems to work well to make people happy, or at least to say that they are satisfied. And 'practice does make perfect' when it comes to both getting the design elements right (i.e. technically perfect, and in keeping with the designer's vision), and also in avoiding mistakes. In these ways the designer's experience and intuition go a long way to improving event experiences. But whatever the design process, there has to be research and feedback from the stakeholders leading to improvement, otherwise the designer is guilty of either taking a 'product orientation' (here is what I offer, it's good for you), or creating art for its own sake (with no problem being solved).

An experience is so highly personal that it cannot be planned, designed or even promised to event-goers. The purpose of any event is to suggest what experiences might be had (through theming and interpretation), facilitate positive experiences (through design of setting, programme, services and consumables) and to enable everyone concerned, as much as possible, to realize their goals (co-creation). On the other hand, design and management also seeks to constrain undesired experiences, including aggression, violence and over-stimulation.

Making meaningful experiences

Diller, Shedroff and Rhea (2006) argued that experiences must have meaning, and that the benefits of meaningful experiences now supersede all other benefits: functional, economic, emotional, identity and status. They specify 15 supposedly universal core meanings that people desire from their experiences, and these are certainly linked to brand values. Event producers and those sponsoring events have to find ways of engaging attendees and ensuring the event's values are communicated. Below are the 15 core meanings, to which comments have been added that we believe are germane to event design.

1 **Accomplishment** – Research clearly shows that the personal accomplishment gained by meeting a physical or mental challenge is a powerful motivator for amateur athletes to participate in events. 'Iconic events' designed to meet the needs of challenge-seekers communicate clear symbolic meanings.

2 **Beauty** – There is beauty expressed in all forms of arts events, but there are also aesthetic elements to be designed into the setting, the programme, staff and volunteers of all events

3 **Community** – Turner's 'communitas' (i.e. belonging and sharing as equals) provides meaning to all forms of celebration; bringing people together is a primary social and cultural justification for public investments in events. Employ symbols of national and community unity, and cultural and social diversity.

4 **Creation** – Foodies, and others with special interests, value hands-on experiences that foster their creativity and appreciation of artistry and crafts; event producers and professionals engage in creativity as they plan and deliver event experiences. Designers facilitate individual creativity.

5 **Duty** – Volunteers often believe they have a civic duty to give their time and skill to the community, the sport or the cause; citizens might feel it is a duty to be tolerant and supportive of diverse expressions of values.

6 **Enlightenment** – Learning is one of the primary motivators for attendees at meetings, expositions and shows. Often the meanings within traditions and performances have to be interpreted for enlightenment to occur, with tools ranging from exhibitions to storytelling.

7 **Freedom** – This defines leisure choices, including the right to attend, create and participate in events. But freedom of expression and activity can be in conflict with the need for regulations and controls, so event designers must balance liberating experiences with responsibility.

8 **Harmony** – This can be an expression of social integration, as expressed through community events; it is also a design principle for artists and event designers. The sustainability paradigm requires that we strive for harmony with the environment, necessitating green practices.

9 **Justice** – Events pursuing social responsibility ensure that everyone is treated the same way, with no exclusions tolerated. Events are often platforms for demonstrations and protests whereby groups seek attention and justice, and these can be destructive, but all event designers can provide the means for freedom of expression.

10 **Oneness** – A spiritual meaning of peace and connectivity that cannot be created, but can be facilitated through event experiences. Pilgrimages and religious events are devoted to the spiritual experience, while other events can encourage participants or guests to seek oneness through mindfulness.

11 **Redemption** – This meaningful experience relates to the idea that people can atone for their self-perceived weaknesses or sins by giving – as volunteers, contributing to community events, or encouraging healthy and sustainable lifestyles. Charitable donations can be a part of any event.

12 **Security** – It goes without saying that providing safe, healthy event experiences is everyone's top priority. There is also the goal of fostering peace and harmony through events as agents of change, in part through education.

13 **Truth** – In an age of 'fake news', events should communicate the essence of authentic cultural experiences; transparency and accountability are needed when it comes to event impacts.

14 **Validation** – All attendees, guests or customers are respected; uniqueness and worthiness can be validated through participation in events. This is in part accomplished through service design, emphasizing how staff and volunteers treat customers and guests.

15 **Wonder** – Surprise, awe, revelation and mystery, can all be facilitated in event experiences; children's festivals in particular aim to stimulate wonder.

The orchestra model

The 'orchestra model' has been proposed by Pearce and Zare (2017) as the basis for teaching tourism experience design. The three experience dimensions are part of the 'orchestra', namely *cognitive* (thinking, choosing, learning, understanding), *affective* (happiness, surprise, fear, love) and conative or *behavioural* (taking photos, texting, activities). Theses are supplemented with two other components, being sensory (seeing, hearing, smelling, touching, tasting) and relationships (guests with service providers, companions, residents and other guests or tourists). A number of design tools are suggested that emphasize the 'emic' perspective, being a full understanding of the consumer, participant or guest leading to co-created experiences. The recommended tools include participant observation, cognitive mapping, service blueprinting and stakeholder mapping.

7.2 RESEARCH NOTE ON THE ORCHESTRA MODEL

Pearce, P. and Zare, S. (2017). The orchestra model as the basis for teaching tourism experience design. *Journal of Hospitality and Tourism Management*, 30, 55–64.

Abstract: The topic of modifying settings and service delivery to enhance consumers' experiences is a potentially distinctive component of tourism hospitality and events education. Nevertheless, educators in these interest areas are faced with a challenging task. The challenge is one of delivering a signature set of learning opportunities which empower graduates with the skills to create superior experiences. Like other key issues in pedagogy, having a conceptual basis for the endeavour is fundamental. This study reviews the conceptual origins of our understanding of tourist experience, considers key directions in the field, and asserts the value of the orchestra model of experience. Key principles of approaching service design tasks are outlined: being emic, considering realistic and sustainable options, using consumer segments and tracking the use of space over time.

The Event Design Collective (https://edco.global/) provides a tool for innovation in event design called the Event Canvass, and a book is available (Frissen *et al.* 2016). Their approach is a mix of 'theory of change' (see the next chapter) and 'return on experience'. The Canvass is intended to be used by teams focusing on the transforming experience an event is intended to co-create.

Creativity and innovation

Jackson *et al.* (2018) have concluded that creativity is under-researched within event studies. In an effort to get festivals and events recognized as part of the 'creative industries', alongside obvious categories like the arts and design, they examined the literature on creativity and determined that it requires attention to both the individual cognitive and emotional processes and to the environment in which it occurs – a position reflecting the view of design as the creation of value systems.

7.3 RESEARCH NOTE ON EVENT CREATIVITY

Jackson, C., Morgan, J. and Laws, C. (2018). Creativity in events: The untold story. *International Journal of Event and Festival Management*, 9(1), 2–19.

Abstract: The purpose of this paper is to report on untold stories that not only illustrate the creativity but also complexity of working in outdoor events. There has been global interest in the creative industries and the creative economy more generally. Events have not been identified or categorised as part of this. Experiences have been identified as part of the creative sectors ... and events are seen as experiences ... There has been little research undertaken about the creative nature of event experiences, especially in how they are created. A theoretical framework was created from literature on creativity more generally to inform the Creativity in Events research project. Interviews with those working in the outdoor events sector were the basis of the qualitative stage of the research project investigating the phenomenon of creativity in events. This paper identifies the core facets of creativity in the management of outdoor events. These were fluency, originality, imagination, elaboration, environment and complexity. A vignette is used to illustrate the intricacy of the nature of creativity in the production of outdoor event experiences. The overall findings were that event management was both creative and pragmatic and that both are necessary. There was a need for a creative environment with processes and familiarity that aided inspiration and originality.

Jackson *et al.* (2018, 11) determined the core facets of creativity for outdoor events to be 'fluency, originality, imagination, elaboration, environment and complexity', and these terms need elaboration. Fluency refers to the background of creative people, often working together: 'There is a pattern to event creation and the power of creativity is dependent upon the experience gained over time.' Changing and adapting yields originality, with events being different each time they are offered. Imagination is inherent in all humans, but often it can be externally stimulated, such as by comparison with other events. New ideas have to be discussed, refined or elaborated, often within a dynamic team, and therefore the organizational or stakeholder environment is important for supporting risk taking, or not, and for inspiring people. The complexity of creative problem solving motivates people, with events being a prime example of producing something meaningful out of chaos.

With whole 'industries' now devoted to creativity and knowledge formation, it is becoming more and more unlikely that individuals will spontaneously generate truly original ideas or non-derivative art. So another approach to creativity becomes more important, and that is to actively search for, discuss and refine new associations between facts and concepts. That is one of the aims of this book – to encourage students, researchers and policy-makers to put things together in new ways – to be creative, to think in different ways, often referred to as 'thinking outside the box'.

Florida's (2002) concept of 'the creative class' is relevant here. According to Florida, creativity is a driving force in economic life, and a key source of competitive advantage. Some cities flourish because of their creative class, and Florida argued that creative-class workers choose cities for their tolerant environments and diverse populations, as well as good jobs. The event sector has to be part of this creativity, and is therefore deserving of attention by both cultural and economic policy-makers. 'Creative capital' has value, and it has to be attracted or nurtured. For example, Prentice and Andersen (2003: 8) examined Edinburgh and its positioning as the world-class 'festival city', saying it has gained 'a unique selling point of creativity as well as heritage'. If the social and political environment is supportive, more people are likely to become artists and inventors; if the learning environment is oriented in such a way, students at all levels can learn to be more creative.

As Franchetti and Page (2009) observed, *innovation* is derived from the Latin term 'innovatio' which means 'to create something new'. In events, this relates to the type of experience being provided. Sundbo and Baerenholdt (2007) observed that innovation normally occurred at the level of the firm, at the level of a network and at a systems level (i.e. within government, institutions and organizations that influence the management and operation of activities). Hjalager (2009) expands upon the typical areas of innovation, basing her observations on the initial work of Schumpeter (1934), which outlined the main areas for industrial innovation. This includes product innovations, process innovations (e.g. new ways of delivering services), market innovations (i.e. new ways of communicating with the customer such as the Internet) and logistical innovations (i.e. innovations in supply chain delivery of services such as vertical integration to deliver a seamless tourism experience). Therefore within an events context, achieving innovation is about organizational culture that fosters innovative (as opposed to more laggard behaviour that resists change) leadership and planning as well as harnessing the raw creativity or design around the staging of events and the experience outcome. To be innovative, event organizers must strive to constantly learn, reform and renew their approach to management and design.

Several research notes illustrate a variety of styles and applications of innovation related to events. Larson (2009a) stressed innovation networks, a view supporting the 'strategic design' paradigm. Hjalager (2009) profiled the innovation system of the Roskilde festival in Denmark. Colombo and Richards (2017) examined the 'innovation capacity' of an event and demonstrated how 'eventful cities' are catalysts for innovation. Woratschek *et al.* (2017) provided a case study of a co-created, 'innovative value proposition', namely the fan zone at sport events.

7.4 RESEARCH NOTES ON INNOVATION

Larson, M. (2009). Festival innovation: Complex and dynamic network interaction. *Scandinavian Journal of Hospitality and Tourism*, 9(2/3), 288–307.

Abstract: Material from case studies of three Swedish festivals showed that innovation takes place in complex networks involving many actors having various interests. Innovation networks are often highly dynamic and changing: innovation often takes place in new partnerships. The innovation work is hard to plan: it is to a large degree an emergent process and sometimes innovation originates from improvisation. Some innovation can, however, become institutionalized and embedded in the routines of the partnership interaction. Festival organizers need to reflect on their network and relate strategically to how their partners can contribute to successful festival innovation.

Hjalager, A. (2009). Cultural tourism innovation systems – the Roskilde Festival. *Scandinavian Journal of Hospitality and Tourism*, 9(2/3), 266–287.

Hjalager wrote:

> [S]ince 1971, Roskilde Festival (Denmark) has developed its role as a leading element in an emerging cultural innovation system. Festival organizers maintain long-term, dense and multi-faceted relations. Funds from the (non-profit) festival are efficiently channelled into cultural and sports facilities, enhancing the attractiveness of the region. To keep ahead in the festival market, innovators in the field of managerial systems, technologies and services are deliberately invited to use the grounds as test benches for new ideas. … Roskilde is not a static event. Since 2001 especially, wider ranging organizational structures have been constructed and politically enforced with the aim of nurturing spin-offs, including strong representation within the educational and research sectors.

Colombo, A. and Richards, G. (2017). Eventful cities as global innovation catalysts: The Sónar Festival network. *Event Management*, 21, 621–634.

Abstract: As the economy becomes more globalized, a growing number of events are exerting an influence on activity and innovation globally in different fields. Therefore, we argue that 'eventful cities' can act as important catalysts for eventfulness in other places as well. This article analyzes the case of the Sónar electronic music festival, an event that originated in Barcelona, Spain, but which now runs different editions in many cities worldwide. This empirical study of the innovation capacity of a cultural event examines how a locally based music festival has transformed itself by using the global 'space of flows' to influence the local 'space of places'. The Sónar Festival has turned itself into a relational hub in a global cultural network, using stylistic innovations to link geographically dispersed nodes in order to create new products, open up new markets, and strengthen its own position as a global source of eventfulness.

Woratschek, H., Durchholz, C., Maier, C. and Stroble, T. (2017). Innovations in sport management: The role of motivations and value cocreation at public viewing events. *Event Management*, 21, 1–12.

Abstract (excerpt): During mega-sport events, such as FIFA World Cup or Olympic Games, Fan Fests and other public viewing events have been developed as an innovative value proposition for watching sports. Those events attract millions of sport spectators worldwide. Event organizers have already realized the tremendous economic potential, yet sport management literature provides little empirical evidence on this innovation in sport management. Therefore, this study investigates motivational drivers for sport consumption of public viewing events and provides a better understanding of innovation-induced value cocreation at sport events. As public viewing represents an innovative mixture of stadium and television, we conduct a literature review of sport spectator motivations and study empirical findings in the stadium, television, and public viewing context.

7.1 EXPERT OPINION

Event design

Dr Steve Brown is an award-winning Australian event designer with a background in both professional practice and academic research, publication and teaching. His most recent project was as a Creative Producer for the Adelaide Symphony Orchestra. His own text, *Event Design: Creating and Staging the Event Experience*, was published in 2010.

I have long held the belief that if one commits to *designing* (as opposed to only managing) an event with the aim of maximizing the experience for the audience, it will lead to a more positive and meaningful experience for them. This, in turn, will increase the effectiveness of communication of the narrative/theme of the event to the audience. An enhanced and targeted experience and a more effective communication method will also increase the likelihood of return business (should the event be staged again) and of meeting the stated objectives of the event whether those objectives be cultural, commercial, personal – or just for fun.

The use of the application of event design principles and techniques to make it better for your audience while increasing the likelihood of meeting your event's objectives would seem an obvious starting point for any event regardless of purpose, budget, scale, style, genre or desired outcome. Indeed, since identifying Event Design as a set of principles and techniques in 2004 – based on my own research and professional practice – I have proof of concept in the staging of a wide range of very successful events for which I have been responsible.

The key to the successful staging of any event is a more complete understanding of your audience and designing the event based on that understanding. Too often event creators (most frequently called 'managers') concentrate their efforts on operational/logistical issues to the exclusion of making their events audience-centric. The first questions an event creator or event organisation need to identify are: the *raison d'être* for the event and its target audience. Once these are known, the event can be designed specifically for that target audience (not 'market'). Events can't be future-proofed or ensured of success even in the short term solely by staging well-managed events for 'everyone'.

Evaluation is a critical component of creating and staging the event experience. Pre-event, evaluation can obtain simple socio-demographic information that informs the event designer about their target audience. During the event, evaluation enables us to identify audience behaviours and how the program elements and the site design works and interacts with the audience. Post-event evaluation can capture spending patterns, recall of information, intention to return and, more importantly, how effectively the event met its desired measurable outcomes.

The Adelaide Symphony Orchestra (ASO) is, like many orchestras, concerned about an ageing audience subscriber base. Their raison d'être for a series of hybrid 'rock band with orchestra' was to attract younger audiences – starting with 'baby boomers' and gradually working younger. The series has included music by Bowie, Queen, Deep Purple, Led Zeppelin, Pink Floyd, Muse and Sigur Rós. To bring younger audiences to traditionally successful concerts there was also a gospel version of Handel's *Messiah*. The programs included innovative staging designed specifically for the target audience to demonstrate the integration of the bands within the orchestra and the power and majesty of orchestral performance – all while playing *their* music. The events have been very well attended and a mix of formal (written) and informal (standing ovations, multiple curtain calls, Facebook, etc.) evaluation has shown that the objectives have been met with increased commitment to return to the ASO for concerts in its 'standard' program.

Event design works. In combination, these simple steps are very powerful and can improve any event. Event designers need to become practiced at these steps and to pursue an event design body of knowledge by studying events and by immersing themselves in the community in which their event will be staged and learning as much as they can about their audience. Only then can an event be called designed and not just managed.

Designing event settings

Setting, services (especially the people component), and theme/programme: these are the three pillars of event design, each of which singly, and synergistically, affect the event experience. The overall aim is to facilitate unique, satisfying and memorable experiences that will attract guests, customers and participants – hopefully creating loyal audiences; this is a 'service proposition' in the language of service-dominant logic. The combination of these three basic elements, within the almost limitless parameters of the elements of style, ensures that every time an event is offered the experiences of those involved will be different.

Nelson (2009) drew upon Goffman's (1959) dramaturgical perspective (see the illustration of dramaturgy in Chapter 6) and the components of atmospherics (Kotler 1973) and servicescape (Bitner 1992). Goffman, according to Nelson, stressed the setting components of furniture, decor, physical layout, and other background items that supply the scenery and stage props. Attendees enter a specially designed setting for the performance of the event. Physical and ambient factors are part of the designer's repertoire: lighting, colour, quality of materials, layout, music, entertainment, fragrance, and room temperature. Signs, symbols and artefacts are also employed to create the right atmosphere and a functional servicescape.

Event settings, first of all, are places that have to be defined as 'special' for the duration of the 'time out of time' that constitutes a planned event. The main initial considerations are location (e.g. centrality and accessibility), site characteristics (is it suitable for the event?) and the social–cultural context (has it historic and cultural meaning?). Infrastructure and management systems then have to be developed or modified, including basic services, theme and programme, amenities and guest services, security and controls. Both site planning and aesthetic design are important.

There are unlimited ways to combine setting, management and people, yielding great opportunities for creative event design. However, each setting poses its own challenges and opportunities, some of which are identified in the ensuing discussion of generic event settings. These are defined by functions, and of course they can be combined.

Generic event settings

(a) Assembly

These are settings for meetings, conventions, concerts, festivals, and spectator sports – any event bringing together large numbers of people where seating, viewing and listening are core design functions. Sports arenas and stadia are mostly outdoors, but not all. Theatres can be stand-alone or part of convention/exhibition centres, arts complexes, educational institutions or commercial resorts and hotels. An event manager can often rent 'assembly' venues that have their own management systems, and those who operate such venues are automatically in the event business.

Purpose-built assembly venues will strive for state-of -the art design to maximize convenience, comfort, safety, visibility and acoustics. Their management systems will likely adhere to various government codes and sustainability standards. But old and non-traditional venues present challenges when it comes to aesthetics, or require substantial modification on technical or creative grounds to suit the event. Opportunities for using unique and even strange venues abound. Meeting planners seek out venues in special places with inspiring or provocative features.

Advice on meeting, convention and exhibition venue design can be found in books by Lawson (2000), and Meeting Professionals International (2003). Party design is covered by Bailey (2002) and by Malouf (2002). There are websites linking users to three-dimensional, computer-assisted design software.

(b) Parade or procession

Parades, flotillas, cavalcades, marches and other similar events are linear, mobile forms of entertainment, spectacle or ritual with special design and management requirements. The audience might be standing, seated or moving along with the procession. The most common linear setting, however, is a street with a static audience along the route. Some processions pass through seating areas and even stadia, where they take on the form of theatre, as in Rio de Janeiro's Carnival.

Logistics for such events are challenging, such as getting everyone in a parade or race mobilized for proper sequencing, the likelihood of causing traffic disruption and congestion, and the fact that most streets are unsuited for spectating. Gregson (1992) gave advice on using pavements, streets and buildings to stage events, noting that architects generally fail to take account of seasonal changes and the needs of public gatherings. There are not many resources on parade planning and design, although many cities publish on their websites the regulations for holding them. One of the few dedicated sources is IFEA's publication *Official Guide to Parades* (2000; editor, Valerie Lagauskas).

(c) Linear-nodal

Many sport events involve races or other linear forms of activity, including long-distance running and auto racing, which combine elements of procession with nodes of activity. Usually the audience congregates at the nodes, such as start, finish and transition points, but could be dispersed along the entire route, like a parade. The event designer will often have to provide live video feeds from the linear portions to the places where fans congregate. Service points for athletes and vehicles are also needed. The establishment of fan zones at major sport events has become a common practice, and this can be viewed as experience augmentation or co-creation. The fan zone experience, as Woratschek *et al.* (2017) concluded, enabled the highly desired benefits of shared experience and the freedom to move around.

(d) Open space

Events make use of parks, plazas and closed-off streets, especially in publicly sponsored events designed to appeal to mass audiences. Free movement is a feature of these settings, but they usually also contain sub-areas for assembly, procession and exhibition/sales. European cities seem to have the advantage in terms of beautiful, culturally significant squares for events, while North American cities tend to have more space, such as waterfronts and natural parks to use for large public gatherings (Getz 2001). Environmental concerns are important in parks, while potential damage to buildings is a concern in urban plazas. Smith (2015) examines both the positives and negatives of utilizing public spaces for events. Outdoor sport facilities of all types serve as event venues, and increasingly sport complexes have been built with sport tourism as a top priority. Just how residents and visitors attending events manage to share such facilities is a challenge for managers. One resource for designers and event managers is the US-based National Council of Youth Sport Events (www.ncys.org).

(e) Exhibition/sales

Purpose-built exhibition and convention centres are the best suited for trade and consumer shows, although any event can incorporate areas for food and beverage or other merchandise sales and demonstrations. These settings are designed to entice entry and circulation, browsing and sales. Sometimes the audience merely views the exhibits; at other venues, sales are made. Since the purpose of these events is usually commerce, a number of principles from environmental psychology have to be applied to the design in order to ensure that interpersonal contacts are facilitated. Good circulation is necessary, but it is also desirable to have people linger and talk. Morrow (1997) examined trade and consumer shows. There is substantial literature on exhibitions within galleries and museums (e.g. Dernie 2006) and many of the principles established for those types of experiences can be applied to other displays and to sales events. A very special case is the outdoor food/beverage event, such as 'taste of …', where sales, consumption, demonstrations and entertainment are often combined, indoors or out.

Events as theatre

Theatre is one form of planned event, and theatres are common event settings, but as already discussed theatre is also a metaphor for performances and events of all kinds. Certainly there is ample scope for the event designer to draw upon theatrical productions to enhance event settings and experiences. Experience design according to Haahti and Komppula (2006) draws heavily on dramaturgy (see Figure 6.10) which is part of theatre and performance studies. They provide examples in which high-contact, high-involvement tourists co-create experiences with professional 'stagers' of facilitators. Ideas for 'manuscripts' and 'staged experiences' have to be generated with the needs and expectations of guests in mind, embodying myths, stories and history from the place or event. 'This enables the creation of a place and a space for being together and the development of a group identity in experiencing' (ibid.: 103). In this approach, the 'stage' is whatever venue the experience takes place in, but it has to be appropriate to the design.

Staging

This is the most fundamental theatrical concept, based on the fact that plays and many other performances are usually produced in a specific (assembly) venue with a stage and an audience. 'Staging' or 'stagecraft' applies to both the layout of this type of setting and to what is done on the stage (or within the entire performance space, whatever it is) to facilitate the performance and enhance the audience's experience. The basic components are illustrated in Figure 7.2.

Brown and James (2004) discussed five specific theatrical applications to events. Scale, shape and focus apply to the setting, whereas timing and build (discussed later) come under the heading of scripting or programming.

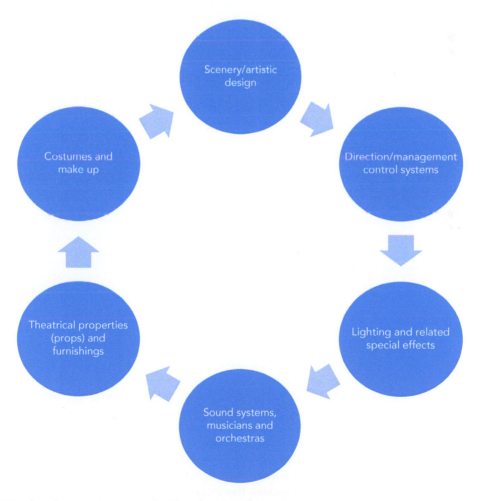

Figure 7.2 The elements associated with enhancing the audience experience

SCALE

It is important to match the scale of the event or activity to the venue, in part to ensure the audience can see and understand what is happening. This principle will affect decisions on whether to stress the visual over the aural, and three-dimensional over two-dimensional. The audience needs enclosure but does not want to feel restricted.

SHAPE

Drawing from environmental psychology, knowledge of how an audience relates to and moves within an environment is essential. Removing visual and tangible clutter or distractions, and keeping things simple and legible, are important design principles for event settings.

FOCUS

The use of blocking techniques from theatre and film direction ensures that the audience concentrates on what the designer/programmer wants it to focus on. Consider how lighting, colour, movement and shape affect people (this draws on both cognitive and environmental psychology).

Sensory stimulation

Research on sensory stimulation at events has been minimal, yet it is clearly an important element in the experience. Biaett (2019: 250) observed from personal experience how the 'infusion of senses and emotions' engaged event attendees. Biaett noted (p. 251): 'At community festivals, the maximized interrelated factors of physical collaborative creative activity, stimulated senses, and cyclically aroused emotions, give rise to highly festive atmospheres during which social capital bonding and bridging flourishes and attendees attain peak levels of liminality with feelings of well-being.' In addition to the traditional five senses, Biaett suggested that attention be given to temperature, vibration and balance. Duffy and Mair (2018) explored how sensual engagement facilitates social engagement, employing and ethnographic methodology and referring to 'sensual geographies' for theoretical support.

7.5 RESEARCH NOTE ON ENGAGING THE SENSES

Duffy, M. and Mair, J. (2018). Engaging the senses to explore community events. *Event Management*, 22, 49–63.

Abstract: Community events are often staged by local authorities as a way to boost the local economy, improve social cohesion, and foster a sense of belonging. However, although it is arguably comparatively straightforward to conceptualize how events may contribute in terms of economic impact, it is much more difficult to understand and assess how events can contribute to feelings of connectedness and belonging. To date, the focus in the event management literature has been very strongly focused on what people think of events; this study instead draws our attention to what people do and how this may provide clues as to how they feel in terms of engagement. Recent studies in tourism, geography, and urban studies have started to explore the role the senses play in our engagement and participation in events. Turning to the senses as a means to explore our bodily engagement with an event provides an opportunity to examine inclusion and exclusion at an event from a new perspective. This article takes an interdisciplinary ethnographic approach to examine a case study of community and the Noosa Jazz Festival in Australia. Findings suggest that festivals, through their embodied participants, can facilitate feelings of inclusion in a community. Sound, vision, and the festival ambience emerged as being of key importance. The research demonstrates the benefits of interdisciplinary research, particularly drawing from sensual geographies, when exploring intangible constructs such as connectedness, inclusion, cohesion, and belonging.

Each of the five senses is not only important in the design of event experiences, constituting some of the elements of style, but also provides the theme for numerous events. Spectacle is by definition a larger than life visual experience (i.e. sight) and is a frequent accompaniment to events in the form of costumes, performances, light shows and fireworks – and these are often stand-alone performances as well. Taste is the essence of food and beverage events, popular the world over, and food and beverage hospitality is an essential component of almost all events that last more than a couple of hours.

The sounds of music are incredibly varied and therefore provide unlimited possibilities for themed events, from popular music to the classics, with either musicians/composers or the style of music being celebrated. Touch, such as hands-on experiences in preparing food, are of great importance to people who want to learn, be creative and gain immediate satisfaction from their work. Perhaps the least utilized sense in event theming is smell, but it does provide the starting point for flower and perfume festivals and, as every restaurateur knows, smells entice people to eat and drink, to enter a venue and linger. Smell also carries the advantage of being associated with memories, so that a smell can, years later, invoke a pleasant or unpleasant experience.

Sight

Lindenberg (2013) noted that lighting is one of a number of sensory cues that can affect human behaviour. Experiments have shown, for example, that lower levels result in greater interpersonal intimacy and quieter or reduced conversation. So event designers reduce lighting just before the curtain rises or the speakers take the stage in order to quiet the audience. On the other hand, soft lighting during a banquet will likely encourage conversation. Lighting also impacts on functionality. If the event purpose is to discuss important topics, dim lighting will be counter-productive. If it requires audience attention on a stage or person, then dim ambient lights plus a spotlight are effective. Light shows, often including lasers, provide a lot of mental stimulation and generate emotional arousal.

Too much light stimulation can be counter-productive if the audience is expected to calm down. Light stimulation generates a lot of brain activity that is difficult to turn off, hence you are wise to avoid watching television before sleep time, and do not want to have a strobe-light effect just before listening to a speaker. People who take their laptops and other devices to bed will find it harder to get a good night's sleep, so imposing a lot of this kind of visual work on event-goers might very well cause stress.

People have colour preferences, and colours affect mood. Colour can be manipulated through lighting or other design features. Perceived spaciousness can be influenced by colours and lighting, helping to reduce feelings of crowding. 'Colour theory' relates to how specific media affect colour appearance (i.e. the effects of context on colour appearance) whereas 'colour psychology' considers the effects of colours on feelings and behaviour (e.g. will a pink room really calm prisoners and a red room increase tension? Does blue make people feel calm and cool?). 'Colour symbolism' is culturally defined, as in whether red suggests heat, anger or danger.

Sound

Desirable sounds motivate event attendance, and people will travel a long way for the right sounds or the musicians who create them. Noise, on the other hand, is undesired sound. We can measure sound by decibels, and when the intensity is high it can cause annoyance or event pain. Pitch, periodicity and duration are also contributors to desirable sounds or unwanted noise (Bilotta and Evans 2013: 29–30).

Persistent, loud noise is universally shunned, as it is both physically bothersome and gets in the way of desired conversations or other interactions (just ask people who live near airports or motorways). Yet loud noise is also expected by many event-goers, so there we also have to consider motivation and the physical characteristics of the listeners (e.g. old versus young, gender and cultural backgrounds) before labelling sounds as unwanted noise. There are huge differences between rock concerts and classical music in terms of who attends, and what sounds they want or noise levels they will tolerate. Quiet, ambient music has been found to be relaxing, although many people are rather sick of the elevator music we are too often subjected to.

Research related to sounds and events has been rare. The paper by Waitt and Duffy (2010) explores 'what ears and listening can add to the understanding of the interconnections between festival spaces and people. This project adopted an interdisciplinary approach that acknowledges listening as simultaneously a neurological, psychological and culturally situated process.' Waitt, Gorman-Murray and Gibson (2011) reported on how '… an embodied sense of rhythm can add to understandings of the relationship between festival spaces and people. Insights are given to how the rhythmic qualities of sound help orientate bodies in festival spaces, and how bodies produce festival space through embodied responses to the rhythmic qualities of sound.'

Smell

Food-service professionals know that their best advertisement is often the smell of cooking. Smells can be strategically intended to get consumers in the mood for shopping. If we are hungry, the right smells can invoke salivation. The wrong smells can make people physically ill. Indeed, the military has experimented with smell as a weapon!

From environmental psychology, we have learned that exposure to nature can be stress reducing, but so too can visual stimulations and olfactory (smells) or auditory stimulation (Joye and van der Berg 2013: 61). This leads us to the possibility that events can be restorative in nature (discussed later).

Taste

Tasting is obviously the critical factor in dining experiences, and tastes can be manipulated in other event environments to stimulate emotional and behavioural responses. The popularity of 'taste of' events, themed with an endless variety of foodstuff, recipes and cultural associations, is universal. This form of taste should not be confused with taste or tastefulness, as in how one dresses or acts, which can be viewed as an element in cultural capital. Everett (2012) used the term 'tastescape' to describe areas that appeal to food tourists on the basis of purity and escape, and in this context both forms of taste and tastefulness are relevant.

From research on foodies and food tourism (Getz *et al.* 2014) it is clear that foodies or food lovers can be defined by a set of attitudes and behaviours that emphasize a love of cooking and strong preferences for quality in the sourcing and preparation of their food. The emphasis on quality leads foodies to markets where fresh and local produce is the appeal, and to seeking authentic food experiences (with special events being highly appealing) as cultural tourists. Some foodies, and many others who would never want to use that term, believe in healthy and sustainable food habits, and this is only in part related to taste or tastefulness. Whatever the perspective taken, there is absolutely no doubt that taste is a major motivator of travel and event attendance.

Touch

Exhibit designers understand that involvement with displays is better than mere visual stimulation. Getting people to touch and try is one key step towards learning or buying. Harvey *et al.* (1998) discovered that they could more than double the time visitors spent at exhibits by making them interactive and multisensory, and providing better lighting and easier-to-read lettering. Visitors felt more immersed in the overall museum experience.

Research on foodies (Getz *et al.* 2014) established the importance of hands-on experiences in motivating food tourism, with events being an important destination attraction. Food tourists value the cultural authenticity, learning, tasting and creativity that accompanies doing – as found in participatory cooking classes with chefs.

Sensory mapping

This is a tool that can be used in conjunction with other methods to evaluate or improve experiences at events (see: service blueprinting and mapping). According to the Sensory Trust UK, 'Sensory mapping is a simple, flexible technique that identifies sensory highlights with a view to creating inclusive and engaging visitor experiences. It essentially consists of individuals or small groups exploring a location and mapping where they encounter particularly strong sensory stimuli, including, but not limited to, sights, sounds, smells, textures and tastes. Mapping can also make note of other things people experience in response to these sensory experiences such as emotions, feelings and memories.' (Source: https://www.sensorytrust.org.uk/information/factsheets/what-is-sensory-mapping.html)

In particular, the visitor experiences of people with special needs, children, the elderly or those unfamiliar with certain environments can benefit from an array of sensory stimulation. Site planning can be modified to maximize exposure to smells, for example, or to minimize them. Combined with service mapping, specific reactions to light, sound, smell, etc. can form part of the evaluation of overall service and programme quality.

Combining sensory data as perceived by users, designers can identify 'hot or cold spots' where stimulation, delight or disgust is concentrated.

Figure 7.3 provides an example of how a sensory map can be linked to service mapping by participant observers, or on the basis of user feedback, during an entire event experience – from entry to the site through various experience opportunities to departure. In this example, the five senses are represented by circles, and these can be enlarged relative to each other depending on their importance in any area or at particular points in time. They could also be colour-coded or substituted with radar graphs. It is possible that all five senses are engaged to some extent all the time, but that is not a given.

The illustration follows the logic of an event experience at a specific venue:

(1) approach and enter the venue: there might be the sights and sounds of traffic

(2) enter the site/venue (reception by staff/volunteers; information provided; initial impressions)

(3) a sit-down meal

(4) spectating a performance or competition

(5) shopping and buying

(6) exiting the site.

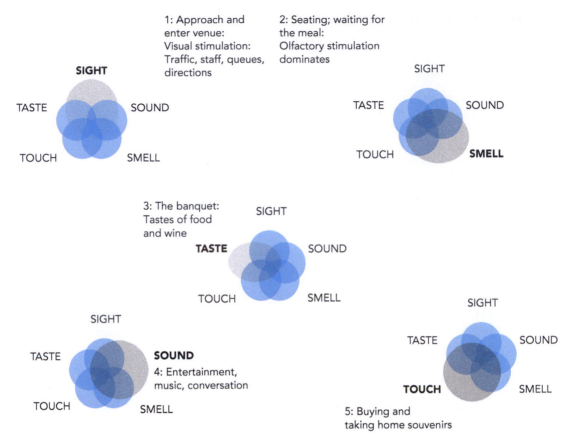

Figure 7.3 Sample sensory map for an event

A combined quantitative/qualitative evaluation is possible, as some things like noise can be measured, whereas taste and smell will vary a great deal among participants. A final summary chart can also be used to approximate the overall perceived (or potential) sensory experience.

Instead of examining the senses within a flow of event experiences, the setting or venue itself can be mapped in advance, leading to design modifications. For example, where (and when in the flow) do you want the visitor to experience that visual 'wow' experience? – at the entrance, or when the entertainment begins and everyone is seated? Where in the large fair site, for example, will smells and tastes be maximized? Combining sensory mapping with cognitive mapping (for wayfaring) should help improve site planning, programming and the overall event experience.

Aesthetics

Aesthetics is 'a branch of philosophy dealing with the nature of beauty, art and taste and with the creation and appreciation of beauty' (Source: https://www.merriam-webster.com/). Aesthetic appeal is usually associated with 'art', but beauty can be manifested through any or all of the five senses. That is why we can talk about culinary arts, visual arts, etc. Aesthetic design elements might also hold symbolic meaning, and this can be manipulated by event designers. For example, certain colours, design features (like expensive art) and shapes or patterns are associated with political ideologies, royalty, lifestyles, social class or other potentially unifying or controversial themes.

Over-stimulation or complexity

The well-known phenomenon of mental fatigue has to be understood by event designers. Viewers, shoppers, listeners and tasters can only devote so much attention before becoming mentally fatigued or experiencing the kind of sensory overload that prevents further enjoyment. If you are tasting wines or food delicacies, there is a limit beyond which discrimination of taste ceases to exist. In a museum, visitors eventually start passing by many exhibits without stopping because they have already absorbed enough.

The same kind of mental fatigue can result in conventioneers skipping sessions, students falling asleep in class (boredom might also be a factor) or visitors to art exhibits merely glancing at outstanding works of art. Event designers can plan their setting to focus attention quickly on the primary exhibits or other features, to reach visitors prior to fatigue setting in. Lecturers and speakers can hit the highlights first, then go on to the mundane details.

Attraction gradients

'Attraction gradient' refers to the ways in which people move in relation to the objects of their attention, or in other words, how do you ensure that what you have to offer or exhibit gets the attendees' attention? Some positions in an exhibition, for example, are better than others. There will be a gradient of high- to low-traffic sites, with those facing the entrance having the highest. Being located next to the free food and drinks helps! Typically exhibition owners charge more for the larger and better-located sites within the venue, based on knowledge of how these factors affect viewing and sales.

The Kaplan (1987) Preference Model for Environments

The Kaplan (1987) model, from environmental psychology, helps to predict people's preferences for various types of environment. There are four basic considerations that can be used as design principles for event settings:

- 'coherence': the scene is organized, everything hangs together;
- 'legibility': we can categorize or understand the setting, everything is clear to us;
- 'complexity': a measure of the number and variety of elements in the setting;
- 'mystery': hidden information is present and we are drawn into the setting to learn more.

Too much complexity or mystery, however, can be a bad thing. Too much mystery can be incompatible with legibility, and can become frightening. If the event designer provides light and dark contrasts, the viewer might be drawn in, whereas too dark a room can be scary and might discourage entry. Also, consider an empty room versus one in which people are present. Are we normally inclined to enter a space in which no other people are present? What appeals to people for meetings, trade shows and learning seminars might be quite different from settings for sports, public celebrations and private parties.

Events as restorative or instorative environments

Can festivals and events be 'restorative' in terms of reducing the stress of daily life, or 'instorative' by way of fostering mood enhancement and improved sense of well-being? Environmental psychologists know that exposure to nature can be restorative (Joye and van den Berg 2013), and that means that holding events in parks and gardens, or in areas with water features, can have positive results. On the other hand, many events held outdoors obviously do not appeal to rest and relaxation, with competitive sports and noisy music concerts being the prime examples. Indoors, the ambient conditions provided by designers (including lighting, layout, temperature, plants, water features, noise suppression, pleasant smells, mystery, etc.), can be restorative through facilitation of physical and psychological comfort and opportunities for reflection, as demonstrated by Packer and Bond (2010) for museums.

Restorative and instorative event settings are not always feasible or desirable, but perhaps some provision can be made within large event settings, or attached to them, for those needing stress reduction. And more events should be designed from the start to provide these benefits – especially to urban dwellers who might have limited opportunities to escape to quiet, natural environments.

The restorative or instorative event environment will be designed with some or all of the following characteristics, keeping in mind that the nature of the event, and the motivations of attendees, will dictate what is appropriate and feasible:

- escape: a setting that is clearly different from one's normal environment, (e.g. Mozart in the mountains) or a retreat within an event setting (e.g. the family rest stations at a fair);
- freedom: a setting conducive to desired experiences (e.g. this is likely to range from a space to experience nature, such as a classical music concert in the city park, to a tolerance of uninhibited behaviour such as at a rock concert in an open field);
- engagement: an interesting and stimulating environment (e.g. hands-on exhibits, participation sports, sensory stimulation through installation art, or discussion circles at conferences);
- coherence and legibility: for some events this means avoiding feelings of crowding or confusion (e.g. at conferences, weddings), but for other events it means providing the right mix of sensory stimulation and intense social interaction (e.g. at concerts, fan zones, sport arenas).

Cognitive mapping and wayfinding

'Cognitive mapping' is the process of acquiring, coding, storing, recalling (and eventually utilizing) information about the environment, such as where things are located, how to get there. We therefore hold mental images, or constructs, of the spatial patterns and relationships that are important to us, based on everyday experience (and perhaps studying maps or searching Google!). 'Wayfinding' is how we navigate, and in novel situations like going to an event for the first time, or into a large venue, we might have difficulty. In unfamiliar surroundings we need information, both graphic and text, as well as other cues as to what movement is either required (such as 'no entry') or optional (such as 'kids' village this way'). 'Cues' can be provided by sensory stimulation (e.g. dark areas discourage traffic) or the organization and design of a venue.

Coherence and legibility are important when it comes to environmental preferences, so how do we translate that into event design, and how does it impact on event experiences? Bateson (1989) said that 'legibility' is crucial in all 'servicescapes', because customers arrive with expectations of how the site will function. These are, of course, social constructs, such as the notion that festival sites should always have a main stage and a food/beverage area.

Lynch (1960) provided the classic approach to cognitive mapping in cities, with implications for event settings. His key principles should be applied to event site planning so that people can easily understand the layout and efficiently navigate within it. The larger and more complex the site, the more important it is to strive for coherence and legibility. Lynch stressed the following features for optimal wayfinding.

- 'nodes': activity places (provide a central stage and entertainment area within a park; arrange the venue to have multiple, easily located focal points);
- 'paths': routes people follow (direction and flow within an event venue has to be controlled; use signs and edges);

- 'landmarks': shapes, signs or symbols that everyone can see and refer to (e.g. every world's fair builds a monument, usually in the centre);
- 'districts': neighbourhoods, shopping centres and other themed areas (group compatible activities together);
- 'edges': perceptual or real barriers between districts (people should recognize where they are in relation to other districts).

Lynch also found age and gender differences in how people wayfare, and there are probably many cultural differences as well. This suggests a research project for application to a variety of event sites. Barker's (1968) behaviour settings can be adapted to fit different circumstances and goals. The three generic means of control pertain to:

- 'access' (who gets in, or under what schedule);
- 'design capacity' (i.e. the numbers allowed; consider peak and average attendance);
- 'flow' (time spent on site; turnover rates). It is also necessary to consider accessibility for persons with physical and other disabilities or special needs (see Fleck 1996).

According to Lask (2011: 48), Lynch's intention with cognitive maps '... was to develop a method that would allow him to understand the subjective feelings that people attach to their built environment.' Lask employed cognitive mapping to determine emotions linked to urban space and suggested this technique can also be applied to special events.

Architecture and settings

Rockwell and Mau (2006: 20) argued that 'The experience of making connections in real time and real space has always fascinated me. Spectacle celebrates events that offer a time and a space for live, shared experience.' Rockwell believes that events provide opportunities for creative risk taking. While architecture has not traditionally been associated with event design, there is plenty of scope for applications.

The affective quality of places

A model by Russell and Lanius (1984), called 'Adaptation level and the affective appraisal of environments' holds the premise that emotional reactions to environments can be described in words along two continua: from pleasant to unpleasant, and from arousing to sleepy. Forty descriptors were developed through research, falling into the four quadrants:

1. highly arousing and highly pleasant (e.g. exciting, exhilarating, interesting)
2. highly arousing and unpleasant (e.g. distressing, frenzied, tense, hectic)
3. unarousing and unpleasant (e.g. dull, dreary, unstimulating)
4. unarousing but pleasant (e.g. serene, tranquil, peaceful, restful).

Is quadrant 1 the 'wow!' factor desired by many event designers? Note that the descriptors are not specifically experiences, only reactions to stimuli.

Russell and Lanius determined through experimentation that the same stimulus (they used photographs) can generate widely different affective appraisals. In other words, setting designers cannot be certain that their work will elicit the intended emotional response. One major reason is that people adapt to the environment and particular stimuli, so they react differently the next time.

Sensation seeking, arousal and optimal stimulation

According to Zuckerman (1979) sensation seeking is a core personality trait, defined by the search for experiences and feelings that are 'varied, novel, complex and intense'. Risk taking is often part of this trait, but so is novelty-seeking without risks. Zuckerman developed the 'sensation seeking scale', and research has demonstrated large differences among people in terms of their preference for sensory stimulation. People who are high sensation seekers, generally more males than females, require a lot of stimulation to reach their personal 'optimal level of arousal'. The components of sensation seeking are thrills and adventure, unconventional experiences, 'disinhibition' (e.g. participation in 'out of control' activities) and intolerance of boredom.

Interpersonal and environmental stimuli cause responses, both physiological and psychological, triggering behavioural responses. Sometimes event designers want to increase arousal, as in fostering celebration or revelry, and at other times they decrease stimulation in order to foster reverence or attentiveness. People have a limited capacity for dealing with a lot of stimulation and can become over-stimulated. When this happens, it can trigger a response such as withdrawal or anxiety, and it will usually result in a filtering of stimuli to focus on the necessary or desirable inputs. Another strategy frequently employed by people is to attempt to eliminate or adjust the stimulus, such as by screening information, turning down noise and light levels, or engaging in conversation in order to mask an annoying or boring speaker.

People have their own ways of finding optimal arousal levels, and this can be accomplished through escaping or seeking stimulation. This is at the core of leisure and travel theory, based on the notion that motivation or need for leisure and travel is a result of simultaneously seeking and escaping (Iso-Ahola 1983). Continuous exposure to simulation can result in 'adaptation', such as people in cities adapting to higher levels of noise or crowding.

Environmental stress

'Environmental stress theory' analyses how stress factors affect people, communities, and cultures, and their responses to stress. Certainly when things feel out of control, beyond our ability to cope, we feel stress. Also when the environment poses danger, or we perceive risks. Event settings or programmes that generate sensory overload, overcrowding, nasty surprises, bad behaviour on the part of other guests, or poorly managed environmental systems can cause stress. A lack of knowledge about what is happening can generate fear and stress, so timely communications are always essential.

According to Bilotta and Evans (2013: 28) chronic environmental stressors cause the greatest harm, such as when people are exposed to continuous noise, or air pollution, whereas acute stressors are those we would expect from temporary events, including crowding, noise, excessive waiting, sensory overloads, overwhelming security or fear of being trapped. Berlonghi (1990: 73) concluded that panic at events is likely to stem from real or perceived threats, and he discussed eight crowd characteristics to help managers or security identify crowd problems and security threats. Freedman (1975) also experimented with 'contagion', which is the rapid spread of emotions or behaviour through a group or crowd. This phenomenon obviously has a direct bearing on events, as in some cases we want to foster positive contagion (especially celebration and humour) and in others it is very bad (fear and fighting).

Personal space

What is the difference between intimacy, personal distance, social distance and public distance? We want intimacy with lovers and family, but not strangers. We tolerate crowds, even seek them out, when a certain atmosphere is desired. At meetings, we might feel uncomfortable if the seats are too close. Hall (1966) identified the four spatial zones, with 'intimate distance' being 0 to 1.5 feet (touching and feeling distance, with lots of contact and various sensory exchanges). 'Personal distance' is 1.5 to 4 feet (mostly verbal and visual contacts; contacts with friends and regular acquaintances). 'Social distance' is 4 to 12 feet (impersonal and business-like eye and voice contacts, no touching, normal voice levels). Fourth, 'public distance' is over 12 feet (formality, as in students' relationship to a lecturer in a classroom; when the need exists for technical assistance or raising one's voice).

Environmental psychologists have studied personal space in various settings, using laboratory experiments and simulations or field methods. For event researchers, field observations and tests will yield the best results. Remember that cultural factors are likely to be important, and that age and gender have to be considered.

'Personal space' can be used by event designers to help achieve goals. For example, it is well known and easily observed that communication effectiveness diminishes with distance from the speaker. That is why classrooms are designed as amphitheatres and not long halls. There have been studies of optimal spacing in learning environments, for professional interaction and for facilitating group processes. 'Sociopetal' distance brings people together, such as the circular or opposite layout of chairs in one's living room, while 'sociofugal' spacing diminishes interaction (e.g. rows of chairs).

A related concept is 'territoriality', which refers to a tendency for similar groups to stick together and apart from other groups. Within- and between-group interactions are easy to observe in most social settings, such as the little cliques that form at parties. If you want people to join in, leave an obvious opening, as in a crescent, but if you feel exclusionary, form a tight little knot with everyone facing inwards. Another form of territoriality occurs when people protect space for themselves or their group, like reserving seats or claiming tables at a banquet. Is this a good or bad thing?

Crowding, crowd management and crowd control

There is a long history of studying crowding within the behavioural sciences such as Psychology, illustrated by Le Bon's (1908) study that is the foundation of many of the subsequent analyses of crowding. More recent studies such as Wynn-Moylan (2017) trace the evolution of thinking on the science of crowding and crowd behaviour pointing to the influential studies such as Berlonghi (1995) on what can cause crowd problems at events (see Figure 7.4). What these studies show is that there are catalysts that can trigger a crowd in crowd behaviour theory. Le Bon (1908) stimulated a debate and research field arguing that through group mind theory, it was evident that individuals in a crowd lost all sense of responsibility, becoming members of the group. Many subsequent studies have questioned these assertions which suggest the context that can trigger these behaviours is also important. For example, Wynn-Moyland (2017) points to the work of Festinger et al. (1952) which suggested deindividuation occurs in crowd settings. This concept suggests that a wider range of behaviours may occur dependent on the context and the individuals involved that can lead in extreme cases to rioting and violence. Other studies have labelled this mob sociology (e.g. Momboisse 1967) suggesting the behaviour is irrational, while Berk (1974) suggested that crowd action was rational and could be modelled. Subsequent research has shown that crowd behaviour is very much based on social identity theory (see Wynn-Moylan 2017) where people act in relation to their own identity and in a socially coherent manner.

Key concepts to understand crowding relate to 'Density' (an objective measure of how many people there are in a given area), where 'crowding' is how people feel about the situation. Studies have shown that in wilderness settings, even the sight of a few other canoeists is crowding. Although a potential problem at events, people often expect crowds and they can even add to our enjoyment (Lee et al. 1997; Wickham and Kerstetter 2000; Mowen et al. 2003).

Some of our reaction to the presence of others is related to the size of the group and our personal space – this is 'social density' (Bell et al. 2001: 296), whereas some of it depends on how much space there

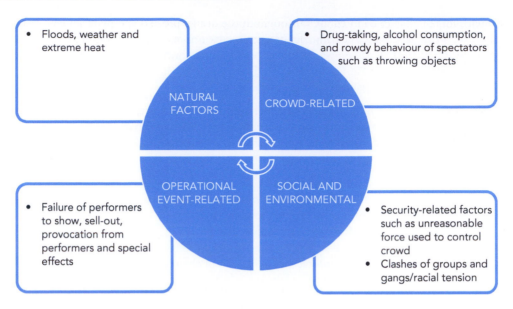

Figure 7.4 Causes of crowd behavioural issues at events

Source: Developed from Berlonghi 1995.

is – that is, 'spatial density'. It is the difference between too many people to interact with, versus not enough space. Freedom to move, perceived control and risks can also be factors. For example, what would happen in a panic – can we escape? Certainly the context also influences our judgement of what is crowding. Researchers have found that males and females are equally affected by high social density, but males suffer more from high spatial density. Friends and social support mitigate stress or anxiety caused by crowding. Evidence linking crowding with aggression or other anti-social behaviour is not clear, especially within event settings.

Bell *et al.* (2001: 315) compared various theoretical models pertaining to crowding. Critical causes of crowding (not of density, but the resultant feeling) have been attributed to excessive social contact and social stimulation, reduced freedom (e.g. to move about), scarcity of resources (bathrooms?), violations of personal space, unwanted contacts (groping?), interference with desired behaviour and lack of privacy. Possible coping mechanisms to crowding include withdrawal, attempts to reduce stimulation/arousal, escape, aggressive behaviour, territoriality and other attempts to maintain freedom, control or privacy. Some of these coping mechanisms might be desirable even if the crowding is considered to be, overall, unavoidable or fun. Cutting across most of these models is the notion of perceived control. If we believe we can take control of the situation, the negative impacts will be diminished.

Freedman's (1975) 'density-intensity model' appears to have great relevance to events, although it has been controversial. His model suggests that density intensifies reactions that would otherwise occur given the particular situation, so that high density heightens the importance of other people and magnifies our reactions to them. High density therefore intensifies the pleasantness of positive situations (e.g. a party or celebration) and intensifies the negativity of situations we would rather avoid. Accordingly, your expectations, desires and mood upon entering an event setting will directly impact on your reaction to density – whether or not you feel crowded. Mowen *et al.* (2003) found that crowding at events is more likely to be a positive factor at the entertainment stage, and negative at food and beverage outlets; it varies by zone and activity.

'Crowd management' has to be integrated throughout the design process and management systems. The purpose is to both prevent problems and facilitate good experiences. 'Crowd control', on the other hand, involves security and other measures that only become necessary when there is a problem and should be handled by experts (Rutley n.d.).

Setting a firm site capacity (or 'design capacity'), in terms of the number of people invited or permitted, is one way to prevent overcrowding and related problems. Similarly, managers can try to regulate the flow and turnover of patrons. Other capacity and crowd management techniques include advance and group ticketing (to avoid bottlenecks), physical barriers and activity spacing, information provision and the management of queues (Mowen *et al.* 2003). See also Ammon and Fried (1998) for advice on event crowd management. In Chapter 9 crowd management and security are discussed further, including an expert opinion by William O'Toole.

Theming, programming and service design

A 'theme' is a unifying idea or concept. It can be a visual or sensory theme, in the realms of decorators and chefs, an activity theme (styles of sport, play, recreation), a fantasy theme (beloved by party planners and usually combining decor and entertainment), an emotional theme (such as a celebration of something of value at a festival or commemoration), or it can be intellectual in nature (such as the conference topic or workshop problem). This interpretation is from the Event Manager Blog:

> *Many event planners find that a theme can help add structure to the décor and activities as well as tie it all neatly together. They can be a great way for your attendees to get involved and it can be a fun participatory activity in itself, while creating plenty of photo opportunities. Themes can also create a buzz prior to the event as guests discuss how they can interpret the theme, what they are going to go as, what their friends are trying and whether they can do joint costumes which can be great corporate team building. Regardless of the event type, there is a theme to transform your event, improve user experience and only make the whole thing better.*
>
> *(https://www.eventmanagerblog.com/100-event-theme-ideas)*

As discussed under 'thematic interpretation', when education is an aim the theme should be stimulating and provocative, embodying tangible and intangible elements. Memorable themes tap into universal belief systems and should provide the take-home message – the moral of the story. Many entertainment or decoration themes do not do that, nor is it necessarily appropriate at concerts, parties and other social gatherings. Whatever goes into the event programme, from sensory stimulation to entertainment and spectacle, should ideally reflect and reinforce the theme.

Festivals can be defined as themed, public celebrations. If it is a Mozart Festival, the theme is fairly obvious, but there might be layers of theming (the grand, unifying theme plus sub-themes), and themes can often be open to interpretation. Superficially the theme might be popular music, but do the attendees see it more as an opportunity for sub-culture celebration involving drinking, drugs or sex? In that case the perceived theme might be completely different from the marketed theme, and an evaluation of motivations and meanings is needed.

Programme planning

A programme is the scheduled or 'scripted' activities for the audience and other participants. A concert programme can be quite simple, consisting of the order of artists or musical pieces. A festival programme might be complex, involving multiple days and venues with numerous activities and performances. Sport events have scheduled times for competitions and award ceremonies. Meetings and conventions typically operate with tight agendas to make sure the programme of speakers, plenary and breakout sessions, meals, coffee breaks and social events keeps to the schedule.

Programme 'portfolios' consist of all the different activities and services provided at events. They have to meet multiple objectives, appeal to diverse audiences and ideally be sustainable. To evaluate feasibility, desirability and continuance requires measures that reflect underlying goals and values. For example, commercial events have to monitor economic demand and profits, while public festivals might be focused on fulfilling social aims, like awareness-building or providing cultural opportunities to specific groups in the community. Other possible values and measures include image, tradition, stakeholder desires, market potential and share, and growth potential.

The 'programme planning process' usually starts with an evaluation of existing programming and/or new idea generation. It is generally wise to test ideas, although for planned events this can be difficult. At a basic level, focus groups can be held to test programme ideas with potential patrons or with stakeholder groups, and at a more costly level mini-events can be held to see if the concept is feasible and satisfies target segments. In terms of evaluation (discussed in the next chapter) this stage is equivalent to 'formative' evaluation.

Life-cycle model

'Life-cycle' considerations are important. Some programmes and services can be slated for a short life expectancy, including planned termination, while others can be allowed to run a full course through growth, maturity and decline. If sales and profits are the primary measure of success, a programme or service will have to be terminated or 'rejuvenated' through reinvestment and re-positioning when profit margins shrink. Community-service and goodwill programmes do not necessarily have to be terminated because of cost and revenue considerations, but their on-going effectiveness has to be demonstrated. Sustaining traditional programmic elements, while innovating regularly to test new ones, is a model followed by many events including the Calgary Stampede (see Getz 1993b, 1997). At some point, changes to programming can be so substantial as to constitute repositioning of the entire event.

The life-cycle concept, whether it is applied to programme elements or the entire life of an event, or to portfolios of events as they evolve, links directly to the evaluation stages called formative, process and summative (see Getz 2018, *Event Evaluation*). Designing, testing and refining are 'formative', and can be based on needs assessments, competitive SWOT analysis, comparisons or benchmarking, and feasibility studies. All too often an event or programme is introduced without such testing and refinement, leading to greater uncertainty and risks. Monitoring value creation (through growth and maturity, then possible decline) is a form of 'process evaluation'. Small, incremental changes can be introduced to correct for problems or improve attractiveness. At some point, 'summative evaluation' is required to determine if goals have been met and to measure impacts. This might lead to termination or come after planned termination. Evaluation can also lead to renewal, or perhaps replacement with another programme/event in the marketing tradition of 'new and improved!'

In product life cycles, the stages are usually linked to sales and/or profit, but this is not suitable for all events. Figure 7.5 shows other possible measures of value, some of which require quantification (attendance, market share, segments reached, revenue, ROI, ROE, satisfaction, loyalty) and some are intangibles (support from stakeholders, institutional status, creation of traditions, needs met, or public good created).

The study of creation, life-cycles, institutionalization process, and failures is not well developed but there are a number of published papers on these subjects, as indicated in Chapters 4 and 9.

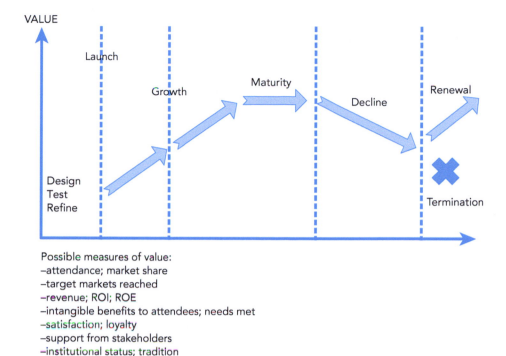

VALUE

Launch

Growth

Maturity

Decline

Renewal

Design
Test
Refine

Termination

Possible measures of value:
–attendance; market share
–target markets reached
–revenue; ROI; ROE
–intangible benefits to attendees; needs met
–satisfaction; loyalty
–support from stakeholders
–institutional status; tradition

Figure 7.5 Life-cycle model for events and event portfolios, with possible value measures

Scripting and choreography

In most forms of theatrical performance, the 'script' is followed to the letter. How appropriate this is at other events is a matter of style and intent. In some respects a schedule of activities, or the event programme, is a script. Specific elements of an event can be scripted while the overall 'performance' is improvised or merely themed. 'Choreography', borrowed from dance, is an alternative approach for events. Here, characters and interactions are suggested through notations, but the actual behaviour of 'performers' is somewhat creative and unpredictable.

Timing and build

'Timing', or scheduling, has to consider the audience's attention span and responses to stimuli, keeping in mind that 'event time is different from real time and audiences respond differently to it'. In general, Brown and James (2004: 61) recommended programming 'tightly' and accurately to maintain 'flow' and contact with the audience. In contrast, 'Build' is the use of time and programming, including ebbs and peaks of intensity, to maximize impact on the audience. There is a skill in using limited resources to achieve great emotional or intellectual stimulation.

Programmic elements of style

'Style' means a characteristic way of doing things to create a unique event or programme, excellence of artistic expression (being a measure of product or programme quality) or fashion (which always changes). We can say that designers have their own style, and that all events are stylistically different. Recall our earlier discussions of aesthetics and beauty, because style is largely subjective and therefore subject to widely different interpretations.

Each 'programmic element of style' has a creative and a technical component. Elements can be combined in unlimited combinations to design a unique event or programme. Generally the elements have to be designed in concert with the setting and implemented through physical development and all the management systems.

Some programmic elements of style are 'hallmarks' of particular types of event. That is, the event form requires it by definition, or, as a social construct, this element is closely associated with it. For example, business and trade events like fairs and trade shows involve commerce by nature. Festivals are celebrations, so they have to incorporate belonging and sharing, emotional stimulation, rituals and symbolism. Sports and recreation must involve games or competition.

Standing alone, one element of style looks bare and will generate a rather narrow range of experiences. Sports are packaged as festivals for a good reason, to expand their appeal and generate additional benefits. Business events are serious, but they almost always base part of their appeal on social and touristic opportunities. The idea of converging forms and functions in the events sector (see Chapter 12) reflects this point.

One way to specify programmic elements of style is to list the actions a programmer or designer can include, or the activities that participants and guests are to engage in (see Table 7.1). These are the main activity elements subject to design, but keep in mind that each one can have varying cognitive and affective outcomes. Refer back to the list for 'making meaningful experiences' and to the Orchestra Model as they are all closely related concepts.

Just about any combination of activities and sensory stimulation can provoke emotional and cognitive responses, but these elements are tried and true in the context of politics, patriotism, religion and affinity groups:

- ritual and symbolism that reflects or suggests cultural and social identity; the display of sacred or respected artefacts;
- direct verbal appeals to loyalty, pride, community or faith (i.e. preaching and propaganda);
- celebrity endorsements and the charisma of speakers, especially from recognized leaders;
- selected information and interpretation (as social marketing and propaganda).

For event designers and programmers, there can be a fine line between emotional or cognitive stimulation and exploitation; between facilitating a powerful, transforming experience or provoking a negative, even violent response. 'Playing with emotions' should always be undertaken with the benefit of research and evaluation, and this has often, sadly, been ignored.

Programme (or 'product') quality

Getz and Carlsen (2006: 146) discussed the main dimensions of event quality. Quality begins with the organization: its mandate and vision, philosophy and customer orientation; the competence of its staff and volunteers; its governance; and effectiveness of its management. Programme (or product) quality is experiential and subject to qualitative evaluation by all the stakeholders. Customers evaluate quality by expressing their level of satisfaction with the event overall, or with the quality of what is being presented to them in the form of sport competition, the musical performance, the speakers at a convention, art at an exhibit, food at a banquet, etc. Product quality can also be assessed through benchmarking against other events, the opinions of expert judges, or through experiential research.

Table 7.1 Programme elements of style and sample associated activities

Programme elements of style (expressed as goals)	Sample associated activities and mediated experiences
Teach, interpret, inform	Engage people in discourse or problem solving; lecture; debate; exhibit
Play, compete and challenge	Games; mental and physical activity; formal competition
Amuse	Humour; surprise
Inspire, stimulate	The example of role models; motivational speakers; opportunities for spiritual reflection or mindfulness
Entertain	Spectacle; performances; costumes
Foster cohesion, togetherness, communitas	Culturally authentic celebrations and rituals; use of unifying symbols
Encourage creativity	Tactile experiences/hands-on (cooking, sculpting, inventing)
Facilitate commerce: buy, sell, trade	Fairs and exhibitions
Consume	Food and drink as the theme or as service
Socialize	Mingling and other social opportunities; people watching; family events
Provide sensory stimulation	Sight, sound, touch, taste, smell; aesthetics
Ensure authenticity	Interpretation of cultural meanings; traditional costumes, recipes, rituals, performances
Maximize hospitality	Connect hosts and guests; personal service; welcoming; guiding; solving problems; meeting basic needs (water, rest, toilets, etc.)
Validate people's worth and identity	Accepting donations for charity; maximizing volunteer benefits; doing community service; social marketing
Provide for behavioural license/liberation/freedom	(Within limits) tolerate dissent, freedom of expression; foster revelry

Love and Crompton (1996) tested the hypothesis, based on the works of Herzberg (1966), that some event elements are 'dissatisfiers' which can undermine the visitor experience, while others are 'satisfiers' which provide benefits. 'Dissatisfiers' are like Herzberg's 'maintenance' factors – they must be provided to expected levels of quality, but in themselves do not satisfy visitors. The researchers argued that most of the physical factors at events, such as parking, rest rooms and information, are dissatisfiers, while ambiance, fantasy, excitement, relaxation, escape and social involvement are satisfiers. High-quality events must meet expectations in both categories, but they are non-compensatory in that a single or small number of attributes can determine perception of overall quality. Tentative support for this model was confirmed, and the researchers believed that certain attributes were perceived to be of so poor or high quality that visitors disregarded or discounted other attributes in giving their overall appraisal.

Baker and Crompton (2000) determined that generic and entertainment features of an event are more likely to generate increased satisfaction and motivate return visits or positive word-of-mouth recommendations. Saleh and Ryan (1993) found that quality of the music programme is the most important service factor in attracting people to jazz festivals. Overall satisfaction levels affected the intention for repeat visits. Similarly, Thrane (2002) explored the link between satisfaction and future intentions of festival-goers. The most important conclusion from his study in Norway was that event managers must try to improve programme quality (in this case music) *and* be concerned with other factors that shape overall satisfaction.

Ryan and Lockyer (2002) studied satisfaction levels of participants in the South Pacific Masters games in New Zealand – a friendly, multi-sport event for older athletes. The results showed that sport-event managers need to pay particular attention to improving items of high importance but low satisfaction. In this sample, the prime motivators – seeking challenge and fun – were found to be satisfied by the event. A factor analysis was also used to identify five components of importance to participants, namely: social (social events plus meeting people); registration (good communications); challenge; after-event communication, and that the competition is both fun and serious.

Service design and quality

Researchers have demonstrated that event satisfaction is primarily dependent upon the core elements of the programme, whether this is music or sport competition, and that is exactly what theme and programme design seeks to accomplish. In this context, the setting, service delivery and consumables are supporting factors. An exception is for food and beverage events, where consumables are the core, or commerce events where people purchase tangible products. Nevertheless, service delivery is important, as bad service easily displeases people. It is a design process because good service is both technical (e.g. no errors made, everything is done on time) and creative/qualitative (staff are friendly and helpful; staff are part of the experience).

There is a huge body of literature on service marketing, quality and delivery, especially for the tourism and hospitality sectors (see, for example, Prideaux *et al.* 2006). Applied to event design, the basic principle is that all management systems, as well as staff and volunteer actions, directly affect the customers' perceptions of quality and therefore their level of satisfaction with the event experience. Drummond and Anderson (2004) discussed the meaning of quality and how service management impacts on events. They explained what has to be done to create a satisfying 'service experience' before, during and after the event. They argued that service enables the guest or customer to more fully enjoy the product or experience. Wicks and Fesenmaier (1993) studied differences between visitors and vendors in their perceptions of service quality at an event. A comparison of alternative approaches to evaluating event quality was undertaken by Crompton and Love (1995).

Service blueprinting and service mapping

'Blueprinting' is a tool with value in all the services, but its application to planned events has been minimal. The idea is to create a chart or 'blueprint' based on the flow of intended visitor activities and experiences, and to show how the experiences are facilitated by the setting (or 'servicescape'), all the management systems and human contacts. The service 'map' is a diagnostic or evaluation tool which can precede blueprinting, or test its effectiveness.

Getz *et al.* (2001) provided two service maps to show the results of a team of nine researchers (the three authors and six trained students) who conducted an on-site evaluation of the event. Triangulation was employed, including (1) direct observation of the site and audience, using standard checklists, (2) a visitor survey, mostly about satisfaction and (3) logbooks reflecting participant observation (i.e. documenting their event experiences).

Stage One provides an overview of the entire event experience, from approach to departure, whereas Stage Two looks at details of the range of possible on-site experiences: consumption, viewing, interacting, essential services. The more complex the event, the more researchers will be needed, and many maps might result. Once the evaluation has been completed, 'blueprints' for the next event can be prepared. Alternatively, the evaluators start with a blueprint to see how well it has been implemented.

Customer actions

The blueprint anticipates the flow of customer actions, starting with approach to the site and ending with departure. If there are many activity options or venues it will be necessary to have multiple blueprints, some in great detail and one for the overall process. Although the blueprint specifies actions in settings, it should consider the intended customer or guest experience. For example, 'viewing art in gallery' can be expanded into 'the guest will enjoy a quiet, aesthetic experience, aided by interactive information about the artists and their displays'. This experiential elaboration will greatly assist in planning the 'physical evidence' and staff–guest interactions.

When doing a service mapping exercise, as evaluation, multiple observers (engaged in direct and participant observation) will be needed to plot the actual flow and activities of guests and to summarize the experiential dimensions.

Tangible evidence of product and service quality

The blueprint specifies all the physical evidence of quality, such as entertainment, the competition, exhibits, facilities, signs, equipment and audio-visual effects, and these are depicted on the diagram in the area above the customer-actions flow chart. Include the hygiene factors like toilets and soap, water and comfort stations. Anticipate everything the guest will need or desire and specify the quality standards. In the case of evaluations, describe gaps and flaws in tangible evidence, such as crowding, unanticipated behaviour, safety and health hazards, obvious customer confusion and inadequate signage or direction. Describe programme or product quality as experienced by observers.

'Hygiene factors' have been found to be extremely important at events, not in motivating people to attend or affecting their assessment of overall programme quality, but in terms of causing dissatisfaction (these include security, cleanliness, comfort). Event quality can also be assessed by reference to its impacts, through measuring the attainment of positive goals and avoidance or amelioration of negative outcomes.

Visible staff contacts

For each customer action, or experience setting, the blueprint has to specify staff or volunteer support that will, or could, involve staff–guest interaction. These also define potential 'critical incidents' where service failure could occur. This line, under the flow chart, also quantifies human resource needs, in terms of staffing levels, duties and necessary training.

Viewed as 'cast members', staff and volunteers have both technical roles to play in delivering essential services, and an experiential role to play in facilitating desired experiences. Their appearance and demeanour are important to theming as well as service. In terms of service marketing theory (i.e. SERVQUAL, developed by Parasuraman et al. 1988), staff and volunteers have to exhibit 'responsiveness' (willingness to help; promptness), 'assurance' (knowledge and courtesy; convey trust and inspire confidence), 'empathy' (caring; providing individual service) and 'reliability' (ability and dependability).

Invisible management processes

The usual practice is to draw a line under the 'visible staff contacts' and in this bottom space on the blueprint to indicate the management systems that have to be in place to support the entire service process (which, at events, inevitably means the programme as well). In evaluations, the observers can work backwards from obvious failures or problems to determine what was missing or flawed in these hidden systems (for example: police should have regulated the approach road).

Importance-performance (IP) measurement

It is one thing to know how satisfied a guest is, another to understand if the items being integrated were important to their decision to attend or their overall satisfaction with the event. Satisfaction usually links to future behaviour such as word-of-mouth recommendations and repeat visits. The IP technique is quite versatile and generates numeric scores and graphics that are fairly easy to interpret and communicate. For example, those attending music concerts can usually be expected to give a high score to the quality and reputation of performers as motivators for attending, and as the main sources of satisfaction or dissatisfaction. Ideally, the manager wants to find out that they performed very well in providing the entertainment that consumers valued the highest. You do not want to find out that toilets were ranked 'very poor' and provided a great source of dissatisfaction. IP grid analysis can be usefully combined with other quantitative techniques. Smith and Costello (2009) used IP in studying culinary tourism, specifically to assist event managers in satisfying customers.

Evidence and research-based design

A purely artistic approach to design is suitable for some performances, but when designing events and event programming it is highly recommended to base goals, design concepts and the evaluation process on available evidence, and that can only be obtained through evaluation and other research. The process is dedicated to basing decisions on credible research and evidence from praxis to achieve desired outcomes. This might involve a client, but certainly there will be a number of key stakeholders to consult. The use of logic and theory of change models, as described in Getz 2019, will facilitate the process.

The example described below is for the design of food and wine events, but the approach is adaptable to many other situations.

Research-based design of wine and food events

At many events, the food and beverage service is incidental to the main theme and programme, and can be considered part of hospitality or service, but at others it is experientially paramount. In particular, research has demonstrated the importance of events in satisfying the special interests of food and wine lovers, whether they stay close to home or travel the globe in search of rewarding gastronomic experiences. Getz *et al.* (2014) provides the research evidence for the design concept that is illustrated here (see Figure 7.6) – also see Getz *et al.* (2013a), Getz and Robinson (2014a, 2014b) and Getz (2013b).

Most food and beverage events are focused on consumption – eating and drinking! Throw in some entertainment (and maybe some family fun) and the typical hedonistic food or beverage event emerges. But this is not what highly involved food and wine lovers want from their event experiences. As a theoretical base, involvement theory (or ego-involvement or leisure involvement) has been employed to identify the core characteristics of being a foodie or a wine lover, and to profile wine and food tourists on the basis of their level of involvement (this being a segmentation method). Attending events has been revealed as being highly attractive in the accumulating body of research. More importantly, the desired experiential components that separate the highly involved from those who attend primarily for consumption or socializing have been identified. This model reflects demand-side thinking in which design follows from market intelligence. Of course many existing food and wine-related events are based on tradition and will not necessarily want to follow this approach; it is highly appropriate for event-tourism purposes and the private sector seeking profit.

Conceptually, Figure 7.6 shows the necessity for positioning food or wine events in such a way that they can attract dedicated food/wine tourists, and not merely provide generic benefits. The designed wine or food event for the highly involved segments can be stand-alone, such as a tasting at a restaurant

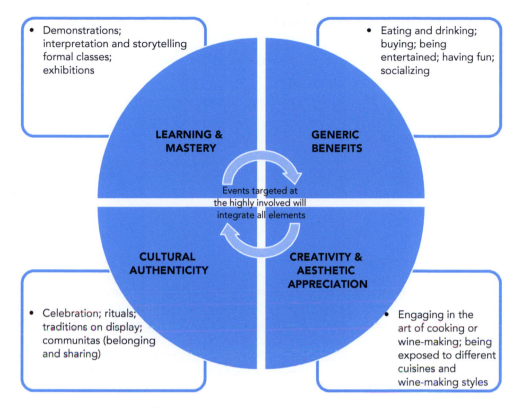

- Demonstrations; interpretation and storytelling formal classes; exhibitions

- Eating and drinking; buying; being entertained; having fun; socializing

LEARNING & MASTERY

GENERIC BENEFITS

Events targeted at the highly involved will integrate all elements

CULTURAL AUTHENTICITY

CREATIVITY & AESTHETIC APPRECIATION

- Celebration; rituals; traditions on display; communitas (belonging and sharing)

- Engaging in the art of cooking or wine-making; being exposed to different cuisines and wine-making styles

Figure 7.6 Design concept for food and wine events

Source: Adapted from Getz *et al.* 2014, 2015.

or demonstrations by experts, or part of a larger festival. The designer starting with this concept can manifest the various core benefits with actual programming. For example, the Learning benefit includes mastery of techniques, leading to cooking classes with chefs or wine blending with the winemaker. The Creativity benefit includes aesthetic appreciation, such as a focus on serving food and wine/food pairings. Making the event culturally authentic can be accomplished through rituals and celebrations with like-minded food and wine lovers (achieving communitas) and through heritage interpretation – telling stories, for example, of why and how various foods have become traditions in local cuisine or of the legendary wine pioneers.

Designing 'slow events'

The 'slow' movement has evolved, and as Page (2015: 129) summarized it:

> *the notion was also popularised at a city-destination level by the Cittaslow (Slow City) movement based on three underpinning concepts:*
>
> *Do things at the right speed*
>
> *Adapt one's attitude towards time and one's use of it*
>
> *The pursuit of quality over quantity.*

Simons (2015) has applied principles from the slow movement to the design of events, stressing that such events should:

- be organized in a bottom-up manner with all stakeholders involved in decision-making;
- ensure that benefits flow to the community;
- be rooted in locality, reflecting a sense of place and providing identity; visitors should be able to connect to locality through stories;
- stress community development, not growth or profit.

Regarding the critical element of time, both frequency and duration of slow events, Simons argued that, 'A slow event takes the time that is necessary for the event to be experienced to the fullest by the people involved in the event as well as by the visitors.'

Liberating versus constraining

Event planning and management can often be described as constraining, that is, we use combinations of setting, programme design and management systems to prevent certain actions (often in the name of safety) or to remove the possibility of distractions and confounding environmental forces like noise. Barriers and gates are erected, flows of people are tightly regulated, security has to be visible and police should be ready to react, schedules must be met, and so on. Do people find this stifling? Does it limit experience to only the manageable and predictable? At some point, event designers and planners must ask themselves if their events have become standardized, contrived, boring or sanitized to the point where innovation and new artistic expression has moved elsewhere. How long can a particular form of event remain popular before it becomes mundane?

Of the three dimensions of experience, the conative (behavioural) is most constrained by event management. The setting constrains movement, the schedule constrains temporal experiences – forcing the guest into the designers' time frame. Of course, people enter into the event space (a time out of time in a special place) willingly, and suspend their normal behaviours in favour of the anticipated experience, but there is no reason why the event time/space cannot also be liberating in particularly pleasant and memorable ways. Let's look at how this can be accomplished.

We can break the spatial constraints by:

- online interconnectivity (have an interactive virtual experience ready for everyone);
- involve the wider community, not just guests/customers (e.g. take aspects of your event to them; outreach programmes to schools);
- site planning that facilitates fluid entrance and exit (also a key safety consideration) and suggests permeability with the wider community and/or natural environment; open the site for wide vistas; make barriers and edges almost invisible; design for extra space and easy movement.

We can break the temporal constraints by:

- co-creation of the event through on-going consultations and feedback;
- encourage participants/customers to take the event experience home with them (e.g. souvenirs, DVDs, follow-up events and real-time communications);
- media coverage, live and delayed.

The cognitive dimensions (i.e. thinking) can also be liberated by being prepared to:

- maximize guests/customers/virtual audiences;
- build in novelty and surprise.

The affective (i.e. emotional) dimensions perhaps require more thought, but are equally amenable to liberating practices whereby we can:

- foster emotional responses that are normally inhibited (e.g. laughter and other verbalizations, tears and other forms of sympathy, surprise and shock, fear and repulsion);
- use sensory stimulation to encourage the formation of permanent and pleasant memories (remember the value of smell in memory formation and recall).

The challenge of enabling or liberating practices is critical. If people fail to get the desired experience in planned events, they are very likely to try others, to give up on the sector altogether or to start inventing their own. Clues to what the future might hold are often apparent online, in blogs and on other social media devoted to event experiences, where members of myriad communities of interest or social worlds interact. A disquieting possibility is that recreational rioting and other forms of anti-social behaviours might become more common as people seek to be liberated from stifling social environments and legal constraints.

Future directions

According to Richards et al. (2014) events should be designed as value creation platforms, and evaluators should judge them according to how well the aims have been met. The study reflected on a number of important design-related themes that require more research and attention, including the somewhat slippery concept of co-creation. While it is true that all events provide some degree of shared experience creation, being social in nature, there are elements of design that can advance this concept and engage visitors even more. Crowther and Orefice (2015) argued strongly for co-creation by design, rather than by default. Technology can enable more before, during and after-event interaction and social media is a vehicle for creating experiences without the direct influence of producers and managers. Taken even further, the concept leads to self-organizing events and liberation, as previously discussed.

Another design theme to explore is 'curation' (Richards et al. 2014). Content curators filter or screen information to reduce volume/flow and make it more targeted to the users' interests and needs; this could apply to messaging, raw data, programming content and other design elements. The time element is always of interest, witness the example of 'slow events' mentioned earlier. Event-related experiences are being extended to the before and after phases, and presumably leading to the next experience! Those enthusiasts pursuing event-tourist careers know this very well. And finally, it is worth mentioning that events are designed at various policy levels, such as being instruments of city design/positioning, and increasingly as assets in broad portfolios. As yet, the design of event portfolios and populations has not been a topic of research.

STUDY GUIDE

Students should start with an appreciation that design is both a technical and creative process to meet goals and solve problems. Event design has most often been associated with form, that is the physical production of event, but has evolved to encompass experience design – these are the main themes of this chapter. However, keep in mind that events have roles to play in value-creation networks, and that too requires action by design.

Experiences are highly personal and therefore cannot be prescribed or guaranteed, so event producers and designers must do their best to specify intended experiences, and to anticipate the motives, needs and desired experiences of all the stakeholders. In terms of the concept of service-dominant logic, experiences are co-created through interactions: designers, producers, guests, the setting and services. Programme and service quality are major factors in engaging and satisfying the participants or customers.

The ensuing study questions address all the learning objectives and provide structure for studying the contents of this chapter. Take particular note of the various theories that inform event design, and the models and methods that can be used by designers and in the evaluation of design.

STUDY QUESTIONS

- Define 'design' and discuss its importance in event studies; consider event form, experiences and value creation through networks
- How can event experiences be made meaningful to different stakeholders?
- What are creativity and innovation, and how can they be fostered?
- Explain the necessity to base event setting design on theory from cognitive and environmental psychology. Give specific applications.
- In what ways can the event designer adapt principles from theatre?
- Give examples of how coherence and legibility can be achieved in event site planning. Provide examples of generic event settings and unique design challenges for each.
- Do people have preferences for event settings? Are these 'social constructs'?
- Discuss how 'crowding' is more than just the number of people at an event; explain dynamic crowd management.
- Define 'restorative and instorative' in the context of different types of planned event
- What are the main tools in crowd management and crowd control?
- Illustrate how various 'programmic elements of style' can be used for learning, sensory and emotional stimulation.
- What is programme and service quality, and how can they be measured or evaluated?
- Describe 'service blueprinting' as an event design tool, and how to convert the blueprint into an evaluation tool.
- What is evidence-based design? Describe market research that can inform the design of an event for a special-interest segment such as foodies or wine lovers.
- How can planned-event experiences be made more liberating? Is this always a good idea?

FURTHER READING

Berridge, G. (2007). *Event Design and Experience*. Oxford: Butterworth Heinemann.

Events Industry Forum, The (2015). *The Purple Guide to Health, Safety and Welfare at Music and Other Events* (https://www.thepurpleguide.co.uk/, accessed 25 September 2018).

Getz, D., Robinson, R., Andersson, T. and Vujicic, S. (2014). *Foodies and Food Tourism*. Oxford: Goodfellow.

Halsey, T. (2010). *Freelancer's Guide to Corporate Event Design*. Oxford: Elsevier.

Lawson, F. (2000). *Congress, Convention and Exhibition Facilities: Planning, Design and Management*. Oxford: Architectural Press.

Meeting Professionals International (2003). *Meetings and Conventions: A Planning Guide*. Mississauga, ON: MPI (https://www.mpiweb.org, accessed 7 June 2019).

Prideaux, B., Moscardo, G. and Laws, E. (eds) (2006). *Managing Tourism and Hospitality Services: Theory and International Applications*. Wallingford: CABI.

Richards, G., Marques, L. and Mein, K. (eds) (2014). *Event Design: Social Perspectives and Practices*. London: Routledge.

Smith, A. (2015). *Events in the City: Using Public Spaces as Event Venues*. London: Routledge.

Chapter **8**

Antecedents and decision-making

Upon completion of this chapter, students should know the following:

- relationships between personal antecedents to event attendance (or participation), the barriers and constraints, decision-making, post-experience evaluation and future decisions;
- differences between motivation in general, and motives to attend specific events;
- differences between intrinsic and extrinsic motives and how they lead to participation in, and travel to attend, events;
- the importance of personality, values and norms, attitudes and lifestyle;
- whether or not events are 'needed'; the hierarchy of needs;
- peak experiences;
- how serious leisure, social worlds and involvement theory apply to event motivation and experiences;
- how the theory of planned behaviour applies to event decisions;
- information and search and use for events;
- the concept of event attractiveness;
- specific constraints influencing the decision to attend different types of events, and how people negotiate through barriers to achieve their goals;
- generic and targeted benefits, and reasons why some people do not attend events;
- how different stakeholders make decisions about attending events, including guest/consumers/participants, organizers and volunteers, sponsors and suppliers;

- the event travel career trajectory (ETCT) and what it means for iconic event design, marketing, and destination event portfolios;
- factors affecting loyalty and future intentions;
- the importance of substitution and what influences choices.

What are antecedents?

Why do people attend events? There are myriad reasons, with both demand and supply factors influencing choices. Event-related behaviour is complex, but there are theoretical perspectives that will help us understand the process and apply this knowledge to all planned events. 'Antecedents' are all those influences that shape knowledge of, interest in, and actual event attendance or participation. We start with needs, which are closely linked to intrinsic (self-directed) and extrinsic (from outside) motives. A discussion of demand takes us from social psychology to economics, then we draw upon consumer research to explore decision-making. Leisure theory provides a solid base for examining barriers and constraints, and how people overcome or negotiate through them to achieve their goals.

To start the discussion, a conceptual model of the main factors shaping participation in, or attendance at, planned events is presented (Figure 8.1). Numerous models and frameworks are available from consumer research in general and, more specifically, tourism (see overviews in Ryan 2002; Crouch *et al.* 2004; Decrop 2006) and leisure (see Walker and Virden 2005; Hinch *et al.* 2006). Benckendorff and Pearce (2012) developed a very useful framework for applying psychological theory to event participation. They considered

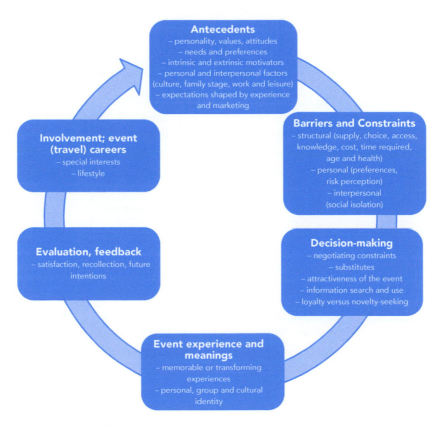

Figure 8.1 Antecedents and decision-making process

pre-event, on-site and post-event experiences, for spectators, attendees, performers and elite participants. They stressed that psychological theory on personality, motivation and involvement are important when looking at antecedents, while role theory, identity, liminality, flow, mindfulness, emotional and performative labour, and experience analysis can be applied to the event experience itself. Satisfaction, loyalty, self-actualization and personal development apply after an event experience, according to Benckendorff and Pearce.

Although this framework is designed as a process, it is not predictive. It shows all the main factors we need to understand, and suggests how they interconnect, but it is not possible to forecast that any particular set of antecedents will result in certain decisions, or that certain experiences lead to predictable future behaviour. The rest of the chapter reflects the main elements of the model, with sections on barriers and constraints, decision-making, evaluation and feedback.

Personality

Personality, values, attitudes and lifestyle preferences are the psychological factors that lie at the foundation of human behaviour. Individuals will show a propensity for certain behaviour as a result of these factors, but that does not necessarily mean they will act, or act consistently on them.

'Personality types' were previously explored, noting that some people have a higher propensity to seek novelty or take risks. Some people, in the terminology of Stanley Plog (1987), are more 'adventuresome' than others, leading them to seek out unique leisure and travel experiences. Others have a greater need for consistency and therefore a higher tolerance of boredom. According to the theory of 'personality-environment congruence', 'extroverted' risktakers will be happy at raucous concerts, but probably shy 'introverts' will not. Events often cater to certain personality types without the organizers being aware of it.

Another theory of potential relevance is that of 'optimal challenge', which suggests that in event programming, the matching of challenges with participants' skills will likely produce the desired 'flow' experience. Csikszentmihalyi (1975, 1990) described 'flow' as a state of absorption characterized by intense concentration, loss of self-awareness, being neither bored nor overwhelmed, and feeling that time is flying. This kind of experience is intrinsically rewarding, meaning that it is valued in itself and not for what it can do, but being able to experience flow might very well help people accomplish their goals. Csikszentmihalyi also concluded that boredom results when challenges are too low, and anxiety stems from challenges that are too great, and this has implications for anyone pursuing self-development.

Values and norms

Values are subjective reactions to, and assessments about, the world. They are deeply held, and in behavioural terms they imply a conscious assessment of the desirability of alternative behaviours, including what is right and wrong. Values are shaped by experience, religious or political affiliations, general social and cultural influences, and perhaps by personality. Do you value freedom of choice? Having decisions made for you by government? Environmental responsibility? How are your personal values different from the important people in your life? And do your values shape your interest in events or tourism?

There are many value perspectives that can be taken on festivals and events, as discussed in the book *The Value of Events* (Lundberg *et al.* 2017). People and organizations value events for different reasons, and use different measures of value or worth. Many believe that events (or certain types) hold 'intrinsic value' because they are important manifestations of culture, promote happiness and healthy lifestyles, or bring communities together. Events valued in this way do not have to be assigned a 'return on investment'. Others prefer 'extrinsic' measures of value or worth, based on the roles of events in fostering economic development, social marketing, or some other benefit that should be measured quantitatively. Events can be valued even when people do not attend them, based on the choices they offer or their perceived contributions to society.

Attitudes and the theory of planned behaviour

Allport (1937) provided the classic definition of attitude as a 'learned predisposition to respond to an object or class of objects in a consistently favorable or unfavourable way'.

Attitudes are theorized to contain 'conative' (action and behavioural intention), 'affective' (evaluation and affect, or emotion) and 'cognitive' (perception and belief) components. Note that this trilogy is also used, in a slightly different way, to describe the dimensions of 'experience'.

Within the context of the 'theory of planned behaviour' (Ajzen 1991), researchers have examined attitudes towards leisure participation. Many other factors influence actual behaviour, but measuring attitudes can be a good predictor if the attitude is linked to specific behaviour, such as 'how do you feel about attending a rock concert/cultural festival/art exhibition in the next 12 months?', as opposed to general behaviour (such as 'how do you feel about attending special events?'). What are the influences shaping attitudes towards planned events? Some combination of personal, social and cultural factors lies at the base of beliefs and predispositions.

Lifestyle

'Lifestyles', as unique patterns of thinking and behaving, arise from personality, values and attitudes. Some researchers refer to these, together, as 'psychographics'. According to Decrop (2006: 11), lifestyles reflect the 'self-concept' of people. Although seldom explored in the context of planned events, as opposed to leisure and travel in general, there are identifiable lifestyles that predispose or facilitate participation in events.

If it is accepted that many people value experiences more than objects and consumables, so that (for example) foodies and food tourists are willing and often eager to pay for rewarding and novel experiences, then consumption of experiences must hold symbolic value. Consistent patterns of symbolic consumption generate and help define discernable lifestyles. In the 'foodie' lifestyle examined by Getz *et al.* (2014; 2015a), events figure prominently in shaping and reinforcing identity, with some specialized events holding high symbolic value and therefore becoming 'iconic' to those with a special interest in food.

But basing lifestyle segmentation on personality and values has become controversial, with more contemporary approaches looking in a more nuanced way at underlying meanings and culture-based value systems, and this perspective links to Bourdeiu and cultural capital. The question is: what are the underlying cultural determinants of lifestyle preferences and choices?

The term 'lifestyle' has a number of possible connotations, including the view that a healthy or moral lifestyle is highly desirable (such as being environmentally and socially responsible), or that some people have enviable or lamentable lifestyles (e.g. lifestyles of the rich and famous). In this context, being a foodie, or demonstrating any other form of lifestyle through leisure and travel, might attract criticism. That is why lifestyle cannot be separated from values and social norms.

Needs and wants

According to Maslow (1954, 1968) 'needs' are both physiological (what we need to live and be safe) and socially learned (what we need to belong and to be happy). The following four were said to be 'deficit' needs, and people instinctively seek to meet them. In times of stress, regression can occur, but people are said to move from the lower- to the higher-order needs in a developmental process:

- physiological: survival needs, including water, food and shelter;
- safety and security needs: stability, order, protection, structure;
- love and belonging needs: social needs, a wish for affection and to show affection, a sense of community;
- esteem needs: hierarchical, with the lower order consisting of respect of others, status and recognition; higher order – self-respect, competence independence, achievement and mastery.

Others have argued that there are additional needs, and that the hierarchical nature of Maslow's theory is unsupportable. However controversial, Maslow's hierarchy of needs have been tremendously influential, and are referenced again in our discussion of volunteer motivation.

Needs get translated into wants, and some of these become economic demand for goods, services and experiences. Needs can therefore activate behaviour (Mannell and Kleiber 1997), and this gives rise to expectation-confirmation theory.

Self-actualization and peak experiences

Maslow's hierarchy is often shown as a pyramid with self-actualization at the top.

Maslow believed that certain people, only 2 per cent of the population, could be called 'self-actualized', and they have many more 'peak experiences' than others. A 'peak experience' is available to all, and self-actualization is 'growth motivation', or a process of seeking.

'Peak experiences' were described as sudden feelings of intense happiness and well-being. They are non-religious, quasi-mystical or mystical in nature, and possibly accompanied by awareness of 'ultimate truth' and the unity of all things. Also accompanying peak experiences is a heightened sense of control over the body and emotions, and a wider sense of awareness. The experience fills the individual with wonder and awe.

Maslow described 'peak experiences' as self-validating, self-justifying moments with their own intrinsic value; never negative, unpleasant or evil; disoriented in time and space (which sounds like the liminal/liminoid zone of Turner, as well as Csikszentimihalyi's 'flow'); and accompanied by a loss of fear, anxiety, doubts and inhibitions. Critics argue that anybody, whether good or evil, could have one of these peak experiences, so it has no moral basis. Others find it unscientific and untestable.

'Benefits' are what people believe they will obtain from consumption or participation, and these are generally expressed in terms related to need fulfilment. For example, of all the benefits provided by leisure services and sport, improved health has to be near the top of the list. People 'want' many things or experiences, but that is not necessarily the same as needing them. Only the individual can decide when a want becomes a need, although society often makes judgements as to what is a basic need. Often potential substitution comes into play, because many needs and wants can be met through different means.

Do people need events?

The answer is yes, sort of! People might not respond to questions by saying they need to attend a party or cultural celebration, but they do need the socializing, relaxation or escapism that events offer. People need to discover, learn and fulfil their aesthetic ambitions, and attending events provides these benefits. Companies have to market and do business, so they need exhibitions and consumer shows. Associations have to meet. Humans need to recreate, leading to sport events. Events of all kinds have been successful because they meet so many fundamental personal, social, cultural and economic needs.

One question that gets at the heart of the issue is this: if all festivals were removed, would people create new ones? If sports events were cancelled, would there be high demand to bring them back? If conferences ceased because of terrorism, how long would it be before companies and associations found alternative ways to get their people together? Clearly, there is demand for events, and history has demonstrated that this growing level of demand reflects underlying, fundamental needs. Individual events may be substitutable, and people have lots of choices, but events do meet basic human needs.

Motivation and motives

'Personality traits' have a rather permanent influence on behaviour, whereas 'motivation' is dynamic, it can and does change. 'Motivation' refers to the process by which people are driven to act in a certain way (Decrop 2006: 9). Iso-Ahola (1980, 1983) took a more comprehensive approach in saying that motivations are internal factors that arouse, direct and integrate behaviour. Another way to look at 'motivation' is to think of a need or 'disequilibrium', which is accompanied by an expectation that action will reduce it. If the expectation is met, satisfaction results. The experience of, or failure to attain, satisfaction, influences future behaviour (i.e. there is a feedback mechanism).

'Motives', by contrast, are specific reasons for doing something, and they have to follow from underlying needs and motivation. For example, people who are 'highly involved' in a sport or lifestyle pursuit (like running) have a strong 'motivation' to attend events where their specific needs can be satisfied. But their 'motives' for deciding to attend a specific event might include consideration of who else is attending, the entertainment opportunities and the attractiveness of the location.

It is common in the tourism literature to use the terms 'push factors' or 'drivers', and 'pull factors' or 'attraction/attractiveness' to cover travel motivation (Dann 1977, 1981; Crompton 1979). When we speak of the interaction of push and pull factors, Iso-Ahola's (1980, 1983; Mannell and Iso-Ahola 1987) 'seeking and escaping' model comes to the fore. Seeking and escaping motivation simultaneously influences our decisions because we are both seeking to find personal and interpersonal rewards and hoping to escape aspects of personal and interpersonal environments that bother us. Both seeking and escaping are forms of intrinsic motivation, or what we want to do for its own sake.

In escaping our everyday environment, we seek change and novelty, especially new experiences. 'Under-' or 'over-arousal' gives rise to this need for escape, but of course we also have to seek out something to alter our arousal levels – hence the need for 'optimal arousal' at events. Motivational studies have been frequent in the events literature (for example: Mohr *et al.* 1993; Uysal *et al.* 1993; Leibold and van Zyl 1994; Backman *et al.* 1995; Scott 1996; Nogawa *et al.* 1996; Crompton and McKay 1997; Oppermann and Chon 1997; Formica and Murrmann 1998; Formica and Uysal 1998; Green and Chalip 1998; Raybould 1998; Pitts 1999; Ngamsom and Beck 2000; Nicholson and Pearce 2001; McGehee *et al.* 2003; Xiao and Smith 2004; Ryan and Trauer 2005; Funk *et al.* 2007) including review articles by Lee *et al.* (2004), Gibson's (2004) review of sport tourism motivation, and reviews by Li and Petrick (2006), Maeng *et al.* (2016), Pilcher and Eade (2016) and Jaimangal-Jones *et al.* (2018).

Li and Petrick (2006) found that most such studies were theoretically grounded in, and gave support to, the 'seeking-escaping' motivation theory, and the similar push/pull model. Benckendorff and Pearce (2012) reviewed motivational studies, with an emphasis on sport spectators and attendees (Parent and Chappelet 2015). Mair (2013) has reviewed the motivational studies conducted on convention attendees. Maeng *et al.* (2016) argued that motivational factors used extensively in the event literature have largely been drawn from tourism studies (the most commonly researched were socialization, family togetherness, escape, novelty, excitement and cultural exploration) and therefore more appropriate factors should be developed.

The event travel career trajectory (ETCT)

This theory-in-development draws from the foundation theories of serious leisure (and the related constructs of active and serious sport tourism), ego- or leisure-involvement, and social worlds (encompassing sub-cultures and to a certain extent lifestyles). The notion of a motivational trajectory in which motivation changes over time, through travel experiences, came from Pearce and Caltabiano (1983) and was later largely refuted by Pearce and Lee (2005), who concluded that multiple, generic motives apply to all leisure travel. However, the trajectory appears to apply much more to special interests than it does to general travel motivation, so it has been hypothesized that motivations should change over time as amateur athletes become more involved (Getz 2008; Getz and McConnell 2011; Getz and Andersson 2010). If this is true, then the motivations of highly involved event tourists should differ significantly from the lesser involved. In particular, the highly involved should stress personal development motives, rather than those relating to the lower-order needs (from Maslow 1954) such as relaxation and socializing.

General pleasure-travel motivation will often be different from special-interest travel. Indeed, a considerable amount of research and theory-building has occurred within the field of sport tourism, with particular relevance to sport-event motivation. Gibson (1998) described 'active sport tourists' as those most likely to travel for participation in favourite pursuits, and they often do this well into retirement. Gibson also referred to involvement and recreation specialization theories to help explain motivation and travel behaviour.

The term 'career' implies 'serious leisure' as theorized by Stebbins. What we want to look for are people who, for reasons of their 'involvement' or 'commitment', not only attend many events but demonstrate a progression or pattern of event participation and attendance that stems from their increasing experience and shifting motivation. Jones and Green (2006: 43) explained the relevance of serious leisure and social worlds to sport tourism studies. They said that (ibid.: 43): 'Serious sport tourism (that is, travel to participate in serious leisure) is able to provide individuals with a positive social identity.' And (ibid.: 44): 'Travel to participate in a sport or leisure activity puts one in an extended contact with other participants … outside of everyday experience, and often includes more experienced members of the subculture' (Jones and Green 2006: 44). In this context, sport events provide spaces for social identity formation and reinforcement.

McGehee *et al.* (2003) found that highly involved recreational runners travelled more on overnight trips to participate in events, compared to medium-involved runners. This confirmed the well-established proposition that greater involvement results in higher levels of participation, and for runners this means participation in competitive events. Although they found that runners did not attend all the races they would have liked to, owing to a number of constraints such as family obligations, they did not examine race characteristics or destination choices. Interestingly, highly involved runners also participated in more races in their own communities. Once attracted, the authors suggested that highly involved recreational runners could become repeat visitors, assuming they had a good overall race and destination experience.

Shipway and Jones (2008) applied the serious leisure framework to runners' experiences at a major marathon. They classified runners as 'serious sport tourists' on the basis of the level of ability needed to compete in a marathon, length of trip and stay necessitated by participation, and relatively high cost of training for the event (ibid.: 65). 'Discussion between participants emphasized the importance of travel, in that races that were held in distant or unusual locations held greater perceived capital than those within the UK' (ibid.: 68). Discussion of past event experiences was very pronounced. Running careers were discussed. The marathon for some was a 'career marker', 'representing a confirmation of their progression to confirmed serious runner' (ibid.: 72). The collection of subculture capital leads to 'the desire to travel and collect places' (ibid.: 72) leading to a lot of storytelling. The durable benefits of running were identified as 'developing and overcoming personal challenges, experiencing a heightened sense of achievement and self-esteem, fun and happiness, healthy living, weight loss and physical well-being, injury rehabilitation' (ibid.: 73).

A related construct is the 'sports tourism demand continuum' developed by Jackson and Weed (2003), in which athletes can progress from incidental participation through sporadic, occasional, regular and committed levels all the way to 'driven'. However, this model is more relevant to professional and elite athletes. In a modification, Weed and Bull (2004) take into account the importance of travel to participants, with those at the 'driven' level taking part in more sport tourism.

Getz and Patterson (2013) explored the travel career in the context of social-world theory and examined its potential applications beyond sports, while Patterson, Getz and Gubb (2016) specifically applied both constructs to yoga practitioners and their travel. Getz *et al*. (2014) examined the travel careers of foodies, and Goh *et al*. (2019) applied the ETCT to artists. Many of the pertinent studies concern runners and triathletes. Shipway and Jones (2007, 2008) examined the careers of amateur distance runners, concluding they collected subculture capital from participation in events, leading to 'the desire to travel and collect places' (2008: 72). Lamont and Kennelly (2011) concluded that various constraints have to be taken into account, as event travel careers are not necessarily linear. Lamont, Kennelly and Wilson (2012) claimed that the choice of events is contingent upon their availability and the intensity of 'the competing priorities' (ibid.: 1071). The highly involved might still participate in local and low-profile events as preparation for more challenging events or as a consequence of 'pulsation' (ibid.: 1077).

Buning and Gibson (2015) proposed an elaboration, reflecting a social-world perspective, being a six-stage model consisting of initiation, introduction, expansion, peak threshold, maintenance and maturity. In support of the ETCT, Buning and Gibson (2016a) studied cyclists and detected '… an escalation in motivation related to intellectual, social, mastery competence, giving back, and competition against others with career progression.' They observed that travel behaviour linked to events changed with career progression, but concluded that '… preferred characteristics related to destinations and travel style remained relatively stagnant.' Buning and Gibson (2016b) concluded that the travel preferences of active cyclists '… vary based on travel conditions and that attractive destinations only become advantageous if event participants are traveling with non-cyclists or on trips involving longer distances.' These findings reflect only one sport, and together indicate the need for ongoing research across a range of sports, events and destinations.

Researching three types of sport tourists, cyclists, runners and triathletes, Newland and Aicher (2018) determined that travel behaviour varied with both the type of sport and the individual athlete's motivation. They pointed out the need for careful targeting of the mix of event and destination-attributes.

Main hypotheses for the ETCT

According to Lee et al. (2016: 493) a number of studies have provided support for the existence of event-travel careers; they concluded that '… these six dimensions of the travel pattern of serious sport participants are widely acknowledged.'

H1 (Motivation): highly involved runners will be motivated significantly more by higher-order needs related to self-actualization. In the context of competitive sport, this translates into personal motivations like meeting challenges and self-improvement, as opposed to social and relaxation motivation; by implication, motivations should be revealed to change over time.

H2 (Travel Style): highly involved runners will be significantly different from others participating in the event. They should travel to more events, possibly more with partners and family, and combine events with general holidays.

H3 (Temporal): the highly involved runners will exhibit less seasonality in their travel, as they seek out specific events; destinations employ events to counter normal demand peaks and troughs.

H4 (Spatial): highly involved runners will travel further, longer and more by air. An advancing career in running should result in higher-level competition at the national and international levels.

H5 (Event Types): highly involved runners will participate in different types of events, related to their prestige, novelty or perceived challenge. Certain events are iconic within social worlds; experienced runners should also be novelty-seekers.

H6 (Destination and Event Choice Criteria): the importance of various criteria when selecting events and destinations will differ significantly between higher- and lesser-involved runners. The ideal holiday destination for the highly involved will provide the opportunity to participate in an event, and to satisfy partners or family members.

Figure 8.2 is supported by research, but remains hypothetical – especially as it might apply to other sports, arts, hobbies and lifestyle pursuits. There is no inevitability to progression, as many people remain at a beginner's level, or they progress then fall back in terms of their commitment and involvement.

Further research is needed to consider the short-term and ultimate goals of highly involved event participants. Do some 'iconic' events compel them forwards, training harder, searching for better performance?

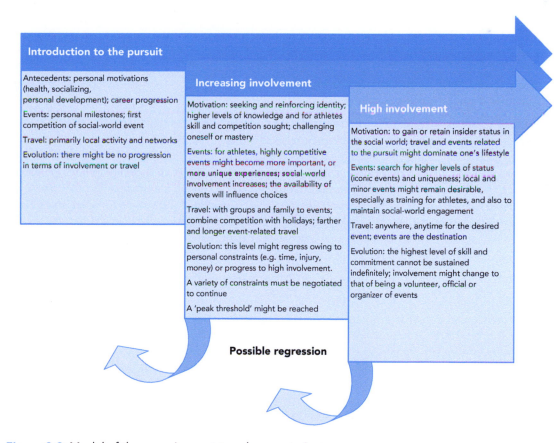

Figure 8.2 Model of the generic event travel career trajectory

How do they combine their interest in running, or art, or any other pursuit with more general leisure and travel preferences? How can event designers maximize the desired experiences of the 'highly involved' as well as those for whom the event is only of general interest?

A study completed for the Swedish Classics tested the ETCT on five different participation sport events and provided additional evidence that the hypotheses are sound, although it was also revealed that there are differences among athletes, types of events and the specific appeal of individual events (see the Swedish Classics website: https://ensvenskklassiker.se/en/our-classics/a-swedish-classic/). The key findings were:

- international event respondents were 'more active' than Swedish participants; that is, they planned to attend more events in the subsequent year;
- participants in the five sports were significantly different in a number of important ways; there are dynamic and diverse styles of event and destination choices in the world of amateur sport event tourists;
- the 'more active' travel to significantly more events and travel longer distances; they are also involved with social worlds and travel to a larger extent with teams or clubs; they have participated in more events and plan to continue this tendency;
- the 'more active' respondents were significantly more motivated by self-development; challenge is important to all, and can be considered a general identifier of the event-sport tourist, and this corroborates earlier data from the Gothenburg half marathon (Getz and Andersson 2010).

8.1 RESEARCH NOTE ON TRAVEL CAREERS

Getz, D. and Andersson, T. (2010). The event-tourist career trajectory: A study of high involvement amateur distance runners. *Scandinavian Journal of Hospitality and Tourism*, 10(4), 468–491.

Abstract: Drawing from theory on serious leisure, social worlds, recreation specialization, ego-involvement, and travel motivation, it is proposed that many people with specific sport or lifestyle interests will develop event-specific careers. These careers will follow a trajectory that can be measured in terms of six dimensions: motivations (especially the pursuit of higher-level personal needs); changing travel styles; spatial and temporal patterns, event and destination choices. As a partial test of the event-tourist career trajectory, a large sample of registrants for a half-marathon in Sweden was questioned in a pre-event survey about their motives, involvement in their sport, and event-related travel. Employing an involvement scale specific to amateur distance runners, analysis revealed that most runners were not highly involved in this sport.

Lamont, M., Kennelly, M. and Wilson, E. (2012). Competing priorities as constraints in event travel careers. *Tourism Management*, 33(5), 1068–1079.

An event travel career is a potentially lifelong pattern of travel to events linked with an individual's preferred leisure activity. This paper applies the concept of an event travel career to non-elite triathletes. For these active sport tourists, ongoing pursuit of an event travel career is arguably constrained by competing priorities that intervene between everyday life and their pursuit of an event travel career. In-depth interviews were conducted with 21 triathletes identified as pursuing an event travel career. Interpretive analysis revealed seven domains of competing priorities that could work to constrain their event travel career aspirations. These domains are familial relationships, domestic responsibilities, sociability, finances, leisure, well-being, and work/education.

Buning, R. and Gibson, H. (2016). Exploring the trajectory of active-sport-event travel careers: A social worlds perspective. *Journal of Sport Management*, 30(3), 265–281

Abstract: Utilizing a social worlds perspective, the study examined active-sport-event travel career progression in the sport of cycling. Event travel careers are considered potentially lifelong patterns of travel to participate in events that evolve through stages with distinct behaviours and motivations. Quantitative methods were used to test tenets of an inductively derived model of the active-sport-event travel career for cyclists. The results depicted an escalation in motivation related to intellectual, social, mastery competence, giving back, and competition against others with career progression.

Getz, D. and McConnell, A. (2014). Comparing trail runners and mountain bikers: Motivation, involvement, portfolios, and event-tourist careers. *Journal of Convention and Event Tourism*, 15(1), 69–100.

Abstract: Amateur trail runners and endurance mountain bikers are compared with regard to motivation, involvement in their sport, competitive-event portfolios, and event-travel careers. Participants in two destination events produced by a for-profit company constitute the sample frame, with the respondents having answered a sub-set of identical questions on an online, post-event evaluation survey. The two 'destination events' differ considerably in terms of the gender of participants, with a much higher proportion of females in the running event. Both samples were revealed to have a fairly high level of involvement in their sport, but a large proportion of participants in both events also participated in a wider portfolio of challenging sports.

Personal and interpersonal factors

Sport, entertainment and business events are an integral part of many cultures. A person's cultural background can have a profound influence on their perceptions of need for, or their interest in, certain types of planned events. In some societies, individuals are encouraged to think in terms of hedonistic consumption, leading to event 'consumption', but in others the collective will or religious/political doctrine generates a quite different pattern of socially acceptable behaviour. There are many common reasons for attending cultural celebrations, including entertainment, spectacle and social, but we also need to focus on the cultural antecedents. For traditional events, people are expected to participate and even organize them because of the cultural norms existing in their communities. How much does social obligation impact on attendance and participation in cultural celebrations? Some take on the status of institutions, thereby attracting volunteers who gain prestige or social standing. Buying tickets to some arts festivals might be considered the thing to do if one is in the higher social classes, while travelling to the annual Wagnerian opera festival in Bayreuth, Germany, might be considered both a pilgrimage and a chance to meet the European elite. Lifestyle is in part a social construct, dependent on other factors such as reference points and participants. Peers are an especially important element in events that have subcultural dimensions, including cultural celebrations and sports.

Expectations

Needs and motives give rise to expectations that certain behaviours will yield desired benefits, and this is the essence of the 'theory of planned behaviour'. Expectations are also shaped by communications (advertising and image-making) on the part of events, and particularly by word-of-mouth recommendations or expressed opinions from valued reference groups. The 'travel career trajectory' is also applicable, as the more experience one has with events (either particular events or events in general), the more it will affect expectations.

Motives for attending festivals

Many of the event motivation studies have examined festivals. Probably the most important conclusion is that generic motives predominate (i.e. family togetherness, socializing, group identity), while event-specific motives (the programme, the art form, uniqueness features) are likely to be important to niche segments and relatively more important for tourists. Certainly festival motivators are primarily intrinsic, that is, for leisure and other personally/socially rewarding reasons, whereas for other types of event extrinsic motivators might also apply (e.g. for work and business). Numerous studies have delineated these motivational factors, suggesting that a core set of drivers for festival attendance exists, including 'cultural enrichment, education, novelty and socialization' (Crompton and McKay 1997: 429). These 'pull factors' should be considered alongside having fun, or hedonism as generic reasons for leisure and travel to events, with the proviso that both seeking and escaping motives are often coincidental. Escaping from boredom and stressful environments is often just as powerful a motivator as the specific attractiveness of events. The importance of socializing has been highlighted by Nordvall *et al.* (2014).

In Figure 8.3 the generic and event-specific motivators, that is, the experiences desired, are combined with essential services to provide a model of value to event designers and marketers. The essential services can be called 'hygiene factors' or 'dissatisfiers' (after Herzberg 1966) because they do not motivate, yet they can dissatisfy customers. Generic benefits attract the widest possible audiences, but are also highly substitutable. Event-specific experiences, or benefits offered, will attract those seeking something special such as unique, one-time-only and high-quality programming. The highly involved are motivated by experiences they can share with others in their social worlds. A mix of generic and targeted benefits, built on a foundation of high-quality service, is essential for events to compete with other events and other forms of entertainment and especially to attract tourists.

There are many types of festivals, so event-specific motivators always have to be considered. A number of research notes have been provided to illustrate some key differences. Perhaps the most challenging type is that of the so-called 'community festival', which often means a multipurpose event intended to appeal to the widest possible audience. While such festivals tend to celebrate the community itself, or have the aim

Figure 8.3 Generic and event-specific motivators, and essential services

of social integration, they might also contain programmic elements that are designed to attract tourists (especially entertainment and participatory sports). Usually they are organized and/or supported by local government, but might be managed by a not-for-profit society or a consortium of local organizations. Jepson and Clarke (2014) and Jepson *et al.* (2013) explore the community festival from the perspective of social inclusion and power relations. Báez-Montenegro and Devesa-Fernández (2017) pointed to festival tourism focused on an interest in cinema, with film festivals attracting aficionados – an observation that reflects both social-world and travel-career perspectives. And, as reflected in research by Podestà and Richards (2017), many such arts or creative-industry festivals have become knowledge hubs, a fact that expands their traditional roles and appeal considerably.

Motivational research on business events

We should expect that motivations to attend meetings and business-related events will be quite different from leisure motivations, specifically that extrinsic motives will often dominate: being required to attend (lack of choice); seeking a reward for attending (learning something useful, developing a personal or business network) and a mix of extrinsic and intrinsic rewards (i.e. combining business with pleasure). Business-event organizers often stress the social programme as well as pre- and post-event tours. Oppermann and Chon (1997) produced a decision-making model for attendees, and subsequent work has expanded our understanding of motives, constraints and choices. Severt *et al.* (2007) examined convention-attendee motivations and identified these: activities and opportunities; networking; convenience of the location; educational benefits; and products and deals. Mair and Thompson (2009) identified two critical factors affecting the decision to attend, namely networking opportunities and costs. In a review article, Elston and Draper (2012) reported that total costs to the attendee was consistently reported to be the main criteria being considered by meeting planners, but they suggested that sustainability and technology should be given more attention by researchers. Mair (2013) reviewed the literature on convention motivation, observing that the main topics explored by researchers were the desire for networking and professional development/education. Constraining factors included cost, timing, accessibility, location attractiveness and health or safety concerns.

Jung and Tanford (2017) conducted a meta-analysis of the convention literature and determined that networking and education are the top contributors to attendee satisfaction, and these generate repeat attendance. However, Kim and Malek (2017) found that motivations to attend a medical conference were somewhat different from other business events, with programming and location being most critical, so a more nuanced approach is needed when examining motivation. Exhibition motivations have been examined by Yi *et al.* (2018) and Fu *et al.* (2019). Exhibitions have to attract exhibitors, and they are primarily motivated by business factors, whereas other attendees will be looking for information, contacts, new ideas and perhaps a good time. Fu *et al.* (2019) emphasized knowledge, social networking and leisure motivations which made exhibitions places of both service and experience. Consumer-show motivations have been studied by Fox and Edwards (2009) and Rittichainuwat and Mair (2012). While these are very diverse in theme, covering such topics as lifestyle, health, leisure and vehicles, a common motivator is to learn and compare, and sometimes to purchase. It can be expected that people with special interests are focusing on shows that cater to their social world or leisure preferences.

Motivational research on sport fans and spectators

In applying psychological ideas to sport event participation, Benckendorff and Pearce (2012: 166) distinguished between spectators and attendees, performers and participants, and elite participants. Fans were considered to be a special segment. Personality, role theory, involvement, motivation and the actual experience plus post-experience are important considerations. Identity theory suggests that people attend sport and other types of event that carry symbolic significance, thereby helping to define themselves. Li and Petrick's (2006) literature review related to sports resulted in several important conclusions. First, a general motivation scale for sport event attendance by fans or spectators has been developed and widely applied (see Wann 1995; Wann *et al.* 1999). Second, studying potential attendees adds to our understanding (as opposed to surveys of actual attendees), and third, travel and event motivation might be different – a finding of significance for sport tourism (also see Parent and Chappelet 2015; Bodet 2015).

Motivational research on sport participation

The event travel career trajectory identified key motives for amateur participation and sport tourism, and in particular the importance of challenging oneself through physical activity. Additional insights can be found in the *Handbook of Sports Event Management* chapter by Young *et al.* (2015) on masters sport perspectives. Prayag and Grivel (2018) have summarized motives for sport participation, noting they have been extensively studied but categorized in different ways – making comparison and replication difficult. The combined evidence from many studies points to these important motivations: escape; socializing or meeting affiliation needs; hedonism, such as fun and thrill seeking; skill development and achievement; learning or exploration, covering both the sport and the destination.

Barriers and constraints

All the antecedents we have considered act together to shape a person's desire and propensity for certain event experiences, but there are often constraints on our actions, especially time and money, and specific barriers to overcome. The next section deals with 'leisure constraint theory' applied to events. There is no comparable theory for extrinsically motivated event participation, but it is probably a combination of intrinsic and extrinsic motivation applied to many business-event decisions (see Figure 8.4).

Leisure constraints theory

Why do some people not participate in events? This question is vital in marketing, but there are also important theoretical considerations that get to the nature of motivation, benefits and the nature of the

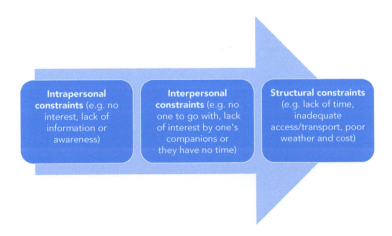

Figure 8.4 Barriers to event attendance

Source: Developed from Lee and Palakurthi (2013).

event experience. In event studies, the challenge is to not only identify constraints on attendance but to examine how people overcome constraints to attend, and how that knowledge might affect both event planning and marketing. In the context of 'serious leisure' or frequent event participation by 'high-involvement' types, we should be studying how constraints are 'negotiated' over a lifetime. Crawford *et al.* (1991) identified three general categories of constraints to participation: 'structural', 'personal' and 'interpersonal'. They are not necessarily hierarchical, and might be interactive. These are set out in Figure 8.4.

Structural constraints

The first and foremost of these is accessibility, which stems from the location and timing of events of all kinds – they are simply not always available, convenient or known by all potential participants. All aspects of supply analysis come into play here, as does marketing and communication. For example, it has long been observed that there is a huge gap between tourists' interest in attending cultural events in other countries and actual participation. Why? Because they have imperfect knowledge of what's available, and are most likely to be in an area when the events are not held. This is also why we are so interested in the 'dedicated event tourist' who travels specifically because of events. Time and cost are always structural constraints. On the one hand we need to identify who is left out of the arts, or sports or any other type of event because they are unable to afford it or cannot make the necessary time. On the other hand, 'not enough time or money' are convenient excuses, and might often mean the person does not assign any priority to a given opportunity. The first is a constraint issue, the second pertains more to preferences.

Age and health are obvious factors to consider. In youth we cannot get about on our own, and until we have income we cannot do what we want. With advancing age and declining health (or at least specific health problems) interest and participation in many leisure and work-related events will likely decline. For events, there is a need to combine both life-cycle and work/career evolutionary approaches.

Personal constraints

These are individual psychological conditions, including personality and moods, that hold us back from participating. Some people are predisposed to social activities, others to introversion. Sometimes we want to mix, at other times we need to be left alone. This category is similar to our earlier discussion of personality, values, attitudes and lifestyle. Risk perception, and tolerance for risk, enters into many leisure and travel decisions. Do we want to have a thrill if it means assuming personal risks, or can we afford to spend time and money on an event that might not satisfy us? How preferences are first formed for events or event experiences has not been researched, but for ongoing participation there are explanations within the concepts of 'serious leisure', 'recreation specialization', 'commitment' and 'involvement'.

Interpersonal constraints

These constraints arise within social contexts, taking into account the influence of others. This might take the form of letting significant others make decisions for us, being influenced by peer pressure (e.g. fear of ridicule), or being subjected to discrimination. Social isolation is often a limitation, especially for certain types of events – after all, who wants to go to a party or celebration alone? On the other hand, events are often great places to meet people.

A lot of research has documented gender differences in travel, leisure and sport, but little of this has been applied to events. More research on why people do not attend events is necessary, such as reported by Miller *et al.* (2004) and Lee and Palakurthi (2013) (also see Mirehie *et al.* 2017; and Mahadevan 2018b).

Constraint negotiation

As constraints almost always exist, how do people who do participate in, or attend, events overcome them? 'Negotiation' of constraints is the individual process of finding ways to do what we want to do. If we really want to attend a concert, how do we get the money, make the time, find someone to go with and book the tickets? The issue of constraints and how you negotiate them to overcome them has been a significant area of research with leisure for over 20 years. The seminal study in the field was by Jackson *et al.* (1993), who discussed generic strategies for negotiating constraints as illustrated in Figure 8.5. What Jackson *et al.* found was that people have to strike a balance between constraints and their motivations to participate; negotiating these barriers or constraints and balancing with motivation results in different strategies being employed.

'Cognitive' strategies are the internal, psychological ways we deal with constraints. For example, the theory of 'cognitive dissonance' can be applied by suggesting that if we cannot attend a concert because of high costs, we will devalue the artist or type of music and do something else that we perceive to provide equal benefits. In this sense, when people say they do not like certain types of events, they might mean they cannot afford them. We all want to feel good about the choices we make, even if they were influenced by constraints.

'Behavioural' strategies include better time management, learning new skills, earning more money, or modifying our routines in order to do what we want to do. Some people turn leisure into work, or vice versa. For 'serious leisure', one generally has to acquire knowledge to get the most out of the experience, and this applies to many volunteers at events. In order to think of oneself as an expert or connoisseur, say for the purpose of getting the most from a wine festival, advanced wine knowledge is essential.

'Time management' is something we all try to improve, particularly in an age when a majority of people complain about time pressures, or lack of time to get active. 'Multi-tasking' (or 'pluriactivity') is the norm for most students, working people and homemakers. Mannell and Zuzanek (1991) reported that even retired seniors felt that a lack of time was a serious leisure constraint.

Setting priorities is the key. Generally, when respondents to a survey say they did not do something because of time or money constraints, they are probably truthful in a general sense. But this common response might very well be hiding a conscious or subconscious prioritization, so they really mean 'attending the event is not high enough on my current list of priorities to justify making the effort or paying the

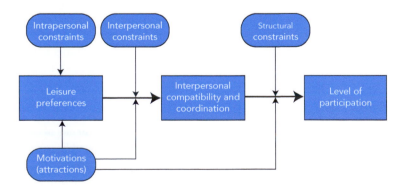

Figure 8.5 Jackson, Crawford and Godbey's balance proposition: leisure anticipation as a product of a balance between constraints and motivations

Source: Jackson *et al.* (1993). Reprinted from *Leisure Sciences*, 15(1), Jackson, E. L., Crawford, D. W. and Godbey, G. Negotiation of leisure constraints, Copyright (1993) with the permission of Taylor and Francis.

price'. So the researcher will have to dig deeper. It seems paradoxical, but the most constrained people are sometimes the most active! How do they manage to engage in preferred leisure pursuits when others give up? The fact is that many people find innovative ways to overcome or negotiate through constraints (see Hinch *et al.* 2006 for a discussion and references).

8.2 RESEARCH NOTE ON CONSTRAINTS

Mahadevan, R. (2018). To attend or not to attend a rural folk festival: Examining nonattendees' behavior using a temporal approach. *Event Management*, 22, 441–452.

Abstract: This article considers a temporal dimension and extends the theoretical framework beyond the leisure constraints theory to incorporate passive use and direct use values for the first time, to examine nonattendees' intention to attend a rural festival. It was found that passive use values affect only the decision to attend but direct use values influence that decision to take place sooner rather than later. Results also support the family life-cycle stage theory for a potential first visit but not the decision to visit soon while the reverse was found for the distance decay theory. Overall, the impact of the various dimensions of the barriers within the leisure constraints theory, the perceived beliefs, and visit motivations differed among would-be visitors and those intending to visit sooner rather than later. Thus, a dual marketing strategy aimed generally at the former, and specifically at the latter, would be effective in attracting new visitors to rural festivals.

Setting affordances

Pertinent to the analysis of antecedents and event studies is 'setting affordances', which are those objective characteristics of the venue or setting that make certain actions and behaviours possible. For example, an attractive, spacious function room presents many social possibilities to dinner guests, but without wheelchair accessibility some people cannot enter. 'Affordance' is also a concept rooted in cognition and environmental psychology, placing the emphasis on 'perceived affordances'. Regardless of the venue manager's or event producer's intentions, people's perception of what is possible, and what is a barrier, can differ greatly.

Decision-making

Negotiation of constraints is both a background antecedent and a key part of specific decision-making processes. Then it is necessary to study how people search for and use information, especially because events are very time-sensitive opportunities. As well, in the context of economic 'demand' for events, we have to consider their 'attractiveness', the possibility of substitute experiences (including competition) and whether or not people are loyal to certain events.

Information search and use

This is a very under-researched area within event marketing, with a majority of related articles dealing with sources used (e.g. Wang and Cole 2016) and not search behaviour. Tasci *et al.* (2018) have reviewed the evidence pertinent to sport tourism. An important consideration is whether the decision is 'routine' or 'unique'. For some sport events and concert series, a consumer can buy season tickets, or multi-day passes, thereby necessitating one big purchase decision – but there will still be a decision required for attending each and every game or concert. Loyal festival fans can also return year after year, in which case most of the same variables enter into the decision. When decision-making becomes 'routine', the person does not need a lot of information (or perceives this to be true), takes less time and already has a predisposition.

Most event opportunities are likely to be 'unique' decision-making episodes, especially when a purchase decision is required. In these cases the consumer needs lots of information and might take a lot of time obtaining it. Part of the appeal of modern Internet marketing is that the time component can be reduced substantially, and research has found that Internet shoppers tend to use only a few sites, thereby limiting their time expenditure. The risk factor also has to be considered, because every new decision to attend or participate in an event poses risks such as wasted time and money, bad experiences, and health and safety concerns.

Demand

'Demand' is often equated with how many people will come to an event, or what they will pay for it. More correctly, in economic terms, it is a function of the relationship between price and the quantity 'demanded' for an event in particular circumstances. For each price, the demand relationship tells the quantity the buyers want to buy at that corresponding price.

Consider other related factors. Usually price is a monetary cost, as in how much an admission ticket costs, but you might also want to put a value on the consumer's time and energy expended, especially if travel is involved. What about 'free' events? For these it is common to measure demand in terms of attendance, but organizers have to be cautious about interpreting this figure. Many people might not pay anything for an event that is currently free. Research on 'willingness to pay' is then required.

Attractiveness of the event and destination

A related concept is 'attractiveness'. This means the 'drawing power' or 'pull' of an event, both its general appeal (generic benefits) and its targeted benefits for specific needs and interests. In the context of economic 'demand', attractiveness could be equated with 'market potential' and measured by 'penetration rates'. That is, within a given market area, how many purchases can be expected, expressed as a percentage of the population (if half the people come twice, that is considered to be 100 per cent)? Different market areas also have to be considered, such as local, regional, national and international zones.

Events contribute to city and destination attractiveness, a fact that helps explain the rise of eventful cities and event portfolio management. Cities that pursue a strategy of maximizing their attractiveness (and in re-positioning and branding in general) invest heavily in event bidding, production, marketing, incentivizing, venues and related infrastructure. Attractiveness also depends on one's point of view, for example, meeting planners versus potential attendees. Crouch *et al.* (2019: 530) determined the top factors influencing international convention site selection for associations. 'The top ten site attributes were (in descending order): the convenience of flight schedules; risk of disruption to the convention; inbound travel barriers or formalities; on-site vs. off-site delegate accommodation; number of available four star hotels; cost of the convention facility; possibility of a subsidy to defray costs; number of available five star hotels; whether or not the association held its convention at the site previously; and domestic air travel costs.' Certainly cost is always a consideration, but not a motivator. Image and attractiveness cannot be separated. An event, venue, destination or city might have everything desirable for general-purpose or event-specific visits but still hold a negative image in the minds of potential clients.

Substitution

Just about every leisure and travel pursuit can be substituted. We do not absolutely need to go to a specific destination or participate in a specific event and (this is assuming free choice) there are always alternative ways to meet our leisure needs. Thinking again of the theory of 'cognitive dissonance', we can easily convince ourselves that one form of music appreciation or sport or hobby is as good as another, even if we were influenced by constraints. If extrinsic motivations to attend an event apply, substitution takes on a different meaning. We might be able to learn what we need to know from different trade shows, or meet the necessary contacts at different conventions, but these choices are less common than in the leisure realm. Many event attendees go to a specific event because it is the only one, or the best one to satisfy their purposes. The theory of 'leisure substitution' suggests that if a person cannot do one thing, he or she will choose another that provides similar psychological experiences, satisfactions and benefits (Brunson and Shelby 1993). This appears to be very true for primarily social experiences, where the activity, setting or event is of secondary concern. Events offering 'targeted benefits' for highly involved persons are less substitutable than those offering only 'generic benefits'.

Decision to attend or participate

Wanting to attend, even planning to, is quite different from going to an event. At some point commitment is made, perhaps money spent on travel or tickets, but something might still intervene to prevent attendance. Researchers therefore seek to discover the links between levels of awareness, interest in attending, forming a specific intention to go and actual attendance.

How are decisions made to attend or travel to events, and what factors are considered? Consider all the contexts and choices we have to understand: decision-making occurs in stages, with feedback called 'post-purchase evaluation'. There is an awareness and opinion-forming stage, which might be combined with information gathering (even if it's no more than asking for someone's advice), during which the consumer forms an intent, rejects the opportunity or waffles indecisively. Reysen *et al.* (2018) employed the theory of planned behaviour to assess the intention to attend a fan convention, finding that attitudes, norms, perceived control, past behaviour and in-group identification each predicted intention to attend. This seems to suggest a social-worlds approach to marketing.

Loyalty versus novelty seeking

Loyalty in the events sector is a complex concept. Except for professional sports and regular theatrical productions, most events are unique opportunities. Numerous event-related decisions are never exactly repeated and people engage in novelty-seeking in travel and leisure, generally preferring something new each time a decision is made. But event loyalty does exist in some forms, as indicated by sport-fan loyalty to teams. Loyalty to periodic conferences and exhibitions exists, both because of the business or professional advantages and the enjoyment of socializing with friends who always meet there. Many people do go to the same festivals year after year, especially those that have become traditions in their home communities. Event loyalty is likely to result from obtaining specific benefits, especially those related to special interests. Loyalty might also be a lifestyle factor stemming from events that fit one's work-life and social calendar.

Evaluation of experience and future intentions

A popular area of research has been to link evaluation of quality (or satisfaction) with future intentions or, more ambitiously, to link antecedents (including expectations of benefits sought, motivation, demographics, involvement, identity) with experiences (e.g. activities, spending, type and level of engagement) to quality evaluations, to satisfaction (reflecting expectancy-disconfirmation) and ultimately to future intentions (i.e. repeat visits, loyalty, recommendations). Structural equation modelling is often the preferred method, and obviously event-visitor data is required. An example is that of the aforementioned study of Kim and Malek (2017). Creating memorable, transforming event experiences is the goal of many event producers, and if people really do enjoy and recollect events they are more likely to return – or seek out comparable experiences. While satisfaction is usually a precondition to loyalty, as confirmed in many studies, the mere realization of expected benefits and satisfaction with service or programme quality is no guarantee of repeat visits. This brings us full circle in the decision-making model, stressing that antecedents include the influence of previous experience. What is not shown are the effects of other kinds of experience on event-related behaviour. Also, broader forces are at work, including a person's experiences with entertainment, sport or business in general.

STUDY GUIDE

Figure 8.1 is a model illustrating the main factors considered in order to understand decisions and choices leading to event attendance, and that is the starting point for studying this chapter. This is partly the realm of psychology and consumer research, but also the economics of supply and demand, and of cultural and social forces. The discussion started with personal factors, specifically personality, values, attitudes and lifestyle. Then needs, motivations and motives were examined, including the event travel career trajectory and how it can help explain event-related behaviour. The ETCT is a relatively new theory, linking to earlier discussions of serious leisure, involvement, commitment and intrinsic motivation. Try to apply it to other leisure pursuits, including different sports, art forms, hobbies and lifestyle interests such as food and wine. Also try to apply the model of basic services, generic and targeted (or specific) benefits to different forms of planned events, from festivals to trade shows.

STUDY QUESTIONS

- Explain how 'personality', 'values', 'attitudes' and 'lifestyle' relate to interest in and demand for event experiences.
- What is the relevance of the theory of planned behaviour in the model of antecedents and decision-making for event attendance?
- What are basic human 'needs', and how do they link to 'motivation'?
- Explain the 'event travel career trajectory' and show how it can be adapted to understanding the antecedents to attending planned events.
- What factors influence event attractiveness?
- How important are 'seeking' versus 'escaping' motivations in explaining event attendance? What have researchers found that confirms or rejects this theory when applied to events?
- Do most people attend festivals for generic or specific benefits? Where do essential services enter the decision-making process?
- How are 'expectations' formed? Consider post-event evaluation.
- Explain 'leisure constraint theory' and how it applies to events. Differentiate between the main types of 'constraints', and give event-specific examples.
- Use the concepts of 'serious leisure', 'commitment', 'ego involvement' and 'recreation specialization' to help explain how people develop event careers and negotiate constraints.
- What are the roles of an event website, and social media, in information searches and the decision to attend an event?
- What is 'demand' for events? How are 'attractiveness' and 'substitution' related to demand?
- What factors help explain the differences between 'loyalty' and 'novelty-seeking' with regard to event behaviour? Where does 'nostalgia' fit in?

NOTE

A hypothesis is an idea or proposition which you construct and test through the research process to assess its validity. The hypothesis may have been constructed to test the existing theories or wisdom on the subject and it follows a scientific process of testing and verification.

FURTHER READING

Decrop, A. (2006). *Vacation Decision Making*. Wallingford: CABI.

Funk, D. (2008). *Consumer Behaviour in Sport and Events: Marketing Action*. Oxford: Butterworth-Heinemann.

Gibson, H. (ed.) (2006). *Sport Tourism: Concepts and Theories*. London: Routledge.

Parent, M. and Chappelet, J.-L. (eds) (2015). *Routledge Handbook of Sports Event Management*. London: Routledge.

Chapter **9**

Event management, planning and marketing

LEARNING OBJECTIVES

Upon completion of this chapter, students should know the foundation concepts and main research approaches to increasing knowledge about the following dimensions of event planning, management and marketing:

- the scope and nature of management theory, marketing theory and planning theory;
- the changing nature of work and how event management will be affected;
- leadership theory, including roles and styles of leadership;
- organizational culture and organizational quality;
- the open-system model;
- ownership and governance;
- inter-organizational behaviour, including organizational structure, coordination, stakeholder management, and institutionalization;
- types of planning (strategic, project, business, portfolio) and decision-making;
- sustainability as a concept and a process;
- operations and logistics (including service quality management);
- human resources, including professionalism, careers, staff and volunteer management;
- resources and financial management, including sponsorship;
- return on investment, return on experience, and return on objectives;
- marketing and communications, including the marketing mix and segmentation;

- risk, health and safety, and dynamic crowd management;
- research, evaluation and information systems.

Introduction

Management is a broad field, encompassing business, not-for-profit and public administration, and planned events fall into all three categories. Most of the management functions associated with events are discussed in this chapter; however, programming and design have already been covered. There is no correct place to start, as all the management functions are crucial, but we have elected to start with leadership, including a discussion of event founders and organizational culture. For each management function, a figure is provided to summarize major themes or topics covered, an indication of the disciplinary foundations for theory and methods, and unique issues or applications for events.

The scope and nature of management studies and theory

'Management' literally means the process of dealing with, or controlling persons and things, although when theory is discussed, it usually refers to the management of organizations and their component parts or management functions. As a noun the word can also refer collectively to the people who run things, as in 'the management of that event is highly competent' or similarly 'their marketing manager is on leave'. The verb *to manage* leads us to the various management functions, as implied in the question 'what are you managing?' (Kessler 2013, xxv) describes the 'unmistakable elements of "management": orientation and direction, coordination and control, authority and responsibility, planning and design, and administration and implementation', and furthermore '… there are countless "theories" (loosely defined as well as loosely connected) of management.' Of note is the omission of 'marketing' in both the list of management functions in the encyclopaedia, and in the categorization of management theories, although the 'product-market differentiation model' is discussed. We are led to believe by this approach that marketing is subsumed by the broad functions of management, although it is – like planning – so important that we treat it separately in this book. In addition to categories pertaining to the management of various aspects of organizations and the people within them, the encyclopaedia also discusses theories pertaining to the nature of management (e.g. scientific versus humanistic), and social and environmental issues (e.g. social responsibility and critical management studies). Anyone seeking theoretical inspiration or guidance about management should consult a reference work (e.g. Kessler), but keep in mind that any knowledge or theory from other disciplines can inform management decisions.

The scope and nature of planning studies and theory

From a management or business perspective, planning is 'a basic management function involving formulation of one or more detailed plans to achieve optimum balance of needs or demands with the available resources'. The planning process:

(1) identifies the goals or objectives to be achieved;

(2) formulates strategies to achieve them;

(3) arranges or creates the means required;

(4) implements, directs, and monitors all steps in their proper sequence.

Source: http://www.businessdictionary.com/definition/planning.html

The main types of plan developed for and by events are discussed in this chapter, including site plans, operational plans, strategic and business plans. But 'planning' has additional and broader applications of interest to event studies: urban and regional planning which affects land use; economic planning which influences the resources available for venues and events; social/cultural planning with its concerns for justice and quality of life; health planning and resulting regulations that govern events, and environmental planning and its emphasis on sustainability.

Planning is a future-oriented process in which organizations set goals and put in place actions to attain them. It is always political, with groups in society or within organizations competing for influence or resources. Although planning by nature should be a rational process, it is clear that decisions in the events sector are often made in an irrational manner (for examples, see Armstrong 1985; Butler and Grigg 1987; Bramwell 1997). Planning is often focused on conflicts and problems, and researchers Phi *et al.* (2014) have examined events in this light using Q method.

The scope and nature of marketing studies and theory

The American Marketing Association has adopted these formal definitions:

> *Marketing is the activity, set of institutions, and processes for creating, communicating, delivering, and exchanging offerings that have value for customers, clients, partners, and society at large.*

> *Marketing research is the function that links the consumer, customer, and public to the marketer through information—information used to identify and define marketing opportunities and problems; generate, refine, and evaluate marketing actions; monitor marketing performance; and improve understanding of marketing as a process. Marketing research specifies the information required to address these issues, designs the method for collecting information, manages and implements the data collection process, analyses the results, and communicates the findings and their implications.*

> *(https://www.ama.org/AboutAMA/Pages/Definition-of-Marketing.aspx)*

Many early definitions of marketing referred to the business of selling things, and to the four Ps (product, price, place/distribution and promotion), or they emphasized the creation and management of exchange relationships. These are all valid, but contemporary marketing theory is mostly about value creation. In this context we examine how events create value, the benefits desired by all the stakeholders, and the vital roles of value co-creation and value networks.

Leadership

The various schools of theory on leadership have been identified by Dulewicz and Higgs (2003), namely:

1: *the trait school*: we can ask, what personality traits are exhibited by people we recognize as leaders in the event management field?

2: *the behavioural school*: what do leaders do that makes them effective?

3: *the contingency school*: are good leaders flexible and adaptable?

4: *the visionary school*: who has a long-term vision for our profession? how is innovation fostered?

5: *the emotional intelligence school*: are good leaders empathetic? team players?

6: *the competency school*: what is the knowledge base, how is it best taught, and what skills are necessary?

Abson (2017) asked: 'What do effective leaders do in the world of festivals and events?' suggesting that effective event leaders perform certain tasks (Figure 9.1).

Figure 9.1 What event managers do (after Abson 2017)

Abson also cautioned:

> *that event managers believe that it is not the technical skills (such as financial planning, event design) that ensure successful event delivery but rather that it is the soft skills and the human resource that drive successful events .... in order to be successful leaders, they also need to work in teams, motivate and empower others, and develop team members.*

Senge (1990) argued that leadership is not about one's position or role; it is not the same as being a boss. Leaders and managers can be two quite different things, although a good manager who is passionate about excellence can also be a leader. 'Leading' literally means to step ahead or move forward (presumably with followers), and Senge equates this with creativity and vision. Leaders have a purpose and are passionate about their work; they care for people. Senge's perspective on leadership reinforces the view of events as agents of change. He points to the importance of community-level leadership, and therefore event managers should look to their broader roles in helping to shape the future.

Leadership roles and styles

In the vast literature on leadership you will find many models, but one that is frequently cited is called full-range leadership (see Avolio 2010). Avolio (2010) suggests that the most effective leaders need a repertoire of styles, and the laissez-faire style (i.e. doing nothing while expecting results) is not an option. Transformational leadership is recommended, but sometimes transactional roles are necessary.

Here are a number of frequently mentioned styles.

Servant leadership

> *Servant leadership is a philosophy and set of practices that enriches the lives of individuals, builds better organizations and ultimately creates a more just and caring world ... A servant-*

leader focuses primarily on the growth and well-being of people and the communities to which they belong. While traditional leadership generally involves the accumulation and exercise of power by one at the 'top of the pyramid', servant leadership is different. The servant-leader shares power, puts the needs of others first and helps people develop and perform as highly as possible.
(*https://www.greenleaf.org/what-is-servant-leadership/*)

This style, or philosophy, seems most appropriate in the not-for-profit event sector, where events and event-producing organizations exist as agents of change or as providers of specific messages and services to communities.

Autocratic leadership

Autocratic leadership is centred on the boss, with the owner or top manager holding all authority and power. Autocratic leaders make decisions without consulting subordinates. We can see this in small and family-owned businesses and it goes with the hands-on, be-my-own-boss attitude of many entrepreneurs.

Charismatic leadership

People follow them because of their personality or attractiveness, or perhaps because of their message; this involves a transformation of followers' values and beliefs. Leaders do not have to be charismatic, but in many circumstances, it helps in attracting followers.

Democratic leadership

In this leadership style, subordinates are involved in making decisions. In some societies consensus-building is essential – no matter how long it takes. This style can be merged with the principles of value co-creation within stakeholder networks.

Transactional leadership

Focusing on the lower-order needs identified by Maslow (1954, 1968), this style of leadership promotes compliance and the status quo. Performance standards will be specified and evaluated and workers will be rewarded or punished as appropriate.

Transformational leadership

Unlike other leadership styles, transformational leadership is all about initiating change in organizations, groups, oneself and others. Transformational leaders motivate others to do more than they originally intended and often even more than they thought possible. They set more challenging expectations and typically achieve higher performance. Transformational leaders empower followers.

Senge (1990) specified three leadership roles necessary for creation of a learning organization (i.e. one that can develop) being the *leader as designer* (i.e. create a common vision with shared values and purpose; design policies, strategies and structures; create the learning processes aimed at fostering continuous improvement), *as teacher* or coach, and *as steward* (similar to the servant leader). These can be framed within transformational leadership theory.

Organizational culture and leadership

Leadership is the pivotal role of managers (Mintzberg 1994) and of boards of directors. Of course, in many small organizations and informal events, everyone chips in as needed, in which case leadership is somewhat of a collective process. Leadership in events requires the setting of a vision, developing strategies and goals, and inspiring everyone to work together towards those goals. Oakley and Krug (1991) believed that creative leaders empower their workers, but also take responsibility for all the decisions made by workers; they focus on goals and results, are both current and future oriented. Group leadership, where no one dominates and all decisions are taken democratically, is an alternative approach, but difficult to implement – especially in projects where rapid decision-making is necessary. Events typically require both artistic and management leadership. An over-emphasis on business might stifle artistic innovation, whereas an over-emphasis on creativity might compromise the event's financial viability.

Leadership ability is essential for owners and founders of events, but leadership skills come to the fore, and have to be learned, as workers become supervisors and progress to become managers. Technical skills and hands-on operations have to give way to people skills such as motivating and problem solving. At the highest management levels, conceptual knowledge (theory) is needed, as well as the ability to formulate visions, goals and strategies, alongside research and evaluation skills. Derrett (2016: xiii) observed that: 'Some practitioners suggest that two vital characteristics of enduring festivals are vision and leadership.' Assuming that many events want to endure, their leadership and culture need to be focused on what it takes to succeed in meeting their most important goals. Other terms that help describe 'enduring' include 'sustainable', 'flourishing', 'resilient' and 'thriving'. Many would insist that 'profitable' or 'competitive' be added to this list. 'Resilience' is a key concept, as many events face crises that threaten their very existence; they must be able to recover or reinvent themselves. Elsewhere in this book we examine the concept of institutionalization, and it is highly relevant to leadership and culture (see Table 9.1).

Power

Power and leadership go together. Owners of companies and events typically have the legal power to compel obedience, just as in the military. Boards of directors can use legal power to enforce their policies. Managers often have 'legitimate' power (Mintzberg 1983) by virtue of their position to direct or coerce the actions of subordinates. Other sources of power identified by Mintzberg include 'reward power' (the ability to bestow or withhold tangible and intangible rewards), 'expert power' (people follow because of superior knowledge or ability), 'information power' (obtained through control of vital information) and 'referent power' (stemming from loyalty and admiration). Power and knowledge are inseparable, according to Stadler (2013) drawing from the theories of Foucault (e.g. 1969, 1982). With regard to community festivals, Clarke and Jepson (2011) looked at how a steering committee exercised power in restricting knowledge within the community; this exercise of power resulted in the communities not being able to feel ownership of the festival.

Entrepreneurs (social and private)

How are events initiated? Somebody, or a group, has to take the initiative, and this leadership can continue well into the lifespan of the event and its organization. The term 'entrepreneur' is not easy to define, and there are two major schools of thought about entrepreneurship: that it is a personality trait held by rather unique persons; or that it is one or more actions that can be observed and measured. Furthermore, entrepreneurship can apply to personal business ventures or to social situations.

The 'personality trait theory' suggests that entrepreneurs are born, not made. Some people are compelled (or have an inborn propensity) to create businesses or events, seek out opportunities that others ignore (especially in terms of finding a niche in the marketplace), pull together resources (often through personal networking), take personal risks and (but not necessarily) create personal wealth. Innovation or creativity is often thought to be inherent in entrepreneurs, and this is certainly evident among those who establish festivals and other events.

Being one's own boss, or wanting to take a hands-on approach to work, is also a personality trait clearly associated with people who start up new businesses or events. Entrepreneurs are not discouraged by failures, and often bounce back from a failure to try again. 'Serial entrepreneurs' keep starting new ventures in a rather restless fashion, which leads some observers to think of them as socially dysfunctional or psychologically disturbed.

If the motivations driving entrepreneurs are mostly personal, or connected to family values and goals, they are clearly within the realm of business and microeconomics. But there is little doubt that 'social entrepreneurs' are very active in the arts, leading to establishment of many not-for-profit festivals and events. A 'social entrepreneur' might also work within governmental or not-for-profit organizations to create profits (or profitable events) to be used for social projects. Cause-related events can be created this way, and 'servant leadership' is a related concept.

'New venture' creation is the starting point for discussing entrepreneurship as observable activity. Starting up an event could be motivated by the desire for profit or social good. Risks are inherent in this process, especially when it comes to acquiring and spending one's own and other people's money. Reputations are also at stake. The entrepreneur's personal network can be vital at this start-up stage and in the subsequent years when vital support and resources have to be sustained through effective stakeholder management.

9.1 RESEARCH NOTE ON EVENT ENTREPRENEURSHIP

Crowther, P., Orefice, C. and Beard, C. (2018). At work and play: Business events as entrepreneurial spaces. *International Journal of Entrepreneurship and Innovation*, 19(2), 90–99.

Abstract: There is inadequate literature examining, and illustrating, the integration of play and business events and how this facilitates entrepreneurial opportunities. Business events are distinct from the patterns of ordinary life and increasingly offer participants an 'invitation to play', encouraging socialization and trust. This paper examines the role of play in the design of business events and how this can enable entrepreneurial outcomes. Through examination of diverse, but related, literature and three contrasting, empirically based case studies, this paper illustrates how event creators take an increasingly entrepreneurial approach.

Intrapreneurship

Within organizations 'intrapreneurship' can be a valuable process, but it usually has to be fostered. Can a whole organization, or a group within, really behave as if they were private entrepreneurs? The object would be to encourage innovation in particular, hopefully leading to higher profits or other forms of corporate effectiveness. In this context it is possible to establish new events, or bid on them, within a government or tourist agency. Another application would be within an event production company that wants to stay ahead of the competition, or within a large corporation that sponsors or produces its own events.

Often it is necessary to set up specific intrapreneurial units to achieve these corporate goals, and such units need leadership. By nature, persons attracted to government and corporate employment might be lacking in those entrepreneurial traits necessary for innovation. Or at least they might lack experience in new venture creation. In such cases there is a serious risk of creating a culture clash!

Organizational culture

Culture in general is based on shared beliefs, values, practices or attitudes, and it is a concept of importance to companies and other organizations. Schein (1985) defined organizational culture as:

> *A pattern of shared basic assumptions that the group learned as it solved its problems of external adaptation and internal integration, that has worked well enough to be considered valid and, therefore, to be taught to new members as the correct way you perceive, think, and feel in relation to those problems.*

In a strong cultural context, everyone works together towards common goals because they share the vision and underlying values of the organization. This is where event founders have the greatest influence, in establishing the 'core values', but this unity of purpose can fade with time. In other organizations, recruitment, indoctrination and compulsory conformity to norms ensures that values are preserved, but at the cost of individual choice and expression. In both situations, if everyone thinks the same way – called 'groupthink' – there is a serious risk that innovation will be stifled.

According to Schein (1985), an observer can assess organizational culture by first identifying superficial but 'tangible attributes' such as facilities, rewards, dress and interactions. The 'professed culture' of an organization is reflected in its mission statements, codes of conduct, public statements, and the expressed values and attitudes of members. At the third and deepest level are an organization's 'tacit or unseen assumptions'. They can be unspoken rules, guiding behaviour and decisions in a taken-for-granted manner. The researcher or member might have to spend a lot of time within an organization to come to any conclusion about its deepest cultural values.

Hofstede (1980) demonstrated that there are national and regional cultural groupings that affect the behaviour of organizations. These five characteristics of culture can be influential in all organizations:

- 'power distance' – refers to the degree to which a society expects that some individuals wield larger amounts of power than others;

- 'uncertainty avoidance' – reflects the extent to which a society accepts uncertainty and risk; this is associated with entrepreneurship;

- 'individualism versus collectivism' – refers to the extent to which people are expected to act on their own versus being a loyal group member;

- 'masculinity versus femininity' – male values supposedly include competitiveness, assertiveness, ambition, and the accumulation of wealth and material possessions;

- 'long- versus short-term orientation' – describes the importance attached to the future (fostering stewardship and sustainable development) versus immediate profit or gratification.

There is no doubt that organizations evolve in terms of their culture, and this affects other management functions in profound ways. Getz (1993a) observed that festival organizations exhibited life-cycle dynamics, and that festival founders did shape their culture. Several festivals in Calgary were seen to have experienced cultural crises, such as changes in strategic direction, which occurred when founders were replaced by newcomers.

O'Toole and Mikolaitis (2002) emphasized the importance of understanding culture when producing corporate events. Such events have to 'fit' in terms of company values, goals, politics and style. But despite the importance of culture within mainstream management theory and practice, there have been few event-related studies published that even mention the concept.

Strategic event creation and public policy

Perhaps the most significant aspect of modern planned events is their elevation from the private, community and institutional domains to a formal incorporation into numerous public policy domains. Events of all kinds are being supported, created and bid on to meet diverse, strategic goals of society. Sharples *et al.* (2014, vii) in their book *Strategic Event Creation* stated:

> *Changes in the wider environment have triggered a new normal for event creation. Heightened attendee expectations, a keener focus upon the return required by funders and wider stakeholders, and, of course, an ever more competitive event marketplace. Couple these with CSR, social media, globalisation and technology and the reasons event creation is now a strategic and multilayered responsibility are clear.*

This has several important implications related to leadership, culture and management. For example, those who plan and produce events are often dealing with a single client but are held accountable to a very wide group of stakeholders. This fact also applies to many events produced for corporations and non-profit societies.

Researchers have examined various policy domains that lead to strategic creation, subsidy or facilitation of planned events and their venues. Strategic tourism roles have been well explored (e.g. Stokes 2008). Swart (2005) argued for strategic planning of sport-event tourism in South Africa. Presenza and Sheehan (2013) commented on the strategic value of a portfolio of sport events in destination development, and it is inevitable that portfolios and populations of events are strategically planned in the future.

Mules (1993) pointed out the roles of events in urban renewal strategies, a theme which has since been expanded to include urban economic and social revitalization and repositioning from a branding perspective (e.g. Duignan 2013). Pugh and Wood (2004) examined multiple reasons for event support in London, including place marketing, pride, and economic development. Cultural development is also a well-explored theme, particularly in the context of cities of culture (Richards 2007a; Richards and Palmer 2010). While in many countries local and regional/state governments and their agencies have been at the forefront, national-level policies and strategies related to events cannot be ignored. Khodr (2012) scrutinized political reasons for Qatar's event strategy, concluding that explanatory factors include economic sustainability and diversification, tourism, and social development strategies; these factors can be viewed in the light of globalization and modernization trends. Houlihan *et al.* (2015) identify reasons why countries host major sport events, including: a desire for increased legitimacy and positive image; boosting sport participation and competitiveness; being a catalyst for urban economic regeneration; economic modernization; allowing for diplomatic initiatives connected to international relations; nation and city identity-building and branding; and fostering social integration.

Resources utilized by events are often heavily competed for, by groups with many legitimate and appealing claims about their cultural, social, economic or environmental benefits. Therefore, the allocation of public resources (including subsidies) to events generally requires their organizers and producers to explicitly justify their public benefits. Those who produce events that are at least partially in the public domain have a far greater planning, control and evaluation challenge than those who produce small, private events. Professionalism and the credentialing of event managers are increasingly demanded by funding agencies because of the need for open, public accountability and for liability reasons. Finally, the sustainability of periodic events is of public interest and is directly linked to specific policies on funding, regulations, subsidies, facility development, etc.

Organizational and inter-organizational behaviour

Organizations are social groups, and therefore sociology and social psychology have made substantial theoretical contributions to our understanding of how they function and change. Microeconomics is also relevant, pertaining especially to how firms acquire and utilize resources. In the research literature, little attention has been paid to event organizations, although some progress has been made in examining events in the context of collaboration and stakeholder management, and regarding human resources and especially volunteers. Ziakas and Costa (2010b) employed network analysis to examine the inter-organizational patterns that shape a host community's capacity to capitalize on its event portfolio. This method allows for the identification of linkages, both strong and weak, central organizations and the nature of interactions. These researchers believe that analysis of inter-institutional networks can suggest a community's capacity for building and managing an event portfolio, and can be used as a strategic tool.

Ownership, governance and organizational structure

There are three generic ownership, or legal, models found in the events world:

1 private, for-profit companies that produce events;
2 government agencies (such as parks and recreation, sport or arts and culture) that produce or facilitate events; and
3 the large not-for-profit sector that includes clubs, charities and event-specific organizations like festival societies.

Andersson and Getz (2009) systematically compared festivals in four countries in terms of their ownership, governance, structure and content. They concluded that although the festivals offered a similar product and had similar mandates, they differed considerably in terms of revenue sources, cost structure, use of volunteers, corporate sponsorship, and decision-making. These differences are potentially important to destinations that view festivals as attractions and use them in place marketing.

There has been little research published on the relative advantages or problems associated with these ownership types, or the business models they follow to provide their 'products' and 'services'. One important question to be addressed is whether or not they are substitutable. For example, in China and other countries, local authorities are the dominant producers of festivals and other events. Can they create private or not-for-profit organizations to take over from the public sector? Clearly legal and cultural constraints exist, especially in societies without a strong volunteering or entrepreneurial tradition.

'Governance' is a large issue. In for-profit companies, there are owners and employees, so the question of who runs the business is generally clear. In government agencies there can be a confusing and stifling bureaucracy to deal with. Within not-for-profit societies, the relationships between boards of directors and professional staff have to be sorted out. Who sits on the board is a major issue, especially in relation to involving key stakeholders. In all-volunteer events, governance and coordination present special challenges, and the organizations can be faced with dissenting opinions within or takeover attempts by organized, external interest groups. Dredge and Whitford (2011) viewed governance as a form of public/private policy-making that requires stakeholders to get together for discussion and to take action to achieve common goals. This approach embodies the notion of collaboration and the process of consensus-building. Stakeholder management, discussed later, is an essential element in this kind of governance.

This entire area of organizational structure and coordination (both internal and external) has largely been untouched by event researchers, although plenty of advice is available through professional associations and books written by experts. It links closely to other topics covered in this chapter, including decision-making and planning. The second level of concern is organizational structure, which has a direct bearing on stakeholder relationships, internal coordination and control. A number of typical structures are illustrated and discussed in Getz (2005), including single and multi-organizational structures. Festivals are often produced by clubs, internally, and by stand-alone not-for-profit societies, but it is also common to find different organizations cooperating to produce events. As well, sport events are frequently produced through formal links between governing bodies and local organizing committees.

Open-system theory and the learning organization

No organization can exist independently of its environment, indeed it has to be 'open' to obtain resources. Its impacts (especially for events) are also felt by the community and environment, giving rise to many stakeholder claims. There is a 'general environment' in which global forces have to be considered through environmental and future scanning, and a 'community context' which includes most event stakeholders and the origin of most 'inputs' (information, support and resources). The 'internal environment' is the organization that produces the event, and all its management systems. In this conceptualization (see Figure 9.2), the event (its theme, programme, facilitated experiences) is a 'transforming process' intended to achieve specific desired outcomes. There can also be unintended 'outcomes', and 'externalities' – like pollution – that are not normally accounted for by the event organizers. However, multiple stakeholders will evaluate the event and its organization, and this process is labelled 'external evaluation'. The 'internal evaluation' process is the task of managers or owners who have to determine if they are meeting their goals (i.e. their effectiveness) and how efficiently they are utilizing their resources. Evaluation and feedback should influence future decision-making through strategic planning.

'Open-system diagnostics' involves using this model to identify problems and to improve both efficiency and effectiveness. 'Effectiveness' means the degree to which goals are obtained or the organization fulfils its mandate. Use of the model helps in identifying how the mandate and goals are externally driven by various stakeholders and environmental forces, and how transforming processes are directed towards achieving those goals. Evaluation systems have to be directed towards identifying goal attainment, although the 'goal-free evaluation' approach sometimes has benefits. 'Efficiency' refers to how well resources are used to generate the desired outcomes. The model suggests ways to improve the flow and use of resources, to

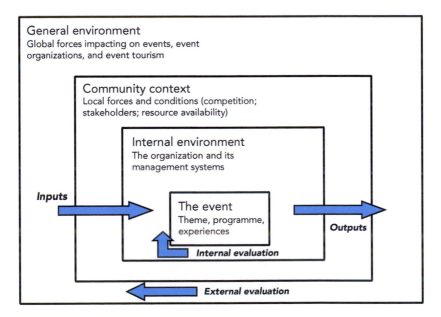

Figure 9.2 Open-system model of event management

Source: Adapted from Getz and Frisby (1998).

cut costs (such as heavy administration costs) and to evaluate outcomes achieved in terms of resources required (i.e. measures of costs and benefits). 'Outcome', 'output', 'impacts' and 'consequences' are often used synonymously. However, the term 'output' is usually reserved for a mechanical or manufacturing process. Elsewhere, we use the term 'impact' in a different sense, stressing that impacts are often perceived or felt in a subjective way.

How do organizations 'learn' and retain memory? Senge (1990: 3) found the 'learning organization' is one in which 'people continuously expand their capacity to create the results they truly desire, where new and expansive patterns of thinking are nurtured, where collective aspiration is set free, and where people are continually learning to learn together' (also see Senge *et al.* 1994). In part, this is a reflection of organizational culture, and in part it can be facilitated through constant research, evaluation and reflection. The open-system model is a good starting point for structuring the learning process.

'Benchmarking' against other events is another way by which managers learn. To a degree, studying other events is both inevitable and good, but it can and does result in copying and standardization. Proper benchmarking looks at the ways successful organizations do things, in other words their processes or 'best practices'. Getz (1998a) studied the searching and sharing practices of festival organizers and classified them as being 'inward or outward-looking organizations'. Searching was either formal or informal in nature, and varied a lot in terms of space (local to international), substance (comparisons with similar festivals versus all events) and theoretical (education) versus experiential (learning through visits and conversations).

Organizational quality and standards

Any discussion of event programme or service quality has to include the 'quality' of the organization producing the event. The people producing events have to demonstrate professionalism and competency, trustworthiness and reliability. Policy on organizational quality is a direct reflection of culture and vision. It will have to cover organizational philosophy, ensure proper documentation in all the management systems, effectively engage all staff and volunteers, and take into account all outcomes. Bowdin and Church (2000) argued that quality programmes cost money, but the investment is quickly recovered by reducing waste and eliminating failures. Over time the costs of auditing and evaluation decline.

Standards prepared for the meetings industry have been developed. These are called MBECS and they have been reviewed by Cecil *et al.* (2013). Professional standards of this kind provide the basis for curriculum design and for continuous learning. They do not (like EMBOK (Event Management Body of Knowledge) and other body-of-knowledge systems) actually provide the knowledge or skills, as that role falls to educators and occurs through real-life experience.

The ISO 20121 standards for 'Sustainable Events Management' (download at www.iso.org) fall into this category as they lay out procedures for event organizations to follow in pursuit of a 'triple-bottom-line' approach to sustainability. These types of standards are intended to lead to improved organization and planning, with the aim of preventing or ameliorating negative impacts and maximizing desired outcomes. They typically include the following:

- designing a sustainability policy;
- issue identification and evaluation;
- stakeholder identification and engagement;
- objectives, targets and plans;
- performance against principles of sustainable development;
- operational controls;
- competence and training;

- supply chain management;
- communication;
- monitoring and measurement;
- corrective and preventive action;
- management system audits;
- management review.

Getz (2018) detailed the establishment of permanent evaluation systems like the Balanced Scorecard and the Event Compass as examples where the focus is on goal-oriented evaluation, the establishment of key performance indicators and evaluation methods.

Evolution, bureaucratization and institutionalization

Organizations have to be created, as in the establishment of a legal corporation or not-for-profit society, or they evolve from informal organizations. For example, many professionally managed festivals and events have evolved from club-produced events. Once established, there can be an evolution towards greater 'formality', emergence of leadership and increasing 'professionalization' (in terms of hiring professional staff and professional conduct) and 'bureaucratization' including formal committee systems and strategic planning (Katz 1981). Frisby and Getz (1989) modelled this hypothetical evolution for festivals, noting that at each evolutionary stage there was a risk of having to return to the previous stage owing to failure or loss of resources. They also suggested that in cities, with larger populations and presumably more resources to draw on, festivals were more likely to professionalize.

Richards and Ryan (2004) adapted the Frisby and Getz (1989) model by suggesting three axes: (1) 'informal/grassroots resource base'; (2) 'organizational age'; and (3) 'organized public and private sector involvement'. They argued (ibid.: 96) that 'being a grassroots event does not preclude the adoption of a formal or professional approach to event organisation'. Professionalism, they said, can be externally imposed on an event organization. Schein's (1985) conceptualization of the evolution of organizational culture, argued that various crises are likely to occur as the organization evolves, linked to leadership changes and value conflicts, particularly as sub-cultures emerge. Richards and Ryan (2004) agreed that various crises will accompany event maturation. In their case study the issues or crises stemmed from the need to achieve financial stability, addressing the festival's cultural orientation and significance, gender issues, the increasing roles of media and sponsors, the representations of groups and regions, and tensions between competitive and performative orientations.

Why do some events, like the Calgary Stampede (profiled in Getz 1993b, 1997 and 2005), become permanent institutions in their communities? Can all events aspire to this status, and should they? One meaning of the word 'institution' is that of 'constraints or rules that induce stability in human interaction' (Voss 2001). These arise because societies face recurrent problems, so that when we call an organization an 'institution', we are saying that it exists to deal with a fundamental – or at least important – social need (including cultural and economic needs). Since not all people can be directly involved in creating institutions, a set of actors, or stakeholders, has to decide on – or establish through repeated interactions or interdependencies – the rules or the organizations to deal with major social problems. Stability in these institutions has direct benefit to the stakeholders, or society as a whole, and should ideally generate increased efficiency in resource use.

The study of institutions is very well established. Selznick (1957) distinguished between institutions as tools to accomplish specific tasks, and institutions to which people formed commitments. Emile Durkheim (as reported in Traugott 1978) argued that sociological analysis should discover the causes, mechanisms and effects of institutions on societal life. Essentially, institutions regularize social life, and may foster cooperation and increase efficiency. Applicable to many festivals, it can also be said that institutions are like 'public goods' in that all members of society may benefit from them, whether or not they contribute to their establishment and upkeep. Coleman (1988, 1990) believed that institutions are part of what is often called 'social capital'. An anthropological perspective (Sahlins 1976) suggests that cultural institutions mainly serve symbolic purposes. Another way of looking at institutions is through the lens of evolutionary game theory. Young (1998) showed that certain institutions arise as equilibria in games played by members of a population of agents who recurrently interact. This ties institutional theory directly to stakeholder and network theory. As well, since powerful agents or special interest groups might create and support institutions, there is a need to take a political science and welfarist approach to their study.

A central focus of the 'old' study of institutions is the evolving relationship between an organization and its environment, which of course includes all its stakeholder interactions. 'New institutionalism', according to Heimer (2001), is an outcome of organizational sociology. It focuses on the process (symbolic reasons are emphasized) by which a practice or structure is diffused, becomes a prerequisite for legitimacy (among key stakeholders), is taken for granted and is expected.

By definition, therefore, an event that becomes an 'institution' exists with a specific mandate or purpose, is permanent, and fulfils an important social role or solves social problems. A community cannot do without its institutions, and when threatened they will receive strong support; if they disappear, others will have to be created to carry on their functions. Very few events fit these criteria, yet recent research involving a survey of festivals in Sweden suggests that many festival managers actually believe their event to be an 'institution' (Getz and Andersson 2008).

Figure 9.3 suggests the process by which an event (as a permanent organization) might evolve or strategically become a permanent institution in its community. The key process is transitioning from an internal to an external orientation, as many events – especially in their early years – are very focused on their internal processes and stakeholders. Relationships with external stakeholders will probably increase in number and complexity over time, and the most important of them can be brought into legal or moral

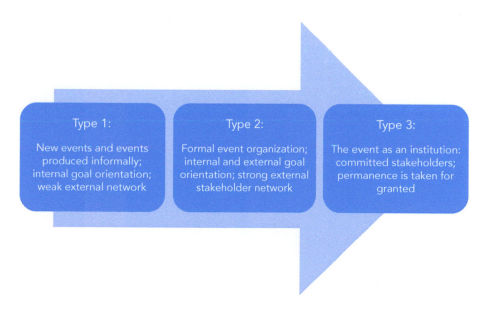

Figure 9.3 Hypothetical institutionalization process for events

Source: Adapted from Getz and Andersson (2008).

'ownership' (through share offerings or board directorships) or other forms of long-term partnership, including sponsorship.

It appears that increasing dependency on committed stakeholders is a large part of becoming an institution. In other words, independence might have to be sacrificed for sustainability. The Stampede reflects this evolution, with the City of Calgary owning the land, having a permanent representative on the Stampede board, and assisting the Stampede in its ongoing development plans.

One-time versus permanent event organizations

There are major differences between permanent event organizations, such as festival societies that produce annual events, and one-time organizations that have to be decommissioned when the event is over. Little attention has been paid to the one-time event organization from a theoretical or even a comparative perspective. Typically established for major sport events or world's fairs, the one-time event organization has to engage in project planning and apply a project management organizational model. One of the unique aspects of permanent event organizations is their 'pulsating' nature (Hanlon and Cuskelly 2002). They need a permanent, small core of volunteers and professionals, but must be able to substantially expand their staff and volunteer force to produce the event. This is examined later in the Human Resources section.

Inter-organizational behaviour and stakeholder management

The need for resources requires that organizations engage with individuals (like customers) and with other organizations. Theories of resource dependency, population ecology, collaboration, network and stakeholder theory are powerful when trying to explain external relationships. Another look at stakeholder theory is warranted here, as some pertinent research has been completed regarding events. Getz *et al.* (2007) described and classified external festival stakeholders based on case studies from Sweden and Calgary. Figure 9.4 shows the resulting conceptualization. The various categories are not mutually

Figure 9.4 Major stakeholder types and roles in festival networks

Source: Adapted from Getz *et al.* (2007).

exclusive, and indeed the research showed clearly that some stakeholders have multiple roles. For example, city government is often simultaneously a 'facilitator' (giving grants and other resources), 'co-producer' (sharing staff and venues), 'owner/controller' (being on the board of directors) and 'regulator', which can make its event-related policies confusing or contradictory.

'Suppliers and venues' are often brought into the festival organization as sponsors; this is generally recognized as being a good strategy for reducing dependency and costs. 'Allies and collaborators' might include marketing partnerships with tourism or the collaborative work of professional and affinity groups. How these stakeholders wield power and negotiate the goals and strategies of the event can be referred to as a 'political market square' (Larson and Wikstrom 2001; Larson 2002; 2009b).

Van Niekerk and Getz (2019) explain stakeholder theory and give details on its applications to event management and event tourism. In their model 'A blended strategy matrix for stakeholder management' they draw upon the seminal work of Savage *et al.* (1991) and others to emphasize the desirability of fostering relationships with potential collaborators as well as identifying and developing appropriate strategies for those external agencies with the power to threaten events.

9.2 RESEARCH NOTE ON COLLABORATION

Schofield, P., Crowther, P., Jago, L., Heeley, J. and Taylor, S. (2018). Collaborative innovation: Catalyst for a destination's event success. *International Journal of Contemporary Hospitality Management*, 30(6), 2499–2516.

Abstract (excerpts): This paper aims to contribute to theory concerning collaborative innovation through stakeholder engagement with reference to Glasgow City Marketing Bureau's (GCMB's) management strategies, which represent UK best practice in events procurement, leveraging and destination branding. GCMB's success results from long-term, extensive, collaborative engagement, a unique institutional structure and sustained political and financial support through to transformational leadership, strategic event selection and targeted marketing through 'earned' distribution channels.

Corporate social responsibility (CSR) and a social licence to operate

Powerful event owners and their backers can usually achieve what they want through the complicity of political and industry collaborators, often resulting in a complete absence of meaningful community input, and, in the worst cases, the actual suppression of dissent. This runs counter to the principles of CSR, in which corporations (including events) should seek a licence to operate from the affected community. For permanent events, this is a matter of stakeholder inclusion and becoming an institution, whereas for one-time events it is a risky proposition.

Planning and decision-making

Are leaders and managers 'rational' when it comes to making decisions? Surely the whole emphasis on planning and research is intended to produce rational decisions that achieve goals, yet Bramwell (1997) concluded that for mega events, there was little evidence of a rigorous application of the full planning cycle as advocated in planning texts. Laybourn (2004) explored theory on decision-making and applied it to the events sector. She found that the generic literature supports the contention that decision-makers are not naturally rational! They tend to use simplifying short-cuts called 'heuristics'. In particular, potential negative impacts are commonly underestimated, which has serious implications for risk assessment and management at events. When people stand to gain from a decision they tend to be more cautious than when they stand to take a loss. And of course everyone notices when something goes wrong, whereas competency and success might be ignored.

Current decisions are strongly influenced by previous decisions, especially when a lot of money has been invested, leading to 'entrapment'. There is a natural tendency to want to recover 'sunk costs' (i.e. money already spent) and maximize return on investments made. This can help explain why risky decisions are made, and the frequent pursuit of losing courses of action, despite obvious and compelling arguments to the contrary. There are always costs of withdrawal to consider, but perhaps more important is 'losing face'.

Laybourn also emphasized that decision-making is affected by personality, perceptions, emotions and moods, social factors, experience, the cost of information, time constraints and gender. There are many constraints on perfect knowledge and perfect judgement, so people should be trained in effective decision-making. A variety of techniques can be used to aid decision-making, including the 'decision tree', or mathematical modelling as found in operations research and management science. But do event planners and managers use them?

Planning theory

'Rational planning' is always future oriented, involving a vision, the setting of goals, consideration of alternative courses of action and their potential consequences, the formulation and implementation of strategies and actions to realize goals, and continuous evaluation and feedback in order to improve the system. It is a process – it is continuously evolving and hopefully learning from past mistakes. Planning is always political, especially when public agencies or public money are involved, but even within organizations 'politics' (that is, the resolution of competing claims and goals) is always a factor.

Not everyone believes in or practises rational planning (for general reviews of planning theory and practice see Mandelbaum *et al.* 1996; Sandercock 1998; Campbell and Fanstein 2003). 'Muddling through' and 'incrementalism' are alternative approaches to managing organizations and events, although few professionals would admit to being 'muddlers'. 'Incrementalism', that is, developing or progressing slowly, in measured steps, is a defensible approach when uncertainty or complexity is high. It does not attempt to be comprehensive, but attacks problems and policy issues with precision instruments rather than broad strategies. It is also closely connected to the notion of a 'political market square', in which decisions are made through bargaining and the exercise of power among all the stakeholders, rather than by professional planners or technocrats. 'Collaborative' or 'consensus-building processes' are similarly intended to involve all parties and points of view, but with the emphasis on formal issue identification and conflict resolution. It is arguable, however, whether rational planning or incrementalism is more democratic or effective.

'Advocacy' is another approach to planning, policy and decision-making that might have relevance to the events sector. Advocacy is based on the premise that disadvantaged and marginalized groups in society are normally left out of planning and policy-making and therefore their interests must be represented by others. To the degree that citizen involvement or 'community-based planning' works, advocacy should not be needed, but that is a seldom-achieved ideal.

Providing opportunities (i.e. events) for a diverse range of business and leisure interests is another approach. In a commercial context it means that companies and organizations respond to expressed demand or felt needs and the government does not intervene. For public agencies it means ensuring that there are sufficient numbers and types of events to please most segments of the population. There is no published evidence that this is part of any government policy, although it is a logical implication of taking a whole-population approach. More likely is the provision of festivals and events for 'deprived' segments of the population (especially those with low incomes) and in areas where better social integration is desired. Those are both needs-based approaches.

In a stakeholder-based or community-development approach, facilities and services – and possibly events – would be planned according to democratic means, from the ground up. A bottom-up approach has the clear advantage of gaining political legitimacy and reflecting the perceived needs and priorities of the residents that are served. In many places this is done indirectly, and incompletely, through the actions of not-for-profit organizations who often claim to meet public needs and fill gaps in government services. Two major issues will arise in the bottom-up approach: where do the resources come from to meet stakeholder demands? And, are all residents and groups equally consulted and served?

From a free-market approach, it could also be suggested that public demand, manifested in ticket sales, should determine what events are held. This could be modified for event tourism as specific target segments are of high value, within the context of a strategic, portfolio approach to bidding on and creating events. That approach is unique to event tourism, as it follows from specific economic and place-marketing goals. If the desired outcomes can be expressed for specific events and whole populations, employing a triple-bottom-line approach, then events planning can devise strategies to achieve these goals. This leads to our later discussions of impact assessments and the difficulty of proving that events achieve certain benefits, or that benefits outweigh costs. The easiest case to prove is that of tourism attractiveness, as event tourists can generally be identified and their economic impacts estimated fairly accurately. Unfortunately, not all costs are considered in many impact studies. One goal, borrowed from leisure, sports and the arts that does make perfect sense for events planning, is that of achieving increases in public participation through the vehicle of providing and hosting events. If there are more participatory events that create leisure, sport and artistic opportunities, then we should see increased participation leading to other benefits. Less certain is the often-made claim that hosting spectator and mega events will generate increased participation. Events as a sector are not generally the subject of direct government planning, as they become subsumed under the headings of sport, arts/culture, leisure or business/trade. Tourism planning for events is at an immature stage in most countries and cities, remaining largely ad hoc and opportunistic.

Project planning and feasibility studies

Rooted in engineering, where it is a vital skill, project planning is applicable to all events – even those produced by permanent organizations that also do strategic planning. The basic nature of events is that they are defined by time (a limited duration) and their schedule is announced and usually fixed well in advance. This necessitates getting all the planning and preparations done according to a fixed and often tight schedule. According to O'Toole (2000), many event projects fail or overrun their budget and schedule, and perhaps this is due to poor planning or control systems.

'Feasibility studies' should ideally precede, or at least accompany, project planning. In a rational planning process, we do not commit to an event until we know it is affordable, desirable, environmentally sound, marketable and manageable. All too often, however, events are bid on and planned without full feasibility studies or cost and benefit forecasts, generally arising from corporate and political influences rather than public input.

O'Toole (2011) and O'Toole and Mikolaitis (2002) examine the specific tools employed in project planning, including project scoping, work breakdown and task analysis, costing, risk analysis, and scheduling and controlling with critical paths. Management of time is critical, and often time pressures lead to modifications or political actions to get the job done. A full life-cycle approach is recommended, including how to wind up the event and deal with the legacy. Far too little attention is given to feasibility within the context of portfolios and populations of events. While a single event can be rationally assessed as to costs and impacts, its effects on other events are harder to evaluate. Long-term feasibility and sustainability of all events presents quite different issues from single-event feasibility.

Business planning

How to prepare and use a business plan for events are outlined in Getz (2005), and Tassiopoulos (2011) explores detailed business planning for new ventures. Unfortunately, the business plan is often overlooked or produced only for show. It is a convenient and useful way to summarize the event concept, its feasibility in financial and marketing terms, and its management. At the core of every business plan is a believable budget, with costs fully estimated and revenues realistically forecast. It is the budget, or financial feasibility, that sinks many events. 'Costs' are viewed as commitments, and the money is spent in preparation for the event. However, 'revenue' forecasts contain a lot of wishful thinking or just plain guesswork. So money gets spent but projected income does not materialize, resulting in shortfalls, debt and ultimately failure. Cash-flow projections and management are also vital components in business plans. Many events have to spend up-front, but earn most of their revenue only at the time of the event through sales – or even afterwards when grants come in.

Strategic planning

Although there is no real evidence to support the claim that strategic planning results in better events or more sustainable organizations, it seems inconceivable that event producers would not want to have a vision, set goals and make strategies for the long term. One-time events also need goals and a plan, and if the planning period is measured in years, it will have strategic elements built in. What separates strategic planning from project planning, in theory, is first of all the principle of 'adaptability'. A project usually has a fixed goal, an event with known form, timing and programme – like a sport competition or exhibition. But permanent events and their organizations have to adapt to changes in their environment – their goals are changeable, and the events evolve. Being a 'learning organization' improves adaptability. Strong external stakeholder relationships help to ensure permanence and diverse inputs. The mandate or mission of the organization needs to be periodically reviewed, leading to a re-assessment of goals and strategies.

'Strategy' is the second main difference, in the sense that a project has a single outcome (the event) whereas strategy to implement goals or fulfil a mandate can evolve and be multidimensional. Perhaps goals can be achieved by changing, terminating or replacing the event. A 'strategy' is defined as an integrated set of policies, programmes and actions intended to fulfil the organization's mandate, realize its vision and achieve its goals.

In contrast to rationally planned strategies, 'emergent strategy' just happens as a consequence of the many decisions taken or untaken, and is often only realized in hindsight. For example, a manager might say 'it was not until years later that I could identify our strategy as one of accommodating and integrating key stakeholders, bringing them in as partners; it just seemed the right way to develop'. Research is fundamental to the process of strategic planning, including 'environmental and future scanning' (forces and trends), 'situation analysis' (where we are, our current situation), stakeholder input and issues identification, and market and consumer research (including strengths, weaknesses, opportunities and threats relative to competitors). Specific outputs in the process typically include a vision statement, goals, strategies, action or implementation plan (actions, costs, schedule and responsibilities defined) and a marketing/communications plan.

Operations and logistics

'Operations' refers to all those systems that must be in place and the actions that have to be taken to produce the event. Clearly these have to be planned well in advance, unless you are doing a 'flash mob'. Operations can also be thought of as the day-to-day decisions and actions within the event organization or company, as opposed to strategic and business-level actions. Operations and logistics generally apply to three subsystems, namely:

1 customer-oriented (traffic, queuing, ticketing, information, essential services, comfort and safety, crowd management);
2 supplier oriented (utilities, infrastructure, technical services, security systems);
3 communications (equipment, procedures, accreditation, hosting the media, scheduling).

Tum *et al.* (2006) provides a more comprehensive event operations model. Its main components are the analysis stage (environmental scanning and situational analysis), the operations planning process – both strategic and detailed – implementation and delivery, and performance evaluation. The basic theory and methods come from 'operations management' and from project planning and management. Tum *et al.* (2006) use the concept of 'transforming processes' (as in our open-systems management model) to describe operations. Resources and other inputs are converted into the desired outputs, namely the event or other services and products. Operations in this context are influenced by four major event characteristics:

1 size and volume of output (how many guests, how many transactions?);
2 complexity and variety of services/products offered to the consumer (size of the site, complexity of the programme);
3 uncertainty (of attendance, costs, time, technical requirements);
4 interactions (extent and nature of contacts between guests and staff).

Logistics

Logistics is how to move people, goods and equipment (even money and tickets) to the right place at the right time. The event producer could take the approach of trying to schedule it all to perfection, as in 'just-in-time delivery', or simply get everything and everyone together at one place at one time and then try to sort it out. Obviously, this latter approach could prove chaotic.

People movement

There has to be a plan for traffic and parking, including policing and security. Site planning takes into account accessibility, flow and emergency evacuation. Queuing and service provision efficiency are related issues. Some event production companies also engage in 'destination management', which in terms of logistics involves greeting and transporting arriving guests/participants, getting them from place to place, and even providing tours and entertainment. Registration and ticketing are key elements; as these often cause bottlenecks, it's best to do them in advance, electronically. Security can be a nightmare if everybody has to be searched, and preventing a crowd-rush to the stage is always necessary.

Queuing theory

For many events, especially meetings and sport competitions, everyone arrives and leaves at roughly the same time, often resulting in traffic congestion and long line-ups. To the extent that arrivals and departures can be staggered, congestion can be reduced. 'Batch' arrivals and departures can be utilized to ease the problem, such as by assembling guests at various external points and then bringing them to the venue in groups. Reservation systems, specifying times and places for guests, are an alternative solution.

How to manage people in queues or line-ups is another management challenge. Theme parks have become skilled at both the psychological and physical management of queues, including offering people the option of paying extra to avoid them! One needs to consider the rate of arrivals and average service time (e.g. how fast are people arriving and how long does it take to get them through the gates?). The resultant measure of 'customer intensity' shows the probability of queuing and queue lengthening.

Critical path analysis

Critical path analysis is the best way to schedule complex projects and event programmes. It starts with the breakdown of the work and task analysis, involves staffing and costing estimates, and works backwards from the event date or programme start time to demonstrate the fastest possible path to getting the necessary tasks accomplished. Detailed examples are provided in Getz (2005) and Tum *et al.* (2006).

Procurement and supply chain management

Many goods and services (including information) have to be purchased or subcontracted, which is 'procurement'. The 'supply chain' refers to how needed information, goods and services flow through the event system, corresponding to the inputs, transforming processes and outputs in the open-systems model. For events, a failure in the supply chain could mean cancellation, programme reduction or quality problems.

Supply chains should be managed to achieve a number of objectives:

- maximize efficiency (no waste or time delays; getting only what was ordered);
- ensure quality (through setting standards and inspections);
- minimize costs (e.g. through competitive bidding);
- bring suppliers into the event as sponsors or partners;
- ensure security (theft protection) and safety;
- benefit the host community (source locally);
- ensure a green event, by requiring all suppliers to conform to environmental management standards.

A key decision for any organization is that of outsourcing versus internal supply. It might look attractive to avoid external supply costs by doing it yourself, but that strategy entails many potential costs and risks. Tum *et al.* (2006: 123) provided an illustration of the 'chain of decisions and decision points' associated with supply chain management. Clearly the process requires a technical knowledge of the event's needs as well as how to work with suppliers.

Capacity management

How much is needed: of food, water, tents, car parking, staff? Being able to forecast attendance and other needs is critical to supply management. It is a very high-risk strategy to allow unlimited access to an event and then try to match supplies to the actual demand. The safer alternative is to establish a 'design capacity', then restrict attendance to numbers that can be accommodated (with reference to both physical capacity and desired level of service quality). Modularization of an event can be used to combine these strategies; set design capacities for critical elements (such as concerts); and allow open attendance at others (e.g. parades).

How long does it take to sell tickets, get people through security, for customers to buy food or to use the toilets? Efficiency studies are often needed to identify bottlenecks and management solutions. Capacity can often be increased, and wait times reduced, by either physical redesign, changes in staffing, or the addition or deletion of certain services within the site or venue.

One of the severe challenges facing many event producers is the fact that if tickets are not sold (for concerts and dinners), the revenue is lost. In technical terms, this kind of capacity cannot be stored, it is 'perishable'. That is why the practice of revenue or yield management is required.

Marketing and communications

Although the practice of marketing is often reduced to, or confused with, advertising and sales, it is better described as the management of the interface (or 'exchange relationships') between an organization and its stakeholders, in pursuit of achieving the organization's goals. The evolution of marketing theory has led to an emphasis on value co-creation within service-dominant logic. Marketing requires research to gain understanding of customers' and other stakeholders' needs, motives and choices, the effectiveness of communications, and the influences of price and supply. Customers are not the only group that requires relationship management – that task starts internally with staff and volunteers and extends externally through 'facilitators' and 'regulators'. The essence of 'exchange relationships' is that the organization offers something of value that others are willing to buy or support; it has to be a voluntary and mutually beneficial process. In our case, events are offered as an experience for consumers to buy or guests to enjoy (i.e. this is a service proposition), a product to be delivered to clients, or a marketing tool for corporations.

The marketing concept: customer versus product orientation

The classic 'marketing' concept embodies the principle of 'customer orientation', which means the organization develops events that are in demand by clearly defined customers or clients. In contrast, a product orientation is often found in the events sector, particularly in the arts, where the event is presented as a work of art that has value on its own, regardless of economic demand or support. Art event producers do not necessarily have to sell their concepts to paying customers, but they do have to 'sell' to public grant-giving agencies and corporate sponsors.

We should add two provisos to customer-orientation attitudes. The first is to argue that the customer is not always right, and event producers should not merely provide the entertainment and spectacle that will generate the highest profit or please the most vocal critics. Customers do need to be educated, and many will be happy to have their tastes modified, their minds stimulated, or their emotions uplifted. And even if customers are happy to pay for unsafe or environmentally destructive events, that is not an adequate reason to provide them.

A second modification is that many events exist in the realm of public policy and do not need to respond only to market forces. But they do need to conduct marketing in the form of relationship management. Mayfield and Crompton (1995) studied the marketing orientation of festivals in Texas, revealing substantial differences. Interestingly, older events tended to have less of a marketing orientation, perhaps reflecting complacency or lack of professionalism compared to younger organizations. A related study was completed by Mehmetoglu and Ellingsen (2005), with the conclusion that there were multiple reasons why none of the small Norwegian festivals in their sample demonstrated a full marketing orientation.

The marketing mix

The 'marketing mix' consists of the elements that can be managed to build and sustain those essential stakeholder relationships. The usual 4 Ps are product, price, place and promotion, whereas the '8 Ps' advocated by of Morrison (1995) cover more ground. We have grouped them into 'experiential' and 'facilitating elements'. The 'product' is in fact the event experience, and marketers have to learn a lot more about experiential marketing through research and theory-building.

The other marketing mix elements that directly affect the experience are 'place' (site, venue or setting), 'programming' (including the theme) and 'people' (interactions among staff, volunteers, guests, participants). Facilitating components consist of 'partnerships', 'promotions' (i.e. communications), 'packaging' (including distribution channels), and 'price'. Partnerships refer to all the external stakeholder relationships that have to be managed.

Packaging, especially in the context of event tourism, can sometimes be thought of as a 'product'. That is because the tourist often prefers to buy travel, accommodation and events all at once. Distribution is the process of communicating with customers and selling the products, including by means of the Internet, social media, in-person sales, and packages sold through agents. Finally, 'price' is a facilitating component because it determines who can, or wants to, make the purchase. Price can also affect the experience in the sense that perceived value for money impacts on a consumer's overall satisfaction.

The communications mix (integrated marketing communications)

Masterman and Wood (2006) not only deal with the traditional 'communications mix' by which the event reaches its targets, but also examine how events are used as communications tools. They emphasize 'integrated marketing communications' (IMC), which has been advanced in response to perceived failures of mass media, new media options and demands from clients for demonstrating the return on investment from marketing efforts. IMC is highly targeted (both customer and multi-stakeholder oriented), combines all the communications tools for consistency and synergy, and stresses relationship and branding goals. Social media not only have an increasing role to play in the communications mix but in co-creation of the experience before, during and after events. Hudson and Hudson (2013), Hudson *et al.* (2015) and Gyimóthy and Larson (2015) have focused on social-media use in the marketing of events, while Devine *et al.* (2017) have provided a social-media strategy for dealing with an event-related crisis.

Research, evaluation and information management for event marketing

Wood (2004) outlined the main marketing information needs for events, starting with setting event objectives. Research and information are also needed in the context of environmental scanning, customer analysis (including segmentation and targeting, satisfaction and expectations), competitor analysis and positioning, tactical marketing decisions, impacts and strategic planning. The main research and data collection tools of event marketers include surveys, interviews, focus groups and observation. Attendance counts (or estimates) and evaluation of marketing effectiveness are important tasks.

Segmentation and target marketing

Segmentation is often tied to motivation studies and has generated a wealth of studies (e.g. Taylor and Shanka 2002; Oakes 2003). Basic variables used in market segmentation for events start with simple geography (market areas), demographics (age and gender) and socio-economics (income and class), and can proceed to more challenging variables including benefits sought (generic versus specific), consumption patterns (what people buy, how and where) and visitation patterns (repeat visits, loyalty, seasonality). Many studies have segmented event visitors on the basis of motivation, including Lee *et al.* (2004)

and Barbieri *et al.* (2008). Interesting variations on segmentation variables include Prentice and Anderson (2003) who segmented visitors to the Edinburgh Festival on the basis of 'tourism styles', which is similar to a benefits-sought approach. Seven clusters of 'consumption style' were identified, reflecting different interest levels in international or Scottish performing arts, and in the historic city.

Segmentation has been based on serious leisure (Mackellar 2009; 2013a), involvement (Robinson and Getz 2013), expenditure (Dixon *et al.* 2012), planned behaviour theory (Horng *et al.* 2013), how stakeholders segment event audiences (Tkaczynski 2013), music genre preferences (Kruger *et al.* 2011), skill and expertise in the context of recreation specialization (Lamont and Jenkins 2013), and leisure benefits (Lyu and Lee 2013). Kruger *et al.* (2018) reviewed the literature on motives-based segmentation and studied a nature-based event. Sharma and Nayak (2018) undertook an emotions-based approach to segment yoga tourists. Tasci *et al.* (2018) segmented sport tourists versus non-sport tourists on the basis of socio-demographic, psychographic and travel-behaviour variables. It should be kept in mind that segmentation is designed to aid marketing, but can also provide new insights on fundamental questions of need, motivation and benefits obtained.

Positioning, branding and co-branding

Although branding is a huge marketing topic, and has been studied in the context of event tourism and destinations (e.g. Chalip and Costa 2006; Chen 2012; Bodet and Lacassagne 2012), little work has been published on branding specific events, examples include art exhibitions (Camarero *et al.* 2010) and the perspective of exhibitors (Jin and Weber 2013). Mossberg and Getz (2006) used case studies to examine a number of concepts and issues involving festival branding. One of the standard approaches is to use a city's name, often in conjunction with specification of the festival genre, as in Calgary Children's Festival. Another common approach, at least in North America, is co-branding with a corporate sponsor including the selling of title rights (e.g. 'TD Canada Trust Calgary International Jazz Festival'). One conclusion of the Mossberg and Getz (2006) study was that festival managers were not fully applying branding theory to their events.

9.3 RESEARCH NOTE ON EVENT BRANDING

Suomi, K., Luonila, M. and Tähtinena, J. (2018). Ironic festival brand co-creation. *Journal of Business Research* (https://doi.org/10.1016/j.jbusres.2018.08.039).

Abstract: This paper embraces the daring use of ironic humor in brand co-creation in festival branding. Innovative branding is an aspiration in the growing festival business. This study explores a unique case: a festival that applies ironic humor in its brand co-creation despite the risks involved. The findings suggest that the use of ironic humor, when made inherent to a festival's brand identity, can increase stakeholders' attention to and awareness of the festival and attract positive media attention. Moreover, the use of ironic humor can prompt stakeholders on social media to share and co-create the festival's brand identity. The study contributes to the literature on festival brand co-creation by demonstrating the use of ironic humor to engage stakeholders in brand co-creation.

Resources and financial management

Little research has been conducted on events as businesses, or from a business and management perspective, so their comparative financial operations are little understood. Perhaps this is because so many events are in the public domain and not subject to normal business management principles, or because not-for-profit event organizations somehow believe they do not have to operate like a business. The basic facts, however, are that all events have to secure, manage and account for their resources, and that financial problems are the main source of business and event failure.

Sponsorship and other sources of revenue

Purely as a business venture, following the usual for-profit business model, events would have to sell products (i.e. merchandise) and services (i.e. admission fees for entertainment) that are in demand in order to generate sufficient revenue to survive, or sufficient profit to justify investment. But many other resources are actually relied upon, including grants and subsidies from public authorities, sponsorship revenue and in-kind support from private sponsors, and fundraising through many activities. For-profit event firms might have a more difficult time getting grants, but might actually have an advantage in obtaining commercial partners.

Sponsorship has received the greatest amount of attention from practitioners and researchers, undoubtedly as a reflection of its global importance in the events sector. It can best be defined in economic and marketing terms as an exchange relationship involving payments made to events by external organizations (these can and do include public agencies) or persons, for specific benefits provided by the events. Advice on event sponsorship can be found in Skinner and Rukavina (2003) and Getz (2005). The International Events Group specializes in seminars and publications on event sponsorship, including a legal guide to sponsorship. Most event associations have publications and hold seminars on sponsorship.

Catherwood and van Kirk (1992) commented on the growth of corporate sponsorship after the commercial success of the Los Angeles Olympic Games. Crompton (1993, 1995) reviewed reasons for sponsorship growth, and examined criteria used by corporations when deciding on what events to sponsor. Weppler and McCarville (1995) conducted research on how corporate decisions on event sponsorship were actually made. Wicks (1995) and Mount and Niro (1995) examined event sponsorship in small communities. In this environment, decisions are often made on the basis of community goodwill and civic duty.

There are numerous issues and risks associated with corporate sponsorship. Events have to worry about 'goal displacement', with the interests of commercial sponsors possibly taking over. Dependency on one or a few sponsors is potentially a problem. Sponsors face risks from 'ambush marketers' and a loss of goodwill if the event goes wrong for them. Indeed, it is a form of co-branding that impacts on both parties.

Research on the effectiveness of event sponsorship has been conducted by Kerstetter and Gitelson (1995) and Coughlan and Mules (2002), examining sponsorship recall among event patrons, revealing that it is not easy to obtain memorable results. The mainstream marketing literature has many more studies on effectiveness, benefits and risks – mostly from the sponsors' points of view. Increasing attention is being given to how sponsors evaluate the effectiveness of their investments in events. Sponsorship research has numerous perspectives including stakeholder management, strategic planning, organizational culture and its evolution, risk management, financial controls, marketing and communications, legal issues and branding. For example, Drengner et al. (2011) researched event-brand congruence, and Andersson et al. (2013) assessed strategies for events to acquire sponsorship revenue. There remains a need for research aimed at improving our understanding of the multidimensional effects of sponsorship in the events world. Maestas (2009) considered return on investment (ROI), return on objectives, media exposure analysis and market value analysis as methods in use. Ballouli et al. (2018) examined the effectiveness of activation through ancillary events to leverage mega events for sponsors.

9.4 RESEARCH NOTE ON EVENT LEVERAGING

Ballouli, K., Koesters, T. and Hall, T. (2018). Leverage and activation of sport sponsorship through music festivals. *Event Management*, 22, 123–133.

Abstract: Research on leverage and activation of sponsorship is an underexplored area in academia, one that is still in its infancy in the event management and sport marketing literature. Much of the existing analyses of sponsorship leverage do not clearly differentiate between activational and nonactivational leverage. It is now common practice for mega-event organizers to create and manage ancillary events for sponsors to leverage and activate sponsorships among attendees. One example is the Austin Fan Fest held each year during the week of the Formula 1 US Grand Prix. However, it remains unclear how leverage differs between main and ancillary events, and what the subsequent impact is on sport consumer behaviour. The purpose of the study was to examine whether sponsorship activation by Austin Fan Fest sponsors would have greater results for these sponsors than for Formula 1 sponsors that were limited to using nonactivational sponsorship (i.e. signage, promotions and public address) during the main event. Results show that activational leverage off site at Austin Fan Fest outperformed on-site nonactivational at the Formula 1 US Grand Prix, as surveyed respondents reported higher ratings on attitudes toward the sponsor, word of mouth, and purchase intentions.

Return on investment, return on experience and return on objectives

The professionals who plan and organize business events, corporations running their own marketing events, and other event planners, often justify the effort and expenditure through estimation of its return on investment (ROI). Phillips *et al.* (2008) deal explicitly with the needs of meeting professionals, as represented by MPI (Meeting Professionals International). Previously, it was adequate to merely document what the event programmed, and the activities undertaken by attendees, while customer or attendee satisfaction was a good-enough measure of value. Phillips *et al.* (2008) provide many measures of impact, not all of which are tangible or measurable in monetary terms. To get the necessary feedback requires detailed research and evaluation. The categories of research and data in their recommended process include the following, and are related to the Kirkpatrick and Kirkpatrick (2007) pyramid model for evaluating training effectiveness (as discussed and illustrated in Getz 2018, *Event Evaluation*).

- Inputs: what the event actually consists of (number of attendees, what they did, etc.);
- reaction and perceived value (were the attendees satisfied and how do they rate their experiences and the programme);
- learning (what did attendees learn);
- application and implementation (what was made of the gained/shared knowledge after the event);
- impact and consequences (effects of the learning on business performance);
- ROI (compares the monetary benefits to the costs of the meeting).

The Kirkpatrick model suggests that reactions to the event or training must be positive, then attitude and behaviour-change must occur before actual work practices are positively impacted. That requires evaluation to be implemented before, during and after business events. Applying this model or the MPI approach to ROI is not necessarily applicable to all events, as it focuses on the roles of events in organizational transformation and productivity. There is a potential problem when destinations and convention centres want more meetings and higher-spending, business-event tourists, and measure only economic impacts from the destination's perspective. They cannot ignore what the meeting organizers want, and should become partners in providing the data and analysis necessary to justify meetings.

ROI has different meanings to other event stakeholders. Tourism officials generally measure their return on investment from events as total economic impact for the destination (which often leads to exaggerations). In social or cultural policy fields, ROI is not usually used, but it could be measured by reference to specific outcomes like changes in awareness and attitude or behaviour.

Return on experience (ROE) is a related concept that can be applied in wider circumstances than training or business events, but it is definitely more challenging. The concept depends on transformational experience design, with goals and performance measures specified clearly, in advance. The essential problem is to predict how a given experience in cognitive, affective and behavioural terms will achieve the goals, and devising appropriate and valid methods and measures. This is where logic and theory-of-change models become necessary.

ROE is increasingly found in the business event sector, including corporate events aimed at team building and motivation, with the idea that a memorable social experience can have more impact than training – although the two approaches are complimentary. This movement can also be seen as a modification of traditional incentive events and travel where rewarding people for performance was the primary consideration. Return on objectives (ROO) links to both ROI and ROE. Rather than insist on a monetary ROI, various qualitative measures of effectiveness can be used. For example, a party aims to give pleasure, a festival to bring people together harmoniously to celebrate, and a participation sport event to challenge people athletically and contribute to their self-defined personal development. Measures of effectiveness start with the attendee/participant and can include simple metrics like satisfaction or more challenging measures of self-reported growth.

Resources and dependency

Theories of the firm were examined in Chapter 4, demonstrating the importance of having a competitive advantage in securing resources and other forms of capital. While it might appear to be desirable in all circumstance to avoid becoming dependent, some degree of dependency on committed stakeholders might actually be a wise strategy to pursue. Indeed, it seems to be a precondition to becoming a permanent institution.

The event as a business venture

Little research exists on events as business ventures, so our knowledge of microeconomics in the events sector is limited. The key question has to be: how effective are events at generating revenues and profits? Wanhill (2006) is one of only a few researchers to have examined event finances.

The study by Andersson and Getz (2007) on a single festival's costs and revenue management, and related issues, showed that strong stakeholders (particularly entertainment booking agents) could inflict higher costs on an event, while the event organizers had the potential to keep costs under control from weak stakeholders (i.e. where choices were available). A related issue is the fact that so many events are produced in the public (governmental) sector and by not-for-profit societies. To some extent they are isolated from market forces, or the normal laws of supply and demand. Government subsidies can support events, for the 'public good', that could not survive on their own. Not-for-profit organizations can sometimes continue to produce events even when in chronic debt because stakeholders, including sponsors, value what they do or trust them.

Revenue or yield management

McMahon-Beattie and Yeoman (2004) discussed revenue management for events. Similar to 'yield management', as practised by hotels and airlines, this financial management approach is suitable for events with a fixed and 'perishable' capacity (i.e. only so many tickets to sell, but if unsold the capacity is wasted) and predictable demand fluctuations (by day, week, hour). Using historical data on demand fluctuations, or forecasts, revenue managers adjust prices or make special offers to entice customers in what would otherwise be low-demand periods. This can affect programming and staffing as well. Season tickets, multi-entry passes, discounts for seniors or other groups, and various other pricing and promotion tactics have to be integrated with revenue management.

Controls and accountability

This is definitely a neglected area of research. Raj (2004) examined the human, or behavioural, aspects of financial management for events. This approach covers not only professionalism but also internal relationships and morale. It was stressed that 'budgeting' is not just financial planning; it is also designed to influence human behaviour and goal-setting. Barbato and Mio (2007) examined accounting practices and the development of management control at the Venice Biennale.

Human resource management

Human resource management for planned events includes the normal considerations of staffing common to all forms of organization, plus several unique challenges. There is the special importance of volunteers and external suppliers or contractors, and unique characteristics of events in terms of how they are governed; the need for project planning and management, and their fluctuating need for workers are special considerations. Lynn Van der Wagen (2006: preface) in the book *Human Resource Management for Events: Managing the Event Workforce*, emphasizes that: 'There is no more challenging environment for human resource management than the event business.' She shows how the challenges stem from a combination of the importance people assign to events, the nature of project planning and management, numerous stakeholders to consider, and the risks associated with every aspect of event production.

Events have unique human resource needs and challenges, especially because of their usual reliance on volunteers. 'Pulsating' event organizations have to manage resources quite differently from permanently staffed organizations. Planned event experiences are also often dependent on staff and volunteers for providing service quality as well as being part of the performance. Sometimes a lack of professionalism is an issue, especially where leadership and organization are informal.

How work is changing and what it means for event management

According to the Education Design Lab (www.edddesignlab.org) several major forces are evident. The first is 'job hopping', meaning that lifelong careers are a thing of the past and workers will have to be prepared to move on frequently. Most good jobs will require university degrees, and even with a degree, many existing job types will be replaced by machines and artificial intelligence. There are two basic personal skills that will always be important: *adaptability* (i.e. the capacity to change, such as working in new ways or for a new purpose, as required by one's environment) and *creativity* (the ability to create meaningful new ideas, to innovate, to solve problems 'outside the box'). Both of these capacities will be crucial for the event professionals of the future.

Management guru Hagel noted in the August 21, 2018, *Harvard Business Review* (online), the nature of work will likely undergo a profound transformation on two fronts:

- First, the machines will take over more and more of the routine tasks that defined work in a standardized, mass market product world.
- Second, the only way to create value in a more differentiated and rapidly changing product world will be to redefine work at a fundamental level to focus on distinctly human capabilities like curiosity, imagination, creativity, and emotional and social intelligence.

There is a very positive thread in Hagel's arguments:

> *We're generally going to see three different categories of work become more and more prominent in a rapidly changing economy. First, we will see more and more business for creators, people who can anticipate the rapidly evolving needs of individual customers and design and deliver creative and highly tailored products and services.*

Creators are those creating innovative new products and services, Hagel (2018) said. Coaches are 'trusted advisors' helping others to become better and faster at what they are doing. 'In a world of increasing performance pressure, those coaches are going to be hugely valuable'. Composers are those who compose experiences. As people get more affluent, they are hungry for experiences rather than products. 'What is an experience that can be much more fulfilling and rich for each of us? The composers of those experiences will be richly rewarded in the future.'

According to Hagel (2018), education institutions have been modelled to prepare people for a certain kind of work in which having skills is paramount – skills to do what you are told efficiently and reliably. But that model is far too limiting for the event professionals and leaders of tomorrow. Today's skills can be made obsolete tomorrow. But the good news is that Hagel, along with other management gurus and futurists, seems to be reinforcing the sustainable value of 'experience designers'. Innovation in the world of planned events will feature new experiences that are better able to anticipate and meet needs for transformation, education, entertainment, socializing and performing. Experts also agree that people with *passion* for their work will be more likely to find success.

Pedagogical theory and experiential learning

There has always been a pedagogical debate on the best ways to prepare students for future careers, and it has been particularly relevant within event management. The trend towards experiential learning has been documented (Sealy 2018), and no doubt this reflects three considerations: the belief that people learn better by doing, student preferences, and feedback from employers as to what they expect from graduates. In light of what Hagel and others have said about the future of work, there can be little doubt that the shift from lecturing and skills training to experiential learning (such as designing, producing and evaluating real events) will help prepare future professionals for sustainable 'creator', 'composer' and 'coach' careers. However, this must not occur without equal attention given to theory, problem solving and management competency.

Research on event careers

Baum *et al.* (2009) was the first to cover research on HR issues in the events sector, and Jago and Mair (2009) discuss career theory applied to major events, referring to McCabe's (2008) identification of a career pattern called 'butterflying'. This term is applicable to convention and exhibition professionals and they noted the difficulties associated with 'pulsating' event organizations and one-time events. Many event professionals, out of preference and necessity, do not stay long in one job and full-time traditional careers are in short supply (this might not hold true for festivals, however). One consequence is the rotating of key staff between major events, and a career pattern that is described as 'episodic' – moving from one major event to another, in sequence. In this way, expertise from the Olympics, for example, gets transferred to the next one. Another trend is for private firms to provide staff to multiple events, or to produce many events professionally, for profit. Stone *et al.* (2017) explored the career preferences and expectations of event-management studies. Despite the fact that the career will neither match the starting salary or lifetime career earnings, or reasonable workload, students are still willing to choose a career in events (see Barron and Ali-Knight 2017 on the career motivations and expectations of event and festival graduates).

Human Resource (HR) planning

Getz (2005) and van der Wagen (2006) both provided detailed HR planning models. Van der Wagen's approach starts with the event's purpose and strategic plan, and integrates HR within project planning and across all the functional areas – from accreditation to workforce planning. Key steps include: an HR strategic plan; work breakdown structure; assessment of labour needs forecast versus supply assessment (considering paid staff, volunteers and contractors); risk assessment; HR operational plan and budget; recruitment and selection; training; staffing logistics; performance management; recognition and reward system; and post-event evaluation.

Hanlon and Stewart (2006) conducted a study of staffing for a major sport-event organization, raising the question of what strategies are best. A mix of full-time, outsourced, seasonal and volunteer personnel might be involved. A complex structural arrangement can exist, numbers fluctuate and everyone is on a defined-term contract. Temporary work teams are one solution. Hanlon and Stewart made a number of recommendations for strategy, documentation and practice. Legal and ethical issues will inevitably arise for events, including laws applying to who can be hired, on what basis applicants can be rejected (certain questions or security checks might not be permitted) or employees terminated. Another common issue is the reality and appearance of discrimination, especially on boards of directors, and the desirability of having staff and volunteers reflect the social and cultural mix of the community.

Motivation

Several theoretical approaches can be applied to the task of recruiting and motivating event workers.

Herzberg's two-factor theory

It is sometimes called the 'motivator-hygiene theory'. Herzberg's workplace studies (1966) caused him to conclude that 'hygiene factors' like salary, security and other benefits, do not motivate people but can cause dissatisfaction. What motivates people to work (or work better) are challenges, recognition and responsibility. One adaptation of this theory is its use to explain customer or guest satisfaction. In this context 'hygiene factors' like inadequate toilets, parking problems or long waits, cause dissatisfaction but do not motivate people to attend events or lead to perceptions of overall quality.

McGregor's Theory X and Theory Y

Managers who believe (consciously or instinctively) in 'Theory X' think that workers are inherently lazy, so structure and discipline (or the threat of punishment) are needed to motivate them. This is in accord with Skinner's (1938) 'behavioural modification' approach, requiring reward and discipline, linking to transactional leadership as discussed previously. McGregor (1960) determined that at higher levels of Maslow's (1954) hierarchy, praise, respect, recognition, empowerment and a sense of belonging are far more powerful motivators than money. Accordingly, the 'Theory Y' manager tries to remove barriers to creativity and self-fulfilment, provide a comfortable work environment, and treat employees or volunteers with a great deal of respect. Transformational leadership is in line with this thinking.

Vroom's expectancy theory

'Expectancy theory' (Vroom 1964) states that workers have a variety of goals (particularly to avoid pain and experience pleasure) and that they can be motivated if they believe that there is a positive correlation between efforts and performance, that favourable performance will result in an outcome, that the outcome's value to the employee can be determined, and the desire to satisfy the need is strong enough to make the effort worthwhile. It is sometimes called 'expectancy-valence theory', where 'valence' refers to the emotional orientations people hold with respect to outcomes.

Professionalism and Professionalization

Professionalism refers to the ways in which people perform their duties or operate their businesses and events, while professionalization describes the process by which 'event management', for example, gets recognized as a legitimate profession. Both are closely associated with university degrees, with most higher-education institutions claiming to prepare graduates for professional life and leadership positions, but it is not the determining factor. We expect both full-time, paid event professionals and unpaid volunteers to behave professionally, acting in accordance with a set of ethical standards and being fully competent to do their jobs. We do not necessarily expect event management and related careers to be accepted as a profession on par with licensed doctors, lawyers or teachers. Getz and Wicks (1994) argued that event management can aspire to quasi-professional status on a par with recreation and leisure managers, but the typical absence of government licensing prevented full professional status. Professionalism remains an important topic. Bladen and Kennell (2014) have considered the necessary pedagogy, while Brown (2014) and Jiang and Schmader (2014) have more examined the case for professionalism from the perspective of practitioners.

Harris (2004: 107) provided a model for professionalization that encompasses three approaches to defining professionals. These are, the 'trait approach' (including skills based on professional, full-time occupation, provision of training, proof of competency, organization, code of conduct and altruistic service), a 'functionalist approach' (systematic knowledge, common interest, recognition by society, control of behaviour, work socialization, system of rewards and community of spirit) and a 'business approach' (commercial vision, effective response to market and client demands, managerial skills, entrepreneurial skills and success through profit). The ethics standards, or codes of conduct, prepared by major international event organizations were documented in Getz (2005), along with advice on how event professionals should create and govern their conduct by their own values and standards. Ethical issues, and how values and ethics are being used in practice throughout the event sector, require research and debate.

As professionalism increases there will be a need for more focused research on what constitutes professionalism, and on the related career issues for practitioners such as leadership (see Tzelepi and Quick 2002; and Hanlon and Cuskelly 2002 on generic induction methods for events, including the need for detailed manuals). Induction and training are particularly crucial for one-time events (also see Sheehan *et al*. 2000 and O'Brien and Shaw 2002 on meeting planners).

The event volunteer

No one would challenge the idea that volunteers have been and will remain absolutely critical in the production of all types of planned events. Even for-profit and corporate events often rely on unpaid workers. Studying event volunteers has been a major theme, with primary topics being volunteer motivation, recruitment and training, managing the volunteer effort, and integrating volunteers with paid staff. Volunteering is not uniformly valued and practiced around the world, being in part a reflection of cultural norms, political systems, economic conditions and living standards. Generic information is available from many countries on who volunteers, why and for what (see, for example: US Department of Labor 2005; Australian Bureau of Statistics; Imagine Canada; UK Institute for Volunteering), which is always a good starting point for any discussion of volunteers. Volunteer management for events requires specialized knowledge within HR, as well as event-specific strategies and practices, reflecting both the size and nature of the event. A lot of research has been conducted on the Olympics, but those findings are not necessarily applicable to small events or other types. Specific to events, a growing body of research evidence exists on volunteer motivation, satisfaction, commitment and experience. Studies include those by: Williams and Harrison (1988); Ryan and Bates (1995); Williams *et al.* (1995); Elstad (1997, 2003, 2009); Farrell *et al.* (1998); Green and Chalip (1998, 2004); Saleh and Wood (1998); Johnston *et al.* (2000); Coyne and Coyne (2001); Strigas and Newton-Jackson (2003); Leigh *et al.* (2013); Ralston *et al.* (2005); Monga (2006); Bendle and Pattersson (2008); Lockstone and Baum (2009); Bang *et al.* (2009); Fairley *et al.* (2013); Neufeind *et al.* (2013); Gallarza *et al.* (2013); Allen and Bartle (2014); Treuren (2014); Bachman *et al.* (2016); Blackman *et al.* (2017); Dickson *et al.* (2017); Holmes *et al.* (2018); Jiang *et al.* (2018); Mahadevan (2018a).

Underlying motivation to volunteer for events can include generic motivations like doing good ('altruism'), looking for social and career benefits (networking), and challenge. Volunteers particularly enjoy the belonging and sharing, or 'communitas' that can occur through their event experiences. Volunteering can also be one manifestation of 'serious leisure', and it is clear that some people volunteer at many events. Those who have a great experience at an event are likely to become motivated to volunteer at others. Involvement in a sport leads to volunteering at sport events of the same type, and that the prestige of an event makes a big difference, with community pride an important factor. Monga (2006) concluded that multiple motivations apply to event volunteers, but that affiliatory reasons, or attachment to the event's theme or activity, are strongest. Indoctrination, training and supervision all have to be directed toward service quality and the participation of all staff, volunteers and suppliers to the facilitation of designed experiences. A serious question to be asked is the degree to which satisfactory staff/volunteer/supplier experiences contribute to guest and other stakeholder experiences. This is much more than a service quality issue, as it gets to the heart of how experiences are shaped.

Risk, health, safety and security

'Health and safety management' aims to ensure that all event participants and attendees, as well as those affected by an event, are protected from threats to their health and safety. It is people-focused, and includes the very important crowd management and security tasks. 'Risk management' can be defined as the process of anticipating, preventing or minimizing potential costs, losses or problems for the event, organization, partners and guests. Ask the question: 'What is at risk? Is it the loss of money, reputation and survival of the event and its organizers, or personal safety and health? Risk, health and safety management has to cut across all the other systems in event management. Figure 9.5 provides an overview of the main areas of risk which affect events. In this section, just the fundamental principles are covered relating to some of the main risks, together with some of the related issues (see Table 9.2), as many books devoted to events and risk now exist (e.g. Wynn-Moylan 2017).

Unique risk elements and challenges for events

Numerous threats or hazards face the event producer, all of which pose risks. Researchers have examined many of these, including: protests (Henderson 2008; Horne and Whannel 2010); terrorism (Toohey 2008); riots (Cunneen and Lynch 1988); health issues (Earl *et al.* 2005; Ahmed *et al.* 2006; Choi and Almanza 2012); crowd problems (Earl 2008); crime (Barker *et al.* 2002; George and Swart 2012; Campaniello 2013; Matheson and Finkel 2013) and alcohol (Pegg *et al.* 2011). Many problems and threats are correlated with the size of events and their ability to attract media coverage. Terrorism and crime in

Figure 9.5 The scope of event risk

Source: Developed from Holmes *et al.* (2015).

particular necessitate high-level security and control measures. Bad weather and unpredictable environmental forces, including the state of the economy, can drastically affect turnout and sales. Attracting the wrong people or incompatible segments could lead to trouble. A number of examples of these issues are illustrated in Figure 9.6.

Within strategic planning, especially for portfolios of events, uncertainty is a major factor. When outcomes cannot be full predicted, risk management becomes an important planning function. In many cases the 'precautionary principle' should apply. Literally, it means that if we do not know exactly what the impacts of our plans, policies and actions will be, don't do it! In reality, that is too limiting. What it should imply is that better impact forecasting and outcome assessment is required, and in some circumstances the risks are too great, compared to the potential rewards, to justify action. Risks also arise from organizational and managerial actions, such as the employment of untrained staff or volunteers, the absence of proper management systems and controls, or a general lack of professionalism. Choosing the wrong setting, such as a sensitive environment or an area known for its natural hazards, can be a serious mistake. The wrong date can lead to competition and conflict, and the wrong price or programme affects image and sales. Quality control is particularly difficult at events, owing to the use of many volunteers, reliance on numerous suppliers, and the difficulty of retaining staff or volunteers. Systems often have to be reinvented annually.

Risk planning and management

Guidance is available from IFA and Argonne Productions (1992), Berlonghi (1996) and textbooks by Tarlow (2002) and Silvers (2008). A very useful manual (*The Event Safety Guide*, revised 1999) on health and

Figure 9.6 The scope of crises which may affect events

Source: Developed from Holmes *et al*. (2015).

safety planning for music events has been prepared in the United Kingdom by the Health and Safety Executive of the central government. In the UK and other jurisdictions, it is a requirement of law for events and facilities to produce a policy and plan for health and safety, and there are government inspectors to ensure compliance with all pertinent laws and regulations. Johnson (n.d.: 71) also called for all events to have a written 'emergency action plan' to ensure that staff and volunteers will respond promptly and adequately to both predictable and unusual problems. The planning process begins with the identification of possible threats and hazards in various risk 'fields', such as finance, health or the environment. This can accompany 'task analysis' in project planning, as recommended by O'Toole and Mikolaitis (2002). Next, an assessment of 'risk probabilities' (how likely are they to occur) and 'severity' (how serious are the consequences) leads to a matrix analysis of probability times severity. Priorities can then be determined, leading to action. Silvers (2008) integrates the risk management process with the various elements of EMBOK (Event Management Body of Knowledge).

According to Berlonghi (1990), there are several generic strategies for events to follow: 'avoidance' (the hazard, such as a programme activity or venue, should be eliminated); 'reduction' (some hazards can be minimized or kept to an acceptable level through better management, training or operations, or actions focused on reducing the potential severity of damage or losses); 'diffusion' (spreading risks among stakeholders or over time and space); 'reallocation' (risks can be reallocated completely, as where a parent body or municipality absorbs risks for specific events; users have to sign waivers). Insurance providers can help in the whole process, as they learn the risks and consequences through experience, and some have developed specific guidelines that event organizers must follow in order to even qualify for insurance. Activities and whole events have been cancelled because of the cost or lack of insurance. Professional associations and cities have resorted to self-insurance schemes just to be able to continue producing events.

Security

Security is a big part of risk planning and a key element in event operations and logistics. Understanding crowd emotions and behaviour is essential for most events, with the threat of terrorism at major events being an added worry. Tarlow (2002: 135) drew attention to the links between events and terrorism; specifically why they make such inviting targets:

- proximity of events and event venues to major transportation routes and centres;
- potentially large-scale business and tourism disruption from cancellation or postponement;
- media attention is immediate, on-site;
- customers at many events are unknown, and anonymous in crowds.

Mastrogiannakis and Dorville (2013) reviewed football-related hooliganism and violence and the roles of technology, such as surveillance, in combatting threats.

Dynamic crowd management (DCM)

The nature of risk and crowd management is changing fast, both in response to the legal and moral consequences of past disasters at events, and because of the enabling effects of technology and AI modelling. Using on-site technology and smart analytic systems, the purpose of DCM is to predict, rather than simply react, and therefor prevent crowd-related problems. This requires constant measurement of size, movement and crowd characteristics linked to environmental conditions. When problems are detected, or better yet anticipated, action is required. Training, risk management and operations can be based on studying past cases and current models.

9.1 EXPERT OPINION

William J. O'Toole: The Australian *Safe and Healthy Crowded Places Handbook*

William O'Toole is an events development specialist (see www.epms.net and https://www.linke din.com/in/william-otoole-events). He wrote the Australian Federal Government's handbook *Safe and Healthy Crowded Places*. The handbook is free online at https://knowledge.aidr.org.au/ resources/handbook-15-safe-and-healthy-crowded-places/

As the events sector matures around the world, it undergoes what can be termed *phase changes*. The latest change concerns the adoption of risk management. Proof of the change is found in the number of public events, such as festivals and parades, that are cancelled due to increased security costs. Reports suggest that the budget for security is now 20 per cent of the whole event budget.

For many years, governments and departments saw events as a source of income, tourist attractors and part of the destination marketing mix. The current focus is for the government and its agencies to regard an event as a crowd of people. This latest phase is a result of the attacks on public events by terrorists and lone shooters combined with the increasing popularity of public festivals and concerts by the new generation. The term used is a *temporary mass gathering*. The risk techniques have been adapted from other types of mass gatherings such as at airports, shopping centres and other transport hubs. The ongoing management of these venues allowed the management team to test and gradually refine their crowd management tools and techniques.

Recognising this change, the Australian Government, through the Australian Institute for Disaster Resilience, decided to update their seminal manual on crowds, originally published in 1999. Called *Safe and Healthy Crowded Places*, the project to write the new handbook gathered numerous agencies together to hear their concerns and techniques. The agencies included representatives of all state and federal police, public health, ambulance services, city authorities, event companies and private security companies. An interesting part of the large project was to discover that, although there are so many agencies dealing with events, they all have similar processes and issues. The standard risk management process was behind all of them. Many of the incidents and issues with crowds could be forecasted. Planning was paramount.

But there were issues with crowds that arose spontaneously and, even with all the planning, could not have been foreseen. First the issue had to be recognised by the on-site event team as a risk. In a complex dynamic entity such as a crowd, what seems to be a small problem can be quickly amplified by the number of people it affects. This introduced the all-important 'situational awareness'. Then the response teams had to use the resources at hand and work rapidly with multiple agencies and volunteers. Decision-making had to be decisive using the knowledge available as time was critical. The handbook was divided into four main topics: Crowd Management, Site and Safety, Health (including Public Health and Medical) and Security. Flowing across these domains were the processes found in risk management, communication and emergency management. This can be illustrated using the EMBOK block model*.

In each of these domains, the agencies had accumulated vast experience and research, honed skills and built heuristics. The problem was that they had worked independently of each other and created their domain-specific terminology. We needed a common handbook that summarized this information from all these agencies and domains.

Dealing with all the agencies and constructing this model led me to realize that there was not a body of work that brought the four areas together. It was obvious there was a common method-

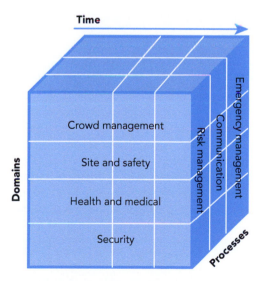

Figure 9.7 Model of the *Safe and Healthy Crowded Places Handbook*, showing the three dimensions of domains, processes and time

ology expressed in very different words. Hence I have asked four on-the-ground experts to write about crowd management from their perspective. This led to the new textbook *Crowd Management: Risk, Security and Health*. The textbook uses the principles of emergence and complexity to describe the management of crowds.

*EMBOK: Event Management Body of Knowledge, developed by a group of international event experts, including William O'Toole, to describe the profession of event management. The three-dimensional model used domains, processes and phases (time). See www.embok.com.

Research, evaluation and information systems

All the management functions have to be supported by research, evaluation and information systems. The open-system model of events illustrates that information is an essential input, and that both internal and external evaluations are crucial for accountability, improvement and learning. Although fundamental research can be useful to managers, they mostly want applied research to solve immediate problems. Increasingly, accountability to external stakeholders is placing heavy information demands on event organizers. 'Pulsating' events have a special challenge to become learning organizations with solid 'memories', as they have only a few permanent staff. Can they develop partnerships for this purpose? All-volunteer event organizations are especially challenged, and probably have to rely on external sources.

The event manager first has to establish an overall process for collecting information and doing research and evaluation (i.e. be a learning organization), then determine how best to analyse, disseminate and utilize it. Storage is an issue, although more from the perspectives of security, access and convenience. Having staff responsible for information management and technology, or outsourcing the work, are options. Numerous software programmes are available for aspects of event information management, especially regarding conference registration, project management and budgeting. As technological advances are frequent, managers and theorists are concerned about how event design, marketing, operations and experiences are being affected. The notion of a technology acceptance model has been examined by Kim *et al.* (2011) and it raises the question of what technology will be used and how it will impact on event studies.

STUDY GUIDE

The context is set with a discussion of theories of management, marketing and planning, leading to consideration of the main management functions – all except design and programming, considered in the previous chapter. This is not a 'how-to' chapter, in fact the emphasis is placed on what we need to know about, and do related research on concerning event management, marketing and planning. Link the discussion of careers and professionalism back to the introductory chapter, and consider how various motivational theories apply to volunteers and professionals – what are the differences? The institutionalization model is a new theory under development for events, related to governance, stakeholder management and dependency theory. Answer the following questions as they cover all the chapter contents.

STUDY QUESTIONS

- Discuss the changing nature of work and careers as it pertains to event professionalism.
- Define 'leadership', 'leadership styles' and 'leadership roles' in the context of planned events.
- Distinguish between 'entrepreneurship' and 'intrapreneurship' as applied to events; how is social entrepreneurship relevant?

- What does 'governance' mean for events and their external relationships?
- How do founders shape 'organizational culture', and why is it important?
- How would you examine and improve 'organizational quality'?
- What are the main differences between governmental, profit and non-profit structures in the events sector? Link ownership to stakeholder theory and resource dependency.
- Explain the interrelationships between the concepts of sustainability, enduring events, and 'institutionalization' for events
- How can events become 'learning organizations'?
- What is 'rational' planning and decision-making, and why is it not always applied to events?
- Distinguish between 'strategic', 'project' and 'business' planning for events.
- Explain the three key operation subsystems for events and discuss key 'logistics' issues.
- What is 'capacity management' for events? Give examples.
- Should the 'marketing concept' always be fully applied to events? Explain in the context of special-interest event tourism and event-related careers.
- How does 'segmentation' and 'target marketing' relate to needs, motives and benefits sought?
- Should all events be run as a 'business'? What exactly would that mean?
- Define and explain the importance of these acronyms: ROI, ROE, and ROO.
- Discuss theories of motivation as they apply to event volunteers and staff.
- Show how to recruit, motivate and keep committed volunteers for specific types of event.
- Why are events unique in terms of the crises they face and their process of risk management? Explain the research and evaluation necessary to support risk planning and management.
- What research, evaluation and information systems should be in place to support event management? Tie your answer to the open-system model.
- What is dynamic crowd management and what kinds of technology support it?

FURTHER READING

Avolio, B. (2010). *Full Range Leadership Development*. Los Angeles: Sage.

Baum, T., Deery, M., Hanlon, C., Lockstone, L. and Smith, K. (2009). *People and Work in Events and Conventions: A Research Perspective*. Wallingford: CABI.

Derrett, R. (2016). *The Complete Guide to Creating Enduring Festivals*. Hoboken, NJ: Wiley.

O'Toole, W. (2011). *Events Feasibility and Development: From Strategy to Operations*. Oxford: Butterworth-Heinemann.

O'Toole, W., Luke, S., Ashwin, P., Tatrai, A. and Brown, J. (2019). *Crowd Management: Risk, Security and Health*. Oxford: Goodfellow Publishers.

Phillips, J., Breining, M. and Phillips, P. (2008). *Return on Investment in Meetings and Events*. Oxford: Elsevier.

Sharples, L., Crowther, P., May, D. and Orefice, C. (2014). *Strategic Event Creation*. Oxford: Goodfellow Publishers.

Silvers, J. (2008). *Risk Management for Meetings and Events*. Oxford: Butterworth-Heinemann.

Tum, J., Norton, P. and Wright. J. (2006). *Management of Event Operations*. Oxford: Butterworth-Heinemann.

Van der Wagen, L. (2006). *Human Resource Management for Events: Managing the Event Workforce*. Oxford: Butterworth-Heinemann.

Van Niekerk, M. and Getz, D. (2019). *Event Stakeholders*. Oxford: Goodfellow Publishers.

The *Journal of Crowd Safety and Security Management* was published for only four volumes (2009–2012), but the articles, many dealing explicitly with events, are available online from: http://www.workingwithcrowds.com/journal-of-crowd-safety-and-security-management/

Outcomes: evaluation and impact assessment

Upon completion of this chapter, students should know the following:

- the 'subjects and objects' of event evaluation and impact assessment;
- setting goals and developing appropriate indicators of outputs and outcomes/impacts;
- multiple perspectives on value and worth; intrinsic versus extrinsic approaches;
- evaluation roles and systems: balanced scorecard;
- the forces-pressure-state-impact-response model; identify forces and stressors which generate event-related outcomes, both intended and unintended;
- 'mitigation' issues and methods for event outputs and impacts;
- the meaning and types of impact assessment (IA), and its relationship with evaluation;
- impact assessment for these five subjects: social, cultural, ecological, built environment and economic;
- specific approaches to evaluating social capital, the direct economic contribution of events, legacy, ecological footprint;
- obtaining valid and acceptable evidence;
- conducting impact assessments and using the Leopold Matrix method;
- logic and theory of change models: construction and applications;
- goals and indicators for ensuring that events contribute positively and comprehensively to sustainable cities or communities;
- consideration of the distribution of benefits and costs (the equity issue) with attention to 'winners and losers'.

Introduction

Planned events always have a purpose and goals. This means that the planning process has to incorporate a system for ensuring that goals are attained, and this necessitates evaluation and impact assessment. It is also possible that unanticipated and negative outcomes are generated, so tunnel vision has to be avoided by evaluators. In this chapter, an overview is provided of the concepts and issues pertaining to evaluation and impact assessment, within the context of event design and planning. The starting point is to define key terms and concepts, including the idea that events can be conceived as agents of change. The bulk of the chapter provides a comprehensive framework for evaluation and impact assessment, including suggested goals across the full range of possible outputs and outcomes.

The subject and objects of evaluation and impact assessment

The mandates and goals of events and event portfolios are very diverse; some are narrowly defined, as in a major-events strategy for tourism development, or very broad as in the portfolios of cities that view events as agents of social, economic, cultural and environmental change. When setting goals, there is a need to consider how realistic they are (i.e. what is the theory or logic that we are following?), feasible (can we meet these goals, and what help do we need?) and demonstrable (can we provide convincing evidence of goal attainment?). The mandate of the organization provides one starting point, suggesting for example that an event should focus on making a profit or bringing diverse social groups together for mutual benefit, but for anyone involved in planning and evaluation there is a need to consider all the possibilities. To that end this chapter provides a framework built around 'subjects and objects'.

The usual focus of event management is on the guest or customer, and what benefits they are to derive from their experiences. They are the 'objects' of our actions and we aim to satisfy them. On a deeper level, we might aim to co-create a transforming experience – giving rise to the expression 'return on experience' as discussed later. Other possible 'objects' are groups, organizations and things we intend to impact. When setting goals and considering outcomes our 'subjects' can be social, cultural, economic, or related to the built environment or nature/ecology. Any combination of these is possible. If events have the mandate to 'improve the quality of life' of residents, then they are all pertinent, but if the mandate is to attract tourists our 'subject' is primarily economics.

This structure is fully developed in Getz (2019). Getz discussed the five subjects listed above for each of eight objects, namely: individuals and families; groups and sub-cultures; events and event organizations; communities and cities; businesses; tourist destinations; politics and government; and society at large or whole nations. Such a matrix can be modified to suit one's purpose and in Table 10.1 we have presented five subject categories and five objects to demonstrate how this approach works.

First and foremost it is a goals-oriented system, with impact assessment and evaluation directed towards determining if and how goals are attained. Beyond that, evaluators have to be concerned with how to avoid 'tunnel vision' and always search for unintended and negative outcomes.

Key terms and concepts

Value and worth

There are many 'value perspectives' taken on events and their outcomes, as discussed by Lundberg *et al.* (2017) and Getz (2018). Some people value events 'intrinsically', meaning they have inherent worth, such as manifestations of culture or as healthy pursuits, and they believe we do not need to justify them through measures of output or impact. Others employ 'extrinsic' measures of value such as economic

Table 10.1 The objects and subjects of event-related goals and impacts

Subjects → / Objects ↓	People – individuals and families; residents; social and cultural groups; attendees and participants	Events – single events, portfolios, populations	Communities and cities – where people live and work	Politics and government – policy and strategy for events; regulations	Business and tourism – venues; tourism; destinations; corporations
Social	– create or improve: leisure opportunities; quality of life; subjective well-being or happiness; health; personal development; family cohesion; learning opportunities; affiliation and identity; social capital – events as agents of change	– work with events as collaborative, network-building institutions. – achieve value-creation networks and event portfolios	– ensure the benefits of events in contributing to community quality of life, community development, health and safety, education, social inclusion and identity	– implement policies and strategies to support events and regulations to ensure health and safety	– foster social tourism linked to event attendance; work to achieve positive host–guest interactions
Cultural	– use events as tools in generating cultural capital, group and national identity, and the legitimation of sub-cultures	– events to be integrated with cultural and artistic institutions and networks	– events designed as authentic cultural expressions; events as art; encourage cultural development; events contributing to cultural appreciation and inter-group cohesion	– maximize government policy and support for culture and the arts	– ensure support for cultural events through sponsorship and marketing
Economic	– support events generating employment and business opportunities for individuals and families; avoid unsafe, exploitative work	– ensure viable events through competent management and sharing within networks	– integrate events, venues and tourism in community economic development strategies	– establish public and private partnerships for event and tourism development	– maximize economic benefits of events and event portfolios to the host community; ensure equitable distribution of costs and benefits

Table 10.1 (continued)

Built environment	– events to enhance housing and neighbourhoods (avoiding inflation and displacement)	– policy to ensure that events, venues and tourism create meaningful places (i.e. healthy, safe communities; aesthetics and amenities; symbolism)	– use events and venues in place making and urban transformation	– integrate events, venues and tourism in physical planning and urban design; use events in making positive contributions to liveable cities	– enhance the roles of events in destination image making and marketing
Ecological; natural environment	– increase appreciation of and access to nature; events to make positive contributions to sustainability	– policy to ensure that events are positive contributors to sustainability; require green events	– ensure events are 'green, relaxing oases'; events as community institutions with sustainable practices	– events should be lobbying for sustainable action	– make events leaders in creating green and sustainable destinations

impacts or profit/revenue generated. Both perspectives can be taken on the same event, reflecting the mandates and goals of multiple stakeholders.

Determining the overall 'worth' of an event is a challenge, and realistically this can only be done when all the stakeholders are agreed upon its goals and its effectiveness. In other words, the worth of an event or event portfolio will of necessity be negotiated.

Evaluation

There are two connotations we need to explore. The first is to put a value on something, as in determining its worth. Event venues will have a monetary value as they can be sold in the real-estate marketplace, but it is much more difficult to say that an event could be sold for a certain amount of money. The real issue is this: does an event have sufficient value to justify the investment of money and effort? The second use of the term evaluation is technical in nature, and sometimes referred to as programme evaluation. This is what most managers do when they collect attendance and spending data from visitors, assess profit and loss, do market research or examine the reasons behind a problem or failure. This form of evaluation is all about supporting the decision-making process and solving problems, and when it comes to impact assessment (IA) the focus is generally on short-term 'outputs' (defined below). A permanent evaluation system is required for every organization. We learn from making mistakes and doing research, but only if the lessons are incorporated into ongoing planning. Two systems are discussed: the balanced scorecard and the Event Compass.

Outputs, outcomes and impacts

The term *'outputs'* is derived from open-system theory wherein 'transforming processes' (i.e. management systems, or the event itself) convert 'inputs' to 'outputs'. In this context outputs are measureable and predicted results, such as attendance, profit or surplus revenue generated, customer satisfaction, and direct economic contribution through event-tourist spending. Using the term 'outputs' this way is an analogy, suggesting how manufacturing turns raw materials into something that can be sold. *'Outcomes' or 'impacts'* (they can be used synonymously) are longer-term consequences that might also reflect the goals of an event or event portfolio, or they might be unexpected and negative. 'Impacts' can also have a more specific meaning, as people and organizations who experience the outcomes of events can feel 'impacted'. They will use this term, for example, to describe how they have been impacted by event experiences, or how the economy has been impacted by event tourism.

Impact assessment

A standard definition of impact assessment comes from the International Association of Impact Assessment:

> **Impact Assessment** *(IA) simply defined is the process of identifying the future consequences of a current or proposed action. The 'impact' is the difference between what would happen with the action and what would happen without it.*
>
> *(https://www.iaia.org/uploads/pdf/Fastips_1%20Impact%20Assessment.pdf)*

Although the forecasting IA is most common (as in 'what will be the impacts or outcomes of an event on the environment?), post-event IAs are often conducted for events, most frequently regarding economic impacts. IA methods are also needed for retrospective assessments of how events and tourism have changed a system (such as: 'Has our portfolio of events improved this city's living conditions?') and for the assessment of potential impacts of policies or strategies by comparing alternatives. Comprehensive impact assessment for events and tourism is rare, being extremely complex to conduct, but with the growing number, size and importance of events – and managed event portfolios – it remains in urgent need of theoretical and methodological development. IA goes hand in hand with evaluation, as there is generally little point in forecasting impacts if outputs and outcomes are not monitored and evaluated, and little point in knowing what impacts have occurred unless something is done about them.

Mitigation

We hope to be able to forecast and prove the attainment of our goals, but what do we do about negative impacts? Mitigation takes on different forms, and as noted by the United States Council on Environmental Quality (1980) it can include:

(a) avoidance (by not doing something);

(b) actions taken to minimize impacts;

(c) repairing damage (or rehabilitation);

(d) reducing or eliminating the undesired outcome over time.

Combining all these could, for example, be incorporated into a plan for the 'greening' of periodic events by:

(a) eliminating all activities that cause air pollution;

(b) setting higher targets each year for waste reduction or energy consumption;

(c) planting trees;

(d) continuously educating visitors about the need for water conservation.

When all else fails, compensation for losses might be needed.

Note the overlaps between mitigation and risk management. All planning and all events entail uncertainty about the future, giving rise to risks. Used this way, a 'risk' is the consequence of something going wrong, or of unpredictable forces; risks might take the form of monetary loss, injury, ecological damage, job losses, or undesired social/cultural change.

Evidence and indicators

What evidence is acceptable to demonstrate goal attainment? To be 'effective' means to achieve one's goals, so when goals are set the means for demonstrating goal attainment are an inherent part of the process. This requires 'performance indicators', and establishment of a method to obtain the evidence. 'Efficiency' is also important, meaning how well we use resources to generate the intended outputs. Efficiency can be improved by achieving more output for less input, such as through productivity gains, reducing costs and waste, or earning more for the same effort. All these need indicators, the things to measure that define efficiency and efficiency gains.

When it comes to events as agents of change, how can we 'prove' that events cause positive or negative impacts? We lack theory that both explains and predicts all potential outcomes, so we are left with compiling evidence and arguing our conclusions, often in a confrontational setting – such as the typical political debates surrounding the advantages and disadvantages of mega events. If all stakeholders can agree upon the goals and related performance and impact indicators, then agree upon methods and measures, impact assessment and evaluation will be easier. What evidence will be accepted by stakeholders is in all likelihood a matter of debate and compromise. Some will want hard numbers only, especially when it comes to economic impacts, while others will be satisfied with hearing the 'voices' of those people and groups who feel they have been impacted.

Goal-free evaluation

Tzelepi and Quick (2002) identified various approaches to evaluating 'effectiveness' that are relevant to events: 'goal attainment' (assuming goals were predetermined), 'systems resource approach' and 'internal process approach' (using the open-system model as a diagnostic tool), 'competing values' (within the organization) and 'strategic constituencies' (considering the views of all stakeholders). Clients and other key stakeholders in events typically want a report on how their resources were used and the degree to which their specific objectives were met. All too often no one is willing to examine 'externalities' – such as impacts on those not directly involved in the event's production, or environmental pollution. A full event evaluation takes into account costs and benefits and their distribution. In 'goal-free evaluation' no assumptions are made about purposes or goals, so evaluators seek to demonstrate what happened, whether intended or unintended. Sometimes this approach is taken when long-term, expensive programmes are evaluated, as in health care and education. Government agencies will want to ensure that major policies are being implemented 'effectively' and 'efficiently', plus they want to avoid negative impacts in other policy fields.

The forces-pressure-state-impact-response model (FPSIR)

This model is adaptable to event impact assessment, and although we do not always have theory to prove cause and effect, if we understand the forces and pressures at work there is a better chance for goal attainment and avoiding negative impacts. A common acronym describing forces is PEST – referring to Political, Economic, Socio-cultural, and Technological forces, and these result in observable trends such as the global legitimation and growth of the events sector. Within a given community or destination it should be possible to identify the forces that give rise to event portfolios, bidding, venues development and tourism. While economic forces tend to dominate, events are now widely utilized across multiple policy fields.

'Pressure' refers to the ways in which events, venues and tourism can cause change. Remember that we conceptualize planned events as agents of change. These pressures include investment in event venues, event production and activities, event tourism and even media coverage can have an impact. Some pressures are rather obvious, such as increased traffic, while others more subtle and open to interpretation, such as the role of media coverage in shifting resident attitudes or how events generate social capital.

When events are viewed as agents of change, the 'state' of the environment, society, culture and the economy is pulled into focus. However, these are all dynamic systems, so establishing a benchmark to assess before and after conditions is often difficult. When assessing impacts, we need to consider if we are making forecasts, looking back at trends, or weighing options. To complete the model, it is necessary to evaluate how people and institutions react to impacts, as the very act of doing an IA or evaluation should lead to changes.

Torres-Delgado and Palomeque (2014) have used the FPSIR model in developing indicators for sustainable tourism. Indicators were recommended for each stage (forces, pressures, state, impacts and responses) then in a TBL (Triple Bottom Line) approach for socio-cultural, economic and environmental impacts. In Table 10.2 a range of forces or pressures is indicated, along with possible impacts and responses. These are intended to show how to develop and use this type of model, as it cannot be comprehensive. Each force or pressure can also be disaggregated, such as for stages of construction.

Leopold Matrix

The objects-subjects matrix is a useful framework at a general level, but in IA forecasting or post-event IA a more refined matrix is often utilized. While the subjects and objects approach can shape an IA matrix, it is designed to included more detailed information. The Leopold Matrix (Leopold *et al.* 1971) is often employed, or some variation of it. It was intended to examine the possible or observed impacts on environmental conditions (i.e. physical and chemical characteristics, biological conditions, cultural factors, ecological relationships) and actions that might cause (or might have caused) impacts. The information has to come from past experience, case studies and comparisons, theory or consultations. These can be called forces or pressures, as indicated in Table 10.2.

In examining the potential environmental impacts of constructing a new arena for major sport events, we need to consider that the planning, design, construction and operation phases will have an impact on the economy, community or natural systems. Previous experience will certainly provide a starting checklist for the matrix, and so will stakeholder consultations. Different kinds of information can be placed in each cell, such as the estimated probability and severity of a forecast impact, or the observed amount of pollution if that information is available in a post-project IA. Opinions can be added, even as simple as a checkmark or X to indicate that residents, through consultation, are concerned about a particular potential consequence.

Logic and theory of change models

Weiss (1972) is generally credited with creation of these models. Advice on the construction and use of logic and theory of change models is provided in Getz (2018, 2019). The models require identification of intended or desired outputs and outcomes, with logic models being more short-term in their orientation and generally appropriate for routine or technical evaluation. TOC models are designed when events or event portfolios are conceived as agents of change. There can be overlap, and combinations are possible.

Table 10.2 Forces and pressures, possible impacts and possible responses

Forces and pressures	Possible impacts	Possible responses
Investment in: – venues – infrastructure – events	Investment: – restructuring of the economy; new or displaced jobs; political debate on priorities	– event-specific policies and strategies, linked to economic development and other policy domains; regulations; demands for public input and demonstration of costs/benefits
Construction – traffic, noise, dust	Construction: – land-use changes – ecological processes altered (drainage, habitat)	– lobbying by special-interest groups; protests against perceived negative impacts
Event production – the programme – visitor activities – management systems	– increased traffic, noise; light, energy, food and water consumption, emissions and waste – related business (supply chain) – social capital formation	– community-level political action; demands for event greening; business opposition or support; police action against bad behaviour; support for social marketing through events
Event experiences: – attendees/guests – staff; volunteers – other participants	– satisfaction or disappointment – learning; personal development; transformation of attitudes or behaviour – social and health benefits	– personal and family support and loyalty; increased voluntarism; formalization of volunteer and training programmes through/with events; increased event tourism and careers
Tourism: – host–guest interactions – related services (accommodation)	– balanced or exploitive relationships	– protests against over-tourism; or commodification; planned renewal of traditions; demands for accountability from industry
Community involvement	– full engagement or exclusion	– community-development initiatives increase; demands for social inclusion and equity
Media coverage	– supportive or negative coverage	– political action stimulated by media coverage
Portfolios of events	– long-term, cumulative impacts on culture, residents, economy, environment	– permanent evaluation and impact assessment system put in place

Figure 10.1 outlines short- and long-term perspectives. The antecedents and preconditions include all past experience, and this is particularly important when theory is absent, or weak, as it is theory that gives credibility to forecasts. Experience will also guide these models, with the assumption that what happened in the past can guide future goal attainment. But if the process planners do not have the theory or experience upon which to base valid pathways the whole process can then be designed as an experiment to help build theory.

There is another side to using TOC models, being the idea that stakeholder collaboration in itself is a major goal. If the intent is to foster social integration and create social capital, what better way than to bring key groups together to plan an event or event portfolio strategy, complete with evaluation indicators and methods?

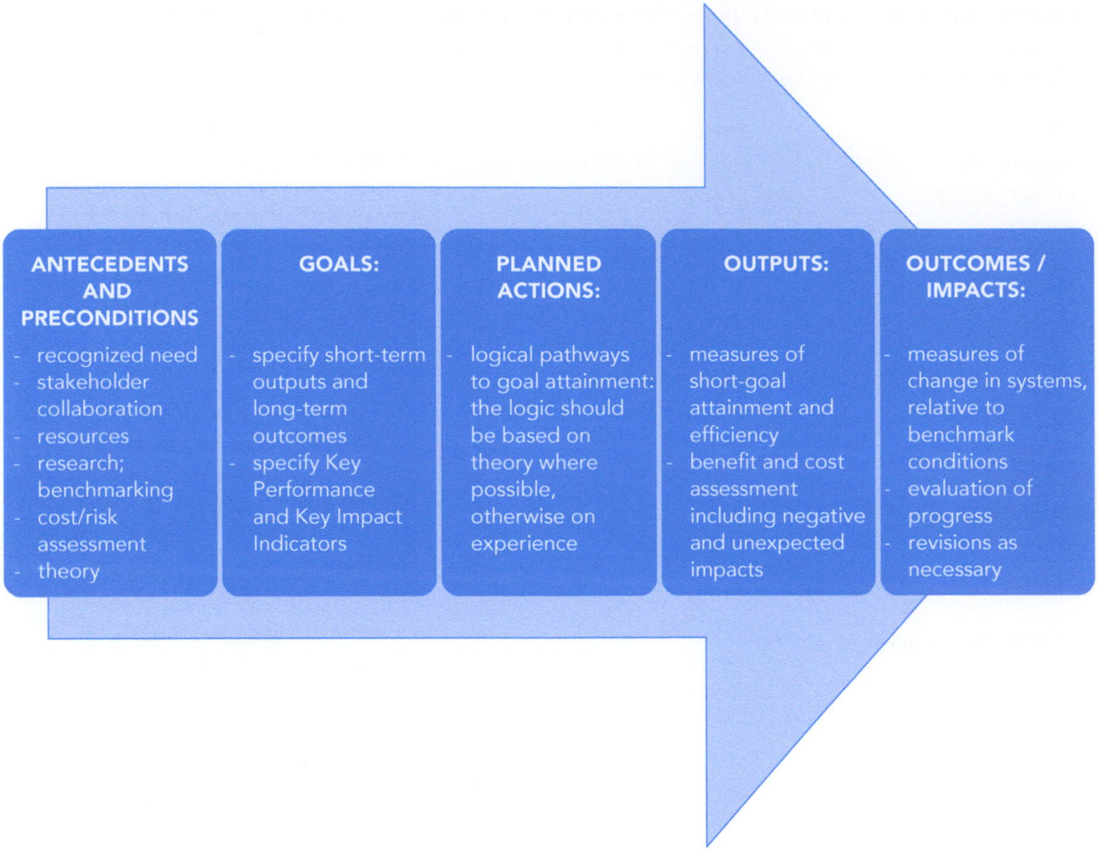

ANTECEDENTS AND PRECONDITIONS
- recognized need
- stakeholder collaboration
- resources
- research; benchmarking
- cost/risk assessment
- theory

GOALS:
- specify short-term outputs and long-term outcomes
- specify Key Performance and Key Impact Indicators

PLANNED ACTIONS:
- logical pathways to goal attainment: the logic should be based on theory where possible, otherwise on experience

OUTPUTS:
- measures of short-goal attainment and efficiency
- benefit and cost assessment including negative and unexpected impacts

OUTCOMES / IMPACTS:
- measures of change in systems, relative to benchmark conditions
- evaluation of progress
- revisions as necessary

Figure 10.1 Logic and theory of change models illustrated

These models are used infrequently, but one example is from Festivals Edinburgh (BOP Consulting 2018), which developed twin logic models for examining the wider impacts of Edinburgh's festivals on Scotland. These employed an 'inputs-activities-outputs-outcomes-impact' path, with the inputs consisting of funding from all sources, resources from partners, stakeholders and staff, and creativity from Scottish and international talent. The measureable outputs for Edinburgh festivals were defined in quantitative terms: events produced and audiences reached, jobs created in the wider economy, Scottish performers, artists and speakers receiving profile and platforms, and networking activities. Outcomes were defined as follows: Edinburgh recognized globally as world's leading festival city; Scotland's creative talent gains profile and opportunity; the festivals facilitate and support sectorial development, and formal and informal education and training opportunities. Finally, impacts included increased confidence and pride, enrichment of the cultural ecosystem and gains for Scottish artists and companies.

Social outcomes

Social-outcome goals are typically made for individuals or families, communities, groups and nations, but we should also examine impacts on businesses, tourism, destinations, politics, government and the events themselves. The challenge is two-fold: (a) provide logic or theory of change models that guide the attainment of these goals, and (b) employ valid and reliable methods and measures to assess and evaluate impacts – positive or negative, intended and unintended. This approach integrates planning, operations, evaluation and IA systems, and also leads to theory development. Each logic or TOC model is somewhat of an experiment designed to test certain hypotheses or informed ideas about what will happen when events are held, and especially when events and tourism are conceived as agents of change.

According to the International Association for Impact Assessment (IAIA.org):

> *Social impact assessment includes the processes of analyzing, monitoring and managing the intended and unintended social consequences, both positive and negative, of planned interventions (policies, programs, plans, projects) and any social change processes invoked by those interventions. Its primary purpose is to bring about a more sustainable and equitable biophysical and human environment.*

Most IAs have been of the forecasting variety, with post-project and longitudinal assessments (especially for events) being largely ignored or unpublished. This gap represents a major impediment to theory development (also see Richards *et al.* 2013 on social impact assessment and Getz 2019 on methods and measures for SIA).

Social pressures and responses

What exactly causes social change is the question at the heart of both planning a logic or theory of change model (TOC), and in IA. There can be general pressures beyond anyone's control that have to be considered, such as globalization, forms of government, cultural norms or the state of the economy, but mostly we will be interested in the event-specific stressors and how to analyse them within a TOC or an IA matrix. Residents, and host communities, experience both direct and indirect event-related stressors. These include changes to the physical environment (e.g. traffic, noise, pollution, transport, infrastructure), to the economy (employment, taxes) and to government and politics (protests, policies, strategy). Residents can decide if they want to attend events, with more choices for entertainment creating a utility value, or they might appreciate events for what they do in the community – this being a non-use value assigned to events. With events designed as agents of change, there is the necessity for specifying the intended consequences, measuring them in ways acceptable to stakeholders, and then taking appropriate action (e.g. mitigation of negative outcomes or reinforcement of positive impacts). In many cases the results of event-related stressors, and what to do about outcomes, will be open to debate.

Personal and family outcomes

If we only want to find out if customers and guests at events are satisfied, that is a simple evaluation problem. We can add Importance-Performance questions, thereby learning more about expectations and quality perceptions. Path analysis or SEM can be used, with appropriate data, to link antecedents, experiences and future intentions or loyalty. But none of these evaluation techniques answer a fundamental question – do events change people? If events are expected to transform visitors, or perhaps other participants and families as well, then some theory must be applicable. We can hypothesize, as is being done by researchers who will be cited, that real change, or transformation, can occur as a result of one or more of the following – singly or in concert.

Activity: Especially in sports, we can expect physical and mental benefits, and this can be augmented by development of serious-leisure careers and event-travel careers.

Emotional engagement: Especially within a festive context, communitas can be fostered. This belonging and sharing experienced by equals in an inclusive setting can foster quality of life improvements (e.g. happiness) or spiritual growth. Even simple entertainment can act as a stress reliever.

Social engagement: Personal and social identity can be fostered or reinforced through social-world activities, or events that otherwise bring diverse people together; social inclusion can ideally foster community-level benefits or social capital; quality-of-life gains can be expected from family togetherness at events; hosts and guests can meet as equals and gain mutual understanding; sub-culture or social-world groups can seek legitimation. Hixson (2014) determined that the more young people participated in a festival, the greater was their identity awareness. Events and family quality of life is a very recent line of research (Jepson and Stadler 2017).

Volunteer engagement or work can lead to networking and career benefits, or satisfy personal needs for belonging and giving. Doherty (2009) employed social exchange theory to examine event volunteers and concluded that their intentions for future volunteering were influenced by experienced benefits of the event, including social enrichment, community contribution and a positive life experience. This and other studies of event volunteers link specifically to volunteering as serious leisure.

Cognitive engagement: If people set out to learn, or get inspired to learn through event programming, attitudes and behaviour might consequently change; this is part of the rationale behind social marketing and a great deal of sponsorship or 'live-experience' marketing by corporations; cultural capital can be gained through improved knowledge and networking.

Inspirational effects: Often cited as a justification of sport events, there is in fact little evidence to suggest that people get more involved or healthy as a result of being exposed to sport events or elite athletes (Sousa-Mast *et al.* 2013; Ramchandani *et al.* 2017). There might be more media engagement, but no lasting, general gains in participation or health.

Social impact scales

Research and theory development regarding social impacts has led to a large body of literature that documents perceived positives and negatives (and grey areas), attitudes towards events and event tourism, and theories of how impacts occur. A well-established theme has focused on resident perceptions of event impacts, both as event participants and general impacts on their communities. This led to development and subsequent testing of social impact scales. The following are some key references on this line of research: Fredline and Faulkner (1998; 2002a; 2002b); Delamere, and Delamere *et al.* (2001); Fredline *et al.* (2003); Small *et al.* (2005); Fredline (2006); Deery and Jago (2010); Yang *et al.* (2010); Lorde *et al.* (2011); Pavlukovic *et al.* (2017), Wallstam *et al.* (2018); Chi *et al.* (2018); Scholtz *et al.* (2019). The paper by Fredline *et al.* (2013) represents a rare case of longitudinal analysis of perceived social impacts surrounding an event.

From the published research, we can identify potential costs and benefits of events for individuals and communities, but it is also inevitable that local variations will occur.

Social exchange theory

Social exchange theory has been a foundation for many social-impact studies (Fredline *et al.* 2013), including a study of the Olympics by Waitt (2003). Gursoy and Kendall (2006) concluded that resident support for the Olympics relied heavily on perceived benefits, confirming social exchange theory. The basic principle of this theory is that reciprocity is sought in human relationships, whether they be economic or social in nature, and therefore if people perceive they gain more from events and tourism than they lose, directly or indirectly, they are more likely to hold positive perceptions of impacts and positive attitudes towards bidding on and holding events in their communities. Other researchers have found that support for mega events varies over time, and a sampling of public opinion after an event will likely reveal a lowered impression of benefits. Euphoria and heavy political support beforehand will persuade many people that the event is worthwhile, but afterwards they look for benefits that might not have accrued (Mihalik 2001). Lorde *et al.* (2011) found significant differences between pre- and post-event perceptions of impacts.

Social representation theory

Social representation theory has also been suggested (Pearce *et al.* 1996), and in this construct it cannot be assumed that people rationally assess the costs and benefits of events or tourism, and they hold representations of these objects based on personal experience and media coverage. The role of media in shaping discourse surrounding mega events in particular has been identified as an issue, with both proponents and opponents attempting to frame convincing arguments through mass and social media. Waitt's (2004) critical examination of the 2000 Sydney Olympic Games provides an example of how 'civic boosterism' was employed to create a dominant, positive representation of the Games, and to exclude or silence its critics. While the Games were used to reposition Sydney in the world context, they also had to be sold to the population through the exploitation of Olympic symbolism and rhetoric, and through promises of major, lasting benefits. *Event Bidding* (2017) by McGillivray and Turner documents how mega-event bids are both 'sold' and resisted.

Negative social impacts

It is possible to predict many possible negative impacts on persons, groups and communities with the research evidence readily available. In general, the bigger the event the more likely that negative impacts will occur. The first comprehensive study of event impacts (Adelaide's Grand Prix, by Burns *et al.* 1986) examined how residents were affected in their homes and while conducting their normal business, such as by increased commuting times. Accident rates were also analysed, revealing a so-called 'hoon effect' attributed to the atmosphere of the races and the nature of those attracted to them. Hall (1992) noted that major events, particularly those with global media coverage, tend to attract potentially violent protests and political demonstrations. Indeed, security has become a dominant theme in event management, and the costs are a deterrent to bidding and hosting major events. A fascinating account of a special event gone wrong was provided by Cunneen and Lynch (1988). They described how the annual Australian Grand Prix Motorcycle Races had become the scene for institutionalized rioting, despite, or perhaps because of, the efforts of organizers and police to control crowd behaviour. After some time, people came for the riots rather than the races. Obviously a major repositioning of the event was necessitated.

Social capital

This has become an important theme in event research and theory development, with samples being: Arcodia and Whitford (2006); Finkel (2010); Pernecky and Luck (2013); Schulenkorf, Thomson and Schlenker (2011); Wilks (2011); Jamieson (2014); Stevenson (2016); Mair and Duffy (2018). The book *Exploring the Social Impacts of Events* (Richards *et al.* 2013) focuses on social capital.

Misener and Mason (2006) concluded that hosting sporting events offers opportunities for generating social capital and community development through building community networks related to events. Arai and Pedlar (2003: 185) believed that public celebrations and other community gatherings engender social capital through enhanced social cohesion, trust, mutuality, cooperation and openness. According to the Social Capital Research website (www.socialcapitalresearch.com), the measurement of social capital, being a complex and debatable construct, has utilized single indicators like 'trust' or indices combining a number of indicators.

> ### 10.1 RESEARCH NOTE ON SOCIAL CAPITAL
>
> Stevenson, N. (2016). Local festivals, social capital and sustainable destination development: Experiences in East London. *Journal of Sustainable Tourism*, 24 (7), 990–1006.
>
> Abstract: This paper explores the nature of social capital arising from engagement in local festivals and the implications of this for the social sustainability of an emerging destination. Two case studies are developed from a longitudinal research project which investigates local festivals staged in the Hackney Wick and Fish Island area adjacent to Queen Elizabeth Olympic Park in East London, UK between 2008 and 2014. This area has been directly affected by extensive development and regeneration efforts associated with the staging of the London 2012 Olympic Games. The two festivals considered here respond to the challenges and opportunities arising for local people as the area changes. One festival aims to foster a sense of community by creating shared experiences and improving communication across diverse groups. The other draws together the cultural community, links them to the opportunities arising as the area emerges as a destination, and attracts visitors. These festivals increase social capital in the area, but its distribution is very uneven. The accrual of social capital exacerbates existing inequalities within the host community, favouring the 'haves' at the expense of the 'have nots'. There are tensions between the development of social capital and social sustainability in this emerging destination.

Cultural outcomes

The United Nations Educational, Scientific and Cultural Organization (UNESCO 2002) defined culture as 'the set of distinctive spiritual, material, intellectual and emotional features of society or a social group, and that it encompasses, in addition to art and literature, lifestyles, ways of living together, value systems, traditions and beliefs'. The term 'heritage' is also relevant, and many festivals and events fall into the category of 'intangible heritage'.

Within the events and tourism literature, there are a number of well-established themes pertaining to cultural issues and impacts, and these are considered below. Many of these come from the anthropology and sociology disciplines, starting with traditional research and theory on rites and rituals. Festivals in particular are generally viewed as being expressions of culture, but the same could be said about all types of events – they reflect values and traditions and communicate important symbols.

Demonstration effects and commodification

To the degree that events generate tourism, then direct and indirect interactions between hosts (residents) and guests (tourists) will result. Many social scientists have argued that tourism in general is a destructive force in cultural terms, and that cultural events in particular are easily 'commodified' as tourist attractions. Many authors have worried about the negative influence of tourism on traditional cultures (e.g. Greenwood 1972; Jordan 1980; Wilson and Udall 1982). Often these effects are most visible in the area of cultural productions such as rituals, music, dance and festivals, and particularly those that incorporate traditional costumes. Residents of destination areas quickly learn that culture can become a 'commodity' for which tourists will pay a great amount, resulting in either the transformation of occasional, sometimes sacred events into regular performances, or the modification of rituals into forms of entertainment that are easier to perform, or please the audiences more. In both cases, the rewards become monetary and divorced from their cultural meanings.

However, there is little agreement on tourism being bad for cultural events, or on how and why negative impacts occur (see, for example, Noronha 1977; Macnaught 1982; Getz 1998b). Some authors have argued that tourism actually helps to preserve or revive traditions and strengthen indigenous cultures (e.g. Boissevain 1979; Cheska 1981), and events are one of the most common mechanisms. Sofield (1991) examined a successful, traditional event in the South Pacific and drew conclusions regarding the analysis and attainment of sustainability for indigenous cultural tourism developments.

Shaw and Williams (2004: 175) modelled 'stages in cultural commodification' for festivals and events affected by tourism, arguing that 'commodification' was part of consumer culture, that commodification and consumerism lead to dependency in tourist destination areas, and that the commodification of social and ritual events leads to 'an erosion of meaning, accompanied by community fragmentation'. The stages are:

- independent travellers take an interest in local events; they observe, but do not necessarily understand meanings;
- growth in organized tourism occurs;
- tour operators market local culture as an attraction;
- events become staged for tourists, leading to a loss of meaning for local people (the event is a commodity) and tourists are observing 'pseudo-events'.

Authenticity

Authentic or genuine cultural experiences motivate cultural tourists, with many events providing the desired experiences. But who is to say that events and their programmes are culturally authentic? Generally this is left up to those who produce events, but increasingly such decisions require broader stakeholder consultations. A 'cultural license to operate' would entail getting the approval and support of cultural groups who believe they have a stake in events and programming. One example of a resident-controlled cultural event is Hoi An, one of Vietnam's most popular destinations. Residents implemented a monthly Lantern Festival that 'ritually refreshes their sense of communitas and reinforces the unique temporality in which they live'. Roemer (2007: 185) studied a Japanese *matsuri* (festival) demonstrating how:

> *ritual participation yields a strong sense of community, and this is connected with several forms of social support ... the main participants in this month of rites and festivities gain a sense of belonging and emotional support based on their roles in this historically and culturally significant shrine-related festival.*

Cultural identity and multiculturalism: integration

In countries like Canada, with increasingly pluralistic cultures, multiculturalism has been institutionalized. The goal is to bring many cultural groups together within one festival to celebrate both diversity and Canadian values. This is official government policy, and not without its critics. Social integration, another goal frequently assigned to events, is made more difficult when diverse cultures interact – sometimes with a troubled history of conflict.

Indigenous cultures

Cultural sensitivity is especially needed when indigenous cultures are showcased, and 'cultural misappropriation' occurs when elements of another culture are used without permission. It has become unacceptable to depict or use indigenous symbols without that kind of 'license'. Laxson (1991) described how Native Americans limited access by tourists to their own pueblo culture, keeping some aspects of their rituals secret. Other native communities have denied access to sacred rituals but have made other performances a regular part of pow-wows that seek to attract tourists. Picard (1996) reported that some Balinese dances performed for tourists are 'staged authenticity' because they do not contain elements that are reserved for authentic rituals.

The arts and culture-led development

Arts festivals are one of the most popular forms, and this genre can be broadly defined to include all music festivals. Development of the fine arts remains a typical public-sector goal, whereas the entertainment industry that controls numerous music events is profit-oriented. In between the two extremes are countless events operated on a not-for-profit basis with dominant goals being the perpetuation and celebration of a form of music, generating revenue for worthwhile causes, and providing social-world meeting places. Cities around the world have pursued culture-led development strategies, encompassing repositioning of cities as places for culture and entertainment. Events of all kinds, and new venues, are manifestations of this instrumentalist approach to events and event tourism.

Methods for cultural IA

Colombo's (2016: 10) model is specifically designed for assessing the cultural impacts of events. Her approach is:

> *based on the perceptions of individuals from a host society, and therefore the results are based on subjective and personal perceptions. Thus individual perceptions are the most appropriate indicator by which to measure cultural impacts, since these impacts, due to their specific characteristics, are more subjective than other impacts such as the economic ones.*

Colombo (2016: 3) listed potential benefits and negatives that should be examined, provided indicators for each, and advocated a method for obtaining resident input on the following:

- *Perceived or not:* yes it is a likely/existing impact, no it is not;
- *Considered positive or negative*: this can be from the individual's or community's perspective;
- *The intensity of the impact on individuals and on the community is evaluated:* on an intensity scale, say from 1–10;
- *Considered intentional or not:* the evaluator could ask respondents if they think an impact was intentional or not, or draw this inclusion from the event organizers or observation and document review.

Measuring the effects of cultural engagement

A schema for assessing the outcomes of cultural engagement has been provided by the Cultural Development Network in Australia. The underlying theory is that exposure, and especially higher levels of engagement in arts and cultural pursuits will lead to greater understanding and appreciation, and possibly to more profound changes that can be termed personal development or self-actualization. (See: http://www.culturaldevelopment.net.au/outcomes.)

Built-environment outcomes

It is useful to distinguish between nature and ecological processes on the one hand and the built environment on the other. By 'built environment' we mean residential neighbourhoods, cities, landscapes modified for agriculture and industrial activities, and all the infrastructure that keeps these systems going. We need 'spaces' in which to hold events, and in doing so we create meaningful 'places'.

Urban development and renewal

Mules (1993) examined how a special event was designed to draw people within the context of urban renewal, and to change the image so that the area would become associated with leisure and tourism. Events as instruments of urban policy has become very widespread, with a number of researchers exploring related themes: Essex and Chalkley (1998); Sadd (2010; Xie and Gu (2015); Pacione (2012); Rogerson (2016). Mega events create special issues, and they are often justified in part on their role in re-shaping and renewing urban environments. The common negative impacts associated with massive construction projects are housing displacement, especially of the poor, and the 'gentrification' of areas so that only the rich can afford to live in the 'renewed' areas. The equity issues and opportunity costs associated with new venues, and especially mega events, are often ignored. One question that should always be asked is this: are residents, and those with special needs, the ones who will benefit from new venues and re-development?

Place making, identity and attachment: civic pride

Richards (2017, p. 12) examined the various elements in place making, arguing that:

> *cities and regions need to think about events in much broader terms than simply economic or image impacts. To have a placemaking effect, events also need to add to the meaning of the location, and creativity needs to be employed to ensure that the meanings developed are embedded in place and appropriate to the needs and capacities of the city or region.*

The existence of events, and engagement with them, can foster a sense of place and help shape the community's identity as perceived by residents. Place making and identity building occurs when residents are encouraged to participate, attend and support events that first and foremost benefit locals, but it can also be combined with developing a positive image for external influence. When people hold positive attitudes about their place of community or country, or feel pride in being citizens, they are more likely to feel an attachment that is difficult to shed. Creative-city and repositioning strategies therefore use events as instruments of policy.

Place marketing and branding

Cities and towns often seek to attract tourists, investment and possibly in-migrants. Events play several roles, as do venues, and improvements in quality of life in general are important. Developing a strong and appealing city or destination brand is essential, and the process of place branding can be considered an exercise in stakeholder collaboration, or of value co-creation.

Chalip and Costa (2006) examined event and destination co-branding and the roles of sports events in the destination event portfolio. The creation of the brand is more than names, logos, symbols or images, but how all of these meaningfully combine in a mental schema. Wang and Jin (2019) examined the roles of mega events in destination marketing and developed a model for event-based destination marketing.

Use and abuse of public places

The 'animation' of public and private spaces with events may be positive but there can also be a downside. Smith (2015; 2017) discusses 'the urbanization of events' when public space is both 'performed and consumed'. Who gains and who loses is an equity issue, and this is especially poignant when peaceful parks are removed from residents' control or use.

10.2 RESEARCH NOTE ON USING PUBLIC SPACE

Smith, A. (2017). Animation or denigration? Using urban public spaces as event venues. *Event Management*, 21, 609–619.

Abstract: City events are increasingly staged outside purpose-built venues in urban public spaces. Parks, streets, and squares have always been used for civic events, but there is now pressure to use them for a wider range of occasions including large-scale, ticketed events. This article identifies why this trend is occurring and outlines the implications for public spaces. The use of London's parks as venues for music festivals, elite sport events, and trade exhibitions is the main focus of the article. These events challenge the established functions and meanings of public parks. Noted positive effects include challenging the rather stiff character of Victorian parks and encouraging different users/uses. However, ticketed events restrict access to parks and various processes currently afflicting urban public spaces—privatization, commercialization, and securitization—are exacerbated when parks are used as event venues. These effects are often dismissed as inherently temporary, but staging events can have enduring effects on the provision and accessibility of public space.

Over-tourism

When residents believe there are too many tourists or events, and when the negative effects are perceived to outweigh the benefits, cries of 'over-tourism' are heard. Activists might be motivated by unaffordable housing, loss of peace and quiet, or damage to heritage sites, but when they start to demand that tourists go home, or chant 'no more events', then sustainability is clearly being compromised. Consider this value chain: the city is successful in bidding on and hosting popular tourist events; more and more residents and investors (some of which are big businesses) convert housing to short-term rental properties aimed at visitors; residents are displaced and take to the streets in protest.

Sustainable cities

While the term 'sustainable development' is still preferred by many in the tourism and economic development sectors, meaning development that goes on forever (or perhaps development with a green touch), it is more important to talk about 'sustainable cities' and how events can be a driving force. This paradigm shift requires that events first be green by regulation, that event portfolios be managed within a triple-bottom-line frame for long-term sustainability, and that the entire event sector (including venues) support all the community's policies and actions on sustainability. Getz (2009; 2017) outlined the ways in which this can be done, indicating for each policy domain the kinds of actions events need to take collaboratively. Table 10.3 summarizes this action plan.

Nature and ecological processes

This remains the least-researched object of event policy and impact assessment, perhaps because economics and social concerns have been favoured because of the educational backgrounds of researchers. The fact that most events are held in built environments, indoors, also contributes to the dearth of knowledge about events and nature. There are impacts of the environment on events, and of events on nature and ecological processes (see Case 2013). Event settings encompass a spectrum of indoor or outdoor spaces from those held in a completely built environment to those held in the wilderness. The relationship

Table 10.3 Action plan for sustainable event cities

City-level policy fields and major goals	Specific concerns and actions for individual events
AIR: Reduce carbon emissions; monitor and improve air quality	Reduce carbon footprint by maximizing use of public mass transit and by careful targeting of tourist segments; events should stress yield over volumes when it comes to design capacity and marketing; adhere to emission standards for all machinery, equipment, and venues
WATER: Conserve supplies; clean water for all citizens; prevent pollution	Reduce consumption; education of guests; avoid pollution; provide clean water as a service
WASTE: Minimize waste; improve recycling and reuse	Implement Reduce, Reuse, Recycle, especially considering supply chain controls, packaging
ENERGY: Reduce consumption; develop alternative, clean sources	Reduce consumption; use alternative clean sources; evaluate all machinery and equipment for efficiency gains; work with venues to be carbon neutral
TRANSPORTATION: Maximize use of public, mass transit; reduce auto use and congestion; use clean fuels	Reduce private-car travel; use shuttle and public mass transit services
NATURE/ECOLOGICAL SYSTEMS: Reduce overall ecological footprint; conserve nature and increase access to nature reserves	Educate guests regarding nature conservation; donate money to conservation projects; plant trees; avoid erosion and land pollution; utilize ecological footprint calculator
BUILT ENVIRONMENT and LIVABILITY: Conserve heritage through the design and use of public spaces; achieve safer, quieter, more liveable communities	Contribute to the liveability of communities through design and heritage conservation initiatives; monitor and reduce light and noise pollution; ensure safety and convenience of residents
ECONOMIC DEVELOPMENT: Foster innovation and entrepreneurship; create and preserve jobs; attract investment; foster a progressive business environment; grow responsible tourism	Develop economic impact strategy and evaluation mechanisms; grow the event and/or expand diversity; become an innovation and creative city leader; add value through supply-chain management, favouring local and regional suppliers
TOURISM: Target high-yield visitors; overcome seasonality of demand; build and maintain a strong reputation and brand; develop a portfolio of events and venues for long-term, sustainable benefits	Carefully target high-yield tourists; favour off-peak timing; cobrand with the city/destination; stress long-term, sustainable value creation within a managed event portfolio; evaluate visitor satisfaction
FOOD: Ensure food supplies; develop urban gardening; preserve traditions and maximize culinary authenticity	Implement a food policy favouring authenticity and local/regional suppliers; integrate with Reduce, Reuse, Recycle actions
EDUCATION/TRAINING: Educate residents and students on sustainability issues and initiatives they can take	Educate guests regarding sustainability issues and practices; train event evaluators
SOCIAL POLICY: Maximize social integration and harmony; foster community development; provide adequate housing for all; build institutions	Set social goals and evaluate outcomes on residents, social groups and the community; engage many stakeholders in social planning

(continued)

Table 10.3 (continued)

City-level policy fields and major goals	Specific concerns and actions for individual events
COMMUNITY DEVELOPMENT: Assist communities in dealing with problems, taking sustainability initiatives and planning their future; ensure leisure opportunities and accessibility for all residents	Develop and manage community stakeholder relations to maximize benefits; increase community self-sufficiency through event production
ARTS AND CULTURAL POLICY: Foster arts appreciation	Utilize local talent; preserve cultural traditions; set and evaluate cultural goals
HEALTH: Maximize accessibility to quality health services; prevent disease and injury; encourage responsible, healthy lifestyles	Provide safe, healthy and secure events; encourage positive lifestyle changes
SAFETY AND SECURITY: Ensure public safety through traffic controls and crime prevention	Work with police and other security-related agencies to ensure a safe event experience for all

Source: Getz (2017).

between events and nature can be exploitive, causing damage, or beneficial through educational and conservation efforts.

The greening of events

There is no lack of knowledge about how to 'green' events, including that available in books such as by Jones (2018). What is difficult to understand is that in many jurisdictions, there is no requirement to impose appropriate regulations, and standards are often merely guidelines.

On the EventImpacts website, advice is given on various categories of, and methods for, event impact assessment. A set of indicators is suggested for environmental sustainability (source: http://www.eventimpacts.com/impact-types/environmental):

- Waste footprint of event-related visitors
- Proportion of waste classified as inert/hazardous
- Changed composition of event-related waste streams
- Changes in amount of waste produced per event-related visitor/participant
- Changes in proportion of waste diverted from landfill (i.e. increase recycling and composting)
- Reduction in waste produced at event site
- Reduction in waste produced per event-related visitor
- Carbon footprint in (CO_2 equivalent) associated with event-related visitation
- Carbon footprint per event-related visitor (CO_2 equivalent)
- Total event carbon footprint (CO_2 equivalent)
- Reductions in personal carbon footprint following events
- Quantity of water used (litres public water supply) at event site
- Changes in the proportion of visitors using public transport to travel to/from event

- Changes in the proportion of visitors driving to/from event by car
- Total distance (miles/km) travelled by visitors to/from the event
- Proportion of visitors using car-sharing schemes
- Quantity of food and drink consumed
- Quantity of food and drink consumed which is organic
- Quantity of food and drink sourced locally (i.e. produced within 100 miles or 160km of the event)
- Quantity of food and drink that is Fair Trade Certified or other eco-certification

From the list of indicators above, it can be seen that 'greening' is not the same as sustainability, nor does the measurement of those indicators constitute a full ecological impact assessment. Sustainable events have to be green – that is a starting point – but they also have to be economically viable, socially responsible and evaluated with regard to their long-term, cumulative impacts.

Carbon calculators and the ecological footprint of events

Carbon calculators are available online, some of which appear to be 'black boxes' with unknown assumptions. Exactly what should be included, and how the data are to be collected, is still an open question. The website greeneventbook (http://www.greeneventbook.com/event-carbon-footprint-possible/) discusses these issues as well as the meaning of carbon offsetting and neutrality. The most important method of reducing the carbon emissions of events is to reduce private automobile use, but there remains a serious issue when it comes to event tourism – it cannot occur without substantial emissions from fossil fuels. That dilemma will not be resolved until alternative, clean energy sources become widespread. The ecological footprint is an attempt to quantify the total demand that people or specific activities like an event make on the earth's resources, thereby demonstrating how 'natural capital' is being depleted (Wackernagel and Rees 1996). The idea is that an event consumes resources and generates wastes that can be converted through a calculator into an area of productive land and water necessary to produce the resources and assimilate the wastes.

Models for calculating the ecological footprint are not widely available, and they have to be customized for particular countries and regions. Collins *et al.* (2005) employed this method in a study of football and found that more than half of the event's footprint was generated by the travel of 73,000 attendees (totalling 2 million kilometres); consumption of food was the second-largest contributor. Andersson and Lundberg (2013), Andersson *et al.* (2013) and Andersson *et al.* (2016) have reported on its use in Sweden. If a carbon calculator is available, it can form the basis of a short-cut footprint analysis. The nature of the event and its setting will dictate what other indicators should form the composite index of ecological impact. For events held indoors key indicators will include energy consumed, the volume and types of wastes and emissions, and of course the numbers of visitors and how they travelled.

10.3 RESEARCH NOTE ON TRIPLE IMPACT ASSESSMENT

Andersson, T., Armbrecht, J. and Lundberg, E. (2016). Triple impact assessments of the 2013 European Athletics Indoor Championship in Gothenburg. *Scandinavian Journal of Hospitality and Tourism*, 16(2), 158–179.

Abstract: This study answers the call for holistic assessments of events' sustainability through testing a model for measuring impacts of a sports tourism event from sustainability perspectives and in a common monetary metric. The aim is to achieve commensurability through integration of economic, socio-cultural and environmental impacts. Concepts such as use- and non-use value, consumer surplus, direct economic impacts, ecological footprint analysis and shadow cost are applied to fulfil this aim. The model is tested on a three-day-long European athletics indoor championship 2013 and the results demonstrate a possibility to produce a sustainability impact analysis in a uniform metric. Measured in monetary terms, sociocultural impacts carry more weight than economic impacts do, whereas environmental impacts have little importance for the total assessment. The assessment of event impacts in one common metric paves the way for destinations to trade-off alternatives and develop clear-cut strategies to increase social, economic and environmental welfare. It is suggested that prices on the market for emission rights severely underestimate environmental costs.

Ecological impact assessment (EIA)

An EIA has to encompass all the greening indicators, and much more. In addition to consumption, emissions and waste generated directly by events, demand by event tourism and the entire supply chain must be considered. Direct and indirect effects on wildlife, habitat, water and drainage, soils and vegetation must be analysed, as well as noise, light, vibrations and other ambient conditions. The EIA might even be extended to cover the potential impacts of new or displaced businesses and related supply-chain activity. The most obvious pressures will arise from construction and subsequent traffic and activity. If events are conceived as agents of change, as in fostering environmental responsibility, then social-marketing evaluation is required.

Although conducting an EIA is in most countries standardized by regulation, it is usually only done for major projects. Under European Union directives, an EIA must provide information in seven key areas:

1 Description of the project or event:
   - breakdown into key components, i.e. construction, operations, decommissioning
   - for each component list all of the sources of environmental disturbance
   - for each component all the inputs and outputs must be listed, e.g. air pollution, noise, hydrology
2 Alternatives considered:
   - e.g. other possible locations; for energy, can wind or solar power be used?
   - opportunity costs: what are the alternatives to the event or venue?
3 Description of the environment:
   - list all aspects of the environment that may be affected by the development, corresponding with elements of the project, in a matrix
   - what are the most likely impacts of construction? of events? of related traffic and visitor activities? what are likely cumulative impacts?
   - consultations should reveal existing issues, fears, and potential impacts
4 Description of the significant effects on the environment:
   - 'significant' must be defined by experts, stakeholders, and through consultations; scales can be used to indicate severity, perceived importance, duration
5 Mitigation:
   - analyse potential ways to avoid or otherwise ameliorate negative impacts
   - consider how events can be moved in space and time, adopt green standards, limit attendance

or types of activity, incorporate educational and social marketing campaigns, raise money for conservation

6 Non-technical summary:

– the EIA is in the public domain and to be used in the decision-making process

7 Lack of know-how/technical difficulties:

– this section is to advise any areas of weakness in knowledge; it can be used to focus areas of future research

Economic impacts

The logic of generating economic impacts from events is well understood, and we know that benefits can be realized from rational development strategies. Appropriate methods are available for impact assessment and obtaining the necessary data is not difficult. But rational planning continues to be shunned, and calls for transparency and accountability disregarded, when it comes to the policies and actions of many politicians and governments around the world – especially regarding mega events. Zimbalist (2015) identifies the fallacy of claims made about the economic benefits of mega events, and McGillivray and Turner (2017) have documented the logic and illogic behind mega-event bidding. Dwyer *et al.* (2010) argues that economic impacts do not equal economic benefits, as proponents of heavy investments often point to the jobs that will be created and the value of tourism that will be facilitated, while ignoring negative impacts, costs and opportunity costs, and their distribution, especially equity issues that arise when the distribution of costs and benefits is evaluated. If debt is incurred, it is passed on to future generations.

Economic value

There are many value perspectives on events and tourism, only one of which is economic in nature. The attraction of tourist spending is one such value, and the related data requirements and estimation methods are detailed later. Here are other possible measures of economic value.

Profit and return on investment

To private investors, the 'ROI' is their measure of value. In other words, for every dollar invested, what are their profits or earnings? In the private sector, the ROI will constitute profit, some or all of which could be reinvested in growth of the event or expansion of the business, raising the matter of short- versus long-term calculations of ROI. Tourism agencies investing in events often equate 'economic impact' with ROI focusing on the numbers of dedicated event tourists attracted (who would not otherwise visit the destination) and what they spent. Strictly speaking this is one impact, and it does not necessarily equal a benefit to everyone. Equity issues have to be considered.

Fostering trade and economic growth

Event portfolios are increasingly important in place marketing, with the aim of attracting investment and stimulating economic growth. The 'leveraging' of events can be applied to creating more business and profit for individual companies, such as hotels, and to regional development (i.e. the spreading out of economic opportunity and jobs throughout a region or country). Mega events are often leveraged to foster international trade, or at least to expose business people to what the host destination has to offer. Measuring these purported benefits is difficult, given there are always many confounding variables.

Consumer surplus and existence values

In this approach an event is worth the value that consumers assign to it in terms of 'willingness to pay'. Their 'utility value' (i.e. benefits gained from the event) might be higher than the cost they have to pay or the value of the resources consumed to produce the event. This approach to valuation is difficult, given that people are possibly unable or unwilling to talk about hypotheticals like 'what would you pay if …?' Andersson and Samuelson (2000) advised on the use of the 'contingent valuation method' for events. Similarly, the 'existence value' of an event could be measured by asking residents what they would pay to create or keep an event, say from their own wallets or in increased taxes. The theory is that people value things even if they do not see or use them. Researchers could also ask who will support or rescue a threatened event; is it worth enough to the community to bail out more than once, and what might the rescue package legitimately cost?

Armbrecht (2014), Andersson and Lundberg (2013) and Andersson and Armbrecht (2014) detail the theory behind and use of contingent valuation and its application to determining various use and non-use values attributable to events. Research clearly reveals that people value events if they do not attend them, as events provide real choices, preserve traditions and enrich communities in different ways. 'Bequest value' pertains to the roles events can play in preserving traditions (to be passed on to future generations) but might also relate to the value of certain events for youth (the next generation). 'Option value' clearly stems from the choices events provide, and most people would agree that communities without events would be very boring! 'Existence value' covers the range of possible social, economic, cultural and environmental benefits that events can bring to communities. However, just because people recognize these values does not necessarily mean they are happy to see governments lavish money on them, or to have their taxes raised to support them – that is a subject for public discourse and political decision-making.

Sponsorship potential

One approach is to determine the value of events to sponsors, as properties for investment and co-branding. In other words, how much will the 'title' and all other sponsors pay (or commit 'in-kind'/'contra') to the event? This is useful because a not-for-profit or public organization can put a commercial value on the event. International Events Group (IEG 1995: 19) advised event owners to consider that qualitative benefits offered to sponsors are more important than the value of tangible things like tickets and gifts. Prestige has a value, but only a surrogate measure of it can be made.

Media value

Many events assign a dollar value to the media coverage they get by valuing the coverage at the same price you would have to pay if it was advertising. For example, news reports about the event could be given a dollar value based on the cost of an equivalent paid advertisement. But this practice ignores the fact that advertising is targeted and usually repetitive, with its timing and reach under control. It also tends to ignore the content by looking mainly at quantity. Finally, it says nothing about the potential effects of the coverage on audiences. Shibli and the Sport Industry Research Centre (2002) took a sample of television viewers in the UK to measure the average and peak size of the live broadcast audience for a snooker championship in Sheffield, England. As well, they determined its television 'rating' (i.e. the percentage of all viewers watching a single programme). The volume of clearly visible or audible exposure for sponsors' logos or messages was calculated using specially trained observers and software, then a cash equivalent value was calculated based on how much it would cost to purchase television advertising in the form of 30-second messages. The same was done for messages about Sheffield. The report emphasized that there is no guarantee that such media exposure is effective.

Psychic benefits

Burns *et al.* (1986) determined that the Adelaide Grand Prix imposed costs and problems on the resident population, but a large majority still thought the event was desirable and should be held again. In other words, it had 'psychic value' for them, which was at least equal to the monetary value of all those personal and community-felt costs.

Legacy

Evaluation of events often has to consider long-term, indirect, and sometimes subtle impacts. The term 'legacy' is neutral: it applies to all that is left over from the event (or events) either as a positive inheritance for future generations, or as problems and costs. For discussions of various event 'legacies' see: Hall 1994b; Andersson *et al.* 1999; Getz 1999; Ritchie 2000; Sadd and Jackson 2006; Preuss 2007; Quinn 2010; Sadd 2010; Rogerson (2016); Blackman *et al.* (2017); Macrae (2017); Malhado and Araujo (2017); Moss *et al.* (2018); Orr and Jarvis (2018).

Sometimes the true value of an element of the legacy will not be clear for a very long time, or a consensus on the value might never be achieved. What usually happens is that mega events are justified in advance in economic and business terms, but a full cost–benefit accounting is never forthcoming, for purely political reasons. Many costs are typically hidden, or treated as externalities, the big items being transportation improvements and security. The so-called induced tourism, supposedly generating a 'quantum leap' in tourist demand (Getz 1999), seldom materializes, and if tourism does flourish in the aftermath it is impossible to prove that it happened because of the event. The concepts of 'net present value' and 'future earnings' can be useful in evaluating the legacy. As pointed out by many economists, the development of new infrastructure for events is a cost of hosting the event, and not a benefit. Any derived, future benefits first have to be justified in terms of future earnings, and then discounted because of depreciation, increasing maintenance costs, and of course normal investment opportunity costs. Many so-called legacies have turned into expensive, useless 'white elephants'.

Economic impact assessment for event tourism

There have been well-documented problems with economic impact assessments for events (Crompton 1999; 2006; Crompton and McKay 1994). Matheson 2002; Matheson and Baade 2003; Getz 2013a), pertaining to both how they are done and the purposes they serve. Dwyer and Jago (2012: 130) identified criticisms associated with the assessment of the economic impacts of events, highlighting the exaggeration of benefits owing to either deliberate manipulation or faulty methods. The state-of-the art in economic impact assessments for events has progressed to the point where we can say there is no excuse for invalid and unreliable studies. The first comprehensive economic assessment of a major Australian event, by Burns *et al.* (1986), laid most of the foundations, including economic cost–benefit evaluation. Burgan and Mules (1992) reported on the economic impacts of sport events, while Crompton's (1999) report for the National Parks and Recreation Association provided specific guidelines for municipalities to conduct valid event impact studies.

Two studies by Dwyer *et al.* (2000a, 2000b) laid out the requirements for assessing and forecasting event impacts; they were based on a meta-analysis of Australian event impact studies, as well as economic theory. The Cooperative Research Centre in Sustainable Tourism in Australia has also published a series on event impacts including *Economic Evaluation of Special Events: A Practitioner's Guide* (Jago and Dwyer 2006) and the ENCORE toolkit for conducting studies (see www.sustainabletourism online.com).

Models and multipliers

Numerous IAs for tourism and events have employed models and multipliers, although we argue this practice has done more harm than good by exaggerating purported benefits and downplaying or ignoring costs. The 'multiplier' effect is mostly expressed in terms of 'income' or 'value added' to the area. Many authors have used multipliers, which are problematic in both theory and practical application (see, for example: Vaughan 1979; Archer 1982; Burns *et al.* 1986; Fleming and Toepper 1990; Crompton and McKay 1994; Crompton 1999; Dwyer *et al.* 2000a, 2000b; Yu and Turco 2000; Tyrrell and Johnston 2001; Jago and Dwyer 2006; Lee *et al.* 2010). Dwyer *et al.* (2006a) have recommended use of 'computable general equilibrium models' for assessing the economic impacts of events beyond the local area, rather than input–output models. The input–output approach, they argued, contains an upward bias if used for broad regions or nations.

Direct economic contribution (DEC)

There is general agreement that the estimation of 'direct economic contribution' is the starting point for all economic IAs for events (Dwyer *et al.* 2010), but we argue that it is all that is needed and desirable. A DEC calculator is provided at the website EventImpacts.com but because nothing is ever as simple as a calculator makes it appear, you MUST read the Guidance Notes (a downloadable PDF) provided by Event Impacts. Getting the right data, avoiding invalid assumptions, and knowing how to interpret forecasts and post-event impact assessments is crucial.

Other considerations

Related measurement issues that have to be considered include the identification of 'time switching' (the visitors would have come to the destination anyway, they merely changed their time to correspond with the event) and 'casual tourists' who travelled for other reasons but also attended the event. 'Displacement' is another issue, as events might attract tourists who take rooms from regular visitors (this happens during peak travel seasons), or residents might refrain from shopping because of congestion associated with the event.

Comprehensive benefit and cost evaluation

If we want to place a value on an event or events, or determine their 'worth', we need to evaluate all costs and benefits. This process will usually begin with a clear statement of goals, or what we want to achieve and to avoid.

Desired benefits

Clear statements of desired and expected benefits are needed, including explicit reference to who will benefit and will pay or experience the negative impacts. The tangible benefits in social, cultural and environmental terms have been discussed in earlier sections, and in economic terms the following are typically the most important: expenditure of sponsors and other investors (e.g. external grants); new facilities and venues (if funded externally); new employment; event tourist expenditures and their direct economic contribution; positive media coverage resulting in tourism gains; general economic growth and trade, and increased capacity (marketing and accommodation) resulting in future tourism growth. Intangible economic benefits include placing a monetary value on the use and non-use values expressed by residents, community pride, cultural renewal, arts development, increased interest and investment in the host community or destination, or enhanced real estate values. Increasingly eventful cities value image or branding benefits as much as direct economic gains, and are emphasizing the non-economic benefits as much as quantifiable, monetary gains. This is a paradigm shift in the making, aided by concerns about over-tourism, climate change and threats to peace and quality of life.

Potential direct and opportunity costs

Tangible economic costs include capital and construction costs, wages, essential services (police, infrastructure) and the long-term maintenance of venues. The harm done to individuals, families and communities is seldom assigned an economic value, but should be. Other intangible costs include: crowding and inconvenience; noise and visual pollution; personal crime and property damage; resident exodus and tourist avoidance of the area.

Externalities and opportunity costs

Costs or problems not taken into the accounts of events are termed 'externalities', and they include indirect and intangible problems like pollution and amenity loss, social and cultural disruption. 'Opportunity costs' are all the alternative uses that could be made of capital, human effort and other resources. If events constitute good investments, it has to be asked if the same resources would generate more benefits when applied to other projects.

Evaluating and weighing benefits versus costs

Getz (2019) presented a BACE model (Benefits and Costs Evaluation). The concept is that evaluation is a step beyond impact assessment and requires much more than measuring goal attainment – even though goals should always be carefully articulated in event and tourism planning. All the tangible and intangible costs and benefits have to be considered and this will be, of necessity, a multi-stakeholder process. Forecasting and measuring costs and benefits is but a step towards reconciling them within sustainability and social equity frames. The model does not permit one subject of impacts assessment or policy domain to dominate, and all possible objects of IA – from individuals to the nation – have to be considered. The distribution of costs and benefits might very well be the most important issue, especially because it often seems that industry and the community's powerful elite realize huge profits at the taxpayer's expense, even while poor people are displaced or the middle class has its taxes increased to pay for the mega event or new event venue. Table 10.4 provides a template for the multi-stakeholder evaluation, and it can be much more detailed than the items shown. In the past, all too often, only the economic winners have been given sufficient attention.

Impact assessment, evaluation and sustainability

Principles of sustainability should be applied to impact assessments and evaluating the worth of events. You need to ask these questions:

- Will the event (or, did the event or events) make it more costly or difficult for future generations to enjoy an equal or better quality of life (that would violate the principle of inter-generational equity)?
- Were irreplaceable resources used up? (Steady-state sustainability requires no net decrease)
- Do events add to global environmental problems, or help solve them? (Events should be a positive force across all dimensions of sustainability)
- Can the long-term and cumulative impacts of an event or portfolios and populations of events be predicted and a favourable benefit-to-cost ration attained? (If not, the precautionary principle should be applied and actions should be limited or closely monitored)
- Where necessary, can (or were, in the past) preventative and ameliorative actions be implemented? (If not, how can development be justified?)

Table 10.4 A framework to identify winners and losers

Types of impact	Examples of stakeholders who win/benefit (specify the benefits)	Examples of stakeholders who lose or experience negative impacts (specify the costs or losses; consider society, culture and the environment to be stakeholders)
Social	New leisure opportunities in venues and at events, for those who can afford them (both residents and tourists)	Social groups excluded from participation owing to financial, physical or social disadvantage
Cultural	Elite groups benefit from investment in 'high culture' events and venues	Sub-cultures reject mainstream cultural events and institutions and usually fail to secure financial support
Ecological; nature	Some interventions can restore habitat, clean up polluted areas and contribute to parks and protected areas	Externalities such as pollution (air, water, land, light, noise), greenhouse gas emissions, and impact on wildlife are seldom considered in formal cost-benefit analyses of events and venues
Built environment	Urban renewal, repositioning of cities, improved infrastructure and services can be benefits of major event and venue projects	Some neighbourhoods are likely to suffer increased traffic and noise, disruption of routines, or amenity losses owing to changes in land use
Economic	Tourism and hospitality sectors almost always gain financially from public investments in events and venues and tourism marketing; property owners, builders and suppliers gain from major venue projects	Small businesses might lose custom temporarily because of an event, or permanently from altered shopping and traffic patterns; new employment for some might be matched by redundancies elsewhere

Source: Getz (2019: 213).

STUDY GUIDE

A starting point for studying outcomes, or for any aspect of evaluation and impact assessment, is to ask the question: who or what is impacted, and in what way? We have indicated five main 'objects', being social, cultural, ecological, economic and built environment, and there are many possible 'subjects' being the people, organizations or things affected. As considered in Table 10.1, 'people' should be the first object of our attention, and this broad category can be disaggregated in many ways, such as by studying participants, guests, volunteers, residents in general or a social or cultural group.

Outcomes should be considered in the context of the open-system model of event organizations. Similar to an industrial process, organizations and events aim to turn inputs into outputs, and in our framework for evaluation and impact assessment these are the short-term and obvious things event producers need to measure such as attendance, revenue generated, customer satisfaction or media coverage. When we think of longer-term outcomes or impacts the theory of change comes into play because we are now viewing the event (or events) as an agent of change. Some outcomes are unintended, and even 'external' to the event and the organization. External stakeholders are likely to focus on these impacts. Those who are 'impacted' by events are legitimate stakeholders, including those who represent environmental, social and cultural concerns.

When conducting impact assessments, or evaluations of outcomes, 'stressors' or 'causal factors' should first be identified. It is not just the event itself that can cause changes, so we have to consider related investments, tourism, physical developments and media effects. The degree to which the community is involved in the event, or in policy formulation related to events, will also have an important bearing on outcomes and on how people feel they have been impacted. Stressors then have to be linked to the full range of potential outcomes, both desired and unintended, internal and external. Whether impacts are positive or negative will depend on one's perspective and on the research and evaluation methods used. This analysis leads to policy, strategy and other possible responses.

A range of models and methods are indicated in this chapter for evaluation and impact assessment, but actually conducting an impact assessment requires substantial knowledge and experience with research and consultations.

STUDY QUESTIONS

- Define outputs and outcomes within the context of a systems model.
- Explain how goals and indicators are the normal basis for evaluation and impact assessment, and how goal-free evaluation is an option.
- What are 'stressors' or 'causal forces'? Work through an example of an event causing impacts to identify the main stressors on people and on nature.
- Identify the key forces that shape personal event outcomes; discuss how and why people might find their event experiences satisfactory or not (or positive/negative).
- How do individuals respond to their direct and indirect event experiences?
- Explain how events can cause social, cultural and political outcomes (i.e. stressors plus potential impacts). Refer specifically to 'exchange theory'.
- What is 'commodification' of culture and how is it related to authenticity in planned events?
- Why and how should we study resident perceptions and attitudes towards events?
- What generates the economic benefits attributed to events? Include 'new money'.
- How do we measure the 'ecological footprints' of events? Is this the same as using a 'carbon calculator'?
- How can events be made 'green'? Is this the same as achieving 'sustainability'?
- What are the roles events should play in achieving sustainable communities and cities?
- What research is required in order to perform an economic impact assessment for an event? What does 'direct economic contribution' mean in this process?
- Provide a detailed explanation of benefit-cost evaluation for events, including discussion of 'opportunity costs' and the 'distribution' of impacts.
- Why are economic impacts not the same as benefits?
- Why is determining the 'winners and losers' an equity issue that must inform determination of the worth or value of an event?
- How would you answer the question: 'what is an event worth?'

FURTHER READING

Getz, D. (2018). *Event Evaluation*. Oxford: Goodfellow Publishers.

Getz, D. (2019). *Event Impact Assessment*. Oxford: Goodfellow Publishers.

Goldblatt, S. and Goldblatt, J. (2011). *The Complete Guide to Greener Meetings and Events*. New York: Wiley.

Jones, M. (2018). *Sustainable Event Management: A Practical Guide* (3rd edn). London: Earthscan.

Lundberg, E., Armbrecht, J., Andersson, T. D. and Getz, D. (eds) (2017). *The Value of Events*. London: Routledge.

McGillivray, D. and Turner, D. (2017). *Event Bidding: Politics, Persuasion and Resistance*. London: Routledge.

Chapter 11

Events and public policy

Public policy and events

The staging of planned events cannot ignore the many public policies and resulting regulations or laws that impact on the event sector. Conversely, policy-makers in many public policy domains have to gain a better understanding of planned events of all types in order to ensure that events can be a sustainable force for cultural, social and economic progress. Ideally, governments at all levels will create a vision and take an integrated approach to events, or at least ensure that policies affecting events are proactive and coordinated. In this chapter, we commence with a discussion of the significance of event policy and how it has developed as a key area along with some of the wider theoretical issues which impact upon the analysis of policy issues in events. This is followed by a discussion of the nature of public policy and the meaning of 'policy domains'. The second section examines justifications for public intervention in the event sector through discussion of the concepts of 'public goods', 'ideology', 'market failure' and 'efficiency'. Then each major policy domain related to planned events receives a more detailed examination, covering economic policy (development, tourism), social (leisure, sport, health and well-being), cultural (arts) and the environment. Finally, the chapter concludes with a look at the policy-making process as applicable to the event sector.

The evolution of policy analysis in events

According to Foley *et al.* (2012), policy analysis in events research has been very limited. It started with a focus on event management and has evolved to encompass the many themes of event studies. Within that transition, policy analysis has focused on a range of issues, including macro-level contextualization, policy dimensions and the impacts of events (see Figure 11.1).

Hall (2014: 188) adopted a more explicit theoretical analysis, noting that 'political analysis is closely related to public policy analysis' and making a case that the political analysis of events does in fact have a much longer pedigree and contribution to the policy debate as noted in Chapter 4. In theoretical terms, Hall (2014) argues that the political analysis of events reflects the wider concern of politics, which is about power and who gets what, where and how, a fundamental concern which was also central in the welfare geography work of D. M. Smith (1977), with an implicit focus on the territorial inequalities that arose from the distribution of goods and benefits in society. In this respect, politics and the analysis of power should be a central concern in event studies as power shapes the public policies and influences the ways in which events are developed and staged, and beneficiaries and losers emerge. This is not deemed to be a popular pastime for researchers, as it often involves critiquing the very bodies funding and hosting events even though there are many good reasons for greater transparency and accountability in event research if events are to benefit the wider public good.

Figure 11.1 Evolution of research on events policy in relation to the transition from event management to event studies

Source: Developed from Foley *et al.* (2012).

What is public policy?

'Public policy' consists of a goal-directed process by governments and their agencies, manifested in laws, regulations, decisions (both actions and inaction) and intentions of governments regarding specific problems or general areas of public concern. Policy can be viewed in terms of 'power', because political parties, special interest groups and their professional lobbyists constantly seek to influence policy.

Political scientists and other researchers can study inequities in who has power, and what interests are actually taken into account when event policy is established. Policies of government are often based on 'ideology', arising from party-political manifestos. However, determining what is a government's policy in many cases has to be deduced from what they do, or avoid doing, and this might simply reflect the dominant values of society at the time. It might also be difficult to discern the rationality behind government actions, and indeed it often appears that there is no coherent policy on events.

A 'policy domain' is a broad area of government responsibility or interest, such as culture, the economy, the environment or health, which usually encompasses a variety of departments, agencies, laws, regulations and programmes. Planned events cross a number of policy fields, often involving two or three levels of government, so it will be necessary to develop liaison between agencies on event-related issues, and to develop integrating policies.

The institutional framework

Hall and Rusher (2004) noted that the policy dimensions related to events include the political nature of the policy-making process, public participation, sources of power, exercise of choice by policy-makers in a complex environment and perceptions of the effectiveness of policy. To study event policy therefore requires knowledge of the various institutions involved, and how they interact and make policy. These include the legislators (elected or otherwise), government agencies (such as culture, tourism, sport and economic development), the courts, law enforcement, public–private partnerships, quasi-governmental organization, regulators, and other organizations with power, such as trade unions and political parties.

Increasingly cities, regions and countries are creating event-specific agencies or companies to bid on, facilitate or produce events. Unfortunately, public policy gets confusing, and perhaps becomes counter-productive, when governments delegate authority to 'independent' agencies. This can result in secrecy, lack of accountability, and decisions made without regard to public needs or preferences. Each policy field will involve a different network of stakeholders, yet tourism, culture, sports, events and other networks of agencies and interests overlap considerably. Finding one's way through these networks can be a challenge. Within them, who has power and how is it used? Intra- and intergovernmental conflicts, or lack of integration, also influence event-related policy. National governments typically promote tourism, but often it is local governments who have to provide the infrastructure; it is their voters who feel the immediate impacts. Sport and events might appear to be perfect partners, but each interest group probably wants something different and might fight over resources.

The concept of 'policy regimes' is of direct relevance, especially when it comes to the very big issues like hosting mega events. Richards *et al.* (2013: 227) noted that 'More recent studies of events have also underlined the importance of policy regimes to provide the "political will" necessary to derive lasting benefits from events.' A 'regime' could be defined by alliances, networks and power brokers. Often there are elite groups in society that have the ability to make things happen because of their collective power.

Governance

Dredge and Whitford (2011) discussed 'governance' as a form of public–private policymaking involving discourse and action among stakeholders towards the achievement of common goals. As such, this relates to stakeholder theory and value co-creation networks; to event portfolios seeking synergies, and to the engagement of all parties and voices in evaluation and impact assessment. While private companies and for-profit entrepreneurs are used to an environment in which decisions are made internally, with the company's goals first and foremost, those organizations in the public and not-for-profit sectors are often inclined towards inclusiveness.

For the purposes of evaluating or planning inclusive governance, Whitford *et al.* (2014) developed a set of indicators covering several important considerations. They recommended indicators of transparency, rule of law, responsiveness, equitable involvement, structures and processes, and accountability. A related issue, also applicable to policy making and stakeholder management in general, is that of legitimacy. Those in power have one kind, while residents and other stakeholder groups might dispute the right of politicians or public agencies to make decisions such as bidding on, funding and hosting events.

A crisis of legitimacy?

The 'legitimation' of events as policy tools and instruments of strategy is now global, but individual events, and specific actions of companies or government are often contested. One of the reasons for widespread adoption of more inclusive governance models is a lack of trust in governments and corporations. The notion of a 'legitimacy crisis' was raised by Habermas (1975) and it applies wherever and whenever the public or key stakeholders question decisions and demand transparency and accountability. Larson *et al.* (2015: 170) argued that festival legitimacy is built and sustained within the culture of a local community, and a festival comes to be regarded as an 'institution' in terms of widespread and permanent legitimacy. The source of this legitimacy can lie in moral authority, commercial success, legal status, and/or strategy. In many ways this is the same as achieving a 'social license'.

Justifying public-sector involvement

At least at election time, most governments try to justify their policies. They also put forward clearly different policy platforms, based on ideology or the need for positioning. Many voters are swayed by specific proposals or measures, while others are impressed more by values and policies that suggest the general direction a government will take. Veal (2006) observed that the critical approach to sociological research and theory has raised many public policy questions. For example, who is being served by public expenditure on festivals? Probably the most obvious public policy that relates to planned events is funding, so what is the case for public funding of events? Practice varies widely, with money coming from a variety of public agencies, all aimed at different outcomes. Increasing scrutiny of policy, or of government inaction, leads to many questions being raised in the media and at the community level.

The main lines of justification for public funding or other forms of intervention (like regulations, direct production of events, or marketing) start with ideology – namely, what is a 'public good'? After that, 'market failure' or market inadequacies are often cited, and achieving greater efficiency is also used as justification. When we addressed possible responses to outcomes and the question of 'what is an event worth' in the previous chapter, we were setting up this discussion of policy justification. Some of it goes back to the disciplinary overview of economics, and there are other threads of justification running throughout the book, including 'leisure benefits'.

The public good argument, and ideology

The key to this powerful argument is to demonstrate important benefits from events that accrue to society as a whole – or to the economy (which should clearly benefit us all) and to the environment (everyone supports a healthier, safer, more sustainable environment). It should also be made clear by policy-makers that the benefits from events can only be achieved through support and investment in events, or at least that the benefits of events are equal to those from other expenditure/investment opportunities. When backed by research, expert testimony and public opinion surveys showing support for events, the 'public good' argument cannot easily be refuted.

Therefore, in order to make the 'public good' argument valid and convincing, the following criteria have to be met:

- events fit into accepted policy domains (culture, health, economics);
- public benefits are substantial (it's worth our while to get involved), inclusive (everyone gains) and they can be demonstrated or proved;
- there are rules and accountability for money spent and other actions taken.

Ideology

Political parties take different approaches to event funding or regulation, and in general to culture, economic development or leisure and sport, based on ideologies. 'Ideology' is rooted in philosophies, value sets and even religious beliefs. Seldom do political parties engage in ideologically based debate over policies towards planned events, but it does happen around specific issues and events – especially for spending on mega events or event venues, and sometimes regarding the funding of festivals and sports. In terms of ideological differences, observers can look for the following indicators of substantial differences between party positions, and then assess how they will affect the events sector:

- a general belief in government intervention, which leads to many programmes of funding as well as to many regulations – versus a general belief in free enterprise, the marketplace and individual rather than collective responsibility;
- policies that result in governments taking a proactive lead, versus a problem-solving approach (e.g. formulating pro-event policy or merely reacting to issues);
- a belief that culture, sport and leisure are matters of health and public welfare, versus the view that they are best left to individual consumption decisions;
- a belief that tourism is business and best left to the industry, rather than being a social, environmental or cultural issue;
- responsiveness to special interest groups (which reveals power bases).

Social equity

The 'social equity' principle is really a part of the 'public good' justification. In the context of planned events it can be stated this way:

> *Where events provide a 'public good' (i.e. benefits accrue to society as a whole), it is justifiable for governments to intervene by way of subsidies (to events or participants) or direct provision of events, in order to ensure that everyone has the means to attend or otherwise benefit from events.*

'Social equity' literally means that access to a public good or service, and to the benefits of public investment, is based on principles of fairness, justice and need. This is not the same as 'equality', wherein everyone gets exactly the same thing. For example, 'equal access' to events or the benefits of events would mean that everyone gets the same, but that principle is not widely held to be feasible or desirable.

Equity is a serious issue for the event sector, particularly because many governments value events in the context of culture, social integration, leisure and health. If left to the free market, it is probable that many people will not be able to participate in some events because of high cost, inaccessibility, or lack of knowledge about opportunities. While the equity principle justifies subsidies and direct provision, the value of events to society can and should be measured. Over-development of economic impact assessment has left us weak on demonstrating social and cultural values. Sometimes government action related to events directly violates the equity principle. We see this occur in the arts sector when heavily subsidized institutions and events (such as symphony, ballet, opera, theatre) still charge high ticket prices, making it impossible for the poor to attend. This contravenes the equity principle and has to be corrected. One solution is to maintain high nominal prices (the rich hardly notice it) but to ensure that low-cost tickets are available to those in need. Another is to proactively take art and events to the people.

Failure (or inadequacies) of the marketplace

This economic justification for public involvement rests on the premise (or ideological belief) that economic development in general is best left in the hands of the private sector, but in some cases the 'free market' does not provide sufficient incentive or reward to stimulate entrepreneurial activity or to generate public goods and services. Accordingly, giving money to tourism marketing organizations, participating in joint ventures with the private sector, or providing tax incentives or subsidies to investors (including events), can all be justified as a necessary means to achieve public policy aims. This argument is sometimes extended to providing assistance for the non-profit sector. For example, non-profit organizations produce many festivals and other events in an inherently risky environment, and so they deserve assistance as long as the public good can be demonstrated.

Why economic 'laws' fail in the event sector

Burgan and Mules (2001) and Mules and Dwyer (2006) argued that fewer sporting venues would be built and fewer events would occur without public support, because 'market forces' will not support them. Yet many of the direct benefits accrue to the hospitality and travel industry, so why should the public sector intervene? The supply of events would eventually reach equilibrium with demand (i.e. what consumers are willing to pay) only if a completely free market existed. At that equilibrium point there would theoretically exist the number and types of events that were 'demanded' by paying customers. But a relatively 'free market' really only exists for certain types of events: those produced by for-profit corporations for companies or consumers that are looking for specific entertainment, learning or marketing opportunities that can only be met by these types of events (perhaps weddings or private parties). But most event entrepreneurs have to compete with subsidized events and event venues in the public or non-profit domains, which distorts the marketplace.

Return on investment and economic efficiency

Governments can make money! Numerous studies have shown that governments at all levels realize substantial tax gains from tourism in general, and event tourism in particular. Events stimulate consumption of goods and services that are heavily taxed. Purely on a profit basis, public-sector investment is thereby justified. However, there has to be proven feasibility, accountability and professional management in place. Increasingly the public sector in many countries has engaged in 'downsizing' and 'outsourcing' to save the taxpayer money. Really this is a way of saying that the services need to be provided, but the private sector can do it more efficiently. Some cities have developed festivals and events, then put them out to tender. Publicly funded facilities are managed, for profit, by private companies that use events to generate both tourism and private profits. Efficiency is also gained when events with surplus capacity are marketed to tourists, and when events are held in public facilities and spaces that both have surplus capacity and need additional revenue. In these cases, spending a little on events can realize important benefits for residents.

Justifications based on intangible benefits (psychic and existence values)

'Psychic benefits' accrue to people when they value something more than its related costs, as was calculated in the landmark event impact study by Burns *et al.* (1986). This is similar to 'consumer surplus', meaning that people are willing to pay more than the actual cost to them.

Researchers might also be able to show that people value an event, even when they do not attend, because it leads to pride in their community or they anticipate indirect benefits. This 'existence' value can be given weight through the use of 'contingent valuation methods'. Andersson (2006) concluded that researchers have generally found citizens to approve of public expenditure on culture, whether or not they are users. Indeed, one of the frontiers in justifying events is that of establishing use and non-use values. Researchers in the Sunshine Coast, Australia, employed the use/non-use methodology pioneered in Sweden by Andersson and Lundberg (2013) and Andersson and Armbrecht (2014), with the aim of valuing the entire population of events within a municipality. Getz *et al.* (2013b) drew a number of conclusions that can help advance this line of research to aid policy-making and strategy for events development (see Events in Focus 11.1).

EVENTS IN FOCUS

11.1 Policy-making and strategy for events development

Selected conclusions from: Getz, D., Gration, D., Raciti, M., Sie, L. and Frost, D. (2013b). *Final Report: Sunshine Coast Event Portfolios Valuation Research*.

The overall purpose of this research was to pilot an innovative approach to determine the value of portfolios of planned events in a community or destination, with implications for policy and strategy making. Both resident and tourist input was obtained. Use and non-use values were examined, attempting to create both an economic valuation in monetary amounts and a social perception of the worth of events. Researchers at both the University of Queensland and the University of the Sunshine Coast collaborated in conducting a pilot survey followed by a large-scale online survey of residents and tourists during 2013. Usable responses to the major online survey were obtained from 1,085 residents and 384 non-residents.

Major conclusions are as follows:

1 Residents of the Sunshine Coast greatly value their planned events, with substantial direct use value accruing from attendance, active participation (e.g. as athletes and artists) and volunteering.

2 Residents gave strong recognition to the economic, personal and social values of planned events, regardless of whether they used them or not.

3 Non-use values recognized by residents include 'option value' (i.e. having more to choose from), 'bequest value' (i.e. valued traditions; creating a legacy for future generations; more for youth to do), and 'existence value' (i.e. events are good for the community in multiple ways).

4 Residents largely believe that planned events are not causing significant social or environmental problems.

5 From a policy perspective, planned events represent a major field in which both economic gain and general public good are being created, with even greater potential to grow.

6 Residents especially support festivals and cultural celebrations, and a range of events and event venues are also supported.

7 There is only limited support among residents to accept tax increases to pay for new events or venues; this could be controversial, and a full justification for new capital expenditures and ongoing support should always be provided to residents.

Implications for policy and strategy

1 Development of a portfolio of planned events and venues should:
   a) maximize the joint value of events and venues for both residents and tourists;
   b) incorporate an events awareness and community benefits communication strategy;
   c) provide a range of celebrations, entertainment, participation and spectator sports that meet contemporary needs and anticipate emerging needs;
   d) facilitate direct involvement of residents as organizers, volunteers, athletes and artists;
   e) develop at least one event into international, hallmark-event status;
   f) provide ongoing evidence of the benefits events and venues bring to residents.

2 A managed portfolio of events for Sunshine Coast should stress balance by types and sizes, and all-year opportunities for celebration and participation.

It is highly desirable to combine regular event visitor surveys with specific questions concerning willingness to pay, perceptions of the overall attractiveness of events in the destination, and ideas for improvements; questions on relationships with residents and the environment would also be useful, in order to identify potential problems. Periodic surveys of residents are important in order to ask questions similar to those included in the current research: willingness to pay; different kinds of engagement with events; events attended; preferences for venues and events; perceptions of positive and negative impacts.

As public authorities, and publicly subsidized events need to demonstrate the creation of 'public goods' (that is, benefits that are realized and appreciated by everyone, or at least by all taxpayers), it is important to be able to show levels of public support and to identify and deal with issues raised; care should be taken to obtain the input of specific segments of the population that might be excluded through typical survey methods, including seniors, youth and economically disadvantaged groups.

The 'health' (or sustainability) of an event population can be measured, in part, by residents' impact perceptions and their changing levels of support for policies and strategies; for tourists, direct measures of demand and expenditure are useful for evaluating overall portfolio health.

The law of the commons

Culture, public lands and facilities, scenery and other natural resources exploited for tourism and events can be considered 'common' assets. Their benefits should accrue to everyone, and they need to be protected (this is the 'stewardship' principle in sustainability theory). Only government policy and action can protect common assets. If 'common' assets are used for tourism or events without regulation, by whoever takes initiative, benefits will accrue only to a few and the resources will potentially be depleted. Accordingly, public policy and action is justified on sustainability grounds, not necessarily in the form of investment, but at least in the form of regulation and, when needed, rationing. This is certainly a good reason for initiating public policy discussions.

Counter-arguments

Counter-arguments are also available. Money given to special interest groups often attracts opposition, especially from groups that do not get similar treatment. Sometimes there are strong cultural or political forces opposing government spending on projects that are claimed to be 'elitist' (e.g. performing arts), 'harmful' (risky sports), 'perverse' (gay or lesbian pride) or 'narrow' (i.e. the benefits accrue only to tourism or to private companies). A lack of involvement with tourism or events might occur because attention is turned elsewhere (so do policy-makers have the facts? Are they effectively lobbied?). And because governments are faced with virtually unlimited spending opportunities, and limits on resources, they have to constantly prioritize. It is certainly reasonable for policy-makers and political parties to say they have more important priorities than planned events, but that is not very convincing when policy already exists for directly related domains like sport, the arts, tourism and economic development.

Why national governments are involved with events

Many governments at all levels are developing policies and strategies regarding the events sector – often with tourism as the main priority, but increasingly adding social, cultural and environmental goals as well. Examples from Scotland and New Zealand can be found in Events in Focus 11.2.

EVENTS IN FOCUS

11.2 Events sector policies and strategies: examples from Scotland and New Zealand

Scotland (www.eventscotland.org).

The Perfect Stage is Scotland's national events strategy which outlines our mission and vision for attracting and hosting events up to 2020. The strategy defines Scotland's key assets, which have made it a world-leading events destination.

Scotland's cultural identity and heritage are strong differentiating factors and the friendliness of our people is renowned throughout the world. Scotland boasts a rich natural landscape as well as impressive architecture and cityscapes and a range of sports facilities and arenas. Scotland has a range of iconic sporting and cultural events, which form the backbone of our events portfolio and reinforce our reputation as a world leading events destination.

The strategy also defines the seven key impacts by which EventScotland will measure the successes of Scotland's events industry: tourism; business; image and identity as a nation; media; participation and development; environment; and social and cultural benefits.

Scotland has earned its place and reputation in hosting major world-class events and, through this visionary and aspirational events strategy, will continue to do so.

Scotland: The Perfect Stage outlines a clear mission and vision for building and strengthening Scotland's events industry and leading that industry into the future.

Major Events New Zealand (www.med.govt.nz/majorevents/new-zealand-major-events/strategy). The New Zealand Government, through New Zealand Major Events, works in partnership with the event sector to support New Zealand's growing reputation as an attractive destination for major events of global significance. The government invests in major events that generate significant immediate and long-term benefits and align with wider government objectives through leverage and legacy opportunities.

'Our vision is that New Zealand becomes a world class event destination where major events generate economic, social and cultural benefits to New Zealand.'

New Zealand Major Events priorities are to attract, retain, grow and enhance tourism.

Major events have the potential to:

- increase tourism revenue
- increase opportunities for New Zealand brand promotion
- create new business and trade opportunities, reinforcing high achievement and increasing participation in sports and arts
- strengthen national pride and identity
- enhance the capability of the events sector.

Over the long term, major event outcomes include:

- a high-value economy
- vibrant communities and culture
- a flourishing events sector.

New Zealand Major Event's priority actions include:

- smart investment of the Major Events Development Fund in events with the most potential for economic return
- continue to ensure that events activate leverage and legacy plans that deliver on wider government objectives
- implement the revised decision-making structure for the Major Events Development Fund – including establishing the Major Events Ministers Group and Major Event Investment Panel
- develop a prospecting plan to enhance New Zealand's ability to attract major events
- develop a stronger model for evaluating the economic, social and cultural benefits of major events
- continue to implement the Business Events Strategic Approach alongside Tourism New Zealand
- more effectively communicate the government's Major Events Strategy to the New Zealand events sector and reinforce New Zealand's reputation as a world-class events destination
- continue to support sector capability building through the Major Events Resource Bank.

In the sections below, we look more closely at the economic, cultural, social and environmental policy domains as they relate to planned events. For each, goals are suggested, then related policy initiatives and appropriate performance measures are discussed.

Economic policy and events

Much of the importance attached to planned events is related to their economic benefits, leading many governments to view event development as a legitimate, strategic policy field. While this has resulted in considerable growth in the events sector, it is a limited view of planned events and does result in some negative consequences (see Table 11.1).

Foster event tourism

Tourism 'boosterism' has led many policy-makers to believe that events are good, and that investment in them is justified, because they attract tourists and media attention. Event tourism clearly can generate foreign currency and enhance a destination's image development, but these benefits cannot be taken for granted. There are too many variables at play to ensure success: witness the downturn in tourist arrivals to Australia following the 2000 Sydney Olympic Games. The Olympics were oversold on the basis of long-term tourism benefits, but who could predict the tragedy of 9/11 the following year? Event tourism is a truly global phenomenon, and is highly competitive, but many destinations and cities do not have a specific policy or strategy for it. Event tourism policy should be fully integrated with policy for venues (e.g. convention centres, sport and cultural facilities) and for place marketing and economic development.

Developing a 'portfolio' of events (see Getz 2005) is a good strategy. At the base of the portfolio 'pyramid' are small, local events which meet resident needs, animate the destination and perhaps have some tourism growth potential. The top of the pyramid should be an occasional mega event, but for most destinations, it is probable that enduring benefits are more attainable through the development of one or more periodic 'hallmark events' that fit the brand and boost the destination's image. As well, many regional-scale events will provide tourism benefits. One essential component of the portfolio approach is to recognize that events have different value (e.g. sustainability, high-yield, growth potential, market share, cost) and that portfolios can be developed for different types of events and for all seasons.

Strategic consideration should also be given to the desirability and means for growing events in size and tourism significance, such as by increased marketing and lengthening of their duration. Some events can be transformed from resident to visitor dominated, although with caution to avoid displacement or disgruntlement of residents. The selection of performance measures is important. Too many tourism organizations rely on volume measures, as if having more tourists is inherently good and without costs. Every destination should instead concentrate on yield and sustainability. Event tourists tend to be high in yield relative to mass, packaged tourists, and this has clearly been documented for convention tourists

Table 11.1 Economic policy and events

Possible goals	Related policy initiatives	Performance measures
Foster event tourism	Establish an event-tourism policy domain	Measure event tourism yield relative to other tourists
Leverage events for general economic development	Develop an event portfolio strategy for the community or destination	
Use events to maximize venue efficiency	Integrate event policy with venue investment and operations	Tourism growth
		Demonstrable 'legacy' benefits
Use events in place marketing (e.g. image enhancement)	Integrate event policy with place marketing and other economic development	Evaluation of image enhancement

and types of participant-sport tourist. The sustainability of tourists in this context refers both to their long-term demand (will they come back?) and their appropriateness in terms of achieving sustainable development goals.

Leverage events for general economic development

Event tourism policy and strategy have been expanding to focus on 'leveraging' events more comprehensively, including using events to foster trade and economic diversification. Plans also have to be in place to realize the potential urban renewal benefits of mega events and to ensure that facilities built for events will remain viable and efficiently utilized in the long term.

The employment-creation potential of most events is small, although mega events can generate substantial short-term growth in construction jobs. To maximize employment benefits, event policy has to be tied closely to tourism, sport and culture/arts development in general, and to venue construction and operations. Suitable performance measures can include jobs created and sustained, the spread of event benefits in time and space, stakeholder satisfaction, new trade and business links formed, and start-up businesses related to events.

Use events to maximize venue efficiency

Funding and building convention and exhibition centres, arts and sports facilities, has a major impact on events and event tourism. What is surprising is that massive infrastructure investments are frequently made without a supporting events policy. It seems to be assumed that cities need impressive facilities, and that most publicly funded event venues will be permanently subsidized by government. How many events are held, and their economic benefits, is one measure of venue efficiency. Building them is expensive, but easy, whereas making good use of facilities in the long-term is the real challenge. A balance between tourist and resident use is also important.

Use events in place-marketing

Exploiting events for image-building, branding, repositioning or place marketing in general requires policy and a strategy. Competitive advantages are being gained by destinations that have the knowledge and vision to integrate events with other place- marketing efforts, including film development, familiarization tours, trade missions, and city or regional branding. As economic impact and growth measures are used, there needs to be more effort expended on developing and testing social, cultural and environmental performance measures in event tourism. Some intangible measures, including image enhancement, are difficult to formulate and research. Even more difficult, both in theoretical and methodological terms, is to prove that image enhancement increases tourism demand.

Cultural policy and events

Next to economics, events are most often seen as being in the domain of cultural policy. This relates mostly to festivals and the arts, but there is no reason why all planned events cannot facilitate cultural experiences and meet other cultural development goals (see Table 11.2).

Foster arts and cultural development

A number of studies have examined the aims or mandates of festivals and events. A survey of Irish festivals (Goh 2003) asked organizers to indicate and prioritize their aims, revealing that the top goal was

Table 11.2 Cultural policy and events

Possible goals	Related policy initiatives	Performance measures
Foster arts and cultural development through investment in events Leverage events for general and traditional/indigenous cultural development Use events to maximize venue efficiency Foster sustainable cultural event tourism	Integrate events in cultural policy and arts development strategies Develop specific event funding programmes Develop cultural themes and programming for all events	Assess the overall effectiveness of arts and cultural development in the community Develop and employ specific measures of cultural event success and its benefits

to promote artistic excellence. This was followed very closely by increasing tourism and area promotion (both place-marketing goals). Other aims (in descending order) were to showcase local heritage or arts, boost the local economy, celebration, encourage social inclusion and education. 'Development' in the arts and cultural domains has to encompass increased awareness of what is available and its benefits to the community, audience-building through direct involvement of people in the arts, generating revenue (such as by facilitating corporate sponsorship and targeting grants), fostering traditional or indigenous talent and expression, and even providing free entertainment for the public.

Radbourne (2002) argued that the most common argument for government involvement is that 'arts and cultural activity enrich a society and that all people have the right of access and participation'. Because public benefits are generated (although these are frequently in dispute), and because the private sector will not provide the necessary supply (a 'failure of the marketplace'), direct government action is needed. Basically this is the 'social equity argument' – that many people cannot afford the arts without government intervention. More recently, claims have been growing that the arts and cultural activity in general make for an attractive living and working environment, stimulating innovation and competitive advantage (e.g. Florida 2002 and the 'creative economy'). All events can provide cultural experiences through appropriate theming and programming. There is no reason why business and political events cannot provide cultural experiences for visitors, such as through authentic entertainment, meaningful host–guest interactions, interpretation, and additional pre- or post-cultural opportunities.

Foster sustainable cultural event tourism

Ali-Knight and Robertson (2004: 8) outlined the Edinburgh Cultural Policy, and the subsequent Festivals Strategy launched in 2001 in tandem with an Events Strategy. These policy initiatives reflected the city's commitment to its positioning as the 'festival city', in recognition of the contribution of events to both the economic and cultural viability of the city. The Festivals Strategy emerged from stakeholder consultations, in both the tourism and festival sectors, discussions with core groups like the Joint Festivals Working Group, and extensive desk research including benchmarking against other cities.

Some of the key goals of the Festivals Strategy were to develop a year-round programme of events, and to ensure their independence and a balance of creativity, social objectives and commercial viability. Other aims covered social inclusion (getting a broad range of residents involved) and securing adequate funding. There will remain, inevitably, many tensions between culture and the growing 'instrumentalist' or 'strategic' approaches to festivals and events. Waterman (1998) highlighted latent tensions between festival as art and economics, between culture and cultural politics. He concluded that support for the arts is part of a process used by elites to establish social distance between themselves and others, and that festival development is related to place promotion, which encourages 'safe' art forms.

Traditional culture

As illustrated in the earlier research note by Xie (2003), official Chinese policy both helped convert the Bamboo-beating dance on Hainan Island to a tourist-oriented spectacle and, ironically, helped turn it into an authentic tradition for the Li people. This aspect of cultural policy is often overlooked in developed countries because traditional events and indigenous peoples are either non-existent or have been marginalized. It is more likely that native celebrations, like the North American pow-wow, will be viewed as tourist attractions and marketed accordingly, rather than viewed as being on a par with opera or theatre.

Social policy and events

Foster social integration

In many communities, including small towns and city neighbourhoods, events can be catalysts for community development. Their organization and revenue-making potential can foster self-sufficiency and pride in accomplishment. Community identity and pride can be heightened through sharing with outsiders. Integration of diverse or conflicted social groups should be a specific aim, to be realized through planning and decision-making, all the way through social interaction and interpretation at events. Public services and resources provided to events (e.g. police, fire, traffic control, transport, physical infra-structure) are often viewed as expenses to be recovered, but should be provided within the context of social and cultural policy. In many cases direct provision of events, and subsidies for using public services, are warranted. Who should have access to public spaces and venues? Many governments license all events and ban or shut down informal gatherings, but does this policy always serve social and other goals? It can certainly be argued that in a free society, people have the right to assemble and hold spontaneous events, although this has to be balanced by responsible behaviour. How should potentially conflicting aims be resolved?

Combat social problems

What constitutes anti-social behaviour versus permissible civil disobedience? Preventing and reacting to social problems at or surrounding events is a matter of social policy. It is not just a security issue, but should integrate public awareness and education, event management including crowd controls, venue design and travel restrictions.

Leverage events for urban renewal

Mega events in particular are viewed as opportunities for large-scale redevelopment or urban renewal projects. Cities create tangible legacies in terms of monuments and landmarks, culture and entertainment precincts, fresh design and aesthetics, and hopefully renewed residential value. History has demonstrated that these benefits must be planned in advance, not left to chance, and that events can be a powerful planning and renewal tool (see Table 11.3).

Use events to enhance health and wellness

Events can be used as social marketing tools (requiring education and thematic interpretation) and to provide activities for encouraging healthy lifestyles. There will be direct tie-ins to sport, parks and recreation. Examples include food and beverage festivals with nutritional themes, sport competitions stressing safe

Table 11.3 Social policy and events

Possible goals	Related policy initiatives	Performance measures
Foster social integration and community development through a programme of public events	Integrate events with urban renewal, social and community development policy	Assess the overall effectiveness of social policy; develop and employ specific measures of event success and its benefits
Combat social problems at and surrounding events (hooliganism, crime)	Integrate events with health and wellness policy	
Leverage events for urban renewal	Integrate events with policy for sport, parks and recreation	
Use events to enhance health and wellness	Provide resources for combating social problems associated with events	
	Formulate policy regarding the use of public spaces for events, both formal and informal	

play, and 'edutainment' events in parks. Health concerns and regulations have to be applied across the spectrum of events and event venues, so why not make them proactive to encourage health and wellness?

'Social tourism' is a related policy field, entailing the subsidization of holidays or other leisure activities, especially for the economically disadvantaged or persons with special needs. 'Sport For All' and sport youth festivals can yield psychological as well as health benefits. Because so many sports glorify violence, policy should be directed towards the counter-message that sport can be safe, friendly and fun. Hooliganism and other social problems associated with certain sport events have to be combated through a multi-dimensional approach including legal prohibitions against travel, public education, venue design, crowd management/controls and security regimes.

Public subsidy for professional sports and private sport venues is controversial. Whilst evidence suggests it is not economically beneficial to cities, typically it is done for reasons of prestige and political expediency. Are there any social benefits that can justify this form of subsidy? Recreation events can be viewed as a public good, particularly when they encompass a variety of social and cultural aims. Events in parks should provide for safe social interaction and should foster environmental responsibility.

Community resilience

Derrett (2008: 107) has developed a model to show how festivals can develop community resilience, defined as the 'future capacity of that community to meet challenges that might beset them'. The key elements in the process are participation (collaboration, engagement from multiple stakeholders), governance (leadership, learning) and the nature and context of the event. The aims are to foster social/cultural well-being, environmental sustainability and economic prosperity. In effect, events are a catalyst in this complex process of community and economic development, in a triple-bottom-line approach. All this should be viewed in the context of development of a sense of place and community.

Social marketing

Many uses of events as policy instruments can be considered as 'social marketing', designed to change attitudes and behaviour of the public – for the better. The focus is on populations, not individuals, and positive results can be very difficult to prove. Probably the best-known examples are from the health policy domain, particularly stop-smoking campaigns. When events are intended to change attitudes and behaviour, new research methods and measures will be required. Lefebvre (2011) outlined a social marketing approach focused on audiences. The four rings of the model have audiences in the middle, and it is essential to specify what are the benefits to the target audience. Benefits should tap into deep motivations. The social context must be understood, both with regard to current attitudes and desired behaviours, and both determinants and consequences of attitudes and behaviour. Methods of branding and positioning should be used to communicate the ideal, in terms that the target audience find appealing. It has to mean something positive to them, such as health, pride, happiness and well-being. The full marketing mix can then be employed, including economic and non-economic aspects of price (such as the cost of social problems in a community).

Environmental policy and events

Case (2013) emphasized the various relationships that have to be considered: the entire supply chain for events; venues, permanent and temporary; micro and macro impacts (from waste and noise to climate change); legacies such as regeneration, and the various environmental constraints and determinants such as weather and landscape. The book covers legislation and standards applicable to the events sector, at various levels of government. One interesting observation made by Case is that small events are not scrutinized in the same way as large events, and perhaps do not even have to account for environmental impacts.

Require green and sustainable events and event venues

The basic policy imperative is to ensure that all events are 'green', meeting the minimum RRR standards (i.e. reduce, reuse, recycle). Integrate events with conservation and environmental management policies, land-use planning and controls, noise and traffic by-laws, and other environmental influencers (see Table 11.4). Beyond that, a policy to foster sustainable events (a 'triple-bottom-line' approach: economic, social, environmental) will go much further to conserve the environment and ensure long-term support for events, although it cannot be expected that all stakeholders will share this comprehensive perspective (Hede 2007).

In the UK, a Sustainable Events Management System has been developed (British Standards Institute 2006) and this suggests a likely global trend. The document provides several reasons for developing standards, including social and client expectations, legislative compliance and the delivery of better outcomes at lower cost. Issues to be considered under the heading of sustainable events are diverse: global climate change; air and water use and quality; land use; biodiversity; heritage; emissions and waste; product

Table 11.4 Environmental policy and events

Possible goals	Related policy initiatives	Performance measures
Require green and sustainable events and event venues	Integrate event policy with planning, land use, and all environmental management systems	Develop comprehensive environmental standards and evaluation measures for events and event venues
Leverage events for environmental education and development	Supply chain controls	Evaluate the social marketing effectiveness of environmental messages at events
Foster events with environmental themes	Full life-cycle accounting	

stewardship (ethics and values); health, safety and comfort. Emphasis is placed on organization and management systems, including risk assessment, working with stakeholders, and supply chain controls.

A related concept is that of 'capacity to absorb' events, or to tolerate change without detrimental impacts on culture or the environment. Each event has potential impacts, but what can we say about cumulative event impacts? Little attention has been paid to this issue. Design capacity for venues is a related concept, and event managers are forced to examine maximum attendance and the activity load of events for safety, health and experiential reasons. The 'precautionary principle' comes up whenever sustainability is discussed, but it is controversial. Some people believe that if we can anticipate that an event might cause negative impacts, we should not produce it. This is an extreme view, as it can be misused to preclude just about any activity or development. In the same way, the principle of 'no irreversible change' is open to considerable misuse as a way to prevent desired and necessary action. The fact is that almost any development results in irreversible changes.

Finally, we have already mentioned economic 'externalities'. A logical response to the externality problem is to require that polluters pay for their actions, and that anyone causing public costs should be held accountable. If this principle gets applied uniformly it will mean that no event organizer will be able to ignore costs and impacts that extend beyond the event. However, this principle can also be abused. Consider that events often result in traffic congestion, albeit temporarily, and some people not attending the event might lose time and money as a consequence. Should they be compensated by the event organizers? What about people impacted by event-caused noise? Certainly it is important to consider all these costs and benefits in the feasibility study and in post-event evaluations, but it is also important to realize that society is almost always paying some price for economic activity; we tolerate congestion and noise as a normal consequence of living in cities and fostering economic growth. The same argument applies to any event that provides a 'public good' – we should be willing to collectively tolerate some degree of inconvenience or amenity loss in pursuit of social and cultural growth. To what extent we tolerate them, and how we deal with externalities, is a matter of debate and public decision-making.

Economic tools exist for influencing the marketplace and fostering sustainable development. Price mechanisms generally work well, either using high prices to discourage consumption or subsidized prices to encourage it. If society believes that attending cultural festivals is a form of sustainable development, but participation in off-road motorcycle races is not, price manipulation can be made through differential taxation, subsidies or other means. Still more effective, of course, is direct prevention of undesirable events through licensing or other regulatory devices.

Leverage events for environmental education and development

Visitors should be made aware of green operations and sustainability principles applied to the event they are attending, and they could also be informed of how to extend these actions to their home and work settings as a social marketing strategy. Events with explicit environmental themes have been growing in number, including global movements like Earth Day and interest-specific themes like bird watching.

Public policy-making

If events are considered a 'public good', on par with – or an element in – social, leisure, health, sport and culture policy, then there should be a planning process in place to ensure adequate provision. The following system could be put in place:

- needs assessment; issues identification; multi-stakeholder input;
- developing a portfolio of events to meet specific needs in specific places;

- setting standards of provision and accessibility;
- funding and facilitation programmes tied to public agencies and venues;
- organizational development to ensure implementation; community capacity-building;
- research, monitoring and impact evaluation;
- review and policy refinement.

It seems likely that most authorities will not develop such an integrated events policy, but within the closely related policy domains, the same planning approach can be applied:

- issues (why are we interested in events? justification for intervention);
- purpose and goals (what we want to accomplish with events – the desired outcomes);
- research, consultations, and the planning process;
- evaluation and accountability (e.g. performance measures, monitoring and feedback);
- implementation: laws and regulations; event development or bidding agencies; event-funding programmes.

Policy considerations

Hall and Page (2006: 335) identified a number of policy-related considerations that should be applied to the events sector.

The policy environment

The basic form of government (is it democratic?), the distribution of power, and how society is structured are determinants of the policy environment as are the values of political parties (i.e. ideology) reflected in the emphasis on a free market versus interventionism. 'Institutional arrangements' are critical, as where an event development agency exists (these are common in Australia and Scotland), or an events office within a city (e.g. in the Chicago Mayor's Office), a consistent message can be provided. This has been viewed against the many voices to be heard, and not all of them are effective in lobbying. Such a situation introduces the notion of a 'policy arena' in which special interest groups engage in lobbying, institutions interact, individuals and groups achieve influence, and leadership might or might not be effective. The notion of a 'political market square' is pertinent, as the various stakeholders have varying degrees of power and influence, form alliances or collaborate, negotiate and seek to influence policy. The openness of this process should be a matter of concern to everyone. In most places the policy arena for events is fractured, consisting of the often-competing voices of sport, arts, heritage, culture and tourism, and further subdivided by professional associations representing specific types of event.

Policies and programmes are formulated for specific purposes, then must be evaluated in terms of their impact, effectiveness and efficiency. Policy should be continuously reviewed and improved, and with full stakeholder input. Finally, there is the important matter of accountability – how are officials and others held accountable for their policies and actions?

Options for events policy and strategy

Getz and Frisby (1991) developed a framework for local government policy-making in the events sector, and their framework can be applied to event-related policy in general. The basic logic also applies to other agencies, such as tourism, with their interconnection with events. Our basic premise is that some level of policy or direct intervention in the events sector is desired and practical. First, several optional roles have to be considered:

- 'direct provision': government or agencies produce and own events;
- 'equity approach': do not produce, but invest in events (in this case 'equity' means the capital invested);
- 'sponsorship': act like corporations and make sponsorship deals for specific benefits (such as image-making, social marketing);
- 'facilitate': through various policy initiatives, facilitate event creation or operations.

The 'facilitation' role leads to various assistance options:

- financial: grants, loans, lines of credit, debt relief, subsidies (e.g. for use of police, traffic services, venues), tax relief, awards and prizes;
- technical: professional advice; training; research and information; office space;
- marketing: overall or event-specific promotions; inclusion in government materials, websites.;
- regulatory: fast-tracking; release from onerous obligations;
- infrastructure: provision and improvement of necessary services (roads, water) and public venues (e.g. theatres, arenas, parks, plazas).

Regulating the events sector

Event producers have to satisfy and manage relationships with numerous regulatory agencies and their officials. A majority of these are at the local level, but sometimes multi-level approvals are needed:

- police: security requirements; police presence;
- traffic: accessibility, parking, public transport, control;
- fire: maximum capacity; accessibility and evacuation procedures; materials;
- health and safety: hazardous materials; fireworks and lasers; food and beverage preparation and storage standards; electricity; waste disposal;
- building inspection: new construction or allowable temporary structures;
- land use: where events can be held; where venues can be built; size limits; site planning requirements;
- noise control: noise levels and dispersion; hours of operation;
- labour: minimum wages; age restrictions; work hours; certification of professionals and trades people;
- environmental: emission standards (smoke, pollutants); recycling; wastes;
- consumer protection: price controls, guarantees, refunds.

Policy formulation at the community level: collaboration and consensus-building

Policy-making for events can range from a top-down approach, led by government or specific agencies, to a bottom-up approach, arising from community needs assessments and the input of many stakeholders. Event tourism policy tends to be top-down (at least in Australia, as demonstrated by Whitford 2004a, 2004b), mainly because it is seen as legitimate economic development, but also because so much bidding on events is opportunistic. When developing policy open to stakeholder input, a number of collaborative, consensus-building approaches can be used. Hall and Rusher (2004: 225) gave an example of effective community involvement in events policy.

Research, evaluation and public policy

What do we need to formulate and effectively administer events-related policy? Both practitioners and academics have a role to play, not just the policy-makers themselves. To analyse policy, or strategy, one should examine the following:

- intention, expressed purpose (is it economic/development-oriented, or community/culture-oriented; goals and performance criteria);
- contents (responsibilities of the agencies involved, types of events covered, applicability in different settings);
- implementation (programmes and schedules, funds allocated, regulations, evaluation and accountability);
- results (multiple, independent evaluations of intended and unintended outcomes; feedback and revisions).

Policy and institutional networks can be important when assessing impacts, as festivals can be catalysts for future action. This creation of social or cultural capital is difficult to measure.

Public discourse and policy

We cannot expect rational and sustainable decision-making until and unless there is a full, open and honest public discourse on events and their cost and impacts. Such a discourse is also essential for the institutionalization of a new paradigm, such as a sustainable events or triple-bottom-line approach. What gets covered in the press, and the issues talked about by residents, constitute important elements in the public discourse. Researchers and practitioners have a moral responsibility to engage politicians and the public, in large part by offering evidence and informed opinions about the impacts of events.

STUDY GUIDE

It is important to all event stakeholders to understand the policy environment in which they operate, and in studying the contents of this chapter it should be remembered that events are heavily regulated, often produced, subsidized or fostered by governments, generally expected to meet diverse policy goals, and are routinely subjected to intense public scrutiny within a political environment.

The nature of public policy was discussed at the beginning of this chapter, leading to an exploration of how public involvement in the events sector can be justified. Specifically this included the 'public good' argument and 'equity principle', which are linked to ideology, and, borrowing from economics, the 'failure of the marketplace' justification. Additional justification is related to 'efficiency', as in getting the most out of public infrastructure and venues, and the intangible or psychic benefits that accrue to people even if they do not attend events.

Increasingly events, and especially funding decisions and bidding on mega events, are highly political in nature. When answering the study questions, keep in mind the potential for controversy, scrutiny (via impact assessments and external evaluations), and how power gets used in the political arena.

STUDY QUESTIONS

- What is 'public policy' and what are 'policy domains'?
- Explain how governmental intervention in the event sector can be justified, including the 'public good' and 'equity' arguments, 'market failure' and 'efficiency'.

- What are the main options for governments, at different levels, when intervening in the events sector?
- Discuss economic, social, cultural and environmental policy domains as they pertain to planned events. Give examples of major possible goals, related policy initiatives and performance measures.
- What factors are important in shaping the policy-making process for events? Include 'ideology' and 'institutional arrangements'.
- What does 'governance' mean in the context of collaboration for the co-creation of value? How is this related to 'legitimacy'?
- What process should governments follow to develop policies for events?

FURTHER READING

Case, R. (2013). *Events and the Environment*. London: Routledge.

Veal, A. (2010). *Leisure, Sport and Tourism: Politics, Policy and Planning* (3rd edn). Wallingford: CABI.

PART IV

Conclusion

Chapter **12**

Science, knowledge and theory for event studies

LEARNING OBJECTIVES

Upon completion of this chapter, students should know the following:

- how knowledge is created in event studies, from disciplines, reflective professionals and other sources;
- the main paradigms of knowledge and knowledge formation;
- how positivism is challenged by alternative paradigms including interpretivism and critical theory;
- the nature and importance of 'discourse';
- the main research methodologies and methods from disciplines and closely related fields;
- quantitative, qualitative and mixed methods;
- how research is justified in applied, theoretical and policy contexts;
- how theory is being developed specifically for event studies, such as the meaning and importance of convergence of forms and functions;
- major knowledge gaps and research priorities in event studies;
- big issues facing the events sector.

A framework for knowledge creation

As argued by Getz (2007) and reiterated by Robertson *et al.* (2018), knowledge creation can be thought of as a pyramid. At the base is applied knowledge about event design and production, with Robertson *et al.* (2018: 866) stating:

At this basic level, knowledge is extensive and well documented, with myriad strategies to ensure good execution through design and production. This is closely related to the second area, that of event management, which builds on the event design and production knowledge with extensions into experience and cohesion, the community aspects of event management.

Theory and discourse lie at the apex, constituting what we mean by 'Event Studies'.

Research lies at the heart of knowledge-creation for the purposes of developing theory, but researchers are not the only ones creating knowledge. Most event-related research has stemmed from sheer curiosity, or from a management or policy need. As event studies is a relatively new field, a lot of pertinent research has been within well-established, disciplinary lines of inquiry. To progress towards interdisciplinarity, wherein event studies will have its own theories and methodologies, we will have to focus more on the core phenomenon and related themes. This is not a chapter on research methods, although many are mentioned. It is intended to provide an overview of the entire knowledge creation and research process, starting with a conceptual model, then proceeding to discussion of basic research paradigms, methodologies and methods. Pertinent books covering research and methods have been written for the events sector (e.g. Fox *et al.* 2014; Veal and Burton 2014; Veal 2011). The books *Event Evaluation* (Getz 2018) and *Event Impact Assessment* (Getz 2019) provide specific research guidance for events and related fields.

Figure 12.1 depicts the various ways in which knowledge can be created and a research project can begin, applied to event studies; each of these is discussed in turn. At the centre is our field of event studies, and we rely on established disciplines and closely related professional fields for ideas, theories and methods.

Disciplinary perspectives

Anyone conducting research on events should view the established disciplinary perspectives as a legitimate starting point. Even if the research problem is rooted in a policy or management need, it is highly possible that sociology, economics or another discipline already provides an answer or a solid foundation for the research. However, within these disciplines, the study of events is often incidental to a broader issue or theoretical problem, or the focus is not on the core phenomenon of the planned event experience.

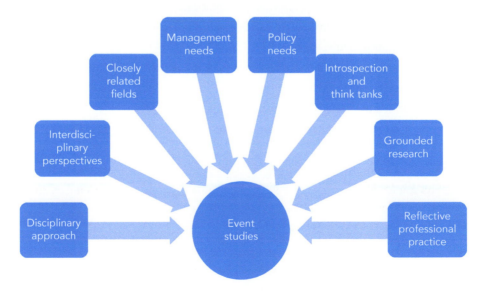

Figure 12.1 Creating knowledge and doing research in event studies

A 2018 review of Australian doctoral dissertations pertaining to planned events by Lockstone-Binney (see the Research Note) found that sociology was providing the most frequent disciplinary foundation, but 51 per cent of the theses studied were multidisciplinary in nature. Lockstone-Binney suggested there was greater scope for drawing from marketing, education, health, environmental and critical studies.

12.1 RESEARCH NOTE ON KNOWLEDGE GENERATION

Lockstone-Binney, L. (2018). Knowledge generation in event studies: What can doctoral research tell us about evolution of the field? *Event Management*, 22, 1047–1056.

The growth path of event studies as an emergent field of study has been documented in a number of reviews and summations of the extant literature to study key topics of research interest, identify gaps in the prevailing research agenda, and map progress towards the field gaining academic legitimacy. These studies have focused on the discourse as generally presented in academic journals. As a marker of maturity, no study has yet to examine the discipline bases, topics studied and methods applied in respect of doctoral research in the field. Content analysis revealed tentative evidence of discipline development in terms of the generation of event-specific knowledge and discipline integration, with sociology the dominant disciplinary influence informing the theses studied. Gaps and opportunities for further advancement of the field are identified.

Interdisciplinary approach

When two or more disciplinary foundations are applied to address a research problem, we enter the realm of interdisciplinary research (see Chapter 1), with the long-term goal being to establish unique, event-specific interdisciplinary theory and knowledge. The term *multidisciplinary* is sometimes used synonymously with interdisciplinary, as in the 'pulling together of a multidisciplinary team to solve a complex problem' but these are distinct. Event studies fits well into the social sciences, mainly because of its heavy reliance on the human and behavioural disciplines, but it also is eclectic in drawing from arts, sciences, engineering and design – really any other area of study can offer something of value. Event management and event tourism, as dominant discourses and professional fields, draw more from mainstream economics, management and marketing theory.

Closely related professional fields

Work being conducted in closely related professional fields, especially leisure studies and tourism, offers a foundation for event studies research. These fields not only have a head start in applying various disciplines to their problems and issues, but events already figure prominently in their contents with their core focus on *visitors* and activities in one's *leisure time*. Patterson and Getz (2013) examine the 'nexus of leisure and event studies' and demonstrate how a considerable amount of disciplinary theory has been adapted by leisure scholars that also has salience for planned events.

Management needs

What producers and managers need to improve events and intended outcomes also drives the global research agenda. Researchers and practitioners have to continue to work together, and to close the natural gap between them, in order to ensure that research is timely and useful. But not all event studies research needs to be, or should be, applied. Ensuring that knowledge grows over time is the aim of a learning organization, and it depends on a formal evaluation system being in place. For one-time events, knowledge transfer is more difficult, as the next organizers might be in a different country, and get started years later. The Olympics Transfer of Knowledge (TOK) programme is designed to build on previous experiences and make it easier to get the mega event produced as promised. Beginning with the Sydney 2000 Olympic Summer Games, the process includes observers who complete reports, visual evidence (videos, photos) and debriefings. Pre-bid research is also conducted according to International Olympic Committee protocols in potential host cities.

Evaluation is also needed on the numerous one-time events that do not have formal requirements for TOK. This should be the role of tourism organizations that bid, and venues that host events. Standard methods and measures are needed to make results comparable.

Getz (2018) has argued that event management cannot be an applied management field without applying mainstream management theory. Management theory is primarily concerned with the management of organizations, enterprise, and persons. It is very broad and fragmented, incorporating foundation theories from traditional disciplines, especially economics, sociology and psychology. Often the management functions are identified when speaking of management theory, but their number and inter-dependencies are open to interpretation: governance, which includes ownership and decision-making; planning; organization and coordination; control; marketing; human resources; financing. Evaluation is a part of several of these functions, and impact assessment is one input to evaluation and planning. Kessler (2013: xxix) advocated that 'it is imperative to recognize that our worldview is shaped by the theories that we employ. Whether we are liberated, or imprisoned, by them is another matter entirely and largely a fate of our choosing.'

Reflective professional practice

It has always proved difficult to get practitioners to contribute research papers or case studies to the academic literature. The starting point is for practitioners to be reflective, not just focused on the tasks at hand, and to use this reflection in part to initiate research projects. Often the applied needs of practitioners can dovetail well with the more theoretical and long-term goals of academic research. *Theory of change models* can be experimental, leading to theory development. Designed when events or portfolios are intended to be agents of change, ideally the valid pathways to goal attainment are informed by theory. But in the absence of predictive theory, which is often the case in event studies, the evaluation of how well the model works to attain goals (as well as consideration of any unintended and negative impacts) will aid theory development. In practice, logic and TOC models are probably going to be based partly on theory and partly on experience, and that is where reflexive praxis enters the picture.

Introspection and think tanks

Knowledge also comes from individual reading and introspection, group brainstorming (the 'think-tank' approach) or pure serendipity (i.e. good luck). When research institutions are established, or groups of academics and research students interact at universities, a lot of new thinking and theorizing occurs almost naturally. To date, only a few such clusters of event scholars have been established. One of their aims has to be a closer link with professional practitioners.

Grounded research

In grounded research we do not start with a problem, theory or hypothesis in mind, but with our interest in the core phenomenon (planned event experiences). The grounded approach rests on the premise that researchers should not carry preconceived notions into their projects, but construct research in such a way that knowledge and theories emerge from data and structured analysis. We always hope that completely fresh insights arise from grounded research.

The central problem with those who attempt this methodology is that they cannot start from scratch; there is always something to guide their thoughts or some parameters already established for the research.

Policy needs

Policy-makers will require a variety of studies – often evaluations – to initiate the policy-making process and, not surprisingly, Best (2009) reported policy-makers are often unhappy about complex theoretical explanations and generally want simplistic answers. Best noted that logic and theory of change models have the potential to bridge the gap.

Philosophy and knowledge

What is knowledge? How do we 'know' anything? These questions are at the heart of epistemology, methodology and ontology. Disciplines have their own perspectives on their desired ways to conduct research, often reflected in one or more research paradigms. Science and the pursuit of knowledge are not the same. 'Scientific method' is all about a prescribed process and theory-building, whereas 'knowledge' can be developed from original thinking (creativity), synthesis (reflective thought by informed, wise people) and serendipity (unplanned discovery). In this section, a number of important terms and concepts are examined so that event-studies researchers will understand where their work fits into the bigger picture of science and knowledge creation. It will become clear that there is a lot of disagreement about the very meaning or usefulness of science and scientific method.

Philosophy of science, epistemology and ontology

Philosophy of science consists of the philosophical foundations, assumptions and implications of natural and social sciences. It seeks to explain such things as the nature of scientific statements and concepts, and the formulation and use of the scientific method.

Epistemology specifically deals with knowledge, the relationships between the 'knower' and 'that which is to be known', and the justification of 'knowledge claims'. Modern science is dominated by 'empiricists' who believe that all knowledge is ultimately derived from some experience that requires research and analysis.

Adapting Tribe's (1997: 639) approach from tourism studies, the 'epistemology of event studies' should be concerned with creating knowledge about planned events, the sources of such knowledge, the validity and reliability of claims of knowledge, the use of concepts, the boundaries of event studies, and the categorization of event studies as a discipline or field. If we limit event studies to the use of 'scientific method', we will miss out on large parts of the world of planned events that are not scientifically quantifiable. Event studies needs greater epistemological breadth, encompassing philosophical, moral, aesthetic, historical and sociological inquiry and discourse.

Ontology is a branch of philosophy concerning the origins, essence and meaning of 'being', or what it means to exist. It can also be defined as dealing with conceptualizations of reality. In research, ontology usually refers to how knowledge is represented and the vocabulary being used to describe it.

In the social sciences there are four main ontological approaches. 'Realism' is based on the idea that 'the truth is out there', or that researchers can indeed discover facts and establish a true picture of reality. For example, marketing researchers might believe they can determine exactly who prefers certain types of events, and why. This leads to 'empirical research', and it can be said that 'empiricism' entails making observations about the real world, which can be evaluated in relation to facts.

Empiricism is what separates 'science' from philosophy or theology. *Positivism* is the scientific approach most associated with experimentation, quantitative techniques and the assumption that researchers are discovering the truth. The fourth ontological approach, *post-modernism*, rejects the notion that we discover the truth through empiricism, and proclaims that every observation or measurement is open to interpretation. Positivism has guided most of the natural sciences and strongly influenced the social sciences, so we will discuss it in greater detail below, along with post-modernism and contemporary discourse on research and knowledge.

Ontological mapping

The literature pertinent to event studies falls into three major subdivisions, as discussed in Chapter 1, and each of these can be considered to be an academic discourse. In this context, ontology refers to the knowledge being created and discussed within event management, event tourism and various disciplines. *Ontological mapping* identifies the main concepts and terminology employed in these discourses so that we can see how they are evolving, how they interconnect, and gaps that need filling. Complete ontological mapping of each discourse, and of event studies in total, is an enormous job and has just begun. This book covers the main concepts and terms being used, but ontological mapping should ideally be based on systematic analysis of all the pertinent literature, and it should be hierarchical in nature. Major concepts are most important, and each can usually be subdivided. The only application in event studies is Singh *et al.* (2008), who employed this method in developing an ontology specific to a knowledge-based system for safe festivals and events.

Discourse

Discourse can be narrowly defined as a conversation, or in a more formalized way as a rule-based dialogue among parties. An event can be interpreted as a discourse or forum for discourses, with Crespi-Vallbona and Richards (2007) viewing festivals as 'arenas of discourse enabling people to express their views on wider cultural, social and political issues'. Foucault (1969) saw discourse as a system of ideas or knowledge, with its own vocabulary; this can result in the power to monopolize communications and debate, and to enforce particular points of view. Following the arguments of Foucault, we can view a discourse as a system, or structured line of reasoning, ideas and approaches to knowledge creation, including theory development and practical applications. Meaning is assigned within a discourse, based on researchers' values, so that the language and concepts define and delimit what is legitimate or expected of those contributing to it.

In academic and political discourse some understandings can be marginalized or ignored completely. For example, Tribe (2004: 57) argued that 'the business discourse' in tourism has 'some coherence and structure, and a framework of theories and concepts (borrowed from the field of business studies)', and that tourism studies tends to crystallize around this interdisciplinary approach. Translated into the subject of this chapter, the business discourse becomes 'event tourism' and is also applicable to the profession of 'event management'. Tribe also argued that the other main area of knowledge creation in tourism studies, undertaken by researchers not interested in the business approach, draws from specific disciplines and leads to interdisciplinarity.

If it is simply asked, 'what is being researched pertaining to planned events?', then the answer is found in an extensive and systematic literature review identifying the terminology and concepts employed by researchers. From reviews conducted by the authors, three discourses were identified, encompassing both the concepts and research themes within event studies and related debate and argument – including contested meanings and the appropriateness of applying particular theories and methodologies. The matter of research and theory-building paradigms comes into question, although individual scholars might never question where they stand on such philosophical issues.

To illustrate, consider that the knowledge domain of event tourism includes considerable attention to economic impact assessment and related issues such as the 'attribution problem' (i.e. what criteria and evidence are necessary to attribute impacts to a particular event?). This is part of the study of event tourism but is neither theoretical nor debated; it simply has to be understood and applied. However, the concept of 'authenticity' is often debated, such as through claims that tourism commodifies festivals and renders them culturally inauthentic. The 'classical' discourse is rooted in social sciences and seems to naturally foster debate and philosophizing, whereas festival tourism and management is much more applied, and less critical. Scholars seeking greater interdisciplinarity are generally responsible for bringing challenging concepts and theoretical/philosophical debate into the tourism and management discourses.

Discourse on any subject, such as a political process for determining support for cultural festivals, involves two-way or multi-stakeholder communications, with the aim of ensuring mutual understanding. It is a rule-based process in which arguments are evaluated for their validity, and it facilitates shared decision-making or consensus-building. Stating one's opinion is not discourse, nor is propaganda and advertising. Argument without rules is not discourse. Allowing statements to be made that cannot be verified as to fact or source violates the principles of discourse. To Jaworski and Pritchard (2005: 1), discourse is 'a semiotic system': textual-linguistic, visual, or any other 'system of signification'. Discourse can mean conversation and language use, whereas 'critical discourse' examines cultural/social practice and processes including politics, values, norms, ideologies (Jaworski and Pritchard 2005: 4). 'Social lives are constructed in and through language/discourse' (Jaworski and Pritchard (2005: 5).

Positivism

Similar to natural scientists, positivists adopt an external (i.e. the researcher's) perspective on discovering the truth and formulating theories that are both explanatory and predictive. Social scientists and management researchers wanting to be more like the 'hard sciences' have adopted a positivistic approach which stresses the 'scientific method' to prove cause and effect, or otherwise employs reliable and valid methods to discover the 'truth' about the world and how people and societies function in it. Positivists separate values from research. Most research done on events has been in this tradition, if only because most event-related research has been concerned with marketing and economics.

When visitor surveys are conducted at events, we will try to obtain a random or systematic sample so that estimates can be made about the whole population of event attendees. Conclusions are drawn regarding average spending and motivations to attend. When a household survey is conducted to assess resident perceptions of, and attitudes towards, events, a similar sampling process occurs and the resulting data are subjected to statistical tests to reveal patterns and explain differences. All of this can be used in theory-building. Researchers assume that they are discovering, measuring or explaining the ways in which real people think and act. Are they wrong to think this?

Experimentation is also at the heart of positivism. Experiments are used to test hypotheses, requiring that controls be put in place to compare cause and effect among groups. While experiments are rare in applied management fields like tourism or events, the method has been widely used in some of the disciplines that contribute to our knowledge of events, especially in psychology and its subdisciplines.

One of the oft-proclaimed advantages of scientific method is the removal of subjectivity and the imposition of strict protocols for data collection and analysis – including ethical research behaviour. For example, no student conducting research for a thesis or dissertation would be allowed to draw conclusions about how events cause economic impacts without convincing supervisors and examiners that data collection and analytical techniques are sound. There is a firm understanding that researchers do not make up results, that studies can be replicated and that conclusions can be tested.

But this scientific 'advantage' also attracts dissatisfaction and criticism when researchers study humans and societies. There is, first of all, real doubt about how well experiments and survey methods reveal the truth, or get at the complexity of individuals and groups. Second, there is a concern that 'objective' research treats people as 'objects', and that the subjects of research should be part of the process and benefit from it. In fact, some research might actually do harm to people either by way of the dynamics of the research (such as observing people and thereby interfering with their lives or work) or its results (such as by exposing divisions and biases).

Schultz and Lavenda (2005) discussed how anthropologists have questioned positivism as the dominant research paradigm. Assumptions about how the world really worked, and about the ethics and politics of their research (particularly about participant observation), started to be challenged in the 1960s and 1970s. As researchers began to de-emphasize scientific detachment and entered into dialogues with informants and respondents, a greater emphasis was placed on interpretation and differences in opinion.

Schultz and Lavenda (2005: 43) argued that collaborative dialogues achieve 'intersubjective meanings' in which researchers and informants gain a new, shared understanding of the world. According to these anthropologists, researchers are to be 'reflexive', or always critically thinking about the experience of research and how it is done. Do researchers and informants share enough, in cultural terms, to really understand each other?

The nature of 'proof', and cause–effect relationships

One of the main tenets of positivism and the scientific method is that we can 'prove' that certain actions cause certain effects. This is not nearly as simple as it sounds, and within event studies there are only a few problems amenable to this application of scientific method. For example, cause-and-effect relationships are demonstrable for economic impacts. A rigorous methodology that incorporates random or systematic sampling of visitors and a theoretically correct attribution of visitor expenditure (based on determination of reasons for travel) is a proven way to show that event tourism makes a direct economic contribution. However, as emphasized by Dwyer and Forsyth (2009), impacts are not the same as benefits. And if a full cost and benefit evaluation is not undertaken, the results of economic impact assessments will be interpreted out of context. Furthermore, it is the distribution of costs and benefits that is often more important, and that is an equity issue.

Similarly, research can prove that events and event tourism cause environmental change, although sometimes interpretation of positive and negative changes will be open to dispute. Clear examples of cause and effect are to be found when crowds at events trample vegetation, or when construction for events pollutes the water or air. But at a macro level, say in a large city, the relative contribution (compared to industry and transport) of events and tourism to air and water pollution might be insignificant.

While considerable progress has been made in evaluating the various positive and negative impacts attributable to events and event tourism, little if anything has been 'proven' of cause and effect in social or cultural terms. There are many confounding variables that could explain why residents perceive good or bad impacts (see social exchange theory and social representation theory). It is too simplistic to argue that a community or city gains specific social benefits like integration or pride from events, as there are clearly many policy and action paths towards the same outcomes. For many purposes, therefore, resident perceptions and attitudes will remain the best indicators of event impacts. That leads us back to the matter of what constitutes appropriate and valid evidence.

Evidence

As covered in the previous chapter within the context of evaluation and impact assessment, the nature of evidence is a critical point. Often it will be a *social construct*, that is an agreed upon set of measures and methods (including key performance and impact indicators) by stakeholders in the evaluation process; these are ideally formulated within logic or theory of change models. Those inclined towards extrinsic valuation, as with the economics of event tourism, usually want quantifiables, often expressed in monetary terms, while those more interested in social and cultural goals and impacts might very well accept the voices of people as valid evidence. These voices can be in the form of opinions, stories, attitudes and arguments.

In terms of theory-building, accumulating evidence will have to be subjected to meta-analysis, and that requires the use of standardized methods and measures. *Meta-analysis* involves statistical analysis of many studies that explore the same phenomenon, and it is the gold standard in medicine and drug testing. To date we have seen limited scope for this methodology in event studies because of a lack of standardization.

Post-modernism

To post-modernists, there is no single truth, and all 'meta-narratives' and 'paradigms' like religion and political doctrine are rejected. Jennings (2006: 3) argued:

> *The postmodern paradigm disputes grand theory and views the world (its ontological perspective) as being constructed of multiple realities and that no one reality has favour over another. A central tenet is the deconstruction of the surface features of phenomena in order to expose the underlying core realities.*

Many observers believe that postmodernism, at least with regard to its manifestations in literature and entertainment, is dead or increasingly irrelevant. The debate in academia will continue.

Theories and models

Klemke *et al.* (1998) asserted that 'theories' have the following properties:

- may be stated as laws or assertions about existence;
- exhibit generality or comprehensiveness;
- explain not one law or phenomenon, but many;
- have explanatory and predictive ability;
- unify diverse phenomena and laws;
- aim at deep understanding of phenomena;
- contain terms referring to unobservable entities or properties.

Klemke *et al.*'s assertions about theory might not be fully applicable to event studies. Much of the so-called 'theory' seen in the academic literature consists not of explanatory and predictive modelling that withstands the test of time (i.e. permanence), as a good physics or chemistry theory would, but of conceptualizations and propositions. Within the social sciences, humanities and management studies, we probably cannot generate explanatory/predictive theory, nor is it necessarily a worthwhile pursuit. A more appropriate approach to theory development comes from Kelly (1987: 2) who argued that all theoretical models share the following:

- they are acts of explanation, communicated to others;
- they are systematic and disclose their presuppositions and evidence;
- they are always subject to question and criticism.

Theory development, to Kelly, is something we do 'whenever we attempt to explain to others the antecedents and conditions of occurrences'. In the context of event studies, each of the chapters on the five themes of event studies contains a lot of theory development. The application of all the theories and models from other disciplines to the study of planned events is also theory development.

Neuman (2003) suggested that a 'conceptual model' is a collection of concepts that together form a web of meaning and represent a simplified description of complex phenomena. Models usually serve to depict the believed or proposed structure of interrelationships of factors which help explain a higher-order concept. Accordingly, theories in our field are never truly complete nor are they completely generalizable, but they do contribute to knowledge-building and stimulate debate. *Thus, we have no distinct theory of planned events*. At this stage we have to reply on borrowing and adapting theories from pertinent disciplines.

Propositions and hypotheses

'Propositions' can form the basis of a conceptual model and can be important in building theory. If we have deep understanding of some aspects of events we can legitimately propose that certain things are true, or will be discovered. Propositions need to be debated or tested, and in that sense they can be turned into 'hypotheses' for other researchers. Propositions are generally stated in the following way:

> *P1: (It is proposed that) what people think of as types or forms of event, such as 'festival', 'convention' or 'sport competition', are social constructs in terms of expected setting and programme, and in terms of their meaning; these constructs will vary from culture to culture and will evolve over time.*

Throughout this book there are other observations or conclusions that can easily be stated as propositions, useful either for generating research hypotheses or policy action.

Research methodologies

Disciplines have their own methods, rules or postulates that together constitute 'methodologies', or accepted ways of conducting research and generating knowledge. Methodology is rooted in philosophical assumptions (i.e. epistemology, ontology) and provides the rationale for conducting research in accepted ways. In 'positivism', reality is assumed to be objective, independent of the researcher/observer, and the truth can be discovered by the methodologies of the 'scientific method' such as experimentation. As discussed earlier, 'science' has been the dominant methodology and it remains the most accepted way of doing things in event studies. Note that many 'qualitative' methods are also part of this tradition, and indeed have considerable credibility within the social 'sciences'.

Deductive research

In the positivistic tradition, the starting point is a proposition or hypothesis, generally derived from previous research and existing theory. Data are collected with the specific intent of testing the hypothesis through statistical techniques, such as comparing means on scores from Likert scales to 'prove' that members of one racial or cultural group hold different attitudes towards an event when compared to another group. This can, indeed, add considerable understanding to our problem of why some events do not engage all members of the community. Whether or not the resultant theory-building is the same, or better/worse than that arising from inductive or grounded research, is difficult to say. In the social sciences there is no real test other than the test of time and criticism.

Inductive and grounded research

The starting point for 'inductive' and 'grounded research' is some kind of observation or data collection, leading to analysis. The researcher is to have no preconceived notion of findings. This leads to explanation or theory-building. In inductive or grounded research, there might emerge many possible explanations for an observed phenomenon, and they all have to be considered. Grounded research draws mostly from the work of Glaser and Strauss (1967). In their approach, various types of coding are employed to reach a 'saturation point' where no additional understanding of relationships or abstractions is gained from the data. Theories are built upon categorized data that help to describe and explain the research focus. It should be said that many researchers find a rigorous application of the Glaser and Strauss methodology to be impractical, but the general principle of working inductively from data in steps that lead to theory is sound. Research by Xiao and Smith (2004) provided an application of this methodology to event studies.

Interpretivism

'Interpretivism' arises from the belief that the study of humans is different from the natural sciences, so positivism is not necessarily the best methodology. Sociology, for example, is split between 'structuralists', who favour positivism and 'interactionists', who favour interpretivism. While positivism views reality as single, objective and tangible, interpretivism believes in multiple, socially constructed realities (Decrop 2006: 47). In other words, your world-view is quite different from mine. Interpretivists seek understanding, but do not make firm predictions (no explanatory/predictive models). Interpretivist research tends to focus on that which is unique, even deviant, rather than seeking global generalizability. The knowledge generated is contextual, being value and culture-bound. Researchers are likely to interact and cooperate with their subjects and to use holistic-inductive methodology (or naturalistic inquiry). 'Naturalistic inquiry' is the non-manipulative study of real-world situations, as opposed to experimentation. A lack of predetermined constraints on findings makes it similar to grounded research.

Social constructivism

Social scientists often engage in debates about the extent to which theories are shaped by their social and political context. In this way 'social constructivism' postulates that social factors play a large role in the acceptance of new scientific theories. Jennings (2006: 3) described it this way: 'Social constructivism has an ontological position that acknowledges the multiple realities of the people (sometimes called actors) participating in the research.' It is contrary to 'postpositivists', who still perceive a reality. 'The epistemological position of social constructivism is a subjective and value-laden one. Moreover, researchers utilize primarily qualitative methodology and engage in an intrinsic, instrumental and transactional axiology' (Jennings 2006: 3).

Semiotics

'Semiotics', or 'semiology', is the study of signs, sign systems and their meanings. 'Signs' are also symbols, standing for something else. For example, semiotics can be applied to words and texts, body movements or the clothes people wear. In contrast, 'communication' is the process of transferring data and is concerned with the media of communication. In both communications and semiotics there is a concern for how receivers interpret and give meaning to signs and communications. According to Echtner (1999), in ontological terms the 'semiotics paradigm' views reality as being socially constructed, and consisting of systems of signs such as language. Semioticians seek to uncover recurring patterns and layers of meanings.

Applied to events, we need to understand interactions among 'signs' (advertisements, branding, theming, explicit and implicit communications about the event and within the event) and the 'interpretants' – those people in attendance, or our target markets. Ryan (2000) believed that tourist space is a locus of selected meanings where the visitor brings their own interpretations. Signs and symbols are interpreted to create meanings, with one implication being that meanings are only in part shaped by the event planner, and another implication being that multiple meanings are often the norm.

Critical theory

In Chapter 1 'critical event studies' was discussed. According to Habermas (1973), the role of the critical researcher is to reveal conflicts and contradictions and help eliminate the causes of alienation or domination. Jennings (2006: 3) described the 'critical theory paradigm' as adopting:

> *an ontological position that the social world is constrained by rules, although these rules can be changed. Its epistemological position is halfway between subjectivism and objectivism. Axiologically, this paradigm should lead to transformational change, as the aim of research in this paradigm is to alter the social circumstances of those being studied.*

Drawing from critical theory, the emergence of critical event studies is noteworthy. A special edition of the journal *Event Management* in 2018 was devoted to this subject. Editors Robertson, Ong, Lockstone-Binney and Ali-Knight framed it this way (2018: 868):

> *this special issue was aimed at challenging the positivist agenda by examining events' role in relation to ethics, governance, and the wider world. The articles included in this special issue challenge the status quo by ascribing meaning to events beyond the neoliberalism that governs the expansionist ambitions of many events.*

One of the papers in the special issue was by Nichols *et al.* (2018) concerning governance, mega events, power and research (see the research note).

12.2 RESEARCH NOTE ON CRITICAL EVENT STUDIES

Nichols, G., Benson, A. and Holmes, K. (2018). Researching mega-events under regulatory capitalism. *Event Management*, 22, 933–943.

A significant legacy of the 2012 Olympic Games was to demonstrate how such an event could be delivered within the governance structure of 'regulatory capitalism'. The delivery of the London 2012 Games was contracted to a private company, the London Organizing Committee of the Olympic Games and Paralympic Games (LOCOG). LOCOG subcontracted packages of work, including Games research, which was conducted by a market research company as 'sponsorship' in kind. Through an autoethnographic account of researching volunteers at these Games, working with the market research company, it is shown how: public accountability was reduced by the selective availability of research results; the access to research became a marketable resource; and research ethics of the private company were inconsistent with those required within a university. Therefore, the delivery of the Games through regulatory capitalism reinforced the unequal power relationships between the different event stakeholders. This leads to a discussion of implications for researching mega-events and the relationship between academic research and commercial researchers. These include the need for researchers to pay for access and to protect their intellectual property.

Research purposes and methods

Veal (2006: 3) provided a typology of research from the perspective of its purpose or utility. 'Exploratory' or 'descriptive' research seeks to uncover facts or describe a situation. This simplest type of research is commonplace in emerging fields like event studies and might consist of inventories, mapping and classifications of events, case histories, profiles of event organizations, or compilations of facts about policies and regulations affecting the event sector. A trend analysis of demand for events is descriptive, whereas an analysis of factors causing the trend is explanatory. 'Explanatory' research seeks understanding. In a positivist tradition, there is often an assumption of cause and effect, such as: the growth in demand for entertainment events is explained by the rise of disposable incomes enabling more people to engage in hedonistic pursuits. If we can explain why something happens, then a predictive model should be possible.

'Evaluative research' is essential in event management and in policy development. 'Internal evaluation' of an organization's effectiveness (in attaining goals) and efficiency (the best use of its resources) is a responsibility of management. 'External evaluation' is conducted by stakeholders who want to know if their 'investment' or support for the event has been worthwhile, or to otherwise examine the impacts of the event. Theory of change models can be used for evaluation and theory-building, with each iteration of the model (incorporating feedback and revisions, new goals and action pathways) contributing to a better understanding of reality.

Quantitative methods

Quantitative methods are associated with positivism, and qualitative with interpretivism, but there is absolutely no reason why both cannot be combined in any given piece of event-related research or evaluation. The difference is not one of good technique, but of what you need to know and how best to find it out. Often an exploratory, qualitative stage, using focus groups, interviews and observation, precedes a more quantitative stage.

Secondary data analysis

Especially when used as a starting point in research projects, existing sources such as large data sets on leisure, travel or consumer behaviour can provide new insights. Have all analytical tools been used on the existing data? Can new hypotheses be tested? It can also be a useful exercise for students to examine general tourism data, for example, to search for event-specific behaviour and motivations.

Systematic observation

As employed in the Getz *et al.* (2001) study of a surfing event, nine trained observers used temporal and areal stratification of an event to observe and record information about the setting and the audience. This is a quantitative method insofar as the data collected can be analysed in the same way as survey data. Remember that observation can also yield qualitative insights.

Questionnaire surveys

These are probably the most popular research method, because you can get lots of data cheaply, and sometimes quickly. In the positivistic tradition a random sample or complete census is necessary to make generalizations about a population. Surveys can follow a number of procedures.

'Self-completion, intercept surveys' are a very common way to get immediate feedback from festival-goers, on site. 'Intercepts' can also be done of cars on roads, or of persons at airports. Usually the researcher wants a random sample (e.g. every n'th person through the gate) but might settle for a 'systematic sample' (such as you can obtain through spatial and temporal stratification).

'Post-event, mail-back' surveys: often a two-stage approach is best (Pol and Pak 1994), such as getting people at the event to provide a little information and having them agree to a postal follow-up. The post-event portion is best for getting more accurate data on total expenditures and an assessment of the overall experience.

The 'telephone survey' is a good way to cover a market area, such as doing a survey of awareness of an event in a city two hours away by car. Sampling problems are common with this method, so often a 'quota' sample is taken (i.e. get so many males, females and families). 'Quota sampling' is useful in market research where you want a balanced response from males and females, or perhaps you only need the opinions of older tourists. Instruct canvassers to obtain a specific number from each target category.

'Convenience sampling' is generally not recommended, but is easy and cheap – just take anybody that you can get to answer your questions. It can be combined with quota sampling, and a useful variation is to sample willing people in a particular location or at an event, which has the advantage of a common frame of reference (the place or the event).

The 'captive sample': this method works well at meetings and other events where participants feel obligated to respond or cannot avoid doing the survey. Students are often a 'captive sample'!

A number of scholars have compared different survey methods applied to events, such as comparing log books with self-completion questionnaires (Faulkner and Raybould 1995; Breen *et al.* 2001). Quite a few studies have been aimed at perfecting attendance counts and improving attendance estimates at events (e.g. Brothers and Brantley 1993; Raybould *et al.* 2000).

Qualitative methods

Qualitative methods generally do not attempt a numerical analysis, and are more focused on discovering people's attitudes, feelings, motives or perhaps meanings attached to an event experience. Often the numbers of respondents involved are small, as the appropriate methods (e.g. participant observation, interviews, focus groups) are time consuming. Of special interest might be the interactions between people in a focus group setting, which need to be recorded and later interpreted, or perhaps the language used by people in a self-reporting situation (e.g. do event-goers use words like 'self-fulfilling' or 'mastery' when describing their event experiences?).

Phenomenology and hermeneutics

'Phenomenology' as a method attempts to obtain a direct description of a person's experience, ignoring for the moment any causation or motivation. 'Hermeneutics' is a Greek word for interpretation. All writing and symbolic communication (including performances and sports) can be viewed as 'text', and that text can be interpreted. Hayllar and Griffin (2004) employed 'hermeneutic phenomenology' to explore tourists' experience of a tourist space, the 'Rocks' in Sydney. They engaged visitors in lengthy, structured interviews about the area and their experiences in it. In effect, visitors interpreted their own experiences, then researchers interpreted the 'text' of those interviews by examining themes in the recounted experiences. The results of such research are insights about experiences, but this is not 'objective' in the positivistic tradition and therefore is regarded as qualitative research. Chen's (2006) use of phenomenology (see Research Note 3.5 in Chapter 3) is one of the few examples specific to events.

Netnography

A possible substitute for field research is to assess the meanings of what people say on web logs, or in other written texts. Netnography is the branch of ethnography that analyses the free behaviour of individuals on the Internet and uses online marketing research techniques to provide useful insights. It provides information on the symbolism, meanings and consumption patterns of consumer or leisure groups (Kozinets 2010). It can be passive and hidden, or researchers can declare their aims and interact openly with online respondents. By way of example of passive netnography, read this first-hand account, taken anonymously from a web posting, from someone who attended a festival.

> *About fifteen years ago I went to my first [festival name and location deleted], and I fell in love with the sacred fire circle and the festival space around it. The strength and magic of this sacred container rocked my world. I can honestly say I have never experienced anything like it in my life. Those 5 days were the most memorable ones I have ever had and cannot wait to return this summer. The festival's an incredible experience. Unbelievable! I just can't explain it! I wouldn't miss it for anything in the World! It keeps me happy! It's a really intense experience if you enjoy the music because there's so much of it! Memories are made here. The kind that really make a difference in your life.*

It appears to have been a truly memorable, even transforming festival experience, and there are clues as to the nature of the experience. But what is really meant by 'magic' and 'intense'? We cannot get clarification from the written text. And how can we interpret the phrase 'rocked my world'? More questions are raised than can possibly be answered.

The following two blog quotations are from marathon runners.

> *I run because it makes me feel alive. It challenges me like nothing else. I have run each decade of my life. The pain brings me a reminder that life is not easy. The feeling when you cross the finish line reminds me that nothing worthwhile in life comes easy.*

> *I ran the first marathon to see if I could do it. I continue to run more marathons to see if I can improve my time, and maybe one day qualify for Boston ... I run to stay in shape, get away for a while, and to compete. Compete against myself to see if I can become a better runner. It's important because it helps keep me in shape and gives me a goal to shoot for. Plus the interaction with other runners is awesome.*

One cannot understand the competitive athlete who participates in many events without paying attention to their fundamental motivations. The quotations suggest that these runners are creating meanings for the events in terms of mastery and self-development, with social or affiliation experiences being important.

This quote is from a student who attended a multicultural youth science forum.

> *Although this trip was academically very enriching, it is the social and cultural exchange along with the bonds we formed that will be cherished forever. This was my first trip to another country as a student and I have certainly gained a lot of confidence from it.*

Clearly 'communitas' was at the core of this event experience, the sense of belonging and sharing reflected in the word 'bonds'. But it was also a learning experience and one of self-growth.

When reading first-person accounts of experiences, a basic interpretive problem is that the researcher had no control over the writer. They might be posturing, lying, exaggerating; who knows? If you take the accounts at face value, they will probably mislead you. If you assume there is some grain of truth in them, collectively, it will probably result in improved understanding and maybe play a part in developing theory. It seems like a good, qualitative starting point for more in-depth phenomenological research. There might be ethical questions to consider when analysing texts. Is it possible to identify the sources of the above blog quotes? Can they be slightly disguised while still retaining their authenticity?

Experiential sampling

Csikszentmihalyi and Csikszentmihalyi (1988) used this method as a means to collect information about the context and content of daily life, or some element of leisure such as event experiences. It can be thought of as 'systematic phenomenology', allowing people to report on the cognitive and affective elements of their lived experiences. It is particularly relevant to event experiences (although we have not found this application reported in the literature) because questions can cover the physical setting, social context, activities, thoughts, feeling, moods and other self-appraisals. Diaries can be used, although there is the problem of recollection bias and memory failure. Getting people to write down or record their thoughts and feelings while engaged in the experience is preferable, but intrusive. Not everyone will agree to participate, and some will either do a poor job or quit. In most experiential sampling projects the respondents have been given a signalling device such as a pager or beeper. Random beeps then trigger self-completion of a brief set of questions, the idea being to intrude as little as possible yet cover the full extent of the experience. Current technology allows for wireless Internet contact and instant communication back to the researchers.

In terms of an event, it would probably be best to start experiential sampling during the anticipation and approach stage, while afterwards it might be better to address experiences through direct debriefing. Here are some ideas on what to ask:

- where are you right now? (perhaps requiring a map of the setting);
- who are you with? (prompt with categories);
- what are you doing? (prompt with categories but allow for the unexpected);
- describe your mood (a seven-point scale with paired opposites describing moods can be used);
- what are you thinking about?
- your level of concentration (e.g. paying attention to the show, or daydreaming);
- perceived control (e.g. are you free to do what you want, or under some obligation).

Larson and Csikszentmihalyi (1983) and Hektner and Csikszentmihalyi (2002) also provided advice on how to conduct experiential sampling, including a draft instrument, and they advised that it is probably best to use this technique in combination with other methods.

Mapping

There are many variations on mapping that have value in event-related research, management and evaluation.

Graphs

In mathematics, mapping is an operation that associates each element of a given set (the domain) with one or more elements of a second set (the range). This kind of 'map' can be a graph showing the relationship between importance and performance (IP) as an evaluative tool. The 'domain' is importance attached to (for example) elements of an event's programme, plotted against a 'range' of performance scores.

Matrices

Matrices, as explained in the book *Event Impact Assessment* (Getz 2019), were devised as a tool for those forecasting the possible impacts of a project, or retrospectively 'mapping' the documented and/or perceived impacts of an event or event portfolio. In a comprehensive matrix, each element of the project (from initiation to completion) is plotted against social, cultural, economic or environmental dimensions of importance.

Geographical mapping

Researchers can use a map to show market areas, traffic patterns, impacts of construction on the environment, or many other spatial elements. An event's site plan is generally done on an accurate, scaled map, but it can also be done artistically using symbols.

Mind mapping

There are software programmes available online to do mind mapping, which is generally described as a technique to aid in the organization of information, such as visualization of complex issues. Mind maps can be used, for example, in impact assessment consultations, either to show people how impacts of various kinds might flow from a project (say, a new arena or mega event) or to gather opinions or questions from those being consulted. Usually symbols are incorporated to summarize complex issues, for example a smiley face to symbolize happy people attending an event, or some other emoji to indicate crime or conflict.

Service mapping and blueprinting

Service 'blueprinting' is done as a design exercise, specifying the various aspects of site, management systems, programme and services (including personnel) that will shape the consumer experience. Service 'mapping' is a depiction of the actual event experience, completed either by participant observation or some other form of attendee feedback (see Getz *et al.* 2001).

Stakeholder mapping

As a mapping exercise, this method can use a sketch or a table to indicate stakeholders (internal and external to the focal organization) and additional information such as the strength of the relationship. The purpose is either to learn about stakeholder networks and relationships or to aid in strategic planning. Mapping can be done in conjunction with a SWOT analysis. Todd *et al.* (2017) mapped stakeholders for the Edinburgh Fringe Festival and documented changing roles over time.

12.3 RESEARCH NOTE ON STAKEHOLDER MAPPING

Todd, L., Leask, A. and Ensor, J. (2017). Understanding primary stakeholders' multiple roles in hallmark event tourism management. *Tourism Management* 59, 494–509.

Abstract: This paper contributes insights into stakeholder theory in hallmark event tourism and the implications for engaging primary stakeholders in further tourism management settings. The tangible and symbolic tourism benefits instilled in destinations by hallmark events are well documented; with destination managers increasingly adopting event portfolio approaches to nurture and develop existing and new hallmark events. Nevertheless, limited understanding exists of how stakeholders engage with hallmark events over time; their lived experiences in event tourism; and consequent management implications. This paper uncovers multiple and shifting roles of primary stakeholders in a long-established hallmark event tourism context (Edinburgh's Festival Fringe). It presents a typology identifying five primary stakeholder roles. Phenomenological interviews with 21 primary stakeholders revealed that most fulfilled multiple roles.

Experience mapping

Experience sampling can be used to construct a spatial map or a quantitative analysis of the relationship between experiences and places. Beard and Russ (2017) adopted a phenomenological approach to exploring an event, with one interpretation consisting of a schematic map to summarize observations.

Personal meaning mapping

This technique was developed for museums and other interpretive experiences to study the learning outcomes and visitor meanings assigned to the experiences. Respondents can be asked for verbal or mind-mapping responses when asked to convey their thoughts about the event experience. Interactions with the researcher lead to discussion or elaboration of those meanings. According to Van Winkle and Falk (2015: 147):

> *Preliminary analysis of the meaning maps completed at … two events revealed that attendees were able to express their thoughts and feelings about diverse aspects of the festival experience including: affective and cognitive elements, functional and hedonistic components, and personal, social, cultural, and physical festival experiences.*

12.4 RESEARCH NOTE

Beard, C. and Russ, W. (2017). Event evaluation and design: Human experience mapping. *Event Management*, 21 (3), 365–374.

Abstract: This article reports a phenomenological evaluation of a small-scale cause-related event. Three complementary methods were applied to the interpretation of data obtained from interviewing participants who took part in an event involving the experience of sleeping on the streets with homeless people in a city in the UK. The participant experience data were first explored by applying a simple multiphasic interpretation. A second layer of exploration involved separating the data into six human experience dimensions. A third and final interpretation method involved the collaborative construction of a schematic map as a composite-summative expression of the data.

Content analysis

What are the newspapers saying about the impacts of an event, or the wisdom of bidding on a world's fair? How have event-goers described their experiences on blogs? Content analysis can employ specific techniques such as hermeneutics to compile and interpret what has been said.

Observation and participant observation

A combination of surveys, systematic observation and participant observation were employed by Getz *et al.* (2001) at an Australian surfing event, representing an application of *triangulation*, or the use of separate methods to examine the same phenomenon. Their direct observation employed checklists and spatially/temporally stratified sampling. Participant observation consisted of each of nine researchers 'enjoying' as much of the event as they could. Each observer then recorded their general observations and impressions, and when these qualitative (and subjective) insights were combined with systematic observation and interviews a *service map* was prepared. Other event-related applications of participant observation include those by Park *et al.* (2010) who combined the technique with photographs and checklists in examining the visitor experience. MacKellar (2013b) argued that this method is suitable for gaining deeper understanding of social dynamics of audiences.

Ethnography and autoethnography

'Ethnography' traditionally involved living in a place, being submersed in a society or cultural group. Favoured by early anthropologists, this obviously time-consuming and challenging research method yields a lot of insights. But there will always be the issues of observer bias, interaction effects (changing what you are observing) and information being withheld and deliberate misrepresentation by the 'observed'. 'Participant observation' can be ethnography at a small scale. Within the positivistic paradigm, the personal involvement of the researchers is taboo; the researcher is to be detached and objective, searching for the truth. But this limits research on experiences, whether they be a transforming event or experiencing the impacts of tourism. Autoethnographic accounts, in which the writer reports on their own experiences, can add insights not otherwise available through traditional – especially quantitative – methods.

Azara *et al.* (2018) based their research in part on an autoethnographic account, describing participant observation as the quintessential ethnographic methodology. Another autoethnographic account by Beer (2018) emphasized *logocentrism* which is 'a philosophy holding that all forms of thought are based on an external point of reference which is held to exist and given a certain degree of authority' (https://www.merriam-webster.com/dictionary/logocentrism).

Interviews and focus groups

One can often learn more from a few interviews than from a large-scale questionnaire, but perhaps both are desirable. 'Formal interviews' are structured, and sometimes it is best for interviewees to know the topics in advance so they can be prepared – especially if they are being consulted because of their professional position. 'Informal interviews' do not have a firm structure, although the topics have to be clear in the mind of the researcher. Interviews can be analysed systematically, using content analysis, or interpreted as to the key points. 'In-depth interviews' are a time-consuming method intended to cover a lot of ground and obtain considerable detail, usually from a few respondents. They are very useful with key informants who know a lot, such as interviewing event managers about their stakeholder relationships and strategies (see Getz *et al.* 2007). This method can be a part of researching the case histories of events or in conducting cross-case analysis.

'Group interviews' and 'focus groups' encourage interaction among respondents within a controlled setting. A synergistic effect is usually desired, such as getting a group of event managers together and asking them to identify all the funding issues faced by the festival sector. However, a strong personality can potentially influence everyone's opinion. Focus groups are a staple in consumer research, but of course you cannot draw generalized conclusions from the input. They are usually the starting point.

Case studies and cross-case analysis

Case study method has seen a massive growth from the initial edition of Yin's (2014) seminal book in the field over 30 years ago. It has been described by Yin (2014) as a key research method to use when seeking to ask questions such as 'How' or 'Why' in social research as well as a technique to gather in-depth knowledge about a specific phenomena. Yet it should not be construed, as Yin (2014) argues, to be a soft approach to research, as one simply associated with the description of events and experiences. The ability to derive generalizations and broader findings from single cases is both challenging and difficult. Getz *et al.* (2007) used the case study method to compare festivals in Canada and Sweden on the topics of stakeholder types, relationships, management and issues. 'Cross-case analysis' is a powerful tool in exploratory research, as it can generate numerous insights. Findings from case studies are not generalizable, but do play an important role in creating new knowledge, generating hypotheses or propositions, and testing existing theory.

Time-budget studies

How much time do people spend attending events of different kinds, or how much time do marathoners use in preparing for and travelling to races? Time is the fundamental determinant of whether people attend planned events and its analysis has largely been undertaken within leisure studies, as Roberts (2006) has demonstrated. The fundamental determinants of whether people actually have time to undertake or attend planned events can be demonstrated in Figure 12.2, which illustrates the three broad categories of time that exist within a given day comprising 1,440 minutes. Current debates around such time-related studies by Gershuny (2011) indicate that trends towards greater time spent on leisure since the nineteenth century have begun to change with greater time pressures on families, households and individuals in many modern societies. Among current research concerns are those related to personal well-being and issues such as work-life balance and greater pressures in balancing the different daily and weekly household obligations as demonstrated in Figure 12.2. This area of research is certainly a fruitful area of inquiry for event studies as the discussion in Tourism in Focus 12.1 shows.

EVENTS IN FOCUS

12.1 The use of time-budget studies in event research: a novel area for research

The importance of events within the everyday lives of people poses a unique research challenge in seeking to utilize a research method or methods that can encapsulate the entirety of an individual's daily/aggregated use of time and how planned events feature in these lives. Within leisure studies research, largely informed by research in sociology, three distinct types of research approach have been used.

Techniques developed in leisure and recreation studies to assess time use

• A continuous record of recreation activities of a sample population for a given time period which involves respondents keeping a diary of activities (the time budget approach). This has a long history of use in social science and leisure research, as outlined by Gershuny (2011), which can be dated to nineteenth-century Russia. Its use in the UK is documented by Pember-Reeves (1913) and in the USSR by Sorokin and Berger (1939). Mass observation in the UK

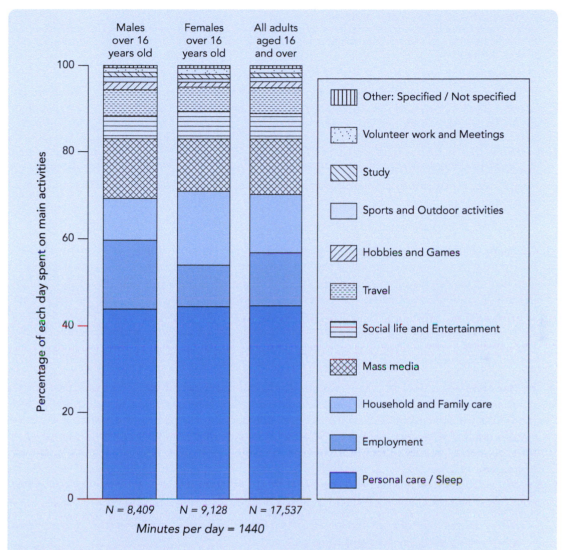

Figure 12.2 Time budgets for males, females and the total population of adults aged 16 and over in 2000

Source: Based on Office for National Statistics, UK 2002 data reproduced with permission from C. M. Hall and S. J. Page (2014).

was conducted between 1937 and 1955, together with more recent studies of leisure such as Zuzanek *et al.*'s (1998) cross-national survey of Dutch and Canadian use of time.

- Questionnaire surveys, which require respondents to recall activities in the form of an individual case study. Such case studies are detailed and sometimes contain both qualitative and quantitative questions, and they are inevitably small-scale due to the time involved in in-depth qualitative interviews.

- Questionnaire surveys which are large scale, enabling statistically significant subsamples to be drawn. Such surveys may be derived using simple and unambiguous questions that focus on a specific recreation activity or one that covers the entire spectrum of leisure activities.

What these studies illustrate is that time budgets record a person's use of time, describing:

- the duration
- sequence and
- timing of a person's activities for a given period, usually of between a *day* and a *week*.

In the analysis of time budgets, Thrift (1977) provided an assessment of three principal constraints on our daily activity patterns, which are:

- comparability constraints (e.g. the biologically based need for food and sleep);
- coupling constraints (e.g. the need to interact and undertake activities with other people);
- authority constraints (e.g. where activities are controlled, not allowed or permitted at a certain point in time).

These need to be superimposed on the three techniques.

Gershuny (2011) has reviewed the scope and scale of time-budget studies undertaken by different countries across the world as well as the differing methods of data collection and analysis used. Two examples that are often referred to are the UK and USA respective studies, which are highlighted. In both cases, planned events as a category are not collated as specific pieces of data and this highlights the importance of further studies which will reveal more specific event-related perspectives around an individual's use of time. Typically data is scattered across different categories of time use, where planned events may be associated with cultural activities, sporting events, socializing and, more broadly, leisure pursuits.

As Hall and Page (2014) illustrated, the UK 2000 Time Use Survey (ONS 2002), which set out to measure how people spent their time, comprised a representative sample of households and individuals within households, based on a household questionnaire survey and diaries, and a one-week work and education time sheet. It was undertaken in 2000–2001 and no further studies have occurred. Therefore, the results can only be indicative of what time use looks like from an aggregated perspective, and they predate the rise of social media and personal technology (e.g. mobile phone and tablet use). As Figure 12.2 shows, time use was calculated over a typical day and it illustrates the following headline statistics based on Hall and Page (2014):

- Almost 44 per cent of male and just over 44 per cent of female time is spent on personal care and sleeping each day, followed by employment.
- Leisure activities (e.g. sport, hobbies, games, social life, entertainment and mass media): the data found that 20 per cent of male and 20.33 per cent of female time is devoted to such pursuits.

Longitudinal data calculated by Gershuny (2011) indicated that ONS studies found that home leisure (of which planned events will feature) grew in the UK from 87 minutes a day in 1961 to 121 minutes in 1983–1984, to 136 minutes in 2000–2001. What time-budget studies do is help us to understand how the prioritization of planned events fits within individual and household time budgets, which is a key starting point for further behavioural studies on individuals to assess the motivations underlying participation in, spectating at and engagement with such events.

Action research

Action researchers' are usually involved in a programme or project that is intended to have specific outcomes, and the entire process continuously needs to be evaluated and revised. There is plenty of scope for learning about what works and what does not, but also the risk of involvement bias. In event studies it can work this way: the researcher joins the team planning and implementing an event, all the while both contributing as an equal and observing/analysing how decisions are made and which stakeholders have the greatest impact. Usually action research is devoted to social causes, so a more typical application would be for the participant/researcher to work with a community group to develop and evaluate a festival intended to solve some local problems. Zigommo and Hull (2011) reported on participatory event design through action research, conducted in Zimbabwe. The research was planned within the frame of critical event studies, using postcolonial theory, where an arts exhibition was conceived as an agent of social change.

Historical research

The history of a specific event or class of event is a subject for historians, yet it has to be put into a social, cultural, environmental and economic context. The historical researcher has to have a point of view, or methodology. For example, how have both politics and technological innovation affected the origin and evolution of international expositions, particularly world's fairs? Why are the Olympics such a sought-after, iconic event? Keep in mind that historiographers will assess the relevance and validity of information used and its analysis within historical research.

Longitudinal research and concatenation

A great deal can be learned by time-sampling, or otherwise studying a phenomenon like an event over a long period of time. This can be an important part of historical research, but just as much an element in policy and programme evaluation. For example, looking at the impacts of event tourism on a community at one point in time is quite limiting, so why not conduct surveys every year for a decade? A linked series of research projects constitutes concatenation, and this will be increasingly important as research centres and consortia focus on particular aspects of event studies. The aim is to build cumulative knowledge and to develop theory. While this can occur by carefully positioning a research project in the context of similar studies by others, it probably works best when the same team undertakes the work.

Futures research

Can we really conduct research on the future? There are trend extrapolation, Delphi panels and future scenarios to help envisage and plan for the future, whereas longitudinal research will tell us if we got it right. Remember that speculation and prophecy are completely different exercises. More and more we will be required to deal with the reality of climate change. If predictions come true, the world will change in profound ways. The various scenarios prepared by experts have to be translated into implications for events, leisure and tourism. Most of the implications will be pessimistic, but the future can also be shaped by policy made today, and we should aim to get certain events considered alongside other important issues. Yeoman *et al.* (2014) summarized contributions to their book by means of a set of cognitive maps that capture core concepts related to the future. An aggregated map demonstrates three general views about where future discourses will lie, pertaining to (a) consumer values and identity, (b) political reasons and power, and (c) the future role of technology.

Meta-analysis

This research method, involving statistical analysis of multiple data sets, has had limited application in the events field, mainly because so few research studies yield comparable data. Dwyer *et al.* (2000a, 2000b) conducted a meta-analysis of impact studies and drew conclusions about both about the methods employed (and how they needed to be improved and standardized) and the nature of event impacts. Our review of review articles (ensuing) could be considered a form of meta-analysis, albeit without statistical analysis of comparable results.

Cross-cultural research

Event studies must also develop through cross-cultural research, and this is rarely attempted. Schneider and Backman (1996) tested a 'Western' motivation scale in Jordan and found that it generally worked well. Kay (2004) conducted a review of research 'of relevance' to cultural event tourism, but that review found that few studies systematically compared or contrasted between cultures. Kay addressed the questions of what should be the focus of cross-cultural research, and how it should be conducted, but the sphere of concern was restricted to gaining improved understanding of who attends events, and why. The greater need is for seeking understanding of all the elements and processes in our event-studies framework within and between different cultures (including countries) and cultural groups in society (including ethnic and affinity groups and subcultures). The vast majority of the available literature is Western, thereby limiting its generalizability, and in this book (and in most pertinent sources) only English-language literature has been considered. When comparing cultures, it is almost certain that the personal and social constructs attached to planned events will be different, giving rise to varying levels of significance assigned to events in a policy context. However, the power of globalization has to be taken into account, particularly through the influence of mass and social media, so we also have to look for diffusion and adaptation within the world of planned events.

Research, knowledge creation and theory development for event studies

In each edition of *Event Studies*, progress in research and theory development is reported, reflecting considerable progress in interdisciplinarity, diversity of perspectives, and in general the healthy growth of this important field of studies. The event-specific literature, both journal articles and books, is now so vast that a complete summary is impossible, and students of the field (including full-time teachers and scholars) cannot possibly access or read it all. The ultimate function of this book, therefore, is to mark progress, summarize major developments, and suggest important questions or research topics that need attention. In this concluding section, we propose a research agenda for knowledge creation that covers both practical and theoretical needs. But first we examine the growing number of reviews of event-specific literature, with a focus on research trends, methods and theory development.

A review of review articles

Periodic reviews of the event-specific literature have been published, each of which provides insights on development of the field and its three main discourses. This supplements the discussion in Chapter 1 of how the field of event studies has evolved, but in this section we are particularly interested in the maturing of research and theory development, with a view to establishing a research agenda. Table 12.1 summarizes the available articles, most being from accessible journals, while a few are from book chapters and conference proceedings. Online sources are provided for those available from conference proceedings. Most of these reviews pertain to planned events in general, and a minority are specific to either festivals or business events. No explicit reviews of research on sport events have been found, although Gibson *et al.* (2018) included sport events in a review of literature in their editorial. The reviews have concentrated on published journal articles, and while that is somewhat of a limitation, it does accurately reflect the research and theory-development dimensions of event studies while omitting the wisdom of book and chapter authors.

Table 12.1 Summary of review articles specific to event studies

Reviews and their coverage	Selected key conclusions
Formica, S. (1998). The development of festivals and special events studies. *Festival Management and Event Tourism, 5* (3), 131–137. – Reviewed 83 articles from 3 tourism journals plus *FMET/Event Management*, covering 1970–1996	– Most research was quantitative (by surveys) or descriptive in nature; mostly North American research – Topics covered: economic/financial impact (15); marketing (13); profile of festival/event sponsorship (10); sponsorship (10); management (10) trends and forecasts (4) – Formica concluded that socio-psychological perspectives had been largely ignored
Carlsen, J. (1999). A review of MICE industry evaluation and research in Asia and Australia 1988–1998. *Journal of Convention and Exhibition Management*, 1 (4), 51–67. Australia and Asia; 1988–1998; unspecified literature review	– Carlsen noted an over-emphasis on economic impact studies – Proposed a research agenda featuring wider management, industrial and technological dimensions
Getz, D. (2000). Developing a research agenda for the event management field. In J. Allen, R. Harris and L. Jago (eds), *Events Beyond 2000: Setting the Agenda, Proceedings of Conference on Event Evaluation, Research and Education*, pp. 10–21. Sydney: Australian Centre for Event Management, University of Technology, Sydney (https://opus.lib.uts.edu.au/handle/2100/430). – Reviewed all *FMET/Event Management* articles from 1993 (issue 1) through Vol. 6 (2)	– Topics covered in the reviewed articles: economic development and economic impacts of events (26 articles); sponsorship and event marketing from the corporate perspective (14); marketing, including segmentation (11); other management topics (9) (by editorial policy business events were not covered during the first 6 volumes) – Getz proposed three major research questions: What are events worth? Is knowledge needed for better marketing? What are critical success factors?
Harris, R., Jago, L., Allen, J. and Huyskens, M. (2000). A rear-view mirror and a crystal ball: Past, present and future perspectives on event research in Australia. In J. Allen, R. Harris and L. Jago (eds), *Events Beyond 2000: Setting the Agenda, Proceedings of Conference on Event Evaluation, Research and Education*, pp. 22–29. Sydney: Australian Centre for Event Management, University of Technology, Sydney (https://opus.lib.uts.edu.au/handle/2100/430). – Also see: Harris, R., Jago, L., Allen, J. and Huyskens, M. (2001). Towards an Australian event research agenda: First steps. *Event Management*, 6 (4), 213–221. – Review of publications listed in event-specific bibliographies, up to 2000; obtained input from 3 stakeholder groups	– Economics and marketing dominated – Government respondents wanted economic and risk-related research; academics wanted more on strategy, value of the event industry, destination image and urban revival; practitioners and associations wanted more on generating funds and the needs of consumer segments

(continued)

Table 12.1 (continued)

Reviews and their coverage	Selected key conclusions
Hede, A., Jago, L. and Deery, M. (2002). Special event research 1990–2001: Key trends and issues. In *Proceedings of International Event Research Conference*, pp. 305–338. Sydney: University of Technology Sydney, Australian Centre for Event Management. – Reviewed 150 articles from 1990–2001 from 13 journals in leisure, tourism, hospitality and event studies plus conference proceedings	– The dominant theme was economic impacts of community, cultural and sport events – There was a trend to more social-impact research and use of triple-bottom-line; more risk management – The authors noted little coverage of commercial, political or religious events
Yoo, J. and Weber, K. (2005). Progress in convention tourism research. *Journal of Hospitality and Tourism Research*, 29 (2), 194–222. – Reviewed 115 articles about convention tourism, 1983–2003	– Marketing and consumer behaviour topics dominated, with a focus on meeting planners; other topics: administration and strategy – The authors said there is a need for more conceptual pieces and a triple-bottom-line approach to impacts
Lee, M. J. and Back, K. J. (2005). A review of convention and meeting management research 1990–2003: Identification of statistical methods and subject areas. *Journal of Convention and Event Tourism*, 7, 1–20. – Reviewed 137 articles from 14 journals, 1990–2003, on conventions and meetings	– The authors noted that descriptive research dominated; major themes were: site selection by associations, destination marketing and economic impacts
Sherwood, P. (2007). *A Triple Bottom Line Evaluation of the Impact of Special Events: The Development of Indicators*. Unpublished Ph.D. thesis, Victoria University, Melbourne (vuir. vu.edu.au/1440/). – Reviewed 224 publications on evaluation and impact assessment plus 85 reports	– The most frequent topic was economic impacts of events (nearly 30%), followed by social impacts (just under 20%), then event management (13.4%) and tourism impacts (13%). He clearly demonstrated the paucity of research and articles on the environmental impacts of events. Sporting events accounted for almost 60% of the papers, while 'cultural events' accounted for 29%
Getz, D. (2008). Event tourism: Definition, evolution, and research. *Tourism Management*, 29 (3), 403–428. – Reviewed previously published reviews	– Developed a chronology of research and conceptual developments related to event tourism, including by event types and themes; identified key research questions and 'possible methods'; the research questions have been modified and expanded in Getz and Page (2016) and in this book, *Event Studies*
Getz, D. (2010). The nature and scope of festival studies. *International Journal of Event Management Research*, 5 (1) (ijemr.org). – Reviewed 423 articles on festivals up to early 2009; derived from a systematic bibliographic search, plus 100% coverage of 17 journals	– Thematic review covering antecedents, planning/management, experiences, outcomes, patterns and processes; thematic review of 3 discourses: festival tourism, festival management, disciplinary perspectives
Page, S. J. and Connell, J. (eds) (2012). *The Routledge Handbook of Events*. London: Routledge. – The editors referred to contents of the Handbook plus previous reviews	– Three themes were identified for research progress: visitor experiences as influenced by changing technology; risk management, and sustainability

Table 12.1 (continued)

Reviews and their coverage	Selected key conclusions
Mair, J. (2012). A review of business events literature. *Event Management*, 16 (2), 133–141. – Reviewed 144 articles on business events, 2000–2009.	– Mair observed a lack of rigour; little research on social or environmental impacts; it remained a problem to get statistics on the MICE sector
Mair, J. and Whitford, M. (2013). An exploration of events research: Event topics, themes and emerging trends. *International Journal of Event and Festival Management*, 4 (1), 6–30. – A literature review generated a list of articles to discern research themes – A panel of experts responded to an online survey using Q-sort	– Results suggested there was already enough research done on definition and typologies of events, logistics and staging – More research was needed on events and public policy, social and environmental impacts, and indigenous events
Kim, J., Boo, S. and Kim, Y. (2013). Patterns and trends in event tourism study topics over 30 years. *International Journal of Event and Festival Management*, 4 (1), 66–83. – Reviewed 178 papers from 3 leading tourism journals, 1980–2010	– Event-tourism articles were dominated by the impact of international-scale sport events – Increased interest was noted in participants, residents, and event tourists – The authors called for more attention to behavioural and psychological factors of event tourism, and for non-economic impact studies
Lee, M. J. and Lee, S. (2014). Subject areas and future research agendas in exhibition research: visitors' and organizers' perspectives. *Event Management*, 18 (3), 377–386. – Reviewed 55 studies on exhibition research from journals and conference proceedings, 1991–2011	– Most research was conducted on trade shows, focusing on exhibitors and organizers; four themes were assessed: motives to attend; role of visitors in the buying centre; service marketing, and site selection criteria – The authors stated the need for more research on visitors and their perceptions of quality
Parent, M. and Chappelet, J-L. (2015). Conclusions and future directions for sport event management scholarship. In Parent, M. and Chappelet, J.-L. (eds) (2015). *Routledge Handbook of Sports Event Management*. London: Routledge. – Comments made in light of articles in the Handbook (this collection takes a stakeholder perspective on sport events)	– More attention is needed by researchers on small-scale and community sport events; critical approaches are required, and more theoretical lenses should be employed
Crowther, P., Bostock, J. and Perry, J. (2015). Review of established methods in event research. *Event Management*, 19, 93–107. – Reviewed 165 selected articles (based on citations) from 6 event-specific and 15 other journals, for a 16-year period up to 2013	– Mostly survey methods were employed; a lack of multiple methods was noted; the authors called for greater use of subjectivist methods; six precepts were stated: 1. Embrace a plurality of methods. 2. Adopt multiple methods within a single study. 3. Liberate multiple stakeholder voices. 4. Reveal the subjective character of events. 5. Use surveys only when they are fit for purpose. 6. Transparency of philosophical viewpoint.

(continued)

Table 12.1 (continued)

Reviews and their coverage	Selected key conclusions
Getz, D. and Page, S. J. (2016). Progress and prospects for event tourism research. *Tourism Management*, 52, 593–631. – Updates the literature review from the 2008 Getz article to 2015	– A substantially extended review; deeper analysis of the field's evolution and development charting the growth of the literature, both chronologically and thematically. A framework for understanding and creating knowledge about events and tourism is presented, forming the basis which signposts established research themes and concepts and outlines future directions for research; also focuses on constraining and propelling forces, ontological advances, contributions from key journals, and emerging themes and issues; presents a roadmap for research activity in event tourism.
Wilson, J., Arshed, N., Shaw, E. and Pret, T. (2017). Expanding the domain of festival research: A review and research agenda. *International Journal of Management Reviews*, 19 (2), 195–213. – Review of festivals research up to 2015; 160 articles covered, the earliest from 1978	– Dominant themes in the literature: motivation; experience; place; impacts, and management of festivals; they note increasing attention to qualitative and mixed methods – The authors call for more of: longitudinal research; paradigmatic diversity; theory building drawing from social sciences; testing and refinement of scales (e.g. social impact); their research agenda has four themes: pre-festival, partnerships, resources and processes in staging festivals
Park, B. and Park, K. (2017). Thematic trends in event management research. *International Journal of Contemporary Hospitality Management*, 29 (3), 848–861. – Reviewed 463 articles, 1998–2013, from 4 event-specific journals and 78 articles from other journals	– The literature has been dominated by research on marketing, destinations and management; in the past there was more research published on volunteers, motivation and economic impacts; more recently there is more on visitor experiences and motivation, satisfaction, behavioural intent – The authors called for more research on trends, planning, evaluation, technology, education and human resources
Kim, Y-H and Kaewnuch, K. (2018). Finding the gaps in event management research: A descriptive meta-analysis. *Event Management*, 22, 453–467. – Reviewed 302 papers from 4 event-specific journals covering 2003–2012	– Used the Balanced Scorecard concept as a framework – The most common methods were quantitative and survey-based – Gaps identified: the infrequent use of financial perspective, which covers research on economic angles, often analysing the potential economic impact of hosting an event; the role of festival and event management in higher education; the role of information technology in managing events and engaging consumers attending events; how events can engage emerging markets and deal with cross-cultural differences; theoretical approach to strengthen event and festival management studies

Table 12.1 (continued)

Reviews and their coverage	Selected key conclusions
Draper, J., Young, L. and Fenich, G. (2018). Event management research over the past 12 years: What are the current trends in research methods, data collection, data analysis procedures, and event types?. *Journal of Convention and Event Tourism*, 19 (1), 3–24.	– Rapid growth in e-data collection, either via email or online surveys, began in 2008 with a decrease in mail and fax survey collection; on-site surveys and interview methods of data collection doubled and continued to grow, starting in 2010
– Reviewed 890 articles; most (69.1%) were from the event-related journals. 22.5% were in the top tourism journals and 8.4% in the top hospitality journals (covering 2004–2016)	– The trend toward more sophisticated statistical procedures was confirmed; top inferential statistical methods were factor analysis/PCA, followed by t-test (14.6%), ANOVA (13.8%) and univariate and multivariate regression (13.7%)
Gouthro, M. and Fox, D. (2019). Methodological approaches to festival research. In J. Mair (ed.), *The Routledge Handbook of Festivals*, pp. 12–21.	– Highlighted the dominance of quantitative methods particularly using surveys to gather data; qualitative methods are receiving greater acceptance
– Reviewed 159 articles on festivals from 2012–16, from 39 journals	

Collectively these reviews shed light on the nature and evolution of event studies, specifying research topics and methods employed, with most authors also identifying perceived gaps and desired lines of research. Unfortunately, there has been little attention given in these reviews to the theories being used in event studies, although the identified research gaps and recommended research topics and methods do suggest avenues of theory development.

As noted by several reviews, the evolution of event studies as an academic field is evident in the literature. There were very few articles specific to events published before 1993, as that year saw the establishment of the journal *Festival Management and Event Tourism* (renamed *Event Management* in 1999). The first review articles were therefore published in the 1990s. Since the year 2000, there has been a documented surge in event-specific articles in both the event-specific journals and elsewhere. The most recent reviews bring us up to literature published in 2016, although in this fourth edition of *Event Studies*, you will find many citations of books and articles up to early 2019. As with new academic fields, the early years were marked by a great number of descriptive studies, as well as quantitative papers with data collection by surveys from single events being common methods. A clear trend is evident towards more qualitative and mixed methods, and greater diversity in the underlying research paradigms and theories informing research.

Summarizing the reviews

Review articles only partially explore the evolution of event studies as texts and other material is generally omitted. As a supplement, it is suggested that a systematic review be conducted of professional and academic associations and their publications, conference proceedings, technical manuals, published and online 'expert' sources (much of which is opinion based on practical experience) and other inputs. There will always be a lag in the published literature, as it can take years to get reviews conducted and published, and it does appear to us that evolution of the field is accelerating in terms of scope and sophistication. Indicators of this acceleration include the growing number and diversity of books, growth in the number of research articles and the journals that accommodate event-themed articles, and the emergence of areas of specialization (or research themes) such as critical event studies.

Here is a summary of key points from the reviews, followed by more focused summaries of reviews that concentrated on festivals, sports, business events and event tourism.

- accelerating growth in the amount of published material on events: from one journal devoted to event studies (launched in 1993) to four operating in 2019; an explosion of published material since 2000; a wider range of journals accepting event-specific research articles; events are now a prominent theme within sport, leisure, tourism and hospitality fields; events remain an important them in the traditional disciplines;
- increasing diversity of topics and methods; from descriptive to more statistical analysis;
- e-methods gaining swiftly (e.g. online surveys);
- recent emergence of new themes or specializations, such as critical event studies.

Festivals

Three of the reviews were confined to festivals, although it is fair to say that literature overlaps in many ways with other types of planned event. The Getz review (2010) was the largest conducted in terms of numbers of journals and articles, systematically covering 17 journals and using bibliographic searches to find articles on festivals wherever they had been published. It was a thematic review, first placing analysis into the categories of antecedents, planning/management, experiences, outcomes, patterns and processes, then into three discourses: festival tourism, festival management and disciplinary perspectives.

The following 'classical' themes were identified, largely drawing from the anthropological and sociological disciplines and applied to festivals to varying extents: myth, ritual and symbolism; ceremony and celebration; spectacle; communitas; host–guest interactions (and the role of the stranger); liminality, the carnivalesque and festivity; authenticity and commodification; pilgrimage; and a considerable amount of political debate over impacts and meanings. Dominating the festival-tourism discourse was the assessment of economic impacts, planning and marketing for destinations, and studies of festival-tourism motivation and various segmentation approaches. The negative impacts of festivals and festival tourism were identified as a more recent line of research.

A number of research gaps were pinpointed, including: cross-case and cross-cultural studies; whole populations of festivals; longitudinal research; experiences or the meanings attached to them; phenomenological (hermeneutics) and experiential assessment; both experimental and participant-observation techniques; using environmental psychology theory; choice modelling. Greater interdisciplinarity in theory development was needed. As well, Getz concluded that the three discourses do not generally inform each other, and cross-over research is rare.

Wilson *et al.* (2017) found the dominant themes in the literature to be motivation, experience, place, impacts, and the management of festivals. They noted increasing attention to qualitative and mixed methods. The authors called for more longitudinal research, paradigmatic diversity, and theory-building drawing from social sciences. More testing and refinement of scales (e.g. social impact) was said to be needed. Wilson *et al.* developed a graphic model for explaining their research agenda, containing four themes: pre-festival, partnerships, resources and processes in staging festivals.

Most recently, Gouthro and Fox (2019) searched the literature on festivals and found that 33 countries were covered in published articles. They noted the dominance of quantitative methods, particularly using surveys to gather data, but showed that qualitative methods are receiving greater acceptance. Some of the 'pioneering' methods being used reflect the trend to incorporate mixed methods in research projects, including elicitation of memories about festival experiences, personal meaning mapping, having respondents write empathy-based stories, role playing, focus groups and netnography pertaining to online communications about events.

As to challenges for festival research, Gouthro and Fox pointed to the requirements for data protection, especially in relation to 'big data', and discussed the ethics of research as this is an issue of increasing concern both to academics and the participants. They also raised concern about how the academic community may be influenced by the demands of governmental monitoring and measurements.

Sports

More thorough reviews of the sport-event literature are definitely needed, as it tends to be a sub-theme within sport management and is only a major theme in the *Journal of Sport & Tourism*. Many research articles published in tourism, hospitality, sport, leisure and event-specific journals pertain to sport events, so the issues cross over many perspectives. There is no argument with the fact that large-scale, international sport events (i.e. mega events) have attracted the most attention, with Olympics-related research arguably being a distinct sub-field.

Parent and Chappelet (2015) based their comments on contents of the Handbook, concluding that more attention is needed by researchers on small-scale and community sport events. They called for more critical approaches, and argued that a greater diversity of theoretical lenses should be employed. That Handbook adopted a stakeholder perspective so is somewhat limited in its coverage.

Gibson (2017) discussed theory development for sport tourism, much of which applies to event studies. She noted (2017: 154):

> Concepts such as leverage (Chalip, 2004), applications of Turner's (1969) theory of ritual process in the form of the social leveraging of communitas (Chalip, 2006), and more recently the concept of the event portfolio (Ziakas, 2010; Ziakas & Costa, 2010a) have been used to build knowledge with a particular focus on events and maximizing the outcomes of events by changing the mindset from 'impact' to a process of maximization of benefit, or what has come to be known as event leverage (Chalip, 2004).

And (Gibson 2017: 155):

> Getz (2008) with an application of serious leisure (Stebbins, 1982 – leisure studies) and the travel career ladder/pattern (Pearce, 1988; Pearce & Lee, 2005 – tourism studies) proposed the idea of an event travel career which has subsequently been used to understand participation in active sport tourism contexts (e.g. Buning & Gibson, 2015; Getz & Anderson, 2010; Getz & McConnell, 2011).

One glaring need identified by Gibson (2017) was research on women's experiences, for which a feminist perspective would be informative.

Gammon *et al.* (2017: 69–70) also commented on sport-tourism theory:

> Whilst inter-disciplinarity is a key feature of sport, tourism and sport tourism research, what is lacking is any significant evidence of theoretical reciprocity from those situated within business schools (e.g. economist, marketing and management scholars), the humanities (geographers and historians) or the social sciences (e.g. psychologists, sociologist, anthropologists).

Gammon also argued that the field of sport tourism has been slow to develop because theories have not been used to reveal something new about the field – a caveat that is certainly applicable to event studies in general. Theories from outside the field should be adapted or augmented, and in turn that will contribute to wider understanding of behaviour and experiences.

Business events

The MICE sector has been a focal area for many researchers, and academically tends to be tied mostly to hospitality and tourism studies. Mair (2012), however, noted that the I in MICE, usually standing for incentive travel, has mostly been ignored by researchers. It should also be remembered that the journal *Festival Management and Event Tourism* excluded business-event papers by editorial policy through five volumes, and only in 2000 – with the new name *Event Management* – did it seek to include all types of planned events.

Carlsen's review (1999) was confined to Asia and Australia. The literature he canvassed was heavily oriented towards economic impact studies, leading Carlsen to propose a more comprehensive research agenda. Subsequent reviews of business-event research by Yoo and Weber (2005) and Lee and Back (2005) were more comprehensive. Yoo and Weber determined that marketing and consumer-behaviour topics dominated, with a focus on meeting planners. Event administration and strategy were other important topics. Those authors said there is a need for more conceptual pieces and a triple-bottom-line approach to impacts. Lee and Back noted that descriptive research had dominated, and major themes in the literature were site selection by associations, destination marketing, and economic impacts.

Mair (2012) observed a lack of rigour in business-event research and lamented there has been little research on social or environmental impacts. One review of exhibition-related research was conducted by Lee and Lee (2014). They noted that most research was conducted on trade shows, focusing on exhibitors and organizers, as opposed to consumer shows. Four themes were assessed: motives to attend, role of visitors in the buying centre, service marketing and site selection criteria. Lee and Lee proclaimed the need for more research on visitors and their perceptions of exhibition quality.

Event tourism

The reviews by Getz (2008) and Getz and Page (2016) covered the event-tourism research literature in depth – conceptually, chronologically and thematically. Getz (2008) identified key research questions and related possible methods. The literature review was updated and expanded by Getz and Page (2016) who utilized the framework for understanding and creating knowledge about events. Particular attention was given to established research themes and concepts, constraining and propelling forces, ontological advances, contributions from key journals, and emerging themes and issues. This review presented a roadmap for research activity in event tourism, and the research questions have been incorporated in this chapter.

A separate review by Kim, Boo and Kim (2013) observed that event-tourism articles were dominated by the impact of international-scale sport events, but increased interest was noted in participants, residents and event tourists. Those authors called for more attention to behavioural and psychological factors of event tourism, and for non-economic impact studies.

An agenda for research and theory development

This section is shaped by our framework for knowledge creation, starting with the experience and followed by antecedents, planning and management, outcomes and the impacts, and finally patterns and processes.

The research agenda shown in Tables 12.1–12.5 builds on those from previous editions of *Event Studies* by incorporating ideas from review articles and our own coverage of the literature. Themes and questions remain important over a long time period, but new ones do keep appearing. Suggested theoretical foundations can apply to more than one of these agendas. New theoretical perspectives and methods also keep appearing, and that is definitely a good sign for advancement of event studies.

A research agenda for planned event experiences and meanings

This is the core of event studies and therefore demands constant attention from researchers and theorists – what separates this from other fields but also brings several closely related fields to the table. According to Borrie and Birzell (2001), there have been four common approaches to studying visitor experiences, namely a focus on satisfaction, benefits, experiences and meanings. The 'satisfaction approach' is really about using surrogate measures, as it asks if people were satisfied with their experiences – not what those experiences were or what they meant. Expectation-disconfirmation theory lies at the heart of this line of research, recognizing that many event attendees (but not all) will have expectations of quality and experiences, and these are shaped by both past experience, marketing, and other personal or cultural antecedents.

An alternative is to indirectly measure satisfaction through observation or technology that permits the monitoring of what people do and where they go – leading to conclusions about what appealed to them and what did not (e.g. hot and cold spots). The literature on services marketing has informed many event-specific studies, the more sophisticated of which employ techniques like importance-performance, service mapping, and technology-based tracking. In line with the generic marketing literature, many papers have been published linking satisfaction with antecedents (i.e. motivations, expectations, involvement, demographics, past event experiences, lifestyle), with quality perceptions and forward to future intentions (i.e. loyalty, repeat visits, personal recommendations). Structural equation modelling has been a favourite tool, but it has to be remembered that this does not develop new theory; it serves to confirm hypotheses that must emerge from theory.

The 'benefits approach' asks respondents to indicate their level of agreement with statements regarding the benefits they might have received, such as to escape, to relax, to learn, etc. It is similar to asking about motivations to attend an event. A priority here is examining and comparing motives/benefits at all types of events, in different cultures and settings. Leisure researchers have paid particular attention to benefits, partly to justify leisure services by demonstrating the personal, social and cultural benefits – and this leads to the issue of how events might be transforming experiences, or to consideration of cumulative impacts. We can also observe this line of research in recent work on event experiences and quality of life, but mostly it is manifested in comprehensive impact assessments that take into account different stakeholders and value perspectives. Asking 'what is the value or worth of this event' brings benefits and meanings to the fore.

'Experience-based' methods involve reporting on thoughts, feelings or moods during daily life, a trip or event. Phenomenological approaches should be a top priority in event studies, particularly for gaining better theoretical understanding of immediate conscious experience. Experiential sampling and the various forms of experience and meaning mapping should be utilized in a variety of event circumstances. Autoethnographic methods have emerged as a way to explore the meanings of experiences. A big question for theorists has been to ask how events can be a transforming experience for attendees and other participants, and that links to involvement, engagement and meanings. A 'meanings-based' approach requires deep insights obtained through participant observation or interviews, or the application of hermeneutic phenomenology; life-enriching stories are elicited. We need considerably more research on social and personal constructs of event meanings, how these vary over time and cross-culturally.

Exchange theory and the convergence of forms and functions

There is an existing multidimensional construct called exchange theory, which answers many fundamental questions about planned events. A common theme in all planned events is exchange, because they are all social experiences with a purpose – whether economic, social, cultural or familial in scope. From an economics perspective we can see planned events as cooperation mechanisms to facilitate necessary exchanges, primarily economic in nature. This especially applies to markets, fairs and exhibitions, but also covers many meetings, conventions, and corporate and political events. Social order arises from the necessity to have such events, and the social conventions associated with them. Festivals and other cultural celebrations appear to conform more to the anthropological approach to exchange theory, as they clearly embody ritual and symbolism, but these elements are found in many events.

In Figure 12.3, four dimensions are shown, based on the premise that any event can potentially embody both economic and social/cultural exchanges, and possess symbolic and ritualistic value. As well, many event experiences are highly personal in nature, pertaining to entertainment at one end and self-development at the other. Planned events both arise from social order and help define and maintain it. Increasingly, we look to planned events as institutionalized forms of business, a means of personal or group expression, social order and celebration. At the innermost zone of convergence, major festivals and events of all forms can possess high value on social, economic, personal and symbolic dimensions. This reflects, in part, their scale and related attractiveness to residents, tourists and the media – they generate substantial economic exchanges even if that is not their goal. Individuals will find ample scope for meeting their self-development needs through volunteering and direct participation. These events – often called mega, iconic, hallmark or signature – are symbols for their host communities/nations and foster pride, identity and cohesion. By their nature, permanent events in this zone tend to become institutions, supported by powerful stakeholders because they perform all these necessary functions. As well, they tend to converge in terms of form, with a high degree of blending of all the elements of style.

At the outermost range of the economic exchange dimension are events – like attending a market to shop, or a consumer show to look around and learn – that are low in social exchange (individuals or small

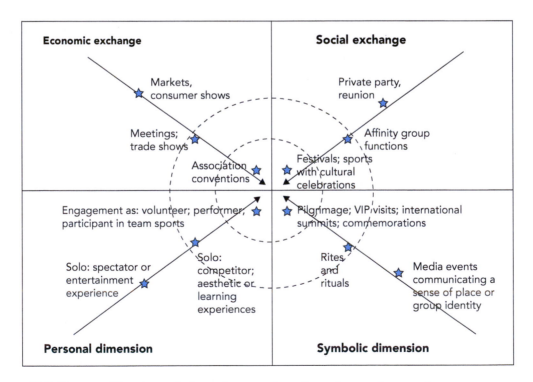

Figure 12.3 Types and functions of planned events: four dimensions and zones of convergence

Note: Events in the inner ring maximally possess a mix of economic, social, personal and symbolic value.

groups attend and group experiences are not facilitated), symbolic value and personal development. But a trade show, while ostensibly all about business for particular industry groups, does also embody social and symbolic dimensions. Although meetings and conventions are often conducted for business reasons, they can also be positioned (alternatively or equally) in the social exchange dimension for purposes of group identity-building and cohesion. Those attending events targeted at specific groups generally experience a sense of communitas.

The social exchange dimension emphasizes the importance of events as both reflections and facilitators of essential social exchanges, the kinds that form and reinforce group identity – from the level of friends and family, through all kinds of affinity groups and subcultures, all the way to city and national identity. Private parties are at the outer range, while public festivals/celebrations are within the inner zone. The largest and most public events also generate economic activity by attracting sponsors, grants and tourists; they are typically high in symbolic value, with the event being iconic within some groups and important to places, as in hallmark events. These planned events typically combine elements such as sports with festivals and exhibitions, or conventions with gala banquets and tours. And they offer many opportunities for personal engagement and growth.

Along the continuum representing the personal dimension, the individual displays a range of levels of involvement or engagement, beginning with being a solo spectator at a sport competition or concert in which entertainment/spectacle prevails. Solo experiences in social events are frequent, such as running in a race or going to an event as a learning or aesthetic opportunity (e.g. art exhibitions). Within the inner zone, the individual experiences a high level of engagement (or involvement), such as in team sports, as a volunteer or performer, and these experiences are associated with both personal development (or self-actualization) and socializing.

All events can hold symbolic value to persons and groups, but many fall primarily within this dimension. Events broadcast to the community or world are often intended to foster a positive image, community pride and group identity; they may be any type of event, or expressly produced as media events with small numbers of direct participants or guests. A panoply of rites and rituals exist that are more social in nature, clearly engaging individuals and groups in symbolic activities: from birthdays and anniversaries to bar mitzvahs and religious processions. Parades, read as social texts, can easily fit into this category. Within the inner zone of convergence are large-scale, social events that also have economic significance, such as pilgrimages, VIP visits, international summits and heritage commemorations. Individuals can experience these events as being spiritually, culturally or intellectually rewarding, and even transforming.

Maximizing the power of planned events

Public policy-makers, corporations and the tourism industry all pursue strategies for augmenting the communicative and instrumentalist power of events; that is, to make them more effective in achieving their varied (and often converging) goals. Larger public and media events are doing this already, combining multiple forms of event, adding symbolic content, and making them meaningful and valuable to many stakeholders. Remember McLuhan's (1964) dictum: the medium – an event – is the message. The powerful event speaks clearly and loudly, it contributes to creativity and innovation in society, and it stands for all things good and wonderful.

But what of small and single-form events? To augment their power, first consider their purpose and strengths. If they are primarily organized for private groups or companies, in what ways can they generate benefits for others? If the event is high on social exchange, organized for example to celebrate belonging and sharing within a social world, to what extent can it become important in an economic sense, such as through event tourism? Wherever possible, maximize the potential for involving individuals in ways that facilitate personal development and socializing.

Perhaps the most neglected power concept is that of deliberately augmenting the symbolic value of events. Many organizers appear to be reluctant to do this, perhaps fearing the alienation of one group when dominant-group symbols are utilized. This can be dealt with in several ways, starting with the planned inclusion of obvious stakeholders and many communities. But symbolism can also be neutral, accepted by most groups through constant media exposure, and universal in meaning. Consider the following examples:

- brands that stand for quality;
- symbols of the nation and the local community (we all live somewhere!);
- symbols associated with charities, good works and fine people;
- rituals that convey gravity, prestige, triumph;
- music and art as a universal language.

Yes, it is likely that somebody will object to every symbol, some group will be offended. It is truly impossible to please everyone all the time. That should not prevent us from trying to enhance the integrative power of events – to bring us all together in communitas.

Themes and questions

In each of the tables constituting our agenda, starting with 12.2 below, there is a list of themes and questions that are either already being addressed by researchers or need to be given more attention. The middle column suggests appropriate theoretical foundations, and they have been discussed in this book. The third column suggests a range of possible methods, but both these and the suggested theoretical foundations have many possible applications – they are not tied to any specific theme.

A research agenda for antecedents and choices

Motivation to attend events and for event tourism has been a well-explored topic, with recent theory development specific to events including a fuller adoption of leisure theory which in turn draws upon social psychology. Consideration of serious leisure, social worlds, ego involvement, identity, and constraint negotiation have informed the Event Travel Career Trajectory. Leisure constraints theory offers considerable scope for examining why some people attend events and others do not. Constraint negotiation applied to intrinsically and extrinsically motivated event attendance should be examined. Economic theories and methods should be applied to gain a better understanding of supply and demand issues that influence event attendance, and particularly willingness to pay and pricing.

Research agenda on outcomes and the impacted

An over-emphasis on the economic impacts of events and event tourism impeded comprehensive theory and methodological development for many years. However, growing acceptance of the sustainability and social responsibility paradigm has led to considerable attention to the greening of events, the meanings of sustainability and how to achieve it, the roles of events in sustainable development or sustainable cities, and new methods for social, cultural, and environmental impact assessment. Claims about the economic benefits of mega-events in particular are no longer accepted on the basis of face value, largely because of a history of unaccountability and no transparency, flawed methodology, and a clear bias on the part of advocates towards development at any cost. More critical examination of costs, benefits and their distribution (i.e. the equity issue) is now an essential task for researchers and practitioners.

Most event-impact-related research to date has been focused on tourism and economics, leaving a huge gap in terms of social, cultural and environmental impact knowledge. Event policy and management cannot advance without addressing this issue. There have been some specific and substantial contributions to

Table 12.2 Research agenda: planned event experience and meanings

Themes and questions	Suggested theoretical foundations	Possible research methods
How do people describe, and assign meaning and value to, various event experiences? Within each of these dimensions: conative (behaviour); affective (emotional) and cognitive	Leisure Theory (mostly from social psychology) on the nature of leisure experiences (e.g. arousal, flow, peak experiences); needs satisfaction; serious leisure; motivation; travel careers; social worlds; play	Hermeneutics (analysis of texts; self-reporting) and Phenomenology (e.g. in-depth interviews at events; recollections and storytelling)
Describe and explain the formation of personal and social constructs regarding event experiences	Identity Theory: personal and social; involvement	Personal or life histories (e.g. how and why athletes get involved); longitudinal
How does level of involvement or engagement affect the event experience?	Quality of Life Theory (e.g. happiness; family quality time)	Direct and participant observation; netnography; autoethnography; attendee tracking; experience mapping
What makes event experiences memorable and transforming?	Lifestyle Theory (e.g. foodies and fans)	Experiential sampling (diary- or time-sampling with standard questions); meaning mapping
How does 'communitas' form at events? Can it be facilitated?	Critical theory (e.g. feminist and post-colonial perspectives)	Life-cycle studies, including documentation of convergence of form and function, and the meanings attached to events
Systematically compare different event experiences (for all stakeholders, from paying customers and guests to the general public, and between types of event, from sport to carnival)	Communitas as a dimension of social identity and group behaviour	Cross-case and cross-cultural comparisons
	Cognition (perception, learning, memory formation and recall)	Longitudinal studies of persons, families, groups
	Stress theory (e.g. emotions, trauma)	Role playing and storytelling about experiences
	Cultural and sub-cultural identity	Visual representations of experiences; photo elicitation
How is quality evaluated?	Exchange Theory (economic, social and symbolic exchanges)	

our understanding of the social and cultural impacts of planned events, but it cannot be said that there is a comprehensive or systematic approach. Anthropologists and sociologists have paid a lot of attention to festivals in particular, and to certain event-related issues, but they have had their own theoretical agendas. Their collective contributions do not constitute sufficient knowledge about the real or potential outcomes of all planned events. The valuation of planned events has to be completely re-evaluated and redirected away from predominantly economic measures. Most planned events, from personal rites of passage to cultural celebrations, from trade shows to world's fairs, meet fundamental social and cultural needs. Who gives value to these meanings and roles?

Research agenda: management, planning, design and operations of events

Getz (2018: viii) has argued that the application of mainstream management theory has been lagging. There has been a tendency to think of 'event management' as the design and production of events, rather than viewing it as an application of management theory to a field of practice where:

Table 12.3 Research agenda: antecedents and choices

Themes and questions	Suggested theoretical foundations	Possible research methods
What are the main cultural variables affecting the perceived value and attractiveness of events?	Motivation (intrinsic vs. extrinsic; seeking and escaping or push-pull; novelty vs. routine)	General consumer and market-area demand surveys
Examine the relative importance and nature of generic versus specific (targeted) needs, motives and benefits that are sought through different planned event experiences. Develop marketing implications.	Needs Hierarchy	Focus groups (within social worlds, clubs, etc.)
	Leisure involvement and specialization; consumption constellations; serious leisure; social worlds; recreation specialization	Supply-demand analyses (measuring opportunity)
Do people believe they 'need' events?		In-depth interviews and life histories examining changes over time in motivation and behaviour
How is economic demand for events shaped by price, competition, substitution, policy and other factors?		
How are event careers developed?	Event Tourist Career Trajectory (six hypotheses)	Time-budget studies; changes in event-related demand and travel; measure constraints as they evolve
In what ways does 'serious leisure' affect events?	Leisure Constraints	
What constraints are most important in shaping demand and attendance at different types of event?	Product involvement and how decisions are made (e.g. routine versus unique)	Comparisons among leisure pursuits, types of sport, types of events
How are constraints negotiated for intrinsically and extrinsically motivated event attendance?		

Event management as a field of study and professional practice has its textbooks with plenty of models and advice, a body of knowledge (EMBOK), competency standards (MBECS) and professional associations with their codes of conduct. But to what extent is it truly an applied management field? In other words, where is the management theory in event management, how is it being used, and what are the practical applications? Event tourism is a related field, one that is defined by the roles events play in tourism and economic development. The primary consideration has always been economic, although increasingly events and managed event portfolios meet more diverse goals for cities and countries. While the economic aspects have been well developed, especially economic impact assessment and forecasting, the application of management theory to event tourism has not received adequate attention.

The very term 'management theory' is problematic, being open to interpretation as to its scope and contents. Kessler (2013, xxv), the editor of the *Encyclopedia of Management Theory*, stated that management, as it is commonly defined in the context of organizations, embodies the management functions of:

orientation and direction, coordination and control, authority and responsibility, planning and design, and administration and implementation ... It should therefore be of little surprise that there are countless 'theories' (loosely defined as well as loosely connected) of management. The study of management is almost as broad and diverse as its practice. It encompasses multiple levels of investigation, a wide array of sub disciplines, hundreds of journals, libraries of books,

Table 12.4 Research agenda: outcomes and the impacted

Themes and questions	Theoretical foundations	Possible research methods
How do people describe and explain why events are satisfying, memorable or transforming?	Personal and social identity (building and reinforcement of identity through social worlds and events)	Consultation and consideration of 'voices': focus groups; in-depth interviews; resident surveys; consumer and social surveys
Value perspectives; intrinsic and extrinsic; quantitative versus qualitative approaches	Kirkpatrick and Kirkpatrick model (experiences leading to attitude and behaviour change)	Media content analysis
What are the personal and social consequences of negative event experiences?		
What performance measures exist and are needed for the social, cultural and environmental policy domains?	Systems Theory (transforming processes; outputs and outcomes)	Stakeholder consultations
How does exchange theory influence various stakeholder perceptions of event impacts?		Ethnography
How are social representations of events formed?	FPSIR (forces, pressures, state, impact and responses) model	Comprehensive cost–benefit evaluations
How does the nature and extent of community involvement influence event success and outcomes?	Theory of Change and Logic Models (as theory-building experiments)	Business surveys
		Market research
Under what circumstances are events commodified and authenticity lost, versus traditions renewed and culture revitalized?	Cumulative impacts (synergistic and other interactive effects; tipping points; feedback mechanisms; limits of acceptable change)	Environmental audits and formal impact assessments
How are the benefits and costs of events distributed through the population? What strategies work best for maximizing local economic benefits?		Valuations of worth
Who are the high-yield event tourists, and how should they be attracted?	Knowledge: explicit, implicit and tacit (as the sources of evidence and opinion)	Logic and Theory of Change Models for planning and evaluation
How can events be made more environmentally sustainable?		
What are the cumulative impacts of an event and events in general, within a community or ecosystem?	Sustainability (sustainable development criteria versus steady-state sustainability)	Matrices (specifying the objects and subjects of impact assessment)
What is the value of any given event?		
How is uncertainty and risk factored into decisions about events? Is the Precautionary principle used in practice?	Social integration and inclusion; social and cultural capital	Baselines and monitoring of changes over time; using key evaluation and impact indicators
What mitigation policies and actions are taken with regard to events and event tourism, and how effective are they?	Social exchange theory	
	Ecological Footprint	

armies of consultants, an eclectic array of researchers and professionals, and diverse education and training programs.

As a reference point for anyone interested in management theory, the *Encyclopedia of Management Theory* (edited by Eric H. Kessler, SAGE Publications, 2013), with about 280 cross-referenced entries, can be somewhat overwhelming. Yet it does not fully answer a critical question: what are *ALL* the theories that can inform event management? That is because economics is excluded, and marketing is barely mentioned. Furthermore, many management theories are rooted in sociology and other disciplines, but they are of necessity absent from the encyclopaedia. For those, we can consult various encyclopaedias of social, behavioural and critical theories. For example, the *International Encyclopedia of the Social and Behavioral Sciences*, edited by Smelser and Baltes (2001) is in 26 volumes, with over 4,000 articles. It covers economics, and the section on Management includes marketing.

In an article in the first issue of the *International Journal of Event and Festival Management*, Getz *et al.* (2010) put forward a very detailed research agenda for festival management studies, and Table 12.5 extends this thinking. A real need was identified for comparative and cross-cultural research, and much of the analysis was based on a four-country comparison employing the same questionnaire for festival managers – research that is summarized in the article. Table 12.5 provides only a starting point, and readers should see the 2010 article for detailed recommendations.

Table 12.5 Research agenda: management, planning, design and operations

Themes and questions	Suggested theoretical foundations	Possible research methods
What leadership styles are most effective for different types of events and event settings?	Design Theory (co-creation of value; experience design)	Case studies and cross-case analysis
How can creativity and management competency be balanced in the event sector?	Portfolio Theory (synergies; management strategies)	Historical research
		Open-system audits
What strategies are most effective in achieving event sustainability and institutional status? Which stakeholder management strategies work best?		Stakeholder mapping
Does rational planning and decision-making work better for events than incrementalism or advocacy? Compare one-time and periodic events.	Population Ecology (dynamics; niche; legitimation)	Organizational ethnography
How do various stakeholders perceive and manage the risks associated with events?	Collaboration Theory	Surveys of owners and managers
What are the potential effects of sensory and emotional stimulation at events?	Stakeholder Theory	Consumer experiments
How can theory from environmental psychology improve event logistics and crowd management?	Resource Dependency	Financial audits and ROI studies
What are the main determinants of customer satisfaction at events?	Organizational Culture	Whole population studies (over time)
	Strategic Planning	
What volunteer careers exist in the event sector, and how do they foster commitment and professionalism?	Competitive Advantages	

Research agenda on patterns and processes

Patterns represent geographical or spatial dimensions, and processes encompass history and policy. The environment in which events and tourism exist is constantly changing, and in turn events and tourism impact upon the environment. A major gap in theory development remains: what are the dynamics of event populations and managed portfolios, and how can policy and strategy achieve their sustainability? So little historical and historiographical research has been undertaken on planned events that it is practically an untouched theme. How has the profession of event management evolved, from the earliest times? The Olympics have been over-analysed, but what about other forms of event that have a long lineage? Multi- and cross-cultural studies are essential.

Histories of individual events are interesting, but only theoretically important if they can be systematically compared and analysed within a theoretical framework such as resource dependency or institutionalism, and Table 12.6 outlines a range of productive lines of inquiry. Historians can also make a major contribution by reassessing history through the lens of major planned events and numerous personal events, as that is how many people remember and give meaning to the flow of time.

Geographical research on planned events has been given a solid foundation by Robert Janiskee and a few others, but there has been no consistent spatial-temporal approach. In cities, what has been the distribution and evolution of events, and how are they to be explained? Have resources, culture or strategy been most responsible for the observable portfolios of events in any given area? When or how does an area or community reach saturation level in terms of the numbers and types of events? How do events interact? What are their cumulative impacts? Some of the answers will assist in event-strategy formulation, policy-making and marketing.

Table 12.6 Research agenda: patterns and processes

Themes and questions	Suggested theoretical foundations	Possible research methods
In what fundamental ways have various types of events evolved, in different cultures?	Innovation diffusion	Document review
Do events progress naturally through life cycles? What factors most shape their evolution?	Product and destination life cycles	Interviews with people who shaped history
Do communities or destinations reach event saturation? What explains different patterns of events in time and space?	Acculturation; demonstration effects (evolutionary perspective on events)	Mapping
What are the forces shaping the future of events? Can they be controlled? How do events adapt?	Central Place Theory	Delphi panels
What are the ways in which stakeholders exercise power, and negotiate, to develop events and event-related policy? Who gets excluded or marginalized?		Trends analysis
How do we know when event policies are effective and efficiently administered?		Scenario-making
Which justifications for public involvement in events are supported, and why?		Policy reviews
What are the ideological foundations of event policy?		

In terms of future studies of planned events, the slate is blank. There has been lots of speculation on how virtual events might evolve, possibly threatening 'live events', but we cannot believe this for a moment.

Future perspectives

There is simply no substitute for 'being there' and for 'live experiences'. However, advances in technology and communications in particular are shaping the events field, and we have to pay attention to these forces and trends. For example, convention centres are now designed as both live and virtual event venues, to reach a global audience. We need 'futurists' in this field. We will play the role, for now, by offering the following propositions, each of which should suggest more than one research project:

FP 1 (Future proposition 1): Planned, live events, both personal and societal in scale and meaning, will always be a prominent feature of civilization, in all societies and cultures.

FP 2: Virtual events will gain in frequency and importance in response to advances in global technology, and because of globalization forces and the costs or risks of travel, but they will be in addition to, and not a substitute for, live event experiences.

FP 3: Corporate influence on the field of planned events will continue to increase, especially in terms of events produced as manifestations of marketing and branding.

FP 4: The strategic justifications for public-sector involvement with events, especially mega events bearing heavy costs, will be increasingly scrutinized and more difficult to defend, while social, cultural and environmental justifications will become more acceptable.

FP 5: Cities and destinations will become more aggressive and sophisticated in creating and managing portfolios of events for multiple purposes, and in facilitating synergies among events, venues, tourism and other policy areas.

FP 6: The event professional of the future will be competent in event management theory and applications, knowledgeable about the importance of events in society, an effective advocate for event-related policy, and a constant learner within the field of event studies. Leaders of the future will be adaptable, creative and devoted to excellence.

FP 7: Even if travel and tourism collapse, possibly because of the cascading effects of global warming, another energy crisis, war, terrorism or global pandemics, events will still remain important globally because they meet fundamental human needs.

Some really big issues

There are many major forces propelling the events sector in terms of growth in numbers and diversity, the attention we pay to them, their perceived value and cumulative impacts. Both supply- and demand-side forces are at work. Leisure and tourism are driven by population and economic growth, especially personal disposable incomes. The all-pervasive and global mass media, more and more the Internet and social media, shape consumer demand for events. Economic growth and the forces of globalization (such as free trade and integrated economies) stimulate more business travel, meetings, conventions and exhibitions. Nations and cities compete heavily to attract and develop events for strategic reasons. But will all these forces continue unabated?

Global warming threatens the world's coastlines and ski resorts, and might very soon alter the ways in which we do business, travel and consume. The very mention of 'global pandemic' sends chills down the collective spines of everyone in the tourism and events industries. Why? Travel and events are the first things to be cancelled when disease breaks out, and dire predictions about the ravages of bird flu, SARS or something else abound. Add the constant threat of wars and terrorism, and the increasing inconveniences caused by security, and the potential for disruption will remain high. If the world is perceived to be unhealthy or unsafe, people will stay at home. And if energy costs continue to accelerate, or shortages are experienced, many will have no choice but to stay close to home. Will that be the end of planned events?

We can foresee a future (this is scenario-making) in which event tourism diminishes greatly because of the counter-forces mentioned above. Whole regions of the planet might lie devastated and mass migrations occur. The economy might suffer and consumerism disappear as a social and economic force. But, perhaps ironically, planned events will then become more important, not less. Instead of event tourism we will have to rely more on media events to stay connected globally. Instead of mega events that move from country to country, each nation, region and community will require its own celebrations, meetings and games to bring people together for live experiences. Because events have met essential needs throughout history, in all civilizations, it is safe to conclude that they will endure and adapt.

Policy questions

A major research priority is to examine how event policy is formulated within the context of power, negotiation, stakeholder and public input. It is equally important to determine why event policy is either not formulated, or is not integrated with other policy fields. Performance evaluation is necessary, including the developing of effectiveness and efficiency measures for policies affecting planned events. Little attention has been given to the justifications used for public-sector involvement with events, including the ideological bases, and how the public perceives the justifications (or value events in general).

Final comments

In this fourth edition of *Event Studies*, we continue to preserve much of the original material while adding new topics and in particular updating references. The field of Event Studies is maturing, judging by the continuous expansion of literature in terms of quantity, quality and scope. As there is so much material available now, we have to be selective; that means we are probably missing some important emerging themes. There will always be people at the cutting edge of research and theory, and by the time fresh ideas get published, some years might have passed. Event studies is one of those fields that will always be open to expansion and innovation, drawing as it must from all the traditional disciplines and many closely related professional fields, as well as from reflective professional practice. It can never have fixed boundaries, and both knowledge creation for, and the nature of, our field has to remain a process of adding, testing and debating.

STUDY GUIDE

Before beginning research, it is important to consider a number of philosophical issues regarding the meaning and creation of knowledge, hence a discussion of epistemology, ontology, positivism and alternative paradigms. Research in event studies should not be confined to any particular research paradigm or methodology, rather it should be inclusive and integrative.

Positivism, associated with quantitative, scientific methods (including experimentation) has led to substantial theory development in the foundation disciplines, much of which is necessary for event studies. Yet the experiential nature of events, and the diverse meanings attached to them, necessitate alternative approaches such as phenomenology, ethnography and inductive, grounded research in general. An interpretivist perspective, recognizing socially constructed realities, will definitely help progress the field.

Research and evaluation purposes and methods were then discussed, revealing the broad range of approaches that can be useful. Throughout the book examples of many methods have been provided, hopefully making it clear that no particular approach or technique should have pre-eminence. Finally, a research agenda for event studies was presented, including key research questions and appropriate methods. This agenda is really just a starting point and is not to limit research. Priorities will be different depending on one's perspective on events, as outlined in our framework for creating knowledge.

As a conclusion to this book, think about the big issues facing events and how the future might unfold. Are you optimistic or pessimistic? Our opinion is that whatever transpires, planned events will always be important in meeting basic human needs.

STUDY QUESTIONS

- Is event studies a 'discipline', 'multidisciplinary' or 'interdisciplinary'? Why?
- Explain the ways in which knowledge can be created for event studies.
- Define these terms and explain how they affect the creation of knowledge: 'epistemology'; 'ontology'; 'positivism'; 'post-modernism'; 'critical theory'.
- Why are 'theories' needed in event studies? How are they developed?
- Show how 'deductive' and 'inductive' methodologies are both appropriate in event studies.
- What are the main purposes and uses of research and evaluation?
- Give examples of established research methods from foundation disciplines that can be applied in event studies.
- Illustrate 'quantitative' and 'qualitative' research that has been applied to the study of planned events.
- Explain 'phenomenology' and why it is important in event studies.
- Suggest gaps and justify research priorities for each of the main themes in event studies.

FURTHER READING

Fox, D., Gouthro, M., Morakabati, Y. and Brackstone, J. (2014). *Doing Events Research: From Theory to Practice*. London: Routledge.

Goodson, L. and Phillimore, J. (eds) (2004). *Qualitative Research in Tourism: Ontologies, Epistemologies and Methodologies*. London: Routledge.

Tribe, J. (ed.) (2009). *Philosophical Issues in Tourism*. Bristol: Channel View.

Veal, A. (2011). *Research Methods for Leisure and Tourism: A Practical Guide* (4th edn). Harlow: Prentice Hall.

Veal, A. and Burton, C. (2014). *Research Methods for Arts and Event Management*. Harlow: Pearson.

Veal, A. and Darcy, S. (2014). *Research Methods in Sport Studies and Sport Management: A Practical Guide*. London: Routledge.

References

Abbott, J. and Geddie, M. (2000). Event and venue management: Minimizing liability through effective crowd management techniques. *Event Management*, 6 (4), 259–270.

Abdulredha, M., Al Khaddar, R., Jordan, D., Kot, P., Abdulridha, A. and Hashim, K. (2018). Estimating solid waste generation by hospitality industry during major festivals: A quantification model based on multiple regression. *Waste Management*, 77, 388–400.

Abrahams, R. (1987). An American vocabulary of celebrations. In A. Falassi (ed.), *Time Out of Time: Essays On the Festival*, pp. 173–183. Albuquerque, NM: University of New Mexico Press.

Abson, E. (2017). How event managers lead: Applying competency school theory to event management. *Event Management*, 21, 403–419.

Addo, P. A. (2009). Anthropology, festival, and spectacle. *Reviews in Anthropology*, 38 (3), 217–236.

Adese, J. (2016). 'You just censored two native artists': Art as antidote, resisting the Vancouver Olympics. *Public*, 27 (53), 35–48.

Adorno, T. (2001). *The Culture Industry: Selected Essays on Mass Culture* (2nd edn). London: Routledge.

Agrusa, J., Maples, G., Kitterlin, M. and Tanner, J. (2008). Sensation seeking, culture, and the valuation of experiential services. *Event Management*, 11 (3), 121–128.

Ahmed, Q., Arabi, Y. and Memish, Z. (2006). Health risks at the Hajj. *The Lancet*, 367 (9515), 1008–1015.

Ahmed, Z. (1991). Marketing your community: Correcting a negative image. *Cornell Quarterly*, 31 (4), 24–27.

AIEST (1987). *Editions AIEST, Vol. 28, The Role and Impact of Mega-Events and Attractions on Regional and National Tourism*. St. Gallen, Switzerland.

Ajzen, I. (1985). From intentions to actions: A theory of planned behaviour. In J. Kuhl and J. Beckmann (eds), *Springer Series in Social Psychology*, pp. 11–39. Berlin: Springer.

Ajzen, I. (1991). The theory of planned behavior. *Organizational Behavior and Human Decision Processes*, 50 (2), 179–211.

Ajzen, I. and Fishbein, M. (1973). Attitudinal and normative variables as predictors of behaviour. *Journal of Personality and Social Psychology*, 27 (1), 41–57.

Al-Kodmany, K. (2013). Crowd management and urban design: New scientific approaches. *Urban Design International*, 18 (4), 282–295.

Al-Tawfiq, J. A. and Memish, Z. A. (2012). Mass gathering medicine: A leisure or necessity? *International Journal of Clinical Practice*, 66 (6), 530–532.

Ali-Knight, J. and Robertson, M. (2004). Introduction to arts, culture and leisure. In I. Yeoman, M. Robertson, J. Ali-Knight, S. Drummond and U. McMahon-Beattie (eds), *Festivals and Events Management*, pp. 3–13. Oxford: Elsevier.

Ali-Knight, J., Robertson, M., Fyall, A. and Ladkin, A. (2008). *International Perspectives of Festivals and Events: Paradigms of Analysis*. Oxford: Butterworth-Heinemann.

Allan, K. (2006). *The Social Lens: An Invitation to Social and Sociological Theory*. London: Sage.

Allen, J. (2008, 2nd edn 2014). *Event Planning: The Ultimate Guide to Successful Meetings, Corporate Events, Fundraising Galas, Conferences and Conventions, Incentives and Other Special Events*. Mississauga, ON: Wiley Canada.

Allen, J. and Bartle, M. (2014). Sport event volunteers' engagement: Management matters. *Managing Leisure*, 19 (1), 36–50.

Allen, J. and Cochrane, A. (2014). The urban unbound: London's politics and the 2012 Olympic Games. *International Journal of Urban and Regional Research*, 38 (5), 1609–1624.

Allen, J., Massiah, C., Cascio, R. and Johnson, Z. (2008). Triggers of extraordinary experiences within a sub-cultural consumption event. *Advances in Consumer Research*, 35, 711–713.

Allen, J., O'Toole W., Harris R. and McDonnell I. (2011). *Festival and Special Event Management* (5th edn). Milton, QLD: John Wiley & Sons Australia.

Allix, A. (1922). The geography of fairs: Illustrated by old-world examples. *Geographical Review*, 12 (4), 532–569.

Allport, G. (1937). *Personality: A Psychological Interpretation*. New York: Holt, Rinehart & Winston.

America's Cup Office (1987). *America's Cup Defence Series, 1986/87: Impact on the Community*. Prepared for Government of Western Australia and Commonwealth America's Cup Support Group, Centre for Applied and Business Research, Nedlands, W.A.

American Anthropological Association (https://www.americananthro.org/, accessed 9 June 2019).

American Historical Association (www.historians.org, accessed 7 June 2019).

American Marketing Association (https://www.ama.org/the-definition-of-marketing/, accessed 9 June 2019).

Ammon, R. and Fried, G. (1998). Crowd management practices. *Journal of Convention and Exhibition Management*, 1 (2/3), 119–150.

Anand, N. and Watson, M. R. (2004). Tournament rituals in the evolution of fields: The case of the Grammy Awards. *Academy of Management Journal*, 47 (1), 59–80.

Ancient Celebration Blogspot (http://ancientcelebration.blogspot.ca/2011/04/grand-procession-of-ptolemy.html).

Andersson, I. and Niedomysl, T. (2010). Clamour for glamour? City competition for hosting the Swedish tryouts to the Eurovision Song Contest. *Tijdschrift voor Economische en Sociale Geografie*, 101 (2), 111–125.

Andersson, T. (2006). The economic impact of cultural tourism. In T. Andersson, B. Holmgren and L. Mossberg (eds), *Cultural Tourism: Visitor Flows, Economic Impact and Product Development*, pp. 33–46. Published for the European Cultural Tourism Network at the School of Business, Economics and Law, University of Gothenburg, Sweden.

Andersson, T. and Armbrecht, J. (2014). Use-value of music event experiences: A 'Triple Ex' model explaining direct and indirect use-value of events. *Scandinavian Journal of Hospitality and Tourism*, 14 (3), 255–274.

Andersson, T., Armbrecht, J. and Lundberg, E. (2016). Triple impact assessments of the 2013 European Athletics Indoor Championship in Gothenburg. *Scandinavian Journal of Hospitality and Tourism*, 16 (2), 158–179.

Andersson, T. and Getz, D. (2007). Resource dependency, costs and revenues of a street festival. *Tourism Economics*, 13 (1), 143–162.

Andersson, T. and Getz, D. (2009). Tourism as a mixed industry: Differences between private, public and not-for-profit festivals. *Tourism Management*, 30 (6), 847–856.

Andersson, T., Getz, D. and Mykletun, R. (2013). Sustainable festival populations: An application of organizational ecology. *Tourism Analysis*, 18, 621–634.

Andersson, T., Getz, D., Mykletun, R., Jaeger, K. and Dolles, H. (2013). Factors influencing grant and sponsorship revenue for festivals. *Event Management*, 17 (3), 195–212.

Andersson, T., Jutbring, H. and Lundberg, E. (2013). When a music festival goes veggie: Communication and environmental impacts of an innovative food strategy. *International Journal of Event and Festival Management*, 4 (3), 224–235.

Andersson, T. and Lundberg, E. (2013). Commensurability and sustainability: Triple impact assessments of a tourism event. *Tourism Management*, 37, 99–109.

Andersson, T., Persson, C., Sahlberg, B. and Strom, L. (eds) (1999). *The Impact of Mega Events*. Ostersund, Sweden: European Tourism Research Institute.

Andersson, T. and Samuelson, L. (2000). Financial effects of events on the public sector. In L. Mossberg (ed.), *Evaluation of Events: Scandinavian Experiences*, pp. 86–103. New York: Cognizant.

Andrews, D. L. (2006). Disneyization, Debord, and the Integrated NBA Spectacle. *Social Semiotics*, 16 (1), 89–102.

Andrews, H. and Leopold, T. (2013). *Events and the Social Sciences*. London: Routledge.

Anheir, H. and Isar, Y. (eds) (2008). *The Cultural Economy*. London: Sage

Anon. (1852). *Statistical Chart of the Great Exhibition. Showing at a view the number and class of visitors on each day and the receipts at the doors*. Weekly Dispatch.

Antchak, V., Ziakas, V. and Getz, D (2019). *Event Portfolio Management: Theory and Methods for Event Management and Tourism*. Oxford: Goodfellow Publishers.

Arai, S. and Pedlar, A. (2003). Moving beyond individualism in leisure theory: A critical analysis of concepts of community and social engagement. *Leisure Studies*, 22 (3), 185–202.

Archer, B. (1982). The value of multipliers and their policy implications. *Tourism Management*, 3 (4), 236–241.

Archibald, M. (2007). An organizational ecology of national self-help/mutual-aid organizations. *Nonprofit and Voluntary Sector Quarterly*, 36 (4), 598–621.

Arcodia, C. and Whitford, M. (2006). Festival attendance and the development of social capital. *Journal of Convention and Event Tourism, 8* (2), 1–18.

Arellano, A. (2011). A history of Quebec–branded: The staging of the New France Festival. *Event Management*, 15 (1), 1–12.

Armbrecht, J. (2014). Use value of cultural experiences: A comparison of contingent valuation and travel cost. *Tourism Management*, 42, 141–148.

Armstrong, J. (1985). International events: The real tourism impact. In *Conference Proceedings of the Canada Chapter, Travel and Tourism Research Association*, pp. 9–37. Edmonton.

Ashworth, G. and Page, S. J. (2011). Urgan tourism research: Recent progress and current paradoxes. *Tourism Management*, 32 (1), 1–15.

Atkinson, M. (2008). Triathlon, suffering and exciting significance. *Leisure Studies*, 27 (2), 165–180.

Australian Bureau of Statistics, Voluntary Work (www.abs.gov.au, accessed 7 June 2019).

Avolio, B. (2010). *Full Range Leadership Development*. Los Angeles: Sage.

Axelsen, M. and Arcodia, C. (2004). Conceptualising art exhibitions as special events: A review of the literature. *Journal of Convention and Event Tourism*, 6 (3), 63–80.

Azara, I., Wiltshier, P. and Greatorex, J. (2018). Against all odds: Embedding new knowledge for event continuity and community well-being. *Event Management*, 22, 25–36.

Babiak, K. and Wolfe, R. (2006). More than just a game? Corporate social responsibility and Super Bowl XL. *Sport Marketing Quarterly*, 15 (4), 214.

Babiak, K. and Wolfe, R. (2009). Determinants of corporate social responsibility in professional sport: Internal and external factors. *Journal of Sport Management*, 23 (6), 717–742.

Bachman, J., Norman, W., Hopkins, C. and Brookover, R. (2016). Examining the role of self-concept theory on motivation, satisfaction, and intent to return of music festival volunteers. *Event Management*, 20, 41–52.

Backman, K., Backman, S., Uysal, M. and Sunshine, K. (1995). Event tourism: An examination of motivations and activities. *Festival Management and Event Tourism*, 3 (1), 15–24.

Báez-Montenegro, A. and Devesa-Fernández, M. (2017). Motivation, satisfaction and loyalty in the case of a film festival: Differences between local and non-local participants. *Journal of Cultural Economics*, 41 (2), 173–195.

Bailey, P. (2002). *Design for Entertaining: Inspiration for Creating the Party of Your Dreams*. Weimar, TX: Culinary and Hospitality Industry Publications Services.

Baker, D. and Crompton, J. (2000). Quality, satisfaction and behavioral intentions. *Annals of Tourism Research*, 27 (2), 785–804.

Baker, S. A. and Rowe, D. (2014). Mediating mega events and manufacturing multiculturalism: The cultural politics of the world game in Australia. *Journal of Sociology*, 50 (3), 299–314.

Bakhtin, M. (1993). *Rabelais and His World*. Translated by H. Iswolsky. Bloomington: Indiana University Press (written in 1941, first published in 1965).

Bale, J. and Dejonghe, T. (2008). Editorial. Sports geography: An overview. *Belgeo. Revue belge de géographie*, (2), 157–166.

Ballantyne, J., Ballantyne, R. and Packer, J. (2014). Designing and managing music festival experiences to enhance attendees' psychological and social benefits. *Musicae Scientiae*, 18 (1), 65–83.

Ballouli, K., Koesters,T. and Hall, T. (2018). Leverage and activation of sport sponsorship through music festivals. *Event Management*, 22, 123–133.

Bandura, A. (1977). Self-efficacy: Toward a unifying theory of behavioral change. *Psychology Review*, 84 (2), 191–215.

Bandura, A. (1986). *Social Foundations of Thought and Action: A Social Cognitive Theory*. Englewood Cliffs, NJ: Prentice-Hall.

Banerjee, S. (2018). Analysis of user-generated comments posted during live matches of the Cricket World Cup 2015. *Online Information Review*, 42 (7), 1180–1194.

Bang, H., Alexandris, K. and Ross, S. D. (2009). Validation of the revised volunteer motivations scale for international sporting events (VMS-ISE) at the Athens 2004 Olympic Games. *Event Management*, 12 (3/4), 119–131.

Bang, H., Won, D. and Kim, Y. (2009). Motivations, commitment, and intentions to continue volunteering for sporting events. *Event Management*, 13 (2), 69–81.

Bao, J., Liu, Y. and Li, X. (2017). Urban spectacles as a pretext: The hidden political economy in the 2010 Asian Games in Guangzhou, China. *Urban Geography*, 1–19.

Barbato, M. and Mio, C. (2007). Accounting and the development of management control in the cultural sphere: The case of the Venice biennale. *Accounting, Business and Financial History*, 17 (1), 187–208.

Barbieri, C., Mahoney, E. and Palmer, R. (2008). RV and camping shows: A motivation-based market segmentation. *Event Management*, 12 (2), 53–66.

Barker, M. (2000). *An Empirical Investigation of Tourist Crime in New Zealand: Perceptions, Victimisation and Future Implications*. Unpublished Ph.D. thesis, Centre for Tourism, University of Otago, Dunedin, New Zealand.

Barker, M., Page, S. and Meyer, D. (2001). Evaluating the impact of the 2000 America's Cup on Auckland, New Zealand. *Event Management*, 7 (2), 79–92.

Barker, M., Page, S. J. and Meyer, D. (2002). Modeling tourism crime: The 2000 America's cup. *Annals of Tourism Research*, 29 (3), 762–782.

Barker, M., Page, S. and Meyer, D. (2003). Urban visitor perceptions of safety during a special event. *Journal of Travel Research*, 41 (4), 355–361.

Barker, R. (1968). *Ecological Psychology: Concepts and Methods for Studying the Environment of Human Behavior*. Stanford, CA: Stanford University Press.

Barnett, R. (1990). *The Idea of Higher Education*. Buckingham: Open University Press.

Barney, J. (1991). Firm resources and sustained competitive advantage. *Journal of Management*, 17 (1), 99–120.

Baron, R. and Byrne, D. (2000). *Social Psychology* (9th edn). Boston, MA: Allyn and Bacon.

Baron, S., Warnaby, G. and Hunter-Jones, P. (2014). Service(s) marketing research: Developments and directions. *International Journal of Management Reviews*, 16 (2), 150–171.

Barrera-Fernández, D. and Hernández-Escampa, M. (2019). Inclusion of people with reduced mobility in festivals: Perceptions and challenges at the Guelaguetza Festival, Mexico. In R. Finkel, B. Sharp and M. Sweeney (eds), *Accessibility, Inclusion and Diversity in Critical Event Studies* (pp. 21–32). London: Routledge.

Barron, P. and Ali-Knight, J. (2017). Aspirations and progression of event management graduates: A study of career development. *Journal of Hospitality and Tourism Management* 30, 29–38.

Barron, P. and Leask, A. (2012). Events management education. In S. J. Page and J. Connell (eds), *The Routledge Handbook of Events*, pp. 473–488. London: Routledge.

Barros, C. P. (2006). Evaluating sport events at European level: The Euro 2004. *International Journal of Sport Management and Marketing*, 1 (4), 400–410.

Bateson, J. (1989). *Managing Services Marketing: Text and Readings*. Chicago, IL: The Dryden Press.

Bathelt, H. and Spigel, B. (2012). The spatial economy of North American trade fairs. *Canadian Geographer*, 56 (1), 18–38.

Batty, M., DeSyllas, J. and Duxbury, E. (2003). The discrete dynamics of small-scale spatial events: Agent-based models of mobility in carnivals and street parades. *International Journal of Geographical Information Science*, 17 (7), 673–697.

Baudrillard, J. (1998). *The Consumer Society: Myths and Structures*. London: Sage.

Baum, J. (1996). Organizational ecology. In S. Clegg, C. Hardy and W. Nord (eds), *Handbook of Organization Studies*, pp. 77–115. London: Sage.

Baum, J. and Oliver, C. (1992). Institutional embeddedness and the dynamics of organizational populations. *American Sociological Review*, 57 (4), 540–559.

Baum, J. and Oliver, C. (1996). Toward an institutional ecology of organizational founding. *Academy of Management Journal*, 39 (5), 1378–1427.

Baum, T. and Lundtorp, S. (eds) (2001). *Seasonality in Tourism*. Pergamon: Oxford.

Baum, T., Deery, M., Hanlon, C., Lockstone, L. and Smith, K. (2009). *People and Work in Events and Conventions: A Research Perspective*. Wallingford: CABI.

Baumann, R., Ciavarra, T., Englehardt, B. and Matheson, V. A. (2012). Sports franchises, events, and city livability: An examination of spectator sports and crime rates. *The Economic and Labour Relations Review*, 23 (2), 83–97.

BBC News Northern Ireland, online service, 14 July 2010 (https://www.pri.org/stories/2010-07-21/recreational-rioting-youth-fad-northern-ireland, accessed 9 June 2019).

Beard, C. and Russ, W. (2017). Event evaluation and design: Human experience mapping. *Event Management*, 21 (3), 365–374.

Becken, S. (2015). *Tourism and Oil: Preparing for the Challenge*. Bristol: Channel View.

Becker, D. (2006). *The Essential Legal Guide to Events: A Practical Handbook for Event Professionals and Their Advisers*. Self-published.

Becker, H. (1960). Notes on the concept of commitment. *American Journal of Sociology*, 66 (1), 32–40.

Beer, S. (2018). Please come, sit, and share my view. *Event Management*, 22, 891–902.

Belghazi, T. (2006). Festivalization of urban space in Morocco. *Critique: Critical Middle Eastern Studies*, 15 (1), 97–107.

Bell, P., Greene, T., Fisher, J. and Baum, A. (2001). *Environmental Psychology* (5th edn). Belmont, CA: Thomson Wadsworth.

Benckendorff, P. and Pearce, P. (2012). The psychology of events. In S. J. Page and J. Connell (eds), *The Routledge Handbook of Events*, pp. 165–185. London: Routledge.

Bendle, L. and Patterson, I. (2008). Serious leisure, career volunteers and the organization of arts events in a regional Australian city. *International Journal of Event Management Research*, 4 (1), 1–11.

Benedict, B. (1983). *The Anthropology of World's Fairs*. Berkeley, CA: Scolar Press.

Bentley, M. (1924). *The Field of Psychology*. London: D. Appleton and Company.

Berk, R. (1974). *Collective Behaviour*. Dubuque, IA: Brown.

Berlonghi, A. (1990). *The Special Event Risk Management Manual*. Self-published (A. Berlonghi, PO Box 3454, Dana Point, California 92629).

Berlonghi, A. (1995). Understanding and planning for different spectator crowds. *Safety Science*, 18 (4), 239–247.

Berlonghi, A. (1996). *Special Event Security Management, Loss Prevention, and Emergency Services*. Self-published (A. Berlonghi, PO Box 3454, Dana Point, California 92629).

Berridge, G. (2007). *Event Design and Experience*. Oxford: Butterworth Heinemann.

Berridge, G. (2010). Event pitching: The role of design and creativity. *International Journal of Hospitality Management*, 29 (2), 208–215.

Berridge, G. (2012a). Event experience: A case study of differences between the way in which organizers plan an event experience and the way in which guests receive the experience. *Journal of Park & Recreation Administration*, 30 (3), 7–23.

Berridge, G. (2012b). Designing event experiences. In S. J. Page and J. Connell (eds), *The Routledge Handbook of Events*, pp. 273–288. London: Routledge.

Berryman, J. (2013). Art and national interest: The diplomatic origins of the 'blockbuster exhibition' in Australia. *Journal of Australian Studies*, 37 (2), 159–173.

Best, J. (2009). What policy-makers want from research: What researchers want to tell them. *Journal of Policy Research in Tourism, Hospitality and Events*, 1 (2), 175–178.

Beverland, M., Hoffman, D. and Rasmussen, M. (2001). The evolution of events in the Australasian wine sector. *Tourism Recreation Research*, 26 (2), 35–44.

Biaett, V. (2019). Festivity and attendee experience: A confessional tale of discovery. In J. Mair (ed.), *The Routledge Handbook of Festivals*, pp. 244–253. London: Routledge.

Billinge, M. (1996). A time and place for everything: An essay on recreation, re-creation and the Victorians. *Journal of Historical Geography*, 22 (4), 443–459.

Billings, A. C., Angelini, J. R. and MacArthur, P. J. (2017). *Olympic Television: Broadcasting the Biggest Show on Earth*. London: Routledge.

Bilotta, E. and Evans, G. (2013). Environmental Stress. In L. Steg, A. van den Berg and J. de Groot (eds), *Environmental Psychology: An Introduction*, pp. 27–35. London: John Wiley & Sons and the British Psychological Society.

Bitner, M. J. (1992). Servicescapes: The impact of physical surroundings on customers and employees. *Journal of Marketing*, 56 (2), 57–71.

Bjorner, E. and Berg, P. O. (2012). Strategic creation of experiences at Shanghai World Expo: A practice of communification. *International Journal of Event and Festival Management*, 3 (1), 30–45.

Blackman, D., Benson, A. and Dickson, T. (2017). Enabling event volunteer legacies: A knowledge management perspective. *Event Management*, 21, 233–250.

Bladen, C. and Kennell, J. (2014). Educating the 21st century event management graduate: Pedagogy, practice, professionalism, and professionalization. *Event Management*, 18 (1), 5–14.

Blaikie, A. (1999). *Ageing and Popular Culture*. Cambridge: Cambridge University Press.

Blake A. (2005). *The Economic Impact of the London 2012 Olympics, Research Report 2005/5*. Christel DeHaan Tourism and Travel Research Institute, Nottingham University.

Bleich, S., Cutler, D., Murray, C. and Adams, A. (2008). Why is the developed world obese? *Annual Review of Public Health*, 29 (1), 273–295.

Blichfeldt, B. S. and Halkier, H. (2014). Mussels, tourism and community development: A case study of place branding through food festivals in rural North Jutland, Denmark. *European Planning Studies*, 22 (8), 1587–1603.

Bloom, B. (ed.) (1956). *Taxonomy of Educational Objectives: The Classification of Educational Goals*. Chicago: Susan Fauer Company.

Bob, U. and Majola, M. (2011). Rural community perceptions of the 2010 FIFA World Cup: The Makhowe community in Kwazulu-Natal. *Development Southern Africa*, 28 (3), 386–399.

Bodet, G. (2015). The spectators' perspective. In M. Parent and J.-L. Chappelet (eds), *Routledge Handbook of Sports Event Management*, pp. 163–180. London: Routledge.

Bodet, G. and Lacassagne, M.-F. (2012). International place branding through sporting events: A British perspective of the 2008 Beijing Olympics. *European Sport Management Quarterly*, 12 (4), 357–374.

Body-Gendrot, S. (2016). *Public Disorder and Globalization*. London: Routledge.

Boggia, A., Massei, G., Paolotti, L., Rocchi, L. and Schiavi, F. (2018). A model for measuring the environmental sustainability of events. *Journal of Environmental Management*, 206, 836–845.

Bohlin, M. (2000). Traveling to events. In L. Mossberg (ed.), *Evaluation of Events: Scandinavian Experiences*, pp. 13–29. New York: Cognizant.

Bohman, J. (2005). Critical theory. In E. Zalta (ed.), *Stanford Encyclopedia of Philosophy* (https://plato.stanford.edu/entries/critical-theory/).

Boissevain, J. (1979). Impact of tourism on a dependent island: Gozo, Malta. *Annals of Tourism Research*, 6 (1), 76–90.

Boissevain, J. (ed.) (1996). *Coping with Tourists: European Reactions to Mass Tourism*. Oxford: Bergahn Books.

Bonthuys, E. (2012). The 2010 Football World Cup and the regulation of sex work in South Africa. *Journal of Southern African Studies*, 38 (1), 11–29.

Boo, S. and Busser, J. (2006). Impact analysis of a tourism festival on tourists' destination images. *Event Management*, 9 (4), 223–237.

Booch, G. (2014). The human and ethical aspects of big data. *IEEE Software*, 31 (1), 20–22.

Boorstin, D. (1961). *The Image: A Guide to Pseudo-Events in America*. New York: Harper and Row.

Booth, A. (2016). Negotiating diasporic culture: Festival collaborations and production networks: Negotiating diasporic culture. *International Journal of Event and Festival Management*, 7 (2), 100–116.

BOP Consulting (2011). Edinburgh Festivals Impact Study 2011 (https://www.edinburghfestivalcity.com/assets/000/000/338/BOP_Edinburgh_Festivals_Impact_-_01.05.11_original.pdf?1411035388, accessed 9 June 2019).

BOP Consulting (2018). *Edinburgh Festivals The Network Effect: The Role of the Edinburgh Festivals in the National Culture and Events Sectors*. Prepared for Festivals Edinburgh.

Borrie, B. and Birzell, R. (2001). Approaches to measuring quality of the wilderness experience. In W. Freimund and D. Cole (eds), *Visitor Use Density and Wilderness Experience: Proceedings*, pp. 29–38. Ogden, UT: US Department of Agriculture, Forest Service, Rocky Mountain Research Station.

Bos, H. (1994). The importance of mega-events in the development of tourism demand. *Festival Management and Event Tourism*, 2 (1), 55–58.

Botterill, D. and Crompton, J. (1996). Two case studies: Exploring the nature of the tourist's experience. *Journal of Leisure Research*, 28 (1), 57–82.

Bouchet, P., LeBrun, A. and Auvergne, S. (2004). Sport tourism consumer experiences: A comprehensive model. *Journal of Sport Tourism*, 9 (2), 127–140.

Bourdieu, P. (1972). *Esquisse d'une théorie de la pratique, précédé de trois études d' ethnologie kabyle* (Outline of a Theory of Practice). Cambridge: Cambridge University Press.

Bourdieu, P. (1986). The forms of capital. In J. Richardson (ed.), *Handbook of Theory and Research in the Sociology of Education*. New York: Greenwald Press.

Bowdin, G., Allen, J., O'Toole, W., Harris, R. and McDonnell, I. (2011). *Events Management* (3rd edn). Oxford: Butterworth-Heinemann.

Bowdin, G. and Church, I. (2000). Customer satisfaction and quality costs: Towards a pragmatic approach for event management. In J. Allen, R. Harris and L. Jago (eds), *Events Beyond 2000 – Setting the Agenda*. Sydney: Australian Centre for Event Management, University of Technology, Sydney.

Bowen, J. P. (2018). A provincial frost fair: Urban space, sociability and spectacle in Shrewsbury during the great frost of 1739. *Midland History*, 43 (1), 43–61.

Boyd, D. and Boyd, L. (1998). The home field advantage: Implications for the pricing of tickets to professional team sporting events. *Journal of Economics and Finance*, 22 (2–3), 169–179.

Bramwell, B. (1997). Strategic planning before and after a mega-event. *Tourism Management*, 18 (3), 167–176.

Bramwell, B. and Lane, B. (1993). Interpretation and sustainable tourism: The potential and the pitfalls. *Journal of Sustainable Tourism*, 1 (2), 71–80.

Brannagan, P. and Rookwood, J. (2016). Sports mega-events, soft power and soft disempowerment: International supporters' perspectives on Qatar's acquisition of the 2022 FIFA World Cup finals. *International Journal of Sport Policy and Politics*, 8 (2), 173–188.

Breen, H., Bull, A. and Walo, M. (2001). A comparison of survey methods to estimate visitor expenditure at a local event. *Tourism Management*, 22 (5), 473–479.

Brennan-Horley, C., Connell, J. and Gibson, C. (2007). The Parkes Elvis Revival Festival: Economic development and contested place identities in rural Australia. *Geographical Research*, 45 (1), 71–84.

Brewster, M., Connell, J. and Page, S. (2009). The Scottish Highland Games: Evolution, development and role as a community event. *Current Issues in Tourism*, 12 (3), 271–293.

Brida, J. G., Disegna, M. and Osti, L. (2013). The effect of authenticity on visitors' expenditure at cultural events. *Current Issues in Tourism*, 16 (3), 266–285.

Brida, J., Meleddu, M. and Tokarchuk, O. (2017). Use value of cultural events: The case of the Christmas markets. *Tourism Management*, 59, 67–75.

Bristow, D. and Sebastion, R. (2001). Holy cow! Wait 'til next year! A closer look at the brand loyalty of Chicago Cubs baseball fans. *The Journal of Consumer Marketing*, 18 (3), 256–275.

British Arts Festivals Association (2000, 2002, 2007). Festivals Mean Business (www.artsfestivals.co.uk, accessed 7 June 2019).

British Columbia Sports Branch (www.tsa.gov.bc.ca/sport, accessed 7 June 2019).

British Standards Institute (2006). *Sustainable Event Management System: Specification with Guidance for Use*. London: BSI.

Britton, S. G. (1982). The political economy of tourism in the Third World. *Annals of Tourism Research*, 9 (3), 331–358.

Brothers, G. and Brantley, V. (1993). Tag and recapture: Testing an attendance estimation technique for an open access special event. *Festival Management and Event Tourism*, 1 (4), 143–146.

Brotherton, B. and Himmetoğlu, B. (1997). Beyond destinations—special interest tourism. *Anatolia*, 8 (3), 11–30.

Broudehoux, A. M. (2017a). Foreword: The politics of event-led urban image construction – notes from Beijing and Rio de Janeiro. In M. Karavatzis, M. Giovanardi and M. Lhrou (eds), *Inclusive Place Branding: Critical Perspectives on Theory and Practice*. London: Routledge.

Broudehoux, A. M. (2017b). *Mega-events and Urban Image Construction: Beijing and Rio de Janeiro*. London: Routledge.

Brown, G., Chalip, L., Jago, L. and Mules, T. (2001). The Sydney Olympics and Brand Australia. In N. Morgan, A. Pritchard and R. Pride (eds), *Destination Branding: Creating the Unique Destination Proposition*, pp. 163–185. Oxford: Butterworth-Heinemann.

Brown, K. (2010). Come on home: Visiting friends and relatives – the Cape Breton experience. *Event Management*, 14 (4), 309–318.

Brown, S. (2010). *Event design: Creating and staging the event experience*. Welland, S. Aust.: Visible Management.

Brown, S. (2014). Emerging Professionalism in the event industry: A practitioner's perspective. *Event Management*, 18 (1), 15–24.

Brown, S. and James, J. (2004). Event design and management: Ritual sacrifice? In I. Yeoman, M. Robertson, J. Ali-Knight, S. Drummond and U. McMahon-Beattie (eds), *Festivals and Events Management*, pp. 53–64. Oxford: Elsevier.

Brunson, M. and Shelby, B. (1993). Recreation substitutability: A research agenda. *Leisure Sciences*, 15 (1), 67–74.

Bruwer, J. and Kelley, K. (2015). Service performance quality evaluation and satisfaction in a USA wine festivalscape: Buying behavioural effects. *International Journal of Event and Festival Management*, 6 (1), 18–38.

Bryan, H. (1977). Leisure value systems and recreation specialization: The case of trout fishermen. *Journal of Leisure Research*, 9 (3), 174–187.

Bryman, A. (2004). *The Disneyization of Society*. London: Sage.

Buck, R. (1977). Making good business better: A second look at staged tourist attractions. *Journal of Travel Research*, 15 (3), 30–31.

Buning, R. and Gibson, H. (2015). The evolution of active-sport-event travel careers. *Journal of Sport Management*, 29, 555–569.

Buning, R. and Gibson, H. (2016a). Exploring the trajectory of active-sport-event travel careers: A social worlds perspective. *Journal of Sport Management*, 30 (3), 265–281.

Buning, R. and Gibson, H. (2016b). The role of travel conditions in cycling tourism: Implications for destination and event management. *Journal of Sport & Tourism*, 20 (3/4), 175–193.

Burdseya, D. (2008). Contested conceptions of identity, community and multiculturalism in the staging of alternative sport events: A case study of the Amsterdam World Cup football tournament. *Leisure Studies*, 27 (3), 259–277.

Bureau International des Expositions (www.bie-paris.org, accessed 7 June 2019).

Burgan, B. and Mules, T. (1992). Economic impact of sporting events. *Annals of Tourism Research*, 19 (4), 700–710.

Burgan, B. and Mules, T. (2001). Reconciling cost-benefit and economic impact assessment for event tourism. *Tourism Economics*, 7 (4), 321–330.

Burns, J., Hatch, J. and Mules, T. (eds) (1986). *The Adelaide Grand Prix: The Impact of a Special Event*. Adelaide: The Centre for South Australian Economic Studies.

Burns, J. and Mules, T. (1989). An economic evaluation of the Adelaide Grand Prix. In G. Syme, B. Shaw, D. Fenton and W. Mueller (eds), *The Planning and Evaluation of Hallmark Events*, pp. 172–185. Aldershot: Gower Publishing Company.

Burr, S. and Scott, D. (2004). Application of the recreational specialization framework to understanding visitors to the Great Salt Lake Bird Festival. *Event Management*, 9 (1/2), 27–37.

Butler, R. (1980). The concept of a tourist area cycle of evolution: Implications for management of resources. *Canadian Geographer*, 24 (1), 5–12.

Butler, R. and Grigg, J. (1987). The hallmark event that got away: The case of the 1991 Pan American Games in London, Ontario. In *PAPER 87, People and Physical Environment Research Conference*. Perth: University of Western Australia.

Butler, R. and Mao, B. (1997). Seasonality in tourism: Problems and measurement. In P. Murphy (ed.), *Quality Management in Urban Tourism*, pp. 9–24, Wiley, Chichester.

Butler, R. W. (2001). Seasonality in tourism: Issues and implications. In S. Lundtorp and T. Baum (eds), *Seasonality in Tourism*, pp. 5–21. Oxford: Pergamon.

Camarero, C., Garrido, M. J. and Vicente, E. (2010). Components of art exhibition brand equity for internal and external visitors. *Tourism Management*, 31 (4), 495–504.

Cameron, C. (1989). Cultural tourism and urban revitalization. *Tourism Recreation Research*, 14 (1), 23–32.

Campaniello, N. (2013). Mega events in sports and crime: Evidence from the 1990 Football World Cup. *Journal of Sports Economics*, 14 (2), 148–170.

Campbell, S. and Fainstein, S. (eds) (2003). *Readings in Planning Theory*. Malden, MA: Blackwell.

Campos, A. C., Mendes, J., do Valle, P. O. and Scott, N. (2018). Co-creation of tourist experiences: A literature review. *Current Issues in Tourism*, 21 (4), 369–400.

Capriello, A. and Rotherham, I. D. (2011). Building a preliminary model of event management for rural communities. *Journal of Hospitality Marketing and Management*, 20 (3/4), 246–264.

Carlsen, J. (1999). A review of MICE industry evaluation and research in Asia and Australia 1988–1998. *Journal of Convention and Exhibition Management*, 1 (4), 51–67.

Carlsen, J., Getz, D. and Soutar, G. (2000). Event evaluation research. *Event Management*, 6 (4), 247–257.

Carnegie, E. and Smith, M. (2006). Mobility, diaspora and the hybridisation of festivity: The case of the Edinburgh Mela. In D. Picard and M. Robinson (eds), *Festivals, Tourism and Social Change: Remaking Worlds*, pp. 255–268. Clevedon: Channel View.

Carnival of Venice (https://venice-carnival-italy.com/services-2/history-venice-carnival, accessed on 9 June 2019).

Carroll, G. (1984). Organizational ecology. *Annual Review of Sociology*, 10, 71–93.

Carroll, G. (1985). Concentration and specialization: Dynamics of niche width in populations of organizations. *American Journal of Sociology*, 90 (6), 1262–1283.

Carroll, G. and Hannan, M. (2000). *The Demography of Corporations and Industries*. Princeton, NJ: Princeton University Press.

Case, R. (2013). *Events and the Environment*. London: Routledge.

Cassinger, C., Eksell, J., Mansson, M. and Thufvesson, O. (2018). The narrative rhythm of terror: A study of the Stockholm terrorist attack and the "Last Night in Sweden" event. *International Journal of Tourism Cities*, 4 (4), 484–494.

Castells, M. (2010). *The Rise of the Network Society*. Malden, MA: Wiley-Blackwell.

Catherwood, D. and van Kirk, R. (1992). *The Complete Guide to Special Event Management*. New York: Wiley.

Cavalcanti, M. (2001). The Amazonian Ox Dance Festival: An anthropological account. *Cultural Analysis*, 2, 69–105.

Cavicchi, A. and Santini, C. (eds) (2014). *Food and Wine Events in Europe: A Stakeholder Approach*. London: Routledge.

Cecil, A., Fenich, G. G., Krugman, C. and Hashimoto, K. (2013). Review and analysis of the new international meeting and business events competency standards. *Journal of Convention and Event Tourism*, 14 (1), 65–74.

Center for Exhibition Industry Research. 26 March 2003, news release. CEIR (www.ceir.org, accessed 7 June 2019).

Chalip, L. (2004). Beyond impact: A general model for sport event leverage. In B.W. Ritchie and D. Adair (eds), *Sport Tourism: Interrelationships, Impacts and Issues*, pp. 226–252. Clevedon, UK: Channel View Publications.

Chalip, L. (2006). Towards social leverage of sport events. *Journal of Sport & Tourism*, 11 (2), 109–127.

Chalip, L. and Costa, C. (2006). Building sport event tourism into the destination brand: Foundations for a general theory. In H. Gibson (ed.), *Sport Tourism: Concepts and Theories*, pp. 86–105. London: Routledge.

Chalip, L., Green, C. and Hill, B. (2003). Effects of sport media on destination image and intentions to visit. *Journal of Sport Management*, 17 (3), 214–234.

Chalip, L. and Leyns, A. (2002). Local business leveraging of a sport event: Managing an event for economic benefit. *Journal of Sport Management*, 16 (2), 132–158.

Chang, J. (2006). Segmenting tourists to aboriginal cultural festivals: An example in the Rukai tribal area, Taiwan. *Tourism Management*, 27 (6), 1224–1234.

Chang, S. and Mahadevan, R. (2014). Fad, fetish or fixture: Contingent valuation of performing and visual arts festivals in Singapore. *International Journal of Cultural Policy*, 20 (3), 318–340.

Chatterjee, K. and Gordon, A. (2006). Planning for an unpredictable future: Transport in Great Britain in 2030. *Transport Policy*, 13 (3), 254–264.

Chen, N. (2012). Branding national images: The 2008 Beijing Summer Olympics, 2010 Shanghai World Expo, and 2010 Guangzhou Asian Games. *Public Relations Review*, 38 (5), 731–745.

Chen, P. (2006). The attributes, consequences, and values associated with event sport tourists' behaviour: A means–end chain approach. *Event Management*, 10 (1), 1–22.

Cheng, T.-M. and Chen, M.-T. (2014). Image transformation for Mazu pilgrimage and festival tourism. *Asia Pacific Journal of Tourism Research*, 19 (5), 1–20.

Cheska, A. (1981). Antigonish Highland Games: An ethnic case study. Paper presented at the North American Society of Sport History, ninth annual convention, Hamilton.

Chi, C., Ouyang, Z. and Xu, X. (2018). Changing perceptions and reasoning process: Comparison of residents' pre- and post-event attitudes. *Annals of Tourism Research*, 70, 39–53.

Chien, P. M., Ritchie, B. W., Shipway, R. and Henderson, H. (2012). I am having a dilemma: Factors affecting resident support of event development in the community. *Journal of Travel Research*, 51 (4), 451–463.

Choi, J.-K. and Almanza, B. (2012). An assessment of food safety risk at fairs and festivals: A comparison of health inspection violations between fairs and festivals and restaurants. *Event Management*, 16 (4), 295–303.

Christou, P., Sharpley, R. and Farmaki, A. (2018). Exploring the emotional dimension of visitors' satisfaction at cultural events. *Event Management*, 22 (2), 255–269.

Chwe, M. (2013). *Rational Ritual: Culture, Coordination, and Common Knowledge*. Princeton: Princeton University Press.

Citrine, K. (n.d.) Site planning for events. In *Event Operations*, pp. 17–19. Port Angeles, WA: International Festivals and Events Association.

Clarke, A. and Jepson, A. (2011). Power and hegemony within a community festival. *International Journal of Event and Festival Management*, 2 (1), 7–19.

Clarke, A. and Jepson, A. (2016). *Managing and Developing Communities, Festivals and Events*. London: Palgrave Macmillan.

Clarke, J. (2003). How journalists judge the 'reality' of an international 'pseudo-event': A study of correspondents who covered the final withdrawal of Vietnamese troops from Cambodia in 1989. *Journalism*, 4 (1), 50–75.

Clawson, M. and Knetsch, J. (1966). *Economics of Outdoor Recreation*. Baltimore: Johns Hopkins.

Club Managers Association of America (www.cmaa.org, accessed 7 June 2019).

Coghlan, A. (2015). Tourism and health: Using positive psychology principles to maximise participants' well-being outcomes – a design concept for charity challenge tourism. *The Journal of Sustainable Tourism*, 23 (3), 382–400.

Coghlan, A. and Filo, K. (2013). Using constant comparison method and qualitative data to understand participants' experiences at the nexus of tourism, sport and charity events. *Tourism Management*, 35, 122–131.

Cohen, E. (1979). A phenomenology of tourist experiences. *Sociology*, 13 (2), 179–201.

Cohen, E. (1988a). Traditions in the qualitative sociology of tourism. *Annals of Tourism Research*, 15 (1), 29–46.

Cohen, E. (1988b). Authenticity and commoditization in tourism. *Annals of Tourism Research*, 15 (3), 371–386.

Coleman, J. (1988). Social capital in the creation of human capital. *American Journal of Sociology*, 94, S95–120. In the Supplement: Organizations and Institutions: Sociological and Economic Approaches to the Analysis of Social Structure.

Coleman, J. (1990). *Foundations of Social Theory*. Cambridge, MA: Belknap Press of Harvard University Press.

Collins, A. and Flynn, A. (2008). Measuring the environmental sustainability of a major sporting event: A case study of the FA Cup Final. *Tourism Economics*, 14 (4), 751–768.

Collins, A., Jones, C. and Munday, M. (2009). Assessing the environmental impacts of mega sporting events: Two options? *Tourism Management*, 30 (6), 828–837.

Collins-Kreiner, N. (2010). Researching pilgrimage: Continuity and transformations. *Annals of Tourism Research*, 37 (2), 440–456.

Colombo, A. (2016). How to evaluate cultural impacts of events? A model and methodology proposal. *Scandinavian Journal of Hospitality and Tourism*, 16 (4), 500–511.

Colombo, A. and Richards, G. (2017). Eventful cities as global innovation catalysts: The Sónar Festival network. *Event Management*, 21, 621–634.

Columbus, G. (2011). *The Complete Guide to Careers in Special Events*. New York: Wiley.

Comas, M. and Moscardo, G. (2005). Understanding associations and their conference decision-making processes. *Journal of Convention and Event Tourism*, 7 (3–4), 117–138.

Connell, J. and Page, S. J. (2005). Evaluating the economic and spatial effects of an event: The case of the world medical and health games. *Tourism Geographies*, 7 (1), 63–85.

Connell, J. and Page, S. J. (eds) (2010). *Event Tourism: Critical Concepts in Tourism. Volumes 1–4*. London: Routledge.

Connell, J. Page, S. J. and Meyer, D. (2015). Visitor attractions and events: Responding to seasonality. *Tourism Management*, 46, 283–298.

Convention Industry Council (www.conventionindustry.org, accessed 7 June 2019).

Coopers and Lybrand Consulting Group (1989). *NCR 1988 Festivals Study Final Report*, Vol. 1. Ottawa: Report for the Ottawa-Carleton Board of Trade.

Cornelissen, S. (2011). Mega event securitisation in a third world setting: Glocal processes and ramifications during the 2010 FIFA World Cup. *Urban Studies*, 48 (15), 3221–3240.

Cornish, E. (2004). Futuring: The exploration of the future. In *Futuring: The Exploration of the Future*. Bethesda, MD: World Future Society.

Coughlan, D. and Mules, T. (2002). Sponsorship awareness and recognition at Canberra's Floriade festival. *Event Management*, 7 (1), 1–9.

Coyne, B. and Coyne, E. (2001). Getting, keeping and caring for unpaid volunteers for professional golf tournament events. *Human Resources Development International*, 4 (2), 199–214.

Craven, J. (1990). *Introduction to Economics: An Integrated Approach to Fundamental Principles*. Oxford: Blackwell.

Crawford, D., Jackson, E. and Godbey, G. (1991). A hierarchical model of leisure constraints. *Leisure Sciences*, 13 (4), 309–320.

Crespi-Vallbona, M. and Richards, G. (2007). The meaning of cultural festivals: Stakeholder perspectives in Catalunya. *International Journal of Cultural Policy*, 13 (1), 103–122.

Crompton, J. (1979). Motivations for pleasure vacation. *Annals of Tourism Research*, 6 (4), 408–424.

Crompton. J. (1993). Understanding a business organization's approach to entering a sponsorship partnership. *Festival Management and Event Tourism*, 1 (3), 98–109.

Crompton, J. (1995). Factors that have stimulated the growth of sponsorship of major events. *Festival Management and Event Tourism*, 3 (2), 97–101.

Crompton, J. (1999). *Measuring the Economic Impact of Visitors to Sports Tournaments and Special Events*. Ashburn, VA: Division of Professional Services, National Recreation and Park Association.

Crompton J. (2006). Economic impact studies: Instruments for political shenanigans? *Journal of Travel Research*, 45, 67–82.

Crompton, J. (2011). Using external reference price to reduce resistance to leisure service pricing increases. *Managing Leisure*, 16 (3), 207–215.

Crompton, J. and Love, L. (1994). Using inferential evidence to determine likely reaction to a price increase at a festival. *Journal of Travel Research*, 32 (4), 32–36.

Crompton, J. and Love, L. (1995). The predictive validity of alternative approaches to evaluating quality of a festival. *Journal of Travel Research*, 34 (1), 11–24.

Crompton, J. and McKay, S. (1994). Measuring the economic impact of festivals and events: Some myths, misapplications and ethical dilemmas. *Festival Management and Event Tourism*, 2 (1), 33–43.

Crompton, J. and McKay, S. (1997). Motives of visitors attending festival events. *Annals of Tourism Research*, 24 (2), 425–439.

Cronin, M. and Adair, D. (2004). *The Wearing of the Green: A History of St Patrick's Day*. London: Routledge.

Cross, G. (1986). The political economy of leisure: Britain and France and the origins of the eight hour day, 1885–1920. *Leisure Studies* (January), 69–90.

Cross, G. (1993). *Time and Money: The Making of Consumer Culture*. London: Routledge.

Crouch, G., Chiappa, G. and Perdue, R. (2019). International convention tourism: A choice modelling experiment of host city competition. *Tourism Management*, 71, 530–542.

Crouch, G., Perdue, R., Timmermans, H. and Uysal, M. (2004). Building foundations for understanding the consumer psychology of tourism, hospitality and leisure. In G. Crouch, R. Perdue, H. Timmermans, and M. Uysal (eds), *Consumer Psychology of Tourism, Hospitality and Leisure*, Vol. III, pp. 1–10. Cambridge, MA: CABI.

Crowther, P., Bostock, J. and Perry, J. (2015). Review of established methods in event research. *Event Management*, 19, 93–107.

Crowther, P. and Donlan, L. (2011). Value-creation space: The role of events in a service-dominant marketing paradigm. *Journal of Marketing Management*, 27 (13–14), 1444–1463.

Crowther, P. and Orefice, C. (2015). Co-creative events: Analysis and illustrations. In G. W. Richards, L. Marques and K. Mein (eds), *Event Design: Social Perspectives and Practices*, pp. 122–136. London: Routledge

Crowther, P., Orefice, C. and Beard, C. (2018). At work and play: Business events as entrepreneurial spaces. *International Journal of Entrepreneurship and Innovation*, 19 (2), 90–99.

Cruikshank, J. (1997). Negotiating with narrative: Establishing cultural identity at the Yukon International Storytelling Festival. *American Anthropologist*, 99 (1), 56–69.

Csikszentmihalyi, M. (1975). *Beyond Boredom and Anxiety: The Experience of Play in Work and Leisure*. San Francisco, CA: Jossey-Bass.

Csikszentmihalyi, M. (1990). *Flow: The Psychology of Optimal Experience*. New York: Harper Perennial.

Csikszentmihalyi, M. and Csikszentmihalyi, I. (1988). *Optimal Experience: Psychological Studies of Flow on Consciousness*. Cambridge, MA. Cambridge University Press.

Cudny, W. (2014). Festivals as a subject for geographical research. *Geografisk Tidsskrift- Danish Journal of Geography*, 114 (2), 132–142.

Cultural Development Network (Australia). *Assessing Cultural Impacts of Events on Individuals and Communities or Society* (http://www.culturaldevelopment.net.au/outcomes)

Cunneen, C. and Lynch, R. (1988). The social meanings of conflict in riots at the Australian Grand Prix Motorcycle Races. *Leisure Studies*, 7 (1), 1–19.

Cusack, C. M. and Digance, J. (2009). The Melbourne Cup: Australian identity and secular pilgrimage. *Sport in Society*, 12 (7), 876–889.

Daniels, M. (2007). Central place theory and sport tourism impacts. *Annals of Tourism Research*, 34 (2), 332–347.

Danish Design Centre (2007). *The Design Ladder*, Danish Business Authority, Copenhagen (http://ddc.dk/en/2015/05/the-design-ladder-four-steps-of-design-use/, accessed 1 June 2019).

Dann, G. (1977). Anomie, ego-involvement and tourism. *Annals of Tourism Research*, 4, 184–194.

Dann, G. (1981). Tourist motivation: An appraisal. *Annals of Tourism Research*, 8 (2), 187–219.

Darcy, S. and Harris, R. (2003). Inclusive and accessible special event planning: An Australian perspective. *Event Management*, 8 (1), 39–47.

Darian-Smith, K. (2011). Histories of agricultural shows and rural festivals in Australia. In C. Gibson and J. Connell (eds), *Festival Places: Revitalising Rural Australia*, pp. 25–43. Bristol: Channel View.

Dashper, K. (2016). Researching from the inside: Autoethnography and critical event studies. In I. Lamond (ed.), *Critical Event Studies. Leisure Studies in a Global Era*, pp. 213–229. London: Palgrave Macmillan.

Dashper, K., Fletcher, T. and McCullough, N. (eds) (2014). *Sports Events, Society and Culture*. London: Routledge.

Dattilo, J. and Howard, D. (1994). The complex and dynamic nature of leisure experience. *Journal of Leisure Research*, 26 (3), 195–211.

Davidson, L. and Schaffer, W. (1980). A discussion of methods employed in analyzing the impact of short-term entertainment events. *Journal of Travel Research*, 28 (3), 12–16.

Davidson, R. (2003). Adding pleasure to business: Conventions and tourism. *Journal of Convention and Exhibition Management*, 5 (1), 29–39.

Davidson, R. and Cope, B. (2003). *Business Travel: Conferences, Incentive Travel, Exhibitions, Corporate Hospitality and Corporate Travel*. Harlow: Pearson.

Davidson, R. and Rogers, T. (2006). *Marketing Destinations and Venues for Conferences, Conventions and Business Events*. Oxford: Butterworth-Heinemann.

Davies, A. (2011). Local leadership and rural renewal through festival fun: The case of SnowFest. In C. Gibson and J. Connell (eds), *Festival Places: Revitalising Rural Australia*, pp. 61–73. Bristol: Channel View.

Davis, J. (1999). *The Great Exhibition*. Thrupp: Sutton Publishing.

Dawson, M. (2011). Putting cities on the map: Vancouver's 1954 British Empire and Commonwealth Games in comparative and historical perspective. *Urban Geography*, 32 (6), 788–803.

Dayan, D. (1994). *Media Events*. Cambridge, MA: Harvard University Press.

De Bres, K. and Davis, J. (2001). Celebrating group and place identity: A case study of a new regional festival. *Tourism Geographies*, 3 (3), 326–337.

De Geus, A. P. (1988). Planning as learning. *Harvard Business Review*, 66 (2), 70–74.

De Grazia, S. (1962). *Of Time, Work, and Leisure*. New York: Twentieth Century Fund.

De Groote, P. (2005). A multidisciplinary analysis of world fairs (expos) and their effects. *Tourism Review*, 60 (1), 12–19.

De Jong, A. (2017). Rethinking activism: Tourism, mobilities and emotion. *Social and Cultural Geography*, 18 (6), 851–868.

De Young, R. (1999). Environmental psychology. In D. Alexander and R. Fairbridge (eds), *Encyclopedia of Environmental Science*. Hingham, MA: Kluwer Academic Publishers.

Dean, D. H. (1999). Brand endorsement, popularity, and event sponsorship as advertising cues affecting consumer pre-purchase attitudes. *Journal of Advertising*, 28 (3), 1–12.

Debord, G. (1983). *Society of the Spectacle*. Translated by Ken Knabb (from the French original of 1967). London: Rebel Books.

Deci, E. and Ryan, R. (1985). *Intrinsic Motivation and Self-Determination in Human Behavior*. New York: Plenum.

Deci, E., and Ryan, R. (2000). The 'what' and 'why' of goal pursuits: Human needs and the self determination of behaviour. *Psychological Inquiry*, 11 (4), 227–268.

Decrop, A. (2006). *Vacation Decision Making*. Wallingford: CABI.

Deery, M. and Jago, L. (2010). Social impacts of events and anti-social behaviour. *International Journal of Event and Festival Management*, 1 (1), 8–28.

Deighton, J. (1992). The consumption of performance. *Journal of Consumer Research*, 19 (3), 362–372.

Delamere, T. (2001). Development of a scale to measure resident attitudes toward the social impacts of community festivals: Part 2: Verification of the scale. *Event Management*, 7 (1), 25–38.

Delamere, T., Wankel, L. and Hinch, T. (2001). Development of a scale to measure resident attitudes toward the social impacts of community festivals: Part 1: Item generation and purification of the measure. *Event Management*, 7 (1), 11–24.

Delbosc, A. (2008). Social identity as a motivator in cultural festivals. *Visitor Studies*, 11 (1), 3–15.

Della Bitta, A., Loudon, D., Booth, G. and Weeks, R. (1977). Estimating the economic impact of a short-term tourist event. *Journal of Travel Research*, 16 (2), 10–15.

Delpy, L. and Li, M. (1998). The art and science of conducting economic impact studies. *Journal of Vacation Marketing*, 4 (3), 230–254.

Deng, Q. and Li, M. (2014). A model of event–destination image transfer. *Journal of Travel Research*, 53 (1), 69–82.

Denton, S. and Furse, B. (1993). Visitation to the 1991 Barossa Valley Vintage Festival: Estimating overall visitor numbers to a festival encompassing several venues and events. *Festival Management and Event Tourism*, 1 (2), 51–56.

Dernie, D. (2006). *Exhibition Design*. London: Laurence King Publishing.

Derrett, R. (2004). Festivals, events and the destination. In I. Yeoman, M. Robertson, J. Ali-Knight, S. Drummond, and U. McMahon-Beattie (eds), *Festivals and Events Management*, pp. 33–50. Oxford: Elsevier.

Derrett, R. (2008). How festivals nurture resilience in regional communities. In J. Ali-Knight, M. Robertson, A. Fyall, and A. Ladkin (eds), *International Perspectives of Festivals and Events: Paradigms of Analysis*, pp. 107–124. Oxford: Butterworth-Heinemann.

Derrett, R. (2016). *The Complete Guide to Creating Enduring Festivals*. Hoboken, NJ: Wiley.

Devine, A., Boluk, K. and Devine, F. (2017). Managing social media during a crisis: A conundrum for event managers. *Event Management*, 21, 375–389.

Dewar, K., Meyer, D. and Li, W. M. (2001). Harbin, lanterns of ice, sculptures of snow. *Tourism Management*, 22 (5), 523–532.

Dickens, C. (1995). *Sketches by Boz*. London: Penguin Classics.

Dickson, T., Darcy, S. and Benson, A. (2017). Volunteers with disabilities at the London 2012 Olympic and Paralympic Games: Who, why, and will they do it again? *Event Management*, 21, 301–318.

Dietz-Uhler, B., Harrick, E., End, C. and Jacquemotte, L. (2000). Sex differences in sport fan behaviour and reasons for being a sport fan. *Journal of Sport Behavior*, 23 (3), 219–231.

Dietz-Uhler, B. and Murrell, A. (1999). Examining fan reactions to game outcomes: A longitudinal study of social identity. *Journal of Sport Behavior*, 22 (1), 15–27.

Digance, J. (2005). Intergovernmental conferences: The CHOGM experience. *Journal of Convention and Event Tourism*, 7 (3/4), 65–68.

Dijck, J. V. (2013). *The Culture of Connectivity: A Critical History of Social Media*. Oxford: Oxford University Press.

Diller, S., Shedroff, N. and Rhea, D. (2006). *Making Meaning: How Successful Businesses Deliver Meaningful Customer Experiences*. Upper Saddle River, NJ: Pearson.

DiMaggio, P. and Mukhtar, T. (2004). Arts participation as cultural capital in the United States, 1982–2002: Signs of decline? *Poetics*, 32 (2), 169–194.

Dixon, A., Backman, S., Backman, K. and Norman, W. (2012). Expenditure-based segmentation of sport tourists. *Journal of Sport & Tourism*, 17 (1), 5–21.

Doherty, A. (2009). The volunteer legacy of a major sport event. *Journal of Policy Research in Tourism, Leisure and Events*, 1 (3), 185–207.

Donaldson, L. (1996). The normal science of structural contingency theory. In S. Clegg, C. Hardy and W. Nord (eds), *Handbook of Organization Studies*, pp. 57–77. London: Sage.

Donaldson, T. and Preston, L. (1995). The stakeholder theory of the corporation: Concepts, evidence, and implications. *Academy of Management Review*, 20 (1), 65–91.

Doshi, J. K., Furlan, A. D., Lopes, L. C., DeLisa, J. and Battistella, L. R. (2014). Conferences and convention centres' accessibility to people with disabilities. *Journal of Rehabilitation Medicine*, 46 (7), 616–619.

Dowse, S. (2016). A qualitative case study of the 2010 Football World Cup in South Africa: Practical considerations and personal dilemmas. In I. Lamond and L. Platt (eds), *Critical Event Studies: Leisure Studies in a Global Era*, pp. 37–57. London: Palgrave Macmillan.

Draper, J., Young, L. and Fenich, G. (2018). Event management research over the past 12 years: What are the current trends in research methods, data collection, data analysis procedures, and event types? *Journal of Convention and Event Tourism*, 19 (1), 3–24.

Dredge, D., Airey, D. and Gross, M. (eds) (2014). *The Routledge Handbook of Tourism and Hospitality Education*. London: Routledge.

Dredge, D. and Whitford, M. (2011). Event tourism governance and the public sphere. *Journal of Sustainable Tourism*, 19 (4/5), 479–499.

Dredge, S. (2014). Facebook closes its $2bn Oculus Rift acquisition. What next? *The Guardian* (http://www.theguardian.com/technology/2014/jul/22/facebook-oculus-rift-acquisition-virtual-reality, accessed 23 August 2014).

Drengner, J., Jahn, S. and Zanger, C. (2011). Measuring event-brand congruence. *Event Management*, 15 (1), 25–36.

Driver, B., Brown, P. and Peterson, G. (eds) (1991). *Benefits of Leisure*. State College, PA: Venture Publishing.

Drummond, S. and Anderson, H. (2004). Service quality and managing your people. In I. Yeoman, M. Robertson, J. Ali-Knight, S. Drummond and U. McMahon-Beattie (eds), *Festival and Events Management*, pp. 80–96. Oxford: Elsevier.

Du Cros, H. and Jolliffe, L. (2014). *The Arts and Events*. London: Routledge.

Duffy, M. (2000). Lines of drift: Festival participation and performing a sense of place. *Popular Music*, 19 (01), 51–64.

Duffy, M. and Mair, J. (2017). *Festival Encounters: Theoretical Perspectives on Festival events*. London: Routledge.

Duffy, M. and Mair, J. (2018). Engaging the senses to explore community events. *Event Management*, 22, 49–63.

Duignan, M. (2013). Events and urban regeneration: The strategic use of events to revitalise cities. *Journal of Policy Research in Tourism, Leisure and Events*, 5 (3), 307–309.

Duignan, M. B., Pappalepore, I. and Everett, S. (2019). The 'summer of discontent': Exclusion and communal resistance at the London 2012 Olympics. *Tourism Management*, 70, 355–367.

Dungan, T. (1984). How cities plan special events. *The Cornell H.R.A. Quarterly* (May): 83–89.

Durant, H. (1938). *The Problem of Leisure*. London: George Routledge and Sons.

Durkheim, E. (1965). *The Elementary Forms of the Religious Life* (written in French in 1912; translated by Joseph Swain in 1915). New York: The Free Press.

Duvignaud, J. (1976). Festivals: A sociological approach. *Cultures*, 3, 13–25.

Dwyer L. and Forsyth, P. (2009). Public sector support for special events. *Eastern Economic Journal*, 35 (4), 481–499.

Dwyer, L., Forsyth, P. and Dwyer, W. (2010). *Tourism Economics and Policy*. Bristol: Channel View.

Dwyer, L., Forsyth, P. and Spurr, R. (2005). Estimating the impacts of special events on the economy. *Journal of Travel Research*, 43, 351–359.

Dwyer, L., Forsyth, P. and Spurr, R. (2006a). Assessing the economic impacts of events: A computable general equilibrium approach. *Journal of Travel Research*, 45 (1), 59–66.

Dwyer, L., Forsyth, P. and Spurr, R. (2006b). Assessing the economic impacts of special events. In L. Dwyer and P. Forsyth (eds), *International Handbook of Tourism Economics*, Edward Elgar, England.

Dwyer, L. and Jago, L. (2012). The economic contribution of special events. In S. J. Page and J. Connell (eds), *The Routledge Handbook of Events*, pp. 129–147. London: Routledge.

Dwyer, L., Mellor, R., Mistillis, N. and Mules, T. (2000a). A framework for assessing 'tangible' and 'intangible' impacts of events and conventions. *Event Management*, 6 (3), 175–189.

Dwyer, L., Mellor, R., Mistillis, N. and Mules, T. (2000b). Forecasting the economic impacts of events and conventions. *Event Management*, 6 (3), 191–204.

Dwyer, L. and Wickens, E. (eds) (2013). *Event Tourism and Cultural Tourism: Issues and Debates*. London: Routledge.

Dyreson, M. (2017). The Super Bowl as a television spectacle: Global designs, glocal niches, and parochial patterns. *International Journal of the History of Sport*, 34 (1–2), 139–156.

Eagleton, T. (1981). *Walter Benjamin: Towards a Revolutionary Criticism*. London: Verso.

Earl, C. (2008). Crowds at outdoor music festivals: An examination of crowd psychology and its implications for the environmental health practitioner. *Environmental Health*, 8 (1), 34–43.

Earl, C., Parker, E. and Capra, M. (2005). Planning and management for public health impacts of outdoor music festivals: An international study. *Environmental Health*, 5 (1), 50–61.

Easto, P. and Truzzi, M. (1973). Towards an ethnography of the carnival social system. *The Journal of Popular Culture*, 6 (3), 550–566.

Echtner, C. (1999). The semiotic paradigm: Implications for tourism research. *Tourism Management*, 20 (1), 47–57.

Echtner, C. and Jamal, T. (1997). The disciplinary dilemmas of tourism studies. *Annals of Tourism Research*, 24 (4), 868–883.

Economic Planning Group and Lord Cultural Resources (1992). *Strategic Directions for the Planning, Development, and Marketing of Ontario's Attractions, Festivals, and Events*. Toronto: Ministry of Culture, Tourism, and Recreation.

Education Design Lab (www.edddesignlab.org).

Edwards, R. (2012). Gympie's country music Muster: Creating a cultural economy from a local tradition. *Journal of Rural Studies*, 28 (4), 517–527.

Ehrenreich, B. (2006). *Dancing in the Streets: A History of Collective Joy*. New York: Metropolitan Books.

Ekman, A. (1999). The revival of cultural celebrations in regional Sweden: Aspects of tradition and transition. *Sociologia Ruralis*, 39 (3), 280–293.

Ellis, M. (1973). *Why People Play*. Englewood Cliffs, NJ: Prentice Hall.

Elstad, B. (1997). Volunteer perceptions of learning and satisfaction in a mega-event: The case of the XVII Olympic Winter Games in Lillehammer. *Festival Management and Event Tourism*, 4 (3/4), 5–83.

Elstad, B. (2003). Continuance commitment and reasons to quit: A study of volunteers at a jazz festival. *Event Management*, 8 (2), 99–108.

Elstad, B. (2009). Kongsberg Jazz Festival, Norway: Motivating and retaining episodic and bounce-back volunteers at an annual festival. In K. Holmes and K. Smith (eds), *Managing Volunteers in Tourism Attractions, Destinations and Events*, pp. 205–214. Oxford: Butterworth-Heinemann.

Elston, K. and Draper, J. (2012). A review of meeting planner site selection criteria research. *Journal of Convention and Event Tourism*, 13 (3), 203–220.

Emery, P. (2001). Bidding to host a major sports event. In C. Gratton and I. Henry (eds), *Sport in the City: The Role of Sport in Economic and Social Regeneration*, pp. 91–108. London: Routledge.

Encyclopaedia Britannica Online. *Economics* (www.britannica.com, accessed 7 June 2019).

End, C., Dietz-Uhler, M. and Demakakos, N. (2003). Perceptions of sport fans who BIRG. *International Sports Journal*, 7 (1), 139–150.

Epting, F. and Neimeyer, R. (1984). *Personal Meanings of Death: Applications of Personal Construct Theory to Clinical Practice*. New York: Hemisphere.

Equations (2010). *Humanity-Equality-Destiny? Implicating Tourism in the Commonwealth Games 2010*. Bengaluru: Equations (www.equitabletourism.org, accessed 5 October 2010).

Essex, S. and Chalkley, B. (1998). Olympic Games: Catalyst of urban change. *Leisure Studies*, 17 (3), 187–206.

European Union. Directives on EIA (http://ec.europa.eu/environment/eia/eia-legalcontext.htm).

Evans, W. D. (2013). *Psychology of Branding*. New York: Nova Science Publishers.

EventImpacts (http://www.eventimpacts.com).

Event Manager Blog (https://www.eventmanagerblog.com/100-event-theme-ideas).

EventScotland (www.eventscotland.org).

Events Industry Forum, The (2015). *The Purple Guide to Health, Safety and Welfare at Music and Other Events* (https://www.thepurpleguide.co.uk/, accessed 25 September 2018).

Everett, S. (2012). Production places or consumption spaces? The place-making agency of food tourism in Ireland and Scotland. *Tourism Geographies*, 14 (4), 535–554.

Fairley, S. (2003). In search of relived social experience: Group-based nostalgia sport tourism. *Journal of Sport Management*, 17 (3), 284–304.

Fairley, S. and Gammon, S. (2006). Something lived, something learned: Nostalgia's expanding role in sport tourism. In H. Gibson (ed.), *Sport Tourism: Concepts and Theories*, pp. 50–65. London: Routledge.

Fairley, S., Lee, Y., Green, B. C. and Kim, M. L. (2013). Considering cultural influences in volunteer satisfaction and commitment. *Event Management*, 17 (4), 337–348.

Falassi, A. (ed.) (1987). *Time Out of Time: Essays on the Festival*. Albuquerque, NM: University of New Mexico Press.

Farber, C. (1983). High, healthy and happy: Ontario mythology on parade. In F. Manning (ed.), *Celebration of Society: Perspectives on Contemporary Cultural Performance*, pp. 33–50. Bowling Green, OH: Bowling Green Popular Press.

Farrell, J., Johnston, M. and Twynam, D. (1998). Volunteer motivation, satisfaction, and management at an elite sporting competition. *Journal of Sport Management*, 12 (4), 288–300.

Faulkner, B., Chalip, L., Brown, G., Jago, L., March, R. and Woodside, A. (2000). Monitoring the tourism impacts of the Sydney 2000 Olympics. *Event Management*, 6 (4), 231–246.

Faulkner, B. and Raybould, M. (1995). Monitoring visitor expenditure associated with attendance at sporting events: An experimental assessment of the diary and recall methods. *Festival Management and Event Tourism*, 3 (2), 73–81.

Federation European Carnival Cities (www.carnivalcities.com, accessed 7 June 2019).

Fenich, G. (2005). *Meetings, Expositions, Events, and Conventions: An Introduction to the Industry*. Upper Saddle River, NJ: Pearson.

Fenich, G., Scott-Halsell, S. and Hashimoto, K. (2011). An investigation of technological uses by different generations as it relates to meetings and events: A pilot study. *Journal of Convention and Event Tourism*, 12 (1), 53–63.

Ferbrache, F. (2013). Le Tour de France: A cultural geography of a mega-event. *Geography*, 98 (3), 144–151.

Ferreira, S. and Donaldson, R. (2013). Global imaging and branding: Source market newspaper reporting of the 2010 Fifa World Cup. *Tourism Review International*, 4, 253–265.

Festinger, L., Pepitone, A. and Newcomb, T. (1952). Some consequences of de-individuation in a group. *The Journal of Abnormal and Social Psychology*, 47 (2), 382–389.

Filep, S. and Pearce, P. (2013). *Tourist Experience and Fulfilment: Insights from Positive Psychology* (Vol. 31). London: Routledge.

Findling, J. E. and Pelle, K. D. (eds) (2008). *Encyclopaedia of World's Fairs and Expositions*. Jefferson, NC: McFarland.

Finkel, R. (2010). Dancing around the ring of fire. Social capital, tourism resistance, and gender dichotomies at Up Helly Aa in Lerwick, Shetland. *Event Management*, 14 (4), 275–285.

Finkel, R., McGillivray, D., McPherson, G. and Robinson, P. (2013). *Research Themes for Events*. Wallingford: CABI.

Finkel, R., Sharp, B. and Sweeney, M. (2019a). Introduction. In R. Finkel, B. Sharp and M. Sweeney (eds), *Accessibility, Inclusion and Diversity in Critical Event Studies* (pp. 1–6). London: Routledge.

Finkel, R., Sharp, B. and Sweeney, M. (eds) (2019b). *Accessibility, Inclusion, and Diversity in Critical Event Studies*. London: Routledge.

Fishbein, M. (1980). A theory of reasoned action: Some applications and implications. In H. Howe and M. Page (eds), *Nebraska Symposium on Motivation*, 27, pp. 65–116. Lincoln, NE: University of Nebraska Press.

Fishbein, M. and Ajzen, I. (1975). *Belief, Attitude, Intention, and Behavior: An Introduction to Theory and Research*. Reading, MA: Addison-Wesley.

Fleck, S. (1996). Events without barriers: Customer service is a key in complying with the Americans With Disabilities Act. *Festivals*, March, pp. 34–35. International Festivals and Events Association.

Fleischer, A. and Felsenstein, D. (2002). Cost-benefit analysis using economic surpluses: A case study of a televised event. *Journal of Cultural Economics*, 26 (2), 139–156.

Fleming, W. and Toepper, L. (1990). Economic impact studies: Relating the positive and negative impacts to tourism development. *Journal of Travel Research*, 29 (1), 35–42.

Flinn, J. and Frew, M. (2014). Glastonbury: Managing the mystification of festivity. *Leisure Studies*, 33 (4), 418–433.

Florida, R. (2002). *The Rise of the Creative Class: And How It's Transforming Work, Leisure, Community and Everyday Life*. New York: Basic Books.

Fola, M. (2011). Athens city branding and the 2004 Olympic Games. In K. Dinnie (ed.), *City Branding: Theory and Cases*, pp. 112–117. London: Palgrave Macmillan.

Foley, M., McGillivray, D. and McPherson, G. (2011). *Event Policy: From Theory to Strategy*. London: Routledge.

Foley, M., McGillivray, D. and McPherson, G. (2012). Policy pragmatism: Qatar and the global events circuit. *International Journal of Event and Festival Management*, 3 (1), 101–115.

Foley, M., McPherson, G. and McGillivray, D. (2008). Establishing Singapore as the events and entertainment capital of Asia: Strategic brand diversification. In J. Ali-Knight, M. Robertson, A. Fyall and A. Ladkin (eds), *International Perspectives of Festivals and Events: Paradigms of Analysis*, pp. 53–64. Oxford: Butterworth-Heinemann.

Ford, R. C. and Peeper, W. C. (2007). The past as prologue: Predicting the future of the convention and visitor bureau industry on the basis of its history. *Tourism Management*, 28 (4), 1104–1114.

Formica, S. (1998). The development of festivals and special events studies. *Festival Management and Event Tourism*, 5 (3), 131–137.

Formica, S. and Murrmann, S. (1998). The effects of group membership and motivation on attendance: An international festival case. *Tourism Analysis*, 3 (3/4), 197–207.

Formica, S. and Uysal, M. (1998). Market segmentation of an international cultural-historical event in Italy. *Journal of Travel Research*, 36 (4), 16–24.

Forsyth, J. (2016). The illusion of inclusion: Agenda 21 and the commodification of Aboriginal culture in the Vancouver 2010 Olympic Games. *Public*, 27(53), 22–34.

Foster, K. and Robinson, P. (2010). A critical analysis of the motivational factors that influence event attendance in family groups. *Event Management*, 14 (2), 107–125.

Foucault, M. (1969). *The Archaeology of Knowledge*. First translated from the French (*L'Archeologie du Savoir*) and published in English in 1972 by Tavistock Publications, London.

Foucault, M. (1982). The subject and power. *Critical Inquiry*, 8 (4), 777–795.

Fourie, J. and Santana-Gallego, M. (2011). The impact of mega-sport events on tourist arrivals. *Tourism Management*, 32 (6), 1364–1370.

Fox, D. and Edwards, J. (2009). A preliminary analysis of the market for small, medium, and large horticultural shows in England. *Event Management*, 12 (3/4), 199–208.

Fox, D., Gouthro, M., Morakabati, Y. and Brackstone, J. (2014). *Doing Events Research. From Theory to Practice*. London: Routledge.

Franchetti, J. and Page, S. J. (2009). Entrepreneurship and innovation in tourism: Public sector experiences of innovation activity in tourism in Scandinavia and Scotland. In A. Ateljevic and S. J. Page (eds), *Tourism and Entrepreneurship: International Perspectives*, pp. 109–130. Oxford: Butterworth-Heinemann.

Frank, S. and Roth, S. (2000). Festivalization and the media: Weimar, culture city of Europe 1999. *International Journal of Cultural Policy*, 6 (2), 219–241.

Fredline, E. (2006). Host and guest relations and sport tourism. In H. Gibson (ed.), *Sport Tourism: Concepts and Theories*, pp. 131–147. London: Routledge.

Fredline, E. and Faulkner, B. (1998). Resident reactions to a major tourist event: The Gold Coast Indy car race. *Festival Management and Event Tourism*, 5 (4), 185–205.

Fredline, E. and Faulkner, B. (2002a). Residents' reactions to the staging of major motorsport events within their communities: A cluster analysis. *Event Management*, 7 (2), 103–114.

Fredline, E. and Faulkner, B. (2002b). Variations in residents' reactions to major motorsport events: Why residents perceive the impacts of events differently. *Event Management*, 7 (2), 115–125.

Fredline, E., Jago, L. and Deery, M. (2003). The development of a generic scale to measure the social impacts of events. *Event Management*, 8 (1), 23–37.

Fredline, L., Deery, M. and Jago, L. (2013). A longitudinal study of the impacts of an annual event on local residents. *Tourism Planning & Development*, 10 (4), 416–432.

Freedman, J. (1975). *Crowding and Behavior*. San Francisco, CA: Freeman.

Freeman, L., White, D. and Romney, A. (1992). *Research Methods in Social Network Analysis*. New Brunswick, NJ: Transaction Publishers.

Freeman, R. (1984). *Strategic Management: A Stakeholder Approach*. Boston, MA: Pitman.

Frew, M. (2014). Events and media spectacle. In R. Finkel, M. McGillivray, G. McPherson and P. Robinson (eds), *Research Themes for Events*. London: CABI.

Fridgen, J. D. (1984). Environmental psychology and tourism. *Annals of Tourism Research*, 11 (1), 19–39.

Frisby, W. and Getz, D. (1989). Festival management: A case study perspective. *Journal of Travel Research*, 28 (1), 7–11.

Frissen, R., Janssen, R. and Luijer, D. (2016). *The Event Design Handbook: Systematically Design Innovative Events Using the Event Canvas*. Amsterdam: Bis B.V., Uitgeverij (BIS Publishers).

Frost, W. and Laing, J. (2013). *Commemorative Events: Memory, Identities, Conflicts*. London: Routledge.

Frost, W. and Laing, J. (2017). *Exhibitions, trade fairs and industrial events*. London: Routledge.

Frost, W., Wheeler, F. and Harvey, M. (2008). Commemorative events: Sacrifice, identity and dissonance. In J. Ali-Knight, M. Robertson, A. Fyall and A. Ladkin (eds), *International Perspectives of Festivals and Events: Paradigms of Analysis*, pp. 161–171. Oxford: Butterworth-Heinemann.

Fu, X., Yi, X., Okumus, F. and Jin, W. (2019). Linking the internal mechanism of exhibition attachment to exhibition satisfaction: A comparison of first-time and repeat attendees. *Tourism Management* 72, 92–104.

Fuller, L. K. (2004). *National Days/National Ways: Historical, Political, and Religious Celebrations Around the World*. Santa Barbara: Praeger.

Funk, D. (2008). *Consumer Behaviour in Sport and Events: Marketing Action*. Oxford: Butterworth-Heinemann.

Funk, D. (2012). *Consumer Behaviour in Sport and Events*. London: Routledge.

Funk, D. and James, J. (2001). The psychological continuum model: A conceptual framework for understanding an individual's psychological connection to sport. *Sport Management Review*, 4 (2), 119–150.

Funk, D. and James, J. (2006). Consumer loyalty: The meaning of attachment in the development of sport team allegiance. *Journal of Sport Management*, 20 (2), 189–217.

Funk, D. C., Mahony, D. F. and Ridinger, L. L. (2002). Characterizing consumer motivation as individual difference factors: Augmenting the Sport Interest Inventory (SII) to explain level of spectator support. *Sport Marketing Quarterly*, 11 (1), 33–43.

Funk, D. C., Ridinger, L. L. and Moorman, A. M. (2003). Understanding consumer support: Extending the Sport Interest Inventory (SII) to examine individual differences among women's professional sport consumers. *Sport Management Review*, 6 (1), 1–31.

Funk, D., Toohey, K. and Bruun, T. (2007). International sport event participation: Prior sport involvement; destination image; and travel motives. *European Sport Management Quarterly*, 7 (3), 227–248.

Gabrenya, W. and Hwang, K. (1996). Chinese social interaction: Harmony and hierarchy on the good earth. In H. Bond (ed.), *The Handbook of Chinese Psychology*, pp. 309–322. Hong Kong: Oxford University Press.

Gallarza, M. G., Arteaga, F. and Gil-Saura, I. (2013). The value of volunteering in special events: A longitudinal study. *Annals of Tourism Research*, 40, 105–131.

Gammon, S. (2004). Secular pilgrimage and sport tourism. In B. Ritchie and D. Adair (eds), *Sport Tourism: Inter-relationships, Impacts and Issues*, pp. 30–45. Clevedon: Channel View.

Gammon, S., Ramshaw, G. and Wright, R. (2017). Theory in sport tourism: Some critical reflections. *Journal of Sport & Tourism*, 21 (2), 69–74.

Gartner, W. and Holocek, D. (1983). Economic impact of an annual tourism industry exposition. *Annals of Tourism Research*, 10 (2), 199–212.

Geertz, C. (1993). *The Interpretation of Cultures*. London: Fontana Press.

Gelder, G. and Robinson, P. (2009). A critical comparative study of visitor motivations for attending music festivals: A case study of Glastonbury and V Festival. *Event Management*, 13 (3), 181–196.

Gelder, G. and Robinson, P. (2011). Events, festivals and the arts. In P. Robinson, S. Heitmann, and P. Dieke (eds), *Research Themes in Tourism*, pp. 128–145. Wallingford: CABI.

George, R. and Swart, K. (2012). International tourists' perceptions of crime-risk and their future travel intentions during the 2010 FIFA World Cup™ in South Africa. *Journal of Sport & Tourism*, 17 (3), 201–223.

Gershuny, J. (2011). Time use surveys and the measurement of national well-being. Centre for Time Use Research, University of Oxford (http://carnivalcities.com/, accessed 9 June 2019).

Getz, D. (1989). Special events: Defining the product. *Tourism Management*, 10 (2), 135–137.

Getz, D. (1991). *Festivals, Special Events, and Tourism*. New York: Van Nostrand Reinhold.

Getz, D. (1993a). Corporate culture in not-for-profit festival organizations: Concepts and potential applications. *Festival Management and Event Tourism*, 1 (1), 11–17.

Getz, D. (1993b). Case study: Marketing the Calgary Exhibition and Stampede. *Festival Management and Event Tourism*, 1 (4), 147–156.

Getz, D. (1997). *Event Management and Event Tourism* (1st edn). New York: Cognizant Communications Corp.

Getz, D. (1998a). Information sharing among festival managers. *Festival Management and Event Tourism*, 5 (1/2), 33–50.

Getz, D. (1998b). Event tourism and the authenticity dilemma. In W. Theobald (ed.), *Global Tourism*, pp. 409–427 (2nd edn). Oxford: Butterworth-Heinemann.

Getz, D. (1999). The impacts of mega events on tourism: Strategies for destinations. In T. Andersson, C. Persson, B. Sahlberg and L. Strom (eds), *The Impact of Mega Events*, pp. 5–32. Ostersund, Sweden: European Tourism Research Institute.

Getz, D. (2000a). Festivals and special events: Life cycle and saturation issues. In W. Garter and D. Lime (eds), *Trends in Outdoor Recreation, Leisure and Tourism*, pp. 175–185. Wallingford: CABI.

Getz, D. (2000b). Developing a research agenda for the event management field. In J. Allen, R. Harris and L. Jago (eds), *Events Beyond 2000: Setting the Agenda, Proceedings of Conference on Event Evaluation, Research and Education*, pp. 10–21. Sydney: Australian Centre for Event Management, University of Technology, Sydney.

Getz, D. (2001). Festival places: A comparison of Europe and North America. *Tourism*, 49 (1), 3–18.

Getz, D. (2002). Why festivals fail. *Event Management*, 7 (4), 209–219.

Getz, D. (2004). Bidding on events: Critical success factors. *Journal of Convention and Exhibition Management*, 5 (2), 1–24.

Getz, D. (2005). *Event Management and Event Tourism* (2nd edn). New York: Cognizant.

Getz, D. (2008). Event tourism: Definition, evolution, and research. *Tourism Management*, 29 (3), 403–428.

Getz, D. (2009). Policy for sustainable and responsible festivals and events: Institutionalization of a new paradigm. *Journal of Policy Research in Tourism, Leisure and Events*, 1 (1), 61–78.

Getz, D. (2010). The nature and scope of festival studies. *International Journal of Event Management Research*, 5 (1) (www.ijemr.org, accessed 7 June 2019).

Getz, D. (2012a). Event studies: Discourses and future directions. *Event Management*, 16 (2), 171–187.

Getz, D. (2012b). *Event Studies: Theory, Research and Policy for Planned Events* (2nd edn). London: Routledge.

Getz, D. (2013a). *Event Tourism: Concepts, International Case Studies, and Research*. New York: Cognizant.

Getz, D. (2013b). Ecotourism Events. In R. Ballantyne and J. Packer (eds), *International Handbook on Ecotourism*. Cheltenham: Edward Elgar.

Getz, D. (2017). The sustainability of eventful cities: Concepts, challenges, and principles. *Event Management*, 21 (5), 575–591.

Getz, D. (2018). *Event Evaluation*. Oxford: Goodfellow Publishers.

Getz, D. (2019). *Event Impact Assessment*, p. 213. Oxford: Goodfellow Publishers.

Getz, D. and Andersson, T. (2008). Sustainable festivals: On becoming an institution. *Event Management*, 12 (1), 1–17.

Getz, D. and Andersson, T. (2010). The event-tourist career trajectory: A study of high-involvement amateur distance runners. *Scandinavian Journal of Hospitality and Tourism*, 10 (4), 468–491.

Getz, D., Andersson, T. and Carlsen, J. (2010). Festival management studies: Developing a framework and priorities for comparative and cross-cultural research. *International Journal of Event and Festival Management*, 1 (1), 29–59.

Getz, D., Andersson, T. and Larson, M. (2007). Festival stakeholder roles: Concepts and case studies. *Event Management*, 10 (2/3), 103–122.

Getz, D., Andersson, T., Armbrecht J. and Lundberg, E. (2017). Definitions and meanings of value. In E. Lundberg, J. Armbrecht, Andersson. T. and D. Getz (eds), *The Value of Events* (pp. 1–9). London: Routledge.

Getz, D., Andersson, T., Vujicic, S. and Robinson, R. (2015). Food events in lifestyle and travel. *Event Management*, 19, 407–419.

Getz, D. and Carlsen, J. (2006). Quality management for events. In B. Prideaux, G. Moscardo, and E. Laws (eds), *Managing Tourism and Hospitality Services*, pp. 145–155. Wallingford: CABI.

Getz, D. and Fairley, S. (2004). Media management at sport events for destination promotion. *Event Management*, 8 (3), 127–140.

Getz, D. and Frisby, W. (1988). Evaluating management effectiveness in community-run festivals. *Journal of Travel Research*, 27 (1), 22–27.

Getz, D. and Frisby, W. (1991). Developing a municipal policy for festivals and special events. *Recreation Canada*, 19 (4), 38–44.

Getz, D., Gration, D., Raciti, M., Sie, L. and Frost, D. (2013b). *Final Report: Sunshine Coast Event Portfolios Valuation Research*. Presented to: Tourism and Events Queensland, Sunshine Coast Council, Sunshine Coast Destination, and Tourism Noosa. University of Queensland and Sunshine Coast University.

Getz, D., Macdonald, D. and Parent, M. (2015b). The sport event owners' perspective. In M. M. Parent and J.-L. Chappelet (eds), *Routledge Handbook of Sports Event Management*, pp. 91–108. London: Routledge.

Getz, D. and McConnell, A. (2011). Event tourist careers and mountain biking. *Journal of Sport Management*, 25 (4), 326–338.

Getz, D. and McConnell, A. (2014). Comparing trail runners and mountain bikers: Motivation, involvement, portfolios, and event-tourist careers. *Journal of Convention and Event Tourism*, 15 (1), 69–100.

Getz, D., O'Neil, M. and Carlsen, J. (2001). Service quality evaluation at events through service mapping. *Journal of Travel Research*, 39 (4), 380–390.

Getz, D. and Page, S. J. (2015). *Event Studies: Theory, Research and Policy for Planned Events* (3rd edn). London: Routledge.

Getz, D. and Page, S. J. (2016). Progress and prospects for event tourism research. *Tourism Management*, 52, 593–631.

Getz, D. and Patterson, I. (2013). Social worlds as a framework for event and travel careers. *Tourism Analysis*, 18 (5), 485–501.

Getz, D. and Robinson, R. N. S. (2014a). Foodies and food events. *Scandinavian Journal of Hospitality and Tourism*, 14 (3), 315–330.

Getz, D. and Robinson, R. N. S. (2014b). Foodies and their travel preferences. *Tourism Analysis*, 19 (6), 659–672.

Getz, D., Robinson, R., Andersson, T. and Vujicic, S. (2014). *Foodies and Food Tourism*. Oxford: Goodfellow Publishers.

Getz, D., Svensson, B., Pettersson, R. and Gunnerval, A. (2013c). Hallmark events: Definition and planning process. *International Journal of Event Management Research*, 7 (1/2).

Getz, D. and Wicks, B. (1994). Professionalism and certification for festival and event practitioners: Trends and issues. *Festival Management and Event Tourism*, 2 (2), 103–109.

Gibson, C. and Connell, J. (eds) (2011). *Festival Places: Revitalising Rural Australia*. Bristol: Channel View.

Gibson, C. and Connell, J. (2012). *Music Festivals and Rural Development in Australia*. Farnham, England: Ashgate Publishing.

Gibson, C. and Davidson, D. (2004). Tamworth, Australia's 'country music capital': Place marketing, rurality, and resident reactions. *Journal of Rural Studies*, 20 (4), 387–404.

Gibson, C., Waitt, G., Walmsley, J. and Connell, J. (2009). Cultural festivals and economic development in nonmetropolitan Australia. *Journal of Planning Education and Research*, 29 (3), 280–293.

Gibson, H. (1998). Sport tourism: A critical analysis of research. *Sport Management Review*, 1, 45–76.

Gibson, H. (2004). Moving beyond the 'what is and who' of sport tourism to understanding 'why'. *Journal of Sport Tourism*, 9 (3), 247–265.

Gibson, H. (ed.) (2006a). *Sport Tourism: Concepts and Theories*. London: Routledge.

Gibson, H. (2006b). Towards an understanding of 'why sport tourists do what they do'. In H. Gibson (ed.), *Sport Tourism: Concepts and Theories*, pp. 66–85. London: Routledge.

Gibson, H. (2017). Sport tourism and theory and other developments: Some reflections. *Journal of Sport & Tourism*, 21 (2), 153–158.

Gibson, H., Lamont, M., Kennelly, M. and Buning, R. (2018). Introduction to the Special Issue – Active Sport Tourism. *Journal of Sport & Tourism*, 22 (2), 83–91.

Gibson, H., Willming, C. and Holdnak, A. (2003). Small-scale event-sport-tourism: Fans as tourists. *Tourism Management*, 22 (3), 181–190.

Gilmore, J. and Pine, J. (2007). *Authenticity: What Consumers Really Want*. Boston, MA: Harvard Business School Press.

Gitelson, R., Kerstetter, D. and Kiernan, N. (1995). Evaluating the educational objectives of a short-term event. *Festival Management and Event Tourism*, 3 (1), 9–14.

Giulianotti, R. and Klauser, F. (2011). Introduction: Security and surveillance at sport mega events. *Urban Studies*, 48 (15), 3157–3168.

Glaser, B. and Strauss, A. (1967). *Discovery of Grounded Theory: Strategies for Qualitative Research*. Chicago, IL: Aldine.

Gleick, J. (2000). *Faster: The Acceleration of Just About Everything*. New York: Pantheon Books.

Glenn, J. and Gordon, T. (eds) (2008). Futures Research Methodology (http://www.millennium-project.org/, accessed 9 June 2019).

Glenn, J., Gordon, T. and Florescu, E. (2014). *2013–14 State of the Future*. Published by the Millennium Project (http://millennium-project.org/millennium/201314SOF.html, accessed 7 June 2019).

Glyptis, S. A. (1981). Leisure life-styles. *Regional Studies*, 15 (5), 311–326.

Godbey, G. and Shim, J. (2008). The development of leisure studies in North America: Implications for China. *Research Journal of Zhejiang University*, July.

Goffman, E. (1959). *The Presentation of Self in Everyday Life*. Garden City, NY: Doubleday.

Goffman, E. (1974). *Frame Analysis: An Essay on the Organization of Experience*. New York: Harper and Row.

Goh, F. (2003). *Irish Festivals – Irish Life: Celebrating the Wealth of Ireland's Festivals. Executive Summary*. Dublin: Association of Irish Festival Events.

Goh, S., Smith, A. and Yeoman, I. (2019). Zooming in: An arts-informed life history approach to the analysis of event travel career narratives. *Event Management, 23 (2)*, 223–238.

Gold, J. (2004). *Cities of Culture: Staging International Festivals and the Urban Agenda, 1851–2000*. London: Routledge.

Gold, J. R. and Gold, M. M. (eds) (2010). *Olympic Cities: City Agendas, Planning, and the World's Games, 1896–2016*. London: Routledge.

Goldblatt, J. (1990). *Special Events: The Art and Science of Celebration*. New York: Van Nostrand Reinhold.

Goldblatt, J. (2004). *Special Events: Event Leadership for a New World*. New York: Wiley.

Goldblatt, J. (2011). *Special Events: A New Generation and The Next Frontier* (6th edn). New York: Wiley.

Goldblatt, J. (2014). *Special Events: Event Leadership for a New World* (7th edn). New York: Wiley.

Goldblatt, S. and Goldblatt, J. (2011). *The Complete Guide to Greener Meetings and Events*. New York: Wiley.

Gong, V. X., Yang, J., Daamen, W., Bozzon, A., Hoogendoorn, S. and Houben, G. J. (2018). Using social media for attendees density estimation in city-scale events. *IEEE Access*, 6, 36325–36340.

Goodson, L. and Phillimore, J. (eds) (2004). *Qualitative Research in Tourism: Ontologies, Epistemologies and Methodologies*. London: Routledge.

Gotham, K. (2005a). Theorizing urban spectacles. *City: Analysis of Urban Trends, Culture, Theory, Policy, Action*, 9 (2), 225–246.

Gotham, K. (2005b). Tourism from above and below: Globalization, localization and New Orleans' Mardi Gras. *International Journal of Urban and Regional Research*, 29 (2), 309–326.

Gottlieb, U., Brown, M. and Ferrier, L. (2013). Consumer perceptions of trade show effectiveness: Scale development and validation within a B2C context. *European Journal of Marketing*, 48 (1/2), 5–5.

Gouthro, M. and Fox, D. (2019). Methodological approaches to festival research. In J. Mair (ed.), *The Routledge Handbook of Festivals*, pp. 12–21. London: Routledge.

Govers, R. and Go, F. (2016). *Place Branding: Glocal, Virtual and Physical Identities, Constructed, Imagined and Experienced.* London: Palgrave Macmillan.

Graham, S., Goldblatt, J. and Delpy, L. (1995). *The Ultimate Guide to Sport Event Management and Marketing.* Chicago, IL: Irwin.

Grant, P. S. (2016). Understanding branded flash mobs: The nature of the concept, stakeholder motivations, and avenues for future research. *Journal of Marketing Communications*, 22 (4), 1–18.

Grant, R. (1996). Toward a knowledge-based theory of the firm. *Strategic Management Journal*, 17 (2), 109–122.

Grappi, S. and Montanari, F. (2011). The role of social identification and hedonism in affecting tourist re-patronizing behaviours: The case of an Italian festival. *Tourism Management*, 32 (5), 1128–1140.

Gratton, C. and Kokolakakis, T. (1997). *Economic Impact of Sport in England 1995.* London: The Sports Council.

Gray, N. and Porter, L. (2014). By any means necessary: Urban regeneration and the 'State of Exception' in Glasgow's Commonwealth Games 2014. *Antipode*, 47 (2), 380–400.

Grayson, R. and McGarry, F. (eds) (2016). *Remembering 1916: The Easter Rising, the Somme and the Politics of Memory in Ireland.* Cambridge: Cambridge University Press.

Green, B. (2018). Whose riot? Collective memory of an iconic event in a local music scene. *Journal of Sociology*, 55 (1), 144–160.

Green, C. and Chalip, L. (1998). Sport tourism as the celebration of subculture. *Annals of Tourism Research*, 25 (2), 275–291.

Green, C. and Chalip, L. (2004). Paths to volunteer commitment: Lessons from the Sydney Olympic Games. In R. Stebbins and M. Graham (eds), *Volunteering as Leisure/Leisure as Volunteering: An International Assessment*, pp. 49–68. Wallingford: CABI.

Greeneventbook (http://www.greeneventbook.com/event-carbon-footprint-possible/)

Greenfield, G. (2010). Reveillon in Rio de Janeiro. *Event Management*, 14 (4), 301–308.

Greenhalgh, P. (2011). *Fair World: A History of World's Fairs and Expositions, from London to Shanghai, 1851–2010.* Winterbourne, Berkshire: Papadakis.

Greenleaf – Robert Greenleaf Center for Servant leadership (https://www.greenleaf.org/what- is-servant-leadership/).

Greenwood, D. (1972). Tourism as an agent of change: A Spanish Basque case study. *Ethnology*, 11 (1), 80–91.

Greenwood, D. (1989). Culture by the pound: An anthropological perspective on tourism as cultural commodification. In V. Smith (ed.), *Hosts and Guests: The Anthropology of Tourism* (2nd edn), pp. 171–185. Philadelphia: University of Pennsylvania Press.

Gregson, B. (1992). *Reinventing Celebration: The Art of Planning Public Events.* Orange, CT: Shannon Press.

Grippo, R. (2004). *Macy's Thanksgiving Day Parade.* Charleston, SC: Arcadia.

Gripsrud, G., Nes, E. and Olsson, U. (2010). Effects of hosting a mega-sport event on country image. *Event Management*, 14 (3), 193–204.

Grix, J. (2013). Sport politics and the Olympics. *Political Studies Review*, 11 (1), 15–25.

Grunwell, S. and Inhyuck, S. (2008). Film festivals: An empirical study of factors for success. *Event Management*, 11 (4), 201–210.

Gumbel, A. (2014). Oculus Rift hands-on: Why the latest version is a watershed moment for gaming. *The Guardian* (http://www.theguardian.com/technology/2014/sep/21/oculus-virtual-reality-headsets-gear-crescent-bay-review, accessed 25 September 2014).

Gunn, C. (1979). *Tourism Planning*. New York: Crane Rusak.

Gursoy, D. and Kendall, K. (2006). Hosting mega events: Modelling locals' support. *Annals of Tourism Research*, 33 (3), 603–623.

Gyimóthy, S. (2009). Casual observers, connoisseurs and experimentalists: A conceptual exploration of niche festival visitors. *Scandinavian Journal of Hospitality and Tourism*, 9 (2–3), 177–205.

Gyimóthy, S. and Larson, M. (2015). Social media cocreation strategies: The 3Cs. *Event Management*, 19 (3), 331–348.

Haahti, A., and Komppula, R. (2006). Experience design in tourism. In D. Buhalis and C. Costa (eds), *Tourism Business Frontiers: Consumers, Products and Industry*, pp. 101–110. Oxford: Elsevier.

Habermas, J. (1973). *The Theory of Communicative Action: Reason and Rationalization of Society*. Boston, MA: Beacon.

Habermas, J. (1975). *Legitimation Crisis*. Boston, MA: Beacon Press.

Hagel, J. (2018). August 21, 2018, Harvard Business Review (https://hbr.org/2018/08/3-kinds-of-jobs-that-will-thrive-as-automation-advances).

Haid, O., Picard, D. and Robinson, M. (2006). Christmas markets in the Tyrolean Alps: Representing regional traditions in a newly created world of Christmas. In D. Picard and M. Robinson (eds), *Festival Tourism and Social Change – Remaking Worlds*, pp. 209–211, Clevedon: Channel View.

Halal, W. and Marien, M. (2011). Global megacrisis: Four scenarios, two perspectives. *The Futurist* (May/June).

Hall, C. M. (1989). The definition and analysis of hallmark tourist events. *GeoJournal*, 19 (3), 263–268.

Hall, C. M. (1992). *Hallmark Tourist Events: Impacts, Management and Planning*. London: Belhaven.

Hall, C. M. (1994a). *Tourism and Politics: Policy, Power and Place*. Chichester: Wiley.

Hall, C. M. (1994b). Mega-events and their legacies. In P. Murphy (ed.), *Quality Management in Urban Tourism: Balancing Business and Environment*, pp. 109–123. Victoria, British Columbia: University of Victoria.

Hall, C. M. (2005). *Tourism: Rethinking the Social Science of Mobility*. Harlow: Pearson.

Hall, C. M. (2006). Urban entrepreneurship, corporate interests and sports mega-events: The thin policies of competitiveness within the hard outcomes of neoliberalism. *The Sociological Review*, 54 (2), 59–70.

Hall, C. M. (2012). Sustainable mega-events: Beyond the myth of balanced approaches to mega-event sustainability. *Event Management*, 16 (2), 119–131.

Hall, C. M. (2012). The political analysis and political economy of events. In S. J. Page and J. Connell (eds), *The Routledge Handbook of Events*, pp. 186–201. London: Routledge.

Hall, C. M. and Page, S. (2006). *The Geography of Tourism and Recreation: Environment, Place and Space* (3rd edn). London: Routledge.

Hall, C. M. and Page, S. J. (2010). The contribution of Neil Leiper to tourism studies. *Current Issues in Tourism*, 13 (4), 299–309.

Hall, C. M. and Page, S. J. (2012). Geography and the study of events. In S. J. Page and J. Connell (eds), *Handbook of Events*. Routledge: London

Hall, C. M. and Page, S. J. (2014). *The Geography of Tourism and Recreation: Environment, Place and Space* (4th edn). London: Routledge.

Hall, C. M. and Rusher, K. (2004). Politics, public policy and the destination. In I. Yeoman, M. Robertson, J. Ali-Knight, S. Drummond and U. McMahon-Beattie (eds), *Festival and Events Management*, pp. 217–231. Oxford: Elsevier.

Hall, C. M. and Selwood, H. J. (1989). America's Cup lost, paradise retained? The dynamics of a hallmark tourist event. In G. J. Syme, B. J. Shaw, D. M. Denton and W. S. Mueller (eds), *The Planning and Evaluation of Hallmark Events*. Avebury: Aldershot.

Hall, C. M., Selwood, J. and McKewon, E. (1995). Hedonists, ladies and larrikins: Crime, prostitution and the 1987 America's Cup. *Visions in Leisure and Business*, 14 (3), 28–51.

Hall, C. M. and Sharples, L. (2008). *Food and Wine Festivals and Events Around the World*. Oxford: Butterworth-Heinemann.

Hall, C. M. and Wilson, S. (2011). Neoliberal urban entrepreneurial agendas, Dunedin Stadium and the Rugby World Cup: Or 'If you don't have a stadium, you don't have a future'. In D. Dredge and J. Jenkins (eds), *Stories of Practice: Tourism Policy and Planning*. Farnham: Ashgate.

Hall, E. (1966). *The Hidden Dimension*. New York: Doubleday.

Halsey, T. (2010). *Freelancer's Guide to Corporate Event Design*. Oxford: Elsevier.

Ham, S., Housego, A. and Weiler, B. (2005). *Tasmanian Thematic Interpretation Planning Manual*. Hobart: Tourism Tasmania.

Handelman, D. (1990). *Models and Mirrors: Towards an Anthropology of Public Events*. Oxford: Berghahn Books.

Hanlon, C. and Cuskelly, G. (2002). Pulsating major sport event organizations: A framework for inducting managerial personnel. *Event Management*, 7 (4), 231–243.

Hanlon, C. and Jago, L. (2012). Staffing for successful events: Having the right skills in the right place at the right time. In S. J. Page and J. Connell (eds), *The Routledge Handbook of Events*, pp. 304–315. London: Routledge.

Hanlon, C. and Stewart, B. (2006). Managing personnel in major sport event organizations: What strategies are required? *Event Management*, 10 (1), 77–88.

Hannam, K., Mostafanezhad, M. and Rickly, J. (2016). *Event Mobilities: Politics, Place and Performance*. London: Routledge.

Hannan, M. and Carroll, G. (1992). *Dynamics of Organizational Populations*. New York: Oxford University Press.

Hannan, M. and Freeman, J. (1977). The population ecology of organizations. *American Journal of Sociology*, 82 (5), 929–964.

Hannan, M. and Freeman, J. (1984). Structural inertia and organizational change. *American Sociological Review*, 49 (2), 149–164.

Hannan, M., Polos, L. and Carroll, G. (2007). *Logics of Organization Theory: Audiences, Code, and Ecologies*. Princeton, NJ: Princeton University Press.

Happel, S. and Jennings, M. (2002). Creating a futures market for major event tickets: Problems and prospects. *Cato Journal*, 21 (3), 443–462.

Harris, M. (2003). *Carnival and Other Christian Festivals: Folk Theology and Folk Performance*. Austin, TX: University of Texas Press.

Harris, R., Jago, L., Allen, J. and Huyskens, M. (2000). A rear-view mirror and a crystal ball: Past, present and future perspectives on event research in Australia. In J. Allen, R. Harris and L. Jago (eds), *Events Beyond 2000: Setting the Agenda, Proceedings of Conference on Event Evaluation, Research and Education*, pp. 10–21. Sydney: Australian Centre for Event Management, University of Technology, Sydney (https://opus.lib.uts.edu.au/handle/2100/430).

Harris, R., Jago, L., Allen, J. and Huyskens, M. (2001). Towards an Australian event research agenda: First steps. *Event Management*, 6 (4), 213–221.

Harris, V. (2004). Event management: A new profession. *Event Management*, 9 (1/2), 103–109.

Hartmann, R. (1986). Tourism, seasonality and social change. *Leisure Studies*, 5 (1), 25–33.

Harvey, M., Loomis, R., Bell, R. and Marino, M. (1998). The influence of museum exhibit design on immersion and psychological flow. *Environment and Behavior*, 30 (5), 601–627.

Hassan, A. and Sharma, A. (eds) (2018). *Tourism Events in Asia: Marketing and Development*. London: Routledge.

Häussermann, H. and Siebel, W. (eds) (1993). *Festivalisierung der Stadtpolitik. Stadtentwicklung durch grosse Projekte*. Leviathan: Sonderheft 13.

Havitz, M. and Dimanche, F. (1999). Leisure involvement revisited: Drive properties and paradoxes. *Journal of Leisure Research*, 31 (2), 122–149.

Hawkins, D. and Goldblatt, J. (1995). Event management implications for tourism education. *Tourism Recreation Research*, 20 (2), 42–45.

Hayllar, B. and Griffin, T. (2004). The precinct experience: A phenomenological approach. *Tourism Management*, 26 (4), 517–528.

Hede, A. (2005). Sports-events, tourism and destination marketing strategies: An Australian case study of Athens 2004 and its media telecast. *Journal of Sport Tourism*, 10 (3), 187–200.

Hede, A. (2007). Managing special events in the new era of the triple bottom line. *Event Management*, 11 (1–2), 13–22.

Hede, A. and Jago, L. (2005). Perceptions of the host destination as a result of attendance at a special event: A post-consumption analysis. *International Journal of Event Management Research*, 1 (1) (an e-journal, online at www.ijemr.org, accessed 7 June 2019).

Hede, A., Jago, L. and Deery, M. (2002). Special event research 1990–2001: Key trends and issues. In *Proceedings of International Event Research Conference*, pp. 305–338. Sydney: University of Technology Sydney, Australian Centre for Event Management.

Hede, A., Jago, L. and Deery, M. (2003). An agenda for special event research: Lessons from the past and directions for the future. *Journal of Hospitality and Tourism Management*, 10 (3), 1–14.

Heimer, C. (2001). Law: New institutionalism. In *International Encyclopedia of the Social and Behavioral Sciences*, pp. 8534–8537. Oxford: Elsevier.

Hektner, J. and Csikszentmihalyi, M. (2002). The experience sampling method: Measuring the context and content of lives. In R. Bechtel and A. Churchman (eds), *Handbook of Environmental Psychology*, pp. 233–243. New York: Wiley.

Henderson, E. and McIlwraith, M. (2013). *Ethics and Corporate Social Responsibility in the Meetings and Events Industry*. Chichester: Wiley.

Henderson, J. (2008). Hosting major meetings and accompanying protestors: Singapore 2006. *Current Issues in Tourism*, 10 (6), 543–557.

Herbert, D. T. (1988). Work and leisure: Exploring a relationship. *Area*, 241–252.

Hereźniak, M. and Florek, M. (2018). Citizen involvement, place branding and mega events: Insights from Expo host cities. *Place Branding and Public Diplomacy*, 14 (2), 89–100.

Hernández-Ehrisman, L. (2008). *Inventing the Fiesta City: Heritage and Carnival in San Antonio*. Albuquerque: UNM Press.

Herzberg, F. (1966). *Work and the Nature of Man*. Cleveland: World Publishing Co.

Hesmondhalgh, D. (2007). *The Cultural Industries*. London: Sage.

Higgins-Desbiolles, F. (2018). Event tourism and event imposition: A critical case study from Kangaroo Island, South Australia. *Tourism Management*, 64, 73–86.

Higham, J. and Hinch, T. (2009). *Sport and Tourism: Globalization, Mobility and Identity*. Oxford: Butterworth-Heinemann.

Hiller, H. (2000a). Toward an urban sociology of mega-events. *Research in Urban Sociology*, 5, 181–205.

Hiller, H. (2012). *Host Cities and the Olympics: An Interactionist Approach*. London: Routledge.

Hilliard, T. (2006). Learning at conventions: Integrating communities of practice. *Journal of Convention and Event Tourism*, 8 (1), 45–68.

Hinch, T. and Delamere, T. (1993). Native festivals as tourism attractions: A community challenge. *Journal of Applied Recreation Research*, 18 (2), 131–142.

Hinch, T., Jackson, E., Hudson, S. and Walker, G. (2006). Leisure constraint theory and sport tourism. In H. Gibson (ed.), *Sport Tourism: Concepts and Theories*, pp. 10–31. London: Routledge.

Hitters, E. (2007). Porto and Rotterdam as European capitals of culture: Towards the festivalisation of urban culture. In G. Richards (ed.), *Cultural Tourism: Global and Local Perspectives*, pp. 281–302. New York: Haworth Hospitality Press.

Hixson, E. (2014). The impact of young people's participation in events: Developing a model of social event impact. *International Journal of Event and Festival Management*, 5 (3), 198–218.

Hjalager, A. (2009). Cultural tourism innovation systems: The Roskilde festival. *Scandinavian Journal of Hospitality and Tourism*, 9 (2/3), 266–287.

Hjorth, D., and Kostera, M. (2007). *Entrepreneurship and the Experience Economy*. Copenhagen Business School Press.

HMSO. (1981). *The Great Exhibition of 1851*. London: HMSO.

Hobsbawm, E. (2010). *The Age of Revolution 1789–1848*. London: Phoenix Press.

Hofstede, G. (1980). *Culture's Consequences: International Differences in Work Related Values*. Beverley Hills, CA: Sage.

Holbrook, M. (1999). *Consumer Value: A Framework for Analysis and Research*. London: Routledge.

Holloway, I., Brown, L. and Shipway, R. (2010). Meaning not measurement: Using ethnography to bring a deeper understanding to the participant experience of festivals and events. *International Journal of Event and Festival Management*, 1 (1), 74–85.

Holloway, L. (2004). Showing and telling farming: Agricultural shows and re-imaging British agriculture. *Journal of Rural Studies*, 20 (3), 319–330.

Holmes, K., Hughes, M., Mair, J. and Carlsen, J. (2015). *Events and Sustainability*. London: Routledge.

Holmes, K., Nichols, G. and Ralston, R. (2018). "It's a once-in-a-lifetime experience and opportunity - deal with it!": Volunteer perceptions of the management of the volunteer experience at the London 2012 Olympic Games. *Event Management*, 22, 389–403.

Hoppen, A., Brown, L. and Fyall, A. (2014). Literary tourism: Opportunities and challenges for the marketing and branding of destinations? *Journal of Destination Marketing and Management*, 3 (1), 37–47.

Horkheimer, M. (1993). *Between Philosophy and Social Science*. Cambridge: MIT Press.

Hormans, G. (1958). Social behaviour as exchange. *American Journal of Sociology*, 63 (6), 597–606.

Horne, J. (2006). The unknown knowns of sports mega-events. In M. Robertson (ed.), *Sporting Events and Event Tourism: Impacts, Plans and Opportunities*. Leisure Studies Association Publication 91, pp. 1–15. Eastbourne: The University of Brighton.

Horne, J. (2015). Assessing the sociology of sport: On sports mega-events and capitalist modernity. *International Review for the Sociology of Sport*, 50 (4–5), 466–471.

Horne, J. and Manzenreiter, W. (2006). An introduction to the sociology of sports mega-events. *Sociological Review*, 54 (issue supplement s2), 1–24.

Horne, J. and Whannel, G. (2010). The 'caged torch procession': Celebrities, protesters and the 2008 Olympic torch relay in London, Paris and San Francisco. *Sport in Society*, 13 (5), 760–770.

Horng, J.-S., Su, C.-S. and So, S.-I. (2013). Segmenting food festival visitors: Applying the theory of planned behaviour and lifestyle. *Journal of Convention and Event Tourism*, 14 (3), 193–216.

Houlihan, B., Tan, T.-C. and Park, J. (2015). The national government's perspective. In M. Parent and J.-L. Chappelet, (eds), *Routledge Handbook of Sports Event Management*, pp. 289–305. London: Routledge.

Hoyle, L. (2002). *Event Marketing: How to Successfully Promote Events, Festivals, Conventions, and Expositions*. New York: Wiley.

Hu, J., Le, D., Funk, M., Wang, F. and Rauterberg, M. (2013). Attractiveness of an interactive public art installation. In N. Streltz and C. Stephanidis (eds), *Distributed, Ambient, and Pervasive Interactions*, pp. 430–438. Berlin: Springer.

Huang, Y., Scott, N., Ding, P. and Cheng, D. (2012). Impression of Liusanjie: Effect of mood on experience and satisfaction. *International Journal of Tourism Research*, 14 (1), 91–102.

Hudson, S. and Hudson, R. (2013). Engaging with consumers using social media: A case study of music festivals. *International Journal of Event and Festival Management*, 4 (3), 206–223.

Hudson, S., Getz, D., Miller, G. and Brown, G. (2004). The future role of sporting events: Evaluating the impacts on tourism. In K. Weiermair and C. Mathies (eds), *The Tourism and Leisure Industry – Shaping the Future*, pp. 237–251. Binghampton, NY: Haworth.

Hudson, S., Roth, M., Madden, T. and Hudson, R. (2015). The effects of social media on emotions, brand relationship quality, and word of mouth: An empirical study of music festival attendees. *Tourism Management*, 47, 68–76.

Hughes, G. (1999). Urban revitalization: The use of festival time strategies. *Leisure Studies*, 18 (2), 119–135.

Hughes, H. (1993). Olympic tourism and urban regeneration. *Festival Management and Event Tourism*, 1 (4), 157–162.

Huizinga, J. (1955). *Homo Ludens: A Study of the Play Element in Culture*. Boston, MA: Beacon Press (first published in German in 1944).

Hull, R. B. (1990). Mood as a product of leisure: Causes and consequences. *Journal of Leisure Research*, 22 (2), 99–111.

Hultkrantz, L. (1998). Mega-event displacement of visitors: The World Championship in Athletics, Goteborg 1995. *Festival Management and Event Tourism*, 5 (1/2).

Hunt, R. (1851). *Synopsis of the Contents of the Great Exhibition of 1851* (5th edn). London: Spicer Bros. and W. Clowes & Sons.

ICCA (2018). *A Modern History of International Association Meetings 1963–2017*. Retrieved from www.icca.org, Amsterdam.

Imagine Canada (www.imaginecanada.ca, accessed 7 June 2019).

International Association for Exhibition Management. Renamed as International Association of Exhibitions and Events in 2006 (www.iaee.com, accessed 14 June 2019).

International Association of Fairs and Expositions (IAFE) (www.fairsandexpos.com, accessed 7 June 2019).

International Association for Impact Assessment (IAIA) (https://www.iaia.org/uploads/pdf/Fastips_1%20Impact%20 Assessment.pdf, accessed 9.June 2019).

International Association of Venue Managers (www.iavm.org, accessed 7 June 2019).

International Events Group (IEG) (1995). *IEG's Complete Guide to Sponsorship*. Chicago, IL: IEG Inc.

International Festivals Association (IFA) and Argonne Productions (1992). *Festival Sponsorship Legal Issues*. Port Angeles, WA.

International Festivals and Events Association (IFEA) (n.d.). *Event Operations*. Port Angeles, WA.

International Festivals and Events Association (IFEA) (2000). *Official Guide to Parades*. Port Angeles, WA. IFEA (www. ifea.com, accessed 14 June 2019).

International Special Events Society (www.ISES.com, accessed 7 June 2019).

International Standards Organisation (www.iso.org).

Iso-Ahola, S. (1980). *The Social Psychology of Leisure and Recreation*. Dubuque, IA: Brown.

Iso-Ahola, S. (1983). Towards a social psychology of recreational travel. *Leisure Studies*, 2 (1), 45–57.

Iso-Ahola, S., Jackson, E. and Dunn, E. (1994). Starting, ceasing and replacing leisure activities over the life-span. *Journal of Leisure Research*, 26 (3), 227–249.

Izzo, F., Bonetti, E. and Masiello, B. (2012). Strong ties within cultural organization event networks and local development in a tale of three festivals. *Event Management*, 16 (3), 223–244.

Jackson, C., Morgan, J. and Laws, C. (2018). Creativity in events: The untold story. *International Journal of Event and Festival Management*, 9 (1), 2–19.

Jackson, E. (ed.) (2005). *Constraints on Leisure*. State College, PA: Venture Publishing.

Jackson, E. L., Crawford, D. W. and Godbey, G. (1993). Negotiation of leisure constraints. *Leisure Sciences*, 15 (1), 1–11.

Jackson, G. and Weed, M. (2003). The sport-tourism interrelationship. In B. Houlihan (ed.), *Sport and Society*. London: Sage.

Jackson, I. (2008). Celebrating communities: Community festivals, participation and belonging. *The Australian Centre, School of Historical Studies*, 161–172.

Jackson, P. (1988). Street life: The politics of Carnival. *Environment and Planning D: Society and Space*, 6 (2), 213–227.

Jaeger, K. and Mykletun, R. J. (2009). The festivalscape of Finnmark. *Scandinavian Journal of Hospitality and Tourism*, 9 (2/3), 327–348.

Jago, L., Chalip, L., Brown, G., Mules, T. and Ali, S. (2002). The role of events in helping to brand a destination. In *Proceedings of International Event Research Conference*, pp. 111–143. Sydney: University of Technology Sydney, Australian Centre for Event Management.

Jago, L., Chalip, L., Brown, G., Mules, T. and Shameem, A. (2003). Building events into destination branding: Insights from experts. *Event Management*, 8 (1), 3–14.

Jago, L. and Dwyer, L. (2006). *Economic Evaluation of Special Events: A Practitioner's Guide*. Gold Coast, Australia: Cooperative Research Centre for Sustainable Tourism.

Jago, L. and Mair, J. (2009). Career theory and major event employment. In T. Baum, M. Deery and C. Hanlon (eds), *People and Work in Events and Conventions: A Research Perspective*, pp. 65–74. Wallingford: CABI.

Jago, L. and Shaw, R. (1999). Consumer perceptions of special events: A multi-stimulus validation. *Journal of Travel and Tourism Marketing*, 8 (4), 1–24.

Jahn, S., Cornwell, T. B., Drengner, J. and Gaus, H. (2018). Temporary communitas and willingness to return to events. *Journal of Business Research*, 92, 329–338.

Jaimangal-Jones, D., Fry, J. and Haven-Tang, C. (2018). Exploring industry priorities regarding customer satisfaction and implications for event evaluation. *International Journal of Event and Festival Management*, 9 (1), 51–66.

Jaimangal-Jones, D., Pritchard, A. and Morgan, N. (2010). Going the distance: Locating journey, liminality and rites of passage in dance music experiences. *Leisure Studies*, 29 (3), 253–268.

Jain, A. (2016). Regional effects: The rise of large-scale art events in South Asia. In R. D'Souza and S. Manghani (eds), *India's Biennale Effect: A Politics of Contemporary Art*. London: Routledge.

Jamal, T. and Getz, D. (1995). Collaboration theory and community tourism planning. *Annals of Tourism Research*, 22 (1), 186–204.

James, J. and Ridinger, L. (2002). Female and male sport fans: A comparison of sport consumption motives. *Journal of Sport Behavior*, 25 (3), 260–278.

James, J. D. and Ross, S. D. (2004). Comparing sport consumer motivations across multiple sports. *Sport Marketing Quarterly*, 13 (1), 17–25.

Jamieson, N. (2014). Sport tourism events as community builders—How social capital helps the "locals" cope. *Journal of Convention and Event Tourism*, 15 (1), 57–68.

Janiskee, R. (1980). South Carolina's harvest festivals: Rural delights for day tripping urbanites. *Journal of Cultural Geography* (October), 96–104.

Janiskee, R. (1985). Community-sponsored rural festivals in South Carolina: A decade of growth and change. Paper presented to the Association of American Geographers, Detroit.

Janiskee, R. (1991). Rural festivals in South Carolina. *Journal of Cultural Geography*, 11 (2), 31–43.

Janiskee, R. (1994). Some macroscale growth trends in America's community festival industry. *Festival Management and Event Tourism*, 2 (1), 10–14.

Janiskee, R. (1996). The temporal distribution of America's community festivals. *Festival Management and Event Tourism*, 3 (3), 129–137.

Janiskee, R. and Drews, P. (1998). Rural festivals and community reimaging. In R. Butler, M. Hall and J. Jenkins (eds), *Tourism and Recreation in Rural Areas*, pp. 157–175. Chichester: Wiley.

Jantzen, C. (2013). Experiencing and experiences: A psychological framework. In J. S. Sundbo and F. Sørensen (eds), *Handbook on the Experience Economy*, pp. 146–170. Cheltenham: Edward Elgar.

Jawahar, I. and McLaughlin, G. (2001). Toward a descriptive stakeholder theory: An organizational life cycle approach. *Academy of Management Review*, 26 (3), 397–414.

Jaworski, A. and Pritchard, A. (eds) (2005). *Discourse, Communication and Tourism*. Clevedon: Channel View.

Jennings, G. (2006). Perspectives on quality tourism experiences: An introduction. In G. Jennings and N. Nickerson (eds), *Quality Tourism Experiences*, pp. 1–21. Oxford: Elsevier.

Jennings, W. (2013). Governing the games: High politics, risk and mega-events. *Political Studies Review*, 11 (1), 2–14.

Jens, C. (2009). *The Business of the Experience Economy*. Aarhus: Aarhus University Press.

Jepson, A. and Clarke, A. (eds) (2014). *Exploring Community Festivals and Events*. London: Routledge.

Jepson, A., Clarke, A. and Ragsdell, G. (2013). Applying the motivation-opportunity-ability (MOA) model to reveal factors that influence inclusive engagement within local community festivals: The case of UtcaZene 2012. *International Journal of Event and Festival Management*, 4 (3), 186–205.

Jepson, A. and Stadler, R. (2017). Conceptualizing the impact of festival and event attendance upon family quality of life (QOL). *Event Management*, 21 (1), 47–60.

Jessop, B. and Sum, N.-L. (2001). Pre-disciplinary and post-disciplinary perspectives. *New Political Economy*, 6(1), 89–101.

Jiang, K., Potwarka,L. and Xiao, H. (2018). Predicting intention to volunteer for mega-sport events in China: The case of Universiade event volunteers. *Event Management*, 21, 713–728.

Jiang, J. and Schmader, S. (2014). Event management education and professionalism: The view from the trenches. *Event Management*, 18 (1), 25–37.

Jin, X. and Weber, K. (2013). Developing and testing a model of exhibition brand preference: The exhibitors' perspective. *Tourism Management*, 38, 94–104.

Jin, X., Weber, K. and Bauer, T. (2010). The state of the exhibition industry in China. *Journal of Convention and Event Tourism*, 11 (1), 2–17.

Jin, X., Weber, K. and Bauer, T. (2012). Impact of clusters on exhibition destination attractiveness: Evidence from mainland China. *Tourism Management*, 33 (6), 1429–1439.

Jóhannesson, G. (2010). Emergent Vikings: The social ordering of tourism innovation. *Event Management*, 14 (4), 261–274.

Johnsen, B. (2009). What a maritime history! The uses of maritime history in summer festivals in southern Norway. *Journal of Tourism History*, 1 (2), 113–130.

Johnson, D. (n.d.). Festival risk management: Success with safety. In *Event Operations*, pp. 71–73. Port Angeles, WA: International Festivals and Events Association.

Johnson, N. (2006). *Britain and the 1918–19 Influenza Pandemic: A Dark Epilogue*. London: Routledge.

Johnston, M., Twynam, G. and Farrell, J. (2000). Motivation and satisfaction of event volunteers for a major youth organization. *Leisure*, 24 (1), 161–177.

Joliffe, L., Bui, H. and Nguyenm, H. (2008). The Buon Ma Thuot coffee festival, Vietnam: Opportunity for tourism? In J. Ali-Knight, M. Robertson, A. Fyall and A. Ladkin (eds), *International Perspectives of Festivals and Events: Paradigms of Analysis*, pp. 125–137. Oxford: Butterworth-Heinemann.

Jones, A. (2015). What's my scene: Festival fandom and the applification of the Big Day out stage. In A. Jones and R. Bennett (eds), *The Digital Evolution of Live Music* (pp. 29–40). Oxford: Elsevier.

Jones, A. and Navarro, C. (2018). Events and the blue economy: Sailing events as alternative pathways for tourism futures – the case of Malta. *International Journal of Event and Festival Management*, 9 (2), 204–222.

Jones, H. (1993). Pop goes the festival. *Marketing Week*, 16 (23), 24–27.

Jones, I. and Green, C. (2006). Serious leisure, social identity and sport tourism. In H. Gibson (ed.), *Sport Tourism: Concepts and Theories*, pp. 32–49. London: Routledge.

Jones, M. (2018). *Sustainable Event Management: A Practical Guide* (3rd edn). London: Earthscan.

Jordan, J. (1980). The summer people and the natives: Some effects of tourism in a Vermont vacation village. *Annals of Tourism Research*, 7 (1), 34–55.

Jordan, L. (2006). Staging the Cricket World Cup 2007 in the Caribbean: Issues and challenges for small island developing states. In M. Robertson (ed.), *Leisure Studies Association No. 91, Sporting Events and Event Tourism: Impacts, Plans and Opportunities*, pp. 17–42. Eastbourne: The University of Brighton.

Joye, Y. and van den Berg, A. (2013). Restorative environments. In L. Steg, A. van den Berg and J. de Groot (eds), *Environmental Psychology: An Introduction*, pp. 57–66. London: John Wiley & Sons and the British Psychological Society.

Jung, M. (2005). Determinants of exhibition service quality as perceived by attendees. *Journal of Convention and Event Tourism*, 7 (3/4), 85–98.

Jung, S. and Tanford, S. (2017). What contributes to convention attendee satisfaction and loyalty? A meta-analysis. *Journal of Convention and Event Tourism*, 18 (2), 118–34.

Jutbring, H. (2014). Encoding destination messages in media coverage of an international event: A case study of the European athletics indoor championships. *Journal of Destination Marketing and Management*, 3 (1), 29–36.

Kachun, M. (2003). *Festivals of Freedom: Memory and Meaning in African American Emancipation Celebrations, 1808–1915*. Amherst, MA: University of Massachusetts Press.

Kaku, M. (2012). *Physics of the Future: The Inventions That Will Transform Our Lives*. London: Penguin Books.

Kang, Y. and Perdue, R. (1994). Long-term impact of a mega-event on international tourism to the host country: A conceptual model and the case of the 1988 Seoul Olympics. In M. Uysal (ed.), *Global Tourist Behavior*, pp. 205–225. New York: International Business Press.

Kaplan, S. (1987). Aesthetics, affect, and cognition: Environmental preference from an evolutionary perspective. *Environment and Behavior*, 19 (1), 3–32.

Kaplanidou, K. and Vogt, C. (2010). The meaning and measurement of a sport event experience among active sport tourists. *Journal of Sport Management*, 24 (5), 544–566.

Katz, A. (1981). Self help and mutual aid: An emerging social movement. *Annual Review of Sociology*, 7, 129–155.

Kay, P. (2004). Cross-cultural research issues in developing international tourist markets for cultural events. *Event Management*, 8 (4), 191–202.

Kelly, G. (1955). *The Psychology of Personal Constructs: Vol. I*. New York: Norton.

Kelly, J. (1987). *Freedom to Be: A New Sociology of Leisure*. New York: Macmillan.

Kendrick, V., Haslam, R. and Waterson, P. (2012). Planning crowd events to achieve high participant satisfaction. *Work: A Journal of Prevention, Assessment and Rehabilitation*, 41 (1), 3223–3226.

Kentucky Derby Festival (http://derbyfestival.org, accessed 7 June 2019).

Kerstetter, D. and Gitelson, R. (1995). Perceptions of sponsorship contributors to a regional arts festival. *Festival Management and Event Tourism*, 2 (3/4), 203–20

Kessler, E. (ed.) (2013). *Encyclopedia of Management Theory*. Sage.

Khodr, H. (2012). Exploring the driving factors behind the event strategy in Qatar: A case study of the 15th Asian Games. *International Journal of Event and Festival Management*, 3 (1), 81–100.

Kim, D.-Y., Jang, S. and Morrison, A. M. (2011). Factors affecting organizational information technology acceptance: A comparison of convention and visitor bureaus and meeting planners in the United States. *Journal of Convention and Event Tourism*, 12 (1), 1–24.

Kim, J., Boo, S. and Kim, Y. (2013). Patterns and trends in event tourism study topics over 30 years. *International Journal of Event and Festival Management*, 4 (1), 66–83.

Kim, J.-H. and Jang, S. (2016). Memory retrieval of cultural event experiences: Examining internal and external influences. *Journal of Travel Research*, 55 (3), 322–339.

Kim, J., Kang, J. and Kim, Y.-K. (2014). Impact of mega sport events on destination image and country image. *Sport Marketing Quarterly*, 23 (3), 161–175.

Kim, S., Ao, Y., Lee, H. and Pan, S. (2012). A study of motivations and the image of Shanghai as perceived by foreign tourists at the Shanghai EXPO. *Journal of Convention and Event Tourism*, 13 (1) 48–73.

Kim, S., Scott, D. and Crompton, J. (1997). An exploration of the relationships among social psychological involvement, behavioral involvement, commitment, and future intentions in the context of birdwatching. *Journal of Leisure Research*, 29 (3), 320–341.

Kim, W. and Malek, K. (2017). Understanding the relationship among motivation to attend, satisfaction, and loyalty of medical convention attendees. *Journal of Convention and Event Tourism*, 18 (4), 282–300.

Kim, Y-H and Kaewnuch, K. (2018). Finding the gaps in event management research: A descriptive meta-analysis. *Event Management*, 22, 453–467.

Kinnunen, M. and Haahti, A. (2015). Visitor discourses on experiences: Reasons for festival success and failure. *International Journal of Event and Festival Management*, 6 (3), 251–268.

Kirkpatrick, D. and Kirkpatrick, J. (2007). *Implementing the Four Levels*. Berrett-Koeler Publishers.

Kleiber, D. A. (1999). *Leisure Experience and Human Development: A Dialectical Interpretation*. New York: Basic Books.

Klemke, E., Hollinger, R. and Rudge, D. (eds) (1998). *Introductory Readings in the Philosophy of Science*. New York: Prometheus Books.

Knox, D. (2008). Spectacular tradition Scottish folksong and authenticity. *Annals of Tourism Research*, 35 (1), 255–273.

Knudsen, B. T., Christensen, D. R. and Blenker, P. (2014). *Enterprising Initiatives in the Experience Economy: Transforming Social Worlds*. London: Routledge.

Ko, Y., Kim, M. K., Kim, Y. K., Lee, J.-H. and Cattani, K. (2010). Consumer satisfaction and event quality perception: A case of US Open Taekwondo Championship. *Event Management*, 14 (3), 205–214.

Koch, N. (2016). *Critical Geographies of Sport: Space, Power and Sport in Global Perspective*. London: Routledge.

Kociatkiewicz, J. and Kostera, M. (2012). The speed of experience: The co-narrative method in experience economy education. *British Journal of Management*, 23 (4), 474–488.

Koenigstorfer, J. and Uhrich, S. (2009). Effects of atmosphere at major sports events: A perspective from environmental psychology. *International Journal of Sports Marketing and Sponsorship*, 10 (4), 56–75.

Kontokosta, C. (2012). The price of victory: The impact of the Olympic games on residential real estate markets. *Urban Studies*, 49 (5), 961–978.

Koo, G. Y. and Hardin, R. (2008). Difference in interrelationship between spectators' motives and behavioral intentions based on emotional attachment. *Sport Marketing Quarterly*, 17 (1), 30.

Kotler, P. (1973). Atmospherics as a marketing tool. *Journal of Retailing*, 4, 48–64.

Kotler, P., Bowen, J. and Maken, J. (1999). *Marketing for Hospitality and Tourism*. New Jersey: Prentice-Hall.

Kotler, P., Haider, D. and Rein, I. (1993). *Marketing Places*. New York: The Free Press.

Kozinets, R. V. (2010). *Netnography. Doing Ethnographic Research Online*. Thousand Oaks, CA: Sage.

Kruger, M., Saayman, M. and Ellis, S. (2011). Segmentation by genres: The case of the Aardklop National Arts Festival. *International Journal of Tourism Research*, 13 (6), 511–526.

Kruger, M., Saayman, M. and Hull, J. (2018). A motivation-based typology for natural event attendees. *Journal of Policy Research in Tourism, Leisure and Events*, 11 (1), 35–53.

Krugman, C. and Wright, R. R. (2006). *Global Meetings and Exhibitions*. Hoboken, NJ: Wiley.

Kurzweil, R. (2008). *The Singularity Is Near: When Humans Transcend Biology*. London: Duckworth Overlook.

Kyle, G. and Chick, G. (2002). The social nature of leisure involvement. *Journal of Leisure Research*, 34 (4), 426–448.

Kyle, G., Absher, J., Norman, W., Hammitt, W. and Jodice, L. (2007). A modified involvement scale. *Leisure Studies*, 26 (4), 399–427.

Laing, J. and Frost, W. (eds) (2014). *Rituals and Traditional Events in the Modern World*. London: Routledge.

Laing, J. and Frost, W. (2017). *Royal Events: Rituals, Innovations, Meanings*. London: Routledge.

Lamond, I. R. and Platt, L. (2016). *Critical Event Studies: Approaches to Research*. London: Palgrave Macmillan.

Lamond, I. and Spracklen, K. (2015). *Protests as Events: Politics, Activism and Leisure*. London: Rowman and Littlefield International.

Lamont, M. and Jenkins, J. (2013). Segmentation of cycling event participants: A two-step cluster method utilizing recreation specialization. *Event Management*, 17 (4), 391–407.

Lamont, M. and Kennelly, M. (2011). I can't do everything! Competing priorities as constraints in triathlon event travel careers. *Tourism Review International*, 14 (2), 85–97.

Lamont, M., Kennelly, M. and Wilson, E. (2012). Competing priorities as constraints in event travel careers. *Tourism Management*, 33 (5), 1068–1079.

Lankford, S. V. (1996) Crime and tourism: A study of perceptions in the Pacific northwest. In A. Pizam and Y. Mansfeld (eds), *Tourism, Crime and International Security Issues*, pp. 51–58. Chichester: John Wiley & Sons.

Lapsley, I. and Rekers, J. V. (2017). The relevance of strategic management accounting to popular culture: The world of West End Musicals. *Management Accounting Research*, 35, 47–55.

Larson, M. (2002). A political approach to relationship marketing: Case study of the Storsjöyran Festival. *International Journal of Tourism Research*, 4 (2), 119–143.

Larson, M. (2009a). Festival innovation: Complex and dynamic network interaction. *Scandinavian Journal of Hospitality and Tourism*, 9 (2/3), 288–307.

Larson, M. (2009b). Joint event production in the jungle, the park, and the garden: Metaphors of event networks. *Tourism Management*, 30 (3), 393–399.

Larson, M., Getz, D. and Pastras, P. (2015). The legitimacy of festivals and their stakeholders: Concepts and propositions. *Event Management, 19*, 159–174.

Larson, M. and Wikstrom, E. (2001). Organising events: Managing conflict and consensus in a political market square. *Event Management*, 7 (1), 51–65.

Larson, R. and Csikszentmihalyi, M. (1983). The experience sampling method. In H. Reis (ed.), *Naturalistic Approaches to Studying Social Interaction*, pp. 41–56. San Francisco, CA: Jossey-Bass.

Lashley, C., Morrisson, A. and Randall, S. (2004). My most memorable meal ever! Hospitality as an emotional experience. In D. Sloan (ed.), *Culinary Taste, Consumer Behaviour in the International Restaurant Sector*, pp. 165–184. Oxford: Butterworth-Heinemann.

Lashua, B., Spracklen, K. and Long, P. (2014). Introduction to the special issue: Music and tourism. *Tourist Studies*, 14 (1), 3–9.

Lask, T. (2011). Cognitive maps: A sustainable tool for impact evaluation. *Journal of Policy Research in Tourism, Leisure and Events*, 3 (1), 44–62.

Laslett, P. (1989). *A Fresh Map of Life: The Emergence of the Third Age*. London: Weidenfeld and Nicolson.

Laurell, C. and Björner, E. (2018). Digital festival engagement: On the interplay between festivals, place brands, and social media. *Event Management*, 22 (4), 527–540.

Lavenda, R. H. (1980). The festival of progress: The globalizing world-system and the transformation of the Caracas Carnival. *The Journal of Popular Culture*, 14 (3), 465–475.

Laverie, D. and Arnett, D. (2000). Factors affecting fan attendance: The influence of identity salience and satisfaction. *Journal of Leisure Research*, 32 (2), 225–246.

Lawson, F. (2000). *Congress, Convention and Exhibition Facilities: Planning, Design and Management*. Oxford: Architectural Press.

Laxson, J. (1991). How 'we' see 'them': Tourism and native American Indians. *Annals of Tourism Research*, 18 (3), 365–391.

Laybourn, P. (2004). Risk and decision making in events management. In I. Yeoman, M. Robertson, J. Ali-Knight, S. Drummond and U. McMahon-Beattie (eds), *Festivals and Events Management*, pp. 286–307. Oxford: Elsevier.

Leapman, M. (2001). *The World for a Shilling: How the Great Exhibition of 1851 Shaped a Nation*. London: Headline.

Le Bon, G. (1908). *The Crowd: A Study of the Popular Mind*. London: Unwin.

Lee, C., Lee, Y. and Wicks, B. (2004). Segmentation of festival motivation by nationality and satisfaction. *Tourism Management*, 25 (1), 61–70.

Lee, C. K., Mjelde, J. W., Kim, T. K. and Lee, H. M. (2014). Estimating the intention– behaviour gap associated with a mega event: The case of the Expo 2012 Yeosu Korea. *Tourism Management*, 41, 168–177.

Lee, D. P. and Palakurthi, R. (2013). Marketing strategy to increase exhibition attendance through controlling and eliminating leisure constraints. *Event Management*, 17 (4), 323–336.

Lee, H., Kerstetter, D., Graefe, A. and Confer, J. (1997). Crowding at an arts festival: A replication and extension of the outdoor recreation crowding model. In W. Kuentzel (ed.), *Proceedings of the 1966 Northeastern Recreation Research Symposium* (USDA Forest Service Ge. Tech. Rep. NE–232), pp. 198–204. Radnor, PA: Northeastern Forest Experiment Station.

Lee, I., Brown, G., King, K. and Shipway, R. (2016). Social identity in serious sport event space. *Event Management*, 20, 491–499.

Lee, J. (1987). The impact of Expo' 86 on British Columbia markets. In P. Williams, J. Hall and M. Hunter (eds), *Tourism: Where Is the Client?* Conference Papers of the Travel and Tourism Research Association, Canada Chapter.

Lee, J. (2014). Visitors' emotional responses to the festival environment. *Journal of Travel and Tourism Marketing*, 31 (1), 114–131.

Lee, J. and Kyle, G. (2013). Segmenting festival visitors using psychological commitment. *Journal of Travel Research*, 53 (5), 656–669.

Lee, J.-E., Almanza, B. and Nelson, D. (2010). Food safety at fairs and festivals: Vendor knowledge and violations at regional festivals. *Event Management*, 14 (3), 215–223.

Lee, J.-S. and Back, K. (2009). Examining the effect of self-image congruence, relative to education and networking, on conference evaluation through its competing models and moderating effect. *Journal of Convention and Event Tourism*, 10 (4), 256–275.

Lee, K. H., Alexander, A. C. and Kim, D. Y. (2013). Motivational factors affecting volunteer intention in local events in the United States. *Journal of Convention and Event Tourism*, 14 (4), 271–292.

Lee, M. J. and Back, K. J. (2005). A review of convention and meeting management research 1990–2003: Identification of statistical methods and subject areas. *Journal of Convention and Event Tourism*, 7, 1–20.

Lee, M. J. and Lee, S. (2014). Subject areas and future research agendas in exhibition research: visitors' and organizers' perspectives. *Event Management*, 18 (3), 377–386.

Lee, S. and Crompton, J. (2003). The attraction power and spending impact of three festivals in Ocean City, Maryland. *Event Management*, 8 (2), 109–112.

Lee, T. H. and Hsu, F. Y. (2013). Examining how attending motivation and satisfaction affects the loyalty for attendees at Aboriginal festivals. *International Journal of Tourism Research*, 15 (1), 18–34.

Lee, Y., Datillo, J. and Howard, D. (1994). The complex and dynamic nature of leisure experience. *Journal of Leisure Research*, 26 (3), 195.

Lefebvre, H. (1991). *The Production of Space*, translated by Donald Nicholson-Smith, originally published in 1974. Oxford: Basil Blackwell.

Lefebvre, R. (2011). An integrative model for social marketing. *Journal of Social Marketing*, 1 (10), 54–72.

Leibold, M. and van Zyl, C. (1994). The Summer Olympic Games and its tourism marketing: City tourism marketing experiences and challenges with specific reference to Cape Town, South Africa. In P. Murphy (ed.), *Quality Management in Urban Tourism: Balancing Business and the Environment, Proceedings*, pp. 135–151. Wellington: University of Victoria.

Leigh, J., Lamont, M. J. and Cairncross, G. (2013). Towards a process model of induction and training for young event volunteers. *International Journal of Event Management Research*, 8 (1), 1–20.

Leiper, N. (1981). Towards a cohesive curriculum in tourism: The case for a distinct discipline. *Annals of Tourism Research*, 8 (1), 69–84.

Leiper, N. (1990). Tourist attraction systems. *Annals of Tourism Research*, 17 (3), 367–384.

Leiper, N. (2008). Why 'the tourism industry' is misleading as a generic expression: The case for the plural variation, 'tourism industries'. *Tourism Management*, 29 (2), 237–251.

Lennon, J. and Foley, M. (2000). *Dark Tourism: The Attraction of Death and Disaster*. London: Continuum.

Leopold, L., Clarke, F., Hanshaw, B. and Balsley, J. (1971). *A Procedure for Evaluating Environmental Impact*. Geological Survey Circular 645. Washington: U.S. Geological Survey.

Leung, R. and Law, R. (2010). A review of personality research in the tourism and hospitality context. *Journal of Travel and Tourism Marketing*, 27 (5), 439–459.

Levermore, R. (2010). CSR for development through sport: Examining its potential and limitations. *Third World Quarterly*, 31 (2), 223–241.

Levy, S. (1959). Symbols for sale. *Harvard Business Review*, 37, 117–124.

Levy, S. (2010). The hospitality of the host: A cross-cultural examination of managerially facilitated consumer-to-consumer interactions. *International Journal of Hospitality Management*, 29 (1), 319–327.

Li, M., Huang, Z. and Cai, L. (2009). Benefit segmentation of visitors to a rural community-based festival. *Journal of Travel and Tourism Marketing*, 26 (5/6), 585–598.

Li, R. and Petrick, J. (2006). A review of festival and event motivation studies. *Event Management*, 9 (4), 239–245.

Li, X. and Vogelsong, H. (2005). Comparing methods of measuring image change: A case 15 study of a small-scale community festival. *Tourism Analysis*, 10 (4), 349–360.

Li, Y. (2000). Geographical consciousness and tourism experience. *Annals of Tourism Research*, 27 (4), 863–883.

Liburd, J. (2008). Tourism and the Hans Christian Andersen bicentenary event in Denmark. In J. Ali-Knight, M. Robertson, A. Fyall, and A. Ladkin (eds), *Perspectives of Festivals and Events: Paradigms of Analysis*, pp. 41–52. Oxford: Butterworth-Heinemann.

Lindenberg, S. (2013). How cues in the environment affect normative behaviour. In L. Steg, A. van den Berg and J. de Groot (eds), *Environmental Psychology: An introduction*, pp. 119–126. London: John Wiley & Sons and the British Psychological Society.

Ling, T. (1998). Exploring the environment for healthcare. *The Madingley Scenarios*.

Locke, M. (2010). A framework for conducting a situational analysis of the meetings, incentives, conventions, and exhibitions sector. *Journal of Convention and Event Tourism*, 11 (3), 209–233.

Lockstone, L. and Baum, T. (2009). 2006 Melbourne Commonwealth Games, Australia: Recruiting, training and managing a volunteer program at a sporting mega event. In K. Holmes and K. Smith (eds), *Managing Volunteers in Tourism Attractions, Destinations and Events*, pp. 215–223. Oxford: Butterworth-Heinemann.

Lockstone-Binney, L. (2018). Knowledge generation in event studies: What can doctoral research tell us about evolution of the field? *Event Management*, 22, 1047–1056.

Lockstone-Binney, L., Whitelaw, P., Robertson, M., Junek, O. and Michael, I. (2014). The motives of ambassadors in bidding for international association meetings and events. *Event Management*, 18 (1), 65–74.

Loeffler, B. and Church, B. (2015). *The Experience: The 5 Principles of Disney Service and Relationship Excellence*: Wiley.

London 2012 (www.london2012.com, accessed 7 June 2019).

Long, P. (2000). After the event: Perspectives on organizational partnership in the management of a themed festival year. *Event Management*, 6 (1), 45–59.

Long, P., Robinson, M. and Picard, D. (2004). Festivals and tourism: Links and developments. In P. Long and M. Robinson (eds), *Festivals and Tourism: Marketing, Management and Evaluation*, pp. 1–14. Sunderland: Business Education Publishers.

Lorde, T., Greenidge, D. and Devonish, D. (2011). Local residents' perceptions of the impacts of the ICC Cricket World Cup 2007 on Barbados: Comparisons of pre- and post-games. *Tourism Management*, 32 (2), 349–356.

Louviere, J. J. and Hensher, D. A. (1983). Using discrete choice models with experimental design data to forecast consumer demand for a unique cultural event. *Journal of Consumer Research*, 348–361.

Love, L. and Crompton, J. (1996). A conceptualization of the relative roles of festival attributes in determining perceptions of overall festival quality. Paper presented to the Research Symposium, annual conference of the International Festivals and Events Association (unpublished).

Lundberg, E., Armbrecht, J., Andersson, T. D. and Getz, D. (eds) (2017). *The Value of Events*. London: Routledge.

Lundman, R. (2018). Spatial responsibilities during informal public events: The case of the Art Slum protestival in Turku, Finland. *City*, 22 (2), 270–284.

Lynch, K. (1960). *The Image of the City*. Cambridge, MA: MIT Press.

Lyu, S. and Lee, H. (2013). Market segmentation of golf event spectators using leisure benefits. *Journal of Travel and Tourism Marketing*, 30 (3), 186–200.

Mabrey, V. and Gerstein, T. (2010). Philadelphia moves to nip flash mobs in bud: Mayor calls for parents to monitor teens' texts after incidents of mob vandalism, 23 April (http://abcnews.go.com, accessed 7 June 2019).

MacAloon, J. (1984). Olympic Games and the theory of spectacle in modern societies. In J. MacAloon (ed.), *Rite, Drama, Festival, Spectacle: Rehearsals Towards a Theory of Cultural Performance*, pp. 241–280. Philadelphia, PA: Institute for the Study of Human Issues.

Macbeth, J., Selwood, J. and Veitch, S. (2012). Paradigm shift or a drop in the ocean? The America's Cup impact on Fremantle. *Tourism Geographies*, 14 (1), 162–182.

MacCannell, D. (1973). Staged authenticity: Arrangements of social space in tourist settings. *American Journal of Sociology*, 79 (3), 589–603.

MacCannell, D. (1976). *The Tourist: A New Theory of the Leisure Class*. New York: Schocken Books.

Mackellar, J. (2009). An examination of serious participants at the Australian Wintersun Festival. *Leisure Studies*, 28 (1), 85–104.

Mackellar, J. (2013a). *Event Audiences and Expectations*. London: Routledge.

Mackellar, J. (2013b). Participant observation at events: Theory, practice and potential. *International Journal of Event and Festival Management*, 4 (1), 56–65.

Mackellar, J. and Nisbet, S. (2014). Sport events and integrated destination development. *Current Issues in Tourism*, 14 (2) 183–189.

Macnaught, T. (1982). Mass tourism and the dilemmas of modernization in Pacific island communities. *Annals of Tourism Research*, 9 (3), 359–381.

Macrae, E. (2017). Delivering sports participation legacies at the grassroots level: The voluntary sports clubs of Glasgow 2014. *Journal of Sport Management,* 31, 15–26.

Madden J. (2006). Economic and fiscal impacts of mega sporting events: A general equilibrium assessment. *Public Finance and Management,* 6 (3), 346–394.

Madrigal, R. (1995). Cognitive and affective determinants of fan satisfaction with sporting event attendance. *Journal of Leisure Research,* 27 (3), 205–207.

Madrigal, R. (2003). Investigating and evolving leisure experience: Antecedents and consequences of spectator affect during a live sporting event. *Journal of Leisure Research,* 35 (1), 23–45.

Maeng, H., Jang, H. and Li, J. (2016). A critical review of the motivational factors for festival attendance based on meta-analysis. *Tourism Management Perspectives,* 17, 16–25.

Maestas, A. (2009). Guide to sponsorship return on investment. *Journal of Sponsorship,* 3 (1), 98–102.

Mahadevan, R. (2018a). Profiling volunteers at a regional folk festival in Australia: Who are they and do they value the festival differently from visitors? *Event Management,* 22, 153–161.

Mahadevan, R. (2018b). To attend or not to attend a rural folk festival: Examining nonattendees' behavior using a temporal approach. *Event Management,* 22, 441–452.

Mahony, D., Madrigal, R. and Howard, D. (1999). The effect of self-monitoring on behavioral and attitudinal loyalty towards athletic teams. *International Journal of Sport Marketing and Sponsorship,* 1, 146–167.

Mahony, D., Madrigal, R. and Howard, D. (2000). Using the psychological commitment to team (PCT) scale to segment sport consumers based on loyalty. *Sport Marketing Quarterly,* 9 (1), 15–25.

Mair, J. (2012). A review of business events literature. *Event Management,* 16 (2), 133–141.

Mair, J. (2013). *Conferences and Conventions: A Research Perspective.* London: Routledge.

Mair, J. (ed.) (2018). *The Routledge Handbook of Festivals.* London: Routledge.

Mair, J. and Duffy, M. (2018). The role of festivals in strengthening social capital in rural communities. *Event Management,* 22, 875–889.

Mair, J., and Thompson, K. (2009). The UK association conference attendance decision-making process. *Tourism Management,* 30 (3), 400–409.

Mair, J. and Whitford, M. (2013). An exploration of events research: Event topics, themes and emerging trends. *International Journal of Event and Festival Management,* 4 (1), 6–30.

Maitland, H. (1999). *A Guide to Audience Development* London: Arts Council.

Major Events New Zealand (www.med.govt.nz/majorevents/new-zealand-major-events/strategy, accessed 14 June 2019).

Mak, J. (2006). Taxation of travel and tourism. In L. Dwyer, and Forsyth, P., (ed.), *International Handbook on the Economics of Tourism* (pp. 251–265). Cheltenham: Edward Elgar.

Malhado, A. and Araujo, L. (2017). Welcome to hell: Rio 2016 Olympics failing to secure sustainable transport legacy. *Event Management,* 21, 523–526.

Mallen, C. and Adams, L. (eds) (2017). *Event Management in Sport, Recreation and Tourism: Theoretical and Practical Dimensions* (3rd edn). London: Routledge.

Malouf, L. (2002). *Parties and Special Events: Planning and Design.* Texas: Culinary and Hospitality Industry Publications Services.

Malouf, L. (2011). *Events Exposed: Managing and Designing Special Events.* Chichester: Wiley.

Mandelbaum, S., Mazza, L. and Burchell, R. W. (eds) (1996). *Explorations in Planning Theory.* New Brunswick, NJ: Center for Urban Policy Research, Rutgers University.

Mannell, R. and Iso-Ahola, S. (1987). Psychological nature of leisure and tourist experiences. *Annals of Tourism Research,* 14 (3), 314–331.

Mannell, R. and Kleiber, D. (1997). *A Social Psychology of Leisure.* State College, PA: Venture Publishing.

Mannell, R. and Zuzanek, J. (1991). The nature and variability of leisure constraints in daily life: The case of the physically active leisure of older adults. *Leisure Sciences*, 13 (4), 337–351.

Manning, F. (ed.) (1983). *The Celebration of Society: Perspectives on Contemporary Cultural Performance*. Bowling Green, OH: Bowling Green University Popular Press.

Mansfield, V. (1998). Time and impermanence in middle way Buddhism and modern physics. Talk at the Physics and Tibetan Buddhism Conference, University of California, Santa Barbara, 30–31 January 1998 (http://www.buddhanet.net/timeimpe.htm, accessed 7 June 2019).

Manthiou, A., Lee, S. A., Tang, L. R. and Chiang, L. (2014). The experience economy approach to festival marketing: Vivid memory and attendee loyalty. *Journal of Services Marketing*, 28 (1), 22–35.

Mariani, M. and Giorgio, L. (2017). The "Pink Night" festival revisited: Meta-events and the role of destination partnerships in staging event tourism. *Annals of Tourism Research*, 62, 89–109.

Markus, H. and Kitayama, S. (1991). Culture and the self: Implications for cognition, emotion, and motivation. *Psychological Review*, 98 (2), 224–253.

Marris, T. (1987). The role and impact of mega-events and attractions on regional and national tourism development: Resolutions of the 37th Congress of the AIEST, Calgary. *Revue de Tourisme*, 42 (4), 3–12.

Marshall, G. (1998). Exchange theory. In *A Dictionary of Sociology* (www.encyclopedia.com/doc/1O88-exchangetheory.html, accessed 24 December 2009).

Martin, A. J., Anderson, M. and Adams, R. J. (2012). What determines young people's engagement with performing arts events? *Leisure Services*, 34 (4), 314–331.

Maslow, A. (1954). *Motivation and Personality* (2nd edn). New York: Harper and Row.

Maslow, A. (1968). *Toward a Psychology of Being* (2nd edn). Toronto: Van Nostrand Rheinhold.

Masterman, G. (2004, 3rd edn 2014). *Strategic Sports Event Management: An International Approach*. London: Routledge.

Masterman, G. and Wood, E. (2006). *Innovative Marketing Communications: Strategies for the Events Industry*. Oxford: Butterworth-Heinemann.

Mastrogiannakis, D. and Dorville, C. (2013). Security and sport mega-events: A complex relation. *Sport in Society*, 16 (2), 133–139.

Matheson, C. and Finkel, R. (2013). Sex trafficking and the Vancouver Winter Olympic Games: Perceptions and preventative measures. *Tourism Management*, 36, 613–628.

Matheson, C. M. (2008). Music, emotion and authenticity: A study of Celtic music festival consumers. *Journal of Tourism and Cultural Change*, 6 (1), 57–74.

Matheson, V. (2002). Upon further review: An examination of sporting event economic impact studies. *The Sport Journal*, 5 (1), 1–3.

Matheson, V. and Baade, R. (2003). Bidding for the Olympics: Fools gold? In C. Barros, M. Ibrahim, and S. Szymanski (ed.), *Transatlantic Sport*. London: Edward Elgar Publishing.

Mattie, E. and George, L. (1998). *World's Fairs*. New Jersey: Princeton Architectural Press.

Mayfield, T. and Crompton, J. (1995). The status of the marketing concept among festival organizers. *Journal of Travel Research*, 33 (4), 14–22.

McCabe, V. (2008). Strategies for career planning and development in the convention and exhibition industry in Australia. *International Journal of Hospitality Management*, 27 (2), 222–231.

McCarthy, M. (2012). *Ireland's 1916 Rising: Explorations of History-Making, Commemorations and Heritage in Modern Times*. Aldershot: Ashgate.

McCartney, G. and Osti, L. (2007). From cultural events to sport events: A case study of cultural authenticity in the dragon boat races. *Journal of Sport & Tourism*, 12 (1), 25–40.

McDowell M. L. and Skillen, F. (2016). The rewards and risks of historical events studies research. In I. Lamond and L. Platt (eds), *Critical Event Studies. Leisure Studies in a Global Era*, pp. 87–107. London: Palgrave Macmillan.

McGehee, N., Yoon, Y. and Cardenas, D. (2003). Involvement and travel for recreational runners in North Carolina. *Journal of Sport Management*, 17 (3), 305–324.

McGillivray, D. (2014). Digital cultures, acceleration and mega sporting event narratives. *Leisure Studies*, 33 (1), 96–109.

McGillivray, D. and Turner, D. (2017). *Event Bidding: Politics, Persuasion and Resistance*. London: Routledge.

McGregor, D. (1960). *The Human Side of Enterprise*. New York: McGraw Hill.

McHenry, J. A. (2011). Rural empowerment through the arts: The role of the arts in civic and social participation in the Mid West region of Western Australia. *Journal of Rural Studies*, 27 (3), 245–253.

McKay, G. (2015). *The Pop Festival: History, Music, Media, Culture*. London: Bloomsbury Publishing.

McKercher, B., Mei, W. and Tse, T. (2006). Are short duration festivals tourist attractions? *Journal of Sustainable Tourism*, 14 (1), 55–66.

McKinnie, M. (2016). Olympian performance: The cultural economics of the opening ceremony of London 2012. *Public*, 27 (53), 49–57.

McLuhan, M. (1964). *Understanding Media: The Extensions of Man*. New York: McGraw Hill.

McMahon-Beattie, U. and Yeoman, I. (2004). The potential for revenue management in festivals and events. In I. Yeoman, M. Robertson, J. Ali-Knight, S. Drummond and U. McMahon-Beattie (eds), *Festivals and Events Management*, pp. 202–214. Oxford: Elsevier.

McPhail, T. (2006). *Global Communication: Theories, Stakeholders, and Trends* (2nd edn). Oxford: Blackwell Publishers.

Meeting Professionals International (2003). *Meetings and Conventions: A Planning Guide*. Mississauga, ON: MPI. (www.mpiweb.org, accessed 7 June 2019).

Mehmetoglu, M. and Ellingsen, K. (2005). Do small-scale festivals adopt 'market orientation' as a management philosophy? *Event Management*, 9 (3), 119–132.

Mehus, I. (2005). Sociability and excitement motives of spectators attending entertainment sport events: Spectators of soccer and ski-jumping. *Journal of Sport Behavior*, 28 (4), 333.

Melton, J. G. (2011). *Religious Celebrations: An Encyclopedia of Holidays, Festivals, Solemn Observances, and Spiritual Commemorations*. Santa Barbara: ABC-CLIO.

Memish, Z. A., Zumla, A., Alhakeem, R. F., Assiri, A., Turkestani, A., Al Harby, K. D. and Al-Tawfiq, J. A. (2014). Hajj: Infectious disease surveillance and control. *The Lancet*, 383 (9934), 2073–2082.

Mendell, R., MacBeth, J. and Solomon, A. (1983). The 1982 world's fair – a synopsis. *Leisure Today, Journal of Physical Education, Recreation and Dance* (April), 48–49.

Merkel, U. (ed.) (2013). *Power, Politics and International Events: Socio-cultural Analyses of Festivals and Spectacles*. London: Routledge.

Merriam Webster Dictionary. *Aesthetics* (https://www.merriam-webster.com/).

Merrilees, B., Getz, D. and O'Brien, D. (2005). Marketing stakeholder analysis: Branding the Brisbane Goodwill Games. *European Journal of Marketing*, 39 (9/10), 1060–1077.

MidSumma (www.midsumma.org.au/, accessed 7 June 2019).

Miffling, K. and Taylor, R. (2007). Investigating the importance of youth culture in successful youth events. *Journal of Contemporary Issues in Business and Government*, 13 (2), 65–80.

Mihalik, B. (1994). Mega-event legacies of the 1996 Atlanta Olympics. In P. Murphy (ed.), *Quality Management in Urban Tourism: Balancing Business and Environment. Proceedings*, pp. 151–162. University of Victoria.

Mihalik, B. (2001). Host population perceptions of the 1996 Atlanta Olympics: Support, benefits and liabilities. *Tourism Analysis*, 5 (1), 49–53.

Mill, R. and Morrison, A. (1985). *The Tourism System: An Introductory Text*. Englewood Cliffs, NJ: Prentice Hall.

Millennium Project (http://millennium-project.org/, accessed 7 June 2019).

Miller, L., Jago, L. and Deery, M. (2004). Profiling the special event nonattendee: An initial investigation. *Event Management*, 8 (3), 141–150.

Miller, R. and Washington, K. (2011). *Consumer Behaviour*. Rockville, MD: Richard K.

Millward, P. (2017). World Cup 2022 and Qatar's construction projects: Relational power in networks and relational responsibilities to migrant workers. *Current Sociology*, 65(5), 756–776.

Milne, G. R. and McDonald, M. A. (1999). *Sport Marketing: Managing the Exchange Process*. Sudbury, MA: Jones & Bartlett Learning.

Mintzberg, H. (1983). *Power In and Around Organizations*. Englewood Cliffs, NJ: Prentice Hall.

Mintzberg, H. (1994). *The Rise and Fall of Strategic Planning*. New York: The Free Press.

Mirehie, M., Buning, R. and Gibson, H. (2017). Participation versus nonparticipation in a charity running event. *Event Management*, 21, 639–652.

Misener, L. and Mason, D. (2006). Creating community networks: Can sporting events offer meaningful sources of social capital? *Managing Leisure*, 11 (1), 39–56.

Misener, L., McGillivray, D., McPherson, G. and Legg, D. (2016). Examining parasport events through the lens of critical disability studies. In I. Lamond (ed.), *Critical Event Studies: Leisure Studies in a Global Era*, pp. 175–192. London: Palgrave Macmillan.

Mishra, D. P., Bobinski Jr, G. S. and Bhabra, H. S. (1997). Assessing the economic worth of corporate event sponsorships: A stock market perspective. *Journal of Market-Focused Management*, 2 (2), 149–169.

Mitchell, R., Agle, B. and Wood, D. (1997). Towards a theory of stakeholder identification and salience: Defining the principle of who and what really counts. *Academy of Management Review*, 22 (4), 853–886.

Mitler, B., van Esterik, P. and van Esterik, J. (2004). *Cultural Anthropology* (2nd Canadian edn). Toronto: Pearson Education, Canada.

Mohr, K., Backman, K., Gahan, L. and Backman, S. (1993). An investigation of festival motivations and event satisfaction by visitor type. *Festival Management and Event Tourism*, 1 (3), 89–97.

Molnár, V. (2014). Reframing public space through digital mobilization: Flash mobs and contemporary urban youth culture. *Space and Culture*, 17 (1), 43–58.

Momboisse, R. (1967). *Riots, Revolts, and Insurrections*. Springfield, IL: Charles C. Thomas.

Monga, M. (2006). Measuring motivation to volunteer for special events. *Event Management*, 10 (1): 47–61.

Monroe, J. and Kates, R. (2005). *Art of the Event: Complete Guide to Designing and Decorating Special Events*. Chichester: Wiley.

Morgan, M. (2008). What makes a good festival? Understanding the event experience. *Event Management*, 12 (2), 81–93.

Morgan, M., Lugosi, P. and Ritchie, J. R. B. (2010). *The Tourism and Leisure Experience: Consumer and Managerial Perspectives*. Bristol: Channel View.

Morgan, M. and Wright, R. (2008). Elite sports tours: Special events with special challenges. In J. Ali-Knight, M. Robertson, A. Fyall, and A. Ladkin (eds), *International Perspectives of Festivals and Events: Paradigms of Analysis*, pp. 187–204. Oxford: Butterworth-Heinemann.

Morgner, C. (2014). The evolution of the art fair. *Historical Social Research*, 39 (3), 318–336.

Morris, M. H., Pryor, C. G. and Schindehutte, M. (2012). *Entrepreneurship as Experience: How Events Create Ventures and Ventures Create Entrepreneurs*. Cheltenham: Edward Elgar.

Morrison, A. (1995). *Hospitality and Travel Marketing* (2nd edn). Albany, NY: Delmar.

Morrow, S. (1997). *The Art of the Show: An Introduction to the Study of Exhibition Management*. Dallas, TX: International Association for Exhibition Management.

Moscardo, G. (2010). The shaping of tourist experience: The importance of stories and themes. In M. Morgan, P. Lugosi and J. R. B. Ritchie (eds), *The Tourism and Leisure Experience: Consumer and Managerial Perspectives*, pp. 43–50. Bristol: Channel View.

Moser, G. and Uzzell, D. (2003). Environmental psychology. In T. Millon and M. Lerner (eds), *Comprehensive Handbook of Psychology: Volume 5: Personality and Social Psychology*. New York: John Wiley and Sons.

Moss, S., Gruben, K. and Moss, J. (2019). An empirical test of the Olympic tourism legacy. *Journal of Policy Research in Tourism, Leisure and Events*. 11 (1), 16–39.

Mossberg, L. (2000). Effects of events on destination image. In L. Mossberg (ed.), *Evaluation of Events: Scandinavian Experiences*, pp. 30–46. New York: Cognizant.

Mossberg, L. (2006). Product development and cultural tourism. In T. Andersson (ed.), *Cultural Tourism: Visitor Flows, Economic Impact and Product Development*, pp. 47–59. Published for the European Cultural Tourism Network at the School of Business, Economics and Law, University of Gothenburg, Sweden.

Mossberg, L. (2008). Extraordinary experiences through storytelling. *Scandinavian Journal of Hospitality and Tourism*, 8 (3), 195–210.

Mossberg, L. and Getz, D. (2006). Stakeholder influences on the ownership and management of festival brands. *Scandinavian Journal of Hospitality and Tourism*, 6 (4), 308–326.

Moufakkir, O. and Pernecky, T. (2014). *Ideological, Social and Cultural Aspects of Events*. Wallingford: CABI.

Mount, J. and Niro, B. (1995). Sponsorship: An empirical study of its application to local business in a small town setting. *Festival Management and Event Tourism*, 2 (3/4), 167–175.

Mowen, A., Vogelsong, H. and Graefe, A. (2003). Perceived crowding and its relationship to crowd management practices at park and recreation events. *Event Management*, 8 (2), 63–72.

Moyer, K. (1968). Kinds of aggression and their physiological basis. *Communications in Behavioral Biology* (Part A), 2 (2), 65–87.

Mueller, J., Taff, B., Wimpey, J. and Graefe, A. (2018). Small-scale race events in natural areas: Participants' attitudes, beliefs, and global perceptions of leave no trace ethics. *Journal of Outdoor Recreation and Tourism*, 23, 8–15.

Mules, T. (1993). A special event as part of an urban renewal strategy. *Festival Management and Event Tourism*, 1 (2), 65–67.

Mules, T. and Dwyer, L. (2006). Public sector support for sport tourism events: The role of cost-benefit assessment. In H. Gibson (ed.), *Sport Tourism: Concepts and Theories*. London: Routledge.

Mules, T. and McDonald, S. (1994). The economic impact of special events: The use of forecasts. *Festival Management and Event Tourism*, 2 (1), 45–53.

Mullan, J. (2001). A brief history of mob rule. *The Guardian*, 28th April (https://www.theguardian.com/education/2001/apr/28/artsandhumanities.higheredu cation).

Müller, M. (2015a). The mega-event syndrome: Why so much goes wrong in mega-event planning and what to do about it. *Journal of the American Planning Association*, 81 (1), 6–17.

Müller, M. (2015b). What makes an event a mega-event? Definitions and sizes. *Leisure Studies*, 34 (6), 627–642.

Müller, M. (2017). Approaching paradox: Loving and hating mega-events. *Tourism Management*, 63, 234–241.

Naik, T. (1948). Aboriginal festivals in Gujarat. *Eastern Anthropologist*, 2 (1), 16–21.

Narasimhan, R. (2018). The fallacy of impact without relevance: Reclaiming relevance and rigor. *European Business Review*, 30(2), 157–168.

National Association for Interpretation (www.interpnet.com, accessed 7 June 2019).

National Association of Sports Commissions (www.sportscommissions.org, accessed 7 June 2019).

National Council of Youth Sport Events (www.ncys.org).

Nelson, K. B. (2009). Enhancing the attendee's experience through creative design of the event environment: Applying Goffman's dramaturgical perspective. *Journal of Convention and Event Tourism*, 10 (2), 120–133.

Neufeind, M., Güntert, S. T. and Wehner, T. (2013). The impact of job design on event volunteers' future engagement: Insights from the European Football Championship 2008. *European Sport Management Quarterly*, 13 (5), 537–556.

Neulinger, J. (1974). *Psychology of Leisure: Research Approaches to the Study of Leisure*. Springfield, IL: Charles C. Thomas.

Neuman, W. (2003). *Social Research Methods: Qualitative and Quantitative Approaches* (4th edn). Boston, MA: Allyn and Bacon.

Newland, B. and Aicher, T. (2018). Exploring sport participants' event and destination choices. *Journal of Sport & Tourism*, 22 (2), 131–149.

Ngamsom, B. and Beck, J. (2000). A pilot study of motivations, inhibitors, and facilitators of association members in attending international conferences. *Journal of Convention and Exhibition Management*, 2 (2/3), 97–111.

Nichols, G., Benson, A. and Holmes, K. (2018). Researching mega-events under regulatory capitalism. *Event Management*, 22, 933–943.

Nicholson, R. and Pearce, D. (2001). Why do people attend events: A comparative analysis of visitor motivations at four South Island events. *Journal of Travel Research*, 39 (4), 449–460.

Nickerson, N. and Ellis, G. (1991). Traveler types and activation theory: A comparison of two models. *Journal of Travel Research*, 29 (3), 26–31.

Nogawa, H., Yamaguchi, Y. and Hagi, Y. (1996). An empirical research study on Japanese sport tourism in Sport-for-All events: Case studies of a single-night event and a multiple-night event. *Journal of Travel Research*, 35 (2), 46–54.

Nordvall, A., Pettersson, R., Svensson, B. and Brown, S. (2014). Designing events for social interaction. *Event Management*, 18 (2), 127–140.

Noronha, R. (1977). Paradise reviewed: Tourism in Bali. In E. de Kadt (ed.), *Tourism: Passport to Development?* pp. 177–204. Oxford: Oxford University Press.

North American Society for Sport Management (www.nassm.com, accessed 7 June 2019).

Nuñez, E. and Vendrell, E. (2016). *Managing Critical Incidents and Large-Scale Event Security*. London: Routledge.

Nurse, K. (2004). Trinidad Carnival: Festival tourism and cultural industry. *Event Management*, 8 (4), 223–230.

Oakes, S. (2003). Demographic and sponsorship considerations for jazz and classical music festivals. *Service Industries Journal*, 23 (3), 165–178.

O'Brien, D. (2005). Event business leveraging: The Sydney 2000 Olympic Games. *Annals of Tourism Research*, 33 (1), 240–261.

O'Brien, E. and Shaw, M. (2002). Independent meeting planners: A Canadian perspective. *Journal of Convention and Exhibition Management*, 3 (4), 37–68.

O'Dell, T. (2005). Management strategies and the need for fun. In T. O'Dell and P. Billing (eds), *Experiencescapes: Tourism, Culture, and Economy*, pp. 127–142. Copenhagen Business School Press.

O'Sullivan, D., Pickernell, D. and Senyard, J. (2009). Public sector evaluation of festivals and special events. *Journal of Policy Research in Tourism, Leisure and Events*, 1 (1), 19–36.

O'Sullivan, E. and Spangler, K. (1998). *Experience Marketing: Strategies for the New Millennium*. State College, PA: Venture Publishing.

O'Toole, W. (2000). The integration of event management best practice by the project management process. *Australian Parks and Leisure*, 3 (1), 4–8.

O'Toole, W. (2011). *Events Feasibility and Development: From Strategy to Operations*. Oxford: Butterworth-Heinemann.

O'Toole, W., Luke, S., Ashwin, P., Tatrai, A. and Brown, J. (2019). *Crowd Management: Risk, Security and Health*. Oxford: Goodfellow Publishers.

O'Toole, W. and Mikolaitis, P. (2002). *Corporate Event Project Management*. New York: Wiley.

Oakley, E. and Krug, D. (1991). *Enlightened Leadership: Getting to the Heart of Change*. New York: Simon and Schuster.

Oakley, K. and O'Connor, J. (eds) (2015). *The Routledge Companion to the Cultural Industries*. London: Routledge.

Office for National Statistics (2002). *Time Use Survey*. London: ONS.

Olberding, J. (2016). *Social Enterprise and Special Events*. London: Routledge.

Olds, K. and Ley, D. (1988). Landscape as spectacle: World's fairs and the culture of heroic consumption. *Environment and Planning D: Society and Space*, 6, 191–212.

Oliver, R. (1977). Effect of expectation and disconfirmation on postexposure product evaluations: An alternative interpretation. *Journal of Applied Psychology*, 62 (4), 480–486.

Oliver, R. (1980). A cognitive model of the antecedents and consequences of satisfaction decisions. *Journal of Marketing Research*, 17 (3), 460–469.

Olsen, K. (2002). Authenticity as a concept in tourism research: The social organization of the experience of authenticity. *Tourist Studies*, 2 (2), 159–182.

Olson, E. D. (2017). An exploration of lesbian, gay, bisexual, and transgender pride festival sponsors. *Journal of Convention and Event Tourism*, 18 (1), 60–73.

Olson, J. and Reynolds, T. (2001). *Understanding Consumer Decision Making: A Means End Approach to Marketing and Advertising Strategy*. Mahwah, NJ: Lawrence Erlbaum Associates.

Ooi, C. (2005). A theory of tourism experiences. In T. O'Dell and P. Billing (eds), *Experience-scapes: Tourism, Culture, and Economy*, pp. 51–68. Copenhagen Business School Press.

Oppermann, M. and Chon, K. (1997). Convention participation decision-making process. *Annals of Tourism Research*, 24 (1), 178–191.

Orefice, C. (2018). Designing for events: A new perspective on event design. *International Journal of Event and Festival Management*, 9 (1), 20–33.

Orr, M. and Jarvis, N. (2018). Blinded by gold: Toronto sports community ignores negative legacies of 2015 Pan Am Games. *Event Management*, 22, 367–378.

Otnes, C. and Pleck, E. (2003). *Cinderella Dreams: The Allure of the Lavish Wedding*. University of California Press.

Pacione, M. (2012). The role of events in urban regeneration. In S. Page and J. Connell (eds), *The Routledge Handbook of Events*, pp. 385–400. London: Routledge.

Packer, J. and Ballantyne, R. (2005). Solitary vs. shared learning: Exploring the social dimension of museum learning. *Curator: The Museum Journal*, 48 (2), 177–192.

Packer, J. and Bond, N. (2010). Museums as restorative environments. *Curator: The Museum Journal*, 53 (4), 421–456.

Page, S. J. (1994). Perspectives on tourism and peripherality: A review of tourism in the Republic of Ireland. In C. Cooper and A. Lockwood (eds), *Progress in Tourism, Recreation and Hospitality Management: Volume 5*, pp. 26–53. London: Belhaven.

Page, S. J. (2009). *Transport and Tourism*. Pearson: Harlow.

Page, S. J. (2019). *Tourism Management* (6th edn). London: Routledge.

Page, S. J. and Connell, J. (2006). *Leisure: Critical Concepts in the Social Sciences, 4 Volumes*. London: Routledge.

Page, S. J. and Connell, J. (2010). *Leisure: An Introduction*. Harlow: Pearson Education.

Page, S. J. and Connell, J. (eds) (2012). *The Routledge Handbook of Events*. London: Routledge.

Page, S. J. and Connell, J. (2014). *Tourism: A Modern Synthesis* (4th edn). Cengage: Andover.

Page, S. J., Yeoman, I., Connell, J. and Greenwood, C. (2010). Scenario planning as a tool to understand uncertainty in tourism: The example of transport and tourism in Scotland in 2025. *Current Issues in Tourism*, 13 (2), 99–137.

Palma, M. L., Palma, L. and Aguado, L. F. (2013). Determinants of cultural and popular celebration abundance: The case study of Seville Spring Fiestas. *Journal of Cultural Economics*, 37 (1), 87–107.

Papastergiadis, N., McQuire, S., Gu, X., Barikin, A., Gibson, R., Yue, A. and Jones, M. (2013). Mega screens for mega cities. *Theory, Culture and Society*, 30 (7–8), 325–341.

Papson, S. (1981). Spuriousness and tourism: Politics of two Canadian provincial governments. *Annals of Tourism Research*, 8 (2), 503–507.

Parasuraman, A., Berry, L. and Zeithaml, V. (1988). SERVQUAL: A multiple-item scale for measuring consumer perceptions of service quality. *Journal of Retailing*, 64 (1), 12–40.

Parent, M. and Chappelet, J.-L. (eds) (2015). *Routledge Handbook of Sports Event Management*. London: Routledge.

Parent, M. and Smith-Swan, S. (eds) (2013). *Managing Major Sports Events: Theory and Practice*. London: Routledge.

Park, B. and Park, K. (2017). Thematic trends in event management research. *International Journal of Contemporary Hospitality Management*, 29 (3), 848–861.

Park, M., Daniels, M., Brayley, R. and Harmon, L. (2010). Analysis of service provision and visitor impacts using participant observation and photographic documentation: The National Cherry Blossom Festival. *Event Management*, 14 (2), 167–182.

Patterson, I. and Getz, D. (2013). At the nexus of leisure and event studies. *Event Management*, 17 (3), 227–240.

Patterson, I., Getz, D. and Gubb, K. (2016). The social world and event travel career of the serious yoga devotee. *Leisure Studies*, 35, 296–313.

Pavlukovic, V., Armenski, T. and Alcantara-Pilar, J. (2017). Social impacts of music festivals: Does culture impact locals' attitude toward events in Serbia and Hungary? *Tourism Management* 63, 42–53.

Pavoni, A. (2018). *Controlling Urban Events: Law, Ethics and the Material*. London: Routledge.

Pearce, P. (1988). *The Ulysses Factor: Evaluating Visitors in Tourist Settings*. New York: Springer.

Pearce, P. (1998). Marketing and management trends in tourist attractions. *Asia Pacific Journal of Tourism Research*, 3 (1), 1–8.

Pearce, P. and Caltabiano, M. (1983). Inferring travel motivation from travelers' experiences. *Journal of Travel Research*, 22 (2), 16–20.

Pearce, P. and Lee, U. (2005). Developing the travel career approach to tourist motivation. *Journal of Travel Research*, 43 (3), 226–237.

Pearce, P., Moscardo, G. and Ross, G. (1996). *Tourism Community Relationships*. Oxford: Pergamon.

Pearce, P. and Zare, S. (2017). The orchestra model as the basis for teaching tourism experience design. *Journal of Hospitality and Tourism Management*, 30, 55–64.

Pearlman, D. and Gates, N. (2010). Hosting business meetings and special events in virtual worlds: A fad or the future? *Journal of Convention and Event Tourism*, 11 (4), 247–265.

Pegg, S. and Patterson, I. (2010). Rethinking music festivals as a staged event: Gaining insights from understanding visitor motivations and the experiences they seek. *Journal of Convention and Event Tourism*, 11 (2), 85–99.

Pegg, S., Patterson, I. and Axelsen, M. (2011). Sporting events and the use of alcohol by university students: Managing the risks. *Event Management*, 15 (1), 63–75.

Penrose, E. (1959). *The Theory of the Growth of the Firm*. New York: Wiley.

People 1st (2010). Labour Market Review of the Events Industry (http:// www.businessvisitsandeventspartner ship.com).

People and Physical Environment Research Conference (1987). Perth: Centre for Urban Research, University of Western Australia.

Pernecky, T. (2016). *Approaches and Methods in Event Studies*. London: Routledge.

Pernecky, T. and Luck, M. (2013). *Events, Society and Sustainability: Critical and Contemporary Approaches*. London: Routledge.

Persson, C. (2002). The Olympic Games site decision. *Tourism Management*, 23 (1), 27–36.

Pettersson, R. and Getz, D. (2009) Event experiences in time and space. A study of visitors to the 2007 World Alpine Ski Championships in Åre, Sweden. *Scandinavian Journal of Hospitality and Tourism*, 9 (2–3), 308–326.

Pettersson, R. and Zillinger, M. (2011). Time and space in event behaviour: Tracking visitors by GPS. *Tourism Geographies*, 13 (1), 1–20.

Pfeffer, J. (1981). *Power in Organizations*. London: Pitman.

Pfeffer, J. and Salancik, G. (1978). *The External Control of Organizations: A Resource Dependence Perspective*. New York: Harper and Row.

Phi, G., Dredge, D. and Whitford, M. (2014). Understanding conflicting perspectives in event planning and management using Q method. *Tourism Management*, 40, 406–415.

Phillips, J., Breining, M. and Phillips, P. (2008). *Return on Investment in Meetings and Events*. Oxford: Elsevier.

Phipps, P. (2011). Performing culture as political strategy: The Garma Festival, northeast Arnhem Land. In C. Gibson and J. Connell (eds), *Festival Places: Revitalising Rural Australia*, pp. 109–122. Bristol: Channel View.

Picard, D. and Robinson, M. (2006a). Remaking worlds: Festivals, tourism and change. In D. Picard and M. Robinson (eds), *Festivals, Tourism and Social Change: Remaking Worlds*, pp. 1–31. Clevedon: Channel View.

Picard, D. and Robinson, M. (eds) (2006b). *Festivals, Tourism and Social Change: Remaking Worlds*. Clevedon: Channel View.

Picard, M. (1996). *Bali: Cultural Tourism and Touristic Culture* (2nd edn). Singapore: Archipelago Press.

Piekarz, M., Jenkins, I. and Mills, P. (2015). *Risk and Safety Management in the Leisure, Events, Tourism and Sports Industries*. Wallingford: CABI.

Pieper, J. (1952). *Leisure: The Basis of Culture*. Translated by Alexander Dru. London: Faber and Faber (originally published as *Muße und Kult*. Munich: Kösel-Verlag, 1948).

Pigram, J. (1983). *Outdoor Recreation and Resource Management*. London: Croom Helm.

Pike, S. and Page, S. J. (2014). Destination marketing organizations and destination marketing: A narrative analysis of the literature. *Tourism Management*, 41, 202–227.

Pilcher, D. and Eade, N. (2016). Understanding the audience: Purbeck Folk Festival. *International Journal of Event and Festival Management*, 7 (1) 21–49.

Pine, B. and Gilmore, J. (1999). *The Experience Economy: Work Is Theatre and Every Business a Stage*. Boston, MA: Harvard Business School Press.

Pitts, B. (1999). Sports tourism and niche markets: Identification and analysis of the growing lesbian and gay sports tourism industry. *Journal of Vacation Marketing*, 5 (1), 31–50.

Pitts, S. (2005). What makes an audience? Investigating the roles and experiences of listeners at a chamber music festival. *Music and Letters*, 86 (2), 257–269.

Pizam, A. (1978). Tourism's impacts: The social costs to the destination community as perceived by its residents. *Journal of Travel Research*, 16 (4), 8–12.

Plog, S. (1972). Why destination areas rise and fall in popularity. Paper presented to the Travel Research Association Southern California Chapter, Los Angeles.

Plog, S. (1987). Understanding psychographics in tourism research. In J. Ritchie and C. Goeldner (eds), *Travel, Tourism and Hospitality Research*, pp. 302–313. New York: Wiley.

Plutschow, H. (2013). *Matsuri: The Festivals of Japan: With a Selection from PG O'Neill's Photographic Archive of Matsuri*. Routledge. (First published in 1996.)

Podestà, M. and Richards, G. (2017). Creating knowledge spillovers through knowledge-based festivals: The case of Mantua, Italy. *Journal of Policy Research in Tourism, Leisure and Events*, 10 (1), 1–16.

Pojani, D. (2014). Urban design, ideology, and power: Use of the central square in Tirana during one century of political transformations. *Planning Perspectives*, 30 (1), 67–94.

Pol, L. and Pak, S. (1994). The use of a two-stage survey design in collecting data from those who have attended periodic or special events. *Journal of the Market Research Society*, 36 (4), 315–326.

Pop, C. (2013). The modern Olympic Games: A globalised cultural and sporting event. *Procedia – Social and Behavioral Sciences*, 92, 728–734.

Porter, M. (1980). *Competitive Strategy: Techniques for Analyzing Industries and Competitors*. New York: The Free Press.

Porter P. (1999). Mega-sports events as municipal investments: A critique of impact analysis. In J. L. Fizel, E. Gustafson and L. Hadley (eds), *Sports Economics: Current Research*, New York: Praeger Press.

Poynter, G. and MacRury, I. (eds) (2009). *Olympic Cities: 2012 and the Remaking of London*. Aldershot: Ashgate Publishing.

Prahalad, C. and Ramaswamy, V. (2004). Co-creation experiences: The next practice in value creation. *Journal of Interactive Marketing*, 18 (3), 5–14.

Prashizky, A. and Remennick, L. (2016). Weddings in the Town Square: Young Russian Israelis protest the religious control of marriage in Tel-Aviv. *City and Community*, 15 (1), 44–63.

Pratt, A. (2008). Locating the cultural economy. In H. Anheir and Y. Isar (eds), *The Cultural Economy*. London: Sage, 42–51.

Prayag, G. and Grivel, E. (2018). Antecedents of sport event satisfaction and behavioral intentions: The role of sport identification, motivation, and place dependence. *Event Management*, 22 (3), 423–439.

Prebensen, N. (2010). Value creation through stakeholder participation: A case study of an event in the high north. *Event Management*, 14 (1), 37–52.

Preda, P. and Watts, T. (2003). Improving the efficiency of sporting venues through capacity management: The case of the Sydney (Australia) Cricket Ground Trust. *Event Management*, 8 (2), 83–89.

Prentice, R. and Anderson, V. (2003). Festival as creative destination. *Annals of Tourism Research*, 30 (1), 7–30.

Presenza, A. and Sheehan, L. (2013). Planning tourism through sporting events. *International Journal of Event and Festival Management*, 4 (2), 125–139.

Preston, C. (2012). *Event Marketing: How to Successfully Promote Events, Festivals, Conventions, and Expositions*. Chichester: Wiley.

Preuss, H. (2004). *The Economics of Staging the Olympics: A Comparison of the Games 1972–2008*. Cheltenham: Edward Elgar.

Preuss, H. (2007). The conceptualisation and measurement of mega sport event legacies. *Journal of Sport & Tourism*, 12 (3/4), 207–228.

Preuss, H. (2009). Opportunity costs and efficiency of investments in mega sport events. *Journal of Policy Research in Tourism, Leisure and Events*, 1 (2), 131–140.

Preuss, H. (ed.) (2013). *Impact and Evaluation of Major Sport Events*. London: Routledge.

Prideaux, B., Moscardo, G. and Laws, E. (eds) (2006). *Managing Tourism and Hospitality Services: Theory and International Applications*. Wallingford: CABI.

Professional Convention Management Association (www.pcma.org, accessed 7 June 2019).

Pugh, C. and Wood, E. (2004). The strategic use of events within local government: A study of London Borough councils. *Event Management*, 9 (1/2), 61–71.

Purbrick, L. (2001). *The Great Exhibition of 1851: New Interdisciplinary Essays*. Manchester: Manchester University Press.

Putnam, R. (2004). *Democracies in Flux: The Evolution of Social Capital in Contemporary Society*. New York: Oxford University Press.

Pyo, S., Cook, R. and Howell, R. (1988). Summer Olympic tourist market – learning from the past. *Tourism Management*, 9 (2), 137–144.

Quinn, B. (2000). Whose festival? Whose place? An insight into the production of cultural meanings in arts festivals turned festival attractions. In M. Robinson, P. Long, N. Evans and R. Sharpley (eds), *Expressions of Culture, Identity and Meaning in Tourism*. Sunderland: Centre for Travel and Tourism Research/Business Education Publishers.

Quinn, B. (2003). Symbols, practices and myth-making: Cultural perspectives on the Wexford Festival Opera. *Tourism Geographies*, 5 (3), 329–349.

Quinn, B. (2006). Problematising 'festival tourism': Arts festivals and sustainable development in Ireland. *Journal of Sustainable Tourism*, 14 (3), 288–306.

Quinn, B. (2010). The European Capital Culture initiative and cultural legacy: An analysis of the cultural sector in the aftermath of Cork 2005. *Event Management*, 13 (4), 249–264.

Quinn, B. (2013). *Key Concepts in Event Management*. London: Sage.

Radbourne, J. (2002). Social intervention or market intervention? A problem for governments in promoting the value of the arts. *International Journal of Arts Management*, 5 (1), 50–61.

Raj, R. (2004). The behavioural aspects of financial management. In I. Yeoman, M. Robertson, J. Ali-Knight, S. Drummond and U. McMahon-Beattie (eds) (2004). *Festival and Events Management: An International Arts and Culture Perspective*, pp. 273–285. Oxford: Elsevier.

Raj, R., Griffin, K. and Blackwell, R. (2015). Motivations for religious tourism, pilgrimage, festivals and events In R. Raj and K. Griffin. (eds), *Religious Tourism and Pilgrimage Management: An International Perspective*, pp. 103–117. CABI.

Raj, R. and Morpeth, N. (eds) (2007). *Religious Tourism and Pilgrimage Festivals Management: An International Approach*. Wallingford: CABI.

Raj, R. and Musgrave, J. (2009). *Event Management and Sustainability*. Wallingford: CABI.

Raj, R., Walters, P. and Rashid, T. (2008). *Event Management: An Integrated and Practical Approach*. London: Sage.

Ralston, L., Ellis, D., Compton, D. and Lee, J. (2007). Staging memorable events and festivals: An integrated model of service and experience factors. *International Journal of Event Management Research*, 3 (2), 24–38.

Ralston, R., Lumsdon, L. and Downward, P. (2005). The third force in events tourism: Volunteers at the XVII Commonwealth Games. *Journal of Sustainable Tourism*, 13 (5), 504–519.

Ramchandani, G., Coleman, R., Davies, L., Shibli, S. and Bingham, J. (2017). Valuing the inspirational impacts of major sports events. In E. Lundberg, J. Armbrecht, T. Andersson and D. Getz (eds), *The Value of Events*, pp. 136–158. London: Routledge.

Ramirez, R. and Mannervik, U. (2008). Designing value-creating systems. In L. Kimbell and V. P. Seidel (eds), *Designing for Services – Multidisciplinary Perspectives*, pp. 35–36. Oxford: University of Oxford.

Ramshaw, G. and Hinch, T. (2006). Place identity and sport tourism: The case of the Heritage Classic Ice Hockey Event. *Current Issues in Tourism*, 9 (4/5), 399–418.

Rapiergroup (2017). *Events 2050: The Future of Events and Exhibitions* (https://www.rapiergroup.com/news/the-next-30-years-of-exhibitions-and-events/).

Rapoport, R., Rapoport, R. N. and Strelitz, Z. (1975). *Leisure and the Family Life Cycle*. London: Routledge & Kegan Paul.

Ravenscroft, N. and Mateucci, X. (2002). The festival as carnivalesque: Social governance and control at Pamplona's San Fermin fiesta. *Tourism Culture & Communication*, 4 (1), 1–15.

Raybould, M. (1998). Participant motivation in a remote fishing event. *Festival Management and Event Tourism*, 5 (4), 231–241.

Raybould, M., Mules, T., Fredline, E. and Tomljenovic, R. (2000). Counting the herd: Using aerial photography to estimate attendance at open events. *Event Management*, 6 (1), 25–32.

Reeves, K., Bird, G., James, L., Stichelbaut, B. and Bourgeois, J. (eds) (2015). *Battlefield Events: Landscape, Commemoration and Heritage*. London: Routledge.

Reic, I. (2016). *Events Marketing Management: A Consumer Perspective*. London: Routledge.

Reid, G. (2006). The politics of city imaging: A case study of the MTV Europe Music Awards in Edinburgh '03. *Event Management*, 10 (1), 35–46.

Reid, S. (2007). Identifying social consequences of rural events. *Event Management*, 11 (1/2), 89–98.

Reisinger, Y. (2006). Travel/tourism: Spiritual experiences. In D. Buhalis and C. Costa (eds), *Tourism Business Frontiers: Consumers, Products and Industry*, pp. 148–167. Oxford: Elsevier.

Reunion Network (www.reunionfriendly.com, accessed 7 June 2019).

Reysen, S., Chadborn, D. and Plante, C. (2018). Theory of planned behaviour and intention to attend a fan convention. *Journal of Convention and Event Tourism*, 19 (3), 204–218.

Rice, E. (1983). *The Grand Procession of Ptolemy Philadelphus*. Oxford: Oxford University Press.

Rich, K., Bean, C. and Apramian, Z. (2014). Boozing, brawling, and community building: Sport-facilitated community development in a rural Ontario community. *Leisure/Loisir*, 38 (1), 73–91.

Richards, G. (1996). European cultural tourism: Trends and future prospects. In G. Richards (ed.), *Cultural Tourism in Europe*, pp. 311–333. Wallingford: CABI.

Richards, G. (2007a). The festivalization of society or the socialization of festivals? The case of Catalunya. In G. Richards (ed.), *Cultural Tourism: Global and Local Perspectives*, pp. 257–269. New York: Haworth.

Richards, G. (2007b). Culture and authenticity in a traditional event: The views of producers, residents, and visitors in Barcelona. *Event Management*, 11 (1–2), 33–44.

Richards, G. (2017). From place branding to place-making: The role of events. *International Journal of Event and Festival Management*, 8 (1), 8–23.

Richards, G. (2018). Cultural tourism: A review of recent research and trends. *Journal of Hospitality and Tourism Management*, 36, pp. 12–21.

Richards, G., de Brito, M. and Wilks, L. (2013). *Exploring the Social Impacts of Events*. Oxford: London.

Richards, G., Marques, L. and Mein, K. (eds) (2014). *Event Design: Social Perspectives and Practices*. London: Routledge.

Richards, G. and Palmer, R. (2010). *Eventful Cities: Cultural Management and Urban Revitalization*. Oxford: Butterworth-Heinemann.

Richards, P. and Ryan, C. (2004). The Aotearoa traditional Maori performing arts festival 1972–2000: A case study of cultural event maturation. *Journal of Tourism and Cultural Change*, 2 (2), 94–117.

Riggio, M. (2004). *Carnival: Culture in Action – The Trinidad Experience*. New York: Routledge.

Rihova, I. (2013). *Customer-to-customer co-creation of value in the context of festivals*. Unpublished Ph.D. thesis, Bournemouth University, Bournemouth.

Ristea, A., Andresen, M. A. and Leitner, M. (2018). Using tweets to understand changes in the spatial crime distribution for hockey events in Vancouver. *Canadian Geographer*, 62 (3), 338–351.

Ritchie, B., Sanders, D. and Mules, T. (2006). Televised events: Shaping destination images and perceptions of capital cities from the couch. In C. Arcodia, M. Whitford and C. Dicksen (eds), *Global Events Congress, Proceedings*, pp. 286–299. Brisbane: University of Queensland.

Ritchie, J. R. B. (1984). Assessing the impacts of hallmark events: Conceptual and research issues. *Journal of Travel Research*, 23 (1), 2–11.

Ritchie, J. R. B. (2000). Turning 16 days into 16 years through Olympic legacies. *Event Management*, 6 (2), 155–165.

Ritchie, J. R. B. and Beliveau, D. (1974). Hallmark events: An evaluation of a strategic response to seasonality in the travel market. *Journal of Travel Research*, 13 (2), 14–20.

Ritchie, J. R. B. and Lyons, M. (1990). Olympulse VI: A post-event assessment of resident reaction to the XV Olympic Winter Games. *Journal of Travel Research*, 28 (3), 14–23.

Ritchie, J. R. B. and Smith, B. (1991). The impact of a mega-event on host region awareness: A longitudinal study. *Journal of Travel Research*, 30 (1), 3–10.

Rittichainuwat, B. and Mair, J. (2012). Visitor attendance motivations at consumer travel exhibitions. *Tourism Management*, 33 (5), 1236–1244.

Rittichainuwat, B., Beck, J. and LaLopa, J. (2001). Understanding motivations, inhibitors, and facilitators of association members in attending international conferences. *Journal of Convention and Exhibition Management*, 3 (3), 45–62.

Roberts, K. (2006). *Leisure in Contemporary Society* (2nd edn). Wallingford: CABI.

Robertson, M., Ong, F., Lockstone-Binney, L. and Ali-Knight, J. (2018). Critical event studies: Issues and perspectives. *Event Management*, 22, 865–874.

Robinson, G. (1990). *Conflict and Change in the Countryside. Rural Society, Economy and Planning in the Developed World.* London: Belhaven Press.

Robinson, L., Chelladurai, P., Bodet, G. and Downward, P. (2013). *Routledge Handbook of Sport Management*. London: Routledge.

Robinson, M., Hums, M., Crow, R. and Philips, D. (2001). *Profiles of Sport Industry Professionals: The People Who Make the Games Happen*. Gaithersburg, MD: Aspen Publishers.

Robinson, M., Picard, D. and Long, P. (2004). Festival tourism: Producing, translating, and consuming expressions of culture(s). *Event Management*, 8 (4), 187–189.

Robinson, R. (2016). *Music Festivals and the Politics of Participation*. London: Routledge.

Robinson, R. N. S. and Clifford, C. (2012). Authenticity and festival foodservice experiences. *Annals of Tourism Research*, 39 (2), 571–600.

Robinson, R. N. S. and Getz, D. (2013). Food enthusiasts and tourism: Exploring involvement dimensions. *Journal of Hospitality and Tourism Research* (first published on September 26, 2013 as doi:10.1177/1096348013503994).

Roche, M. (1992). Mega-events and micro-modernization: On the sociology of the new urban tourism. *The British Journal of Sociology*, 43 (4), 563–600.

Roche, M. (1994). Mega-events and urban policy. *Annals of Tourism Research*, 21 (1), 1–19.

Roche, M. (2000). *Mega-Events and Modernity: Olympics and Expos in the Growth of Global Culture*. London: Routledge.

Roche, M. (2006). Mega-events and modernity revisited: Globalization and the case of the Olympics. *Sociological Review*, 54 (2), 25–40.

Roche, M. (2017). *Mega-events and Social Change: Spectacle, Legacy and Public Culture*. Manchester: Manchester University Press.

Rockwell, D. and Mau, B. (2006). *Spectacle*. London: Phaidon Press.

Roemer, M. (2007). Ritual participation and social support in a major Japanese festival. *Journal for the Scientific Study of Religion*, 46 (2), 185–200.

Rogers, A. (2012). Geographies of the performing arts: Landscapes, places and cities. *Geography Compass*, 6 (2), 60–75.

Rogers, E. (1995). *Diffusion of Innovations*. New York: The Free Press.

Rogers, T. (1998). *Conferences: A Twenty-First Century Industry*. Harlow: Addison Wesley Longman.

Rogers, T. (2013). *Conferences and Conventions: A Global Industry* (3rd edn). Oxford: Butterworth-Heinemann.

Rogerson, R. (2016). Re-defining temporal notions of event legacy: Lessons from Glasgow's Commonwealth Games. *Annals of Leisure Research, 19* (4), 497–518.

Rojek, C. (1995). *Decentring Leisure*. London: Sage.

Rojek, C. (2005). *Leisure Theory: Principles and Practice*. Basingstoke: Palgrave Macmillan.

Rojek, C. (2012). *Fame Attack: The Inflation of Celebrity and Its Consequences*. London: Bloomsbury Publishing.

Rojek, C. (2013). *Event Power: How Global Events Manage and Manipulate*. London: Sage.

Rojek, C. and Urry, J. (eds) (1997). *Touring Cultures: Transformation of Travel and Theory*. London: Routledge.

Rosenfield, P. L. (1992). The potential of transdisciplinary research for sustaining and extending linkages between the health and social sciences. *Social Science & Medicine*, 35 (11), 1343–1357.

Rota, F. S. and Salone, C. (2014). Place-making processes in unconventional cultural practices. The case of Turin's contemporary art festival Paratissima. *Cities*, 40, 90–98.

Rotenberg, R. L. and McDonogh, G. W. (1993). *The Cultural Meaning of Urban Space*. Toronto: ABC-CLIO.

Roth, S. and Frank, S. (2000). Festivalization and the media: Weimar, cultural capital of Europe 1999. *International Journal of Cultural Policy*, 6 (2), 219–224.

Rothman, R. A. (1978). Residents and transients: Community reaction to seasonal visitors. *Journal of Travel Research*, 16 (winter), 8–13.

Rothman, R. A., Donnelly, P. G. and Tower, J. K. (1979). Police departments in resort communities: Organisational adjustments to population undulation. *Leisure Sciences*, 2, 105–118.

Rowland, D. (2012). *Population Aging*. Dordrecht: Springer.

Rowntree, B. S. and Lavers, G. R. (1951). *English Life and Leisure: A Social Study*. London: Longmans, Green.

Rozin, S. (2000). The amateurs who saved Indianapolis. *Business Week*, 10 April.

Ruperto, A. and Kerr, G. (2009). A study of community events held by not-for-profit organizations in Australia. *Journal of Nonprofit & Public Sector Marketing*, 21 (3), 298–308.

Russell, J. (2004). Celebrating culture, energising language, transforming society. In M. Robinson, *Conference Proceedings, Journeys of Expression III*. Centre for Tourism and Cultural Change, Sheffield-Hallam University (Compact Disc).

Russell J. and Lanius, U. (1984). Adaptation level and the affective appraisal of environments. *Journal of Environmental Psychology*, 4 (2), 119–135.

Rutley, J. (n.d.). Security. In *Event Operations*, pp. 75–83. Port Angeles, WA: International Festivals and Events Association.

Ryan, C. (2000). Tourist experiences, phenomenographic analysis, post positivism and neural network software. *International Journal of Tourism Research*, 2 (2), 119–131.

Ryan, C. (2002). *The Tourist Experience* (2nd edn). London: Continuum.

Ryan, C. (2012). The experience of events. In S. J. Page and J. Connell (eds), *The Routledge Handbook of Events*. London: Routledge.

Ryan. C. and Bates, C. (1995). A rose by any other name: The motivations of those opening their gardens for a festival. *Festival Management and Event Tourism*, 3 (2), 59–71.

Ryan, C. and Lockyer, T. (2002). Masters' Games: The nature of competitors' involvement and requirements. *Event Management*, 7 (4), 259–270.

Ryan, C., Smee, A., Murphy, S. and Getz, D. (1998). New Zealand events: A temporal and regional analysis. *Festival Management and Event Tourism*, 5 (1/2), 71–83.

Ryan, C. and Trauer, B. (2005). Sport tourist behaviour: The example of the Masters Games. In J. Higham (ed.), *Sport Tourism Destinations: Issues, Opportunities and Analysis*. Oxford: Elsevier.

Rybczynski, W. (1991). *Waiting for the Weekend*. New York: Viking.

Sadd, D. (2010). What is event-led regeneration? Are we confusing terminology or will London 2012 be the first games to truly benefit the local existing population? *Event Management*, 13 (4), 265–275.

Sadd, D. (2014). The future is virtual. In I. Yeoman, M. Robertson, J., Ali-Knight, S. Drummond, and U. McMahon-Beattie (eds), *The Future of Events and Festivals*, pp. 209–218. London: Routledge.

Sadd, D. and Jackson, C. (2006). Planning for resort regeneration. In M. Robertson (ed.), *Sporting Events and Event Tourism: Impacts, Plans and Opportunities*, pp. 43–64. Leisure Studies Association Publication 91. Eastbourne: University of Brighton.

Safe and Healthy Crowded Places Handbook (2018). Canberra: Australian Institute for Disaster Resilience.

Saget, A. (2006). *The Event Marketing Handbook: Beyond Logistics and Planning*. Chicago, IL: Dearborn Trade Publishing.

Sahlins, M. (1976). *Culture and Practical Reason*. Chicago, IL: University of Chicago Press.

Salamone, F. (2004). *Routledge Encyclopedia of Religious Rites, Rituals and Festivals*. London: Routledge.

Salazar, N. B., Timmerman, C., Wets, J., Gato, L. G. and Van den Broucke, S. (2016). *Mega-Event Mobilities: A Critical Analysis*. London: Routledge.

Saleh, F. and Ryan, C. (1993). Jazz and knitwear: Factors that attract tourists to festivals. *Tourism Management*, 14 (4), 289–297.

Saleh, F. and Wood, C. (1998). Motives and volunteers in multi-cultural events: The case of Saskatoon Folkfest. *Festival Management and Event Tourism*, 5 (1/2), 59–70.

Sandercock, L. (ed.) (1998). *Making the Invisible Visible, A Multicultural Planning History*. Berkeley, CA: University of California Press.

Santos, J. (2014). Brazil: An emerging power establishing itself in the world of international sports mega-events. *International Journal of the History of Sport*, 31 (10), 1312–1327.

Savage, G., Nix, T., Whitehead, C. and Blair, J. (1991). Strategies for assessing and managing organizational stakeholders. *Academy of Management Executive*, 5 (2), 61–75.

Scannell, L. and Gifford, R. (2010). Defining place attachment: A tripartite organizing framework. *Journal of Environmental Psychology*, 30 (1), 1–10.

Schechner, R. (1988). *Performance Theory*. New York: Routledge.

Schechner, R. (2002, 2013 3rd edn). *Performance Studies: An Introduction*. London: Routledge.

Schein, E. (1985). *Organizational Culture and Leadership*. San Francisco, CA: Jossey-Bass.

Scheyvens, R. (2002). *Tourism for Development*. Harlow: Prentice-Hall.

Schlenker, K., Edwards, D. and Wearing, S. (2012). Volunteering and events. In S. J. Page and J. Connell (eds), *The Routledge Handbook of Events*. London: Routledge.

Schlentrich, U. (2008). The MICE industry: Meetings, incentives, conventions and exhibitions. In B. Brotherton and R. Wood (eds), *The Sage Handbook of Hospitality Management*, pp. 400–420. London: Sage.

Schmidt, E. and Cohen, J. (2013). *The New Digital Age: Reshaping the Future of People, Nations and Business*. London: John Murray.

Schneider, I. and Backman, S. (1996). Cross-cultural equivalence of festival motivations: A study in Jordan. *Festival Management and Event Tourism*, 4 (3/4), 139–144.

Schnell, T. and Pali, S. (2013). Pilgrimage today: The meaning-making potential of ritual. *Mental Health, Religion & Culture*, 16 (9), 887–902.

Schofield, P., Crowther, P., Jago, L., Heeley, J. and Taylor, S. (2018). Collaborative innovation: Catalyst for a destination's event success. *International Journal of Contemporary Hospitality Management*, 30 (6), 2499–2516.

Scholtz, M., Slabbert, E. and Saayman, M. (2019). I like you. I like you not. Dynamic social impact perceptions of an international sporting event. *Event Management*, 23, 149–164.

Schulenkorf, N., Thomson, A. and Schlenker, K. (2011). Intercommunity sport events: Vehicles and catalysts for social capital in divided societies. *Event Management*, 15 (2), 105–119.

Schultz, E. and Lavenda, R. (2005). *Cultural Anthropology: A Perspective on the Human Condition*. Oxford: Oxford University Press.

Schumpeter, J. (1931). *Theorie der wirtschaftlichen Entwichlung*, Munich and Leipzig: Dunker und Humblat.

Schumpeter, J. (1934). *The Theory of Economic Development*. Cambridge, MA: Harvard University Press.

Schybergson, O. (2014). The generation raised on touchscreens will forever alter tech design. *Wired* (http://www.wired.com/2014/06/generation-moth/, accessed 30 June 2014).

Scotinform Ltd. (1991). *Edinburgh Festivals Study 1990–91: Visitor Survey and Economic Impact Assessment, Final Report*. Edinburgh: Scottish Tourist Board.

Scott, D. (1995). A comparison of visitors' motivations to attend three urban festivals. *Festival Management and Event Tourism*, 3 (3), 121–128.

Scott, D. (1996). A comparison of visitors' motivations to attend three urban festivals. *Festival Management and Event Tourism*, 3 (3), 121–128.

Scott, J. (2000). *Social Network Analysis: A Handbook* (2nd edn). London: Sage.

Scott, W. (2001). *Institutions and Organizations*. Thousand Oaks, CA: Sage.

Sealy, W. (2018). Vocationalizing event management degrees. *Event Management*, 22, 469–482.

Seguin, B., Parent, M. M. and O'Reilly, N. (2010). Corporate support: A corporate social responsibility alternative to traditional event sponsorship. *International Journal of Sport Management and Marketing*, 7 (3), 202–222.

Selznick, P. (1957). *Leadership in Administration*. Evanston, IL: Row, Peterson.

Senge, P. (1990). *The Fifth Discipline: The Art and Practice of the Learning Organization*. New York: Doubleday.

Senge, P, Roberts, C., Ross, R., Smith, B. and Kleiner, A. (1994). *The Fifth Discipline Fieldbook: Strategies and Tools for Building a Learning Organization*. New York: Doubleday.

Sensory Trust UK (n.d.). What is sensory mapping? (https://www.sensorytrust.org.uk/information/factsheets/what-is-sensory-mapping.html).

Severt, D., Wang, Y., Chen, P. and Breiter, D. (2007). Examining the motivation, perceived performance, and behavioural intentions of convention attendees: Evidence from a regional conference. *Tourism Management*, 28 (2), 399–408.

Shackley, M. (2001). *Managing Sacred Sites: Service Provision and Visitor Experience*. London: Continuum.

Shaffer, M., Greer, A. and Mauboules, C. (2003). *Olympic Costs and Benefits*. Canadian Centre for Policy Alternatives Publication, February.

Sharma, P. and Nayak, J. (2018). An analysis on the emotional approach to segmentation: A study of yoga tourism. *Journal of Convention and Event Tourism*, 20 (1), 1–23.

Sharples, L., Crowther, P., May, D. and Orefice, C. (2014). *Strategic Event Creation*. Oxford: Goodfellow Publishers.

Shaw, G. and Williams, A. (2004). *Tourism and Tourism Spaces*. London: Sage.

Shedroff, N. (2001). *Experience Design*. Indianapolis, IN: New Riders.

Sheehan, A., Hubbard, S. and Popovich, P. (2000). Profiling the hotel and conference center meeting planner: A preliminary study. *Journal of Convention and Exhibition Management*, 2 (2/3), 11–25.

Sherwood, P. (2007). *A Triple Bottom Line Evaluation of the Impact of Special Events: The Development of Indicators*. Unpublished Ph.D. thesis, Victoria University, Melbourne.

Shibli, S. and the Sport Industry Research Centre (2002). *The 2002 Embassy World Snooker Championship, An Evaluation of the Economic Impact, Place Marketing Effects, and Visitors' Perceptions of Sheffield*. For Sheffield City Council.

Shinde, K. (2010). Managing Hindu festivals in pilgrimage sites: Emerging trends, opportunities, and challenges. *Event Management*, 14 (1), 53–67.

Shipway, R. and Fyall, A. (eds) (2012). *International Sports Events: Impacts, Experiences and Identities*. London: Routledge.

Shipway, R. and Jones, I. (2007). Running away from home: Understanding visitor experiences and behaviour at sport tourism events. *International Journal of Tourism Research*, 9 (5), 373–383.

Shipway, R. and Jones, I. (2008). The great suburban Everest: An 'Insiders' perspective on experiences at the 2007 Flora London Marathon. *Journal of Sport & Tourism*, 13 (1), 61–77.

Shone, A. and Parry B. (2004). *Successful Event Management: A Practical Handbook* (2nd edn). London: Continuum.

Short, A. (1966). Workers under glass in 1851. *Victorian Studies*, 10 (2), 193–202.

Silvers, J. (2004). *Professional Event Coordination*. Hoboken, NJ: Wiley.

Silvers, J. (2008). *Risk Management for Meetings and Events*. Oxford: Butterworth-Heinemann.

Silvers, J., Bowdin, G., O'Toole, W. and Nelson, K. (2006). Towards an international event management body of knowledge (EMBOK). *Event Management*, 9 (4), 185–198.

Simon, L. (2014). *The Greatest Shows on Earth: A History of the Circus*. Reaktion Books, distributed by University of Chicago Press.

Simons, I. (2015). How to slay a dragon slowly: Applying slow principles to event design. In G. W. Richards, L. Marques and K. Mein (eds), *Event Design: Social Perspectives and Practices*, pp. 78–91. London: Routledge.

Singh, N., Racherla, P. and Hu, C. (2008). Knowledge mapping for safe festivals and events: An ontological approach. *Event Management*, 11 (1/2), 71–80.

Singh, R. (2006). Pilgrimage in Hinduism: Historical context and modern perspectives. In D. Timothy and D. Olsen (eds), *Tourism, Religion and Spiritual Journeys*, pp. 220–236. London and New York: Routledge.

Sit, J. K. and Birch, D. (2014). Entertainment events in shopping malls: Profiling passive and active participation behaviors. *Journal of Consumer Behaviour*, 13 (6), 383–392.

Skinner, B. (1938). *The Behavior of Organisms*. New York: Appleton-Century-Crofts.

Skinner, B. and Rukavina, V. (2003). *Event Sponsorship*. New York: Wiley.

Slack, T. and Thurston, A. (2014). The social and commercial impact of sport, the role of sport management. *European Sport Management Quarterly*, 14 (5), 454–463.

Slater, L. (2010). 'Calling our spirits home': Indigenous cultural festivals and the making of a good life. *Cultural Studies Review*, 16 (1), 143–154.

Small, K., Edwards, D. and Sheridan, L. (2005). A flexible framework for evaluating the socio-cultural impacts of a (small) festival. *International Journal of Event Management Research*, 1 (1), 66–77.

Smelser, N. and Baltes, P. (eds) (2001). *International Encyclopedia of Social and Behavioral Sciences*. London: Pergamon.

Smidt-Jensen, S., Skytt, C. B. and Winther, L. (2009). The geography of the experience economy in Denmark: Employment change and location dynamics in attendance-based experience industries. *European Planning Studies*, 17 (6), 847–862.

Smit, B. and Melissen, F. (2018). *Sustainable Customer Experience Design: Co-creating Experiences in Events, Tourism and Hospitality*. London: Routledge.

Smith, A. (2008). Using major events to promote peripheral urban areas: Deptford and the 2007 Tour de France. In J. Ali-Knight, M. Robertson, A. Fyall, and A. Ladkin (eds), *International Perspectives of Festivals and Events: Paradigms of Analysis*, pp. 3–19. Oxford: Butterworth-Heinemann.

Smith, A. (2009). Spreading the positive effects of major events to peripheral areas. *Journal of Policy Research in Tourism, Leisure and Events*, 1 (3), 231–246.

Smith, A. (2012). *Events and Urban Regeneration: The Strategic Use of Events to Revitalise Cities*. London: Routledge.

Smith, A. (2014). 'Borrowing' public space to stage major events: The Greenwich Park controversy. *Urban Studies*, 51 (2), 247–263.

Smith, A. (2015). *Events in the City: Using Public Spaces as Event Venues*. London: Routledge.

Smith, A. (2017). Animation or denigration? Using urban public spaces as event venues. *Event Management*, 21, 609–619.

Smith, D. M. (1977). *Human Geography: A Welfare Approach*. Oxford: Edward Arnold.

Smith, E. and Mackie, D. (2000). *Social Psychology* (2nd edn). New York: Worth Publishers.

Smith, K., Lockstone-Binney, L., Holmes, K. and Baum, T. (eds) (2014). *Event Volunteering: International Perspectives on the Event Volunteering Experience*. London: Routledge.

Smith, M. (2005). Spotlight events, media relations, and place promotion: A case study. *Journal of Hospitality and Leisure Marketing*, 12 (1/2), 115–134.

Smith, M. (2006). Entertainment and new leisure tourism. In D. Buhalis and C. Costa (eds), *Tourism Business Frontiers: Consumers, Products and Industry*, pp. 220–227. Oxford: Elsevier.

Smith, S. and Costello, C. (2009). Culinary tourism: Satisfaction with a culinary event utilizing importance-performance grid analysis. *Journal of Vacation Marketing*, 15 (2), 99–110.

Smith, S. and Godbey, G. (1991). Leisure, recreation and tourism. *Annals of Tourism Research*, 18 (1), 85–100.

Snaith, T. and Haley, A. (1999). Residents' opinions of tourism development in the historic city of York, England. *Tourism Management*, 20 (5), 595–603.

Social Capital Research (www.socialcapitalresearch.com).

Sociology (www.sociology.org.uk, accessed 7 June 2019).

Sofield, T. (1991). Sustainable ethnic tourism in the South Pacific: Some principles. *Journal of Tourism Studies*, 1 (3), 56–72.

Sofield, T. and Li, F. (1998). Historical methodology and sustainability: An 800-year-old festival from China. *Journal of Sustainable Tourism*, 6 (4), 267–292.

Sofield, T. and Sivan, A. (2003). From cultural festival to international sport – the Hong Kong Dragon Boat Races. *Journal of Sport Tourism*, 8 (1), 9–20.

Solis, B. (2013). *What's the Future of Business: Changing the Way Businesses Create Experiences*. New Jersey: John Wiley & Sons.

Solomon, J. (2002). *An Insider's Guide to Managing Sporting Events*. Champaign, IL: Human Kinetics.

Sonder, M. (2003). *Event Entertainment and Production*. New York: Wiley.

Song, H. J., Ahn, Y. J. and Lee, C. K. (2014). Examining relationships among Expo experiences, service quality, satisfaction, and the effect of the Expo: The case of the Expo 2012 Yeosu Korea. *Asia Pacific Journal of Tourism Research*, 1–20.

Sousa-Mast, F. R., Reis, A. C., Gurgel, L. A. and Duarte, A. F. P. (2013). Are cariocas getting ready for the Games? Sport participation and the Rio de Janeiro 2016 Olympic Games. *Managing Leisure*, 18 (4), 331–335.

Soutar, G. and McLeod, B. (1993). Residents' perceptions on impact of the America's Cup. *Annals of Tourism Research*, 20 (3), 571–582.

Spencer, D. M. and Holecek, D. F. (2007). Basic characteristics of the fall tourism market. *Tourism Management*, 28 (2), 491–504.

Spencer, J. P. and Steyn, J. N. (2017). Logistical management of iconic sporting events. *African Journal of Hospitality, Tourism and Leisure*, 6 (1).

Spiller, J. (2002). History of convention tourism. In K. Weber and K. Chon (eds), *Convention Tourism: International Research and Industry Perspectives*, pp. 3–20. Binghampton, NY: Haworth.

Spilling, O. (1998). Beyond intermezzo? On the long-term industrial impacts of mega-events: The case of Lillehammer 1994. *Festival Management and Event Tourism*, 5 (3), 101–122.

Spiropoulos, S., Gargalianos, D. and Sotiriadou, K. (2006). The 20th Greek Festival of Sydney: A stakeholder analysis. *Event Management*, 9 (4), 169–183.

Sport Business (www.sportbusiness.com, accessed 7 June 2019).

Sports Business Market Research Inc. (2000–2006). *Sports Business Market Research Handbook*. New York: EPM Communications Inc.

Spracklen, K. (2014). Leisure studies education: Historical trends and pedagogical futures in the United Kingdom and beyond. *Journal of Hospitality, Leisure, Sport and Tourism Education*, 15 (1), 20–23.

Spracklen, K. and Lamond, I. R. (2016). *Critical Event Studies*. London: Routledge.

Stadler, R. (2013). Power relations and the production of new knowledge within a Queensland Music Festival community cultural development project. *Annals of Leisure Research*, 16 (1), 87–102.

Stadler, R., Jepson, A. S. and Wood, E. H. (2018). Electrodermal activity measurement within a qualitative methodology: Exploring emotion in leisure experiences. *International Journal of Contemporary Hospitality Management*, 30 (8).

Stadler, R., Reid, S. and Fullagar, S. (2013). An ethnographic exploration of knowledge practices within the Queensland Music Festival. *International Journal of Event and Festival Management*, 4 (2), 90–106.

Stallworth, H., Harris, L. and Wise, G. (n.d.). *The Economics of Sustainability*. Watershed Academy Web, US EPA. (http://cfpub.epa.gov/watertrain/pdf/economics_of_sustainability.pdf, accessed 7 June 2019).

Stebbins, R. (1982). Serious leisure: A conceptual statement. *Pacific Sociological Review*, 25 (2), 251–272.

Stebbins, R. (1992). *Amateurs, Professionals, and Serious Leisure*. Montreal, QC: McGill-Queen's University Press.

Stebbins, R. (2001). *New Directions in the Theory and Research of Serious Leisure*. Lewiston, NY: Edwin Mellen.

Stebbins, R. (2006). *Serious Leisure: A Perspective for Our Time*. Somerset, NJ: Aldine Transaction Publications.

Stebbins, R. A. and Graham, M. (eds) (2004). *Volunteering as Leisure/Leisure as Volunteering: An International Assessment*. Wallingford: Cabi.

Stein, A. and Evans, B. (2009). *An Introduction to the Entertainment Industry*. New York: Peter Lang.

Stember, M. (1991). Advancing the social sciences through the interdisciplinary enterprise. *The Social Science Journal*, 28 (1), 1–14.

Stevens, Q. and Shin, H. R. (2014). Urban festivals and local social space. *Planning Practice and Research*, 29 (1), 1–20.

Stevenson, N. (2016). Local festivals, social capital and sustainable destination development: Experiences in East London. *Journal of Sustainable Tourism*, 24 (7), 990–1006.

Stockdale, J. E. (1985). *What Is Leisure? An Empirical Analysis of the Concept of Leisure and the Role of Leisure in People's Lives*. London: Sports Council and Economic and Social Research Council.

Stokes, R. (2004). A framework for the analysis of events-tourism knowledge networks. Journal of Hospitality and Tourism Management, 11 (2), 108–123.

Stokes, R. (2008). Tourism strategy making: Insights to the events tourism domain. *Tourism Management*, 29 (2), 252–262.

Stokes, R. (2012). The private sector and events. In S. J. Page and J. Connell (eds), *The Routledge Handbook of Events*, pp. 215–233. London: Routledge.

Stone, C. (2008). The British pop music festival phenomenon. In J. Ali-Knight, M. Robertson, A. Fyall, and A. Ladkin (eds), *International Perspectives of Festivals and Events: Paradigms of Analysis*, pp. 205–224. Oxford: Butterworth-Heinemann.

Stone, M., Padron, T., Wray, M., La Lopa, J. and Olson, E. (2017). Career desires and expectations of event management students. *Journal of Hospitality and Tourism Management*, 32, 45–53.

Stott, C., Hutchison, P. and Drury, J. (2001). 'Hooligans' abroad? Inter-group dynamics, social identity and participation in collective 'disorder' at the 1998 World Cup Finals. *British Journal of Social Psychology*, 40 (3), 359–384.

Stricklin, M. and Ellis, G. (2018). Structuring quality experiences for event participants. *Event Management*, 22 (3), 353–365.

Strigas, A. and Newton-Jackson, E. (2003). Motivating volunteers to serve and succeed: Design and results of a pilot study that explores demographics and motivational factors in sport volunteerism. *International Sports Journal*, 7 (1), 111–123.

Suarez-Villa, L. (2009). *Technocapitalism: A Critical Perspective on Technological Innovation and Corporatism*. Philadelphia: Temple University Press.

Sugathan, P., Ranjan, K. and Mulky, A. (2017). An examination of the emotions that follow a failure of co-creation. *Journal of Business Research*, 78, 43–52.

Sundbo, J. and Bærenholdt, J. O. (2007). Indledning: Den mangfoldige oplevelsesøkonomi. In J.O. Bærenholdt and J. Sundbo (eds), *Oplevelsesøkonomi: Produktion, forbrug, kultur*, pp. 9–25. Frederiksberg: Samfundslitteratur.

Sundbo, J., Orfila-Sintes, F. and Sørensen, F. (2007). The innovative behaviour of tourism firms—Comparative studies of Denmark and Spain. *Research Policy*, 36 (1), 88–106.

Sundbo, J. and Sørensen, F. (eds) (2013). *Handbook on the Experience Economy*. Cheltenham: Edward Elgar.

Suomi, K., Luonila, M. and Tähtinena, J. (2018). Ironic festival brand co-creation. *Journal of Business Research* (https://doi.org/10.1016/j.jbusres.2018.08.039)

Swart, K. (2005). Strategic planning – implications for the bidding of sport events in South Africa. *Journal of Sport & Tourism*, 10 (1), 37–46.

Swedish Classics (https://ensvenskklassiker.se/en/our-classics/a-swedish-classic/)

Syme, G., Shaw, B., Fenton, D. and Mueller, W. (eds) (1989). *The Planning and Evaluation of Hallmark Events*. Aldershot: Avebury.

Taks, M., Chalip, L. and Green, B. C. (2017). *Impacts and Strategic Outcomes from Non-mega Sport Events for Local Communities*. London: Routledge.

Tang, T. and Cooper, R. (2018). The most social games: Predictors of social media uses during the 2016 Rio Olympics. *Communication and Sport*, 6 (3), 308–330.

Tapp, A. (2004). The loyalty of football fans – we'll support you evermore? *Journal of Database Marketing and Customer Strategy Management*, 11 (3), 203–215.

Tarlow, P. (2002). *Event Risk Management and Safety*. New York: Wiley.

Tasci, A., Hahm, J. and Terry, D. (2018). Sports tourists and non-sports tourists: *Event Management*, 22, 303–315.

Tassiopoulos, D. (2011). *New Tourism Ventures: An Entrepreneurial and Managerial Approach* (2nd edn). Claremont, South Africa: Juta and Company

Taylor, P. and Gratton, C. (1988). The Olympic Games: An economic analysis. *Leisure Management*, 8 (3), 32–34.

Taylor, R. and Shanka, T. (2002). Attributes for staging successful wine festivals. *Event Management*, 7 (3), 165–175.

Taylor, R. and Shanka, T. (2008). Cause for event: Not-for-profit marketing through participant sports events. *Journal of Marketing Management*, 24 (9–10), 945–958.

Taylor, T. and Toohey, K. (2011). Ensuring safety at Australian sport event precincts: Creating securitised, sanitised and stifling spaces? *Urban Studies*, 48 (15), 3259–3275.

Teigland, J. (1996). *Impacts on Tourism From Mega-Events: The Case of Winter Olympic Games*. Sogndal: Western Norway Research Institute.

Terzi, M., Sakas, D. and Seimenis, I. (2013). International Events: The Impact of the Conference Location. *Procedia – Social and Behavioral Sciences*, 73, 363–372.

Testa, A. (2014). Rethinking the festival: Power and politics. *Method and Theory in the Study of Religion*, 26 (1), 44–73.

The Event Design Collective (https://edco.global/).

Theilmann, J. (1987). Medieval pilgrims and the origins of tourism. *Journal of Popular Culture*, 20 (4), 93–102.

Theodoraki, E. (2007). *Olympic Event Organization*. Oxford: Butterworth-Heinemann.

Therkelsen, A. (2010). Rethinking place brand communication: From product oriented monologue to consumer engaging dialogue. In M. Kavaratzis, Warnaby, G and Ashworth, G. (ed.), *Rethinking Place Branding: Comprehensive Brand Development for Cities and Regions*, pp. 159–174. Dordrecht: Springer.

Thrane, C. (2002). Music quality, satisfaction, and behavioral intentions within a jazz festival context. *Event Management*, 7 (3), 143–150.

Thrift, N. (1977). *An Introduction to Time Geography*. Norwich: Catmog.

Tilden, F. (1957). *Interpreting Our Heritage*. Chapel Hill, NC: University of North Carolina Press.

Timothy, D. and Boyd, S. (2006). Heritage tourism in the 21st century: Valued traditions and new perspectives. *Journal of Heritage Tourism*, 1 (1), 1–16.

Timothy, D. and Olsen, D. (eds) (2006). *Tourism, Religion and Spiritual Journeys*. London and New York: Routledge.

Tkaczynski, A. (2013). A stakeholder approach to attendee segmentation: A case study of an Australian Christian music festival. *Event Management*, 17 (3), 283–298.

Tkaczynski, A. and Rundle-Thiele, S. (2013). Understanding what really motivates attendance: A music festival segmentation study. *Journal of Travel and Tourism Marketing*, 30(6), 610–623.

Tkaczynski, A. and Stokes, R. (2010). FESTPERF: A service quality measurement scale for festivals. *Event Management*, 14 (1), 69–82.

Todd, L., Leask, A. and Ensor, J. (2017). Understanding primary stakeholders' multiple roles in hallmark event tourism management. *Tourism Management*, 59, 494–509.

Tomlinson, A. (2014). Olympic legacies: Recurrent rhetoric and harsh realities. *Contemporary Social Science*, 9 (2), 137–158.

Tomlinson, G. (1986). The staging of rural food festivals: Some problems with the concept of liminoid performances. Paper presented to the Qualitative Research Conference on Ethnographic Research, University of Waterloo.

Toohey, K. (2008). Terrorism, sport and public policy in the risk society. *Sport in Society*, 11 (4), 429–442.

Toohey, K. and Veal, T. (2007). *The Olympic Games: A Social Science Perspective*. Wallingford: CABI.

Toraldo, M. (2013). Mobilising the cultural consumer through the senses: Festivals as sensory experiences. *International Journal of Work Organisation and Emotion*, 5 (4), 384–400.

Torres-Delgado, A. and Palomeque, F. (2014). Measuring sustainable tourism at the municipal level. *Annals of Tourism Research*, 49, 122–137.

Trail, G. and James, J. (2001). The motivation scale for sport consumption: Assessment of the scale's psychometric properties. *Journal of Sport Behavior*, 24 (1), 109–127.

Traugott, M. (editor and translator) (1978). *Emile Durkheim on Institutional Analysis*. Chicago, IL: University of Chicago Press.

Travel and Tourism Research Association Canada Chapter (1986). *Conference Proceedings of the Canada Chapter*, Travel and Tourism Research Association, Edmonton.

Travel Industry Association of America (1999). *Profile of Travelers Who Attend Sports Events*. Washington DC: TIAA.

Treuren, G. (2014). Enthusiasts, conscripts or instrumentalists? The motivational profiles of event volunteers. *Managing Leisure*, 19 (1), 51–70.

Tribe, J. (1997). The indiscipline of tourism. *Annals of Tourism Research*, 24 (3), 638–657.

Tribe, J. (2002). The philosophic practitioner. *Annals of Tourism Research*, 29 (2), 338–357.

Tribe, J. (2004). Knowing about tourism – epistemological issues. In L. Goodson and J. Phillimore (eds), *Qualitative Research in Tourism: Ontologies, Epistemologies and Methodologies*, pp. 46–62. London: Routledge.

Tribe, J. (2005). *The Economics of Recreation, Leisure and Tourism* (3rd edn). Oxford: Elsevier.

Tribe, J. (2006). The truth about tourism. *Annals of Tourism Research*, 33 (2), 360–381.

Tribe, J. (ed.) (2009). *Philosophical Issues in Tourism*. Bristol: Channel View.

Tribe, J. (2014). The curriculum: A philosophic practice? In D. Dredge, D. Airey and M. Gross (eds), *The Routledge Handbook of Tourism and Hospitality Education*. London: Routledge.

Tsouros, A. and Efstathiou, P. (eds) (2007). *Mass Gatherings and Public Health: The Experience of the Athens 2004 Olympics*. Copenhagen: World Health Organization, Europe.

Tum, J. (2012). Managing uncertainty: (Re)conceptualising aspects for operations for events. In S. J. Page and J. Connell (eds), *The Routledge Handbook of Events*, pp. 212–312. London: Routledge.

Tum, J., Norton, P. and Wright. J. (2006). *Management of Event Operations*. Oxford: Butterworth-Heinemann.

Turner, E. (2012). *Communitas: The Anthropology of Collective Joy*. Basingstoke: Palgrave Macmillan.

Turner, J. (1997). The policy process. In B. Axford, G. Browning, R. Huggins, B. Rosamond and J. Turner (eds), *Politics: An Introduction*, pp. 409–439. London: Routledge.

Turner, V. (1969). *The Ritual Process: Structure and Anti-structure*. New York: Aldine de Gruyter.

Turner, V. (1974). Liminal to liminoid, in play, flow and ritual: An essay in comparative symbology. In E. Norbeck (ed.), *The Anthropological Study of Human Play*, Vol. 60, pp. 53–92. Rice University Studies.

Turner, V. (1979). *Process, Performance, and Pilgrimage: A Study in Comparative Symbology*. New Delhi: Concept.

Turner, V. (ed.) (1982). *Celebration: Studies in Festivity and Ritual*. Washington DC: Smithsonian Institution Press.

Turner, V. and Turner, E. (1978). *Image and Pilgrimage in Christian Culture*. New York: Columbia University Press.

Tyrrell, T. and Johnston, R. (2001). A framework for assessing direct economic impacts of tourist events: Distinguishing origins, destinations, and causes of expenditures. *Journal of Travel Research*, 40 (1), 94–100.

Tyrrell, T. and Johnston, R. (2012). A spatial extension to a framework for assessing direct economic impacts of tourist events. In S. J. Page and J. Connell (eds), *The Routledge Handbook of Events*. London: Routledge.

Tyson, B., Jordan, L. A. and Truly, D. (2016). *Sports Event Management: The Caribbean Experience*. London: Routledge.

Tzanelli, R. (2015). *Socio-Cultural Mobility and Mega-Events: Ethics and Aesthetics in Brazil's 2014 World Cup*. London: Routledge.

Tzelepi, M. and Quick, S. (2002). The Sydney organizing committee for the Olympic Games (SOCOG) 'Event Leadership' training course – an effectiveness evaluation. *Event Management*, 7 (4), 245–257.

UK Health and Safety Executive (1999). *The Event Safety Guide* (www.hsebooks.com, accessed 7 June 2019).

UK Institute for Volunteering (www.ivr.org.uk, accessed 7 June 2019).

United Nations Educational, Scientific and Cultural Organization (2002). *Guidelines for the Establishment of Living Human Treasures Systems*. Paris: UNESCO.

United States Council on Environmental Quality (1980). *Environmental Quality: The Eleventh Annual Report of the Council on Environmental Quality*. Washington, DC: Council on Environmental Quality.

Unruh, D. (1980). The nature of social worlds. *The Pacific Sociological Review*, 23 (3), 271–296.

Urry, J. (1990). *The Tourist Gaze: Leisure and Travel in Contemporary Societies*. London: Sage.

Urry, J. (1995). *Consuming Places*. London: Routledge.

Urry, J. (2002). *The Tourist Gaze: Leisure and Travel in Contemporary Societies* (2nd edn). London: Sage.

US Department of Labor (2005). *Volunteering in the United States, 2005* (www.bls.gov/news.release/volun.nr0.htm, accessed 7 June 2019).

Uysal, M. and Li, X. (2008). Trends and critical issues in festival and event motivation. In A. Aktas, *International Cultural and Event Tourism: Issues and Debates*, pp. 10–20. Ankara, Turkey: Detay Yayincilik.

Uysal, M., Gahan, L. and Martin, B. (1993). An examination of event motivations: A case study. *Festival Management and Event Tourism*, 1 (1), 510.

Van der Auwera, S. and Schramme, A. (2014). Commemoration of the Great War: A global phenomenon or a national agenda? *Journal of Conflict Archaeology*, 9 (1), 3–15.

Van der Wagen, L. (2006). *Human Resource Management for Events: Managing the Event Workforce*. Oxford: Butterworth-Heinemann.

Van der Wagen, L. (2008). *Event Management for Tourism, Cultural, Business and Sporting Events* (3rd edn). Frenchs Forest, NSW: Pearson Education Australia.

Van Der Wagen, L. and White, L. (2014). *Human Resource Management for the Event Industry*. London: Routledge.

Van Gennep, A. (1909). *The Rites of Passage* (1960 translation by M. Vizedom and G. Coffee). London: Routledge and Kegan Paul.

Van Limburg, B. (2008). Innovation in pop festivals by co-creation. *Event Management*, 12 (2), 105–117.

Van Niekerk, M. and Getz, D. (2019). *Event Stakeholders*. Oxford: Goodfellow Publishers.

Van Riper, C. J., van Riper III, C., Kyle, G. T. and Lee, M. E. (2013). Understanding how social networking influences perceived satisfaction with conference experiences. *Annals of Leisure Research*, 16 (1), 103–114.

Van Winkle, C. and Backman, K. (2009). Examining visitor mindfulness at a cultural event. *Event Management*, 12 (3/4), 163–169.

Van Winkle, C. M. and Bueddefeld, J. N. H. (2016). Service-dominant logic and the festival experience. *International Journal of Event and Festival Management*, 7 (3), 237–254.

Vanhamme, J. and Snelders, D. (2001). The role of surprise in satisfaction judgments. *Journal of Consumer Satisfaction Dissatisfaction And Complaining Behavior*, 14, 27–45.

Vanhove, D. and Witt, S. (1987). Report of the English-speaking group on the conference theme. *Revue de Tourisme*, 4, 10–12.

Vanwynsberghe, R., Surborg, B. and Wyly, E. (2013). When the games come to town: Neoliberalism, mega-events and social inclusion in the Vancouver 2010 Winter Olympic Games. *International Journal of Urban and Regional Research*, 37 (6), 2074–2093.

Vargo, S. L. and Lusch, R. F. (2004). Evolving to a new dominant logic for marketing. *Journal of Marketing*, 68 (1), 1–17.

Vargo, S. L. and Lusch, R. F. (2006). Service-dominant logic: What it is, what it is not, what it might be. In S. L. Vargo and R. F. Lusch (eds), *The Service-Dominant Logic of Marketing: Dialog, Debate, and Directions*, pp. 43–56. Armonk, NY: M. E. Sharpe.

Vargo, S. L. and Lusch, R. F. (2008). Service-dominant logic: Continuing the evolution. *Journal of the Academy of Marketing Science*, 36 (1), 1–10.

Vaughan, R. (1979). *Does a Festival Pay? A Case Study of the Edinburgh Festival in 1976*. Tourism Recreation Research Unit, Working Paper 5, University of Edinburgh.

Veal, A. (2006). *Research Methods for Leisure and Tourism: A Practical Guide* (3rd edn). Harlow: Prentice Hall.

Veal, A. (2010). *Leisure, Sport and Tourism: Politics, Policy and Planning* (3rd edn). Wallingford: CABI.

Veal, A. (2011). *Research Methods for Leisure and Tourism: A Practical Guide* (4th edn). Harlow: Prentice Hall.

Veal, A. and Burton, C. (2014). *Research Methods for Arts and Event Management*. Harlow: Pearson.

Veal, A. and Darcy, S. (2014). *Research Methods in Sport Studies and Sport Management, A Practical Guide*. London: Routledge.

Veblen, T. (1899). *The Theory of the Leisure Class* (Penguin twentieth-century classics, 1994). New York: Penguin Books.

Verhoven, P., Wall, D. and Cottrell, S. (1998). Application of desktop mapping as a marketing tool for special events planning and evaluation: A case study of the Newport News Celebration in Lights. *Festival Management and Event Tourism*, 5 (3), 123–130.

Verleye, K. (2015). The co-creation experience from the customer perspective: Its measurement and determinants. *Journal of Service Management*, 26 (2), 321–342.

Victorian Auditor General (2007). *State Investment in Major Events*. Victorian Government Printer, Victoria, Australia, May.

Viehoff, V. and Poynter, P. G. (2015). *Mega-event Cities: Urban Legacies of Global Sports Events*. Basingstoke: Ashgate.

Viol, M., Todd, L., Theodoraki, E. and Anastasiadou, C. (2018). The role of iconic-historic commemorative events in event tourism: Insights from the 20th and 25th anniversaries of the fall of the Berlin Wall. *Tourism Management*, 69, 246–262.

Voss, T. (2001). Institutions. In *International Encyclopedia of the Social and Behavioral Sciences*, pp. 7561–7566. Oxford: Elsevier.

Vroom, V. (1964). *Work and Motivation*. New York: Wiley.

Wackernagel, M. and Rees, W. (1996). *Our Ecological Footprint: Reducing Human Impact on the Earth*. Gabriola Island, BC: New Society Publishers.

Waitt, G. (2003). Social impacts of the Sydney Olympics. *Annals of Tourism Research*, 30 (1), 194–215.

Waitt, G. (2004). A critical examination of Sydney's 2000 Olympic Games. In I. Yeoman, M. Robertson, J. Ali-Knight, S. Drummond and U. McMahon-Beattie (eds), *Festivals and Events Management*, pp. 391–408. Oxford: Elsevier.

Waitt, G. and Duffy, M. (2010). Listening and tourism studies. *Annals of Tourism Research*, 37 (2), 457–477.

Waitt, G., Gorman-Murray, A. and Gibson, C. (2011). Bodily rhythms: Corporeal capacities to engage with festival spaces. *Emotion, Space and Society*, 4 (1), 17–24.

Waitt, G. and Stapel, C. (2011). 'Fornicating on floats'? The cultural politics of the Sydney Mardi Gras Parade beyond the metropolis. *Leisure Studies*, 30 (2), 197–216.

Walker, G., Deng, J. and Dieser, R. (2005). Culture, self-construal, and leisure theory and practice. *Journal of Leisure Research*, 37 (1), 77–99.

Walker, G. and Virden, R. (2005). Constraints on outdoor recreation. In E. Jackson (ed.), *Constraints to Leisure*, Chapter 13. State College, PA: Venture Publishing.

Walker, R. A. (2013). Fill/flash/memory: A history of flash mobs. *Text and Performance Quarterly*, 33 (2), 115–132.

Walle, A. (1994). The festival life cycle and tourism strategies: The case of the Cowboy Poetry Gathering. *Festival Management and Event Tourism*, 2 (2), 85–94.

Wallstam, M., Ioannides, D. and Pettersson, R. (2018). Evaluating the social impacts of events: In search of unified indicators for effective policymaking. *Journal of Policy Research in Tourism, Leisure and Events*.

Walmsley, D. J., Boskovic, R. M. and Pigram, J. J. (1983). Tourism and crime: An Australian perspective. *Journal of Leisure Research*, 15 (2), 136–155.

Walters, T. and Jepson, A. S., (eds) (2019). *Marginalisation and Events*. London: Routledge.

Walton, J. (1999). *Chartism*. London: Routledge.

Walvin, J. (1984). *English Urban Life 1776–1851*. London: Routledge.

Wang, F., Wang, K. and Wang, L. (2018). An examination of a city greening mega-event. *International Journal of Hospitality Management*, 77, 538–548.

Wang, M. and Bao, H. (2018). Mega-event effects on the housing market: Evidence from the Beijing 2008 Olympic Games. *Cities*, 72, 207–216.

Wang, N. (1999). Rethinking authenticity in tourism experience. *Annals of Tourism Research*, 26 (2), 349–370.

Wang, P. and Gitelson, R. (1988). Economic limitations of festivals and other hallmark events. *Leisure Industry Report*, August: 4–5.

Wang, W. and Cole, S. (2016). A comparative analysis of event attendees' spending behaviors, satisfaction, and information search patterns by event types at a midwestern college town. *Event Management*, 20, 3–10.

Wang, Y. and Jin, X. (2019). Event-based destination marketing: The role of mega-events. *Event Management*, 23, 109–118.

Wanhill, S. (2006). Some economics of staging festivals: The case of opera festivals. *Tourism, Culture and Communication*, 6 (2), 137–149.

Wann, D. (1995). Preliminary validation of the sport fan motivation scale. *Journal of Sport and Social Issues*, 19 (4), 377–396.

Wann, D. (1997). *Sport Psychology*. Upper Saddle River, NJ: Prentice Hall.

Wann, D. and Branscombe, N. (1993). Sport fans: Measuring degree of identification with their team. *International Journal of Sport Psychology*, 24 (1), 1–17.

Wann, D., Royalty, J. and Rochelle, A. (2002). Using motivation and team identification to predict sport fans' emotional responses to team performance. *Journal of Sport Behavior*, 25 (2), 207–216.

Wann, D., Schrader, M. and Wilson, A. (1999). Sport fan motivation: Questionnaire validation, comparisons by sport, and relationship to athletic motivation. *Journal of Sport Behaviour*, 22 (1), 114–139.

Warf, B. (2008). *Time–Space Compression: Historical Geographies*: London: Routledge.

Waterman, S. (1998). Carnivals for elites? The cultural politics of arts festivals. *Progress in Human Geography*, 22 (1), 54–74.

Waters, H. (1939). *History of Fairs and Expositions*. London, Canada: Reid Brothers.

Watson, R. and Yip, P. (2011). How many were there when it mattered? *Significance*, 8 (3), 104–107.

Watt, J. (2014). Brazil 2014: World Cup where politics and social media invaded the pitch. *The Guardian* (http://www.theguardian.com/football/world-cup-2014, accessed 15 September 2014).

Weber, K. and Ladkin, A. (2005). Trends affecting the convention industry in the 21st century. *Journal of Convention and Event Tourism*, 6 (4), 47–63.

Weed, M. (2008). *Olympic Tourism*. Oxford: Butterworth-Heinemann.

Weed, M. (2012). *Olympic Tourism* (2nd edn). Oxford: Butterworth-Heinemann.

Weed, M. and Bull, C. (2004). *Sports Tourism: Participants, Policy and Providers*. Oxford: Elsevier.

Weidenfeld, A., Butler, R. and Williams, A. (eds) (2015). *Visitor Attractions and Events: Locations and Linkages*. London: Routledge.

Weiss, C. (1972). *Evaluation Research. Methods for Assessing Program Effectiveness*. Englewood Cliffs, New Jersey: Prentice-Hall,

Weller, S. (2013). Consuming the city: Public fashion festivals and the participatory economies of urban spaces in Melbourne. *Urban Studies*, 50 (14), 2853–2868.

Weppler, K. and McCarville, R. (1995). Understanding organizational buying behaviour to secure sponsorship. *Festival Management and Event Tourism*, 2 (3/4), 139–148.

Westerbeek, H., Turner, P. and Ingerson, L. (2002). Key success factors in bidding for hallmark sporting events. *International Marketing Review*, 19 (3), 303–322.

White, L. (2011). The Sydney 2000 Olympic Games bid: Marketing Indigenous Australia for the Millennium Games. *International Journal of the History of Sport*, 28 (10), 1447–1462.

White, L. (2013). Cathy Freeman and Australia's indigenous heritage: A new beginning for an old nation at the Sydney 2000 Olympic Games. *International Journal of Heritage Studies*, 19 (2), 153–170.

Whitehead, J. and Wicker, P. (2018). Estimating willingness to pay for a cycling event using a willingness to travel approach. *Tourism Management*, 65, 160–169.

Whitfield, J. (2009). Why and how UK visitor attractions diversify their product to offer conference and event facilities. *Journal of Convention and Event Tourism*, 10, 72–88.

Whitford, M. (2004a). Regional development through domestic and tourist event policies: Gold Coast and Brisbane, 1974–2003. *UNLV Journal of Hospitality, Tourism and Leisure Science*, 2, 1–24.

Whitford, M. (2004b). Event public policy development in the Northern Sub-Regional Organisation of Councils, Queensland Australia: Rhetoric or realisation? *Journal of Convention and Event Tourism*, 6 (3), 81–99.

Whitford, M., Phi, G. and Dredge, D. (2014). Principles to practice: Indicators for measuring event governance performance. *Event Management*, 18, 387–403.

Whitford, M. and Ruhanen, L. (2013). Indigenous festivals and community development: A sociocultural analysis of an Australian indigenous festival. *Event Management*, 17 (1), 49–61.

Whitson, D. and Macintosh, D. (1996). The global circus: International sport, tourism, and the marketing of cities. *Journal of Sport and Social Issues*, 20 (3), 275–295.

Wickham, T. and Kerstetter, D. (2000). The relationship between place attachment and crowding in an event setting. *Event Management*, 6 (3), 167–174.

Wicks, B. (1995). The business sector's reaction to a community special event in a small town: A case study of the Autumn on Parade Festival. *Festival Management and Event Tourism*, 2 (3/4), 177–183.

Wicks, B. and Fesenmaier, D. (1993). A comparison of visitor and vendor perceptions of service quality at a special event. *Festival Management and Event Tourism*, 1 (1), 1926.

Wicks, B. and Fesenmaier, D. (1995). Market potential for special events: A midwestern case study. *Festival Management and Event Tourism*, 3 (1), 25–31.

Wikipedia articles (www.wikipedia.org):

- G20 Toronto Summit Protests (accessed 7 June 2019)
- Performance Studies (accessed 7 June 2019)
- Experience Design (accessed Feb. 25, 2019)
- Civil Society
- Future Studies

Wilks, L. (2011). Bridging and bonding: Social capital at music festivals. *Journal of Policy Research in Tourism, Leisure and Events*, 3 (3), 281–297.

Williams, K., Laing, J. and Frost, W. (2013). *Fashion, Design and Events*. London: Routledge.

Williams, P., Dossa, K. and Tompkins, L. (1995). Volunteerism and special event management: A case study of Whistler's Men's World Cup of Skiing. *Festival Management and Event Tourism*, 3 (2), 83–95.

Williams, P. and Harrison, L. (1988). *A Framework for Marketing Ethnocultural Communities and Festivals*. Unpublished report to the Secretary of State Multiculturalism, Ottawa.

Williams, P. W. and Elkhashab, A. (2012). Leveraging tourism social capital: The case of the 2010 Olympic tourism consortium. *International Journal of Event and Festival Management*, 3 (3), 317–334.

Williamson, M. (2016). *Celebrity: Capitalism and the Making of Fame*. Chichester: Wiley.

Wilson, J., Arshed, N., Shaw, E. and Pret, T. (2017). Expanding the domain of festival research: A review and research agenda. *International Journal of Management Reviews*, 19 (2), 195–213.

Wilson J. and Udall, L. (1982). *Folk Festivals: A Handbook for Organization and Management*. Knoxville, TN: University of Tennessee Press.

Wiscombe, C. (2019). Agricultural shows – The challenge of accessibility. In R. Finkel, B. Sharp and M. Sweeney (eds), *Accessibility, Inclusion and Diversity in Critical Event Studies* (pp. 65–78). London: Routledge.

Wise, N. and Harris, J. (2017). *Sport, Events, Tourism and Regeneration*. London: Routledge.

Wood, D. and Gray, B. (1991). Toward a comprehensive theory of collaboration. *The Journal of Applied Behavioural Science*, 27 (1), 3–22.

Wood, E. (2004). Marketing information for the events industry. In I. Yeoman, M. Robertson, J. Ali-Knight, S. Drummond and U. McMahon-Beattie (eds), *Festival and Events Management: An International Arts and Culture Perspective*, pp. 130–157. Oxford: Elsevier.

Wood, E. H. and Kenyon, A. J. (2018). Remembering together: The importance of shared emotional memory in event experiences. *Event Management*, 22 (2), 163–181.

Wooten, M. and Norman, W. (2008). Interpreting and managing special events and festivals. In A. Woodside and D. Martin (eds), *Managing Tourism: Analysis, Behavior and Strategy*, pp. 197–217. Wallingford: CABI.

Woratschek, H., Durchholz, C., Maier, C. and Stroble, T. (2017). Innovations in sport management: The role of motivations and value cocreation at public viewing events. *Event Management*, 21, 1–12.

Wuensch, U. (2008). *Facets of Contemporary Event Communication – Theory and Practice for Event Success*. Bad Honnef, Germany: K. H. Bock.

Wuensch, U. (ed.) (2015). Atmosphären des Populären, Berlin.

Wuensch, U. (2015). *Handbuch Event-Kommunikation*, second newly edited edition, Berlin.

Wundt, W. (1896). *Grundriss der Psychologie*. Leipzig: Wilhelm Engelmann.

Wynn-Moylan, P. (2017). *Risk and Hazard Management for Festivals and Events*. London: Routledge.

Xiao, H. and Smith, S. (2004). Residents' perceptions of Kitchener-Waterloo Oktoberfest: An inductive analysis. *Event Management*, 8 (3), 161–175.

Xie, P. (2003). The bamboo-beating dance in Hainan, China: Authenticity and commodification. *Journal of Sustainable Tourism*, 11 (1), 5–16.

Xie, P. (2004). Visitors' perceptions of authenticity at a rural heritage festival: A case study. *Event Management*, 8 (3), 151–160.

Xie, P. and Gu, K. (2015). The changing urban morphology: Waterfront redevelopment and event tourism in New Zealand. *Tourism Management Perspectives* 15, 105–114.

Xue, K., Chen, X. and Yu, M. (2012). Can the World Expo change a city's image through foreign media reports? *Public Relations Review*, 38 (5), 746–754.

Yang, J., Zeng, X. and Gu, Y. (2010). Local residents' perceptions of the impact of 2010 Expo. *Journal of Convention and Event Tourism*, 11 (3), 161–175.

Yeoman, I., Robertson, M., Ali-Knight, J., Drummond, S. and McMahon-Beattie, U. (eds) (2004). *Festival and Events Management: An International Arts and Culture Perspective*. Oxford: Elsevier.

Yeoman, I., Robertson, M., McMahon-Beattie, U., Backer, E. and Smith, K. (eds) (2014). *The Future of Events and Festivals*. London: Routledge.

Yi, X., Fu, X., Jin, W. and Okumus, F. (2018). Constructing a model of exhibition attachment: Motivation, attachment, and loyalty. *Tourism Management*, 65, 224–236.

Yin, R. (2014). *Case Study Research: Design and Methods* (5th edn). Beverly Hills, CA: Sage.

Ying-Chih, D. (2016). Space and memory in the Huashan event. In I. Lamond (ed.), *Critical Event Studies. Leisure Studies in a Global Era*, pp. 109–130. London: Palgrave Macmillan.

Yolal, M., Cetinel, F. and Uysal, M. (2009). An examination of festival motivation and perceived benefits relationship: Eskisehir International Festival. *Journal of Convention and Event Tourism*, 10 (4), 276–291.

Yoo, J. and Weber, K. (2005). Progress in convention tourism research. *Journal of Hospitality and Tourism Research*, 29 (2), 194–222.

Yoon, S., Spencer, D., Holecek, D. and Kim, D. (2000). A profile of Michigan's festival and special event tourism market. *Event Management*, 6 (1), 33–44.

Young, B., Bennett, A. and Seguin, B. (2015). Masters sport perspectives. In M. Parent and J.-L. Chappelet (eds), *Routledge Handbook of Sports Event Management*, pp. 139–162. London: Routledge.

Young, H. (1998). *Individual Strategy and Social Structure*. Princeton, NJ: Princeton University Press.

Yu, Y. and Turco, D. (2000). Issues in tourism event economic impact studies: The case of Albuquerque International Balloon Fiesta. *Current Issues in Tourism*, 3 (2), 138–149.

Zaichkowsky, J. (1985). Measuring the involvement construct. Journal of Consumer Research, 12 (3), 341–352.

Zelinsky, W. (1994). Conventionland USA: The geography of a latterday phenomenon. *Annals of the Association of American Geographers*, 84 (1), 68–86.

Ziakas, V. (2010). Understanding an event portfolio: The uncovering of interrelationships, synergies, and leveraging opportunities. *Journal of Policy Research in Tourism, Leisure and Events*, 2 (2), 144–164.

Ziakas, V. (2013). *Event Portfolio Planning and Management: A Holistic Approach*. London: Routledge.

Ziakas, V. (2014). Planning and leveraging event portfolios: Towards a holistic theory. *Journal of Hospitality Marketing and Management*, 23 (3), 327–356.

Ziakas, V. and Boukas, N. (2013). Extracting meanings of event tourist experiences: A phenomenological exploration of Limassol carnival. *Journal of Destination Marketing and Management*, 2 (2), 94–107.

Ziakas, V. and Boukas, N. (2014). Contextualizing phenomenology in event management research: Deciphering the meaning of event experiences. *International Journal of Event and Festival Management*, 5 (1), 56–73.

Ziakas, V. and Costa, C. (2010a). 'Between theatre and sport' in a rural event: Evolving unity and community development from the inside-out. *Journal of Sport & Tourism*, 15 (1), 7–26.

Ziakas, V. and Costa, C. (2010b). Explicating inter-organizational linkages of a host community's events network. *International Journal of Event and Festival Management*, 1 (2), 132–147.

Zimbalist, A. (2015). *Circus Maximus: The Economic Gamble Behind Hosting the Olympics and the World Cup*. Washington D.C.: Brookings Institution Press

Zuckerman, M. (1979). *Sensation Seeking: Beyond the Optimal Level of Arousal*. Hillsdale, NJ: LEA.

Zuzanek, J., Robinson, J. P. and Iwasaki, Y. (1998). The relationships between stress, health, and physically active leisure as a function of life-cycle. *Leisure Sciences*, 20 (4), 253–275.

Index